T0181717

Foundations of Computational Linguistics

Roland Hausser

Foundations of Computational Linguistics

Human-Computer Communication in Natural Language

Third Edition

 Springer

Roland Hausser
Abteilung für Computerlinguistik (retired)
Friedrich-Alexander-Universität
    Erlangen-Nürnberg
Erlangen, Germany

ISBN 978-3-662-49600-8   ISBN 978-3-642-41431-2 (eBook)
DOI 10.1007/978-3-642-41431-2
Springer Heidelberg New York Dordrecht London

Preface to the Third Edition

The Third Edition has been gently modernized, leaving the overview of traditional, theoretical, and computational linguistics, analytic philosophy of language, and mathematical complexity theory with their historical backgrounds intact. The format of the empirical analyses of English and German syntax and semantics has been adapted to current practice. Sects. 22.3–24.5 have been rewritten to focus more sharply on the construction of a talking robot.

Because the Second Edition is quite long, one aim of the present edition has been to shorten the number of pages. Little is lost, however, because later publications make up for a reduction of about 10 percent. The broad, leisurely style induced by the book's origin as material for a four semester introductory lecture course, however, has been preserved.

Special thanks to Ronan Nugent, Senior Editor of Computer Science at Springer, for his continued support.

Erlangen, Germany   Roland Hausser
June 2013

Remark on the Use of *Risci*

Science books often use a menagerie of tables, graphs, examples, definitions, theorems, lemmata, schemata, etc., which are either (i) not numbered or (ii) use different counters for each kind. For the author, (i) makes it difficult to refer to a particular item. For the reader, (ii) makes it difficult to find the item.

As a remedy, we use a uniform container called *riscus*[1] to hold any of such items. A riscus begins with a numbered head line and ends when normal text resumes. In this book, the number of a riscus consists of three parts, e.g., 3.2.1, which specify the location in terms of the chapter within the text, the section within the chapter, and the riscus within the section.

Independently of the riscus numbering, the head line may classify and number the item contained, as in the following fictitious example:

3.2.1   THEOREM 9: THE POLYNOMIAL COMPLEXITY OF CF LANGUAGES

Content of the theorem followed by the proof.

Elsewhere in the text, the above riscus may be referred to with something like As shown in 3.2.1, ... or In Theorem 9 (3.2.1) ... . In this way, the riscus numbering allows the author to be brief yet precise because the reader may be guided to a more detailed presentation given in another place. The method works regardless of whether the book is a hard copy or an eBook.

The numbering of a riscus may be provided automatically, for example, by using the LATEX \subsection command for riscus headings. The riscus numbering, like that of chapters and sections, may be hooked up with automatic cross-referencing, for example, by adding \usepackage{hyperref} to the LATEX preamble of the text.

As a result, the reader of an eBook may click on a three part number to be transported automatically to the riscus in question, and may get back to the earlier position with a simple command like cntrl [. The comfort of accessing a riscus directly, instead of having to leaf through the chapter and the section as in a hard copy, is perhaps not the least advantage added by the transition from a hard copy to an eBook.

Erlangen, Germany   Roland Hausser

---

[1] *riscus <i> m,* is the Latin word for suitcase. A riscus was made of woven willow branches covered with fur.

Preface to the First Edition

The central task of a future-oriented computational linguistics is the development of cognitive machines which humans can freely talk with in their respective natural language. In the long run, this task will ensure the development of a functional theory of language, an objective method of verification, and a wide range of applications.

Natural communication requires not only verbal processing, but also non-verbal recognition and action. Therefore the content of this textbook is organized as a theory of language for the construction of talking robots. The main topic is the *mechanism of natural language communication* in both the speaker and the hearer.

The content is divided into the following parts:

    I.   Theory of Language
    II.   Theory of Grammar
    III. Morphology and Syntax
    IV. Semantics and Pragmatics

Each part consists of 6 chapters. Each of the 24 chapters consists of 5 sections. A total of 797 exercises help in reviewing key ideas and important problems.

Part I begins with current applications of computational linguistics. Then it describes a new theory of language, the functioning of which is illustrated by the robot CURIOUS. This theory is referred to with the acronym SLIM, which stands for *Surface compositional Linear Internal Matching*. It includes a cognitive foundation of semantic primitives, a theory of signs, a structural delineation of the components syntax, semantics, and pragmatics, as well as their functional integration in the speaker's utterance and the hearer's interpretation. The presentation refers to other contemporary theories of language, especially those of Chomsky and Grice, as well as to the classic theories of Frege, Peirce, de Saussure, Bühler, and Shannon and Weaver, explaining their formal and methodological foundations as well as their historical background and motivations.

Part II presents the theory of *formal grammar* and its methodological, mathematical, and computational roles in the description of natural languages. A description of Categorial (C) Grammar and Phrase Structure (PS) Grammar is combined with an introduction to the basic notions and linguistic motivation of generative grammar. Further topics are the declarative vs. procedural aspects of parsing and generation, type transparency, as well as the relation between formalisms and complexity classes. It is shown that the principle of possible *substitutions* causes empirical and mathematical problems for the description of natural language. As an alternative, the principle of possible *continuations* is formalized as LA Grammar. LA stands for the left-associative derivation order which models the time-linear nature of language. Applications of LA Grammar to relevant artificial languages show that its hierarchy of formal languages is orthogonal to that of PS Grammar. Within the LA hierarchy, natural language is in the lowest complexity class, namely the class of C1 languages which parse in linear time.

Part III describes the *morphology* and *syntax* of natural language. A general description of the notions word, word form, morpheme, and allomorph, the morphological processes of inflection, derivation, and composition, as well as the different possible methods of automatic word form recognition is followed by the morphological analysis of English within the framework of LA Grammar. Then the syntactic principles of valency, agreement, and word order are explained within the left-associative approach. LA Grammars for English and German are developed by systematically extending a small initial system to handle more and more constructions such as the fixed vs. free word order of English and German, respectively, the structure of complex noun phrases and complex verbs, interrogatives, subordinate clauses, etc. These analyses are presented in the form of explicit grammars and sample derivations.

Part IV describes the *semantics* and *pragmatics* of natural language. The general description of language interpretation begins by comparing three different types of semantics, namely those of logical languages, programming languages, and natural languages. Based on Tarski's foundation of logical semantics and his reconstruction of the Epimenides paradox, the possibility of applying logical semantics to natural language is investigated. Alternative analyses of intensional contexts, propositional attitudes, and the phenomenon of vagueness illustrate that different types of semantics are based on different ontologies which greatly influence the empirical results. It is shown how a semantic interpretation may cause an increase in complexity and how this is to be avoided within the SLIM theory of language. The last two chapters, 23 and 24, analyze the interpretation by the hearer and the conceptualization by the speaker as a time-linear navigation through a database called *word bank*. A word bank allows the storage of arbitrary propositional content and is implemented as a highly restricted specialization of a classic (i.e., record-based) network database. The autonomous navigation through a word bank is controlled by the explicit rules of suitable LA Grammars.

As supplementary reading the *Survey of the State of the Art in Human Language Technology*, Ron Cole (ed.) 1998 is recommended. This book contains about 90 contributions by different specialists giving detailed snapshots of their research in language theory and technology.

Erlangen, Germany   Roland Hausser
June 1999

Contents

Part III. Morphology and Syntax

Abbreviations Referring to Preceding and Subsequent Work

Preceding Work

SCG   Hausser, R. (1984) *Surface Compositional Grammar*, München: Wilhelm Fink Verlag, pp. 274

NEWCAT   Hausser, R. (1986) *NEWCAT: Natural Language Parsing Using Left-Associative Grammar*, Lecture Notes in Computer Science, Vol. 231, Springer, pp. 540

CoL   Hausser, R. (1989a) *Computation of Language: An Essay on Syntax, Semantics and Pragmatics in Natural Man-Machine Communication*, Symbolic Computation: Artificial Intelligence, Springer, pp. 425

TCS   Hausser, R. (1992) "Complexity in Left-Associative Grammar," *Theoretical Computer Science* 106.2:283–308

Subsequent Work

AIJ   Hausser, R. (2001c) "Database Semantics for Natural Language." *Artificial Intelligence* 130.1:27–74

NLC   Hausser, R. (2006) *A Computational Model of Natural Language Communication – Interpretation, Inferencing, and Production in Database Semantics*, Springer, pp. 365

L&I   Hausser, R. (2010) "Language Production Based on Autonomous Control – A Content-Addressable Memory for a Model of Cognition," *Language and Information* 11:5–31

CLaTR   Hausser, R. (2011) *Computational Linguistics and Talking Robots, Processing Content in Database Semantics*, Springer, pp. 286

Introduction

I. Basic Goal of Computational Linguistics

Transmitting information by means of a natural language like Chinese, English, or German is a real and well structured procedure. This becomes evident when we attempt to communicate with people who speak a foreign language. Even if the information we want to convey is completely clear to us, we will not be understood by our hearers if we fail to use their language adequately. Conversely, even if our foreign language partners use their language as they always do, and without any problems, we will not understand them.

The goal of computational linguistics is to reproduce the natural transmission of information by modeling the speaker's production and the hearer's interpretation on a suitable type of computer. This amounts to the construction of autonomous cognitive machines (robots) which can freely communicate in natural language.

The development of speaking robots is not a matter of fiction, but a real scientific task. Remarkably, however, theories of language have so far avoided a functional modeling of the natural communication mechanism, concentrating instead on peripheral aspects such as methodology (behaviorism), innate ideas (nativism), and scientific truth (model theory).

II. Turing Test

The task of modeling the mechanism of natural communication on the computer was described in 1950 by ALAN TURING (1912–1954) in the form of an 'imitation game' known today as the Turing test. In this game, a human interrogator is asked to question a male and a female partner in another room via a teleprinter in order to determine which answer was given by the man and which by the woman.[1] The people running the test count how often the interrogator classifies his communication partners correctly and how often he is wrong.

Then one of the two humans is replaced by a computer. The computer passes the Turing test if the man or the woman replaced by the computer is simulated so well that the guesses of the human interrogator are just as often right and wrong as with

---

[1] As a corresponding situation in real life consider an author wondering about the gender of the anonymous copyeditor courteously provided by the publisher.

the earlier natural partner. In this way Turing wanted to replace the question "Can machines think?" with the question "Are there imaginable digital computers which would do well in the imitation game?"

III. Eliza Program

In its original intention, the Turing test requires the construction of an artificial cognitive agent with a language behavior so natural that it cannot be distinguished from that of a human. This presupposes complete coverage of the language data and of the communicative functions in real time. At the same time, the test tries to avoid all aspects not directly involved in human language behavior.[2]

However, the Turing test does not specify what cognitive structure the artificial agent should have in order to succeed in the imitation game. It is therefore possible to misinterpret the aim of the Turing test as fooling the human interrogator rather than providing a functional model of communication on the computer. This was shown by the Eliza program of Weizenbaum (1965).

The Eliza program simulates a psychiatrist encouraging the human interrogator, now in the role of a patient, to talk more and more about him- or herself. Eliza works with a list of words. Whenever one of these words is typed by the human interrogator/patient, Eliza inserts it into one of several prefabricated sentence templates. For example, when the word mother is used by the human, Eliza uses the template Tell me more about your ___ to generate the sentence Tell me more about your mother.

Because of the way in which Eliza works, we know that Eliza has no understanding of the dialog with the interrogator/patient. Thus, the construction of Eliza is not a model of communication. If we regard the dialog between Eliza/psychiatrist and the interrogator/patient as a modified Turing test, however, the Eliza program is successful insofar as the interrogator/patient *feels* him- or herself understood and therefore does not distinguish between a human and an artificial communication partner in the role of a psychiatrist.

The Eliza program is the prototype of a *smart* solution (Sect. 2.3) in that it exploits the restrictions of a highly specialized application to achieve a maximal effect with a minimum of effort. The goal of computational linguistics, however, is a *solid* solution in science: it must (i) explain the mechanism of natural communication theoretically and (ii) verify the theory with an implementation (software machine) which may be loaded with the language-dependent lexicon and compositional operations of any natural language. The speak and the hear mode of the implementation must work in any practical application for which free natural language communication between humans and machines is desired (15.1.3).

---

[2] As an example of such an aspect, Turing (1950), p. 434, mentions the artificial recreation of human skin.

IV. MODELING NATURAL COMMUNICATION

Designing a talking robot provides an excellent opportunity for systematically developing the basic notions as well as the philosophical, mathematical, grammatical, methodological, and programming aspects of computational linguistics. This is because modeling the mechanism of natural communication requires

- a theory of language which explains the natural transfer of information in a way that is functionally coherent and mathematically explicit,
- a description of language data which is empirically complete for all components of this theory of language, i.e., the lexicon, the morphology, the syntax, and the semantics, as well as the pragmatics and the representation of the internal context, and
- a degree of precision in the description of these components which supports a straightforward computational implementation running in real time.

Fulfilling these requirements will take hard, systematic, goal-oriented work, but it will be worth the effort.

For theory development, the construction of talking robots is of interest because an electronically implemented model of communication may be tested both in terms of the language behavior observed externally, and internally via direct access to its cognitive states via the service channel. The work towards realizing unrestricted human-computer communication in natural language is facilitated by the fact that the functional model may be developed incrementally, beginning with a simplified, but fully general system to which additional functions as well as additional natural languages are added step by step.

For practical purposes, unrestricted communication with computers and robots in natural languages will make the interaction with these machines maximally user friendly and permit new, powerful ways of information processing. The use of artificial programming languages may then be limited to specialists developing and servicing the machines.

V. USING PARSERS

Computational linguistics analyzes natural languages automatically in terms of software programs called parsers. The use of parsers influences the theoretical viewpoint of linguistic research, distribution of funds, and everyday research practice as follows:

- *Competition*
  Competing theories of grammar are measured with respect to the new standard of how well they are suited for efficient parsing and how well they fit into a theory of language designed to model the mechanism of natural language communication.

– *Funding*

Adequate parsers for different languages are needed for an unlimited range of practical applications, which has a major impact on the inflow of funds for research, development, and teaching in this particular area of the humanities.

– *Verification*

Programming grammars as parsers allows testing their empirical adequacy automatically on arbitrarily large amounts of real data in the areas of word form recognition and synthesis, syntactic analysis and generation, and the semantic-pragmatic interpretation in both the speak and the hear mode.

The verification of a theory of language and grammar by means of testing an electronic model in real applications is a new approach which clearly differs from the methods of traditional linguistics, psychology, philosophy, and mathematical logic.

VI. THEORETICAL LEVELS OF ABSTRACTION

So far there are no electronic systems which model the functioning of natural communication so successfully that one can talk with them more or less freely. Furthermore, researchers do not agree on how the mechanism of natural communication really works. One may therefore question whether achieving a functional model of natural communication is possible in principle. I would like to answer this question with an analogy[3] from the recent history of science.

Today's situation in computational linguistics resembles the development of mechanical flight before 1903.[4] For hundreds of years humans had observed sparrows and other birds in order to understand how they fly. Their goal was to become airborne in a similar manner. It turned out, however, that flapping wings did not work for humans. This was taken by some as a basis for declaring human flight impossible in principle, in accordance with the pious cliché "If God had intended humans to fly, He would have given them wings."[5]

---

[3] See also CoL, p. 317.

[4] In 1903, the brothers Orville and Wilbur Wright succeeded with the first manned motorized flight.

[5] Irrational reasons against a modeling of natural communication reside in the subconscious fear of creating artificial beings resembling humans and having superhuman powers. Such *homunculi*, which occur in the earliest of mythologies, are regarded widely as violating a tabu. The tabu of Doppelgänger-similarity is described in Girard (1972).

Besides dark versions of homunculi, such as the cabalistically inspired Golem and the electrically initialized creature of the surgeon Dr. Victor Frankenstein, the literature provides also more lighthearted variants. Examples are the piano-playing doll automata of the 18th century, based on the anatomical and physical knowledge of their time, and the mechanical beauty singing and dancing in *The Tales of Hoffmann*. More recent is the robot C3P0 in George Lucas' film *Star Wars*, which represents a positive view of human-like

Today human air travel is commonplace. Furthermore, we now know that a sparrow remains air-borne in accordance with the same aero-dynamic principles as a jumbo jet. Thus, there is a certain level of abstraction at which the flights of sparrows and jumbo jets function in the same way.

Similarly, the modeling of natural communication requires an abstract theory which applies to human and artificial cognitive machines alike. Thereby, one naturally runs the risk of setting the level of abstraction either too low or too high. As in the case of flying, the crucial problem is finding the correct level of abstraction.

A level of abstraction which is too low is exemplified by closed signal systems such as vending machines. Such machines are inappropriate as a theoretical model because they fail to capture the diversity of natural language use, i.e., the characteristic property that one and the same expression may be used meaningfully in different contexts.

A level of abstraction which is too high, on the other hand, is exemplified by naive anthropomorphic expectations. For example, a notion of 'proper understanding' which requires that the computational system be subtly amused when scanning *Finnegans Wake* is as far off the mark as a notion of 'proper flying' which requires mating and breeding behavior from a jumbo jet.[6]

VII. ANALYZING HUMAN COGNITION

The history of mechanical flight shows how a natural process (bird flight) poses a conceptually simple and obvious problem to science. Despite great efforts it was un-solvable for a long time. In the end, the solution turned out to be a highly abstract mathematical theory. In addition to being a successful foundation of mechanical flight, this theory is able to explain the functioning of natural flight as well.

This is why the abstract theory of aero-dynamics has led to a new appreciation of nature. Once the development of biplanes, turboprops, and jets resulted in a better the-oretical and practical understanding of the principles of flight, interest was refocussed again on the natural flight of animals in order to grasp their wonderful efficiency and power. This in turn led to major improvements in artificial flight, resulting in less noisy and more fuel-efficient airplanes.

Applied to computational linguistics, this analogy shows that our abstract and tech-nological approach does not imply a lack of interest in the human language capacity. On the contrary, investigating the particular properties of natural language communi-cation by humans is meaningful only *after* the mechanism of natural language com-munication has been understood in principle, modeled computationally, and proven successful in concrete applications on massive amounts of data.

---

robots.

[6] Though this may seem reasonable from the viewpoint of sparrows.

VIII. Internal and External Truths

In science we may distinguish between internal and external truths. Internal truths are conceptual models, developed and used by scientists to explain certain phenomena, and held true by relevant parts of society for limited periods of time. Examples are the Ptolemaic (geocentric) view of planetary motion or Bohr's model of the atom.

External truths are the bare facts of external reality which exist irrespective of whether or not there are cognitive agents to appreciate them. These facts may be measured more or less accurately, and explained using conceptual models.

Because conceptual models of science have been known to change radically in the course of history, internal truths must be viewed as *hypotheses*. They are justified mainly by the degree to which they are ably to systematically describe and explain large amounts of real data.

Especially in the natural sciences, internal truths have improved dramatically over the last five centuries. This is shown by an increasingly close fit between theoretical predictions and data, as well as a theoretical consolidation exhibited in the form of greater mathematical precision and greater functional coherence of the conceptual (sub)models.

In contrast, contemporary linguistics is characterized by a lack of theoretical consolidation, as shown by the many disparate theories of language[7] and the overwhelming variety of competing theories of grammar.[8] As in the natural sciences, however, there is external truth also in linguistics. It may be approximated by completeness of empirical data coverage and functional modeling.

IX. Linguistic Verification

The relation between internal and external truth is established by means of a *verification method*. The verification method of the natural sciences is the repeatability of experiments. This means that, given the same initial conditions, the same measurements must result again and again.

On the one hand, this method is not without problems because experimental data may be interpreted in different ways and may thus support different, even conflicting, hypotheses. On the other hand, the requirements of this method are so minimal that by now no self-respecting theory of natural science can afford to reject it. Therefore

---

[7] Examples are nativism, behaviorism, structuralism, speech act theory, model theory, as well Givón's (1985) iconicity, Lieb's (1992) neostructuralism, and Halliday's (1985) systemic approach.

[8] Known by acronyms such as TG (with its different manifestations ST, EST, REST, and GB), LFG, GPSG, HPSG, CG, CCG, CUG, FUG, UCG, etc. These theories of grammar concentrate mostly on an initial foundation of internal truths such as 'psychological reality,' 'innate knowledge,' 'explanatory adequacy,' 'universals,' 'principles,' etc., based on suitably selected examples. Cf. Sect. 9.5.

the repeatability of experiments has managed to channel the competing forces in the natural sciences in a constructive manner.

Another aspect of achieving scientific truth has developed in the tradition of mathematical logic. This is the principle of formal consistency, as realized in the method of axiomatization and the rule-based derivation of theorems.

Taken by itself the quasi-mechanical reconstruction of mathematical intuition in the form of axiom systems is separate from the facts of scientific measurements. As the logical foundation of natural science theories, however, the method of axiomatization has proven to be a helpful complement to the principle of repeatable experiments.

In linguistics, corresponding methods of verification have sorely been missing. To make up for this shortcoming there have been repeated attempts to remodel linguistics into either a natural science or a branch of mathematical logic. Such attempts are bound to fail, however, for the following reasons:

– The principle of repeatable experiments can only be applied under precisely defined conditions suitable for measuring. The method of experiments is not suitable for linguistics because the objects of description are *conventions* which have developed over the course of centuries and exist as the intuitions ("Sprachgefühl") of the native speaker-hearer.
– The method of axiomatization can only be applied to theories which have consolidated on a high level of abstraction, such as Newtonian mechanics, thermodynamics, or the theory of relativity. In today's linguistics, there is neither the required consolidation of theory nor completeness of data coverage. Therefore, any attempt at axiomatization in current linguistics is bound to be empirically vacuous.

Happily, there is no necessity to borrow from the neighboring sciences in order to arrive at a methodological foundation of linguistics. Instead, theories of language and grammar are to be implemented as electronic models which are tested automatically on arbitrarily large amounts of real data as well as in real applications of spontaneous human-computer communication. This method of verifying or falsifying linguistic theories objectively is specific to computational linguistics and may be viewed as the counterpart of the repeatability of experiments in the natural sciences.

X. EMPIRICAL DATA AND THEIR THEORETICAL FRAMEWORK

The methodology of computational linguistics presupposes a theory of language which defines the goals of empirical analysis and provides the framework into which components are to be embedded without conflict or redundancy. The development of such a framework can be extraordinarily difficult, as witnessed again and again in the history of science.

For example, in the beginning of astronomy scientists wrestled for centuries with the problem of providing a functional framework to explain the measurements that had been made of planetary motion and to make correct predictions based on such a framework. It was comparatively recently that Copernicus (1473–1543), Kepler

(1571–1630) and Newton (1642–1727) first succeeded with a description which was both empirically precise and functionally simple. This, however, required the overthrow of clusters of belief held to be true for millennia.

The revolution affected the *structural hypothesis* (transition from geo- to heliocentrism), the *functional explanation* (transition from crystal spheres to gravitation in space), and the *mathematical model* (transition from a complicated system of epicycles to the form of ellipses). Furthermore, the new system of astronomy was constructed at a level of abstraction where the dropping of an apple and the trajectory of the moon are explained as instantiations of one and the same set of general principles.

In linguistics, a corresponding scientific revolution has long been overdue. Even though the empirical data and the goals of their theoretical description are no less clear in linguistics than in astronomy, linguistics has not achieved a comparable consolidation in the form of a comprehensive, verifiable, functional theory of language.[9]

XI. Principles of the Slim Theory of Language

The analysis of natural communication should be structured in terms of methodological, empirical, ontological, and functional principles of the most general kind. The SLIM theory of language presented in this book is based on *Surface compositional, Linear, Internal Matching*. These principles are defined as follows.

1. *Surface compositional* (methodological principle)
   Syntactic-semantic composition assembles only concrete word forms, excluding all operations known to increase computational complexity to exponential or undecidable, such as using zero-elements, identity mappings, or transformations.
2. *Linear* (empirical principle)
   Interpretation and production of utterances are based on a strictly time-linear derivation order.
3. *Internal* (ontological principle)
   Interpretation and production of utterances are analyzed as cognitive procedures located inside the speaker-hearer.
4. *Matching* (functional principle)
   Referring with language to past, current, or future objects and events, relations, and properties is modeled in terms of pattern matching between language meaning and a context, defined as content in a speaker-hearer internal database.

These principles originate in widely different areas (methodology, ontology, etc.), but within the SLIM theory of language they interact very closely. For example, the functional principle of (4) matching can only be implemented on a computer if the overall

---

[9] From a history of science point of view, the fragmentation of today's linguistics resembles the state of astronomy before Copernicus, Kepler, and Newton.

system is handled ontologically as (3) an internal procedure of the cognitive agent. Furthermore, the methodological principle of (1) surface compositionality and the empirical principle of (2) time-linearity can be realized within a functional mechanism of communication only if the overall theory is based on internal matching (3,4).

In addition to what its letters stand for, the acronym SLIM is motivated as a word with a meaning like *slender*. This is so because detailed mathematical and computational investigations have proven SLIM to be efficient in the areas of syntax, semantics, and pragmatics – both relatively in comparison to existing alternatives, and absolutely in accordance with the formal principles of mathematical complexity theory.

XII. CHALLENGES AND SOLUTIONS

The SLIM theory of language is defined on a level of abstraction at which the mechanism of natural language communication in humans and in suitably constructed cognitive machines is explained in terms of the same principles of surface compositional, linear, internal matching.[10] This is an important precondition for unrestricted human-computer communication in natural language. Its realization requires general and efficient solutions in the following areas.

First, SLIM must model the hearer's *understanding* of natural language. This process is realized as the automatic reading-in of propositions into a database and – most importantly – determining the correct place for their storage and retrieval. The semantic primitives are defined as the artificial or natural agent's basic recognition and action procedures (and not as truth conditions).

Second, SLIM must model the speaker's *production* of natural language. This includes determining the content to be expressed in language, traditionally called *conceptualization*. In its simplest form, it is realized as an autonomous navigation through the propositions of the agent-internal database. Thereby speech production is handled as a direct reflection (internal matching) of the navigation path in line with the motto: *speech is verbalized thought*.

Third, SLIM must derive blueprints for action by means of *inferences*. The autonomous control of the agent's actions is driven by the principle of maintaining the agent in a state of balance vis-à-vis a continuously changing external and internal environment. Inferencing also plays an important role in the pragmatics of natural language, both in the hear and the speak mode.

---

[10] Moreover, the *structural hypothesis* of the SLIM theory of language is a regular, strictly time-linear derivation order – in contrast to grammar systems based on constituent structure. The *functional explanation* of SLIM is designed to model the mechanism of natural communication as a speaking robot – and not some tacit language knowledge innate in the speaker-hearer which excludes language use (performance). The *mathematical model* of SLIM is the continuation-based algorithm of LA-grammar, and not the substitution-based algorithms of the last 50 years.

CONCLUDING REMARK

In summary, the vision of unrestricted natural language communication between humans and machines is like the vision of motorized flight a 110 years ago: largely solved theoretically, but not yet realized in practical systems. At this point, all it will take to really succeed in computational linguistics is a well-directed, concentrated, sustained effort in cooperation with robotics, artificial intelligence, and psychology.

Part I

Theory of Language

1. Computational Analysis of Natural Language

Computational linguistics may be defined as an application of computer science to modeling natural language communication as a software system. This includes a linguistic analysis of natural language using computers. Given that the natural languages are based on social conventions, computational linguistics is located at the historical divide between the natural sciences and mathematics,[1] on the one hand, and the humanities and social sciences, on the other. In the beginnings of computer science in the 1940s, this divide opened as the distinction between numerical and non-numerical computation.

Numerical computation specializes in the calculation of numbers. In the fields of physics, chemistry, astronomy, etc., it has led to a tremendous expansion of scientific knowledge. Also many applications like banking, air travel, stock inventory, manufacturing, etc., depend heavily on numerical computation. Without computers and their software, operations could not be maintained in these areas.

Non-numerical computation deals with the phenomena of perception and cognition. Despite hopeful beginnings, non-numerical computer science soon lagged behind the numerical branch. In recent years, however, non-numerical computer science has made a comeback as artificial intelligence and cognitive science. These new, interdisciplinary fields investigate and electronically model natural information processing.

Computational linguistics is presented here as an application of non-numerical computer science to the analysis of natural language communication in the form of a talking robot. The goals of the computational model are completeness of function and of data coverage as well as processing in real time. Central notions are external interface, functional flow, component structure, data structure, database schema, and algorithm. Our approach draws from traditional and theoretical linguistics, lexicography, corpus linguistics, the psychology of language, analytic philosophy and logic, text processing, and the interaction with databases in natural language.

---

[1] In German, mathematics and the natural sciences are combined in the notion mathematisch-naturwissenschaftliche Fächer.

R. Hausser, *Foundations of Computational Linguistics*,
DOI 10.1007/978-3-642-41431-2_1, © Springer-Verlag Berlin Heidelberg 2014

1.1 Human-Computer Communication

In fiction, there are artificial cognitive agents (robots) which a human can talk with as with another human. This is called *nonrestricted* human-machine communication in natural language. It requires modeling the functioning of natural language communication and constitutes the ultimate standard for a successful computational linguistics.

Today, however, human-machine communication is still limited to highly *restricted* forms. Consider, for example, the interaction between the user and a standard computer, such as a PC or a workstation. The main input and output devices are the keyboard and the screen for the transfer of alphanumerical sequences.[2] Therefore, computers are convenient for entering, editing, and retrieving natural language, at least in the medium of writing, thus replacing electric typewriters.

For utilizing the computers' abilities beyond word processing, however, commands using artificial languages must be applied. These are called programming languages, and are especially designed for controlling the computer's electronic operations. In contrast to natural languages, which are flexible and rely on the seemingly obvious circumstances of the utterance situation, common background knowledge, the content of earlier conversations, etc., programming languages are inflexible and refer directly, explicitly, and exclusively to operations of the machine.

For most potential users, a programming language is difficult to handle because (a) they are not familiar with the operations of the computer, (b) the expressions of the programming language differ from those of everyday language, and (c) the use of the programming language requires great precision. Consider, for example, a standard database[3] which stores information about the employees of a company in the form of records:

---

[2] For simplicity, we are disregarding additional input and output devices, such as mouse and loud-speakers, respectively.

It is conceivable that one could expand the notion of human-machine communication to machines which do not provide general input-output components for language signs. Consider, for example, the operation of a contemporary washing machine. Leaving aside the loading of laundry and the measuring of detergent, the 'communication' consists in choosing a program and a temperature and pushing the start button. The machine 'answers' by providing freshly cleaned laundry once the program has run its course.

Such an expanded notion of human-machine communication should be avoided, however, because it fosters misunderstandings. Machines without general input-output facilities for language constitute the special case of *nonlanguage* human-machine communication.

[3] As introductions to databases see Elmasri and Navathe (2010), Date (2003). We will return to this topic in Chap. 22 in connection with the interpretation of natural language.

1.1.1 EXAMPLE OF A RECORD-BASED DATABASE

	last name	first name	place	...
A1	Schmidt	Peter	Bamberg	...
A2	Meyer	Susanne	Nürnberg	...
A3	Sanders	Reinhard	Schwabach	...
	⋮	⋮	⋮	

The rows, named by different attributes like first name, last name, etc., are called the fields of the record type. The lines A1, A2, etc., each constitute a record. Based on this fixed record structure, the standard operations for the retrieval and update of information in the database are defined.

To retrieve the name of the representative in, for example, Schwabach, the user must type in the following commands of the programming language (here, a query language for databases) without mistake:

1.1.2 DATABASE QUERY

Query:
```
select A#
where city = 'Schwabach'
```
Result:
```
result: A3 Sanders Reinhard
```

The correct use of commands such as `select` initiates quasi-mechanical procedures which correspond to filing and retrieving cards in a filing cabinet with many compartments. Compared to the nonelectronic method, the computational system has many practical advantages. The electronic version is faster, the adding and removing of information is simpler, and the possibilities of search are much more powerful because various different keywords may be logically combined into a complex query.[4] Is it possible to gradually extend such an interaction with a computer to natural language?

Standard computers have been regarded as general-purpose machines for information processing because any kind of standard program can be developed and installed on them. From this point of view, their capabilities are restricted only by hardware factors like available speed and memory. In another sense, the information processing of standard computers is not general-purpose, however, because their input and output facilities are restricted to alphanumerical sequences.

A second type of computer not subject to this limitation is autonomous[5] robots. In contradistinction to standard computers, the input and output of autonomous robots is not restricted to alphanumerical sequences. Instead they are designed to recognize their environment and to act in it.

---

[4] See also Sect. 2.1.

[5] Today three different generations of robots are distinguished. Most relevant for computational linguistics are robots of the third generation, which are designed as autonomous agents. See Wloka (1992).

Corresponding to the different technologies of standard computers and robots, there have evolved two different branches of artificial intelligence. One branch, dubbed classic AI by its opponents, is based on standard computers. The other branch, which calls itself nouvelle AI,[6] requires the technology of robots.

Classic AI analyzes intelligent behavior in terms of manipulating abstract symbols. A typical example is a chess-playing program.[7] It operates in isolation from the rest of the world, using a fixed set of predefined pieces and a predefined board. The search space for a dynamic strategy of winning in chess is astronomical. Yet the technology of a standard computer is sufficient because the world of chess is closed.

Nouvelle AI aims at the development of autonomous agents. In contrast to systems which respond solely to a predefined set of user commands and behave otherwise in isolation, autonomous agents are designed to interact with their real-world environment. Because the environment is constantly changing in unpredictable ways they must continually keep track of it by means of sensors.

For this, nouvelle AI uses the strategy of task level decomposition (Brooks 1986). Rather than building and updating one giant global representation to serve as the basis of automatic reasoning, nouvelle AI systems aim at handling their tasks in terms of many interacting local procedures controlled by perception. Thereby inferencing operates directly on the local perception data.

A third type of machine processing information – besides standard computers and robots – is systems of virtual reality (VR).[8] While a robot analyzes its environment in order to influence it in certain ways (such as moving in it), a VR system aims at creating an artificial environment for the user. Thereby the VR system reacts to the movements of the user's hand, the direction of his gaze, etc., and utilizes them in order to create as realistic an environment as possible.

The different types of human-computer communication exemplified by standard computers, robots, and VR systems may be compared schematically as follows:

1.1.3 THREE TYPES OF HUMAN-COMPUTER INTERACTION

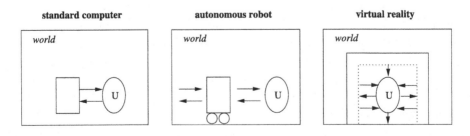

---

[6] See for example Maes (ed.) (1990).

[7] Newell and Simon (1972), Reddy et al. (1973).

[8] For an introduction see Wexelblat (ed.) (1993).

The ovals represent the user who faces the respective systems in the world. The arrows represent the interaction of the systems with their environment and the user.

A standard computer interacts solely with its user, who initiates the communication. A robot interacts autonomously with its environment and its user. A VR system does not interact with its environment, but rather creates an artificial environment for the user. In robots and VR systems, communication with the user in terms of language is optional and may be found only in advanced systems. These systems must always have an alphanumerical 'service channel,' however, for the installation and upgrading of the system software.

1.2 Language Sciences and Their Components

A speaker of English knows the meaning of a word like red. When asked to pick the red object among a set of non-red objects, for example, a competent speaker-hearer will be able to do it. A standard computer, on the other hand, does not 'understand' what red means, just as a piece of paper does not understand what is written on it.[9]

In the interaction with a standard computer, the understanding of natural language is restricted largely[10] to the user. For example, if a user searches in a database for a red object, he understands the word red before it is put into – and after it is given out by – the standard computer. But inside the standard computer, the word red is manipulated as a sign which is uninterpreted with respect to the color denoted.

What is true for standard computers does not apply to human-computer communication in general, however. Consider for example a modern robot which is asked by its master to get an object it has not previously encountered, for example, the new blue and yellow book on the desk in the other room.[11] If such a robot is able to spontaneously perform an open range of different tasks like this, it has an understanding of language which at some level may be regarded as functionally equivalent to the corresponding cognitive procedures in humans.

The communication with a robot may be based on either artificial or natural language. The use of natural language is more challenging, however, and preferable in many situations. As a first step towards achieving unrestricted human-computer communication in natural language, let us consider the current state of linguistics.

---

[9] This fact has been misunderstood to imply that a modeling of understanding in AI is impossible in principle. An example which is as prominent as it is mistaken is the 'Chinese room argument' in Searle (1992).

[10] Even a standard computer may interpret certain structural aspects of language, however, such as the categories of the word forms.

[11] Reference to objects removed in time and/or space is called *displaced reference*.

In this field of research, three basic approaches to natural language analysis may be distinguished, namely (i) traditional grammar, (ii) theoretical linguistics, and (iii) computational linguistics. They differ in their methods, goals, and applications.

1.2.1 THREE APPROACHES TO ANALYZING NATURAL LANGUAGE

I *Traditional Grammar*
- (a) uses the method of informal classification and description based on tradition and experience,
- (b) has the goal to collect and classify the regularities and irregularities of the natural language in question as completely as possible, and
- (c) is applied mostly in the teaching of languages (originally Latin).

While traditional grammar has long been shunted aside by theoretical linguistics, it has been of great interest to computational linguistics because of its wealth of concrete data. The notions of traditional grammar will be discussed in detail in Part III.

II *Theoretical Linguistics*
- (a) uses the method of mathematical logic to describe natural languages by means of formal rule systems intended to derive all and only the well-formed expressions of a language (explicit hypothesis formation instead of the informal descriptions of traditional grammar),
- (b) has pursued the goal of describing the 'innate human language ability' (competence), whereby aspects of language use in communication (performance) have been excluded, and
- (c) has had rather limited applications because of its computational inefficiency and because of its fragmentation into different schools.

Theoretical linguistics is relevant to computational linguistics in the area of formal language analysis and mathematical complexity theory. Formal language theory will be discussed in detail in Part II.

III *Computational Linguistics*
- (a) combines the methods of traditional grammar and theoretical linguistics with the method of effectively verifying explicit hypotheses by implementing formal grammars as efficient computer programs and testing them automatically on realistic – i.e., large – amounts of real data,
- (b) has the goal of modeling the mechanism of natural language communication – which requires a complete morphological, lexical, syntactic, semantic, and pragmatic analysis of a given natural language within a functional framework, and
- (c) has applications in all instances of human-computer communication far beyond letter-based 'natural language processing' (NLP).

Despite their different methods, goals, and applications, the three variants of language science described divide the field into the same components, namely phonology, morphology, lexicon, syntax, semantics, and the additional field of pragmatics.

The roles played by these components and the methods in which they are handled scientifically differ, however, within the three approaches.

1.2.2 THE COMPONENTS OF GRAMMAR

Phonology: Science of language sounds

    I In traditional linguistics, phonology is the study of historical changes as well as synchronic alternations in the spoken surface of word forms, such as trisyllabic laxing in English (sincere/sincerity) or final devoicing in German (König, Könige) by informal description.

    II In theoretical linguistics, phonology is concerned with the systematic organization of sounds in a language. Regarding phonology as a microcosm of the human language ability, nativism has attempted to use the same formal constructs such as distinctive features and constraints in phonology and in syntax.

    III In computational linguistics, the role of phonology is marginal because spoken language is just one modality besides written and signed language. Instead, the emphasis is on analyzing natural language at a level of abstraction which is independent of any particular medium of manifestation (modality, e.g., sound, Sect. 1.4).

One might conceive of using phonology in peripheral cognition for automatic speech recognition and synthesis, but the appropriate science is in fact phonetics. Phonetics investigates the (i) articulatory, (ii) acoustic, and (iii) auditive processes of speech. In contrast to phonology, phonetics is traditionally not considered part of the grammar and justly so because phonetics is explicitly limited to the sensory modality of sound.

Morphology: Science of word form structure

    I In traditional grammar, morphology classifies the words of a language according to their part of speech (category) and other properties such as gender, number, case, and tense, and describes the structure of word forms in terms of inflection/agglutination, derivation, and composition. To traditional grammar, morphology has long been central, as shown by the many paradigm tables in grammars of Latin.

    II In theoretical linguistics, morphology has played a minor role. Squeezed between phonology and syntax, morphology has been used mostly to exemplify principles of either or both of its neighboring components.

    III In computational linguistics, morphology is used in automatic word form recognition. Based on an online lexicon and a morphological parser, (i) each word form is related to its base form (lemmatization) and (ii) characterized in terms of its morpho-syntactic properties (categorization).

In computational linguistics, automatic word form recognition is fundamental. Required for the syntactic and semantic parsing in the hear mode, the morphological analyses are re-used for language production in the speak mode.

Lexicon: Listing analyzed words

    I In traditional grammar, the words of a language are collected and classified in lexicography and lexicology. Lexicography deals with the principles of coding and structuring lexical entries, and is a practically oriented border area of natural language science. Lexicology investigates semantic relations in the vocabulary of a language and is part of traditional philology.

    II In theoretical linguistics, interest in the lexicon has steadily increased, focusing on the distributed nature of compositionality in natural language.[12]

    III In computational linguistics, electronic lexica combine with morphological parsers in the task of automatic word form recognition. The goal is maximal completeness of data coverage with fast access and low space requirements. For building online lexica, the knowledge contained in traditional lexica has proved to be most valuable ('mining of dictionaries').

With the advent of computers, the building of electronic lexica for different natural languages has been assisted by the building of larger and larger corpora in corpus linguistics (Chaps. 13–15).

Syntax: Science of assembling word forms into sentences

    I In traditional linguistics, certain syntactic constructions such as the AcI in Latin are described informally, using examples.

    II In theoretical linguistics, syntactic analysis has concentrated on a description of grammatical well-formedness. The problem with analyzing well-formedness in isolation is that any finite set of sentences may be described by a vast multitude of different grammars. In order to select the one type of description which turns out to be correct in the long run, theoretical linguistics has vainly searched for 'universals' supposed to characterize the 'innate human language faculty.'

    III In computational linguistics, the syntax must be suitable to serve as a component in an artificial cognitive agent *communicating* in natural language. This constitutes a more realistic and effective standard than intuitions of well-formedness alone, because the descriptive and functional adequacy of the grammar system may be tested automatically on the full range of natural language data. The parsing algorithm must be input-output-equivalent with the mechanism of natural language and be of low mathematical complexity.

In communication, the task of syntax is the composition of meanings via the composition of word forms surfaces.[13] One aspect of this is characterizing well-formed compositions in terms of grammatical rules. The other is to provide the basis for a simultaneous semantic interpretation.

---

[12] Bresnan (ed.) (1982), Pustejovsky (1995).

[13] Sect. 19.1.

Semantics: Science of literal meanings

    I The beginning of traditional Western grammar contributed considerably to the theory of semantics, for example, Aristotle's distinction between subject and predicate. However, these contributions were passed on and developed mostly within philosophy of language. In the teaching of traditional grammar, the treatment of semantics did not reach beyond the anecdotal.

    II In theoretical linguistics, semantics was initially limited to characterizing syntactic ambiguity and paraphrase. Subsequently, truth-conditional semantics has been applied to natural language: using a metalanguage, natural language meanings are defined relative to a formal model based on set-theory.

    III Computational linguistics uses a procedural semantics instead of a metalanguage-based logical semantics. The semantic primitives of a procedural semantics are based on the elementary operations of recognition and action by the cognitive agent (grounding). The procedural semantics is designed to be used by the pragmatics in an explicit modeling of the information transfer between speaker and hearer (24.2.3).

The field is naturally divided into (i) lexical semantics, describing the meaning of words, and (ii) compositional semantics, describing the composition of meanings in accordance with the syntax. In the hear mode, the task of semantics is a systematic conversion of the syntactically analyzed expression into a semantic representation based on the functor-argument and coordination.

Pragmatics: Science of using language expressions relative to a context of use

    I In traditional grammar, the phenomena of pragmatics have been handled in the separate discipline of rhetoric. This has been an obstacle to integrating the structural analysis of language signs (grammar) and their use (pragmatics) into a functional model of communication.

    II In theoretical linguistics, the distinction between semantics and pragmatics has evolved only haltingly. Because theoretical linguistics has not been based on a functional model of communication, pragmatics has served mostly as the proverbial 'wastebasket' (Bar-Hillel 1971, p. 405).

    III In computational linguistics, the need for a systematic theory of pragmatics became most obvious in natural language generation – as in dialog systems or machine translation, in which the system has to decide what to say and how to say it in a rhetorically acceptable way.

While the *theory of grammar* is limited to the structural analysis of the language signs, i.e., words, word forms, and sentences in isolation, the *theory of language* includes (i) the theory of grammar, (ii) the explicit definition of the context of use, and (iii) the pragmatics describing the interaction between the language expressions and the context of use in an *utterance*.

That the different approaches of traditional grammar, theoretical linguistics, and computational linguistics use the same set of components to describe the phenomena of natural language – despite their different methods and goals – is due to the fact that the division of phenomena underlying these components is based on different structural aspects, namely *sounds* (phonology), *word forms* (morphology), *sentences* (syntax), literal *meanings* (semantics), and their *use* in communication (pragmatics).

1.3 Methods and Applications of Computational Linguistics

Computational linguistics uses parsers for the automatic analysis of language. The term 'parser' is derived from the Latin word *pars* meaning part, as in 'part of speech.' Parsing in its most basic form consists in the automatic

1. *decomposition* of a complex sign into its elementary components,
2. *classification* of the components[14] via lexical lookup, and
3. *composition* of the classified components by means of rules in order to arrive at an overall grammatical analysis of the complex sign.[15]

Methodologically, the implementation of natural language grammars as parsers is important because it allows one to test the descriptive adequacy of formal rule systems automatically, and therefore reliably objectively, on real data. This new method of verification is as characteristic for computational linguistics as the method of repeatable experiments is for natural science.

Practically, the parsing of natural language may be used in different applications.

1.3.1 PRACTICAL TASKS OF COMPUTATIONAL LINGUISTICS

(a) *Indexing and retrieval in textual databases*

Textual databases electronically store texts such as publications of daily newspapers, medical journals, and court decisions. The user of such a database should be able to find exactly those documents and passages with ease and speed which are relevant for the specific task in question. The World Wide Web (WWW) may also be viewed as a large, unstructured textual database, which demonstrates daily to a growing number of users the difficulties of successfully finding the information desired. Linguistic methods for optimizing retrieval are described in Sect. 2.2.

(b) *Machine translation*

Especially in the European Union, currently with 24 official languages, the potential utility of automatic or even semi-automatic translation systems is tremendous. Different approaches to machine translation are described in Sects. 2.4 and 2.5.

(c) *Automatic text production*

Large companies which continually bring out new products such as motors, CD players, farming equipment, etc., must constantly modify the associated product descriptions and maintenance manuals. A similar situation holds for lawyers, tax

---

[14] By assigning, for example, the part of speech.

[15] Including assignment of the part of speech.

accountants, personnel officers, etc., who must deal with large amounts of correspondence in which most of the letters differ only in a few, well-defined places.
Here techniques of automatic text production can help, ranging from simple templates to highly flexible and interactive systems using sophisticated linguistic
knowledge.

(d) *Automatic text checking*

Applications in this area range from simple spelling checkers (based on word
form lists) via word form recognition (based on a morphological parser) to syntax
checkers based on syntactic parsers which can find errors in word order, agreement, etc.

(e) *Automatic content analysis*

The letter-based information on this planet has been said to double every ten
years. Even in specialized fields such as natural science, law, and economics, the
constant stream of relevant new literature is so large that researchers and profes-
sionals do not nearly have enough time to read it all. A reliable automatic content
analysis in the form of brief summaries would be very useful. Automatic content
analysis is also a precondition for concept-based indexing, needed for accurate
retrieval from textual databases, as well as for adequate machine translation.

(f) *Automatic tutoring*

There are numerous areas of teaching in which much time is spent on drill exercises such as the more or less mechanical practicing of regular and irregular
paradigms in foreign languages. These may be done just as well on the computer,
providing the students with more fun (if they are presented as a game, for example) and the teacher with additional time for other, more sophisticated activities
such as conversation.

Furthermore, these systems may produce automatic protocols detailing the most
frequent errors and the amount of time needed for various phases of the exercise.
This constitutes a valuable heuristics for improving the automatic tutoring system
ergonometrically. It has led to a new field of research in which the 'electronic text
book' of old is replaced by new teaching programs utilizing the special possibilities of the electronic medium to facilitate learning in ways never explored before.

(g) *Automatic dialog and information systems*

These applications range from automatic information services for train schedules
via queries and storage in medical databases to automatic tax consulting.

This list is by no means complete, however, because the possible applications of computational linguistics include all areas in which humans communicate with computers
and other machines of this level, today and in the future.

1.4 Electronic Medium in Recognition and Synthesis

The signs of natural language may be realized in different modalities, such as the
sounds of spoken language, the *letters* of handwritten or printed language, and the

gestures of signed language. Spoken and signed languages in their original forms have a fleeting existence, while written language is the traditional method of storing information more permanently, e.g., on stone, clay, wood, papyrus, parchment, or paper.

A modern form of storing information is the electronic medium. It codes information abstractly in terms of numbers which are represented magnetically. In contrast to the traditional means of storage, the electronic medium has the advantage of great flexibility: the data may be copied, edited, sorted, reformatted, and transferred at will.

The electronic medium may represent language in a modality-independent or a modality-dependent form. The modality-independent form represents language as abstract *types*, coded digitally as electronic sign sequences, e.g., in ASCII[16] or Unicode. The modality-dependent form reproduces accidental properties of *tokens* in a certain modality, such as a tape recording of spoken language, a bitmap of written language, or a video recording of signed language. As types,[17] the signs may be recognized unambiguously by suitable machines, copied without loss of information, and realized as token surfaces in any imaginable variant in any of the language modalities.

In communication, there is a constant transfer between modality-dependent and modality-independent representations. During recognition in the hear mode, modality-dependent tokens are mapped into the modality-independent types (d$\Rightarrow$i transfer). The technology for written language is called optical character recognition (OCR); for spoken language, it is called speech recognition.

During production in the speak mode, modality-independent types are mapped into modality-dependent tokens (i$\Rightarrow$d transfer). The technology of mapping types of language signs into spoken language is called speech synthesis and presents the challenge of achieving the appropriate realization for a wide range of different utterance situations; for print, the analogous mapping is into the appropriate fonts.

Especially, automatic speech recognition has been the subject of an intensive worldwide research effort. There are many users and many circumstances of use for which input to a computer based on spoken language would be considerably more user friendly than typing on a keyboard. The projects range from an "electronic secretary" capable of taking dictation to telephone-based automatic information systems (e.g., for train schedules) to Verbmobil.[18]

The quality of automatic speech recognition should be at least equal to that of an average human hearer. This leads to the following desiderata:

---

[16] ASCII stands for *American Standard Code for Information Interchange*.

[17] Each instance of such a type is coded identically to any other instance of the same type. For further discussion of the type-token distinction, see Sect. 3.3.

[18] Verbmobil (Wahlster 1993) was designed to allow speakers of German or Japanese with only a passive knowledge of English to arrange meetings. By translating German or Japanese input into English, Verbmobil allows the hearer to understand the output of the system, and the speaker to check whether the system has translated as intended (Sect. 2.5).

1.4.1 DESIDERATA OF AUTOMATIC SPEECH RECOGNITION

(a) *Speaker independence*
   The system should understand the speech of an open range of speakers with varying dialects, pitch, etc. – without the need for an initial learning phase to adapt
   the system to one particular user.

(b) *Continuous speech*
   The system should handle continuous speech at different speeds – without the
   need for unnatural pauses between individual word forms.

(c) *Domain independence*
   The system should understand spoken language independently of the subject matter – without the need to tell the system in advance which vocabulary is to be
   expected and which is not.

(d) *Realistic vocabulary*
   The system should recognize at least as many word forms as an average human.

(e) *Robustness*
   The system should recover gracefully from interruptions, contractions, and slurring of spoken language, and should be able to infer the word forms intended.

Today's continuous speech systems can achieve speaker independence only at the
price of domain dependence. The prior restriction to a certain domain – for example,
train schedules, or when and where to meet – facilitates recognition by drastically
reducing the number of hypotheses about the word forms underlying a given sound
pattern.[19]

The vocabulary of speaker-independent continuous speech recognition systems is
still limited to no more than 1 000 word forms. An average speaker, however, uses
about 10 000 words – which in English corresponds to about 40 000 word forms.
A speaker's passive vocabulary is about three to four times as large. Therefore a
speech recognition system for English would have to recognize 120 000 word forms in
order to be in the same class as an average speaker.[20] Accordingly, Zue et al. (1995)[21]
estimate that "It will be many years before unlimited vocabulary, speaker-independent
continuous dictation capability is realized."

Speech recognition will be fully successful only if the technological side is supplied
continuously with small bits of highly specific data from large stores of domain and

---

[19] Utilizing domain knowledge is crucial for inferring the most probable word sequence from
the acoustic signal in both human and artificial speech recognition. The point is that the system should be capable to determine the current domain automatically, instead of designing
the system for one specific domain only or requiring the user to preselect a domain.

[20] Based on (i) a training phase to adapt to a particular user and (ii) pauses between each word
form, the IBM-VoiceType system can recognize up to 22 000 different word forms.

[21] In Cole (ed.) (1998), p. 9.

language knowledge. These bits are needed only momentarily and must be provided very fast in order for the system to work in real time.

Therefore, the crucial question for designing truly adequate speech recognition is:

How should the domain and language knowledge best be organized?

The answer is obvious:

Within a functional theory of language which is mathematically and computationally efficient.

The better natural communication is modeled on the computer, the more effectively speech recognition can be supplied with the necessary bits of information. Conversely, the better the functioning of speech recognition, the easier the d⇒i transfer and thus the supply of knowledge needed for understanding during human-computer dialog.

1.5 Second Gutenberg Revolution

The first Gutenberg revolution[22] was based on the technological innovation of printing with movable letters. It made it possible to reproduce books inexpensively and in great numbers, making a wealth of information available to a broader public for the first time. This led to a rapid expansion of knowledge which in turn was stored and multiplied in the form of even more books.

Due to quickly expanding amounts of information being made freely available, it became increasingly difficult to *find* the relevant information for a given purpose. Today the accumulated wealth of printed information far exceeds the capacity of a human life span, even in narrowly defined subdomains of scientific research.

This is to be remedied by what has been called the second Gutenberg revolution (e.g., Howell (ed.) 1990), based on the technological innovation of the electronic medium. The automatic processing of natural language on the computer facilitates access to specific pieces of information in such a way that huge amounts of text can be searched quickly and comfortably, producing accurate and complete results.

The second Gutenberg revolution is supported by the fact that today's publications originate primarily in the electronic medium, making a d⇒i modality transfer from the conventional print media unnecessary. When texts are typed directly into the com-

---

[22] Named after Johannes Gutenberg, 1400?–1468?, who invented printing with movable type in Europe. This technique had been discovered earlier in China by Bi Sheng between 1041 and 1048 (Chen 1988, p. 121) and in Korea, probably around 1234 (Kim 1981; Park 1987).

One reason why the earlier discovery of this technique did not prevail is the great number of Chinese characters, which are not as suitable for printing as the roughly 40 characters of the Latin alphabet (the Korean alphabet *Hangul* was designed much later, in 1446). The other is that the early printing in Asia was done by hand only, whereas Gutenberg – presumably inspired by the wine presses of his time – integrated the printing blocks into a mechanism which facilitated and sped up the printing of pages, and which could be combined with an engine to run automatically.

puter, the traditional print medium becomes a secondary medium into which the electronic versions are converted only on demand.

Even texts which have long existed in the traditional print medium are nowadays being transferred into the electronic medium in order to make them susceptible to the methods of electronic processing. Examples are the complete texts of classical Greek and Latin, the complete Shakespeare, and the Encyclopædia Britannica, which are now available electronically.

Compared to the printed version of a multi-volume edition, the electronic medium has the advantage of compactness, ease of use, and speed. Instead of one having to haul several volumes from the shelf and leaf through hundreds of pages by hand in order to find a particular passage, the electronic version merely requires typing in a few keywords.

Given suitable software, it is also possible to search using combinations of words, enabling the retrieval of all passages in which, for example, painter, Venice, and 16th century occur within a certain interval of text. These methods of search can be life-saving, for example, when a textual database is used for diagnosing a rare disease, or for choosing a particular medication.

Another advantage of the electronic medium is the editing, formatting, and copying of text. In the old days, newspaper articles were put together with mechanical typesetting machines. Information coming in from a wire service had to be typeset from the ticker tape letter by letter. To make room for some late-breaking piece of news, the printing plate had to be rearranged by hand.

Today the production of newspapers is done primarily online in *soft copy*. Contributions by wire services are not delivered on paper, but by email. The form and contents of the online newspaper can be freely reformatted, copied, and edited, and any of these versions can be printed as *hard copies* without additional work.

The form of a newspaper article, like any text, is based on such structural features as title, name of author, date, section headers, sections, paragraphs, etc. In the electronic medium, this textual structure is coded abstractly by means of control symbols.

1.5.1 Newspaper Text with Control Symbols

```
<HTML>
<HEAD>
<TITLE>9/4/95 COVER: Siberia, the Tortured Land</TITLE>
</HEAD>
<BODY>
<!-- #include "header.html" -->
<P>TIME Magazine</P>
<P>September 4, 1995 Volume 146, No. 10</P>
<HR>
Return to <A href="../../../../../time/magazine/domestic/toc/
950904.toc.html">Contents page</A>
<HR>
<BR>
<!-- end include -->
```

```
<H3>COVER STORY</H3>
<H2>THE TORTURED LAND</H2>
<H3>An epic landscape steeped in tragedy, Siberia suffered
grievously under  communism. Now the world's capitalists covet
its vast riches </H3>
<P><EM>BY <A href="../../../../../time/bios/eugenelinden.html">
EUGENE LINDEN</A>/YAKUTSK</EM>
<P>Siberia has come to mean a land of exile, and the place
easily fulfills its reputation as a metaphor for death and
deprivation. Even at the peak of midsummer, a soul-chilling
fog blows in off the Arctic Ocean and across the mossy tundra,
muting the midnight sun above the ghostly remains of a
slave-labor camp. The mist settles like a shroud over broken
grave markers and bits of wooden barracks siding bleached
as gray as the bones of the dead that still protrude through
the earth in places. Throughout Siberia, more than 20 million
perished in Stalin's Gulag.     ...
```

To be positioned here, the text was copied electronically from a publication of TIME magazine available on the Internet. The example contains control symbols of the form <...>, which specify the formatting of the text in print or on the screen. For example, <P>September 4, 1995 Volume 146, No. 10</P> is to be treated in print as a paragraph, and <H2>THE TORTURED LAND</H2> as a header.

At first, different print shops used their own conventions to mark the formatting instructions, for which reason the control symbols had to be readjusted each time a text was moved to another typesetting system. To avoid this needless complication, the International Standards Organization (ISO) developed the SGML standard.

1.5.2 SGML: *Standard Generalized Markup Language*

> A family of ISO standards for labeling electronic versions of text, enabling both sender and receiver of the text to identify its structure (e.g., title, author, header, paragraph, etc.)
>
> Dictionary of Computing, p. 416 (Illingworth et al. (eds.) 1990)

Meanwhile, the SGML language,[23] exemplified in 1.5.1, has been replaced by an easier to use subset, called XML (for eXtensible Markup Language).[24] Use of a common markup language has the advantage that formatting instructions can be automatically interpreted by other users.

In addition to the standardized coding of textual building blocks such as header, subtitle, author, date, table of contents, paragraph, etc., there is the question of how different types of text, such as articles, novels, theater plays, and dictionaries, should best be constructed from these building blocks. For example, the textual building blocks of a theater play, i.e., the acts, the scenes, the dialog parts of different roles, and the stage descriptions, can all be coded in XML. Yet the general text structure of a play

---

[23] See Goldfarb (1990), van Herwijnen (1990).

[24] See St. Laurent (1998), Bray et al. (eds.) (2008), Salminen and Tompa (2011).

as compared to a newspaper article or a dictionary entry goes beyond the definition of the individual building blocks.

In order to standardize the structure of different types of texts, the International Standards Organization (ISO) began in 1987 to develop the TEI Guidelines. TEI stands for *Text Encoding Initiative* and defines a DTD (*Document Type Definition*) for the markup of different types of text in XML.[25]

XML and TEI specify the markup at the most abstract level insofar as they define the text structure and its building blocks in terms of their function (e.g., header), and not in terms of how this function is to be represented in print (e.g., bold face, 12 pt.). For this reason, texts conforming to the XML and TEI standards may be realized in any print style of choice without additional work.

An intermediate level of abstraction is represented by the formatting systems developed as programming languages for typesetting only a few years earlier. Widely used in academic circles are TEX, developed by Knuth (1984), and its macro package LATEX (Lamport 1986). Since they were first introduced in 1984 they have been used by scientists for preparing camera-ready manuscripts of research papers and books.

At the lowest level of abstraction are menu-based text processing systems on PCs, such as MS Office Word. They are initially easy to learn, but their control is comparatively limited, and they may have difficulty handling longer documents. Also, transferring text from one PC text processing system to another is difficult to impossible.

In summary, XML and TEI focus on defining the abstract structure of the text, TEX and LATEX focus on control of the print, and PC systems focus on the ease and comfort of the user. Thereby the higher level of abstraction, e.g., XML, can always be mapped onto a lower level, e.g., LATEX. The inverse direction, on the other hand, is not generally possible because the lower level control symbols have no unambiguous interpretation in terms of text structure.

XML/TEI and TEX/LATEX have in common that their control symbols are placed into the text's source code (as shown in 1.5.1) by hand; then they are interpreted by a program producing the corresponding print. PC systems, on the other hand, are based on WYSIWYG (*what you see is what you get*), i.e., the look of the print is manipulated by the user on the screen. In this process, the software automatically floods the text's source code with cryptic control symbols.

For authors, the production of camera-ready manuscripts on the computer has many practical advantages. With this method, called *desktop publishing* (DTP), the author can shape the form of the publication directly and there are no galley proofs to be corrected. Also, the time between text production and publication may be shortened, and the publication is much less expensive than with conventional typesetting.

For linguists, online texts have the advantage that they can be analyzed electronically. With most current publications originating in the electronic medium it is only

---

[25] A description of TEI Lite and bibliographical references may be found in Burnard and Sperberg-McQueen (1995).

a question of access and copyright to obtain arbitrarily large amounts of online text such as newspapers, novels, or scientific publications in various domains.

One linguistic task is to select from the vast amounts of electronically stored text a representative and balanced sample of the language (corpus construction, Chap. 15). Another is to analyze the texts in terms of their lexical, morphological, syntactic, and semantic properties. In either case, linguists are not interested in a text because of its content or layout, but as a genuine ("real") instance of natural language at a certain time and place – in contrast to the invented examples of "armchair linguistics."

There are many possibilities for processing an online text for linguistic analysis. For example, using some simple commands one may easily remove all control symbols from the text in 1.5.1 and then transform it into an alphabetical list of word forms.

1.5.3 ALPHABETICAL LIST OF WORD FORMS

10	in	STORY
146	in	suffered
1995	in	sun
20	its	than
4	its	that
a	LAND	The
a	land	the
a	landscape	the
a	like	the
a	LINDEN	the
above	Magazine	the
across	markers	the
and	mean	the
and	metaphor	the
and	midnight	the
and	midsummer	the
Arctic	million	through
as	mist	Throughout
as	more	to
barracks	mossy	to
bits	muting	TORTURED
bleached	No	tragedy
blows	Now	tundra
bones	of	vast
broken	of	Volume
camp	of	wooden
capitalists	of	world's
come	of	An
communism	off	as
Contents	page	at
covet	peak	COVER
dead	perished	EUGENE

death	place	fulfills
deprivation	places	ghostly
earth	protrude	in
easily	remains	Ocean
epic	reputation	over
Even	riches	Return
exile	settles	September
fog	shroud	Siberia
for	Siberia	Stalin's
grave	Siberia	THE
gray	siding	TIME
grievously	slave-labor	under
Gulag	soul-chilling	/YAKUTSK
has	steeped	

In this list, word forms are represented as often as they occur in the text, thus providing the basis for word form statistics. It would be just as easy, however, to create a unique list in which each word form is listed only once, as for lexical work. Another approach to analyzing an online text for linguistic purposes is measuring the co-occurrence of word forms next to each other, based on bigrams and trigrams.

These methods all have in common that they are *letter-based*.[26] They operate with the abstract, digitally coded signs in the electronic medium, whereby word forms are no more than sequences of letters between spaces. Compared to nonelectronic methods – such as typewriting, typesetting, card indexing, searching by leafing and/or reading through documents, or building alphabetical word lists by hand – the electronic computation on the basis of letters is fast, precise, and easy to use.

At the same time, the letter-based method is limited inasmuch as any grammatical analysis is by definition outside of its domain. Letter-based technology and grammatical analysis may work closely together, however. By combining the already powerful letter-based technology with the concepts and structures of a functional, mathematically efficient, and computationally suitable theory of language, natural language processing (NLP) may be greatly improved.

---

[26] In the sense of alphanumeric, i.e., including numbers and punctuation signs.

Exercises

Section 1.1
1. Describe three different variants of human-computer interaction.
2. In what sense is the interaction with a contemporary washing machine a special case of human-machine communication, and why is it not in the domain of computational linguistics?
3. Why is it difficult to get accustomed to programming languages, as in the interaction with a database?
4. Why is a standard computer a universal machine for processing information, yet at the same time of limited cognitive capacity in comparison to a robot?
5. Describe two different branches of artificial intelligence.
6. What is the difference in principle between a robot and a VR system?

Section 1.2
1. Why is the development of talking robots of special interest to the theoretical development of computational linguistics?
2. Compare three different approaches to language analysis and describe their different methods, goals, and applications.
3. What are the components of grammar and what are their respective functions?
4. Why do different approaches to language analysis use the same kinds of components, dividing the phenomena in the same way?

Section 1.3
1. Classify computational linguistics as a science. Explain the notions numerical, non-numerical, cognitive science, and artificial intelligence.
2. What sciences are integrated into computational linguistics in an interdisciplinary way?
3. What are the methodological consequences of programming in computational linguistics?
4. Describe the practical applications of computational linguistics.

Section 1.4
1. What are the different modalities in which the expressions of natural language can be realized?
2. Explain the distinction between a modality-dependent and a modality-independent storage of information.
3. Does communication require constant $d \Rightarrow i$ and $i \Rightarrow d$ transfers only in artificial cognitive agents or also in humans?
4. Explain the notion OCR software.
5. What are the desiderata of automatic speech recognition?
6. What will be required for automatic speech recognition to eventually become successful?

Section 1.5
1. What is the second Gutenberg revolution and how does it differ from the first?
2. Explain the technological advantages of the electronic medium.
3. Explain the terms SGML, XML, DTD, and TEI.
4. What is the role of computers in DTP?
5. Explain the notions *hard copy* and *soft copy*.
6. What are the possibilities and the limitations of a purely technology-based natural language processing?

2. Smart vs. Solid Solutions

For computational applications, two approaches may be generally distinguished: smart solutions and solid solutions. Smart solutions use special properties of the particular application to obtain a sufficient result at a minimum of cost. Solid solutions, in contrast, analyze the application at a more general level such that they can be used for a whole class of applications. By maintaining and extending a solid solution, it may be re-used again and again, thus saving time and money in the long run.

For computational linguistics, the most general solid solution is a general theory of how natural language communication works. To give an idea of the kinds of applications such a solid solution may be used for, Sect. 2.1 explains the structures underlying the use of textual databases. Section 2.2 shows how linguistic methods can improve the retrieval from textual databases. Section 2.3 shows how different applications require linguistic knowledge to different degrees in order to be practically useful. Section 2.4 explains the notion of language pairs in machine translation and describes the *direct* and the *transfer* approaches. A third approach to machine translation, the *interlingua* approach, as well as computer-based systems for aiding translation, are described in Sect. 2.5.

2.1 Indexing and Retrieval in Textual Databases

A textual database is an arbitrary collection of electronically stored texts. In contrast to a classic, record-based database like the one in 1.1.1, no structural restrictions apply to a textual database. Thus, the individual texts may be arranged, for example, in the temporal order of their arrival or according to their subject matter, the name of their author(s), their length, or no principle at all.

The search for a certain text or text passage is based on the standard, letter-based indexing of the textual database.

2.1.1 STANDARD INDEXING OF A TEXTUAL DATABASE (INVERTED FILE)

The indexing of a textual database is based on a table, called inverted file, which specifies for each letter all the positions (place numbers) where it occurs in the storage medium of the database.

R. Hausser, *Foundations of Computational Linguistics*,
DOI 10.1007/978-3-642-41431-2_2, © Springer-Verlag Berlin Heidelberg 2014

The electronic index (inverted file) of a textual database functions in many ways like a traditional library catalog of alphabetically ordered file cards.

Each traditional file card contains a *keyword*, e.g., the name of the author, and the associated *address*, e.g., the shelf where the book of the author may be found. While the file cards are ordered alphabetically according to their respective keywords, the choice of the addresses is initially free. Once a given book has been assigned a certain address and this address has been noted in the catalog, however, it is bound to this address.

In an unordered library without a catalog, the search for a certain book requires looking through the shelves (linear search). In the worst case, the book in question happens to be on the last of them. A library catalog speeds up such searching because it replaces a linear search by specifying the exact address(es) of the physical location. Thus, a book may be found using the alphabetical order of the file cards, irrespective of how the actual locations of the books are arranged.

The electronic index of a textual database uses the letters of the alphabet like the keywords of a library catalog, specifying for each letter all its positions (addresses) in the storage medium. The occurrences of a certain word form, e.g., sale, is then computed from the intersection of the position sets of s, a, l, and e. The electronic index is built up automatically when the texts are read into the database, whereby the size of the index is roughly equal to that of the textual database itself.

The search for relevant texts or passages in the database is guided by the user on the basis of words he considers characteristic of the subject matter at hand. Consider for example a lawyer interested in legal decisions dealing with warranties in used car sales. After accessing an electronic database in which all federal court decisions since 1960 are stored, he specifies the words warranty, sale, and used car. After a few seconds the database returns a list of all the texts in which these words occur. When the user clicks on a title in the list the corresponding text appears on the screen.

The user might well find that not all texts in the query result are actually relevant for the purpose at hand. It is much easier, however, to look through the texts of the query result than to look through the entire database.

Also, the database might still contain texts which happen to be relevant to the subject matter, yet are not included in the query result. Such texts, however, would have to deal with the subject matter without mentioning the query words, which is unlikely.

The use of an electronic index has the following advantages over a card index:

2.1.2 ADVANTAGES OF AN ELECTRONIC INDEX

(a) Power of search
    Because the electronic index of a textual database uses the letters of the alphabet as its keys, the database may be searched for any sequence of letters, whereas the keys of a conventional catalogue are limited to certain kinds of words, such as the name of the author.

(b) Flexibility
   (i) General specification of patterns
       An electronic index makes it possible to search for patterns. For example, the pattern[1] in.*i..tion matches all word forms of which the first two letters are in, the seventh letter from the end is i and the last four letters are tion, as in inhibition and inclination.
   (ii) Combination of patterns
       The electronic index allows to search for the combination of several word forms, whereby a maximal distance for their co-occurrence may be specified.
   Though it is theoretically possible to create a conventional card index for the positions of each letter of the books in a library, this would not be practical. Therefore searching with patterns or the combination of keywords and/or patterns is not technically feasible with a conventional card index.
(c) Automatic creation of the index structure
   The electronic index of a textual database is generated automatically during the reading-in of texts into the database. In a conventional card index, on the other hand, each new keyword requires making a new card by hand.
(d) Ease, speed, and reliability
   While an electronic search is done automatically in milliseconds, is error free, and is complete, a conventional search using a card index requires human labor, is susceptible to errors, and may take anywhere from minutes to hours or days. The advantages of electronic search apply to both the *query* (input of the search words) and the *retrieval* (output of the corresponding texts or passages).
   (i) Query
       An electronic database is queried by typing the search patterns on the computer, while the use of a card index requires picking out the relevant cards by hand.
   (ii) Retrieval
       In an electronic database, the retrieved texts or passages are displayed on the screen automatically, while use of a conventional card index requires going to the library shelves to get the books.

The quality of a query result is measured in terms of recall and precision.[2]

2.1.3 DEFINITION OF RECALL AND PRECISION

Recall measures the percentage of relevant texts retrieved as compared to the total of relevant texts contained in the database.

---

[1] A widely used notation for specifying patterns of letter sequences are *regular expressions* (RegEx) as implemented in Unix.

[2] See Salton (1989), p. 248.

For example: a database of several million pieces of text happens to contain 100 texts which are relevant to a given question. If the query returns 75 texts, 50 of which are relevant to the user and 25 irrelevant, then the recall is $50 : 100 = 50\,\%$.

Precision measures the percentage of relevant texts contained in the result of a query.

For example: a query results in 75 texts of which 50 turn out to be relevant to the user. Then the precision is $50 : 75 = 66.6\,\%$.

Experience has shown that recall and precision are not independent of each other, but inversely proportional: a highly specific query will result in low recall with high precision, while a loosely formulated query will result in high recall with low precision.

High recall has the advantage of retrieving a large percentage of the relevant texts from the database. Because of the concomitant low precision, however, the user has to work through a huge amount of material most of which turns out to be irrelevant.

High precision, on the other hand, produces a return most of which is relevant for the user. Because of the concomitant low recall, however, the user has to accept the likelihood that a large percentage of relevant texts remain undiscovered.

Measuring recall is difficult in large databases. It presupposes exact knowledge of all the texts or passages which happen to be relevant for any given query. To measure the recall for a given query, one would have to search the entire database manually in order to objectively determine the complete set of documents relevant to the user's question and to compare it with the automatic query result.

Measuring precision, on the other hand, is easy, because the number of documents returned by the system in response to a query is small compared to the overall database. The user need only look through the documents in the query result in order to find out which of them are relevant.

In a famous and controversial study, Blair and Maron (1985) attempted to measure the average recall of a commercial database system called STAIRS.[3] For this purpose they cooperated with a large law firm whose electronic data comprised 40 000 documents, amounting to a total of 350 000 pages. Because of this substantial, but at the same time manageable, size of the data it was possible to roughly determine the real number of relevant texts for 51 queries with the assistance of the employees.

Prior to the study, the employees subjectively estimated an electronic recall of 75 %. The nonelectronic verification, however, determined an average recall of only 20 %, with a standard deviation of 15.9 %, and an average precision of 79.0 %, with a standard deviation of 22.2 %.

---

[3] STAIRS is an acronym for *Storage and Information Retrieval System*, a software product developed by IBM and distributed from 1973 to 1994.

2.2 Using Grammatical Knowledge

The reason for the surprisingly low recall of only 20 % on average is that STAIRS uses only technological, i.e., letter-based, methods. Using grammatical knowledge in addition, recall could be improved considerably. Textual phenomena which resist a technological treatment, but are suitable for a linguistic solution, are listed below under the heading of the associated grammatical component.

2.2.1 PHENOMENA REQUIRING LINGUISTIC SOLUTIONS

(a) *Morphology*

A letter-based search does not recognize words. For example, the search for sell will overlook relevant forms like sold.

A possible remedy would be a program for word form recognition which automatically assigns to each word form the corresponding base form (lemmatization). By systematically associating each word form with its base form, all variants of a search word in the database can be found. A program of automatic word form recognition would be superior to the customary method of truncation – especially in languages with a morphology richer than that of English.

(b) *Lexicon*

A letter-based search does not take semantic relations between words into account. For example, the search for car would ignore relevant occurrences such as convertible, pickup truck, station wagon, etc.

A lexical structure which automatically specifies for each word the set of equivalent terms (synonyms), of the superclass (hypernyms), and of the instantiations (hyponyms) can help to overcome this weakness, especially when the domain is taken into account.[4]

(c) *Syntax*

A letter-based search does not take syntactic structures into account. Thus, the system does not distinguish between, for example, teenagers sold used cars and teenagers were sold used cars.

A possible remedy would be a syntactic parser which recognizes different grammatical relations between, for example, the subject and the object. Such a parser, which presupposes automatic word form recognition, would be superior to the currently used search for words within specified maximal distances.

---

[4] Some database systems already use *thesauri*, though with mixed results. Commercially available lexica are in fact likely to lower precision without improving recall. For example, in *Webster's New Collegiate Dictionary*, the word car is related to vehicle, carriage, cart, chariot, railroad car, streetcar, automobile, cage of an elevator, and part of an airship or balloon. With the exception of automobile and perhaps vehicle, all of these would only lower precision without improving recall.

(d) *Semantics*

A letter-based search does not recognize semantic relations such as negation. For example, the system would not be able to distinguish between selling cars and selling no cars. Also, equivalent descriptions of the same facts, such as A sold x to B and B bought x from A, could not be recognized.

Based on a syntactic parser and a suitable lexicon, the semantic interpretation of a textual database could analyze these distinctions and relations, helping to improve recall and precision.

(e) *Pragmatics*

According to Blair and Maron (1985), a major reason for poor recall was the frequent use of context-dependent formulations such as concerning our last letter, following our recent discussion, as well as nonspecific words such as problem, situation, or occurrence.

The treatment of these frequent phenomena requires a complete theoretical understanding of natural language pragmatics. For example, the system will have to be able to infer that, for example, seventeen-year-old bought battered convertible is relevant to the query used car sales to teenagers.

In order to improve recall and precision, linguistic knowledge may be applied in various different places in the database structure. The main alternatives are whether improvements in the search should be based on preprocessing the query, refining the index, and/or postprocessing the result. Further alternatives are an automatic or an interactive refinement of the query and/or the result, as described below.

2.2.2 LINGUISTIC METHODS OF OPTIMIZATION

A Preprocessing the query
1. Automatic query expansion
    (i) The search words in the query are automatically 'exploded' into their full inflectional paradigm and the inflectional forms are added to the query.
    (ii) Via a thesaurus the search words are related to all synonyms, hypernyms, and hyponyms. These are included in the query – possibly with all their inflectional variants.
    (iii) The syntactic structure of the query, e.g., A sold x to B, is transformed automatically into equivalent versions, e.g., B was sold x by A, x was sold to B by A, etc., to be used in the query.
2. Interactive query improvement
    The automatic expansion of the query may result in an uneconomic widening of the search and considerably lower precision. Therefore, prior to the search, the result of a query expansion is presented to the user to eliminate useless aspects of the automatic expansion and to improve the formulation of the query.

B Improving the indexing
  1. Letter-based indexing
     This is the basic technology of search, allowing one to retrieve the positions of each letter and each letter sequence in the database.
  2. Morphologically based indexing
     A morphological analyzer is applied during the reading in of texts, relating each word form to its base form. This information is coded into an index which for any given word (base form) allows one to find the associated word forms in the text.
  3. Syntactically based indexing
     A syntactic parser is applied during the reading in of texts, eliminating morphological ambiguities and categorizing phrases. This information is coded into an index on the basis of which all occurrences of a given syntactic construction may be found.
  4. Concept-based indexing
     The texts are analyzed semantically and pragmatically, whereby the software eliminates syntactic and semantic ambiguities and infers special uses characteristic of the domain. This information is coded into an index on the basis of which all occurrences of a given concept may be found.
C Postquery processing
  1. The low precision resulting from a nonspecific formulation of the query may be countered by an automatic processing of the data retrieved. Because there is only a small amount of raw data retrieved, as compared to the database as a whole, it may be parsed after the query and checked for their content. Then only those texts are displayed which are relevant according to this postquery analysis.

The ultimate goal of indexing textual databases is a concept-based retrieval founded on a complete morphological, syntactic, semantic, and pragmatic analysis of the texts.

2.3 Smart vs. Solid Solutions in Computational Linguistics

Which of the alternatives mentioned above is actually chosen in the design of a textual database depends on the amount of data to be handled, the available memory and speed of the hardware, the users' requirements regarding recall, precision, and speed of the search, and the designer's preferences and abilities. At the same time, the alternatives of 2.2.2 are not independent from each other.

For example, if an improvement of recall and precision is to be achieved via an automatic processing of the query, one can use a simple indexing. More specifically, if the processing of the query explodes the search words into their full inflectional paradigm for use in the search, a morphological index of the database would be superfluous. Conversely, if there is a morphological index, there would be no need for exploding the search words.

Similarly, the automatic expansion of queries may be relatively carefree if it is to be scrutinized by the user prior to search. If no interactive fine-tuning of queries is provided, on the other hand, the automatic expansion should be handled restrictively in order to avoid a drastic lowering of precision.

Finally, the indexing of texts may be comparatively simple if the results of each query are automatically analyzed and reduced to the most relevant cases before being output to the user. Conversely, a very powerful index method, such as concept-based indexing, would produce results with such high precision that there would be no need for an automatic postprocessing of results.

The different degrees of using linguistic theory for handling the retrieval from textual databases illustrate the choice between smart versus solid solutions. Further examples are the following:

2.3.1 SMART SOLUTIONS IN COMPUTATIONAL LINGUISTICS

Smart solutions avoid difficult, costly, or theoretically unsolved aspects of natural communication, as in

(a) Weizenbaum's Eliza program, which appears to understand natural language, but doesn't (cf. the Introduction in the Frontmatter)
(b) direct and transfer approaches in machine translation, which avoid understanding the source text (Sects. 2.4 and 2.5), and
(c) finite state technology (Sect. 13.5) and statistics (Sect. 15.5) for tagging and probabilistic parsing.[5]

Initially, smart solutions seem cheaper and quicker, but they are costly to maintain and their accuracy cannot be substantially improved. The alternative is solid solutions:

2.3.2 SOLID SOLUTIONS IN COMPUTATIONAL LINGUISTICS

Solid solutions aim at a complete theoretical and practical understanding of natural language communication. Applications are based on ready-made off-the-shelf components such as

(a) online lexica,
(b) rule-based grammars for the syntactic-semantic analysis of word forms and sentences,

---

[5] These methods may seem impressive because of the vast number of toys and tools assembled in the course of many decades (Jurafsky and Martin 2000). But they do not provide an answer to the question of how natural language communication works. Imagine that the Martians came to Earth and modeled cars statistically: they would never run. What is needed instead is a functional reconstruction of the engine, the transmission, the steering mechanism, etc., i.e., a solid solution.

(c) parsers and generators for running the grammars in the analysis and production of free text, and

(d) reference and monitor corpora for different domains, which provide a systematic, standardized account of the current state of the language.

Solid solution components are an application-independent long-term investment. Due to their systematic theoretical structure they are easy to maintain, can be improved continuously, and may be used again and again in different applications.

Whether a given task is suitable for a smart or a solid solution depends to a great extent on whether the application requires a perfect result or whether a partial answer is sufficient. For example, a user working with a giant textual database will be greatly helped by a recall of 70 %, while a machine translation system with 70 % accuracy will be of little practical use.

This is because a 70 % recall in a giant database is much more than a user could ever hope to achieve with human effort alone. Also, the user never knows which texts the system did not retrieve.

In translation, in contrast, the deficits of an automatic system with 70 % accuracy are painfully obvious to the user. Furthermore there is an alternative available, namely professional human translators. Because of the costly and time-consuming human correction required by today's machine translation, the user is faced daily with the question of whether or not the machine translation system should be thrown out altogether in order to rely on human work completely.

Another, more practical factor in the choice between a smart and a solid solution in computational linguistics is the off-the-shelf availability of grammatical components for the natural language in question. Such components of grammar, e.g., automatic word form recognition, syntactic parsing, etc., must be developed independently of any specific applications as part of basic research – solely in accordance with the general criteria of (i) their functional role as components in the mechanism of natural communication, (ii) completeness of data coverage, and (iii) efficiency.

Modular subsystems fulfilling these criteria can be used in practical applications without any need for modification, using their standard interfaces. The more such modules become available as ready-made, well-documented, portable, off-the-shelf products for different languages, the less costly will be the strategy of solid solutions in practical applications.

The main reason for the long-term superiority of solid solutions, however, is quality. This is because a 70 % smart solution is typically very difficult or even impossible to improve to 71 %.

2.4 Beginnings of Machine Translation

The choice between a smart and a solid solution is exemplified by machine translation. Translation in general requires understanding a text or utterance in a certain language (interpretation) and reconstructing it in another language (production).

On the one hand, translation goes beyond the general repertoire of natural communication. Superficially, it may seem related to bilingual communication. Bilingualism, however, is merely the ability to switch between languages, whereby only *one* language is used at any given time – in contradistinction to translation.

On the other hand, translation offers the facilitating circumstance that a coherent source text is given in advance – in contrast to automatic language production, which has to grapple with the problems of 'what to say' and 'how to say it'. A given source text can be utilized to avoid the really difficult problems of interpretation (e.g., a language-independent modeling of understanding) and production (e.g., the selection of content, the serialization, the lexical selection) in order to automatically translate large amounts of nonliterary text, usually into several different languages at once.

The administration of the European Union,[6] for example, must publish every report, protocol, decree, law, etc., in the 24 different languages of the member states (as of 2013). For example, a decree formulated in French under a French EU presidency would have to be translated into the following 22 languages.

French → Bulgarian	French → Irish
French → Czech	French → Latvian
French → Danish	French → Lithuanian
French → Dutch	French → Maltese
French → English	French → Polish
French → Estonian	French → Portuguese
French → Finnish	French → Slovene
French → German	French → Slovak
French → Greek	French → Spanish
French → Hungarian	French → Swedish

Under a Danish EU presidency, on the other hand, a document might first be formulated in Danish. Then it would have to be translated into the remaining EU languages, resulting in another set of 22 language pairs.

The total number of language pairs for a set of different languages is determined by the following formula:

2.4.1 FORMULA TO COMPUTE THE NUMBER OF LANGUAGE PAIRS

$n \cdot (n-1)$,   *where n = number of different languages*

For example, an EU with 23 different languages has to deal with a total of $23 \cdot 22 = 506$ language pairs.

In a language pair, the source language (SL) and the target language (TL) are distinguished. For example, 'French→Danish' and 'Danish→French' are different language pairs. The source language poses the task of correctly *understanding* the meaning, taking into account the domain and the context of utterance, whereas the target language poses the task of *formulating* the meaning in a rhetorically correct way.

---

[6] Another example is the United Nations, which generates a volume of similar magnitude.

The first attempts at machine translation tried to get as far as possible with the new computer technology, avoiding linguistic theory as much as possible. This resulted in the smart solution of 'direct translation', which was dominant in the 1950s and 1960s.

Direct translation systems assign to each word form in the source language a corresponding form of the target language. In this way the designers of these systems hoped to avoid a meaning analysis of the source text, while arriving at translations which are syntactically acceptable and express the meaning correctly.

2.4.2 SCHEMA OF DIRECT TRANSLATION

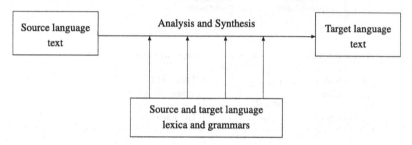

Each language pair requires the programming of its own direct translation system.

Direct translation is based mainly on a differentiated dictionary, distinguishing many special cases for a correct assignment of word forms in the target language. In the source language, grammatical analysis is limited to resolving ambiguities as much as possible; in the target language, it is limited to adjusting the word order and handling agreement.

The methodological weakness of direct translation systems is that they do not systematically separate source language analysis and target language synthesis. Consequently one is forced with each new text to add new special cases and exceptions. In this way the little systematic structure which was present initially is quickly swept away by a tidal wave of exceptions and special cases.

Even though representatives of the direct approach asserted repeatedly in the 1950s that the goal of machine translation, namely

FULLY AUTOMATIC HIGH QUALITY TRANSLATION (FAHQT)

was just around the corner, their hopes were not fulfilled. Hutchins (1986) provides the following examples to illustrate the striking shortcomings of early translation systems:

2.4.3 EXAMPLES OF AUTOMATIC MIS-TRANSLATIONS

Out of sight, out of mind. ⇒ *Invisible idiot.*

The spirit is willing, but the flesh is weak. ⇒ *The whiskey is all right, but the meat is rotten.*

La Cour de Justice considère la création d'un sixième poste d'avocat général. ⇒ *The Court of Justice is considering the creation of a sixth avocado station.*

The first two examples are apocryphal, described as the result of an automatic translation from English into Russian and back into English. The third example is documented in Lawson (1983) as output of the SYSTRAN system.

An attempt to avoid the weaknesses of direct translation is the transfer approach:

2.4.4 SCHEMA OF THE TRANSFER APPROACH

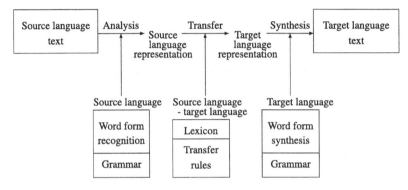

The transfer approach is characterized by a modular separation of

1. source language analysis and target language synthesis, of
2. linguistic data and processing procedures, and of the
3. lexica for source language analysis, target language transfer and target language synthesis.

The result is a clearer structure as compared to the direct approach, facilitating debugging and upscaling. Implementing the different modules independently of each other and separating the computational algorithm from the language-specific data also makes it possible to re-use parts of the software when adding another language pair.

For example, given a transfer system for the language pair A-B, adding the new language pair A-C will require writing new transfer and synthesis modules for language C, but the analysis module of the source language A may be re-used. Furthermore, if the language-specific aspects of the new transfer and synthesis modules are written within a prespecified software framework suitable for different languages, the new language pair A-C should be operational from the beginning.

The three phases of the transfer approach are illustrated below with a word form.

2.4.5 THREE PHRASES OF A WORD FORM TRANSFER *English-German*

1. Source language analysis:

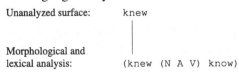

| Unanalyzed surface: | knew |

| Morphological and lexical analysis: | (knew (N A V) know) |

The source language analysis produces the syntactic category (N A V) of the inflectional form (categorization) and the base form know (lemmatization).

2. Source-target language transfer:
   Using the base form resulting from the source language analysis, a source-target language dictionary provides the corresponding base forms in the target language.

```
know  ⟹   wissen
          kennen
```

3. Target language synthesis
   Using the source language category (resulting from analysis) and the target language base forms (resulting from transfer), the desired target language word forms are generated based on target language morphology.

```
wußte        kannte
wußtest      kanntest
wußten       kannten
wußtet       kanntet
```

The transfer of a syntactic structure functions similarly to the transfer of word forms. First, the syntactic structure of the source language sentence is analyzed. Second, a corresponding syntactic structure of the target language is determined (transfer). Third, the target language structure is supplied with the target language word forms (synthesis), whereby correct handling of agreement, domain-specific lexical selection, correct positioning of pronouns, rhetorically suitable word order, and other issues of this kind must be resolved.

Due to similarities between the direct and the transfer methods, they have the following shortcomings in common:

2.4.6 SHORTCOMINGS OF THE DIRECT AND THE TRANSFER APPROACH

1. Each language pair requires a special source-target component.
2. Analysis and synthesis are limited to single sentences.
3. Semantic and pragmatic analyses are avoided, by attempting automatic translation without understanding the source language.

Thus, the advantage of the transfer approach over the direct approach is limited to the re-usability of certain components, specifically the source language analysis and the target language synthesis for additional language pairs.

2.5 Machine Translation Today

The importance of language *understanding* for adequate translation is illustrated by the following examples:

2.5.1 SYNTACTIC AMBIGUITY IN THE SOURCE LANGUAGE

1. Julia flew and crashed the airplane.

   Julia (flew and crashed the airplane)
   (Julia flew) and (crashed the airplane)
2. Susanne observed the yacht with a telescope.
   Susanne observed the man with a beard.
3. The mixture gives off dangerous cyanide and chlorine fumes.

   (dangerous cyanide) and (chlorine fumes)
   dangerous (cyanide and chlorine) fumes

The first example is ambiguous between using the verb fly transitively (someone flies an airplane) or intransitively (someone/-thing flies). The second example provides a choice between an adnominal and an adverbial interpretation of the prepositional phrase (Sect. 12.5). The third example exhibits a scope ambiguity regarding dangerous. A human translator recognizes these structural ambiguities, determines the intended reading, and recreates the proper meaning in the target language.

A second type of problem for translation without understanding the source language arises from lexical differences between source and target language:

2.5.2 LEXICAL DIFFERENCES BETWEEN SOURCE AND TARGET

1. The men killed the women. Three days later they were caught.
   The men killed the women. Three days later they were buried.
2. know: wissen savoir
           kennen connaître
3. The watch included two new recruits that night.

When translating example 1 into French, it must be decided whether they should be mapped into ils or elles – an easy task for someone understanding the source language. Example 2 illustrates the phenomenon of a *lexical gap*: whereas French and German distinguish between savoir–wissen and connaître–kennen, English provides only one word, know. Therefore a translation from English into French or German makes it necessary to choose the correct variant in the target language. Example 3 shows a language-specific lexical homonymy. For translation, it must decided whether watch should be treated as a variant of clock or of guard in the target language.

A third type of problem arises from syntactic differences between the source and the target language:

2.5.3 SYNTACTIC DIFFERENCES BETWEEN SOURCE AND TARGET

1. German:
   Auf dem Hof sahen wir einen kleinen Jungen, der einem Ferkel nachlief.
   Dem Jungen folgte ein großer Hund.

2. English:

   In the courtyard we saw a small boy running after a piglet.
   (a) A large dog followed the boy.
   (b) The boy was followed by a large dog.

German with its free word order can front the dative dem Jungen in the second sentence, providing textual cohesion by continuing with the topic. This cannot be precisely mirrored by the English translation because of its fixed word order. Instead, one can either keep the active verb construction of the source language in the translation (a), losing the textual cohesion, or one can take the liberty of changing the construction into passive (b). Rhetorically the second choice would be preferable in this case.

A fourth type of problem is caused by the fact that sequences of words may become more or less stable in a language, depending on the context of use. These fixed sequences range from frequently used 'proverbial' phrases to collocations and idioms.

2.5.4 COLLOCATION AND IDIOM

   strong current | high voltage (but: *high current | *strong voltage)
   bite the dust | ins Gras beißen (but: *bite the grass | *in den Staub beißen)

For adequate translation, colloquial and idiomatic relations such as those above must be taken into account.

The problems illustrated in 2.5.1–2.5.4 cannot be treated within morphology and syntax alone. Thus, any attempt to avoid a semantic and pragmatic interpretation in machine translation leads quickly to a huge number of special cases. As a consequence, such systems cannot be effectively maintained.

In light of these difficulties, many practically oriented researchers have turned away from the goal of fully automatic high quality translation (FAHQT) to work instead on partial solutions which promise quick help in high volume translation.

2.5.5 PARTIAL SOLUTIONS FOR PRACTICAL MACHINE TRANSLATION

1. *Machine-aided translation* (MAT) supports human translators with comfortable tools such as online dictionaries, text processing, morphological analysis, etc.
2. *Rough translation* – as provided by an automatic transfer system – arguably reduces the translators' work to correcting the automatic output.
3. *Restricted language* provides a fully automatic translation, but only for texts which fulfill canonical restrictions on lexical items and syntactic structures.

Systems of restricted language constitute a positive example of a smart solution. They utilize the fact that the texts to be translated fast and routinely into numerous different languages, such as maintenance manuals, are typically of a highly schematic nature. By combining aspects of automatic text generation and machine translation, the structural restrictions of the translation texts can be exploited in a twofold manner.

First, an online text processing system helps the authors of the original text with highly structured schemata which only need to be filled in (text production). Second, the online text system accepts only words and syntactic constructions for which correct translations into the various target languages have been carefully prepared and implemented (machine translation).

The use of restricted language may be compared to the use of a car. To take advantage of motorized transportation, one has to stay on the road. In this way one may travel much longer distances than one could on foot. However, there are always places a car cannot go. There one can leave the car and continue by walking.

Similarly, due to their automatic input restrictions, systems of restricted language provide reliable machine translation which is sufficiently correct in terms of form and content. If the text to be translated does not conform to the restricted language, however, one may switch off the automatic translation system and look for a human translator.

Besides these smart partial solutions, the solid goal of fully automatic high quality translation (FAHQT) for nonrestricted language has not been abandoned. Today's theoretical research concentrates especially on the interlingua approach, including knowledge-based systems of artificial intelligence. In contrast to the direct and the transfer approach, the interlingua approach does not attempt to avoid semantic and pragmatic interpretation from the outset.

The interlingua approach is based on a general, language-independent level called the interlingua. It is designed to represent contents derived from different source languages in a uniform format. From this representation, the surfaces of different target languages are generated.

2.5.6 SCHEMA OF THE INTERLINGUA APPROACH

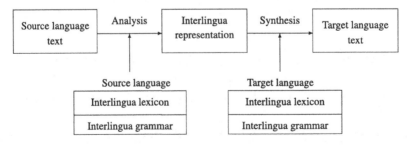

An interlingua system handles translation in two independent steps. The first step translates the source language text into the interlingua representation (analysis). The second step maps the interlingua representation into the target language (synthesis).

It follows from the basic structure of the interlingua approach that for $n(n-1)$ language pairs only $2n$ interlingual components are needed (namely n analysis and n synthesis modules), in contrast to the direct and the transfer approach which require $n(n - 1)$ components. Thus, as soon as more than three languages ($n > 3$) are involved, the interlingua approach has a substantial advantage over the other two.

The crucial question, however, is the exact nature of the interlingua. The following interlinguas have been proposed:

1. an artificial logical language,
2. a semi-natural language like Esperanto which is man-made, but functions like a natural language,
3. a set of semantic primitives common to both the source and the target language, serving as a kind of universal vocabulary.

Closer inspection shows, however, that these proposals have not yet resulted in theoretically and practically acceptable results. Existing interlingua systems are highly experimental, usually illustrating theoretical principles by translating tiny amounts of data by means of huge systems.

The experimental character of these attempts is not surprising because a general solution to interlingua translation may almost be equated with modeling the mechanism of natural language communication. After all, interlingua translation requires (i) a language-independent representation of cognitive content in the interlingua, (ii) the automatic translation of the natural source language into the language-independent content representation, and (iii) the automatic generation of the natural target language from the language-independent content representation.

Conversely, as soon as natural communication has been modeled on the computer in a general way, fully automatic high quality translation (FAHQT) is within reach. At the same time, all the other applications of computational linguistics mentioned in 1.1.2, such as human-computer communication in natural language, a concept-based indexing of textual databases with maximal recall and precision, etc., can be provided with solid solutions as well, using available off-the-shelf modules.

These applications are one reason why the SLIM theory of language aims from the outset at modeling the mechanism of natural language communication in general. Thereby verbal and nonverbal contents are represented alike as concatenated propositions, defined as sets of bidirectionally connected *proplets* in a content-addressable database. Though partially language-independent, these contents may differ from language to language in terms lexicalization and agreement information.

Exercises

Section 2.1

1. Explain the notions recall and precision using the example of a database containing 300 texts relevant for a given query, whereby 1000 texts are retrieved, of which 50 turn out to be relevant.

2. What are the weaknesses of purely technology-based indexing and retrieval in textual databases?

3. Give examples in which truncation retrieves irrelevant and misses relevant word forms.

4. Read Chap. 11, *Language Analysis and Understanding*, in Salton (1989) (pp. 377–424). Give a written summary of three to five pages of the linguistic methods for improving information retrieval described there.

Section 2.2

1. Which components of a textual database system are susceptible to linguistically based optimization?

2. What is the difference between on-the-fly processing and batch mode processing? Illustrate the difference using the examples of query expansion, indexing, and processing of a query result.

3. Why is high quality indexing better suited for fast search than preprocessing the query or postprocessing the retrieved data?

4. What is the cost of high quality indexing as compared to preprocessing the query or postprocessing the retrieved data?

5. Investigate whether the thesaurus of *WordNet* raises or lowers precision.

Section 2.3

1. What are the different ways of improving retrieval from a textual database, and how are they connected with each other?

2. Describe the different advantages and disadvantages of smart versus solid solutions in applications of computational linguistics.

3. What kinds of applications are not suitable for smart solutions?

4. Call up the Eliza program in the Emacs editor with 'meta-x doctor' and check it out. Explain why the Eliza program is a smart solution. What is the function of grammatical components in Eliza?

Section 2.4

1. Describe the differences between the direct and the transfer approach to machine translation.

2. What is the ultimate goal of machine translation?

3. In 1995, the EU was expanded from 12 to 15 member states, increasing the number of different languages from nine to 11. How many additional language pairs resulted from this expansion?

4. Which components of a transfer system can be re-used, and which cannot? Explain your answer with the example of six language pairs for the languages English, French, and German. Enumerate the components necessary in such a system.

Section 2.5

1. Which phenomena of language use make an understanding of the source language necessary for adequate translation?
2. It is sometimes pointed out that English has no word corresponding to the German Schadenfreude. Does this mean in your opinion that the corresponding concept is alien to speakers of English and cannot be expressed? Provide two further examples of *lexical gaps* relative to language pairs of your choice.
3. Provide two examples of collocations.
4. Where in MT could one use off-the-shelf components of grammar?
5. What linguistic insights could be gained from building a system of controlled language?
6. Why is machine translation with controlled language an example of a smart solution?
7. What is an interlingua?
8. How many additional components are needed when adding three new languages to an interlingua system?

3. Cognitive Foundations of Semantics

Modeling the mechanism of natural communication in terms of a computationally efficient, general theory has a threefold motivation in computational linguistics. First, theoretically it requires discovering how natural language actually works – surely an important problem of general interest. Second, methodologically it provides a unified, functional viewpoint for developing the components of grammar on the computer and allows objective verification of the theoretical model in terms of its implementation. Third, practically it serves as the basis for solid solutions in advanced applications.

The mechanism of natural communication is described in Chaps. 3–6 in terms of constructing a robot named CURIOUS. The present chapter prepares the ground by describing how CURIOUS perceives and cognitively processes its immediate environment. The result is a preliminary version of the robot functioning without language, but suitable for adding a language component in Chap. 4.

Section 3.1 describes the cognitive abilities of CURIOUS in relation to its task environment. Section 3.2 explains how CURIOUS recognizes simple geometric objects. Section 3.3 defines the notions of the internal *context* and its *concepts*. Section 3.4 describes how the analysis of the task environment results in the automatic derivation of context propositions. Section 3.5 integrates the components of CURIOUS into a functioning system and defines a program which controls the construction and the updating of the robot's internal representation of its external task environment.

3.1 Prototype of Communication

The question of how natural language functions in communication may seem complicated because there are so many different ways of using language. Consider the following examples:

3.1.1 VARIANTS OF LANGUAGE COMMUNICATION

– two speakers are located face to face and talk about concrete objects in their immediate environment

R. Hausser, *Foundations of Computational Linguistics*,
DOI 10.1007/978-3-642-41431-2_3, © Springer-Verlag Berlin Heidelberg 2014

- two speakers talk on the phone about events experienced together in the past
- a merchant writes to a company to order merchandise in a certain number, size, color, etc., and the company responds by filling the order
- a newspaper article reports a planned extension of public transportation
- a translator reconstructs an English short story in German
- a teacher of physics explains the law of gravitation
- a registrar issues a marriage license
- a judge announces a sentence
- a conductor says: End of the line, everybody please get off!
- a sign reads: Don't walk on the grass!
- a professor of literature interprets an expressionistic poem
- an author writes a science fiction story
- an actor speaks a role

These different variants are not *per se* an insurmountable obstacle to designing a general model of natural language communication. They merely require finding a basic mechanism which works for all of them while accommodating their respective differences.

The SLIM theory of language proceeds on the hypothesis that there is a basic prototype which includes all essential aspects of natural language communication. This prototype is defined as follows:

3.1.2 PROTOTYPE OF COMMUNICATION

> The basic prototype of natural language communication is the direct face-to-face discourse of two partners talking about concrete objects in their immediate environment.

Possible alternatives would be approaches which take as their basic model, for example, complete texts or the signs of nature, such as smoke indicating fire.

The prototype hypothesis is proven in two steps. First, a robot is described which allows unrestricted natural human-computer communication within the basic prototype. Second, it is shown that all the other variants are special cases or extensions which can easily be integrated into the cognitive structure of the robot.

Realizing the prototype of communication as a functioning robot requires an exact definition of the following components of basic communication:

3.1.3 THREE COMPONENTS OF THE COMMUNICATION PROTOTYPE

- Specification of the *task environment*[1]

---

[1] The notion *task environment* was introduced by Newell and Simon (1972). It refers to the robot's external situation. The robot-internal representation of the task environment is called the *problem space*.

– Structure of the *cognitive agent*
– Specification of the *language*

The task environment of the robot CURIOUS is a large room with a flat floor. Distributed randomly on the floor are objects of the following kinds:

3.1.4 OBJECTS IN THE WORLD OF CURIOUS

– triangles (scalene, isosceles, etc.)
– quadrangles (square, rectilinear, etc.)
– circles and ellipses

These objects of varying sizes and different colors are elements of the real world.

The robot is called CURIOUS[2] because it is programmed to constantly observe the state of its task environment. The task environment keeps changing in unforeseeable ways because the human 'wardens' remove objects on the floor, add others, or change their position in order to test CURIOUS' attention.

CURIOUS knows about the state of its task environment by exploring it regularly. To avoid disturbing the objects on the floor, CURIOUS is mounted on the ceiling. The floor is divided into even-sized fields which CURIOUS can visit from above.

The basic cognition of CURIOUS includes an internal map divided into fields corresponding to those on the floor and a procedure indicating its current external position on the internal map. Furthermore, CURIOUS can specify a certain goal on its internal map and then adjust its external position accordingly.

When CURIOUS finds an object while visiting a certain field, the object is analyzed and the information is stored as, for example, Isosceles red triangle in field D2. By systematically collecting data of this kind for all fields, CURIOUS is as well-informed about its task environment as its human wardens.

3.2 From Perception to Recognition

The first crucial aspect of this setup is that the task environment is an *open* world: the objects in the task environment are not restricted to a fixed, predefined set, but can be processed by CURIOUS even if some disappear and new ones are added in unpredictable ways.

The second crucial aspect is that the task environment is part of the *real* world. Thus, for the proper functioning of CURIOUS a nontrivial form of reference must be implemented, allowing the system to keep track of external objects.

---

[2] CURIOUS is an advanced variant of the COLOR READER described in CoL, pp. 295f.

The cognitive functioning of CURIOUS presupposes the real external world as a given.[3] Its internal representations do not attempt to model the external world completely, but are limited to properties necessary for the intended interaction with the external world, here the perception and recognition of two-dimensional geometric objects of varying colors.

The performance of the system is evaluated according to the following two criteria:

3.2.1 CRITERIA FOR EVALUATING CURIOUS

– *Behavior test*: measuring active and reactive behavior
– *Cognition test*: measuring cognitive processing directly

The behavior test is the conventional method of observing actions and reactions of cognitive agents in controlled environments. If only behavior tests are available – as is normally the case with natural cognitive agents – the examination of cognitive functions is limited.[4]

The cognition test consists in evaluating the cognitive performance of a system directly. This kind of test presupposes that the internal states can be accessed and accurately interpreted from the outside.[5]

A cognitive agent interacts with the world in terms of recognition and action. Recognition is the process of transporting structures of the external world into the cognitive agent. Action is the process of transporting structures originating inside the cognitive agent into the world.

The processes of recognition and action may be described at different levels of abstraction. Modeling vision, for example, is complicated by such problems as separating objects from the background, completing occluded portions, perception of depth, handling reflection, changes in lighting, perception of motion, etc.[6]

For purposes of grounding a semantics procedurally, however, a relatively high level of abstraction may be sufficient. As an illustration consider a robot without language observing its environment by means of a video camera. The robot's recognition begins with an unanalyzed internal image of the object in question, e.g., a blue square.

---

[3] This is in accordance with the approach of nouvelle AI (Sect. 1.3), which is based on the motto *The world is its own best model* (Brooks 1986).

[4] Behavior tests with humans may include the use of language by interviewing the subjects about their experience. This however, (i) introduces a subjective element and (ii) is not possible with all kinds of cognitive agents.

[5] While we can never be sure whether our human partners see the world as we do and understand us the way we mean it, this can be determined precisely in the case of CURIOUS because its cognition may be accessed directly via the service channel. Thus, the problem of *solipsism* may be overcome in CURIOUS.

[6] For a summary of natural vision, see Nakayama et al. (1995). A classic treatment of artificial vision is Marr (1982). For summaries see Anderson (1990), pp. 36f., and the special issue of *Cognition*, Vol. 67, 1998, edited by Tarr and Bülthoff.

3.2.2 INTERNAL BITMAP REPRESENTATION OF EXTERNAL OBJECT

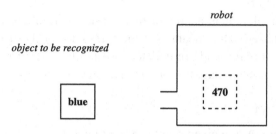

Inside the robot, the blue square is represented as a bitmap outline and its color as the electromagnetic frequency measured, e.g., 470 nm. Just as an OCR system[7] analyzes bitmap structures to recognize letters, the robot recognizes the form of objects in its task environment by matching their bitmap structures with corresponding patterns.

The recognition of geometric forms may be viewed as a three-step process. First, a suitable program approximates the bitmap outline with movable bars resulting in a reconstructed pattern:

3.2.3 ANALYSIS OF AN INTERNAL BITMAP REPRESENTATION

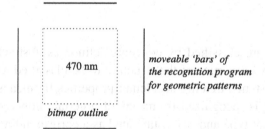

Second, the reconstructed pattern is logically analyzed in terms of the number of corners, their angles, the length of the edges, etc. In our example, the logical analysis results in an area enclosed by four lines of equal length forming four right angles.

Third, the logical analysis is classified in terms of abstract concepts, to be discussed in the following section. The classification results in the recognition of the object in question.[8] The basic recognition procedure illustrated above with the example *square*

---

[7] OCR or optical character recognition systems are used with scanners to recognize printed text. See Sect. 1.4.

[8] For the sake of conceptual simplicity, the reconstructed pattern, the logical analysis, and the classification are described here as separate phases. In practice, these three aspects may be closely interrelated in an incremental procedure. For example, the analysis system may measure an angle as soon as two edges intersect, the counter for corners may be incremented each time a new corner is found, a hypothesis regarding a possible matching concept may be formed early so that the remainder of the logical analysis is used to verify this hypothesis, etc.

may be extended to other types of geometric objects, to properties like colors, and to relations such as A being contained in B.[9]

When a system like CURIOUS is alert it is anchored in its task environment by means of its perception and recognition. This means that the relevant aspects of its task environment are represented internally and are updated constantly. The current internal representation is called the (nonlanguage)[10] *context* of a cognitive agent.

3.2.4 DEFINITION OF THE CONTEXT

The context of a cognitive agent CA at a given point of time t includes
1. the total of all current cognitive parameter values CA_t,
2. the logical analyses of the parameter values and their combinations (reconstructed patterns),
3. the conceptual structures used to classify the reconstructed patterns and their combinations.

The cognitive processing of CURIOUS described so far illustrates the difference between perception and recognition. The raw data provided by the video camera are what CURIOUS perceives. Their classification with respect to geometric shape and color constitute what CURIOUS recognizes.

3.3 Iconicity of Formal Concepts

Logical analyses as the one in 3.2.3 are classified by concepts defined as abstract types.[11] A type specifies the necessary properties of the structure to be classified as a constellation of parameters and constants, treating accidental properties by means of variables. When a logical analysis is recognized by means of a certain concept type, the analysis is (i) classified by that type and (ii) instantiated as a corresponding concept token.

---

[9] See also Langacker (1987/1991) , who analyzes *above* vs. *below*, pp. 219, 467; *before*, p. 222; *enter*, p. 245; *arrive*, p. 247; *rise*, p. 263; *disperse*, p. 268; *under*, pp. 280, 289; *go*, p. 283; *pole climber*, p. 311; and *hit*, p. 317. These may be regarded as logical analyses in our sense.

[10] In the following, we will avoid the term '(non)verbal' as much as possible because of a possible confusion with the part of speech 'verb.' Instead of 'nonlanguage cognition' we will use the term 'context-based cognition.' Instead of 'verbal cognition' we will use the term 'language-based cognition.'

[11] The type/token distinction was introduced by the American philosopher and logician Charles Sanders PEIRCE (1839–1914), see CP, Vol. 4, p. 375. An example of a token is the actual occurrence of a sign at a certain time and a certain place, for example the now following capital letter: A. The associated type, on the other hand, is the abstract structure underlying all actual and possible occurrences of this letter. Realization-dependent differences between corresponding tokens, such as size, font, place of occurrence, etc., are not part of the associated type.

A concept type is defined as a combination of constants and variables. The variables enable the type to *match* arbitrarily many concept tokens. A concept token shares the constants with its type, but instantiates the variables as constants as well. In this way, a given type matches an open number of different logical analyses of the same kind. Consider the following example:

3.3.1 CONCEPT TYPE OF *square*

$$
\begin{bmatrix}
\text{edge 1} : \alpha \text{ cm} \\
\text{angle 1/2} : 90° \\
\text{edge 2} : \alpha \text{ cm} \\
\text{angle 2/3} : 90° \\
\text{edge 3} : \alpha \text{ cm} \\
\text{angle 3/4} : 90° \\
\text{edge 4} : \alpha \text{ cm} \\
\text{angle 4/1} : 90°
\end{bmatrix}
$$

This concept type is defined as a feature structure. The necessary properties of the concept are represented by eight attribute-value pairs (avp), four of which specify the edges and four the angles. Also, the values of the angles are specified as the constant 90°. The accidental property, in contrast, is the edge length, specified as the variable α.[12] Instances of the same variable in a concept must all take the same value. The variable makes the concept type applicable to an open number of squares of any size.

3.3.2 DEFINITION: CONCEPT TYPE

A concept type is the structural representation of a characteristic logical analysis, whereby accidental properties are defined as variables.

When the concept type is matched onto the logical analysis in 3.2.3, the variables are bound to a particular edge length, here 2 cm, resulting in the instantiation of a token$_{loc}$.

3.3.3 CONCEPT TOKEN$_{loc}$ OF A *square*

$$
\begin{bmatrix}
\text{edge 1} : 2 \text{ cm} \\
\text{angle 1/2} : 90° \\
\text{edge 2} : 2 \text{ cm} \\
\text{angle 2/3} : 90° \\
\text{edge 3} : 2 \text{ cm} \\
\text{angle 3/4} : 90° \\
\text{edge 4} : 2 \text{ cm} \\
\text{angle 4/1} : 90°
\end{bmatrix}_{loc}
$$

---

[12] Technically, this example would require an operator – for example a quantifier – binding the variables in its scope.

The feature *loc* specifies when and where the token was recognized, i.e., the spatio-temporal location.

3.3.4 DEFINITION: CONCEPT TOKEN$_{loc}$

A concept token$_{loc}$ results from successfully matching a concept type onto a corresponding logical analysis of a parameter constellation at a certain spatio-temporal location.

Concept types are usually defined for subsets of the available parameters and their possible values. For example, the concept in 3.3.1 applies to a certain constellation of visual parameter values. Other parameters, e.g., color values, are disregarded by the type *square*. It is possible, however, to define elementary concepts which apply to a multitude of different parameters. For example, *situation* could be defined as the elementary concept type which matches the totality of current parameter values.

Elementary concept types may be defined only for those notions for which the corresponding parameters have been implemented. For example, the concepts for *warm* and *cold* may be defined only after (i) the robot has been equipped with suitable sensors for temperature and (ii) the resulting measurements have been integrated into the robot's conceptual structure.

The constellation of parameter values, concept types, and concept tokens$_{loc}$ provides not only for an abstract characterization of recognition, but also of action. Thereby recognition and action differ in the direction of the respective procedures.

3.3.5 ABSTRACT CHARACTERIZATION OF RECOGNITION AND ACTION

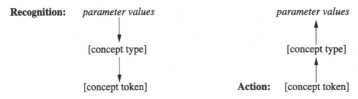

Recognition begins with the incoming parameter values which are logically analyzed and classified by means of a matching concept type. A successful matching binds the variables to particular values and results in a corresponding concept token$_{loc}$. In this way constellations of perception parameters are individuated into concept tokens$_{loc}$.

Action begins with a certain concept token$_{loc}$ which is to be realized as a specific outgoing parameter constellation by means of a corresponding concept type. Consider for example a robot equipped with a gripping device wanting to pick up a glass. For this, a certain concept token$_{loc}$ is realized as a gripping action (token) with the help of the concept type (general procedure). Thereby distance, size, firmness, etc., of the object are determined via the robot's recognition and integrated into the planned action.

The natural evolution of concept types can be analyzed as an abstraction over logically similar parameter constellations, whereby the accidental aspects of constellations are represented by variables. Thus the types originate as the formation of classes over sets of similar raw data of perception or unconscious action. Only after the formation of types can individual tokens be instantiated on the basis of these types.[13]

A set of similar parameter values may result in an abstract type for different reasons: frequent occurrence, rare occurrence, simple logical (e.g., geometrical) structure, pleasant or unpleasant feeling, etc. For example, geometric shapes (visual parameter values) which are logically similar in that they consist of three straight, intersecting lines may be summarized as an abstract concept type which speakers of English happen to call a triangle. Once the concept type is available it can be applied to newly encountered parameter values resulting in individualized concept tokens$_{loc}$ of triangles. Correspondingly, electromagnetic frequencies which are similar in that they fall into the same narrow range may result in the abstract concept type of a certain color.[14]

Our analysis of concept type formation and concept type use is an *iconic* theory. The notion of iconicity derives from the classical Greek word for image (ikon). Intuitively, iconicity means the following:

3.3.6 ASPECTS OF ICONICITY

– The parameter values of the internal context are images insofar as they reflect the corresponding structures of the real world.

---

[13] In the course of evolution, the concept types and concept tokens$_{loc}$ of recognition and action have acquired additional functions: concept tokens$_{loc}$ are used for storing content in the cognitive agent's memory, while concept types serve as language meanings.

Our analysis of language evolution, beginning here with non-verbal cognition based on concept types and concept tokens$_{loc}$ and continuing in the following chapters by our analyzing their functional interaction, is of a logical nature. Other approaches to human language evolution are concerned with quite different questions such as

– Why do humans have language while chimpanzees do not?
– Did language arise in 'male' situations such as *Look out, a tiger!*, in 'female' situations of trust-building during grooming, or out of chanting?
– Did language evolve initially from hand signs or was the development of a larynx capable of articulation a precondition?

For further discussion of these questions, which are not addressed here, see Hurford et al. (1998).

[14] This abstract description of visual recognition is compatible with the neurological view. For example, after describing the neurochemical processing of photons in the eye and the visual cortex, Rumelhart (1977), pp. 59f., writes:

These features which are abstracted from the visual image are then to be matched against memorial representations of the possible patterns, thus finally eliciting a name to be applied to the stimulus pattern, and making contact with stored information pertaining to the item.

– The reconstructed patterns (concept tokens$_{loc}$) are images of parameter values because they are logical analyses of parameter values.
– The concept types of the internal context are images insofar as they (i) originate as abstractions over similar parameter constellations and (ii) characterize associated classes of reconstructed patterns.

That the recognition of CURIOUS is iconic follows quite simply from the requirement that the system should perceive its task environment correctly. For example, if an external triangle is represented internally as the outline of a quadrangle, then the system is obviously deficient.

The same holds for action. Assume that CURIOUS is equipped with a gripping device and wants to move an object from field A2 into field A4. If the external action of the gripping device is not iconic with respect to the internal presentation of the movement in question and the object is moved instead into field A5, then the system obviously does not function correctly.

In the literature, the properties and the status of iconicity have long been controversial and were, for example, at the core of the debate between the naturalists and the conventionalists in ancient Greece (Sect. 6.4). The often fierce opposition to iconic constructs[15] stems from misunderstanding iconicity in the sense of naive little pictures. That this is not meant at all is illustrated by the examples in 3.3.3 (parameter constellation, concept token$_{loc}$) and 3.3.1 (concept type), which use an abstract coding. The notion of an icon must be understood in the mathematical sense of a *homomorphism* (Sect. 21.3), that is, as a structure-preserving representation.

For example, if the photograph of a familiar face is scanned into the computer and ultimately coded as a sequence of 0s and 1s, this coding is iconic in our sense because the original image can be recreated from it on the screen. This point of view was taken by the English philosopher John LOCKE (1632–1704). Locke (1690) said that a person seeing a tree has an image of that tree in his head – which is shown by the fact that the person can later make a drawing.

There are basically three arguments against iconicity, which seem to be as popular as they are misguided. The first one is based on the claim that if one were to surgically search the brain of a person who has seen a tree, one would not find such an image.

In reply we point out that this method is much too crude. After all, in the analogous case of a computer it is not certain that a thorough investigation of the hardware would discover an image that had been scanned in – even though the computer is a man-made machine and as such is completely understood. Furthermore, modern research has shown that the optical cortex does indeed exhibit *'iconic representations'* such as

---

[15] For example, Ogden and Richards (1923) call the use of icons or images in the analysis of meaning 'a potent instinctive belief being given from many sources' (p. 15) which is 'hazardous,' 'mental luxuries,' and 'doubtful' (p. 59). In more recent years, the idea of iconicity has been quietly rehabilitated in the work of Chafe (1970), Johnson-Laird (1983) pp. 146f., Givón (1985) p. 189, Haiman (ed.) (1985a), Haiman (1985b), and others.

"the line, edge, and angle detectors discovered by Hubel and Wiesel (1962) and the iconic or sensory memories proposed by Sperling (1960) and Neisser (1967)"[16] from which the internal representations of the images are built up.

The second argument was used in the famous controversy among the British empiricists regarding the (non)existence of abstract ideas. Locke (1690) took the view that recognition is based on abstract concepts or 'ideas' in the head of the perceiving person. He said that a person recognized, for example, a triangle on the basis of an internal concept (idea) of a triangle.

A generation later this analysis was attacked by Berkeley (1710). George BERKELEY (1685–1753), a bishop by profession,[17] regarded Locke's approach as naive and tried to reduce it to absurdity by asking what *kind* of triangle the concept should be *exactly*: isosceles, scalene, right-angled?

CURIOUS, however, shows Berkeley's argument to be a fallacy. CURIOUS uses an abstract concept of a triangle based on a formal definition involving three straight, intersecting lines forming three angles which together add up to 180 degrees. This concept is realized procedurally as part of a pattern recognition program which may be demonstrated as recognizing *all* possible kinds of triangles (analogous to 3.2.3).[18]

The third argument is the homunculus argument, which was used by David HUME (1711–1776) two generations after Locke. Hume's (1748) argument goes like this: if there are pictures in the mind, then there must be someone to see them. Yet postulating a little man (homunculus) in the head to see the images would not do because the little man would have images in his little head in turn, requiring another homunculus, and so on. Since postulating a homunculus is of no help for understanding the interpretation of images, the images themselves are concluded to be superfluous.

CURIOUS, however, shows Hume's argument to be a fallacy as well. CURIOUS uses two kinds of iconic structures: concept types and concept tokens$_{loc}$. Neither of them is intended to be seen by any CURIOUS-internal homunculus. Instead the concept types are matched with parameter values, whereby their external origin ('Urbild') is classified and instantiated as a concept token$_{loc}$ (3.3.5).

---

[16] Palmer (1975).

[17] Peirce (1871) writes about Berkeley:

> Berkeley's metaphysical theories have at first sight an air of paradox and levity very unbecoming to a bishop. He denies the existence of matter, our ability to see distance, and the possibility of forming the simplest general conception; while he admits the existence of Platonic ideas; and argues the whole with a cleverness which every reader admits, but which few are convinced by.

[18] The program may even be expanded to recognize bitmap outlines with imprecise or uneven contours by specifying different degrees of granularity. Cf. Austin's (1962) example *France is hexagonal*.

3.4 Context Propositions

In order to perform its task, CURIOUS must (i) move through its environment, (ii) analyze each current field, (iii) represent the objects found there internally, and (iv) integrate the results into a correct cognitive representation of the overall situation. To this purpose, the concept tokens$_{loc}$ derived are combined into elementary *propositions*.

In accordance with the classic view since ARISTOTLE (384–322 B.C.), propositions are simple representations of what is. Propositions are so general and abstract that they have been regarded as both the states of real or possible worlds and the meanings of language sentences.

In logic, propositions are built from three basic kinds of elements, called *arguments*, *functors*, and *modifiers*. An elementary proposition consists of one functor which combines with a characteristic number of arguments. Modifiers are optional and may apply to functors as well as to arguments.

In philosophy, the arguments are the *objects* in the world, the functors are the (intrapropositional) *relations*, and the modifiers are the *properties*. These constitute a simple ontology – in contradistinction to other possible ontologies, such as that of physics (based on atoms, gravity, etc.), biology (based on metabolism, reproduction, etc.), or economy (based on markets, inflation, interest rates, etc.).

In linguistics, the arguments are the *nouns*, the functors are the *verbs* (16.2.1), and the modifiers are the *adjectives* (whereby adnominals modify nominals and adverbs modify verbs). They comprise the content words of a language, form the open word classes (13.1.9), and are called the parts of speech.

This plurality of terminology may be summarized as follows:

3.4.1 DIFFERENT NAMES FOR THE THREE ELEMENTS OF BASIC PROPOSITIONS

	(a) *logic*	(b) *philosophy*	(c) *linguistics*
1.	argument	object	noun
2.	functor	relation	verb
3.	modifier	property	adjective

For simplicity, we choose *noun, verb*, and *adj* of grammar, with the possible abbreviations N, V, and A. However, because we use these notions at the language as well as the context level, they are interpreted ontologically and called *core attributes* instead of "parts of speech."

The core attributes are used in flat, ordered feature structures,[19] called *proplets*.[20] As examples of isolated (unconnected, lexical) proplets consider the following examples:

---

[19] As shown in 3.3.1 and 3.3.3, but at the next higher level of grammatical complexity.

[20] The term *proplet* is coined in analogy to *droplet* and refers to the basic parts of an elementary proposition. Superficially, proplets may seem to resemble the feature structures of HPSG. The latter, however, are recursive feature structures with unordered attributes. Intended to be part of a phrase structure tree rather than a database, they encode functor-

3.4.2 LEXICAL ITEMS OF A PROPOSITION

$$
\begin{bmatrix} \text{noun: field} \\ \text{arg:} \\ \text{place:} \\ \text{prn:} \end{bmatrix}
\begin{bmatrix} \text{verb: contain} \\ \text{fnc:} \\ \text{time:} \\ \text{pc:} \\ \text{prn:} \end{bmatrix}
\begin{bmatrix} \text{noun: square} \\ \text{arg:} \\ \text{place:} \\ \text{prn:} \end{bmatrix}
$$

The ordered attributes of the rightmost proplet, for example, are noun, arg, place, and prn. The value of the core attribute is called the *core value*. Here it is *square*, explicitly defined as the name of the concept type defined in 3.3.1. The proplets shown above are lexical because except for the core attributes they have no values yet.

The elements of a proposition may be connected by five kinds of basic semantic relations, namely (1) subject-predicate, (2) object-predicate, (3) adnominal-noun, (4) adverbial-verb, and (5) conjunct-conjunct. We code these relations as proplet values, defined as addresses and implemented as pointers.

For example, the content corresponding to English

The field contains a triangle and (the field contains) a square

is coded as the following set of proplets:

3.4.3 ADDRESSES ESTABLISHING INTER-PROPLET RELATIONS

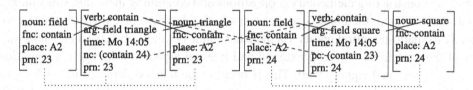

The intrapropositional relations are indicated by the diagonal "—" lines; the distinction between a subject, a direct object, and an indirect object is indicated by the order of the values in the verb's arg attribute. The expropositional relation between the two propositions is indicated by the diagonal "− − −" lines between the verbs. The proplets of each proposition are held together by a common proposition number (prn value), here 23 and 24, indicated by the "..." lines.

By coding the semantic relations between proplets and between propositions solely by means of addresses, proplets are *order-free* in that the relations are maintained regardless of how the proplets are arranged in two- or three-dimensional space. This is important for the storage and retrieval of proplets in a database. For linguistic intuitions, however, we represent the semantic relations graphically using characteristic lines (edges) for (1) subject/predicate, (2) object\predicate, (3) adnominal|nominal,

---

argument structure in terms of embedding rather than by address, do not concatenate propositions in terms of extrapropositional relations, and do not provide a suitable basis for a time-linear navigation and storage in a database.

(4) adverbial|predicate, and (5) conjunct−conjunct (Sect. 23.3). Accordingly, the above set of proplets may be represented graphically as follows:

3.4.4 AN EXAMPLE OF TWO CONTEXTUAL PROPOSITIONS

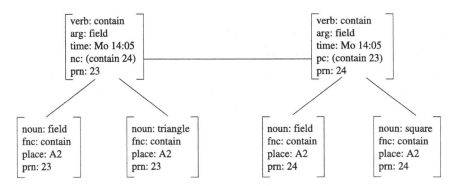

This example illustrates an automatic analysis of a situation in which CURIOUS finds a triangle and a square in field A2 at the time Mo 14:05.

The coherence of context propositions and their connections follows from the coherence of the external world which they reflect (Sect. 24.5). This coherence is maintained by the system-internal algorithm which interprets the input parameters by automatically constructing elementary propositions and combining them into subcontexts.

On the one hand, the context propositions in the database of CURIOUS relate concretely to spatio-temporal reality via the place values of their objects and the time values of their relations. Thereby external and internal aspects of the agent's cognition may be represented equally well. This is because the method depicted in 3.3.5 is just as suitable for analyzing internal parameters (such as hunger or the loading state of the robot's battery) as for analyzing external parameters (such as visual perception).[21]

On the other hand, the context propositions constitute an autonomous system-internal abstract representation which may be processed independently of the spatio-temporal reality in which they originated. For example, the context propositions may represent information not only about current states, but also about past and possible future states of the task environment, which can be compared with each other, etc. The abstract processing of propositions may result in actions, however, which again relate meaningfully to the spatio-temporal reality.

The contextual aspects of the external world, e.g., the number of planets in the solar system, the atomic structure of the elements, the colors, etc., are inherently nonlinguis-

---

[21] In analytic philosophy, internal parameters – such as an individual toothache – have been needlessly treated as a major problem because they are regarded as a 'subjective' phenomenon which allegedly must be made objective by means of indirect methods such as the *double aspect* theory. See in this connection the treatment of propositional attitudes in Sect. 20.3, especially footnote 9.

tic in nature. To call these structures a 'language' is inappropriate because it would stretch the notion of a language beyond recognition.

The essentially nonlinguistic nature of the external originals holds also for their internal representations in the cognitive agent. Higher nontalking animals like a dog are able to develop concept types, to derive concept tokens, to combine them into elementary context propositions, to concatenate these into subcontexts, and to draw inferences. These cognitive structures and procedures are not explicitly defined as a language, however, but evolve solely as physiologically grown structures.

The contextual structures of a nontalking natural cognitive agent acquire a language aspect (i.e., description) only if and when they are analyzed theoretically. Corresponding artificial systems, on the other hand, usually begin with a language-based definition which is then realized in terms of the hardware and software of the implementation. However, even in artificial systems the language aspect may be completely ignored once a system is up and running: on the level of its machine operations the cognitive procedures of a nontalking robot are just as nonlinguistic as those of a corresponding natural agent.

The correlation between the nonlanguage and the language level in the description of a nontalking natural cognitive agent and its artificial model may be described schematically as follows:

3.4.5 ARTIFICIAL MODELING OF NATURAL COGNITION

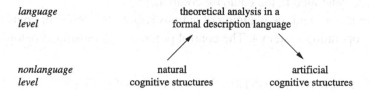

language *level*	theoretical analysis in a formal description language	
nonlanguage *level*	natural cognitive structures	artificial cognitive structures

The point is that modeling the representation of context within a robot in terms of propositions based on feature structures and defining the procedures operating on these context structures in terms of a formal grammar is not in conflict with the essentially nonlanguage character of these phenomena. Instead, feature structures and grammatical algorithms are general abstract formalisms which may be used as much for the modeling of nonlanguage structures as for the description of natural or artificial languages. Furthermore, once the nonlanguage structures and the associated inferences have been implemented as electronic procedures, they function without any recourse to the language that was used in their construction.

3.5 Recognition and Action

The cognitive representation of the task environment in the database of CURIOUS as well as the cognitive derivation of action schemata and their realization are based on five components which interact in well-defined procedures:

3.5.1 SCHEMATIC STRUCTURE OF CONTEXT-BASED COGNITION

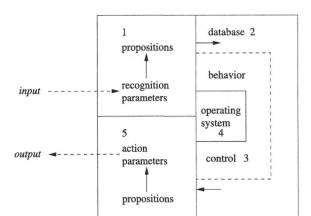

The recognition component 1 analyzes a field of CURIOUS's task environment by matching concept types with constellations of incoming parameter values. These are instantiated as concept tokens (cf. recognition in 3.3.5), automatically combined into concatenated context propositions (3.4.4), and stored in the database component 2.

A planned change of the task environment is realized by means of the action component 5. Thereby concept tokens$_{loc}$ are realized with the help of concept types as outgoing parameter constellations (action in 3.3.5). The action schemata are based on propositions which are generated in the database component 2.

The storing of recognitions and the planning of actions require the behavior control component 3 and the operating system 4. The control program 3 is illustrated below.

3.5.2 EXAMPLE OF A BEHAVIOR CONTROL PROGRAM FOR CURIOUS

1. Primary analysis of the current task environment:
   (a) Move into the start field A1.[22]
   (b) Analyze the current field:
       (i) Approximate bitmap outline with edge program.
       (ii) Measure color value inside the bitmap outline.
       (iii) Derive proposition.
   (c) Write proposition at index P-0.1 (present) into the database.
   (d) If current field is not D4, move into the next field and enter state b. Otherwise go to 2.
2. Secondary analysis of current task environment (inferences):
   (a) Count all triangles, rectangles, squares, red triangles, etc., in the primary analysis P-0.1 and write the result at index P-0.2 into the database.

---

[22] The formulation in 3.5.2 assumes that the task environment is divided into 16 fields, named A1, A2, A3, A4, B1, B2 etc., up to D4.

    (b) Compare the current secondary analysis P-0.2 with the previous secondary analysis P-1.2 and write the result (e.g., 'number of red triangles increased by 2') at index P-1.3 into the database.

3. Wait for 10 minutes.
4. Return to state 1.

This sketch must still be realized in a suitable programming language. Furthermore, notions like 'move into the next field', 'measure the color value', or 'wait for 10 minutes', require technical components (such as a system-internal clock) which realize these notions as corresponding operations. Neither would be a problem with existing technology.

The components of context-based cognition are in close interaction. For example, the behavior control guides the recognition and ensures that the resulting propositions are stored by the operating system at the correct index in the database. Then the behavior control determines the name of the next field and executes the command 'move into the next field' with the help of the operating system and the action component.

In the sense of nouvelle AI, CURIOUS exemplifies the notion of an *autonomous agent* because its symbolic processing is connected to its recognition and action.

> Without a carefully built physical grounding any symbolic representation will be mismatched to its sensors and actuators. These groundings provide the constraints on symbols necessary for them to be truly useful.
>
> Brooks (1990), p. 6

In the sense of classic AI, CURIOUS exemplifies also the notion of a *physical symbol system*:

> The total concept [of a physical symbol system] is the join of computability, physical realizability (and by multiple technologies), universality, the symbolic representation of processes (i.e., interpretability), and finally, symbolic structure and designation.
>
> Newell and Simon (1975), p. 46

The combination of an autonomous agent and a physical symbol system allow CURIOUS to recognize its task environment and to act in it. In addition, CURIOUS can refer to past and possible states of its task environment and compare them with the current state. These inferences operate meaningfully with internal states which may be completely independent of the current state of the concrete outside world.

As a purely contextual cognitive system, the current version of CURIOUS properly belongs in the domain of AI and robotics. Yet its cognitive mechanism – based on parameter values, concept types, concept tokens, propositions, the automatic analysis of artificial perception in the form of concatenated context propositions and the realization of context propositions in the form of artificial action – is an essential foundation of language-based cognition in computational linguistics.

This is firstly because in talking cognitive agents the contextual (nonlanguage) cognitive system functions as the *context* of language interpretation and production. Secondly, in the extension to language, the concept types serve an additional function as the literal *meanings* of the sign kind symbol. Thirdly, the analysis of context-based cognition is needed in order to explain the phylo- and ontogenetic development of natural language from earlier evolutionary and developmental stages without language.

Exercises

Section 3.1

1. Describe how the uses of natural language in 3.1.1 differ.
2. What are the communication components within the prototype hypothesis?
3. Explain the notions task environment and problem space.
4. Compare the description of natural visual pattern recognition (Rumelhart 1977; Anderson 1990) with electronic models (e.g., Marr 1982). Bring out the differences on the level of hardware and common properties on the logical level between the two types of system. Refer in particular to the section *Template-Matching Models* in Anderson (1990), pp. 58f.

Section 3.2

1. What criteria can be used to measure the functional adequacy of CURIOUS?
2. What is the problem of solipsism and how can it be avoided?
3. When would CURIOUS say something true (false)?
4. Describe the SHRDLU system of Winograd (1972). Discuss its critique in Dreyfus (1981).
5. Why is SHRDLU a closed system – and why is CURIOUS an open system?
6. Does SHRDLU distinguish between the task environment and the problem space?
7. What is the definition of the system-internal *context*. How does it relate to the notions of task environment and problem space?

Section 3.3

1. Explain the notions of type and token, using the letter A as the example.
2. What is the relation between the external object, the parameter values, the concept type and the concept token of a certain square?
3. How does a type originate in time?
4. Why does a token presuppose a type?
5. What is iconicity? What arguments have been made against it?
6. In what sense is the cognitive theory underlying CURIOUS iconic?

Section 3.4

1. What are the three basic elements from which propositions are built?
2. Which language categories do the basic elements of propositions correspond to?
3. How do the propositions of the internal context relate to the external reality?
4. Why do the propositions of the internal context form an autonomous system?
5. What is the role of language in the modeling of context-based cognition?
6. Why is the use of a grammar for modeling cognitive processes not in conflict with their essentially contextual (nonlanguage) nature?

Section 3.5

1. Describe the schematic structure of CURIOUS. Why are its components self-contained modules and how do they interact functionally?
2. Does CURIOUS fulfill the definition of a physical symbol system?
3. What are the operations of CURIOUS and are they decidable? How are these operations physically realized?
4. Explain how the concepts *left, right, up, down, large, small, fast, slow, hard, soft, warm, cold, sweet, sour*, and *loud* could be added to CURIOUS.
5. How would you implement the concept *search* in CURIOUS?
6. Would it be possible to add the command *Find a four-cornered triangle* to the behavior control 3.5.2? If so, what would happen? What is the logical status of the notion of a four-cornered triangle?

4. Language Communication

This chapter describes the functioning of natural language. To this purpose, the robot CURIOUS – introduced in Chap. 3 as an artificial cognitive agent without language – is equipped with additional components needed for natural language communication between the robot and its wardens.

Section 4.1 describes the components of language-based cognition as phylo- and ontogenetic specializations of the corresponding components of context-based (non-language) cognition, whereby the language-based components are arranged as a second level above the contextual components. Section 4.2 reconstructs language-based reference as an interaction between the levels of language and context. Section 4.3 explains the distinction between the literal meaning$_1$ of language signs and the speaker meaning$_2$ of utterances. Section 4.4 describes Frege's principle, and shows why the phenomena of ambiguity and paraphrase are, properly analyzed, no exceptions to it. Section 4.5 presents the principle of surface compositionality as a strict interpretation of Frege's principle and explains its functional and methodological role within the SLIM theory of language.

4.1 Adding Language

Communication between humans and machines requires a common language. At present, it is not yet possible to use natural language for this purpose. Instead, it is necessary to devise programming languages which adapt to the primitive communication capabilities of current machines. This has the disadvantage that the users have to learn the special commands of an artificial language.

The construction of machines which can communicate freely in a preexisting natural language (e.g., English) is the task of computational linguistics. This requires a modeling of cognitive states and procedures.[1] More specifically, a model of the speak

---

[1] Traditional grammar and theoretical linguistics (1.2.1) avoid the modeling of cognition. Their analyses are purely *sign-oriented* and concentrate on the structural properties of expressions such as word forms, sentences, or texts. For this, dictionaries have been compiled listing the words of a language; generative syntax grammars have been developed which try to formally distinguish between well-formed and ill-formed sentences; and the meanings

R. Hausser, *Foundations of Computational Linguistics*,
DOI 10.1007/978-3-642-41431-2_4, © Springer-Verlag Berlin Heidelberg 2014

mode must describe the internal procedures which map meanings to signs of natural language. Correspondingly, a model of the hear mode must describe the internal procedures which map the signs of natural language to the intended meanings.

Language understanding and language production have in common that they may be divided into two subprocedures, namely (i) sign *processing* and (ii) sign *interpretation*. They differ, however, in that they apply these subprocedures in opposite directions.

4.1.1 TWO SUBPROCEDURES OF LANGUAGE USE

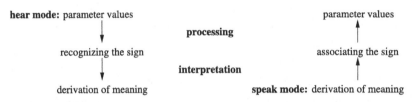

Language understanding (hear mode) begins with sign processing as a precondition for sign interpretation. Language production (speak mode) begins with the linguistic interpretation of what is meant as a precondition for sign processing.

By analogy to the analysis of contextual recognition and action in terms of characteristic constellations of parameters, concept types, and concept tokens (3.3.5), the linguistic recognition and action (synthesis) of language signs is based on corresponding correlations of parameters, surface types, and surface tokens:

4.1.2 PROCESSING OF LANGUAGE SIGNS

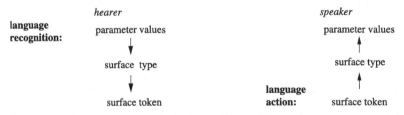

In the hear mode, language *input* is processed. It consists of incoming parameter values in the acoustic or visual medium to which surface types are applied. In the case of a successful matching, a corresponding surface token is derived and the lexical entry corresponding to the surface type is retrieved.

---

of sentences have been characterized in logical semantics as relations between expressions and the world – omitting the cognitive structure of the speaker-hearer. When the goal is to model successful language *use*, however, an *agent-oriented* approach cannot be avoided. It must provide a computational reconstruction of the cognitive processing in the speak and hear modes which is functionally equivalent to the natural prototype.

In the speak mode, language *output* is processed, yielding the surface token of a word form. It is realized with the help of the associated surface type as outgoing parameter values in the medium of choice, e.g., speech, writing, signing.

Integrating the components of language processing into the nonlanguage version of CURIOUS shown in 3.5.1 results in the following overall structure:

4.1.3 EXPANDED STRUCTURE OF CURIOUS

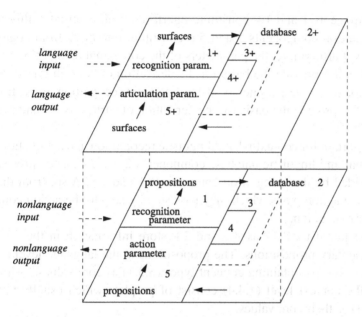

The lower level of the diagram shows the structure 3.5.1 of the contextual version of CURIOUS, though slanted to give a three-dimensional overall view. The upper level has the same structure as the lower level and contains the new components of language recognition 1+ and language synthesis 5+, as well as counterparts of the components 2, 3, and 4.

Phylogenetically and ontogenetically the components of the language level may be viewed as specializations which co-evolved with the corresponding components of the contextual level. Thus, component 1+ of word form recognition is a special function of the general component 1 for recognizing the task environment: just as CURIOUS recognizes, for example, a square by matching the concept type onto parameter values, thus forming a concept token (3.3.3 and 3.3.5, recognition), the expanded version recognizes a language surface by matching a suitable surface type onto language-based input parameters, resulting in a surface token (4.1.2, hearer).

Furthermore, component 5+ of language synthesis is a special function of the general component 5 for controlling action parameters. Just as CURIOUS can, for example, change its position from one field to another by realizing the concept tokens of an action proposition with the help of the associated concept types and its electro-motors as output parameter values (3.3.5, action), it can realize the surface tokens of language signs with the help of the associated surface types and the associated articulation as language-based output parameters (4.1.2, speaker).

4.2 Modeling Reference

The recognition components 1 and 1+ constitute interfaces from external reality to cognition, while the action components 5 and 5+ constitute interfaces from cognition to external reality. Furthermore, the parameters of the contextual recognition and action components 1 and 5 provide the basis for the derivation of concept types and concept tokens (3.3.5), while the parameters of the linguistic recognition and action components 1+ and 5+ provide the basis for the derivation of surface types and surface tokens (4.1.2).

At least equally important for contextual and linguistic recognition and action, however, are the contextual and linguistic database components 2 and 2+. They process the information provided by the recognition components 1 and 1+. Also, from this information they derive action plans which they pass step by step to the action components 5 and 5+ for realization.

The contextual and linguistic databases 2 and 2+ store information in the form of concatenated elementary propositions. The propositions at the language level are composed of proplets (3.4.3) containing concept types (3.3.1) as core values,[2] while the propositions at the context level (3.4.4) consist of proplets which usually take concept tokens (3.3.3) as their core values.

In the speak mode, content is communicated by mapping a subcontext of the database 2 into language. Thereby, the propositions (tokens) of the subcontext are matched by language propositions (types) generated in the database 2+. These language propositions are realized as language surfaces by means of the lexicon and the grammar.

In the hear mode, the content coded by the speaker into a language expression is reconstructed in the hearer's database 2. Thereby the incoming surfaces are assigned literal meanings by the lexicon and combined into language propositions of the database 2+ by means of the grammar. The speaker's subcontext is reconstructed either by matching these language propositions onto existing propositions in a corresponding subcontext of the database 2 or by storing the language propositions in the subcontext as new context propositions.

The matching process underlying language production and language understanding requires that the language propositions (types) and the context propositions (tokens)

---

[2] In addition to the concepts of *symbols* (Sect. 6.2), language propositions contain the pointers of *indexicals* (Sect. 6.3) as well as *names* (Sect. 6.4).

be properly positioned relative to each other. The conceptually simplest solution is to treat the language and the context database as two parallel layers,[3] as in 4.1.3.

In summary, the SLIM theory of language reconstructs the basic communication mechanism of natural language as an agent-internal matching between concept types at the language level and concept tokens at the context level. This differs from the approach of analytic philosophy and symbolic logic, which treat the central notion of *reference* as a direct relation between a language sign and an object in the world, defined in a metalanguage:

4.2.1 THE EXTERNAL VIEW OF REFERENCE IN ANALYTIC PHILOSOPHY

language sign: Look, a square!

reference:

object in the world:

This way of treating reference is independent of any communicating agents.

In communication, however, there is nothing in reality corresponding to the dotted line between the word square and the referential object. Any theory trying to explain reference functionally by postulating any such external connection between the sign and its referent trivializes reference by relying on a fictional construct.[4]

The SLIM alternative of reconstructing reference cognitively as an automatic agent-internal type/token matching is illustrated by the following example, which uses the type defined in 3.3.1 and the token defined in 3.3.3. The example is simplified in that (i) the embedding of core values into the feature structure of proplets (3.4.2) and thus (ii) any semantic relations to other proplets (3.4.3) are omitted.

---

[3] For the purpose of programming, this solution has turned out to be insufficient (CLaTR'11, Chap. 4).

[4] Without detracting from their merits in other areas, such a trivialized treatment of reference may be found in SHRDLU (Winograd 1972) and in Montague grammar (Montague 1974). Winograd treats an expression like blue pyramid by 'gluing' it once and for all to a corresponding construct in the toy world of the SHRDLU program. Montague defines the denotation of a predicate like sleeps in the metalanguage via the denotation function F for all possible worlds and moments of time. In either case, no distinction is made between the meanings of language expressions and corresponding sets of objects in the world.

Binding language expressions to their referents in terms of definitions (in either a logical or a programming language) has the short term advantage of (i) avoiding a semantic analysis of language meaning and (ii) treating reference as an external connection – like the dotted line in 4.2.1. The cost for this is high indeed: such systems are in principle limited to being closed. See Chaps. 19–22, especially Sect. 20.3, for a detailed discussion.

4.2.2 COGNITIVE 2 + 1 LEVEL ANALYSIS OF REFERENCE

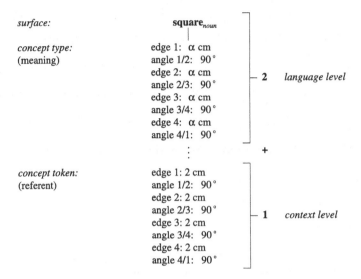

The 2 in the 2 + 1 structure represents the language level as a surface-meaning pair. The 1 represents the context level as a referent.

At the level of language, the word square is lexically analyzed as a fixed constellation of a surface (here the letter sequence s, q, u, a, r, e), subscripted with the category *noun*, and a literal meaning (here the concept type defined in 3.3.1). At the context level, the referent is the concept token defined in 3.3.3.

In CURIOUS, the fixed connection between a surface and its literal meaning is established by the designers, using a programming language. In humans, this connection is established by means of conventions which each speaker-hearer has to learn (de Saussure's first law, 6.2.2).

The speaker-hearer may use (tokens of) the same sign to refer to ever new objects in ever varying situations. Assume, for example, that two people land on the planet Mars for the first time and both see a rock shaped like a mushroom. If one says Look, a Mars mushroom! the other will understand.

This situation provides no occasion to establish – prior to the utterance – an external relation between the spontaneous ad hoc expression Mars mushroom and the intended referent. Thus, any attempt to explain successful reference in terms of an external relation between the signs and the referential objects, as in shown in 4.2.1, is unrealistic.

Instead, the successful reference of the expression Mars mushroom is based on the analyzed word forms Mars and mushroom, available to speaker and hearer as predefined, internal linguistic entities consisting of a surface, a category, and a minimal literal meaning (analogously to the analysis of the word form square shown in 4.2.2). Furthermore, their context must (i) indicate where they presently are, and (ii) represent the same characteristic rock formation in their respective fields of vision.

4.3 Using Literal Meaning

Depending on whether or not the relevant context of use is the current task environment, immediate and mediated[5] reference are to be distinguished:

4.3.1 IMMEDIATE AND MEDIATED REFERENCE

- *Immediate reference* is the speaker's or hearer's reference to objects in the current task environment.[6]
- *Mediated reference* is the speaker's or hearer's reference to objects which exist in memory, but not in the current task environment.[7]

Immediate reference and mediated reference have in common that they are based on internal cognitive procedures. They differ only in that in immediate reference the speaker-hearer interacts with the task environment at both the contextual and the linguistic level. Mediated reference, on the other hand, relates solely to structures of the internal database, for which reason the speaker-hearer interacts with the task environment at the linguistic level alone.

The following schema of immediate reference shows CURIOUS' linguistic and contextual interaction with the current task environment:

4.3.2 INTERNAL AND EXTERNAL ASPECTS OF IMMEDIATE REFERENCE

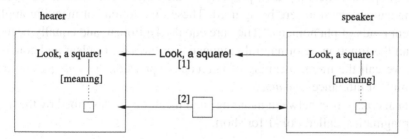

In this analysis, reference is reconstructed as a purely cognitive procedure, without any relation between the external sign [1] and its external referent [2]. Language

---

[5] Translated from German unmittelbar (*immediate*) and mittelbar (*mediated*). Wahrig (1986/1989) defines unmittelbar as 'ohne örtl. od. zeitl. Zwischenraum' (*without spatial or temporal distance*).

[6] Immediate reference may occur outside the communication prototype 3.1.2, for example, when a hearer finds a note on her desk, saying: Have you found the cookies in the right-hand drawer?

[7] For example, when speaker and hearer talk about the person of J.S. Bach (1685–1750), they refer to a contextual structure for which there is no counterpart in the current real world. Another form of mediated reference is CURIOUS' reference to objects in a state which was current in the past, as in How many red triangles did you find yesterday?

meanings are treated solely as mental constructs in the cognition of the language users.

The reason why such a cognitive analysis of reference has been rejected in analytic philosophy is the irrational fear that without an external reference relation (as shown in 4.2.1) cognitive agents might take the liberty to attach their own 'private' meanings to the surfaces of natural language.[8] There is no cause for concern, however: the alleged misuse is never committed because it would break the most elementary functional principle of communication, namely the *conventional* connection between the surface and its meaning.

For example, anyone who decides to use the word table for label and vice versa, should not be surprised if unprepared partners do not understand. Furthermore, if concerned partners were to catch up and join the game, this would amount to a highly local (and usually temporary) change in the convention-based connection between a language surface and its meaning. At any rate, postulating an external 'real' relation between a language expressions and its referent is not effective and does not contribute to making the meanings of language "objective" or "real."

The conventions connecting language surfaces to their literal (lexical) meanings have to be learned (i.e., agent-internally established) by every member of the language community. The conventions are maintained by their constant use and whoever does not master them has a problem with communication.

In addition to the notion of literal meaning as a property of expression types, there is the notion of speaker meaning as a property of utterances, i.e., actions in which tokens of language expressions are being used. These two notions of meaning apply to two different kinds of phenomena.[9] They are equally legitimate and equally necessary to explain the functioning of natural language. For the sake of clear and concise terminology, we call the literal meaning of language expressions $meaning_1$, and the speaker meaning of utterances $meaning_2$.

The functional connection between $meaning_1$ and $meaning_2$ is described by the first principle of pragmatics, called PoP-1 for short.[10]

---

[8] These concerns underlie the laborious arguments guarding against possible accusations of 'psychologism' in the writings of Frege, among others.

[9] One might argue that Wittgenstein concentrated on the first notion in his early (1921) work and on the second notion in his late (1953) philosophy. Rather than functionally integrating expression meaning into utterance meaning, as in PoP-1 (4.3.3), Wittgenstein opted to abandon his first approach. See also the discussion of ordinary language philosophy as exemplified by Grice in Sect. 4.5 and the discussion of semantic ontologies in Chap. 20.

[10] A preliminary version of PoP-1 may be found in Hausser (1980), where the distinction between $meaning_1$ and $meaning_2$ is already used. In CoL, p. 271, the first principle is published as one of altogether seven principles of pragmatics (see 5.3.3, 5.4.5, 6.1.3, 6.1.4, 6.1.5, and 6.1.7).

4.3.3 FIRST PRINCIPLE OF PRAGMATICS (PoP-1)

The speaker's utterance meaning$_2$ is the use of the sign's literal meaning$_1$ relative to an internal context.

The meaning$_1$ (concept type) of an expression exists independently of any contextual substructures (concept tokens) that might match it. Conversely, the contextual substructures exist independently of any corresponding meaning$_1$ of the language.[11] The meaning$_2$ derived by the hearer is nevertheless called the speaker meaning because the hearer's interpretation is successful only if the speaker's subcontext is reconstructed correctly.[12]

4.4 Frege's Principle

A clear distinction between meaning$_1$ and meaning$_2$ allows us to strictly maintain Frege's principle in the syntactic and semantic analysis of natural language. This principle is named after Gottlob FREGE (1848–1925), mathematician, philosopher, and one of the founders of modern mathematical logic. Though it was not stated explicitly in Frege's writings, the principle may be formulated as follows:

4.4.1 FREGE'S PRINCIPLE

The meaning of a complex expression is a function of the meaning of its parts and their mode of composition.

That the meaning of the parts influences the meaning of the whole is demonstrated by the comparison of the syntactically similar sentences a and b:

- *a.* The dog bites the man
- *b.* The dog bites the bone

---

[11] For example, the meaning$_1$ of the word **square** defined in 4.2.2 is a concept type which exists independently of any possible referents, in either the agent-internal context or the agent-external task environment. Correspondingly, the square objects in the world and their reflexes in the cognitive agents' context do not depend on the existence of a word with a corresponding meaning$_1$ – as demonstrated by the nonlanguage version of CURIOUS in Chap. 3.

This independence between concept types and corresponding concept tokens holds only for the secondary use of concept types as language meanings$_1$ which are lexically bound (by convention) to the surface types of symbols, as shown in 4.2.2. In their primary function as contextual types for certain parameter constellations, in contrast, concept types are the precondition for the derivation of concept tokens (3.3.5).

[12] See the definition of successful communication in 4.5.5 as well as the schemata of language interpretation in 5.4.1 and production in 5.4.2.

The sentences *a* and *b* have different meanings because they differ in one of their parts (i.e., the respective last word).

That the syntactic composition influences the meaning of the whole is demonstrated by the following sentences *a* and *a'*, which are composed from exactly the same word forms (parts):

a. The dog bites the man

a'. The man bites the dog

The sentences *a* and *a'* have different meanings because they differ in their mode of composition (exchange of the nouns dog and man).

Frege's principle is intuitively obvious, but it has often been misunderstood. This is caused by a failure to clearly decide whether the notion of 'meaning' should be the meaning$_1$ of expressions or the meaning$_2$ of utterances.

Consider, for example, the meaning$_1$ of The weather is beautiful! This expression may be used literally on a sunny summer day or ironically on a dark, wet day in November (northern hemisphere). In the second case, the meaning$_2$ may be paraphrased as *The weather is disgusting.* Thus, one sign (type) is related in two different utterances to two different contexts of use, resulting in two different meanings$_2$.

If Frege's principle is applied – erroneously – to a meaning$_2$ (e.g., what has been paraphrased as *The weather is disgusting* in the above example), then the meaning of the whole does not follow from the meaning of the parts (i.e., the words The weather is beautiful). Examples of this type have been used repeatedly to cast Frege's principle into doubt. In reality, however, these apparent counterexamples are fallacious because of confusing meaning$_1$ and meaning$_2$.

If Frege's principle is applied – correctly – to meaning$_1$, then it serves to characterize the functional relation between syntax and semantics: by putting together the word surfaces in the syntax, the associated meanings$_1$ are composed simultaneously on the level of the semantics. Thus, the meaning of complex expressions is derived compositionally via the composition of word forms whose surface and meaning$_1$ are in a fixed constellation (4.2.2). A completely different matter is the use of a complex meaning$_1$ relative to a context. This aspect lies entirely outside Frege's principle, namely in the domain of pragmatics, which is the theory of correlating the meaning$_1$ of language and the context of use.

Our standard interpretation of Frege's principle implies that two complex expressions with different surfaces must have different meanings$_1$. Correspondingly, two complex expressions with the same surface must have the same meaning$_1$.

4.4.2 STANDARD INTERPRETATION OF FREGE'S PRINCIPLE

There are two apparent exceptions to the standard interpretation, however, namely syntactic[13] ambiguity and syntactic paraphrase.

A surface is called syntactically ambiguous if it can be assigned two or more meanings$_1$. For example, the adjective good in

They don't know how good meat tastes

can be interpreted as an adverbial modifying taste or as an adnominal modifying meat. These alternative syntactic analyses come out quite clearly in the intonation.

Conversely, different surfaces constitute a set of syntactic paraphrases if their meanings$_1$ turn out to be equivalent. For example, the sentences

The dog bit the man (active)
The man was bitten by the dog (passive)

may be considered to have equivalent meanings$_1$.

As apparent exceptions to the standard interpretation of Frege's principle, syntactic ambiguity and paraphrase may be analyzed superficially as follows:

4.4.3 APPARENT EXCEPTIONS (Incorrect Analysis)

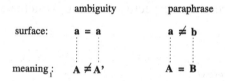

	ambiguity	paraphrase
surface:	a = a	a ≠ b
meaning$_i$	A ≠ A'	A = B

In the representation of ambiguity, two different meanings$_1$, A and A', seem to have the same surface, while in the representation of paraphrase two different surfaces seem to have the same meaning$_1$. Both representations seem to disagree with the standard interpretation 4.4.2 of Frege's principle.

However, for a proper understanding of Frege's principle we must recognize the distinction between an unanalyzed and a grammatically analyzed surface. Consider the following simplified example:

4.4.4 AMBIGUOUS UNANALYZED SURFACE AND ITS ANALYZED SURFACES

unanalyzed surface:
They don't know how good meat tastes

analyzed surface, reading 1:
They don't know how good$_{adn}$ meat tastes

analyzed surface, reading 2:
They don't know how good$_{adv}$ meat tastes

---

[13] See Sect. 6.5 for a distinction between syntactic, semantic, and pragmatic ambiguities.

Clearly, only the unanalyzed surface is ambiguous, while the analyzed surfaces are disambiguated by the grammatical subscripts of good$_{adn}$ and good$_{adv}$.

While syntactic ambiguity applies only to unanalyzed surfaces, Frege's principle applies only to analyzed surfaces. Thus, 4.4.3 must be reanalyzed as follows:

4.4.5 SYNTACTIC AMBIGUITY (Correct Analysis)

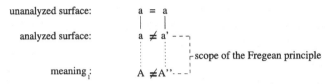

As a property of the unanalyzed surface, syntactic ambiguity is outside of the domain of Frege's principle; therefore syntactic ambiguity is no exception to its standard interpretation.

Another important aspect which 4.4.3 fails to express is that the meanings$_1$ of different complex surfaces can at best be equivalent, but never identical. In arithmetic, for example, no one in his right mind would express the semantic equivalence of $2+4$ and $3+3$ in terms of an identical 'underlying form' (e.g., 6). Instead, the correct way of treating paraphrase is to show the equivalence of the respective meaning$_1$ structures.

4.4.6 SYNTACTIC PARAPHRASE

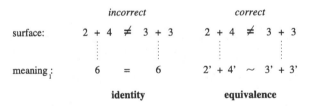

According to the correct analysis, paraphrases are no exception to the standard interpretation of Frege's principle: even though the meanings$_1$ turn out to be equivalent, they are not identical (Sect. 23.4).[14]

4.5 Surface Compositionality

In its standard interpretation, Frege's principle corresponds to the principle of surface compositionality.[15]

---

[14] The need to distinguish between identity and equivalence has been a topic of philosophy at least since the Middle Ages. A classic treatment of this subject as applied to intensional contexts (Sects. 20.1 and 20.2) is Barcan-Marcus (1960).

[15] The SC-I principle was first described in Hausser (1978). As shown in SCG, it may be interpreted formally as restricting Montague's homomorphism condition regarding the relation

4.5.1 SURFACE COMPOSITIONALITY I (SC-I PRINCIPLE)

An analysis of natural language signs is surface compositional if it uses only concrete word forms as building blocks, such that all syntactic and semantic properties of a complex expression derive systematically from (i) the lexical properties of the isolated word forms and (ii) their standard syntactic-semantic composition.

For linguistic analysis, surface compositionality has far-reaching methodological, mathematical, and functional consequences:

– Methodology: syntactic analyses are *maximally concrete* because no kind of zero surface or underlying form may be used;
– Mathematics: syntactic and semantic analyses are of the *lowest complexity* (12.5.7 and 21.5.2, respectively);
– Function: the internal matching between meaning$_1$ and context is extended from single words (4.2.2) to the systematic syntactic-semantic *combination* of expressions.

The principles of internal matching and surface compositionality – represented by the letters IM and S, respectively, in the SLIM acronym – presuppose each other in the following way. Internal matching is a precondition for a strictly compositional analysis in syntax and semantics, because it moves all aspects of meaning$_2$ into the pragmatics, where they belong. Conversely, surface compositionality provides the systematically derived meaning$_1$ needed for internal matching with the context.

While functionally integrated into the mechanism of natural language communication, surface compositionality is primarily a methodological standard for ensuring concreteness in the empirical analysis of natural language syntax and semantics. To show the consequences of violating this standard, let us consider two examples, namely generative grammar within nativism, and speech act theory within ordinary language philosophy. A third example from yet another tradition is Montague grammar; for a detailed analysis see SCG.

Violating Surface Compositionality: EXAMPLE I
Generative grammar within nativism began with transformational grammar (TG). TG dominated theoretical linguistics between 1957 and 1981, and is still influential in current theories[16] – protestations to the contrary notwithstanding. Transforma-

_____

between a categorial syntax and a formal semantics based on a typed lambda calculus. The relation between the SC-I principle and the mathematical notion of a homomorphism is described in Sect. 21.3, in which the informal, intuitive version of 4.5.1 is supplemented by the formal variant SC-II (21.3.6).

[16] A description of the post-transformational systems of GB, LFG, and GPSG may be found in Sells (1985). Yet another variant of nativism is HPSG as the continuation of GPSG.

tional grammar aims at characterizing the innate linguistic knowledge of the speaker-hearer.

In TG, deep structures defined as context-free constituent structures (Chap. 8) are mapped to surface structures by means of transformations. Since Katz and Postal (1964), deep and surface structures have been assumed to be semantically equivalent, i.e., the transformations are 'meaning preserving.'

The correlation between semantically equivalent deep and surface structures in TG is illustrated by the following examples:

4.5.2 EXAMPLES OF 'CLASSICAL' TRANSFORMATIONS

DEEP STRUCTURE: SURFACE STRUCTURE:

Passive:
Peter closed the door $\Rightarrow$ The door was closed by Peter

Do-support:
Peter not open the door $\Rightarrow$ Peter didn't open the door

Reflexivization
Peter$_i$ shaves Peter$_i$ $\Rightarrow$ Peter shaves himself

There-insertion
A hedgehog is in the garden $\Rightarrow$ There is a hedgehog in the garden

Pronominalization
Peter$_i$ said that Peter$_i$ was tired $\Rightarrow$ Peter said that he was tired

Relative clause formation
Peter [Peter was tired] $\Rightarrow$ Peter, who was tired

Main clause order in German
Peter die Tür geschlossen hat $\Rightarrow$ Peter hat die Tür geschlossen

Object raising[a]
Peter persuaded Mary [Mary sleep] $\Rightarrow$ Peter persuaded Mary to sleep

Subject-raising
Peter promised Mary [Peter sleep] $\Rightarrow$ Peter promised Mary to sleep

---

[a]A lexical treatment of so-called *subject raising* and *object raising* may be found in SCG, p. 254.

The transformational derivation of surface structures from deep structures has no functional role in communication.[17] Instead, transformations are intended to express linguistic generalizations at the level of competence.[18]

Transformations violate surface compositionality because they treat the concrete parts of the surface and their mode of composition as irrelevant for the resulting meaning. The properties distinguishing a surface from its semantically equivalent deep structure have been belittled as *syntactic sugar.*

TG's violation of surface compositionality is illustrated by the passive sentence

The door was closed by Peter.

Here transformations change the word order (mode of composition) on the way from the deep structure to the surface. Furthermore, the word forms was and by are not treated as meaningful elements in their own right, but smuggled into the surface by transformations (Sect. 21.3).

From the viewpoint of surface compositionality it is therefore no surprise that the presumed meaning equivalence between active and passive has turned out to be spurious. For example, there is general agreement that the active sentence

Everyone in this room speaks at least two languages

and the corresponding passive sentence

At least two languages are spoken by everyone in this room

differ in meaning. The passive has the dominant reading that there are two languages (e.g., English and French) which everyone speaks. The active only says that each person speaks two languages, which may differ from person to person.[19] Because of the lack of meaning equivalence illustrated by these examples, the passive transformation was later abandoned in nativist grammar.

The purpose of transformations was to characterize the innate human language faculty. There is a general law of nature, however, that the form of innate structures follows their function. For example, in an aquatic bird such as a duck the form of the feet is clearly innate. This innate structure can be described in many different ways,

---

[17] Some followers of Chomsky have recognized this as a weakness. However, their belated attempts to provide transformations with a genuine functional role have not been successful. Chomsky has always rejected such attempts as inappropriate for his nativist program (e.g., Chomsky 1965, p. 9).

[18] Transformations were later replaced by similar mechanisms. When asked in 1994 about the frequent, seemingly radical, changes in his theories, Chomsky pointed out that the 'leading ideas' had never changed (personal communication by Prof. Dong-Whee Yang, Seoul, Korea 1995). See also Chomsky (1981), p. 3, in the same vein.

[19] The surface compositional treatment is based on separate derivations of the active and the passive. If they happen to be paraphrases, this may be expressed by establishing semantic equivalence on the level of meanings$_1$ (4.4.6).

but its scientific analysis in biology must explain the relation between the specific form (webbed toes) and the specific function (locomotion in water by paddling).

The same holds for innate cognitive structures. In particular, the human language capacity may be described in many different ways, but its scientific analysis in linguistics must explain the relation between the specific form of natural language surfaces and their specific function in the time-linear coding and decoding of content.

There may be innate structures whose function has either not yet been discovered, is of seemingly little importance (as the wing pattern of butterflies), or has been lost during evolution (as in the rudimentary pelvis bones of whales). Natural language communication, however, is neither a minor nor a lost function.

Consequently, any structure alleged to be part of the innate human language faculty is implausible if it cannot be demonstrated to have a functional role in the mechanism of natural communication. We formulate this conclusion as a cognitive variant of *Ockham's razor* – a rule of science named after William of OCKHAM (1270–1347).

4.5.3 COGNITIVE VARIANT OF OCKHAM'S RAZOR

> Entities or components of grammar should not be postulated as innate if they have no clearly defined function within natural communication.

The cognitive razor applies to transformational grammar as well as to all later variants of nativism including LFG,[20] GPSG,[21] and HPSG.[22] Like transformational grammar, their linguistic generalizations are nonfunctional with respect to communication and inherently in violation of surface compositionality (21.3.4 and 21.3.5). It is no accident that their computational complexity turned out to be similar to that of transformational grammar (Sect. 8.5), namely computationally intractable.

Violating Surface Compositionality: EXAMPLE II
A second example of a non-surface-compositional approach is the definition of meaning by Paul GRICE (1913–1988). It is in the tradition of Ludwig WITTGENSTEIN's (1889–1951) ordinary language philosophy and John Langshaw AUSTIN's (1911–1960) speech act theory, specifically Wittgenstein (1953) and Austin (1962).[23] This philosophical tradition has a considerable following because it provides an intention-

---

[20] Bresnan (ed.) (1982).

[21] Gazdar et al. (1985).

[22] Pollard and Sag (1987, 1994).

[23] According to Levinson (1983), pp. 227f.

> there are strong parallels between the later Wittgenstein's emphasis on language usage and language-games and Austin's (1962:147) insistence that "the total speech act in the total speech situation is the *only actual* phenomenon which, in the last resort, we are engaged in elucidating". Nevertheless Austin appears to have been largely unaware of, and probably quite uninfluenced by, Wittgenstein's later work, and we may treat Austin's theory as autonomous.

based alternative to the logical definition of meaning in terms of truth conditions (Chaps. 19–21).

4.5.4 DEFINITION OF MEANING BY GRICE

> Definiendum: U meant something by uttering x.
> Definiens: For some audience A, U intends his utterance of x to produce in A some effect (response) E, by means of A's recognition of the intention.[24]

The speaker (utterer) U conventionally uses x with a certain intention. Given a token of x, the hearer (audience) A recognizes the intention because A has gotten used to associating x with this particular intention type of U. Knowledge of the type enables the hearer A to recognize the intention of the speaker U, because the speaker *habitually intends* for the sentence to have a certain effect.

In this way, the sentence meaning is defined as the type of a convention, while the corresponding utterance meanings are defined as tokens of this type. By reducing sentence meaning to a conventional habit,[25] an explicit representation of literal word meanings and their composition based on syntactic analysis is avoided.

As has been pointed out repeatedly,[26] however, Grice's construction is not suitable to explain the evolution of natural language communication. How are the sentence meanings (types) supposed to originate in the language community so that the corresponding utterance meanings (tokens) can have their intended effect? For the hearer, the type must already exist as a convention in order to be able to recognize a corresponding token. The point is that convention cannot be used to establish a certain type of intention, because for starting the convention by recognizing the first token, the type must already be in place.

Another problem for Grice is nonstandard uses of language, such as metaphor or irony. After all, tokens of a purely convention-based sentence meaning can only be recognized by the audience if they comply with the standard, habitual use.

That Austin, who was 22 years younger than Wittgenstein, was "largely unaware" of Wittgenstein's writings, is attributed by Levinson to their teaching at different universities: Austin was at Oxford and Wittgenstein 66 miles away at Cambridge. The train once connecting the towns via Bletchley was known as the "brain line."

[24] Grice (1957, 1965).

[25] This reduction is epitomized by ordinary language philosophy's imprecise and misleading formula

MEANING IS USE.

The SLIM theory of language is also based on use, but on the use of literal expression meanings$_1$ relative to a context of interpretation, resulting in the speaker's utterance meaning$_2$ (PoP-1, 4.3.3).

[26] See for example Searle (1969), pp. 44f.

In order to nevertheless handle spontaneous metaphors and other nonstandard uses, Grice proposed another theory, based on violating conventions and known as conversational implicature. Conversational implicature formulates common sense principles for making sense of the exception to the rule.[27]

Thus, Grice simultaneously uses two opposite methods for realizing intentions. One is his standard method of *using conventions*, the other is his nonstandard method of *violating conventions*. Neither method is surface compositional because neither is based on the structure of the signs and their literal meaning$_1$.

Conveying intentions by either conforming to habit, or violating it selectively, may succeed for utterer U and audience A if they have been familiar with each other for the better part of a lifetime in highly ritualized situations. For better or worse, however, this is not language communication in the normal sense.

For explaining the interpretation of, for example, an average newspaper editorial with ironic innuendos and metaphoric insinuations, Grice's meaning definition does not suffice. This is because it does not take into account the differentiated syntactic-semantic structure of natural language signs by means of which an infinite variety of complex meaning structures may be encoded.[28]

Apart from the internal problems of Grice's theory, the notions 'recognition of the intention,' 'producing some effect,' and 'intending for some audience' of his meaning definition are not sufficiently algebraic[29] for a computational model of natural com-

---

[27] See also Austin (1962), pp. 121f.

[28] Rather than applying the type/token distinction to conventions, the SLIM theory of language applies it to recognition and action. In contextual recognition, for example, the types arise as classes of similar parameter constellations. Once a type has evolved in this way it is used to classify corresponding constellations of parameter values, resulting in tokens instantiating the type.

In the extension to language, the types are used in a secondary function, namely as the meaning$_1$ of symbols. The interpretation of symbols is based on matching these meanings$_1$ (concept types) with contextual referent structures (concept tokens).

The principle of internal matching between concept types and concept tokens aims from the outset at handling the spontaneous use of language to express new meanings$_2$ relative to new contexts. Conventions are used only for fixing the relation between the language surfaces and their meaning$_1$ inside the speaker-hearer (in agreement with de Saussure's first law, 6.2.2).

This straightforward explanation of the primary origin and function of types and tokens on the contextual level and the secondary functioning of the types as the word meanings$_1$ of language surfaces cannot be transferred to Grice's speech act theory. The reason is that the speaker's intentions are not accessible to the hearer's recognition as characteristic parameter constellations – in contradistinction to the SLIM-theoretic meaning$_2$ derivation based on lexical types and contextual tokens.

[29] Regarding its mathematical properties, a formal definition of Grice's approach has yet to be provided. What such a formalization could look like is indicated by another system of ordinary language philosophy and speech act theory, namely that of Searle and Van-

munication. For this, a functional theory of language is required which explains the understanding and purposeful use of natural language in terms of explicit procedures.

This is a clear and simple goal, but for theories not designed from the outset to effectively model natural language communication, it is practically out of reach. Hypothetically, it could turn out in hindsight that a nonfunctional theory – such as structuralism, behaviorism, speech act theory, nativism, model theory, stratificational grammar, meaning-text theory, etc. – happens to be functionally suitable anyway. This, however, would constitute a historically unique scenario: a nonfunctional theory turns out to be of such profound correctness regarding interfaces, components, basic elements, functional flow, etc., that it can be used by later generations as an adequate functional model – without any need for major corrections. Such a stroke of luck has not occurred in linguistics, and is probably without precedent in the whole history of science.

In conclusion we turn to the notion of *successful communication* within the SLIM theory of language. In human-human dialog, it is impossible to determine for sure whether the hearer understands precisely in the way the speaker intended (solipsism, Sect. 3.2). In human-machine dialog, in contrast, direct access to the internal cognitive processing of the machine makes it possible to reconstruct this notion objectively:

4.5.5 SUCCESSFUL NATURAL HUMAN-COMPUTER COMMUNICATION

Let L be an established natural language, SH a human speaker-hearer of L, and CA an artificial cognitive agent (e.g., an advanced version of CURIOUS).

– *Successful natural language interpretation*
CA communicates successfully in the hear mode, if CA understands the L-utterance in the way intended by SH. In technical terms this means that CA correctly recreates the speaker meaning$_2$ of the L-utterance in its database. The developers of CA can verify the procedure because (i) they themselves can understand the utterance in L, and (ii) they can view the interpretation directly in the database of CA.

– *Successful natural language production*
CA communicates successfully in the speak mode, if CA formulates the content to be transmitted in L in a way that SH can understand. This requires technically that CA map a certain content in its database to an L-expression from which this content may correctly be reconstructed by SH. The developers of CA can verify the procedure because (i) they have direct access to the database content to be communicated, and (ii) they themselves can understand the surface in L.

derveken (1985). Depending on one's approach, this formalization either may be shown to be too imprecise for drawing any firm mathematical conclusions, or some particular aspect of it may be isolated for demonstrating high complexity.

The logical structure of the database and the procedures of reading-in (hear mode) and -out (speak mode) are described in more detail in Chaps. 22–24.

Exercises

Section 4.1

1. What components are required to extend the nonlanguage version of CURIOUS presented in Chap. 3 into a robot communicating in natural language?
2. In what sense are the components of language processing in CURIOUS a specialization of its contextual cognitive components?
3. What is the relation between natural language defined as a set of grammatically analyzed expressions, and the cognitive structure of the speaker-hearer using the language? Explain your answer in three to four pages.
4. Why does the construction of artificial cognitive agents have a methodological impact on the formation of linguistic theory?

Section 4.2

1. What is the internal aspect of reference?
2. Explain the cognitive [2 + 1] level structure of reference in natural language.
3. On what basis does the hearer establish reference if the speaker uses an expression not heard before (e.g., Mars mushroom) to refer to an object not seen before?
4. Why is the handling of reference nontrivial in the case of CURIOUS, but trivial in the case of SHRDLU? How does this difference depend on the distinction or nondistinction between task environment and problem space?
5. In what respect can SHRDLU do more than CURIOUS in its present form? What would be required to combine the different merits of the two systems?

Section 4.3

1. Explain which letters in the acronym of the SLIM theory of language relate directly or indirectly to the [2 + 1] level structure of reference?
2. What is the difference between immediate and mediated reference?
3. Describe the connection between reference and cognitive processing.
4. What is the difference between the speak mode and the hear mode in natural language communication?

5. Describe the connection between the literal meaning$_1$ of a language expression and the speaker meaning$_2$ of an utterance.

6. Given that the time linearity of natural language signs is represented from left to right, can you explain why the hearer is placed to the left of the speaker in 4.3.2 and 5.2.1?

Section 4.4

1. Who was Frege and when did he live? Explain the principle that carries his name.

2. Does Frege's principle relate to the speaker's utterance meaning$_2$ or the expression's literal meaning$_1$?

3. Why are ambiguity and paraphrase apparent exceptions to Frege's principle? Which properties of the analysis make it possible to eliminate these exceptions? Explain your answer using concrete examples of ambiguity and paraphrase.

4. Name other areas in which confusing identity and equivalence has led to problems (cf. Barcan-Marcus 1960).

5. What is the relation between the principle of surface compositionality and Frege's principle?

Section 4.5

1. Give nine different examples of transformations and show how they violate surface compositionality.

2. Why can Frege's principle be applied only to the deep structures of transformational grammar, but not to the surface structures?

3. What is a methodological objection to applying Frege's principle to deep structures?

4. Describe the definition of meaning by Grice and explain why it is not suitable for computational linguistics.

5. Compare the analysis of meaning in the theory of Grice and the SLIM theory of language. Explain the different uses of the *type/token* distinction and the different definitions of sentence and utterance meaning in the two theories.

6. What can a concrete implementation of CURIOUS as a talking robot do for an improved understanding of natural language communication?

7. Explain the criteria for successful human-computer communication in natural language.

8. Compare the language processing of Eliza, SHRDLU and CURIOUS.

5. Using Language Signs on Suitable Contexts

The crucial question for the interpretation of natural language is: how does the relation between the sign and the intended referent come about? Chapters 3 and 4 investigated this question in the context of designing the talking robot CURIOUS. This design is simplified in that cognition and language are limited to triangles, quadrangles, and circles of various sizes and colors. Nevertheless, CURIOUS models the general functioning of natural language insofar as the system can talk not only about new objects of a known kind, but also about situations outside its current task environment, such as past or future situations.

This chapter investigates principles which allow the natural or artificial hearer to *find* the correct subcontext such that the internal matching between the expression used and the subcontext selected results in successful communication as defined in 4.5.5. This leads to a further differentiation of the SLIM theory of language and an extension of CURIOUS to general phenomena of natural language pragmatics.

Section 5.1 compares the structure of CURIOUS with Bühler's organon model and Shannon and Weaver's information theory. Section 5.2 demonstrates, with an example of nonliteral use, why the precise delimitation of the internal subcontext is crucial for the correct interpretation of natural language signs. Section 5.3 describes the four parameters which define the origin of signs (STAR) and specify the correct subcontext for interpretation. Section 5.4 explains the function of the time-linear order of the signs for production and interpretation, as well as de Saussure's second law. Section 5.5 describes the conceptualization underlying language production as an autonomous navigation through the propositions of the internal database.

5.1 Bühler's Organon Model

A theory of pragmatics analyzes the general principles of purposeful action. It describes how a cognitive agent can achieve certain goals by using certain means in certain situations. Examples of pragmatic problems are the use of a screwdriver to fasten a screw, the use of one's legs to go from *a* to *b*, the scavenging of food from the refrigerator in the middle of the night to fix a BLT and satisfy one's hunger, or the request that someone fix and serve the sandwich.

R. Hausser, *Foundations of Computational Linguistics,*
DOI 10.1007/978-3-642-41431-2_5, © Springer-Verlag Berlin Heidelberg 2014

Depending on whether or not the means employed are signs of language, we speak of linguistic and nonlinguistic pragmatics. Just as language recognition and articulation may be analyzed as phylo- and ontogenetic specializations of contextual (nonlanguage) recognition and action, respectively (Sect. 4.1), linguistic pragmatics may be analyzed as phylo- and ontogenetic specializations of nonlanguage pragmatics.

This embedding of linguistic pragmatics into nonlinguistic pragmatics was recognized by PLATO (427?–347 BC), who pointed out the *organon* character of language in his dialog Kratylos. In modern times, the tool character (*Werkzeugcharakter*) of language was emphasized by Karl BÜLER (1879–1963):

> Die Sprache ist dem Werkzeug verwandt; auch sie gehört zu den Geräten des Lebens, ist ein Organon wie das dingliche Gerät, das leibesfremde Zwischending; die Sprache ist wie das Werkzeug ein *geformter Mittler*. Nur sind es nicht die materiellen Dinge, die auf den sprachlichen Mittler reagieren, sondern es sind die lebenden Wesen, mit denen wir verkehren.
>
> [Language is akin to the tool: language belongs to the instruments of life, it is an organon like the material instrument, a body-extraneous hybrid; language is – like the tool – a *mediator designed for a specific purpose*. The only difference is that it is not material things which react to the linguistic mediator, but living beings with whom we communicate.]
>
> Bühler (1934), p. xxi

Bühler summarized his analysis in terms of the well-known organon model. In addition to the function of language *representation*, the organon model includes the functions of language *expression* and language *appeal*:

5.1.1 BÜHLER'S ORGANON MODEL

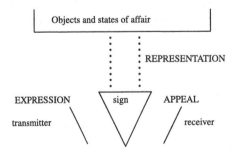

REPRESENTATION refers to the language-based transfer of information. EXPRESSION refers to the way the transmitter produces the sign. APPEAL refers to the way the sign affects the receiver beyond the bare content of the sign.

At first glance the relation between the organon model and the CURIOUS model (4.1.3) is not obvious. This is because the organon model describes the communication prototype (3.1.2) from the viewpoint of an external observer – like 4.2.1. The CURIOUS model, in contrast, describes the internal mechanism of natural language communication. As a consequence, the organon model is limited to immediate reference, while the CURIOUS model can also handle mediated reference (4.3.1) to subcontexts of past, future, and other nonactual modalities.

Upon closer investigation, however, the following correlations between the organon model and the CURIOUS model may be established. The function of *expression* in 5.1.1 is to be located in component 5+ (language synthesis) of 4.1.3. The function of *appeal* is to be located in component 1+ (language recognition). The function of *representation* is performed by means of lexical, syntactic, and semantic components in the language-based database structure 2+ and interpreted in relation to the contextual database structure 2.

Thus, the organon model and CURIOUS are compatible, though the organon model applies only to the communication prototype of 3.1.2, and is limited to an external, noncognitive viewpoint. This limitation is reflected in Bühler's terminology: the notions transmitter and receiver are more appropriate for the transmission of surfaces (signals) than for modeling the cognitive processing in the speak and the hear mode.

The mathematical theory of signal transmission was presented in 1949 by Shannon and Weaver as *information theory* – 15 years after Bühler's 'Sprachtheorie.' Information theory investigates the conditions under which the transmission of electric and electronic signals is of sufficient quality. Central notions of information theory besides transmitter and receiver are the bandwidth of the channel, the redundancy and relative entropy of the codes, and the noise in the transmission.

The laws of information theory hold also in everyday conversation, but impairments of the transmission channel such as background noises, slurring of speech, hearing loss, etc., are hardly components of the natural language communication mechanism. The latter must be based on a model of cognitive agents – which requires the definition of interfaces, components, surface-meaning mappings, etc., and goes far beyond the long-distance transmission and reception of surfaces.[1]

5.2 Pragmatics of Tools and Pragmatics of Words

A theory of nonlinguistic pragmatics must describe the structure of the tools, of the objects to be worked on, and of the user's strategies in applying a tool to an object in order to realize a certain purpose. Analogously, a theory of linguistic pragmatics requires an explicit definition of meaning$_1$ (tool), of the interpretation context (object to be worked on), and of the strategies for relating a meaning$_1$ and a context such that the intended meaning$_2$ is communicated. Just as a tool is positioned at a specific

---

[1] Nevertheless there have been repeated attempts to glorify the mechanics of code transmission into an explanation of natural communication. A case in point is Eco (1975), whose theory of semiotics within the framework of Shannon and Weaver's information theory begins with the example of a buoy which 'tells' the engineer about dangerous elevations of the water table. Other cases are Grice's (1957) 'bus bell model' and Dretske's (1981) 'doorbell model.'

spot of the object to be worked on and then manipulated in a purposeful way, a suitable meaning$_1$ is positioned relative to a certain subcontext in order to represent it linguistically (speak mode) or to insert it into the proper subcontext (hear mode).

The analogy between an external tool like a screwdriver and a cognitive tool like the word table shows up in their respective literal and nonliteral uses. While the 'literal use' of a screwdriver consists in the fastening and unfastening of screws, it also has a multitude of 'nonliteral uses,' such as for punching holes into juice cans, as a doorstop, as a paperweight, etc. Because these nonliteral uses depend on the momentary purpose and the properties of the current context, it is impossible to provide a valid enumeration[2] of all the possible uses (i.e., all the different possible instances of meaning$_2$) of a screwdriver.

Instead the user infers the most effective application of the tool for each new context and for each new purpose via general principles of pragmatics. These refer to (i) the structure of the tool with its well-known shape and properties of material (constituting the screwdriver's meaning$_1$) and (ii) the current properties of the object to be worked on (constituting the 'context of use').

By analogy, a word like table may be used not only to refer to prototypical tables. Assume that the hearer is in a room never seen before with an orange-crate in the middle. If the speaker says Put the coffee on the table!, the hearer will understand that table refers to the orange-crate. Given this limited context of use, the minimal meaning$_1$ of the word table best fits the structure of the orange-crate (*best match*).

5.2.1 NONLITERAL USE OF THE WORD table

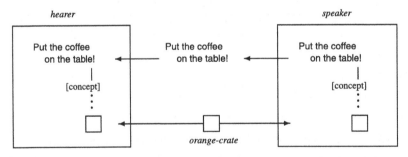

However, if a prototypical table were placed next to the orange-crate, the hearer would interpret the sentence differently, putting the coffee not on the orange-crate, but on the table. This is not caused by a change in the meaning$_1$ of table, but by the fact that the context of use has changed, providing an additional candidate for best match.

The principle of best match can only function properly if the choice of possible candidates is restricted. Therefore the selection and delimitation of the subcontext is crucial for the successful interpretation of natural language. This leads to a central question of linguistic pragmatics:

---

[2] This is another problem for the speech act theory of Austin, Grice, and Searle (Sect. 4.5).

How does the speaker code the selection and delimitation of the subcontext used into the sign and how can these be correctly inferred by the hearer?

The internal database of a speaker-hearer comprises all the episodic and theoretical facts accumulated in the course of a lifetime. To correctly find the small, delimited subcontext required for each interpretation of language in this huge database is not trivial. It is particularly challenging in the case of mediated reference (4.3.1), in which the context of use does not correspond to the current task environment.

5.3 Finding the Correct Subcontext

As an example of mediated reference consider a postcard, i.e., a sign whose places of origin and of interpretation are far apart in time and space. On a beach in New Zealand on a hot day in February 2013, the 'hearer' Heather is reading a postcard with the Statue of Liberty on one side and the following text on the other:

5.3.1 POSTCARD EXAMPLE

New York, December 1, 2012

Dear Heather,

Your dog is doing fine. The weather is very cold. In the morning he played in the snow. Then he ate a bone. Right now I am sitting in the kitchen. Fido is here, too. The fuzzball hissed at him again. We miss you.

Love,

Spencer

Which structural properties of the sign enable Heather to select from all her stored knowledge the one subcontext which is correct for the interpretation of this text?

Like all human artifacts the postcard (as a handwritten sign) has a point of origin. In signs this origin is defined by the following parameters:

5.3.2 PARAMETERS OF ORIGIN OF SIGNS (STAR)

S = the **S**patial place of origin
T = the **T**emporal moment of origin
A = the **A**uthor
R = the intended **R**ecipient.

The parameters S, T, A, and R have their values defined automatically during production and constitute the STAR of a sign.[3] All meaningful utterances have their unique STAR which is a necessary property of sign *tokens*.

---

[3] Following a suggestion by Brian MacWhinney, Carnegie Mellon University, in 2000, the earlier naming convention of 'STAR point' (Hausser 1989a) is changed to simply 'STAR'.

In some respects the STAR resembles Bühler's (1934) notion of *origo*. However, the STAR is defined as a property of the (token of the) sign, whereas the *origo* seems to refer to the spatio-temporal coordinates and gestures of the speaker-hearer during the utterance.

The spatio-temporal location specified by a STAR may be interpreted rather loosely. Even in spoken language the temporal origin is strictly speaking an interval rather than a point. In writing, this interval may be of considerable length.

Apart from the parameters of origin of a sign there are the parameters of its interpretation. The latter are called ST_{inter} because they consist of (1) a spatial location S and (2) a moment of time T. Just as the STAR is fixed automatically by the origin, an ST_{inter} is defined whenever a sign is interpreted.[4]

While the STAR is unique for any given sign (token) and defined once and for all, the number of its possible ST_{inter} is open. For example, a postcard which is lost in the mail may not have any ST_{inter} at all, whereas a letter published in *The New York Times* will have many ST_{inter}.

The ST_{inter} is known to each single hearer or reader: it equals his or her current circumstances. Yet the correct interpretation of a sign depends mostly on the knowledge of its STAR, which may be difficult to infer.[5] Consider a clay tablet found in an archaeological dig in Mesopotamia. The ST_{inter} of the various interpretation attempts by various scientists make no difference as to what the tablet really means. What is crucial are the place of origin (S), the correct dynasty (T), the writer (A), and the addressee (R) of the clay tablet.[6]

---

[4] Many different constellations between STAR and ST_{inter} are possible. For example, in someone talking to himself the S and T parameters of the STAR and ST_{inter} are identical. Furthermore, the A value and the R value of the STAR are equal.

If two people talk to each other in the situation of the communication prototype, the T parameter values in the STAR and ST_{inter} are practically the same, while the S values are significantly different. Furthermore, in a dialog the R value of the STAR equals the hearer, while in the case of someone overhearing a conversation, this person will be distinct from the R value of the STAR.

[5] In logical semantics the speaker – and thus the origin of signs – is not formally treated. For this reason, the model-theoretic interpretation can only be defined relative to an (arbitrary) ST_{inter}. This is of no major consequence in the case of eternally true sentences. In the extension of logical semantics to contingent sentences, however, the formal interpretation relative to ST_{inter} is plainly in conflict with the empirical facts of communication.

Similarly, speech act theory has attempted to represent the speaker's intention and action in terms of performative clauses like *I request, I declare*, etc. These are subscripted to the language expression and treated as part of the type (sentence meaning). Thereby the utterance-dependent interpretation of *I*, of the addressee, of the moment of time, and of the place is left untreated. This may seem acceptable for the communication prototype (3.1.2), but for the interpretation of a postcard, a theoretical treatment of the STAR as a property of the utterance cannot be done without.

[6] The importance of the STAR is also shown by the question of whether the tablet is real or fake. While the glyphs remain unaffected by this question, the different hypotheses regarding authenticity lead to different interpretations. Another example is an anonymous letter whose threatening quality derives in large part from the fact that it specifies the recipient R without revealing the author A.

Only face-to-face communication – as in the communication prototype – provides the hearer with the STAR directly. Therefore, the pragmatic interpretation of natural language is especially easy in those situations. In contrast, signs not intended for face-to-face communication must ensure their correct contextual positioning by an explicit or implicit specification of their STAR.

The role of the STAR is described by the second principle of pragmatics:

5.3.3 Second Principle of Pragmatics (PoP-2)

The STAR of the sign determines its primary positioning in the database by specifying the *entry context* of interpretation.

The need for primary positioning is especially obvious in the case of mediated reference, as in Heather's interpretation of Spencer's postcard.

5.3.4 Primary Positioning in Terms of the STAR

Heather's cognitive representation:

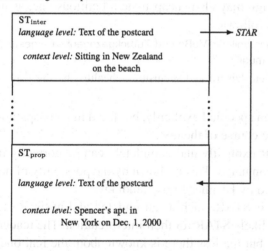

Heather's current situation is stored at the ST_{inter}: sitting on the beach she is looking at the postcard. The signs of the postcard, however, are not matched to the subcontext of the ST_{inter}, but rather to a subcontext called ST_{prop}, which is determined by means of the STAR.

Accordingly, Heather does not object to the statement The weather is very cold by pointing to the hot New Zealand summer. Based on the STAR, she knows that the words of the postcard refer to New York in winter.

Similarly, when the nosy landlady secretly reads Spencer's postcard she is not surprised by Your dog is doing fine, given that she has no dog. Based on the STAR, she knows full well that the words of the postcard refer to Heather's dog.

For the hearer, PoP-2 determines the subcontext where the interpretation begins. But it makes no demands on its contents, which depend solely on the person who interprets the sign. A subcontext of interpretation may contain personal memories, factual information, etc., but it may also be completely empty.

In Heather's case, the subcontext *Spencer's apt. in New York on December 1, 2012* is richly filled insofar as Heather is Spencer's friend and knows his apartment from personal experience. In contrast, the corresponding subcontext of Heather's landlady is initially a new, empty file. Yet the landlady's interpretation is successful insofar as she reads the postcard text into this file, making sense of it via her acquaintance with Heather (pragmatic anchoring).

The function of the STAR is twofold. On the one hand, it regulates the reference to content already present (as in the case of Heather). On the other hand, it is the basis for integrating new information so that it may be retrieved correctly on later occasions (as in the case of the landlady, but also in the case of Heather).

Thus the landlady may smile knowingly when Heather later announces an impending visit from New York. This knowledge is based not only on the text of the postcard, but also in large part on the explicitly specified STAR which allowed the landlady to put the content into a correct subcontext.

In addition to its real STAR, a sign may also encapsulate a fictitious one, as in the novel *Felix Krull*, which begins as follows.

> Indem ich die Feder ergreife, um in völliger Muße und Zurückgezogenheit – gesund übrigens, wenn auch müde, sehr müde...
>
> [While I seize the pen in complete leisure and seclusion – healthy, by the way – though tired, very tired...]

Here the fictitious STAR is not even specified explicitly, but filled in inconspicuously, piece by piece, by the author in the course of the text.[7]

Signs which provide their STAR explicitly and completely can be correctly interpreted by anyone who speaks the language. This is shown by the possibility of nonintended interpretations, as illustrated by Heather's nosy landlady.

Signs which do not provide their STAR, such as an undated and unsigned letter, require at least a *hypothesis* of the likely STAR for their interpretation. The reader can always provide a tentative STAR, but the less there is known about the real one, the less sense he can make of the content coded by the writer.

5.4 Language Production and Interpretation

The STAR of a sign provides the entry context for the speaker's language production and the hearer's interpretation. From there, however, an unlimited variety of other

---

[7] In a novel, the real STAR may be of little or no interest to the average reader. Nevertheless it is explicitly specified. The name of the author, Thomas Mann, is written on the cover. The intended recipient is the general readership as may be inferred from the text form 'book'. The year of the first printing and the place of publication are specified on the back of the title page.

subcontexts may be accessed and traversed. The time-linear coding of the subcontexts into language surfaces during production and their decoding during interpretation is based on the [2+1] level structure (4.2.2) of the SLIM theory of language.

In language interpretation, the navigation through the subcontexts is controlled by the language signs: the hearer follows the surfaces of the signs, looks up their meanings$_1$ in the lexicon, and matches them with suitable subcontexts.

5.4.1 SCHEMA OF LANGUAGE INTERPRETATION (ANALYSIS)

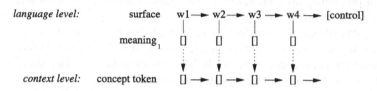

In language production, the navigation control is located in the subcontexts of the speaker. Each content unit traversed is matched with the corresponding meaning$_1$ of a suitable word form. Utterance of the word form surfaces allows the hearer to reconstruct the speaker's time-linear navigation path.

5.4.2 SCHEMA OF LANGUAGE PRODUCTION (GENERATION)

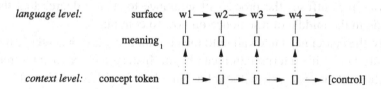

The two schemata agree with the view that interpretation ($\downarrow$) and production ($\uparrow$) are inverse vertical procedures. Nevertheless, interpretation and production have their main direction in common, namely a horizontal time-linear structure ($\rightarrow$).

5.4.3 THE TIME-LINEAR STRUCTURE OF NATURAL LANGUAGE SIGNS

The basic structure of natural language signs is their *time-linear order*. This holds for the sentences in a text, the word forms in a sentence, and the allomorphs in a word form.

Time-linear means:

LINEAR LIKE TIME AND IN THE DIRECTION OF TIME.

This formulation may be regarded as a modern version of Ferdinand DE SAUSSURE's (1857–1913) second law.

5.4.4 DE SAUSSURE'S SECOND LAW: *linear character of signs*

SECOND PRINCIPE; CARACTÈRE LINÉAIRE DU SIGNIFIANT.

Le signifiant, étant de nature auditive, se déroule dans le temps seul et a les caractères qu'il emprunte au temps: a) *représente une étendue*, et b) *cette étendue est mesurable dans une seule dimension*: c'est une ligne.

Ce principe est évident, mais il semble qu'on ait toujours négligé de l'énoncer, sans doute parce qu'on l'a trouvé trop simple; cependent il est fondamental et les conséquences en sont incalculables; son importance est égale à celle de la première loi. Tout le mécanisme de la langue en dépend.

[The designator, being auditory in nature, unfolds solely in time and is characterized by temporal properties: (a) *it occupies an expansion*, and (b) *this expansion is measured in just one dimension*: it is a line.

This principle is obvious, but it seems that stating it explicitly has always been neglected, doubtless because it is considered too elementary. It is, however, a fundamental principle and its consequences are incalculable. Its importance equals that of the first law. All the mechanisms of language depend on it.]

de Saussure (1972), p. 103

The failure pointed out so politely by de Saussure in 1913 has continued until today. C Grammar (Chap. 7) and PS Grammar (Chap. 8) are based on two-dimensional trees called *constituent structures* (8.4.3), and treat surface order as the 'problem of linearization.' Only LA Grammar (Chap. 10) uses a time-linear derivation order as the common backbone for language production and interpretation.

The time-linear structure of natural language is so fundamental that a speaker cannot but utter a text sentence by sentence, and a sentence word form by word form. Thereby the time-linear principle suffuses the process of utterance to such a degree that the speaker may decide in the middle of a sentence on how to continue.

Correspondingly, the hearer need not wait until the utterance of a text or sentence has been finished before her or his interpretation can begin. Instead the hearer interprets the beginning of the sentence (or text) without knowing how it will be continued.[8]

In spoken language, the time-linear movement of the navigation must be maintained *continuously* during production and interpretation. If a speaker pauses too long, (s)he ceases to be a speaker. If a hearer stops following the words as they are being spoken and starts to think of something else, (s)he ceases to be a hearer.

The function of time linearity is described by the third principle of pragmatics.

5.4.5 THIRD PRINCIPLE OF PRAGMATICS (POP-3)

The matching of word forms with their respective subcontexts is incremental, whereby in production the elementary signs follow the time-linear order of

---

[8] Hearers are often able to continue incoming sentences, especially if the speaker is slowly producing well-ingrained platitudes describing widespread beliefs. This phenomenon shows again that the principle of possible continuations permeates the interpretation of language as well.

the underlying thought path, while in interpretation the thought path follows
the time-linear order of the incoming elementary signs.

The third principle presupposes the second. The initial step in the interpretation of a
natural language sign is to determine the entry context as precisely as possible via the
STAR (PoP-2). The next step is to match the complex sign word form by word form
with a sequence of subcontexts. PoP-3 goes beyond 5.4.3 and de Saussure's second
law in that PoP-3 emphasizes the role of the time-linear structure for the incremental
matching between the signs' meaning$_1$ and the subcontexts within the [2+1] level
structure of the SLIM theory of language.

5.5 Thought as the Motor of Spontaneous Production

According to the SLIM theory of language, what is said is a direct reflection of what
is thought. Thus, the once famous motto of behaviorism

Thought is nonverbal speech

is flipped around into

Speech is verbalized thought.

Behaviorism wanted to avoid a definition of thought by attempting to reduce thought
to speech. The SLIM theory of language, on the other hand, models thought explicitly
as an autonomous navigation through the internal database.[9]

The navigation is implemented computationally as a focus point moving through
the concatenated propositions. Its momentary direction is controlled by (i) the connections between the propositions traversed, (ii) internal contextual influences such
as hunger, (iii) external contextual influences (sensory input), and (iv) language input.

The navigation provides a basic handling of *conceptualization*. This notion is used
in conventional systems of natural language generation for choosing the contents to be
expressed (what to say), in contradistinction to the notion of *realization*, which refers
to the way in which a chosen content is represented in language (how to say it).

That the SLIM theory of language treats conceptualization as thought itself, and
realization as a simultaneous assignment of language surfaces, is in concord with the
fact that spontaneous speech is not based on a conscious choice of content or style.
A representative example of spontaneous speech is an eyewitness report after a recent
shock experience. The horrified witness' description gushes out automatically without
any stylistic qualms or hesitation about what to say or how to say it. For better or
worse, the same is true for most situations of normal everyday life.

---

[9] The SLIM-theoretic model of thought may be viewed as a formal realization of spreading
activation theories in cognitive psychology. Different versions may be found in Collins and
Loftus (1975), Anderson and Bower (1980), Anderson (1990), Rumelhart et al. (1986b),
and others.

That a person will sometimes speak slowly and deliberately, sometimes fast and emotionally, sometimes formally and politely, and sometimes in dialect or slang, is a direct reflection of the current navigation through the subcontexts and an indirect reflection of the internal and external factors modifying the state of the database and thus the course of the navigation. Internal factors are the current mood and intention of the cognitive agent, while external factors are the status of the hearer, the presence or absence of a third party, and the events taking place at the time.

The navigation through subcontexts (i.e., the thought path) is independent of language insofar as it often occurs without a concomitant verbalization.[10] When language is produced, however, it is usually a completely automatic process in which order and choice of the words are a direct reflection of the underlying navigation.

> Speech is irreversible. That is its fatality. What has been said cannot be unsaid, except by adding to it: to correct here is, oddly enough, to continue.
>
> Barthes (1986), p. 76

Even in written language the realization of time-linear navigation shows up at least partially in that the word and sentence order are fixed. For example, Spencer decided to describe events in their temporal order:

In the morning he played in the snow. Then he ate a bone.

In the medium of writing, the order of the two sentences can be inverted, i.e.,

*Then he ate a bone. In the morning he played in the snow.

but this would destroy the intended interpretation of then.

Alternatively Spencer could have depicted the events as follows:

In the morning Fido ate a bone. Before that he played in the snow.

This anti-temporal sequencing represents an alternative thought path through the contextual database and has the stylistic effect of emphasizing the eating of the bone. Here a later inversion would likewise destroy textual cohesion.

There are also examples in which a later change of sequencing does not destroy cohesion, but 'only' modifies the interpretation:

a. 1. In February, I visited the Equator. 2. There it was very hot. 3. In March, I was in Alaska. 4. There it was very cold.

b. 3. In March, I was in Alaska. 2. There it was very hot. 1. In February, I visited the Equator. 4. There it was very cold.

The four sentences in *a* and *b* are the same, but their order is different. The interpretation differs with the orderings because there obviously refers to the subcontext (Alaska/Equator) that was traversed most recently. This holds for both the reader and

---

[10] Whether thought is *influenced* by one's language is another question which has been hotly debated through the centuries. According to the Humboldt-Sapir-Whorf Hypothesis the thought of humans is indeed influenced by their respective languages.

the writer. According to our knowledge of the world, example *b* is highly unlikely, yet a sincere interpretation cannot but navigate a corresponding thought.[11]

In summary, the time-linear structure of natural language underlies written language as much as it underlies spoken language. The only difference is that written signs are more permanent than spoken ones (if we disregard recordings) for which reason

- a writer can correct and/or modify a given text without having to add more sentences, and
- a reader can leaf through a text, going forward or backward, without being bound to the linear order of the word forms.

These are additional possibilities, however, which in no way change the essential time-linear structure of written signs.[12]

Exercises

Section 5.1

1. Explain the relation between nonlinguistic and linguistic pragmatics.
2. Who was Karl Bühler, and when did he live?
3. What are the three functions of language specified by Bühler's organon model?
4. What do the CURIOUS model and the organon model have in common and how do they differ?
5. Which components of the CURIOUS model 4.1.3 treat *expression* and *appeal*, respectively?
6. Who first presented information theory, what are its tasks, and what are its central notions?
7. Is information theory suitable to explain the mechanism of communication?

---

[11] The question of trustworthiness, seriousness, etc. of a sign's author is discussed in CoL, pp. 280f.

[12] Even hypertexts, with their various options of continuation, are designed for a time-linear consumption by the reader. There are, however, special kinds of books, e.g., dictionaries, in which the entries are ordered alphabetically for the sake of a specialized access (though the entries are of a conventional time-linear structure). Characteristically, dictionaries – like telephone books, inventory lists, bank accounts, relational databases, and other non-time-linear language structures – are not regarded as 'normal' texts of natural language.

Section 5.2

1. How does the view of language as an organon affect the theoretical development of linguistic pragmatics?
2. Why does PoP-1 presuppose the view of language as a tool?
3. Name and explain two analogies between the use of nonlinguistic and linguistic pragmatics.
4. Why is determining the correct context of use a central problem of linguistic pragmatics? Is this problem addressed in linguistic mainstream pragmatics (e.g., Levinson 1983)?

Section 5.3

1. Explain the roles of the STAR and the ST_{inter} in the interpretation of linguistic signs.
2. Why is it necessary for the STAR to specify also the intended recipient (example)? Why does this not hold for the ST_{inter}?
3. How is the STAR specified in Spencer's postcard?
4. What is the entry context and why is its specification important?
5. Is it possible to interpret a sign relative to an empty subcontext? What would be the purpose of this?
6. Consider a lawn with the sign Keep off the grass! Define the STAR of this sign (CoL, p. 280.)
7. The novel *A Clockwork Orange* is written in the first person: There was me, that is Alex, and my three droogs... How does the reader distinguish between the author Anthony Burgess and Alex? Explain the notion of an auxiliary STAR.

Section 5.4

1. Why is the [2+1] level structure of the SLIM theory of language crucial for the interpretation and production of natural language?
2. What exactly is meant by the notion *time-linear*? How does it differ from the notion *linear time* in complexity theory?
3. Explain the time-linear structure of natural language in terms of the speaker's production and the hearer's interpretation.
4. Who was de Saussure, when did he live, and what is his second law?
5. Why does PoP-3 presuppose PoP-2?
6. Is there a difference between PoP-3 and de Saussure's second law?

Section 5.5

1. What is the difference between spoken and written language regarding production and interpretation? Is written language time-linear as well?
2. What is the difference in how spoken vs. written language is corrected?
3. In the production of language, is there an intermediate state which is not time-linear?

4. What are the three basic problems of production in constituent-structure-based grammars? How are they avoided in the SLIM theory of language?
5. Is the late phylo- and ontogenetic acquisition of reading and writing an argument for or against treating them as central cases of language use?
6. How deliberately are style and topic chosen in spontaneous speech?
7. How does the speaker control what she or he says?

6. Structure and Functioning of Signs

The semantic and pragmatic functioning of complex expressions is based on individual words. These correspond to different sign kinds with different mechanisms of reference. The classification and analysis of words as sign kinds belongs traditionally in the philosophical domain of the *theory of signs*. For the modeling of natural communication in computational linguistics, a theory of signs is an obvious necessity.

Section 6.1 shows with an example in telegram style that complex meanings can be transmitted simply by means of the time-linear order and the meaning$_1$ of the signs, without the usual grammatical composition, and explains how the iconic, indexical, and name-based reference mechanisms work. Section 6.2 describes the sign kind symbol and how it is used by the speaker and hearer to refer. Section 6.3 investigates the phenomenon of repeating reference. Section 6.4 discusses two exceptions to de Saussure's first law, namely the sign kinds icon and name. Section 6.5 explains the evolution of icons from pictures and describes the development of modern writing systems as a gradual transition from pictures via visual icons (pictograms) to symbols.

6.1 Reference Mechanisms of Different Sign Kinds

The functioning of natural language communication as described so far is based on the following pragmatic mechanisms:

1. The use of language expressions is handled as an internal matching between the expression's meaning$_1$ and a subcontext (PoP-1, Sect. 4.3).
2. The entrance subcontext is determined by the sign's STAR (PoP-2, Sect. 5.3).
3. In complex expressions, the reference relation between word forms and their context of interpretation is based on a time-linear derivation order (PoP-3, Sect. 5.4).

PoP-1, PoP-2, and PoP-3 are rooted so deeply in the basic functioning of natural language communication that their fundamental role shows up in each and every instance of meaningful language production and interpretation. Even though their elementary structure and function are "obvious, ... it seems that stating [them] explicitly has always been neglected, doubtlessly because [they are] considered too elementary" – to borrow de Saussure's formulation quoted in 5.4.4 and extend it to pragmatics.

R. Hausser, *Foundations of Computational Linguistics*,
DOI 10.1007/978-3-642-41431-2_6, © Springer-Verlag Berlin Heidelberg 2014

Based on PoP-1, PoP-2, and PoP-3, we are now at the point where the individual signs are positioned more or less precisely opposite the correct internal subcontext. From here our analysis may continue in two different directions. One is to describe the horizontal relation of the individual signs to each other, i.e., the principles of time-linear syntactic-semantic composition. The other is to analyze the vertical relation of individual signs to the subcontext, i.e., reference. The correlation of these two structural aspects may be shown schematically as follows:

6.1.1 ALTERNATIVES OF DESCRIPTION

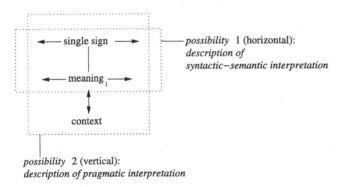

Of these alternatives, we choose the second, because the vertical pragmatic interpretation is possible even in the case of single signs, as shown by the phenomenon of the one-word sentence. Moreover, the horizontal syntactic-semantic composition is rather complex in the natural languages and requires a separate, detailed analysis. This will be provided in Parts III (Morphology and Syntax) and IV (Semantics and Pragmatics).

Ignoring for the moment the role of syntax in the pragmatic interpretation of complex signs, let us begin with a special type of communication, e.g., the telegram style and similar variants,[1] in which the function of the syntax is minimal:

6.1.2 EXAMPLE WITH MINIMAL SYNTAX

Me up. Weather nice. Go beach. Catch fish. Fish big. Me hungry. Fix breakfast.
Eat fish. Feel good. Go sleep.

There is no doubt that this kind of language works. Though it is syntactically simplified, even ungrammatical, it is well-suited to convey nonelementary content. This is based solely on (i) the linear order and (ii) the meaning$_1$ of the individual words. A good theory of language should therefore be able to explain a fully developed syntax as a refinement of communication with little or no grammar.

For this, the semantic-pragmatic functioning of individual words must be explained. In referring expressions, analytic philosophy distinguishes the sign kinds of *symbol*,

---

[1] A typical example is the simplification in the discourse with foreigners: Me Tarzan, you Jane.

indexical,[2] and *name*. The SLIM theory of language explains their different reference mechanisms in terms of their characteristic internal structures.

6.1.3 FOURTH PRINCIPLE OF PRAGMATICS (POP-4)

The reference mechanism of the sign kind **symbol** is based on a meaning$_1$ which is defined as a concept type. Symbols refer from their place in a positioned sentence by matching their concept type with suitable contextual referents (concept tokens).

The reference mechanism of symbols is called iconic because the functioning of symbols and icons is similar: both can be used to refer spontaneously to new objects of a known kind. The difference resides in the relation between the meaning$_1$ (concept type) and the surface, which is "arbitrary" in the case of symbols, but "motivated" in the case of icons. Examples of symbols in are the nouns weather, beach, and fish, the verbs go, catch, and eat, and the adjectives nice, big, and hungry.

6.1.4 FIFTH PRINCIPLE OF PRAGMATICS (POP-5)

The reference mechanism of the sign kind **indexical** is based on a meaning$_1$ which is defined as a pointer. An indexical refers by pointing from its place in the positioned sentence to appropriate parameter values.

Indexical reference is illustrated by the adverbs here and now, which point to the spatial and temporal parameter values of an utterance, respectively, and the pronouns I and you, which point to the author and the intended recipient, respectively.[3]

Names have no meaning$_1$ distinct from their surface, in contrast to symbols and indexicals. Instead, the surface serves to match a corresponding marker in the cognitive representation of the named item:

6.1.5 SIXTH PRINCIPLE OF PRAGMATICS (POP-6)

The reference mechanism of the sign kind **name** is based on an act of naming which consists in adding a name-marker to the internal representation of the individual or object in question. Reference with a name consists in matching the name surface and the corresponding marker.[4]

As an example of name-based reference consider meeting a stranger who introduces his dog as Fido. Afterwards, our internal representation of this particular dog as a

---

[2] The term 'indexical' as a sign kind is distinct from the term 'index' used in the domain of databases (2.1.1). Both terms have in common, however, that they are based on the notion of a pointer.

[3] As content units, indexical pointers are restricted to view-dependent representations such as language meanings and task analyses. Symbols and names, in contrast, may be used for representing both view-dependent and view-independent representations of content.

[4] In analytic philosophy, names have long been a puzzle. Attempts to explain their functioning range from *causal chains* to *rigid designators* (Kripke 1972).

contextual referent comprises not only properties like size, color, etc., but also the name marker Fido.[5]

The respective structural basis of iconic, indexical, and name-based reference is illustrated in the following schematic comparison in which the three sign kinds are used to refer to the same contextual object, i.e., a red triangle.

6.1.6 COMPARING ICONIC, INDEXICAL, AND NAME-BASED REFERENCE

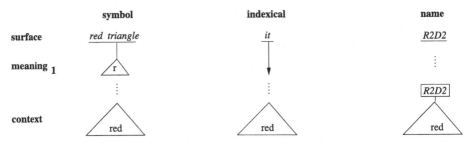

The symbol red triangle refers on the basis of the type/token relation: the concept type matches a corresponding concept token in a limited range of contextual candidates. The indexical it refers on the basis of pointing: the characteristic pointer points at the referential object within an associated parameter (here, third person, i.e., everything that is neither author nor addressee). The name R2D2 refers on the basis of a marker: the name surface is matched with an identical marker which is part of the contextual referent and is attached to it in an act of naming.

Names fit into the basic [2+1] level structure of the SLIM theory of language. However, while symbols and indexicals establish a fixed connection between the surface and the meaning$_1$, names establish a fixed relation between the name-marker and the contextual referent. Accordingly, in names the matching is between the name surface and the name marker (Sect. 6.4).

All three mechanisms of reference must be analyzed as internal, cognitive procedures. This is because it would be ontologically unjustifiable to locate the fixed connections between surface and meaning$_1$ (symbols and indexicals) and between marker and contextual referent (names) in the external reality.[6]

For explaining the phylo- and ontogenetic development of natural language it is of interest that the basic mechanisms of iconic, indexical, and name-based reference constitute the foundation of nonlanguage and prelanguage communication as well. Thereby

1. nonlanguage iconic reference consists in spontaneously imitating the referent by means of gestures or sounds,
2. nonlanguage indexical reference consists in pointing at the referent, and

---

[5] Apart from explicit acts of naming, names may also be inferred implicitly, for example, when we observe an unknown person being called by a certain name.

[6] See Sect. 4.2 as well as the discussion of four possible semantic ontologies in Sect. 20.4.

3. nonlanguage name-based reference consists in pointing at the referent while simultaneously pronouncing a name.

While largely limited to the communication prototype 3.1.2, these nonlanguage mechanisms of reference may be quite effective. By doing without conventionally established surfaces, nonlanguage reference allows spontaneous communication in situations in which no common language is available.

The distinction between the different *sign kinds*, i.e., symbol, index, and name, is orthogonal to the distinction between the main *parts of speech*, i.e., noun, verb, and adjective, as well as to the corresponding distinction between the basic *elements of propositions*, i.e., argument, functor, and modifier (3.4.1).

6.1.7 SEVENTH PRINCIPLE OF PRAGMATICS (POP-7)

The sign kind *symbol* occurs as noun, verb, and adjective. The sign kind *indexical* occurs as noun and adjective. The sign kind *name* occurs only as noun.

The orthogonal correlation between sign kinds and parts of speech described in PoP-7[7] may be represented graphically as follows:

6.1.8 RELATION BETWEEN SIGN KINDS AND PARTS OF SPEECH

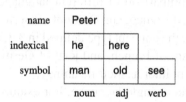

The sign kind which is the most general with respect to the parts of speech is the symbol, while the name is the most restricted. Conversely, the part of speech (and, correspondingly, the propositional element) which is the most general with respect to sign kinds is the noun (object), while the verb (relation) is the most restricted.

6.2 Internal Structure of Symbols and Indexicals

As signs, the symbols and indexicals of natural language have an internal structure which is composed of the following components:

6.2.1 INTERNAL COMPONENTS OF THE SIGN KINDS SYMBOL AND INDEXICAL

– The *surface* is constrained by acoustic articulation, i.e., pronounceability, in the original medium of spoken language.

---

[7] While CoL presented preliminary versions of PoP-1 to PoP-5 as the first to fifth principle of pragmatics, respectively, PoP-6 and PoP-7 are defined here for the first time.

– The *category* reflects the combinatorial properties of the part of speech and the inflectional/agglutinative class to which the sign belongs.
– The *meaning*$_1$ reflects the conceptual structures of the internal context and/or contains characteristic pointers to certain contextual parameters.
– The *glue* connecting surface, category, and meaning$_1$ consists of conventions which must be learned by each member of the language community.

The convention-based nature of the glue, particularly between surface and meaning$_1$, is the subject of de Saussure's first law:

6.2.2 *De Saussure*'s First Law

PREMIER PRINCIPE; L'ARBITRAIRE DU SIGNE.
Le lien unissant signifiant au signifié est arbitraire, ou encore, puisque nous entendons par signe le total résultant de l'association d'un signifiant à un signifié, nous pouvons dire plus simplement: *le signe linguistique est arbitraire.*
[THE FIRST LAW: ARBITRARINESS OF SIGNS
The link connecting the designator and the designated is arbitrary; and since we are treating a sign as the combination which results from connecting the designator with the designated, we can express this more simply as: *the linguistic sign is arbitrary.*]

de Saussure (1972), p. 100

The arbitrariness of signs may be seen in the comparison of different languages. For example, the symbols square of English, carré of French, and Quadrat of German have different surfaces, but the same meaning$_1$ (i.e., the concept type defined in 3.3.3). Similarly, the indexicals now of English, maintenant of French, and jetzt of German have different surfaces, but use the same indexical pointer as their meaning$_1$.

The arbitrariness of signs may also be seen within a single language. For example, the surface of the symbol square contains nothing that might be construed as indicating the meaning$_1$ of an equal-sided quadrangle with 90 degree angles. Similarly, nothing in the surface of indexical now might be construed as indicating the meaning$_1$ of a temporal pointer. Thus, the surface-meaning$_1$ relation in the sign kinds symbol and indexical is what de Saussure's calls *unmotivated*.

In natural communication, symbols can have the following functions:

6.2.3 POSSIBLE FUNCTIONS OF THE SIGN KIND SYMBOL

1. *Initial* reference to objects which have not been mentioned so far (4.3.2).
2. *Repeating* reference to referents which have already been introduced linguistically (6.3.3 and 6.3.7).
3. *Metaphorical* reference to partially compatible referents (5.2.1), both in initial and repeating reference.

These different functions are based on

– the minimal meaning$_1$ structure of symbols (concept types), and
– the limited selection of compatible referents available in the subcontext.

Consider, for example, the word table. The multitude of different possible referents, e.g., dining tables, kitchen tables, garden tables, writing tables, card tables, picnic tables, operating tables, etc., of various brands, sizes, colors, locations, etc., is not part of the meaning$_1$ of this word. The referents arise only at the level of the internal context, whereby, for example, different kinds of tables are distributed over the subcontexts of the cognitive agent in accordance with previous and current experience.

Yet a minimal meaning$_1$ structure of the word table is sufficient to refer properly, provided that the subcontext is sufficiently limited in terms of the STAR and the time-linear order of the sign. If there are no standard referents, a word like table can even refer to an orange-crate (5.2.1). Furthermore, the speaker may differentiate the meaning$_1$ structure of the referring expression by integrating additional symbolic content into the sign, e.g., the table, the garden table, the green garden table, the small green garden table, the round small green garden table, the round small green garden table near the pool, etc.

Reference with a symbol will not succeed if the activated subcontext contains several similar candidates, e.g., several prototypical tables, and the speaker fails to provide additional symbolic characterization or a pointing gesture to single out the one intended. This problem would arise not only for an artificial cognitive agent like CURIOUS, but for a human hearer as well. Cases of uncertain reference are common in daily life. When they occur, it is normal for the hearer to request clarification.

In the hear mode, the concept type of a symbol may not only be matched with an existing concept token in a subcontext, but may also introduce a new one. For example, when a buyer goes through a house saying, for example, living room in room$_1$, dining room in room$_2$, etc., the associated properties are inserted into the respective representations of the hearer-internal context structure. This process differs from naming in that not just markers, but concepts are added to the internal representations:

6.2.4 CHARACTERIZING OBJECTS SYMBOLICALLY

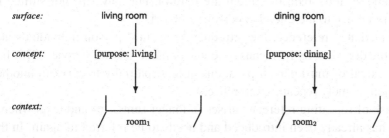

Externally there is nothing changed in room$_1$, but speaker and hearer can leave the house, the town, or the country, and talk without any problem about the living room in the context of their new house.[8]

---

[8] Should the buyer and his companion decide later to make room$_2$ into the living room instead, this will require an explicit agreement to ensure the functioning of communication.

6.3 Repeating Reference

Words exemplifying the sign kind indexical are here, now, I, and you. Their meaning$_1$ consists of pointers at the parameters S, T, A, and R, respectively. Thus, these four indexicals are well suited to position a sign in accordance with its STAR.

In the speak mode, the characteristic pointers of indexical words may be easily implemented. Within a robot like CURIOUS, for example, here (S) points to the center of the on-board orientation system, now (T) to the current value of the on-board clock, I (A) to CURIOUS as the author of any language signs to be produced, and you (R) to the current partner in discourse.

The pointer of an indexical word may combine with grammatical and symbolic components of meaning which help to support and refine the process of reference. How much symbolic support is required by an indexical for successful reference depends on how many potential candidates are provided by the currently activated subcontext.

Indexical words which contain no additional grammatical or symbolic meaning components are called *pure indexicals*. If the speaker wishes additional precision or emphasis when using a pure indexical like here, now, and you,[9] this may be expressed compositionally as in up here, right now, you there, etc.

Examples of non-pure indexicals, on the other hand, are the first person pronouns I, me, we, and us in English. They incorporate the symbolic-grammatical distinction between singular (I) and plural (we), and the grammatical distinction between nominative case (I, we) and oblique case (me, us). Thus, even though the pronouns of first person in English all share the same pointer to the parameter A, they differ in their symbolic-grammatical meaning components and are therefore not pure indexicals.

The pointing area of pronouns of third person, finally, is outside the STAR parameters and comprises all objects and persons that have been activated so far and are neither the speaker nor the hearer. Depending on the subcontext, this pointing area may be very large, for which reason gender-number distinctions in third person pronouns like he, she, it, they, him, her, them are helpful, but may still not suffice to achieve correct reference to the intended person or object.

Especially in mediated reference, the introduction of third person individuals and objects is therefore done mostly by means of iconic or name-based reference. This has freed up the indexical of third person pronouns at least partially to serve in another important function, namely repeating reference.

The special task of repeating reference arises in longer sentences and texts when a certain referent has already been introduced and needs to be referred to again. In the SLIM theory of language, repeating reference is analyzed as the return to a contextual object that has been recently traversed.

---

[9] In German, the second person pronoun is not a pure index. For a detailed discussion of the personal pronouns of English in connection with their role as nominal fillers see Sect. 17.2. The corresponding analysis for German is in Sect. 18.2.

From the viewpoint of a time-linear coding and decoding of meaning it would be cumbersome if reference to an object already introduced always required the use of a complex noun phrase or a name. Instead, third person pronouns are ideally suited for a brief, precise, and versatile handling of repeating reference because of their grammatical differentiation and the general nature of their pointing.

The following example illustrates a case of repeating reference in which a complex symbolic noun phrase is followed by a third person pronoun. As indicated by the arrows, reference by the noun phrase is taken up again by the pronoun.

6.3.1 COREFERENTIAL PRONOUN REPEATING REFERENCE

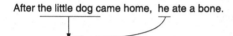

After the little dog came home, he ate a bone.

To connect this and the following examples pragmatically beyond their role as linguistic examples in this chapter, let us assume that the little dog is called Fido and that Fido lives in Peter's house together with a big dog named Zach.

Reference to Fido is established initially by means of the symbolic meaning$_1$ of the complex noun phrase the little dog. Use of the pronoun he allows repeating reference to Fido with minimal effort. In traditional grammar, the pronominal reference illustrated above is called *anaphoric*. The 'full' noun phrase preceding the pronoun is called the *antecedent* and is coreferential with the pronoun. In traditional analysis, anaphoric interpretations are limited to individual sentences.

In addition to the anaphoric (i.e., reference repeating) interpretation, the pronoun he may also be interpreted noncoreferentially.

6.3.2 INDEXICAL PRONOUN WITHOUT COREFERENCE

After the little dog came home, he ate a bone.

The surface is the same as in 6.3.1. Yet the complex noun phrase and the pronoun refer to different individuals, e.g., Fido vs. Zach.

According to a surface compositional analysis, the difference between 6.3.1 and 6.3.2 is neither syntactic nor semantic. Instead, it resides in the pragmatics, i.e., the relation between the meaning$_1$ (here, specifically the pointer of he) and the context. Which interpretation is intended by the speaker and which is chosen by the hearer depends solely on the content of the respective subcontexts.

Under certain circumstances it may be desirable to establish initial reference with a third person pronoun and then return to that referent using a (definite) complex noun phrase or a name.[10]

---

[10] This type of repeating reference is relatively rare. In spoken language, it must be supported by a characteristic intonation. Stylistically it may create an expectation in the hearer who

6.3.3 Symbolically Repeating Reference I

After he came home,   the little dog ate a bone.

In traditional grammar this pronominal reference is called *cataphoric*. The 'full' noun phrase following the pronoun is called the *postcedent* and is coreferential with the pronoun.

In addition to the cataphoric (i.e., reference repeating) interpretation, the noun phrase the little dog may also be interpreted noncoreferentially.

6.3.4 Symbolic Reference Without Coreference

After he came home,   the little dog ate a bone.

The surface is the same as in 6.3.3, but the pronoun and the noun phrase refer to different individuals. Without special contextual priming, the interpretation 6.3.4 is in fact more probable than 6.3.3.

A coreferential interpretation presupposes that the two nominals involved are grammatically and conceptually compatible. For example, if he were replaced by they in 6.3.1 or 6.3.3, an interpretation of repeating reference to Fido would not be possible because of the incompatibility of number. Instead, an indexical interpretation of the pronoun – as in 6.3.2 or 6.3.4 – would be the only possibility.

A pronoun-based return to a noun phrase referent or a noun-phrase-based return to a pronoun referent may also be restricted by the sentence structure, as shown by the following examples. They express the intended coreference in terms of equal subscripts (e.g., Peter$_k$, he$_k$) – a notational convention borrowed from theoretical linguistics.

6.3.5 Sentence Structure Blocking Repeating Reference
1. Anaphorical positioning:
   After Peter$_i$ came home he$_i$ took a bath.
   Peter$_i$ took a bath after he$_i$ came home.
   %! Near Peter$_i$ he$_i$ saw a snake.[11]
2. Cataphorical positioning:
   After he$_i$ came home Peter$_i$ took a bath.
   %! He$_i$ took a bath after Peter$_i$ came home.[12]
   Near him$_i$ Peter$_i$ saw a snake.

is uncertain of the pronoun referent and who must wait for the following noun phrase to support or specify the interpretation.

[11] Lakoff (1968).

[12] Langacker (1969). However, MacWhinney (1999) shows that this construction allows a coreferential interpretation if the preceding main clause is marked as background information by particles:
She$_i$ had *just* returned home when Mary$_i$ saw that the mailbox was open.

The examples marked with '%!' are grammatically well-formed, but the co-indexed nominals cannot be interpreted as coreferential – despite their closeness of position and despite grammatical and conceptual compatibility.

In communication, repeating reference is also needed across sentence boundaries.

6.3.6 CROSS-SENTENTIAL COREFERENCE

> Peter$_k$ wanted to drive into the countryside. He$_k$ waited for Fido$_i$. When the little dog$_i$ came home he$_k$ was glad.

This example shows that of several coreferential candidates it is not always the one closest to the pronoun or the one in the same sentence which is the most plausible. For example, the third sentence taken alone would suggest coreference between the little dog and he. The content of the wider linguistic context, however, makes Peter a more probable antecedent of the second he than the the little dog, even though the latter is positioned closer to the pronoun.

Repeating reference with a complex noun phrase is also possible if the initial reference is based on a proper name:[13]

6.3.7 SYMBOLICALLY REPEATING REFERENCE II

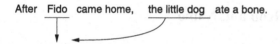

Like 6.3.3 and 6.3.4, the surface of this example permits both a coreferential and a noncoreferential interpretation.

Examples like this lead to the generalization that all three sign types may be used for initial reference.

6.3.8 INITIAL REFERENCE ESTABLISHED BY SYMBOL, INDEX, AND NAME

>   the little dog
> After   he   came home, he slept.
>   Fido

Furthermore, all three sign kinds may be used for repeating reference.

---

[13] Instead of a proper name, repeated reference may be by a noun phrase, as in the following example by Jackendoff (1972):

> My neighbor went on vacation, but the idiot forgot his credit cards.

Jackendoff called the second noun phrase a *pronominal epithet*, based on the mistaken view that the noun phrase the idiot is "pronominalized" via coreference with the antecedent my neighbor.

6.3.9 REPEATING REFERENCE USING SYMBOL, INDEX, AND NAME

	the little dog	
After he came home,	he	slept.
	Fido	

All instances in 6.3.8 and 6.3.9 permit a coreferential and a noncoreferential interpretation. Which interpretation is intended by the speaker and chosen by the hearer is a question of pragmatics.

Therefore the noun phrase the little dog maintains its symbolic character, the pronoun he maintains its indexical character, and Fido maintains its character as a name – irrespective of whether these signs are used for repeating reference or not. Postulating two different lexical entries for he, for example, one for each use, violates surface compositionality.

Unfortunately, nativism has a long tradition[14] of assigning special morphosyntactic analyses to the anaphoric and cataphoric interpretations of third person pronouns, based on stipulated coreference within the sentence boundary.[15] This is not justified because the personal pronouns form a uniform class not only morphologically and syntactically, but also semantically: they are all of the sign kind index. This indexical character is as inherent in third person pronouns as it is in first or second person pronouns, regardless of whether or not such pronouns are used for repeating reference.

6.4 Exceptional Properties of Icon and Name

There are two important and interesting exceptions to de Saussure's first law, namely the sign kinds icon and name. Typical icons are signs with pictorial representations. For example, in the Dutch city of Amsterdam one will find the following street sign:

6.4.1 EXAMPLE OF AN ICON (STREET SIGN)

Positioned at parking places between the street and the canal (Gracht) this sign says something like "Attention: danger of driving car into water!"

---

[14] Beginning with Lees' (1960) transformational analysis of reflexive pronouns. A more recent example may be found in Pollard and Sag (1994).

[15] One likely reason for this mistake is that nativism overlooked the need for a theory of signs.

Foreigners who speak no Dutch and see this sign for the first time can infer the intended meaning₂ directly from the surface of the sign and its positioning – via pragmatic inferences which are obviously not language dependent. Thus the crucial property of icons is that they can be understood spontaneously without the prior learning of a specific language. For this reason, icons are widely used in multilingual applications such as international airports, programming surfaces, manuals, etc.

Icons occur in all media of language such as vision, sound, and gesture. Sound-based icons in natural language are called onomatopoeia. An example in English is the word cuckoo: the sound form of the surface is in a meaningful (motivated, iconic) relation to the sound of the bird in question.

That the meaning₁ of icons may be understood independently of any particular language comes with a cost, however. Depending on the modality, there is only a limited number of concepts suitable[16] for iconic representation. For this reason, new icons must be designed and positioned very carefully to ensure proper understanding.

De Saussure viewed onomatopeia mostly as an exception to his first law.[17] He pointed out, first, that the number of onomatopoeic words is much smaller than 'generally assumed.' Second, they are only partially motivated because they differ from language to language (e.g., glug-glug in English, glou-glou in French, and gluck-gluck in German). Third, the onomatopoeic word forms are subject to morphological processes, for which reason they may become demotivated over time.

Regarding the synchronic functioning of a fully developed natural language, one may agree with de Saussure that onomatopeic words are indeed of secondary importance. The main interest of icons as a basic sign kind, however, arises with the question of how natural language developed during evolution. In this context, de Saussure's position must be seen against the background of the age-old controversy between the *naturalists* and the *conventionalists*:

> [The naturalists] maintained that all words were indeed 'naturally' appropriate to the things they signified. Although this might not always be evident to the layman, they would say, it could be demonstrated by the philosopher able to discern the 'reality' that lay behind the appearance of things. Thus was born the practice of conscious and deliberate etymology. The term itself (being formed from the Greek stem *etymo-* signifying 'true' or 'real') betrays its philosophical origin. To lay bare the origin of a word and thereby its 'true' meaning was to reveal one of the truths of 'nature'.
>
> Lyons (1968), pp. 4f.

---

[16] For example, the sound form cuckoo is considerably more distinctive and thus more suitable for use as an icon than a visual icon for this bird, recognition of which would require above-average ornithological knowledge. Conversely, it would be very hard to find an acoustic counterpart of the well-known nonsmoking sign consisting of the schematic representation of a burning cigarette in a circle crossed by a diagonal bar – whereby the latter components are symbolic in character.

[17] Cf. de Saussure (1967), pp. 81f.

The prototypical sign kind of naturalists is the icon, that of conventionalists the symbol.

The naturalists recognized the spontaneous understanding of icons as an important functional aspect of sign-based communication. This insight, however, is not applicable to signs in which the relation between the surface and the concept type is based on convention, as in symbols, or in which there is no concept type at all, as in indexicals and names.

The conventionalists recognized that most signs have surfaces which – in the terminology of de Saussure – are unmotivated. This insight, however, is no reason to downplay iconic reference as a phenomenon.

According to the SLIM theory of language, the sign kinds icon and symbol function in terms of the same *iconic* reference mechanism.

6.4.2 COMPARING THE STRUCTURE OF SYMBOL AND ICON

Symbol and icon share the same two-level structure with a fixed connection between the surface and the concept type. The difference between the two sign kinds is in their respective *surfaces* and the *kind* of connection between the two levels.

In symbols, the surface is unmotivated and the connection between the levels of the surface and the concept type is based on the glue of convention. In icons, the surface is motivated and the connection between the two levels is based ideally on their equality.

This analysis explains why icons, but not symbols, can be understood spontaneously, independently of any specific language. Icons use iconic reference directly, because their meaning$_1$ is apparent in the surface – for which reason icons can be understood without having to learn a convention. Symbols, on the other hand, use iconic reference indirectly, because the connection between the concept type and the surface is convention-based – for which reason symbols cannot be understood without the prior learning of the convention.

By relating symbols and icons in a coherent theoretical manner within the [2+1] level structure of the SLIM theory of language, the controversy between the conventionalists and the naturalists is amicably resolved. Furthermore, the theory explains why symbols can be used to refer spontaneously to objects never encountered before (as in the Mars mushroom example in Sect. 4.2), namely because symbols and icons function on the basis of the same iconic mechanism of reference.

Gradual changes in the surface (e.g., simplification) or the concept type (e.g., semantic reinterpretation) turn icons quasi-automatically into symbols. These processes of demotivation destroy the spontaneous understandability of the original icons, but have the advantage of achieving a new level of generality. Once the concept has become independent of the surface it is not constrained by the surface's modality any more. The expressive power of symbols is much greater than that of icons because symbols may build their meaning$_1$ by combining elementary as well as complex concept types from different modalities and may include logical concepts like negation.

Another exception to de Saussure's first law besides icons is proper names. Because names have no meaning$_1$[18] (PoP-6 in 6.1.5), their initial choice is free.[19] Once a name has been given, however, it becomes a fixed property of its referent. The effective use of a name requires that it be known to the speaker and the hearer.

A name like R2D2 is certainly 'arbitrary' in de Saussure's sense. Names are an exception to his first law, however, because they do not establish a convention-based relation between a surface and a meaning. Rather, in names the matching frontier is directly underneath the surface, in contradistinction to all the other sign kinds.

6.4.3 COMPARING THE STRUCTURE OF ICON AND NAME

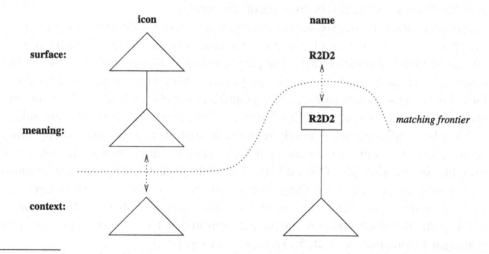

<hr />

[18] It is possible and common to use symbols as names, e.g., Miller, Walker, Smith, Goldsmith, or Diamond. In such a case, the symbolic meanings are only *connotative*. As a mechanism of reference, name-based reference is independent of any symbolic connotations connected to the marker used. In daily life, advertising, or art, however, the connotation of a name may be of importance.

For example, Act I of Walküre (Valkyrie) by Richard WAGNER (1813–1883) devotes more than forty minutes (depending on the conductor) to the question of which name the stranger should take from the lady of the house who is also his long lost sister and very soon to be lover. The stage direction at the end of Act I says Vorhang fällt schnell, which Schopenhauer annotated in the margin of his dedicated score with Denn es ist hohe Zeit.

[19] This allowed Giacomo CASANOVA (1725–1798) to give a detailed explanation of why he chose Chevalier de Seingalt as his self-given title of nobility (Casanova de Seingalt 1963, Vol. II, pp. 728f.). Sign-theoretically the free choice of names is in contrast to the absence of such a choice in the other sign kinds of natural language. See in this connection Sect. 4.3 as well as Wittgenstein (1953) on *private language*.

Icons are special signs in that their *meaning doubles as the surface* (↑). The theoretical distinction between the surface and the meaning₁ in icons allows their gradual demotivation and their transformation into symbols.

Names are special signs in that their *surface doubles as a marker* (↓) at the level of the contextual referent. The theoretical distinction between the surface and the marker in names allows for reference to different persons having the same name, depending on the context of use.[20]

6.5 Pictures, Pictograms, and Letters

In conclusion, let us consider the origin of icons from pictures and the gradual transition from pictures via visual icons (pictograms) to the ideographic,[21] syllabic,[22] and alphabetic writing systems. Pictures are cognitively basic in that they arise in early childhood and at the earliest beginnings of humankind.

Though pictures are not signs, they have the sign-theoretically interesting property that they can refer. For example, Heather spontaneously recognizes the Statue of Liberty on Spencer's postcard (5.3.1). The picture refers to the statue because the viewer establishes a relation to the statue via the picture. This relation is based on the similarity between the picture (here, a photograph) and the object depicted. If the picture showed something else, e.g., the Eiffel Tower, reference would be to a different object.

Taken by itself, a picture is purely representational. If its positioning is taken into account, however, a picture may be used with a certain communicative intention. For example, the photograph of an ashtray filled with disgusting cigarette butts placed prominently on the wall of a waiting room in a hospital may be viewed as a mere picture. When the viewer begins to consider why this particular photograph was placed in this particular place, however, the picture turns into an icon. Thereby linguistic and nonlinguistic pragmatics (Sect. 5.1) have not yet separated.

The iconic use of a picture does not indicate explicitly whether a communicative purpose is intended or not. Moreover, a successful iconic interpretation depends not only on the disposition, but often also on the knowledge of the viewer. For example, paintings from the European Middle Ages are usually loaded with iconic messages the understanding of which requires a considerable degree of specialized knowledge.[23]

---

[20] The crucial problem in the classic AI systems' handling of natural language is the 'gluing' of surfaces to machine internal referents, based on a [−sense, +constructive] ontology. See Sect. 20.4.

[21] E.g., Chinese.

[22] E.g., Japanese *kana*.

[23] For example, when an *Annunciation* by the Flemish painter Rogier VAN DER WEYDEN (1399?–1464) shows a glass of water through which there falls a beam of light, this may seem accidental to the uninitiated. A more literate viewer will interpret it as an allegory of

In addition to the iconic use of a genuine picture there are icons as a sign kind. An icon results from a picture by simplifying it into a basic schema, whereby the loss of detail (i) generalizes the content and (ii) explicitly marks a communicative purpose. The schematic nature of an icon in conjunction with its relevant positioning invites the viewer to infer the author's intended message.

Using a picture as an icon is like using a rock as a hammer. Modifying the rock to make it better suited for a specialized task is like schematizing a picture into an icon. Just as handle and hitting side of a modified stone (e.g., a paleolithic wedge) are different sides of the same object, the surface (handle) and the meaning of an icon are different sides of the same concept.

In other words, a paleolithic wedge and a random rock differ in that the wedge – but not the rock – provides for a clear distinction between the handling side and the working side. The same is true for an icon in comparison to a picture: only the icon – but not the picture – provides for a distinction between the levels of the surface and the meaning.

This distinction is the basis for an independent development of surfaces and concepts in signs, allowing a process of demotivation – and thus generalization – which considerably improves expressive power.

6.5.1 TRANSITION FROM PICTURE TO ICON TO SYMBOL

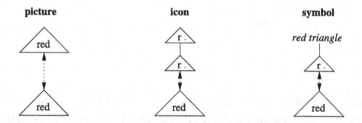

According to this analysis, the iconic reference mechanism originated with pictures. This process of generalization via icons to symbols occurs in all modalities of language.

In the *acoustic* modality, the development begins with, for example, imitating the call of a bird. The process continues with a simplified icon, e.g., cuckoo, and may end with a demotivated symbol.

---

the Holy Ghost, however, because it is known that clerical scripture viewed the Immaculate Conception as similar to light passing through a glass without causing material change.

This example shows once again that the positioning of signs in general, and icons in particular, is of the greatest importance for the interpretation. Positioning the glass with light passing through it in a painting of the Annunciation starts thought processes in the educated viewer which go far beyond the purely representational aspect of this part of the picture.

In the *gestural* modality, the development begins with imitating a certain activity such as harvesting or threshing grain. Such imitations are often schematized and ritualized into traditional dances. In sign languages the process of demotivating gestures results in true symbols.[24]

In the *visual* modality, the development begins with the picture of, for example, a bull and continues with a simplified icon, e.g., Ɐ. At this point two different kinds of writing systems may evolve. Ideographic writing systems use the icon directly as a pictogram. For example, the meaning 'six bulls' may be expressed in such a system by drawing, painting, or chiseling a sequence of six bull icons: ɅɅɅɅɅɅ.

Letter- or syllable-based writing systems turn the pictogram into a letter by substituting the original meaning with the characteristic sound of the corresponding word in the language. For example, in Hebrew, the word for bull or cattle has the sound form 'lf (= alf).[25] The letter *aleph* or *alpha* resulted from replacing the meaning of the icon Ɐ with the sound form of the word with this meaning. This was accompanied by typographical considerations such as looks (letting the icon stand squarely on its 'feet' as A) and maximizing the distinction to other letters. This transition may be viewed as a process of rotation:

6.5.2 ROTATION PRINCIPLE UNDERLYING TRANSITION FROM ICON TO LETTER

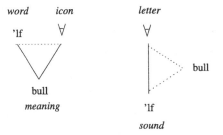

The word 'lf and the corresponding icon Ɐ are cognitively related because they have the same meaning. This amounts to a meaning-based equivalence relation between the word's acoustic surface and the icon's graphical surface (dotted line on the left). The icon turns into a letter representing the sound if this dotted line between the surfaces evolves into the main bond (solid line on the right). Thereby, the respective relations to the meaning, which motivated the correlation between word and icon in the first place, become obsolete and are forgotten.

The evolution of letters or ideographs as symbols for sounds[26] permits representing natural language in writing. The elementary symbols of the writing system, e.g., the

---

[24] The notion of a 'symbolic gesture' in the SLIM theory of signs is related to, but pragmatically different from, the common use of this term.

[25] Givón (1985), pp. 193–195.

[26] Highly developed ideographic writing systems such as Egyptian hieroglyphs or Chinese pictograms annotate icons with the sound form of corresponding words to overcome the inherent limitations of iconic representation.

letters, are combined into letter sequences which denote word surfaces. The surfaces in turn denote the meanings$_1$. Aristotle put it this way:

> Spoken words are the signs of mental experience and written words are the signs of spoken words.

Aristotle, DE INTERPRETATIONE, 1

For example, the sequence of letter symbols s, q, u, a, r, and e denotes the surface of the symbol square. This surface, which may also be represented acoustically, denotes the concept defined in 3.3.3. The gradual demotivation in the evolution of language symbols – affecting spoken word surfaces as well as letters or signs – is a process of the motivational chain becoming longer and longer until the original motivation has become irrelevant and is forgotten.

Exercises

Section 6.1

1. Is there a theory of signs included in nativism, model theory, or speech act theory?
2. Explain the functioning of iconic, indexical, and name-based reference.
3. Which indexical words refer to the four parameters of the STAR? What is their syntactic category? How pure are they?
4. Explain the use of here in the postcard example 5.3.1. Is it an example of immediate or a mediated reference? Do you require different answers for the speaker and the hearer?
5. How would you implement the meaning$_1$ of yesterday, tomorrow, in three minutes, to my right, to your right, above me, and behind you in CURIOUS?
6. Explain the indexical, symbolic, and grammatical components in the word forms me, my, mine, our, us, ours.
7. Why does a coherent treatment of language and nonlanguage reference require a cognitive approach describing the internal states of the agents involved? Give detailed reasons, with examples of symbols, indexicals, and names.
8. Describe the language of the bees and explain how it handles *displaced reference* (CoL, pp. 281f.).
9. Why are PoP-1 – PoP-3 presupposed by PoP-4 – PoP-6?

In the modality of gestures, the Marx Brothers use the same principle for comical purposes. In the movie *Love Happy* (1949), Harpo gestures the name of Madame Egelichi by pantomiming eagle and itchy.

10. Summarize the linguistic universals that have been proclaimed within nativism by making a list of those in Chomsky (1957, 1965, 1981), as well as in LFG (Bresnan (ed.) 1982), GPSG (Gazdar et al. 1985), and HPSG (Pollard and Sag 1987, 1994). Compare their empirical content and their functionality. How do they characterize the innate human language faculty?

Section 6.2

1. Which four ingredients make up the internal structure of symbols and indexicals?
2. Describe de Saussure's first law and illustrate it with examples from different languages. Why does it apply to symbols as well as indexicals?
3. Name three possible functions of symbols, and explain the difference between the speak and hear modes with examples.
4. Why can the meaning$_1$ of symbols be minimal? Are the different shades of the color red part of the meaning of the word red?
5. What is the difference between the index of a textual database (2.1.1) and the sign kind of an indexical? What is their common conceptual root?

Section 6.3

1. Compare the pointing areas of first, second, and third person.
2. What is repeating reference and how can it be achieved in natural language?
3. Explain the anaphoric and the cataphoric use of a third person pronoun.
4. Which syntactic structures can block anaphoric or cataphoric interpretations?
5. Can a third person pronoun refer without an antecedent or a postcedent?
6. What did Jackendoff mean by his notion *pronominal epithet*?

Section 6.4

1. What is the characteristic property of an icon, and how can it be practically used?
2. Why are icons an exception to de Saussure's first law?
3. Why are onomatopeic words a kind of icon?
4. How does de Saussure view the role of onomatopeia in the natural languages?
5. Explain the viewpoints of the naturalists and the conventionalists.
6. What are the specific strengths and weaknesses of the icon as a sign kind?
7. Why can demotivation increase the expressive potential of a sign?
8. Would you classify de Saussure's approach as naturalist or conventionalist?

Section 6.5

1. Compare the structure and functioning of icon and name.
2. Why are names an exception to de Saussure's first law?
3. Why is a name like Peter less general than a symbol like table or an indexical like here? What is the great advantage of name-based reference?
4. How does Peirce define the difference between symbols, indexicals, and icons? Can this definition be used in computational linguistics? (CoL, pp. 276–280.)
5. Why is a picture not a sign? How can a picture be used as a sign?

6. Explain the gradual development of symbols from pictures.
7. What is the difference between ideographic- and letter-based writing systems?
8. Why are letters symbols? What is their meaning$_1$?
9. What is the difference between letter symbols and word symbols?
10. Explain the rotation principle in the evolution of letters from icons.

Part II

Theory of Grammar

7. Formal Grammar

Part I has explained the mechanism of natural communication, based on the [2+1] level structure of the SLIM theory of language and different kinds of language signs. Part II turns to the combinatorial building up of complex signs within the grammar component of syntax. The methods are those of formal language theory, a wide field reaching far into the foundations of mathematics and logic. The purpose here is to introduce the linguistically relevant concepts and formalisms as simply as possible, explaining their historical origin and motivation as well as their different strengths and weaknesses. Formal proofs will be kept to a minimum.

Section 7.1 explains the formal notion of a language as a subset of the free monoid over a finite lexicon. Section 7.2 describes the mathematical, empirical, and computational reasons for using formal grammars in the linguistic description of natural language. Section 7.3 shows that using formal grammar is a methodologically necessary condition for natural language analysis, but it is not sufficient to ensure that the grammar formalism of choice will be structurally suitable for an empirically successful analysis in the long run. Section 7.4 introduces the historically first formal grammar for natural language, namely categorial grammar or C Grammar. Section 7.5 presents a formal application of C Grammar to a small 'fragment' of English.

7.1 Language as a Subset of the Free Monoid

Formal language theory works with mathematical methods which treat the empirical contents of grammatical analysis and the functioning of communication as neutrally as possible. This is apparent in its abstract notion of language:

7.1.1 DEFINITION OF LANGUAGE

A language is a set of finite word sequences (sentences).

This set (in the sense of set theory) is unordered. Each element of the set, however, consists of an ordered sequence of words.

The most basic task in defining a formal language is to characterize the grammatically well-formed sequences. Thereby the words are usually treated as simple surfaces with no category, no morphological variation, no special base form, and no meaning$_1$.

R. Hausser, *Foundations of Computational Linguistics*,
DOI 10.1007/978-3-642-41431-2_7, © Springer-Verlag Berlin Heidelberg 2014

For example, the words a and b constitute the word set $LX = \{a, b\}$, i.e., the lexicon (or alphabet[1]) of a formal language to be defined below. The elements of LX may be combined into infinitely many different word sequences (provided there is no limit on their length). Such an infinite set of all possible sequences is called the *free monoid* produced from a finite lexicon.

7.1.2 ILLUSTRATION OF THE FREE MONOID OVER $LX = \{a, b\}$

ε

a, b

aa, ab, ba, bb

aaa, aab, aba, abb, baa, bab, bba, bbb

aaaa, aaab, aaba, aabb, abaa, abab, abba, abbb . . .

. . .

The free monoid over LX is also called the *Kleene closure* (Kleene 1952) and denoted by LX^*. The free monoid without the neutral element ε (also called empty sequence or zero sequence) is called the *positive closure* and is denoted by LX^+.[2]

The concept of a free monoid is applicable to artificial and natural languages alike. The lexica of natural languages are comparatively large: if all the different word forms are taken into account, they may contain several million entries. In principle, however, the lexica of natural languages are like those of artificial languages in that they are finite, whereas the associated free monoids are infinite.

Because a free monoid contains all possible word sequences, many of them will not be grammatical relative to a given language. In order to filter out the grammatically correct word sequences, a formal criterion is required to distinguish the grammatically well-formed sequences from the ill-formed ones.

In an artificial language, the specification of grammatical well-formedness is not difficult. It is defined by those who invented the language. For example, one has defined the artificial language $a^k b^k$ (with $k \geq 1$) as the set of expressions which consist of an arbitrary number of the word a followed by an equal number of the word b. This language is a proper subset of the set of sequences over $\{a, b\}$ sketched in 7.1.2.

According to the informal description of $a^k b^k$, the following expressions

a b, a a b b, a a a b b b, a a a a b b b b, etc.,

are well-formed. All the expressions of the free monoid not complying with this structure, such as

a, b, b a, b b a a, a b a b, etc.,

---

[1] In formal language theory, the lexicon of an artificial language is sometimes called the *alphabet*, a word a *letter*, and a sentence a *word*. From a linguistic point of view this practice is unnecessarily misleading. Therefore a basic expression of an artificial or a natural language is called here uniformly a *word* (even if the word consists of only a single letter, e.g., a) and a complete well-formed expression is called here uniformly a *sentence* (even if it consists only of a sequence of one-letter-words, e.g., aaabbb).

[2] In other words: the free monoid over LX equals $LX^+ \cup \{\varepsilon\}$ (Harrison 1978, p. 3).

are not well-formed expressions of the language $a^k b^k$. Analogously to $a^k b^k$ we may invent other artificial languages such as $a^k b^k c^k$, $a^k b^m c^k d^m$, etc.

It is not only the free monoid over a finite lexicon which contains infinitely many expressions, but the possible languages – as subsets of the free monoid – also usually comprise infinitely[3] many well-formed expressions or sentences. Therefore the criterion for filtering a language from a free monoid must be more than just a list.[4]

What is needed instead is a principled structural description of the well-formed expressions which may be applied to infinitely many (i.e., ever new) expressions. In formal language theory, these structural descriptions are specified as *recursive rule systems* which were borrowed from logic.

The following example of a formal grammar for the artificial language $a^k b^k$ uses a formalism known today as PS Grammar.[5]

7.1.3 PS GRAMMAR FOR $a^k b^k$

$\quad$ S → a S b

$\quad$ S → a b

This kind of grammar is called a *generative grammar* because it generates all well-formed expressions of the language from a single start symbol, here the S node. A generative grammar is based on the principle of possible substitution, i.e., the sign on the left of a rule arrow is substituted by the signs on the right.

Consider for example the derivation of the string a a a b b b. First the rule S → a S b is applied, replacing the S on the left of the arrow by the signs on the right. This produces the string

$\quad$ a S b.

Next, the first rule is applied again, replacing the S in the expression just derived by a S b. This produces the new string

$\quad$ a a S b b.

Finally, the S in this new string is replaced by a b using the second rule, resulting in

$\quad$ a a a b b b.

In this way the string in question may be derived formally using the rules of the grammar, thus proving that it is a well-formed expression of the language $a^k b^k$.

---

[3] The subsets of infinite sets may themselves be infinite. For example, the even numbers, e.g., 2,4,6, ... form an infinite subset of the natural numbers 1,2,3,4,5, ... The latter are formed from the finite lexicon of the digits 1,2,3,4,5,6,7,8,9, and 0 by means of concatenation, e.g., 12 or 21.

[4] This is because an explicit list of the well-formed sentences is finite by nature. Therefore it would be impossible to make a list of, for example, all the natural numbers. Instead the infinitely many surfaces of possible natural numbers are *produced* from the digits via the structural principle of concatenation.

[5] A detailed introduction to PS Grammar is given in Chap. 8.

Even though the grammar uses the finite lexicon {a, b} and a finite number of rules, it generates infinitely many expressions of the language $a^k b^k$. The formal basis for this is the *recursion* of the first rule: the variable S appears both on the left and on the right of the rule arrow, thus allowing a reapplication of the rule to its own output. The second rule, on the other hand, is an example of a nonrecursive rule in PS Grammar because its right-hand side does not contain a variable.

While all generative grammars are formal rule systems, not all formal grammars are generative grammars. A generative grammar proves the well-formedness of an expression indirectly by showing that it can be generated from an initial S node, computing possible substitutions. It is also possible, however, to establish well-formedness directly by going from left-to-right through an input expression, computing possible continuations.[6]

Today we are confronted with hundreds of different grammar formalisms. Most of these are formalisms which are derived from the first two of the following three elementary grammar formalisms:

7.1.4 ELEMENTARY GRAMMAR FORMALISMS

1. Categorial or C Grammar
2. Phrase-structure or PS Grammar
3. Left-associative or LA Grammar

These elementary formalisms differ in the form of their respective categories and rules (10.1.3, 10.1.4, and 10.1.5) as well as in their conceptual derivation orders (10.1.6). The formal basis of an elementary formalism is its *algebraic definition*.

7.1.5 ALGEBRAIC DEFINITION

The algebraic definition of a formal grammar[7] explicitly enumerates the basic components of the system, defining them and the structural relations between them using notions of set theory only.

An elementary formalism requires, furthermore, that its most relevant mathematical properties have been determined. These are in particular the hierarchy of language classes accepted by subtypes of the formalism and their complexity. Also, the formal relations between different elementary formalisms must be established.[8]

The reason for the many derived formalisms existing today is the attempt to overcome inherent weaknesses of the underlying elementary formalism. Some examples

---

[6] This latter approach is taken by Left-Associative grammar (LA Grammar, Chap. 10).

[7] An algebraic definition of C Grammar is provided in 7.4.2, of PS Grammar in 8.1.1, and of LA Grammar in 10.2.1, respectively.

[8] The relation between C and PS Grammar is described in Sect. 9.2. The different language hierarchies of PS and LA Grammar are compared in Chap. 12.

of derived formalisms which have enjoyed wider popularity at one time or another may be enumerated as follows:

7.1.6 Derived Formalisms of PS Grammar

Syntactic Structures, Generative Semantics, Standard Theory (ST), Extended Standard Theory (EST), Revised Extended Standard Theory (REST), Government and Binding (GB), Barriers, Generalized Phrase Structure Grammar (GPSG), Lexical Functional Grammar (LFG), Head-driven Phrase Structure Grammar (HPSG)

7.1.7 Derived Formalisms of C Grammar

Montague grammar (MG), Functional Unification Grammar (FUG), Categorial Unification Grammar (CUG), Combinatory Categorial Grammar (CCG), Unification-based Categorial Grammar (UCG)

It was even proposed that PS and C Grammar be combined into a derived formalism to compensate for their weaknesses and to benefit from their respective strengths.

The mathematical properties of derived formalisms must be characterized just as explicitly and precisely as those of the underlying elementary formalism. At first, derived formalisms seem to have the advantage that the known properties of their respective elementary formalisms would facilitate their analysis. In the long run, however, the mathematical analysis of derived formalisms has turned out to be at least as difficult as that of elementary formalisms. Often taking decades, this analysis has frequently been subject to error.[9]

In addition to elementary and derived formalisms there also exist *semi-formal systems* of grammar, the description of which has not been underpinned by an algebraic definition. Examples are dependency grammar (Tesnière 1959), systemic grammar (Halliday 1985), and stratificational grammar (Lamb 1996). In such systems one tries to get by, to a certain degree, with *conjectures* based on similarities with properties of known formalisms. For example, there is a structural resemblance between dependency grammar and C Grammar.

For systematic reasons, the analysis of mathematical properties and empirical suitability will concentrate here mainly on the elementary formalisms. The question is which of them is suited best (i) for the linguistic analysis of natural language and

---

[9] For example, Chomsky originally thought that the *recoverability condition* of deletions would keep transformational grammar decidable (see Sect. 8.5). However, Peters and Ritchie proved in 1972 that TG is undecidable despite this condition.

When Gazdar (1981) proposed the additional formalism of metarules for context-free PS Grammar, he formulated the *finite closure condition* to ensure that metarules would not increase complexity beyond that of context-free. However, the condition was widely rejected as linguistically unmotivated, leading Uszkoreit and Peters (1986) to the conclusion that GPSG is in fact undecidable.

(ii) for being implemented as automatic parsers. Also, the formal and conceptual reasons for why some elementary formalisms have been producing ever new derived formalisms will be explained.

7.2 Methodological Reasons for Formal Grammar

In contrast to artificial languages like $a^k b^k$ and $a^k b^k c^k$, which were invented for certain purposes (particularly complexity-theoretic considerations), natural languages are given by their respective language communities. This means that the decision of whether or not a natural language expression is grammatically well-formed depends on the language intuition of the native speakers. For example, the grammatical correctness of expression of English is noncontroversial:

7.2.1 GRAMMATICALLY WELL-FORMED EXPRESSION

the little dogs slept soundly

The following expression, on the other hand, will be rejected as ungrammatical by any competent speaker of English.

7.2.2 GRAMMATICALLY ILL-FORMED EXPRESSION

*[10]Soundly slept dogs little the

The second example resulted from inverting the order of the first.

Based on the distinction between well-formed and ill-formed expressions, formal grammars may also be written for natural languages. Just as the laws of physics allow one to precompute the location of a celestial body at a certain time, the rules of a descriptively adequate formal grammar should make it possible to *formally* decide, for any arbitrary expression, whether or not it is grammatically well-formed.

At first glance this goal of theoretical linguistics may look rather academic. In fact, however, the use of strictly formalized grammars is indispensable for modern linguistic methodology:

7.2.3 METHODOLOGICAL CONSEQUENCES OF FORMAL GRAMMAR

– *Empirical*: formation of explicit hypotheses
    A formal rule system provides explicit hypotheses about which input expressions are considered well-formed and which are not. The comparison of the hypotheses of the formal system with the intuitions of the native speaker provides clarity about where the formal grammar is empirically inadequate – which is essential for an incremental improvement of the grammar.

---

[10] In linguistics, examples of ungrammatical structures are marked with an asterisk *, a convention which dates back at least to Bloomfield (1933).

– *Mathematical*: determining the formal properties
  Only strictly formalized descriptions allow us to analyze their mathematical properties[11] such as decidability, complexity, and generative capacity. The mathematical properties of a grammar formalism in turn determine whether it is suitable for empirical description and computational realization.
– *Computational*: declarative specification of the parser
  Only a formal rule system may be used as a declarative specification[12] of the parser, characterizing its necessary properties in contrast to accidental properties stemming from the choice of the programming environment, etc. A parser in turn provides the automatic language analysis needed for the verification of the individual grammars written within the formalism of choice.

Compared to traditional grammar (1.2.1), a formal grammar provides an explicit description of a language's regular structures, and not only the exceptions and irregularities. However, for the initial analysis of a given natural language many different formal grammars may be defined; they may all be equally well formalized and each may offer a confusing mix of different merits and weaknesses. This raises the question of which of these formalisms will turn out best empirically in the long-term upscaling of a natural language's description.

In summary, the definition of a formal grammar is a necessary, but not a sufficient, condition for an adequate linguistic analysis of a natural language. If a grammar formalism may be shown to be suboptimal by means of mathematical analysis, this is not the fault of the formal method. Conversely, if no such conclusions can be drawn because of insufficient formalization, this is not a merit of the grammar formalism.

7.3 Adequacy of Formal Grammars

A formal grammar is called descriptively adequate for a given natural language if it accepts all and only the well-formed expressions of the language. An inadequate grammar is either incorrect, incomplete, or both. A grammar is incorrect if it accepts expressions which are not well-formed (overgeneration). A grammar is incomplete if there are well-formed expressions it does not accept (undergeneration).

Let us assume, for example, that there is a formal grammar for a natural language we do not speak, e.g., Quechua,[13] and we would like to check whether a certain expression

---

[11] The mathematical properties of informal descriptions, on the other hand, cannot be investigated because their structures are not sufficiently clearly specified.

[12] Programs which are not based on a declarative specification may still run. However, as long as it is not clear which of their properties are theoretically necessary and which are an accidental result of the programming environment and the programmer's idiosyncrasies, such programs – called hacks – are of little theoretical interest. From a practical point of view, they are difficult to scale up and hard to debug. The relation between grammar systems and their implementation is further discussed in Sect. 15.1.

[13] Quechua is a language of South-American Indians.

is well-formed. For this, we assign to the word forms their respective categories using the lexicon of our formal Quechua grammar. Then we attempt to derive the resulting sequence of analyzed word forms using the formal grammar rules. According to the formal grammar, the expression is well-formed if such a derivation exists.

However, in natural language such a formal derivation is a reliable criterion of well-formedness only if the formal grammar is known to be descriptively adequate. As long as there is any doubt about the grammar in question, all accepted and rejected expressions must be presented to native speakers for deciding whether the grammar has correctly distinguished between well-formed or ill-formed input (correctness). Also, any new Quechua expressions must be checked as to whether or not the grammar will accept them (completeness).

Determining whether a given expression is in fact accepted by the formal grammar may take long – in fact, infinitely long – even if the check is done automatically on a supercomputer. This is the case whenever the grammar formalism used is of high mathematical complexity. The mathematical complexity of a formal grammar is measured as the maximal number of rule applications (worst case) relative to the length of the input (Sect. 8.2).

Within nativism, systems of generative grammar for natural language are of high mathematical complexity while attempting to characterize grammatical well-formedness without a functional theory of communication. To avoid these shortcomings, the syntactic analysis of natural language should be

- defined *mathematically* as a formal theory of low complexity,
- designed *functionally* as a component of natural language communication, and
- realized *methodologically* as an efficiently implemented computer program in which the properties of formal language theory and of natural language analysis are represented in a modular and transparent manner.

These desiderata must pursued simultaneously. After all, what use is a pleasantly designed syntax, if its complexity turns out to be undecidable or exponential? What is the purpose of a mathematically well-founded and efficient formalism, if it turns out to be structurally incompatible with the mechanism of natural communication? How reliable is a mathematically and functionally well-suited grammar, if it has not been computationally verified on realistic, i.e., very large, amounts of data?

7.4 Formalism of C Grammar

The historically first elementary grammar formalism was categorial grammar or C grammar. It was invented by the Polish logicians Leśniewski (1929) and Ajdukiewicz (1935) in order to avoid the Russell paradox in formal language analysis. C Grammar was first applied to natural language by Bar-Hillel (1953).[14]

---

[14] A good intuitive summary may be found in Geach (1972). See also Lambek (1958) and Bar-Hillel (1964), Chap. 14, pp. 185–189.

The origin of C Grammar in the context of the Russell paradox resulted from the outset in a logical semantic orientation (Sect. 19.3). The combinatorics of C Grammar is based on the functor-argument structure of a mathematical function. A functor denotes a function which maps suitable arguments to values. A mathematical function consists of a 1. *name*, a specification of the 2. *domain* (i.e., the set of arguments), a specification of the 3. *range* (i.e., the set of values), and a specification of the 4. *assignment* which associates each argument with at most one value.

7.4.1 STRUCTURE OF A MATHEMATICAL FUNCTION

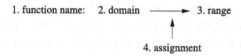

1. function name: 2. domain ————▶ 3. range

↑

4. assignment

A simple example of a function is the squaring of natural numbers. The name of this function is square_number, the domain is the set of natural numbers, the range is likewise the set of natural numbers, and the assignment provides for each possible argument, e.g., 1, 2, 3, 4, 5,..., exactly one value, i.e., 1, 4, 9, 16, 25,....[15]

The role of functors and arguments in C Grammar is formally reflected in the definition of its categories and rules. This is shown by the following algebraic definition:[16]

7.4.2 ALGEBRAIC DEFINITION OF C GRAMMAR

A C Grammar is a quintuple <W, C, LX, R, CE>.

1. W is a finite set of word form surfaces.
2. C is a set of categories such that
   (a) *basis*
       u and v $\in$ C,[17]
   (b) *induction*
       if X and Y $\in$ C, then also (X/Y) and (X\Y) $\in$ C,
   (c) *closure*
       Nothing is in C except as specified in (a) and (b).
3. LX is a finite set such that LX $\subset$ (W $\times$ C).
4. R is a set comprising the following two rule schemata:
   $$\alpha_{(Y/X)} \circ \beta_{(Y)} \Rightarrow \alpha\beta_{(X)}$$
   $$\beta_{(Y)} \circ \alpha_{(Y\backslash X)} \Rightarrow \beta\alpha_{(X)}$$
5. CE is a set comprising the categories of *complete expressions*, with CE $\subseteq$ C.

---

[15] In contrast, square_root is not a function, but called a relation because it may assign more than one value to an argument in the domain. The root of 4, for example, has two values, namely 2 and −2.

[16] An alternative algebraic definition of C Grammar may be found in Bar-Hillel (1964), p. 188.

[17] The names and the number of elementary categories (here, u and v) are in principle unrestricted. For example, Ajdukiewicz used only one elementary category, Geach and Montague used two, others three.

In accordance with the general notion of an algebraic definition (7.1.5), the basic components of C Grammar are first enumerated in the quintuple <W, C, LX, R, CE>. Then these components are set-theoretically characterized in clauses 1–5.

More specifically, the set W is defined as a finite, unordered enumeration of the basic surfaces of the language to be described. For example, in the case of the artificial language $a^k b^k$ the set W would contain a and b.

The set C is defined recursively. Because the start elements u and v are in C, so are (u/v), (v/u), (u\v), and (v\u), according to the induction clause. This means in turn that also ((u/v)/v), ((u/v)\v), ((u/v)/u), ((u/v)\u), (u/(u/v)), (v/(u/v)), etc., belong to C. C is infinite because new elements can be formed recursively from old ones.

The set LX is a finite set of ordered pairs such that each ordered pair is built from (i) an element of W and (ii) an element of C. Notationally, the second member of the ordered pair, i.e., the category, is written as a subscript to the first as in, for example, $a_{((u/v)\backslash v)}$. Which surfaces (i.e., elements of W) take which elements of C as their categories is specified in LX by explicitly listing the ordered pairs.

The set R contains two rule schemata. They use the variables α and β to represent the surfaces of the functor and the argument, respectively, and the variables X and Y to represent their category patterns. The first schema combines functor and argument in the order $\alpha\beta$, whereby the Y in the category of the functor α is canceled by the corresponding symbol in the category of argument β. The second schema combines functor and argument in the inverse order, i.e., $\beta\alpha$. The alternative ordering is formally triggered by the backslash '\' (instead of the slash '/') in the category of α. This kind of C Grammar has been called bidirectional C Grammar by Bar-Hillel because the two rule schemata permit placing a functor either before or after the argument.

The set CE, finally, describes the categories of those expressions which are considered complete. Depending on the specific C Grammar and the specific language, this set may be finite and specified in terms of an explicit listing, or it may be infinite and characterized by patterns containing variables.

Whether two categorized language expressions may be legally combined depends on whether their categories can be pattern-matched with a suitable rule schema. This process of matching is traditionally handled implicitly in C Grammar because there are only the following two rule schemata, one for combining a functor-argument pair, the other for combining an argument-functor pair:

7.4.3 IMPLICIT PATTERN MATCHING IN COMBINATIONS OF C GRAMMAR

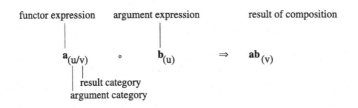

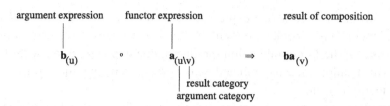

Like PS Grammar, C Grammar is based on possible substitutions: the expression to the left of the arrow is replaced by the expression to the right. However, while the derivation order of PS Grammar is top-down, that of C Grammar is bottom-up.

In contrast to PS Grammar, which codes the combinatorics into a multitude of rules, C Grammar codes the combinatorics into the category structures: a language is completely specified by defining (i) the lexicon LX and (ii) the set of complete expressions CE. This is illustrated by the following definition of the artificial language $a^k b^k$, familiar from its PS Grammar analysis 7.1.3:

7.4.4 C GRAMMAR FOR $a^k b^k$

$$LX =_{def} \{a_{(u/v)}, b_{(u)}, a_{(v/(u/v))}\}$$
$$CE =_{def} \{(v)\}$$

The word a has two lexical definitions with the categories (u/v) and $(v/(u/v))$, respectively, for reasons apparent in the following derivation tree:

7.4.5 EXAMPLE OF $a^k b^k$ DERIVATION, FOR $k = 3$

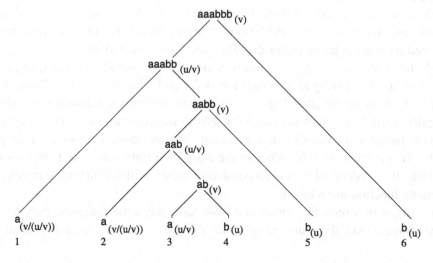

The derivation begins with the combination of words 3 and 4. Only this initial composition uses the categorial reading (u/v) of word a. The result is the expression ab of category (v). This would be a complete expression according to the definition of CE in 7.4.4, provided there were no other words in the input string. Next, word 2 is combined with the result of the last combination, producing the expression aab with the category (u/v). This result is in turn combined with word 5, producing the expression aabb with the category (v), etc.

In this way complete expressions of category (v) may be derived, each consisting of arbitrarily many words a followed by an equal number of words b. Thus, a finite definition generates infinitely many expressions of the artificial language $a^k b^k$.

7.5 C Grammar for Natural Language

C Grammar is the prototype of a lexicalist approach: all the combinatorial properties of the language are coded into the categories of its basic expressions. This is as apparent in the C grammatical definition of the artificial language $a^k b^k$ as it is in the following definition of a tiny fragment[18] of English:

7.5.1 C GRAMMAR FOR A TINY FRAGMENT OF ENGLISH

$$LX =_{def} \{W_{(e)} \cup W_{(e \backslash t)}\}, \text{ where}$$
$$W_{(e)} = \{\text{Julia, Peter, Mary, Fritz, Susanne, } \ldots\}$$
$$W_{(e \backslash t)} = \{\text{sleeps, laughs, sings, } \ldots\}$$
$$CE =_{def} \{(t)\}$$

Compared to 7.4.4, this grammar exhibits two notational modifications.

First, the lexical entries are assembled into word classes W_{cat}. This notation, which originated with Montague, makes the writing of lexica simpler because the categories are specified for whole classes rather than for each single word form.

Second, the elementary categories, called u and v, are renamed as e and t, respectively. According to Montague, e stands for *entity* and t for *truth value*. Thus, the category (e\t) of sleeps, laughs, sings, ... is motivated not only syntactically, but also semantically: (e\t) is interpreted as a characteristic function from entities into truth values. The characteristic function of, for example, sleeps determines the set of sleepers by checking each entity e for whether the associated truth value t is 1 (true) or 0 (false). Thus, the set denoted by sleeps consists of those entities which the equivalent characteristic function maps into 1.

Because different words like sleep and walk have the same category, they have the same domain and the same range. The difference in their meaning resides

---

[18] The term *fragment* is used to refer to that subset of a natural language which a given formal grammar is designed to handle.

solely in their different assignments (4 in 7.4.1). How to define these different assignments in a nontrivial way (i.e., *not* in terms of explicitly listing ordered pairs in the model definition) is one of the basic problems of model-theoretic semantics.[19]

The semantic interpretation of the C grammatically analyzed sentence Julia sleeps relative to some model $\mathcal{M}$ is defined as follows: The sentence is true if the denotation of sleeps maps the denotation of Julia into 1, and false otherwise.

7.5.2 SIMULTANEOUS SYNTACTIC AND SEMANTIC ANALYSIS

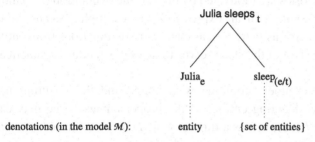

According to the equivalent set-theoretic view, the sentence is true if the denotation of Julia in $\mathcal{M}$ is an element of the set denoted by sleeps in $\mathcal{M}$.

Based on the method of categorization outlined above, a sentence like The little black dogs sleep may be analyzed as in the following derivation tree.

7.5.3 C ANALYSIS OF A NATURAL LANGUAGE SENTENCE

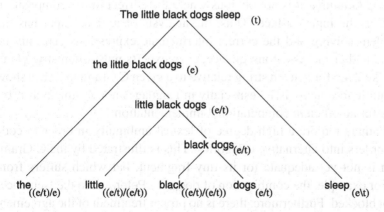

As in the previous examples 7.4.4 and 7.5.1, the C Grammar analyzing or generating this example consists only of the lexicon LX and the set CE.

---

[19] Sect. 19.4 and CoL, pp. 292–295.

7.5.4 C GRAMMAR FOR EXAMPLE 7.5.3

$\text{LX} =_{def} \{W_{(e)} \cup W_{(e\setminus t)} \cup W_{(e/t)} \cup W_{((e/t)/(e/t))} \cup W_{((e/t)/t)}\}$, where

$\quad W_{(e)} = \{\text{Julia, Peter, Mary, Fritz, Susanne}, \ldots\}$

$\quad W_{(e\setminus t)} = \{\text{sleeps, laughs, sings}, \ldots\}$

$\quad W_{(e/t)} = \{\text{dog, dogs, cat, cats, table, tables}, \ldots\}$

$\quad W_{((e/t)/(e/t))} = \{\text{little, black}, \ldots\}$

$\quad W_{((e/t)/t)} = \{\text{a, the, every}, \ldots\}$

$\text{CE} =_{def} \{(t)\}$

In this C Grammar, the categories are motivated by both (i) the denotation (semantics) and (ii) the combinatorics (syntax) of an expression. For example, because nouns denote sets they are categorized[20] as (e/t), i.e., as characteristic functions from entities to truth values, whereby the slant of the slash serves to distinguish nouns syntactically from intransitive verbs.

Furthermore, because determiners combine with nouns and the resulting noun phrases may be regarded as denoting entities – like proper names – one may categorize the determiner as $((e/t)/e)$, i.e., as a functor which takes a noun (e/t) to make something like a name (e). Adjectives, on the other hand, take a noun to make a noun, which may be expressed by categorizing adjectives as $((e/t)/(e/t))$. From this structure follows the possibility of stacking modifiers recursively. It follows that a noun may take an unlimited number of adjectives.

In theory, such a high degree of motivation and the constraints following from it are generally regarded as highly desirable in science. The idea is: the better constrained the theory, the better the guidance for empirical work. This presupposes, however, that the theory in question doesn't suffer from any fatal flaws.

For example, in C Grammar it is not obvious where the correct initial composition should take place in the input surface. Thus, the analysis of a given input has the character of problem solving and the correct intermediate expressions can only be discovered by trial and error. As a consequence, even experts must often struggle to find a derivation like 7.4.5 for a given string relative to a given C Grammar (or to show that such a derivation does not exist) – especially in languages not as simple as $a^k b^k$. This is unsuitable for an efficient computational implementation.

Second, C Grammars require a high degree of lexical ambiguity in order to code alternative word orders into alternative categories. This is illustrated by the C Grammar 7.5.4, which is not yet adequate for its tiny fragment, but which suffers from overgeneration. For example, the combination of $\text{dog}_{(e/t)} \circ \text{Peter}_{(e)}$ into the 'sentence' *$\text{dogPeter}_{(t)}$ is not blocked. Furthermore, there is no proper treatment of the agreement

---

[20] For simplicity and consistency, our notation differs from Montague's in that the distinction between syntactic categories and semantic types is omitted, with arguments positioned before the slash.

between determiners and nouns, allowing the generation of ungrammatical combinations like *every dogs and *all dog.

In theory, each such difficulty could be handled by a seemingly minor extension of the formalism. In practice, however, the extensions necessary for even moderately sized descriptive work[21] quickly turn the conceptually transparent and mathematically benign elementary formalism of C Grammar into derived systems of high complexity. The need for ever more ad hoc solutions and the concomitant loss of transparency make C Grammar an unlikely candidate for reaching the goal of theoretical linguistics, namely a complete formal description of at least one natural language.

Exercises

Section 7.1

1. How is the notion of a language defined in formal grammar?
2. Explain the notion of a free monoid as it relates to formal grammar.
3. What is the difference between positive closure and Kleene closure?
4. In what sense can a generative grammar be viewed as a filter?
5. Explain the role of recursion in the derivation of aaaabbbb using definition 7.1.3.
6. Why is PS Grammar called a *generative grammar*?
7. What is an algebraic definition and what is its purpose?
8. What is the difference between elementary, derived, and semi-formal formalisms?
9. What is the reason for the development of derived formalisms?

Section 7.2

1. Explain the difference in the well-formedness for artificial and natural languages.
2. Why is a formal characterization of grammatical well-formedness a descriptive goal of theoretical linguistics?
3. Name three reasons for using formal grammar in modern linguistics.
4. Why is the use of formal grammars a necessary, but not a sufficient, condition for a successful language analysis?

---

[21] For an attempt see SCG.

Section 7.3

1. Under what circumstances is a formal grammar descriptively adequate?
2. What is meant by the mathematical complexity of a grammar formalism and why is it relevant for practical work?
3. What is the difference between functional and nonfunctional grammar theories?
4. Which three aspects should be jointly taken into account in the development of a generative grammar and why?

Section 7.4

1. Who invented C Grammar, when, and for what purpose?
2. When was C Grammar first applied to natural language and by whom?
3. What is the structure of a logical function?
4. Give an algebraic definition of C Grammar.
5. Explain the interpretation of complex C Grammar categories as functors.
6. Why is the set of categories in C Grammar infinite and the lexicon finite?
7. Name the formal principle allowing the C Grammar 7.4.4 to generate infinitely many expressions even though its lexicon and its rule set are finite.
8. Why is the grammar formalism defined in 7.4.4 called *bidirectional* C Grammar?
9. Would it be advisable to use C Grammar as the syntactic component of the SLIM theory of language?

Section 7.5

1. Why is C Grammar prototypical of a lexical approach?
2. What is meant by a fragment of a natural language in formal grammar?
3. Explain the relation between a functional interpretation of complex categories in C Grammar and the model-theoretic interpretation of natural language.
4. Explain the recursive structure in the C Grammar 7.5.4.
5. Explain how the semantic interpretation of C Grammar works in principle.
6. Extend the C Grammar 7.5.4 to generate the sentences The man sent the girl a letter, The girl received a letter from the man, The girl was sent a letter by the man. Explain the semantic motivation of your categories.
7. Why are there no large-scale descriptions of natural language in C Grammar?
8. Why are there no efficient implementations of C Grammar?
9. Why is the absence of efficient implementations a serious methodological problem for C Grammar?
10. Does C Grammar provide a mechanism of natural communication? Would it be suitable as a component of such a mechanism?

8. Language Hierarchies and Complexity

The historically second elementary grammar formalism was published in 1936 by the American logician Emil POST (1897–1957). Known as *rewrite systems* or *Post production systems*, they originated in the mathematical context of recursion theory and are closely related to automata theory and computational complexity theory.

Rewrite systems were first applied to natural language by Chomsky (1957) under the new name of *phrase structure grammars*[1] and the general heading of *generative grammar*. Based on PS Grammar, Chomsky and others developed a series of derived formalisms initially called transformational grammars.

Section 8.1 provides an algebraic definition of PS Grammar and restrictions on the form of PS rules which result in regular, context-free, context-sensitive, and unrestricted PS Grammars. Section 8.2 explains four basic degrees of complexity and relates them to different kinds of PS Grammar. Section 8.3 illustrates the notion of generative capacity with applications of PS Grammar to artificial languages. Section 8.4 applies context-free PS Grammar to natural language and defines the linguistic concept of constituent structure. Section 8.5 explains the constituent structure paradox and shows why adding transformations makes the resulting PS Grammar formalism undecidable.

---

[1] Apparently, Chomsky forgot to mention Post's contribution. This was commented on by Bar-Hillel (1964) as follows:

> This approach [i.e., rewriting systems] is the standard one for the combinatorial systems conceived much earlier by Post [1936], as a result of his penetrating researches into the structure of formal calculi, though Chomsky seems to have become aware of the proximity of his ideas to those of Post only at a later stage of his work.
>
> Bar-Hillel (1964), p. 103

This is remarkable insofar as Chomsky's thesis advisor Harris and Bar-Hillel had been in close scientific contact since 1947. Moreover, Bar-Hillel and Chomsky discussed "linguistics, logic, and methodology in endless talks" beginning in 1951 (Bar-Hillel 1964, p. 16).

R. Hausser, *Foundations of Computational Linguistics*,
DOI 10.1007/978-3-642-41431-2_8, © Springer-Verlag Berlin Heidelberg 2014

8.1 Formalism of PS Grammar

The algebraic definition of PS Grammar resembles that of C Grammar (7.4.2) insofar
as it enumerates the basic components of the system and characterizes each in terms
of set theory.

8.1.1 ALGEBRAIC DEFINITION OF PS GRAMMAR

A PS Grammar is a quadruple $<V, V_T, S, P>$ such that

1. V is a finite set of signs,
2. V_T is a proper subset of V, called *terminal symbols*,
3. S is a sign in V minus V_T, called the *start symbol* , and
4. P is a set of rewrite rules of the form $\alpha \rightarrow \beta$, where α is an element of V^+ and β
   an element of V^*.[2]

The basic components of PS Grammar are the sets V, V_T, and P, plus the start symbol S. The terminal symbols of V_T are the word surfaces of the language. The nonterminal symbols of V minus V_T are called the variables. We will use Greek letters to
represent sequences from V^*, uppercase Latin letters to represent individual variables,
and lowercase Latin letters to represent individual terminal symbols.

A PS Grammar generates language expressions by means of rewrite rules, whereby
the sign sequence on the left-hand side is replaced (substituted) by that on the right.
For example, if $\alpha \rightarrow \beta$ is a rewrite rule in P and γ, δ are sequences in V^*, then

$$\gamma\alpha\delta \Rightarrow \gamma\beta\delta$$

is a direct substitution of the sequence $\gamma\alpha\delta$ by the sequence $\gamma\beta\delta$. In other words, by
applying the rule $\alpha \rightarrow \beta$ to the sequence $\gamma\alpha\delta$ there results the new sequence $\gamma\beta\delta$.

The general format of rewrite rules in PS Grammar suggests systematic restrictions
of the following kind, whereby the numbering used here follows tradition:

8.1.2 RESTRICTIONS OF PS RULE SCHEMATA

0. Unrestricted PS rules:
   The left- and right-hand sides of a type 0 rule each consist of arbitrary sequences
   of terminal and nonterminal symbols.
1. Context-sensitive PS rules:
   The left- and right-hand sides of a type 1 rule each consist of arbitrary sequences
   of terminal and nonterminal symbols, whereby the right-hand side must be at
   least as long as the left.
   Example: A B C $\rightarrow$ A D E C

---

[2] V^+ is the positive closure and V^* is the Kleene closure of V (Sect. 7.2).

2. Context-free PS rules:
   The left-hand side of a type 2 rule consists of exactly one variable. The right-hand side of the rule consists of a sequence from V^+.
   Examples: A → BC, A → bBCc, etc.[3]
3. Regular PS rules:
   The left-hand side of a type 3 rule consists of exactly one variable. The right-hand side consists of exactly one terminal symbol and at most one variable.[4]
   Examples: A → b, A → bC.

Because the rule types become more and more restrictive – from type 0 to type 3 – the rules of a certain type obey all restrictions of the lower rule types. For example, the regular type 3 rule

A → bC

complies with the lesser restrictions of the rule types 2, 1, and 0. The context-free type 2 rule

A → BC

on the other hand, while not complying with the type 3 restriction, complies with the lesser restrictions of the lower rule types 1 and 0, and similarly for type 1 rules.

The different restrictions on the PS Grammar rule schema result in four different kinds of PS Grammars. PS Grammars which contain only type 3 rules are called regular, those which contain at most type 2 rules are called context-free, those which contain at most type 1 rules are called context-sensitive, and those which have no restrictions on their rules are called unrestricted PS Grammars.

These four kinds of PS Grammar generate in turn four different classes of languages. They are the regular languages generated by the regular PS Grammars, the context-free languages generated by the context-free PS Grammars, the context-sensitive languages generated by the context-sensitive PS Grammars, and the recursively enumerable languages generated by the unrestricted PS Grammars.

The different language classes are properly contained in each other. Thus, the class of regular languages is a proper subset of the class of context-free languages, which in turn is a proper subset of the class of context-sensitive languages, which in turn is a proper subset of the class of recursively enumerable languages.

---

[3] Context-free grammar sometimes uses so-called 'epsilon rules' of the form A → ε, where ε is the empty string. However, epsilon rules can always be eliminated (Hopcroft and Ullman 1979, p. 90, Theorem 4.3). We specify the right-hand side of type 2 rules as a nonempty sequence in order to formally maintain the context-free rules as a special form of the context-sensitive rules (subset relation).

[4] This is the definition of *right linear* PS Grammars. PS Grammars in which the order of the terminal and the nonterminal symbols on the right-hand side of the rule is inverted are called *left linear*. Left and right linear grammars are equivalent (Hopcroft and Ullman 1979, p. 219, Theorem 9.2).

The differences in the language classes result from differences in the generative capacity of the associated kinds of PS Grammar. The generative capacity of a grammar kind is high if a corresponding grammar is able not only to recursively generate many formal language structures, but can at the same time *exclude* those which are not part of the language. The generative capacity of a grammar kind is low, on the other hand, if the grammar allows only limited control over the structures to be generated.[5]

8.2 Language Classes and Computational Complexity

Associated with the generative capacity of a grammar kind and its language class is the degree of computational complexity, i.e., the amount of computing time and/or memory space needed to analyze expressions of a certain language class. The computational complexity increases systematically with the generative capacity.

In short, different restrictions on a grammatical rule schema result in

- different *kinds of grammar*, which have
- different *degrees of generative capacity* and generate
- different *language classes*, which in turn exhibit
- different *degrees of computational complexity*.

This structural correlation is not limited to PS Grammar, but holds in any well-defined grammar formalism (8.2.3, 11.5.10).

The complexity of a grammar formalism is traditionally measured on the basis of an algorithm which implements the grammar formalism as an operational procedure on an abstract automaton (e.g., a Turing machine, a linearly bounded automaton, a push-down automaton, a finite state automaton, etc.). The complexity of the algorithm is computed as the number of *primitive operations*[6] required to analyze an arbitrary input expression in the worst possible case (upper bound).[7] Thereby

---

[5] For example, the generative capacity of the PS Grammar 7.1.3 for the artificial language $a^k b^k$ is higher than that of a regular PS Grammar 8.3.2 for the free monoid over $\{a,b\}$ (7.1.2). The free monoid contains all the expressions of $a^k b^k$, but its regular PS Grammar is unable to *exclude* the expressions which do not belong to the language $a^k b^k$.

[6] Earley (1970) characterizes a primitive operation as "in some sense the most complex operation performed by the algorithm whose complexity is independent of the size of the grammar and the input string." The exact nature of the primitive operation varies from one grammar formalism to the next.

For example, Earley chose the operation of *adding a state to a state set* as the primitive operation of his famous algorithm for context-free grammars (Sect. 9.3). In LA Grammar, on the other hand, the subclass of C LAGs uses a *rule application* as its primitive operation (Sect. 11.4).

[7] We are referring here to time complexity.

the number of primitive operations is counted in relation to the length of the input.

In elementary grammar formalisms, complexity is usually determined for well-defined subtypes such as the regular, context-free, context-sensitive, and unrestricted subtypes of PS Grammar, or the C1, C2, C3, B, and A LAGs of LA Grammar. Furthermore, the complexity of a language class is equated with that of the associated grammar kind. For example, one says the context-free languages have a complexity of n^3 because there exists a known algorithm which for any arbitrary context-free PS Grammar can analyze any arbitrary input using at most n^3 primitive operations, where n is the length of the input.

There are the following four basic degrees of computational complexity, where n is the length of the input:

8.2.1 BASIC DEGREES OF COMPLEXITY

1. *Linear complexity*
   n, 2n, 3n, etc.
2. *Polynomial complexity*
   n^2, n^3, n^4, etc.
3. *Exponential complexity*
   2^n, 3^n, 4^n, etc.
4. *Undecidable*
   $n \cdot \infty$

To get an idea of how these complexity degrees affect practical work, consider the Limas corpus[8] of German. The average sentence length in the Limas corpus is 17.54 word forms (including punctuation marks). Thus, a linear $3 \cdot n$ algorithm will require at most 51 operations for the analysis of an average sentence (with $n = 17$), a polynomial n^3 algorithm will require at most 4 913 operations, an exponential 3^n algorithm will require at most 127 362 132 operations, and an undecidable algorithm will require at most $17 \cdot \infty$ $(=\infty)$ operations.

Garey and Johnson (1979) compare the time needed for solving a problem of n^3 (polynomial) and 2^n (exponential) complexity relative to different problem sizes as follows:

---

[8] As explained in Sect. 15.3, the Limas corpus was built in analogy to the Brown and the LOB corpora, and contains 500 texts of 2000 running word forms each. The texts were selected at random from roughly the same 15 genres as those of the Brown and LOB corpora in order to come as close as possible to the desideratum of a *balanced* corpus which is *representative* of the German language in the year 1973.

8.2.2 TIMING OF POLYNOMIAL VS. EXPONENTIAL ALGORITHMS

time complexity	problem size n		
	10	50	100
n^3	0.001 seconds	0.125 seconds	1.0 seconds
2^n	0.001 seconds	35.7 years	10^{15} centuries

In this example, Garey and Johnson use *adding the next word* as the primitive operation of their algorithm.

Of a total of 71 148 sentences in the Limas corpus, there are exactly 50 which consist of 100 word forms or more, whereby the longest sentence in the whole corpus consists of 165 words.[9] Thus, if we apply the measurements of Garey and Johnson to the automatic analysis of the Limas corpus, an exponential 2^n grammar algorithm, though decidable, could take longer than 1 000 000 000 000 000 centuries in the worst case. This amount of time is considerably longer than the existence of the universe and could not be reduced to practical levels by faster machines.

In the case of PS Grammar, the correlation between rule restrictions, grammar kinds, language classes, and complexity is as follows:

8.2.3 PS GRAMMAR HIERARCHY OF FORMAL LANGUAGES

rule restrictions	types of PS–grammar	language classes	degree of complexity
type 3	regular PSG	regular languages	linear
type 2	context–free PSG	context–free languages	polynominal
type 1	context–sensitive PSG	context–sensitive lang.	exponential
type 0	unrestricted PSG	recursively enum. lang.	undecidable

The above considerations of polynomial and exponential complexity lead to the conclusion that only regular and context-free PSGs are computationally suitable for a description of language. As an alternative to the PS Grammar hierarchy, also called the Chomsky hierarchy, the LA Grammar hierarchy is defined in Chap. 11.

---

[9] These data were provided by Schulze at CLUE (Computational Linguistics at the University of Erlangen Nürnberg).

8.3 Generative Capacity and Formal Language Classes

From a linguistic point of view, the question is whether or not there is a kind of PS Grammar which generates exactly those structures which are characteristic of natural language. Let us therefore take a closer look at the structures generated by different kinds of PS Grammar.

The kind of PS Grammar which has the most restricted rules, the lowest generative capacity, and the lowest computational complexity is regular PS Grammar.[10] The generative capacity of a regular PS Grammar permits the recursive repetition of single words, but without any recursive correspondences.

For example, expressions of the regular language ab^k consist of one a, followed by one, two, or more b. A (right linear) PS Grammar for ab^k is defined as follows:

8.3.1 REGULAR PS GRAMMAR FOR ab^k ($k \geq 1$)

$$V \quad =_{def} \{S, B, a, b\}$$
$$V_T =_{def} \{a, b\}$$
$$P \quad =_{def} \{S \rightarrow a\,B,$$
$$\qquad\quad B \rightarrow b\,B,$$
$$\qquad\quad B \rightarrow b\}$$

Another example of a regular language is the free monoid over $\{a, b\}$ minus the zero-element, which is generated by the following PS Grammar:

8.3.2 REGULAR PS GRAMMAR FOR $\{a, b\}^+$

$$V \quad =_{def} \{S, a, b\}$$
$$V_T =_{def} \{a, b\}$$
$$P \quad =_{def} \{S \rightarrow a\,S,$$
$$\qquad\quad S \rightarrow b\,S,$$
$$\qquad\quad S \rightarrow a,$$
$$\qquad\quad S \rightarrow b\}$$

That a regular PS Grammar cannot generate systematic correspondences of arbitrary number is illustrated by the contrast between the already familiar context-free language $a^k b^k$ and the regular language $a^m b^k$.

---

[10] The class of regular languages is not part of the hierarchy of LA Grammar, though it may be reconstructed in it (CoL, Theorem 3, p. 138). Instead the LA Grammar hierarchy provides the alternative linear class of C1 languages. As shown in Sects. 11.5 ff., the class of C1 languages contains all regular languages, all deterministic context-free languages which are recognized by an epsilon-free DPDA, as well as many context-sensitive languages.

8.3.3 REGULAR PS GRAMMAR FOR $a^m b^k$ ($k, m \geq 1$)

$V \ =_{def} \{S, S_1, S_2, a, b\}$
$V_T =_{def} \{a, b\}$
$P \ =_{def} \{S \rightarrow a\, S_1,$
$\qquad\qquad\ S_1 \rightarrow a\, S_1,$
$\qquad\qquad\ S_1 \rightarrow b\, S_2,$
$\qquad\qquad\ S_2 \rightarrow b\}$

The language $a^m b^k$ is regular because the number of a and the number of b in $a^m b^k$ is open – as indicated by the use of the two superscripts ^{m} and ^{k}. The language $a^k b^k$, on the other hand, exceeds the generative capacity of a regular PS Grammar because it requires a correspondence between the number of a and the number of b – as indicated by their having the same superscript ^{k}.

The characteristic limitation in the generative capacity of regular PS Grammars follows in an intuitively obvious way from the restrictions on the associated rule type: Because the right-hand side of a type 3 rule consists of one terminal and at most one variable it is impossible to recursively generate even pairwise correspondences – as would be required by $a^k b^k$.

The formal proof of the lower generative capacity of regular PS Grammars as compared to the context-free PS Grammars is not trivial, however. It is based on the *pumping lemma* for regular languages,[11] which formally shows that there are languages that may not be generated by regular PS Grammars.

A pumping lemma for a certain language class shows which structures it can have. This is done by explicitly listing the basic structural patterns of the language class such that the infinite set of additional expressions can be pumped, i.e., they can be shown to consist only of repetitions of the basic structural patterns.

The next grammar kind in the PS Grammar hierarchy is that of context-free PS Grammars. Examples of context-free languages are $a^k b^k$ (for which a PS Grammar is defined in 7.1.3 and a C Grammar in 7.4.4) and $a^k b^{3k}$ defined below.

8.3.4 CONTEXT-FREE PS GRAMMAR FOR $a^k b^{3k}$

$V \ =_{def} \{S, a, b\}$
$V_T =_{def} \{a, b\}$
$P \ =_{def} \{S \rightarrow a\, S\, b\, b\, b,$
$\qquad\qquad\ S \rightarrow a\, b\, b\, b\}$

This kind of grammar is called context-free because the left-hand side of a type 2 rule consists by definition of a single variable (8.1.2) – without a surrounding 'context' of other signs.[12]

---

[11] Hopcroft and Ullman (1979), pp. 55f.

[12] This notion of 'context' is peculiar to the terminology of PS Grammar and has nothing to do with the speaker-hearer-internal *context of use* (Chaps. 3–6).

The context-free rule format results in another restriction on generative capacity: context-free grammars may recursively generate correspondences, but only those of the type *inverse pair* like a b c ... c b a.[13]

This inverse pair structure characteristic of context-free languages shows up clearly in the derivation of context-free expressions. Consider, for example, the context-free language WW^R, where W represents an arbitrary sequence of words, e.g., abcd, and W^R stands for the inverse sequence,[14] e.g., dcba.

8.3.5 CONTEXT-FREE PS GRAMMAR FOR WW^R

$$V \quad =_{def} \{S, a, b, c, d\}$$
$$V_T =_{def} \{a, b, c, d\}$$
$$P \quad =_{def} \{S \rightarrow a\,S\,a,$$
$$S \rightarrow b\,S\,b,$$
$$S \rightarrow c\,S\,c,$$
$$S \rightarrow d\,S\,d,$$
$$S \rightarrow a\,a,$$
$$S \rightarrow b\,b,$$
$$S \rightarrow c\,c,$$
$$S \rightarrow d\,d\}$$

The increased generative capacity of the class of context-free languages as compared to the class of regular languages is associated with an increase in computational complexity. While the class of regular languages parses in linear time, the class of context-free languages parses in polynomial time (8.2.3).

The generative capacity of context-free PS Grammars is still rather limited.[15] As a classic example of a language exceeding the generative capacity of context-free PS Grammar, consider a^{k}b^{k}c^k. Expressions of this language consist of three equally long sequences of a, b, and c, for example, as in

a b c, a a b b c c, a a a b b b c c c, etc.

The language a^{k}b^{k}c^k cannot be generated by a context-free PS Grammar because it requires a correspondence between three different parts – which exceeds the *pairwise* reverse structure of the context-free languages such as the familiar a^{k}b^k and WW^R.

---

[13] Each context-free language is homomorphic with the intersection of a regular set and a semi-Dyck set (Chomsky-Schützenberger Theorem). See Harrison (1978), pp. 317f.

[14] The superscript ^{R} in WW^R stands mnemonically for *reverse*.

[15] The class of context-free languages is not part of the hierarchy of LA Grammar, though it may be reconstructed in it (CoL, Theorem 4, pp. 138). See also Sect. 12.3, footnote 10. Instead the LA Grammar hierarchy provides the alternative polynomial class of C2-languages. As shown in Sect. 12.4, the class of C2-languages contains most, though not all, context-free languages, as well as many context-sensitive languages.

Another language exceeding the generative capacity of context-free PS Grammars is WW, where W is an arbitrary sequence of words. While the context-free language WW^R defined in 8.3.5 consists of expressions like

aa

abba

abccba

abcddcba

. . .

which have a pairwise *reverse* structure, the context-sensitive language WW consists of expressions like

aa

abab

abcabc

abcdabcd

. . .

which do not. Thus, despite the close resemblance between WW^R and WW, it is simply impossible to write a PS Grammar like 8.3.5 for WW.

While a^{k}b^{k}c^k and WW show in an intuitively obvious way that there are languages which cannot be generated by context-free PS Grammar, the formal proof is by no means trivial. As in the case of the regular languages, it is based on a pumping lemma, this time for the context-free languages.[16]

The next larger language class in the PS Grammar hierarchy is the context-sensitive languages, which are generated by PS Grammars using type 1 rules.

> Almost any language one can think of is context-sensitive; the only known proofs that certain languages are not CSL's are ultimately based on diagonalization.[17]
>
> Hopcroft and Ullman (1979), p. 224

Because it is impossible to exhaustively list the basic patterns of practically all structures "one can think of," there is no pumping lemma for the class of context-sensitive languages.

The structure of a type 1 or context-sensitive rule is as follows:

8.3.6 STANDARD SCHEMA OF CONTEXT-SENSITIVE RULES

$\alpha_1 A \alpha_2 \rightarrow \alpha_1 \beta \alpha_2$,   where β is not the empty sequence.

In PS Grammar, the term *context-sensitive* is interpreted in contrast to the term *context-free*. While a context-free type 2 rule allows nothing but a single variable

---

[16] Hopcroft and Ullman (1979) , pp. 125f.

[17] One of the earliest and simplest examples of diagonalization is the Ackermann Function (Ackermann 1928).

on the left-hand side, a context-sensitive type 1 rule may surround the variable with other symbols. As illustrated in 8.3.6, a type 1 rule is context-*sensitive* because the variable A may be rewritten as β only in the specific 'context' $\alpha_1\_\alpha_2$.

The possibility of specifying a particular environment (context) for the variable on the left-hand side of a type 1 rule greatly increases the control and thus the generative power of the context-sensitive PS Grammars. This is illustrated in the following PS Grammar for $a^k b^k c^k$:

8.3.7 PS GRAMMAR FOR CONTEXT-SENSITIVE $a^k b^k c^k$

$V =_{def} \{S, B, C, D_1, D_2, a, b, c\}$
$V_T =_{def} \{a, b, c\}$
$P =_{def} \{S \rightarrow a\, S\, B\, C, \qquad rule\ 1$
$\qquad\quad S \rightarrow a\, b\, C, \qquad\qquad rule\ 2$
$\qquad\quad C\, B \rightarrow D_1\, B, \qquad\quad rule\ 3a$
$\qquad\quad D_1\, B \rightarrow D_1\, D_2, \qquad rule\ 3b$
$\qquad\quad D_1\, D_2 \rightarrow B\, D_2, \qquad rule\ 3c$
$\qquad\quad B\, D_2 \rightarrow B\, C, \qquad\quad rule\ 3d$
$\qquad\quad b\, B \rightarrow b\, b, \qquad\qquad rule\ 4$
$\qquad\quad b\, C \rightarrow b\, c, \qquad\qquad rule\ 5$
$\qquad\quad c\, C \rightarrow c\, c\} \qquad\qquad rule\ 6$

The rules 3a–3d jointly have the same effect as the (monotonic)

$rule\ 3 \qquad C\, B \rightarrow B\, C.$

The above PS Grammar uses the rules 3a–3d because the equivalent rule 3 does not comply with the simplifying assumption that only *one* variable on the left-hand side of a context-sensitive rule may be replaced.

The crucial function of the context for controlling the three correspondences in the expressions of $a^k b^k c^k$ is shown in the following derivation of a a a b b b c c c. For simplicity, the rules 3a–3d are combined into the equivalent rule 3.

8.3.8 DERIVATION OF a a a b b b c c c

	intermediate chains	rules
1.	S	
2.	a S B C	(1)
3.	a a S B C B C	(1)
4.	a a a b C B C B C	(2)
5.	a a a b B C C B C	(3)
6.	a a a b B C B C C	(3)
7.	a a a b B B C C C	(3)
8.	a a a b b B C C C	(4)
9.	a a a b b b C C C	(4)
10.	a a a b b b c C C	(5)
11.	a a a b b b c c C	(6)
12.	a a a b b b c c c	(6)

The high generative capacity of the context-sensitive PS Grammars is based on the possibility of *changing the order* of sequences already derived. The reordering of sequences takes place in the transition from the intermediate sequence 4 to 7.

The possibility of context-sensitively changing the order of sequences provides for a degree of control which is much higher than in context-free PS Grammars. The cost, however, is a high degree of computational complexity. In order to correctly reconstruct automatically which sequence of context-sensitive rule applications resulted in a given expression, a potentially exponential number of reordering possibilities must be checked.

This kind of search space is so large that there exists no practical parsing algorithm for the class of context-sensitive PS Grammars. In other words, the class of context-sensitive languages is computationally intractable.

The context-sensitive languages are a proper subset of the recursive languages.[18] The class of recursive languages is not reflected in the PS Grammar hierarchy. This is because the PS rule schema does not provide a suitable restriction (8.1.2) such that the associated PS Grammar class would generate exactly the recursive languages.[19]

A language is recursive if and only if it is decidable, i.e., if there exists an algorithm which can determine in finitely many steps for arbitrary input whether or not the input belongs to the language. An example of a recursive language which is not context-sensitive is the Ackermann function.[20]

The largest language class in the PS Grammar hierarchy is the recursively enumerable languages, which are generated by unrestricted or type 0 rewrite rules. In unrestricted PS Grammars, the right-hand side of a rule may be shorter than the left-hand side. This characteristic property of type 0 rules provides for the possibility of *deleting* parts of sequences already generated and is the source of undecidability. The decision of whether or not an expression of a recursively enumerable language is well-formed may thus take not just a very long time (8.2.2), but forever.[21]

8.4 PS Grammar for Natural Language

A simple application of PS Grammar to natural language is illustrated in the following definition. In order to facilitate comparison, it generates the same sentence as the C Grammar 7.5.4.

---

[18] Hopcroft and Ullman (1979), p. 228, Theorem 9.8.

[19] In the hierarchy of LA Grammar, in contrast, the class of recursive languages is formally defined as the class of A-languages, generated by unrestricted LA Grammars (11.2.2). Furthermore, the class of context-sensitive languages is formally defined as the class of B languages, generated by *bounded* LA Grammars.

[20] Hopcroft and Ullman (1979) , p. 175, 7.4.

[21] The class of recursively enumerable languages is not part of the LA Grammar hierarchy, though it may be reconstructed in it (footnote 10 at the end of Sect. 11.2).

8.4.1 PS GRAMMAR FOR EXAMPLE 7.5.3

V $=_{def}$ {S, NP, VP, V, N, DET, ADJ, black, dogs, little, sleep, the}
V_T $=_{def}$ {black, dogs, little, sleep, the}
P $=_{def}$ {S → NP VP,
           VP → V,
           NP → DET N,
           N → ADJ N,
           N → dogs,
           ADJ → little,
           ADJ → black,
           DET → the,
           V → sleep}

The form of this PS Grammar is context-free: it is not yet context-sensitive because the left-hand side of the rules consists of only one variable; it is not regular any more because the right-hand side of some rules contains more than one variable.

Like the C Grammar derivation 7.5.3, the corresponding derivation based on the above PS Grammar derivation can be represented as a tree:

8.4.2 PS GRAMMAR ANALYSIS OF EXAMPLE 7.5.3

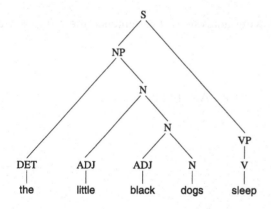

Such trees are called phrase structures in PS Grammar. The category symbols in a phrase structure tree are called nodes. There are two formal relations between nodes: *dominance* and *precedence*. For example, the node S dominates the nodes NP and VP in accordance with the rule S → NP VP. At the same time this rule specifies precedence: the NP node is located in the tree to the left of the VP node.

In comparison to C Grammar, which codes the combinatorics of a language into the complex categories of its word forms and uses only two rule schemata for composition, PS Grammar uses only elementary categories the combinatorics of which are expressed in terms of a multitude of rewrite rules.

Even the lexicon, which is treated in C Grammar as categorized sets of word forms (7.5.4), is handled in PS Grammar by certain rewrite rules. They are called terminal rules because they have a terminal symbol (word) on their right-hand side. The remaining rules, called nonterminal rules, generate the sentence frames of the PS Grammar, into which the terminal rules insert various word forms.

In addition to the formal differences between C and PS Grammar, their respective analyses of natural language are linguistically motivated by different empirical goals. The goal of C Grammar is to characterize the *functor-argument structure* of natural language, whereas PS Grammar aims to represent the *constituent structure* of natural language.

Constituent structure represents linguistic intuitions about which parts in a sentence belong most closely together semantically. The principle of constituent structure is defined as a formal property of phrase structure trees.

8.4.3 DEFINITION OF CONSTITUENT STRUCTURE

1. Words or constituents which belong together semantically must be dominated directly and exhaustively by a node.
2. The lines of a constituent structure may not cross (*nontangling condition*).

According to this definition, the following analysis of the sentence the man read a book is linguistically correct:

8.4.4 CORRECT CONSTITUENT STRUCTURE ANALYSIS

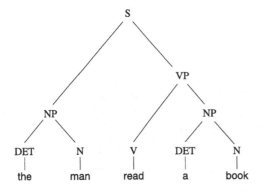

The following analysis, in contrast, violates the definition of constituent structure:

8.4.5 INCORRECT CONSTITUENT STRUCTURE ANALYSIS

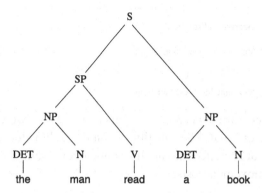

While formally possible, this analysis is incorrect linguistically because according to the PS Grammarians' intuition read and a book belong semantically together and thus must be dominated directly and exhaustively by a node (as illustrated by the correct analysis).

Historically, the notion of constituent structure is quite recent. It evolved from the *immediate constituent analysis* of the American structuralist BLOOMFIELD (1887–1949) and the distribution tests of his student Harris. In Bloomfield's main work *Language* of 1933, immediate constituents do not take center stage, however, and are mentioned on only four of 549 pages. They are briefly sketched on pages 161 and 167 using simple sentences and later applied to morphology (op.cit., pp. 209f., 221f.).

> The principle of immediate constituents will lead us, for example, to class a form like gentlemanly not as a compound word, but as a derived secondary word, since the immediate constituents are the bound form -ly and the underlying form gentleman.
>
> Bloomfield (1933), p. 210

This statement may be translated into the following tree structures:

8.4.6 IMMEDIATE CONSTITUENTS IN PS GRAMMAR

correct: incorrect:

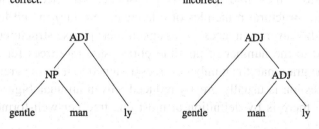

The example gentlemanly is also discussed in Harris (1951), pp. 278–280, where the methodological innovation of distribution tests is introduced.

Distribution tests are realized either as substitution tests or as movement tests. Their goal is to distinguish grammatically correct from grammatically incorrect substitutions or movements.

8.4.7 SUBSTITUTION TEST

correct substitution: incorrect substitution:

Susanne has [eaten] an apple   Susanne has [eaten] an apple

      ↓   ↓

      [cooked]   *Susanne has [desk] an apple

The substitution on the left is considered correct because it results in a sentence which is grammatically as well formed as the original. The substitution on the right is incorrect because it turns a well-formed input sentence into an ungrammatical result.

Analogous considerations hold for movement tests:

8.4.8 MOVEMENT TEST

correct movement:

    Susanne [has] eaten an apple   ⟶   [has] Susanne eaten an apple (?)

incorrect movement:

    Susanne has eaten [an] apple   ⟶   *[an] Susanne has eaten apple

For the linguists of American structuralism, the distribution tests were important methodologically in order to objectively support their intuitions about the *correct segmentation* of sentences. The segmentation of sentences and the concomitant hypotheses about more or less closely related subparts were needed in turn to distinguish between linguistically correct and incorrect phrase structure trees.

Such a distinction seemed necessary because for any finite string the number of possible phrase structures is infinite.[22] This constitutes an embarrassment of riches: the possible phrase structures should not all be equally correct linguistically.

The huge variety of possible trees holds primarily for isolated sentences outside a formal grammar. Once the structural principles of a language are known and formulated as a PS Grammar, however, sentences are assigned their phrase structure(s) by the grammar. Compared to the number of possible phrase structure trees for an isolated sentence outside the grammar, the number of trees assigned to it by the grammar for the language in question is usually greatly reduced. Given an unambiguous PS Grammar, for example, there is by definition at most one tree per well-formed sentence.

---

[22] Even if phrase structures of the form A–B–C...A are excluded, the number of different phrase structure trees still grows exponentially with the length of the input. From a formal as well as an empirical point of view, however, structures like A–B–C...A are legitimate in phrase structure grammar.

In the case of context-free artificial languages, the structural principles are sufficiently simple to allow for the definition of adequate formal PS Grammars (e.g., 8.3.1,
8.3.2, 8.3.3, 8.3.4, 8.3.5). When there are several essentially different PS Grammars
which are equally adequate for the same context-free language, there is no rational
reason to argue about which of them assigns the 'correct' phrase structure trees.

In the case of natural languages, on the other hand, the structural principles are
still unknown. Thus it is an open question which PS Grammar for a single sentence or
small set of sentences might turn out to be best suited for the correct extension to cover
the whole language. In order to guide the long-term development of PS Grammars for
natural language, an empirical criterion was needed.

For this, the intuitive principle of constituent structure was chosen, supported by the
associated substitution and movement tests. It has not prevented, however, a constant
debate within nativism over which phrase structures for natural language are linguistically correct and why.

From the viewpoint of formal language theory, the cause of this fruitless linguistic
debate is the lack of complete PS Grammars – either elementary or derived. That over
forty years of substantially funded research has not produced a complete formal grammar for a single natural language might perhaps be taken as a hint that the approach
of constituent structure in combination with PS Grammar may not be quite optimal.

8.5 Constituent Structure Paradox

From the viewpoint of the SLIM theory of language, there are several objections to
the principle of constituent structure (8.4.3). First, constituent structure and the distribution tests claimed to support it run counter to the time-linear structure of natural
language. Second, the resulting phrase structure trees have no communicative purpose. Third, the principles of constituent structure cannot always be fulfilled.

This is because the conditions of constituent structure require that the parts which
belong together semantically are positioned right next to each other in the natural
language surface. Yet there are expressions in natural language – called *discontinuous
elements* – in which this is not the case.

For example, there is general agreement that in the sentence

Peter looked the word up.

the discontinuous elements looked and up are more closely related semantically than
either the adjacent expressions looked – the word or the word – up.

Discontinuous elements are the structural reason why the principle of constituent
structures cannot always be fulfilled in context-free PS Grammars for natural language. This structural problem has been called the *constituent structure paradox*.[23] It
is illustrated by the following alternative tree structures:

---

[23] CoL, p. 24.

8.5.1 VIOLATING THE SECOND CONDITION OF 8.4.3

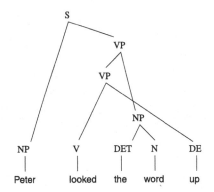

Here the semantically related subexpressions looked and up are dominated directly and exhaustively by a node, thus satisfying the first condition of 8.4.3. The analysis violates the second condition, however, because the lines in the tree cross.

8.5.2 VIOLATING THE FIRST CONDITION OF 8.4.3

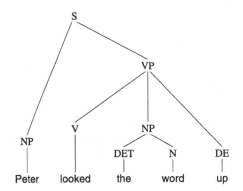

Here the lines do not cross, satisfying the second condition. The analysis violates the first condition, however, because the semantically related expressions looked – up, or rather the nodes V and DE dominating them, are not *exhaustively* dominated by a node. Instead, the node directly dominating V and DE also dominates the NP the word.

From the viewpoint of formal language theory, the constituent structure paradox is caused by the fact that the generative power of context-free PS Grammars is insufficient to handle discontinuous elements in the fashion prescribed by the conditions of 8.4.3. This empirical problem has been known since the early 1950s.[24]

---

[24] Bar-Hillel wrote in 1960 (Bar-Hillel 1964, p. 102) that he had abandoned his 1953 work on C Grammar because of analogous difficulties with the discontinuous elements in sentences like He gave it up.

All natural languages have discontinuous elements of one kind or another. In order to nevertheless maintain the principle of constituent structure as much as possible, Chomsky (1957) turned Harris' methodologically motivated substitution and movement tests into generative rules called transformations, which he claimed to be innate (Chomsky 1965, pp. 47f.).

A transformation rule takes a phrase structure tree as input and produces a modified phrase structure tree as output. In transformational grammar, many transformations are ordered into a transformational component and applied one after the other to the phrase structure of the input. The input and output conditions of a transformation are formally specified as patterns with variables, which are called indexed bracketings.

8.5.3 EXAMPLE OF A FORMAL TRANSFORMATION

$$[[V\ DE]_{V'}\ [DET\ N]_{NP}]_{VP} \Rightarrow [V\ [DET\ N]_{NP}\ DE]_{VP}$$

An application of this transformation is illustrated as follows:

8.5.4 APPLYING THE TRANSFORMATION 8.5.3

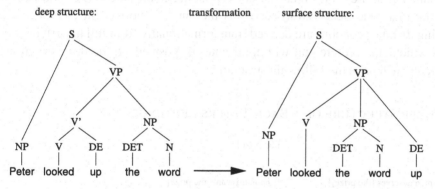

In Standard Theory (ST, Chomsky 1965), the input to the transformational component is generated by a context-free PS Grammar. These 'deep structures' must satisfy the conditions 8.4.3 of constituent structure, but need not correspond to a grammatical sequence (as in the tree on the left).

If the input pattern (indexed bracketing) of a transformational rule has been matched successfully onto a phrase structure, it is mapped to another phrase structure in accordance with the output pattern of the transformation. After the application of one or more transformations, a surface structure is obtained. The phrase structure of the surface must correspond to a grammatical sequence, but need not fulfill the conditions of constituent structure (as in the tree on the right.)

Transformations like the one illustrated above are regarded as 'meaning preserving' – just like the examples in 4.5.2. This approach is supposed to characterize the innate human language faculty even though the transformations do not have any communicative function.

From a mathematical viewpoint, a mechanism designed to recursively modify an open set of input structures always results in high degrees of complexity. This has been demonstrated with the PS Grammar 8.3.7 for the simple context-sensitive language $a^k b^k c^k$. Yet, while context-sensitive languages are 'only' exponential, transformational grammar is equivalent to a Turing machine, generates the recursively enumerable languages, and is therefore undecidable.

Initially, Chomsky had hoped to avoid this consequence by imposing a formal restriction called *recoverability of deletions*. According to this condition, a transformation may delete a node only if it can be reconstructed (recovered) via well-defined access to a copy of the node and the subtree dominated by it.

The so-called Bach-Peters sentences showed, however, that the recoverability of deletions does not always have the desired effect.

8.5.5 Example of a Bach-Peters Sentence

The man who deserves it will get the prize he wants.

This sentence contains two noun phrases with relative clauses. Each clause contains a pronoun (i.e., it, he) for which the corresponding noun phrase (i.e., the prize he wants, the man who deserves it) serves as the ante- or postcedent (see Sect. 6.2). Assuming that the pronouns are derived transformationally from full underlying noun phrases which are coreferential with their ante- or postcedent, the deep structure of the sentence will have the following structure:

8.5.6 Deep Structure of a Bach-Peters Sentence

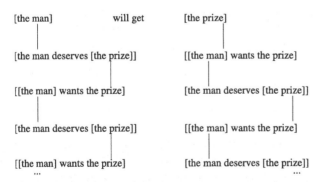

Given the surface of the sentence, the transformational algorithm is supposed to produce a deep structure from which this surface may be correctly derived transformationally. Due to the structure of the example, the algorithm will consider larger and larger deep structures while observing the recoverability of deletions.

For example, the algorithm will postulate the full noun phrase [the man who deserves it] as the deep structure and antecedent of the pronoun he. This deep structure in turn contains the pronoun it, for which the algorithm will postulate the full noun phrase [the price which he deserves] as postcedent. This deep structure in turn contains the pronoun he, etc.

This procedure can be continued indefinitely in both relative clauses without ever stopping (the halting problem). The formal proof that transformational grammar is undecidable and generates the class of the recursively enumerable languages was established 1969 by Peters and Ritchie[25] and published in 1973.

Later variants of nativism, such as LFG, GPSG, and HPSG, do without transformations, trying to deal with the constituent structure paradox in other ways. In these derived formalisms of PS Grammar, the conditions of constituent structure need only be fulfilled when permitted by the language input. Otherwise (as in cases of discontinuous elements) the intuitions about what is most closely semantically related are not expressed in terms of PS trees, but alternatively in terms of feature structures.

In this way, constituent structures have failed to maintain their alleged status as a universal, innate characteristic of human language and as a methodologically meaningful principle. Therefore, one may well ask why systems like GPSG, LFG, and HPSG continue to hang on to constituent structure as a central principle of their theories. Furthermore, in terms of complexity these later systems are no improvement over transformational grammar: they generate the class of recursively enumerable languages and are undecidable.[26]

Exercises

Section 8.1
1. State an algebraic definition of PS Grammar.
2. What is the difference between terminal and nonterminal symbols in PS Grammar?
3. By whom and when was PS Grammar invented, under what name, and for what purpose?

---

[25] In active consultation with Chomsky (personal communication by Bob Ritchie, Stanford, 1983).

[26] Cf. Barton et al. (1987). If context-free rule loops like A → B → ... → A are forbidden, the complexity of LFG is exponential. However, because such loops are formally legal within context-free PS Grammar, this restriction is not really legitimate from the viewpoint of complexity theory. Besides, even an exponential complexity is much too high for computational applications.

4. By whom and when was PS Grammar first used for describing natural language?
5. Describe the standard restrictions on the rules of PS Grammar.
6. Explain the term generative capacity.

Section 8.2

1. Explain the relation between special kinds of PS Grammar, formal language classes, and different degrees of complexity.
2. Name the main classes of complexity. Why are they independent of specific formalisms of generative grammar?
3. What is the complexity of language classes in the PS hierarchy?
4. What is the average sentence length in the Limas corpus?
5. What is the maximal sentence length in the Limas corpus?
6. How much time would an exponential algorithm require in the worst case to parse the Limas corpus?
7. Explain the PS Grammar hierarchy of formal languages.
8. Which language classes in the PS Grammar hierarchy are of a complexity still practical for computational linguistics?

Section 8.3

1. Define a PS Grammar which generates the free monoid over $\{a, b, c\}$. Classify this language, called $\{a, b, c\}^+$, within the PS Grammar hierarchy. Compare the generative capacity of the grammar for $\{a, b, c\}^+$ with that for $a^k b^k c^k$. Which is higher and why?
2. Where does the term context-free come from in PS Grammar?
3. What kinds of structures can be generated by context-free PS Grammars?
4. Name two artificial languages which are not context-free. Explain why they exceed the generative power of context-free PS Grammars.
5. Define a PS Grammar for $a^k b^{2k}$. Explain why this language fulfills the context-free schema pairwise inverse.
6. Define a PS Grammar for $ca^m dyb^n$. What are examples of well-formed expressions of this artificial language? Explain why it is a regular language.
7. Why would 8.3.6 violate the definition of context-sensitive PS Grammar rules if β were zero?
8. What is a pumping lemma?
9. Why is there no pumping lemma for the context-sensitive languages?
10. Are the recursively enumerable languages recursive?
11. Name a recursive language which is not context-sensitive.

Section 8.4

1. State the definition of constituent structure.
2. Explain the relation between context-free PS Grammars and phrase structure trees.
3. Describe how the notion of constituent structure developed historically.

4. Name two kinds of distribution tests and explain their role for finding correct constituent structures.
5. Why was it important to American structuralists to segment sentences correctly?

Section 8.5

1. Describe the notion of a discontinuous element in natural language and explain why discontinuous elements cause the constituent structure paradox.
2. How does transformational grammar try to solve the problem caused by discontinuous elements?
3. Compare the goal of transformational grammar with the goal of computational linguistics.
4. What is the generative capacity of transformational grammar?
5. Explain the structure of a Bach-Peters sentence in relation to the recoverability of deletions condition. Which mathematical property was shown with this sentence? Is it a property of natural language or of transformational grammar?

9. Basic Notions of Parsing

This chapter investigates which formal properties make a formal grammar suitable for automatic language analysis and which do not. For this purpose, context-free PS Grammar and its parsers will be used as our main example.

Section 9.1 describes the basic structure of parsers and explains how the declarative-procedural distinction applies to the relation between formal grammars and parsers. Section 9.2 discusses the relation between context-free PS Grammar and standard C Grammar, and summarizes the relations between the notions of language, formal grammars, subtypes of grammars, subclasses of languages, parsers, and complexity. Section 9.3 explains the principle of type transparency and illustrates with an Earley algorithm analysis of $a^k b^k$ that context-free PS Grammar is not type-transparent. Section 9.4 shows that the principle of possible substitutions, on which derivations in PS Grammar are based, does not permit input-output equivalence of PS Grammar with either its parsers or the speaker-hearer. Section 9.5 explains the mathematical, computational, and psychological properties which an empirically adequate formal grammar for natural language must have.

9.1 Declarative and Procedural Aspects of Parsing

Parsers[1] for artificial languages are used in computer science for transforming one programming level into another, for example in compilation. Parsers for natural languages are used for automatic word form recognition as well as automatic syntactic and semantic analysis. Accordingly, one may distinguish between morphology parsers, syntax parsers, and semantic parsers.

Morphology parsers (Chaps. 13–15) take a word form as input and analyze it by (i) segmenting its surface into allomorphs, (ii) characterizing its syntactic combinatorics (categorization), and (iii) deriving the base form (lemmatization). Syntax parsers (Chaps. 16–18) take a sentence as input and render as output an analysis of its grammatical structure, e.g., the constituent structure in PS Grammar or the time-linear buildup and canceling of valency positions in LA Grammar. Semantic parsers

---

[1] As explained in Sect. 1.3, a parser is a computer program which takes language expressions as input and produces some other representation, e.g., a grammatical analysis, as output.

R. Hausser, *Foundations of Computational Linguistics*,
DOI 10.1007/978-3-642-41431-2_9, © Springer-Verlag Berlin Heidelberg 2014

(Chaps. 22–24) complement the syntactic analyses by deriving associated semantic representations.

For modeling the mechanism of natural language communication on the computer, these different kinds of parsers need to be integrated into an overall functional system. For example, syntax parsers presuppose automatic word form recognition and thus require a morphology parser of some kind. Semantic parsers presuppose syntactic analysis and thus require a syntax parser (unless syntactic and semantic parsing are combined, as in the SLIM theory of language).

Common to all kinds of parsers is the distinction between (i) the *structural description* of the expressions to be analyzed and (ii) the *computational algorithm* of the automatic analysis procedure. In modern parsers, these two aspects are separated systematically by treating the structural description by means of a formal grammar which is interpreted and applied by the computational algorithm.

In other words, a modern parser may load one of the arbitrary formal grammars G_i, G_j, G_k of a certain formalism[2] and analyze a language L_j by interpreting the associated grammar G_j. In the automatic analysis of L_j expressions, a clear distinction is made between the contributions of (i) the grammar G_j and (ii) the parser for the whole class of formal grammars G_i, G_j, G_k.[3]

The separate handling of the grammar and the parsing algorithm corresponds to a distinction which is aspired to in computer science in general, namely the systematic separation of the *declarative specification* and the *procedural implementation* in the solution of a computational problem.

9.1.1 DECLARATIVE AND PROCEDURAL ASPECTS IN LINGUISTICS

– The *declarative* aspect of computational language analysis is represented by a formal grammar, written for the specific language to be analyzed within a general, mathematically well-defined formalism.
– The *procedural* aspect of computational language analysis comprises those parts of the computer program which interpret and apply the general formalism in the automatic analysis of language input.

---

[2] For example, a context-free PS Grammar like 7.1.3, 8.3.4, 8.3.5, or a C LAG like 10.2.2, 10.2.3, 11.5.1, 11.5.2, 11.5.4, 11.5.6–11.5.8.

[3] There is general agreement that the formal rules of a grammar should not be formulated in the programming language directly. Such an implicit use of a formal grammar has the disadvantage that the resulting computer program does not show which of its properties are theoretically accidental (reflecting the programming environment or stylistic idiosyncrasies of the programmer) and which are theoretically necessary (reflecting the formal analysis of the language described). Another disadvantage of failing to separate between the formal grammar and the parsing algorithm is that the software works only for a single language rather than a whole subtype of formal grammars and their languages.

The distinction between the declarative and procedural aspects of a parser is especially clear if the formal grammar leaves open certain properties which an automatic parser must decide one way or another.

Consider, for example, the following context-free PS Grammar.

rule 1: A → B C
rule 2: B → c d
rule 3: C → e f

The distribution of variables ensures implicitly that, in a top-down derivation, rule 1 is applied before rule 2 and rule 3. However, the decision of whether rule 2 should be applied before rule 3, or rule 3 before rule 2, or both at once, remains open.

For the declarative specification of context-free PS Grammars, such a partial rule ordering is sufficient. For a computer program, however, a complete rule ordering must be decided explicitly – even if it may be irrelevant from a theoretical point of view. Those ordering decisions which go beyond the declarative specification of a formal grammar, or which – for reasons of the parsing algorithm – run counter to the conceptual derivation order of the grammar (9.3.4), are called procedural.

For a given formalism (e.g., context-free PS Grammar) different parsing algorithms may be developed in different programming languages. The result is different procedural realizations which take the same declarative grammars as input. For example, two parsing algorithms (e.g., the Earley algorithm and the CYK algorithm) implemented in two programming languages (e.g., Lisp and C, respectively) will produce results for (i) the same grammar (e.g., 7.1.3 for $a^k b^k$) and (ii) the same language input (e.g., aaabbb) which are identical from a declarative point of view.

General parsers are practical for a given grammar kind only, however, if its complexity is not too high. Therefore, there exist general parsers for the classes of regular and context-free PS Grammars, while no practical parsers can be written for the classes of context-sensitive and, a fortiori, unrestricted PS Grammars.

9.2 Fitting Grammar onto Language

Deciding where in the PS hierarchy (8.2.3) the natural languages might belong is not only of academic interest, but determines whether or not the natural languages may be parsed efficiently within PS Grammar. For reasons of efficiency it would be optimal if the natural languages could be shown to belong in the class of regular languages – because then their PS Grammar analyses could be parsed in linear time.

There are, however, natural language structures in which the surface is obviously context-free rather than regular, e.g., center-embedded relative clauses in German.

9.2.1 CONTEXT-FREE STRUCTURE IN GERMAN

Der Mann,		schläft.
(the man)		*(sleeps).*
der die Frau,		liebt,
(who the woman)		*(loves)*
die das Kind,		sieht,
(who the child)		*(sees)*
das die Katze	füttert,	
(who the cat)	*(feeds)*	

The structure of this sentence corresponds to the abstract schema 'noun_phrase$_1$ noun_phrase$_2$ ... verb_phrase$_2$ verb_phrase$_1$', which in turn corresponds to abc... cba. The structure is context-free because there is no grammatical limit on the number of embeddings. Given that context-free PS Grammars are of n^3 complexity (Earley 1970), a PS grammatical analysis of natural language is at least polynomial.

The next question is whether or not natural language can be shown to belong in the PS Grammar class of context-free languages. The answer to this question is less clear than in the case of the regular languages.

Chomsky (1957) and (1965) expanded context-free PS Grammar into the derived formalism of transformational grammar by arguing that PS Grammar alone was insufficient to formulate what he considered "linguistic generalizations" (4.5.2, 8.5.4). In addition, Shieber (1985) presented sentences from Swiss German with the context-sensitive structure of WW', which were intended to prove – in analogy to 9.2.1 – that the natural languages are at least context-sensitive.

9.2.2 CONTEXT-SENSITIVE STRUCTURE IN SWISS GERMAN

mer em Hans es huus hälfed aastriiche
we the Hans the house help paint

The formal structure of this example is analyzed as a b a' b' (with a = the Hans, b = the house, a' = help, and b' = paint). This is not context-free because it doesn't have an *inverse* structure – like the context-sensitive language WW. If this argument is accepted, the PS grammatical analysis of natural language is at least context-sensitive. It is thus of exponential complexity and requires billions and billions of centuries for the analysis of longer sentences in the worst case (8.2.2).

To avoid this implausible conclusion, Harman (1963) and Gazdar (1982) each presented sizable PS Grammar systems intended to show that there are no structures in natural language which could not be handled in a context-free fashion. Harman's proposal came at a time when complexity-theoretic considerations were not widely understood and transformational grammar was pursued with undiminished enthusiasm. Also, Harman did not provide a detailed linguistic motivation for his system.

At the time of Gazdar's proposal, on the other hand, awareness of complexity-theoretic considerations had increased. Also, Gazdar did not employ context-free PS Grammar directly, but used the additional mechanism of *metarules* to define the derived PS Grammar formalism of GPSG. The purpose of the metarules was to combine huge numbers of context-free PS rules,[4] in order to formulate the linguistic generalizations which he and others considered important at the time.

In order to ensure that metarules would not increase the complexity of GPSG, Gazdar formulated the *finite closure condition*. This condition, however, was rejected as a linguistically unmotivated formal trick[5] – and without it GPSG is not context-free, but rather recursively enumerable and therefore undecidable.

If the natural languages are not context-free – and the majority of theoretical linguists takes this view – what other formal language class does natural language belong to? Here we should remember that the class of context-free languages is the result of using a certain *rule type* (i.e., type 2) of a certain *formalism* (i.e., PS Grammar).

On the one hand, there is no reason why this particular formalism and this particular rule type – resulting in the pairwise inverse structure of context-free languages – should be characteristic of natural language. On the other hand, the context-free languages are the largest class offered by PS Grammar with a mathematical complexity which is sufficiently low to be of any practical interest.

The assumption that the natural languages are not context-free implies one of the following two conclusions:

1. PS Grammar is the only elementary formalism of formal grammar, for which reason one must accept that the natural languages are of high complexity and thus computationally intractable.
2. PS Grammar is not the only elementary formalism of formal grammar. Instead, there are other elementary formalisms which define other language hierarchies whose language classes are orthogonal to those of PS Grammar.

In light of the fact that humans process natural language in a highly efficient manner, the first conclusion is implausible. The second conclusion, on the other hand, raises the question of what concrete alternatives are available.

From a historical point of view, a natural first step in the search for new formal language classes is to analyze the generative capacity and complexity of C Grammar (Sect. 7.4). For this, the easiest strategy is a comparison of the formal properties of C and PS Grammar, whereby one of the following three possible relations must hold:

9.2.3 POSSIBLE RELATIONS BETWEEN TWO GRAMMAR FORMALISMS

– *No equivalence*
   Two formalisms are not equivalent if they accept different language classes; this
   means that the formalisms have different generative capacities.

---

[4] "Literally trillions and trillions of rules," Shieber et al. (1983).

[5] Uszkoreit and Peters (1986).

– *Weak equivalence*
   Two formalisms are weakly equivalent if they accept the same language classes;
   this means that the formalisms have the same generative capacity.
– *Strong equivalence*
   Two formalisms are strongly equivalent if they are (i) weakly equivalent, and moreover (ii) produce the same structural descriptions; this means that the formalisms
   are no more than *notational variants*.

Historically, it would have been desirable for the development of modern linguistics
if the elementary formalisms of C and PS Grammar had turned out to be not equivalent
because in this way one would have had a true alternative to the class of context-
free languages. In fact, however, it was discovered early on that C Grammar and PS
Grammar are *weakly equivalent*.

> The problem arose of determining the exact relationships between these types of
> [PS]grammars and the categorial grammars. I surmised in 1958 that the BCGs [Bidi-
> rectional Categorial Grammar *à la* 7.4.2] were of approximately the same strength [as
> context-free phrase structure grammars]. A proof of their equivalence was found in
> June of 1959 by Gaifman. ... The equivalence of these different types of grammars
> should not be too surprising. Each of them was meant to be a precise explicatum
> of the notion *immediate constituent grammars* which has served for many years as
> the favorite type of American descriptive linguistics as exhibited, for instance, in the
> well-known books by Harris (1951) and Hockett (1958).
>
> Bar-Hillel (1964), p. 103

The fact that C and PS Grammar are equivalent only in certain subtypes, namely
bidirectional C Grammar and context-free PS Grammar, was eclipsed by context-
free grammars generating the largest language class which is still computationally
tractable. The fact that bidirectional C Grammar and context-free PS Grammar are
only weakly equivalent was studiously ignored as well.

These oversights gave rise to the erroneous belief that PS Grammar and its formal
language hierarchy are somehow given by nature and that it is the only formal system
of artificial and natural languages. However, the existence of LA Grammar (TCS'92)
shows that there may be elementary grammar formalisms which divide the set of
artificial languages into language classes different from those of PS Grammar.[6]

The notions of languages, formal grammars, subtypes of grammars, classes of languages, parsers, and complexity are related as follows:

– *Languages*
   Languages exist independently of formal grammars. This is shown not only by the
   natural languages, but also by artificial languages like $a^k b^m$, $a^k b^k$, $a^k b^k c^k$, $a^k b^k c^k d^k$,
   $\{a^k b^k c^k\}*$, WW^R, WW, WWW, etc. Their traditional names characterize the respec-

---

[6] For example, context-free $a^k b^k$ (7.1.3, 10.2.2) and context-sensitive $a^k b^k c^k$ (8.3.5, 10.2.3)
are classified in LA Grammar as elements of the same linear class of C1 LAGs. Correspondingly, context-free WW^R (8.3.5, 11.5.4) and context-sensitive WW (11.5.6) are classified in
LA Grammar as elements of the same polynomial (n^2) class of C2 LAGs.

tive languages sufficiently well as to allow writing down and recognizing their well-formed expressions.

The definition of an explicit grammar within a given grammar formalism for a natural or artificial language constitutes a second step which usually is not trivial at all. That a given language may be described by different formal grammars of different grammar formalisms is shown by the comparison of the C and PS Grammar analysis of $a^k b^k$ in 7.4.4 and 7.1.3, respectively.

– *Formal grammars*

On the one hand, a formal grammar is a general framework; on the other, it is a specific rule system defined for describing a specific language within the general framework. For example, PS Grammar as a general framework is formally defined as the quadruple $<V, V_T, S, P>$, with certain additional conditions on its elements. Within this general formalism, specific PS Grammars may be defined for generating specific languages such as $a^k b^k$ (7.1.3).

– *Subtypes of formal grammars*

Different restrictions on a formal grammar framework may result in different grammar kinds. In this way, the subtypes of regular, context-free, context-sensitive, and unrestricted PS Grammars are defined in PS Grammar, and the subtypes of C1, C2, C3, B, and A LAGs are defined in LA Grammar. The various restrictions do not exist absolutely, but depend on formal properties of the particular grammar framework employed (especially its rule structure).

– *Language classes*

The subtypes of a formal grammar may be used to divide the set of possible languages into different language classes. Because the subtypes depend on the formalism used, the associated language classes do not exist absolutely, but instead reflect the formal properties of the grammar formalism employed. For example, the pairwise inverse structure characteristic of context-free languages follows directly from the specific restrictions on the rule structure of context-free PS Grammars.

Nota bene: *languages* exist independently of the formal grammars which may accept them. The *language classes*, on the other hand, do not exist independently, but result from particular restrictions on particular grammar formalisms.

– *Parsers*

Parsers are programs of automatic language analysis which are defined for whole subtypes of formal grammars (e.g., context-free PS Grammars or the C LAGs). Thus, the problem with a context-sensitive language like $a^k b^k c^k$ (8.3.7) is not that one could not write an efficient analysis program for it, but rather that no practical parser can be written for the class of context-sensitive PS Grammars in general.

– *Complexity*

The complexity of a subtype of formal grammar is determined over the number of primitive operations needed by an equivalent abstract automaton or parsing program for analyzing expressions in the worst case. The complexity of individual languages is usually determined over the complexity of their respective classes. Because language classes depend on the particular formalism employed, a language like $a^k b^k c^k$ belongs in PS Grammar to the class of context-sensitive languages, which is of exponential complexity, but in LA Grammar to the class of C1 LAGs, which is of linear complexity.

Besides studying the complexity of a language in terms of its class, one may also investigate the *inherent* complexity of individual languages. In this case one uses the specific structural properties of the language (independent of any particular grammar formalism) to show how many operations its analysis would require in the worst case, on an abstract machine (e.g., a Turing or register machine). For example, languages like 3SAT and Subset Sum (Sect. 11.5) are inherently complex. Therefore, these languages will necessarily be in a high complexity class (here, exponential) in any possible grammar formalism.

The inherent complexity of individual languages is an important tool for determining the minimal complexity of language classes. This form of analysis occurs on a very low level, however, corresponding to machine or assembler code. For this reason, the complexity of artificial and natural languages is usually analyzed at the abstraction level of grammar formalisms, whereby complexity is determined for the grammar kind and its language class as a whole.

9.3 Type Transparency Between Grammar and Parser

The simplest and most transparent use of a grammar by a parser consists in the parser merely applying the formal grammar mechanism in the analysis of the input. This natural view of the parser as a simple motor or driver of the grammar was originally intended also in PS Grammar.

> Miller and Chomsky's original (1963) suggestion is really that grammars be realized more or less directly as parsing algorithms. We might take this as a methodological principle. In this case we impose the condition that the logical organization of rules and structures incorporated in the grammar be mirrored rather exactly in the organization of the parsing mechanism. We will call this *type transparency*.
>
> Berwick and Weinberg (1984), p. 39

The following definition specifies the notion of *absolute type transparency* (Berwick and Weinberg (1984), p. 41, in a precise, intuitively obvious, and general way.

9.3.1 DEFINITION OF ABSOLUTE TYPE TRANSPARENCY

– For any given language, parser and generator use the *same* formal grammar,
– and the parser/generator applies the rules of the grammar *directly*.
– This means in particular that the parser/generator applies the rules in the *same order* as the grammatical derivation,
– that in each rule application the parser/generator takes the *same input* expressions as the grammar, and

– that in each rule application the parser/generator produces the *same output* expressions as the grammar.

In PS Grammar, it soon turned out that a direct application of the grammar rules by a parser is inherently impossible (see below). The historical background for this is that Post (1936) developed his production or rewrite system to mathematically characterize the notion of *effective computability* in recursion theory.[7] In this original application, a derivation order based on the substitution of signs by other signs is perfectly natural.

When Chomsky (1957) borrowed the Post production system under the name of PS grammar for analyzing natural language, he inherited its substitution-based derivation order. Because a parser takes terminal strings as input, while a PS Grammar starts from a start symbol, PS Grammars and their parsers are not *input-output equivalent* – which means that a parser able to apply the rules of PS Grammar directly cannot exist.

The structural problem of using context-free PS Grammar for parsing is illustrated by the following step-by-step derivation of a a a b b b based on the PS Grammar 7.1.3 for $a^k b^k$:

9.3.2 *Top-down* DERIVATION OF a a a b b b

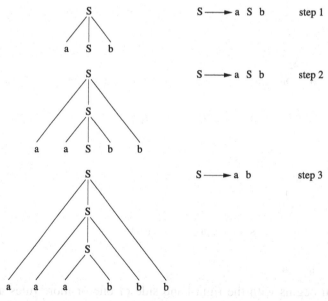

In this substitution-based derivation , the variable S on the left-hand side of the rules is repeatedly replaced by the signs on the right-hand side of the rules. The derivation begins with the variable S and ends when all variables have been replaced by terminal signs. This expansion of variables is called a *top-down* derivation.

---

[7] See for example Church (1956), p. 52, footnote 119.

A computational procedure cannot apply the derivational mechanism of PS Grammar directly in the analysis of the input a a a b b b, because PS Grammar always inserts terminal symbols in two different locations into the output string. In contrast to PS Grammar, the computer program has to deal with the unanalyzed terminal string, and there the structural relation between two locations of arbitrary distance is not at all obvious.

The only possibility for using the grammatical top-down derivation directly for the automatic analysis of input would be a systematic derivation of all outputs (beginning with the shortest), hoping that the string to be analyzed would at some point show up in the set of outputs. In the case of $a^k b^k$ this would succeed fairly easily, but for the whole class of context-free PS Grammars this approach would be no solution. For example, in the case WW^R, the number of possible outputs may grow exponentially with their length, for which reason the method of generating all possible strings would quickly become prohibitively inefficient.

Alternatively, one may try to apply PS Grammar in a *bottom-up* derivation.

9.3.3 *Bottom-up* DERIVATION OF a a a b b b

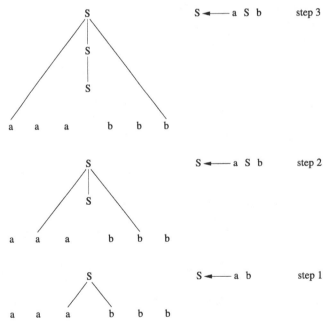

A bottom-up derivation begins with the right-hand side of one or more rules and replaces them with the variable of their left-hand side. These variables are matched to the right-hand sides of other rules and replaced by their respective left-hand sides. This type of bottom-up derivation may be stopped whenever only one rule is active and its right-hand side is replaced by the start symbol S.

The weakness of a bottom-up derivation in context-free PS Grammar is that it requires the program to find the theoretical center of the pairwise inverse structures.

This is a problem because the program has to deal with arbitrary unanalyzed input strings in which the theoretical center is not marked.

In the case of a^kb^k, the program could use the border between the a and b words to determine the center, but this would be no solution for context-free PS Grammar in general. The language WW^R, for example, contains strings like a a a a a a and a a a a a a a a, where the center can only be determined via the length. Length, however, is not a general criterion either, because there are context-free languages like a^kb^{3k} (8.3.4) where the center of the derivation is not located at half the length of the input.

In order to show how a parser may overcome the difficulties with the logical derivation order of context-free PS Grammar in a generally valid manner, let us consider an analysis within the Earley algorithm, which according to Hopcroft and Ullman (1979), p. 145, "is the most practical, general, context-free recognition and parsing algorithm." The main purpose of the following example is to illustrate the restructuring of PS Grammar rules necessary for the general parsing of context-free languages.

9.3.4 THE EARLEY ALGORITHM ANALYZING a^kb^k

```
.aaabbb

.S
 |        a.aabbb
 |
.ab   -> a.b
.aSb  -> a.Sb
          |        aa.abbb
          |
        a.abb   -> aa.bb
        a.aSbb  -> aa.Sbb
                    |        aaa.bbb      aaab.bb
                    |
                  aa.abbb   -> aaa.bbb   -> aaab.bb-> ...
                  aa.aSbbb  -> aaa.Sbbb
```

The Earley[8] algorithm uses three operations which are not part of the algebraic definition of PS Grammar (8.1.1), namely the *predictor-*, *scan-* and *completor-*operation (Earley 1970). With these operations, the input to 9.3.4 is analyzed from left to right, whereby a dot indicates how far the analysis has proceeded.

At the beginning of the analysis, the dot is placed before the input string

.a a a b b b

which is interpreted as corresponding to the state

.S

As a variable, S cannot have a counterpart in the input string, for which reason the *scan-*operation cannot apply.

---

[8] Jay Earley developed his parsing algorithm for context-free PS Grammars in his dissertation at the Computer Science Department of Carnegie Mellon University in Pittsburgh, USA. After this achievement he became a clinical psychologist specializing in group therapy and Internal Family Systems Therapy (IFS).

However, using the two rules S → a b and S → a S b of the PS Grammar for $a^k b^k$, the *predictor*-operation produces two new states, namely

.a b

.a S b

which are added to the *state set* of the parsing algorithm.

In the next cycle of the algorithm, the dot is moved one position to the right (*completor*-operation), both in the input string, i.e.,

a. a a b b b

and in the states, i.e.,

a. b

a. S b

The *scan*-operation checks whether the sign before the dot in the states corresponds to the sign before the dot in the input string. This is successful in both cases.

In the next cycle, the dot is again moved one position to the right, resulting in the input string

a a. a b b b

and in the states

a b.

a S. b

Because the first state has a terminal symbol preceding the dot, namely b, the *scan*-operation is attempted. This is not successful, however, because the terminal preceding the dot in the input string is an a.

The second state, on the other hand, has an S preceding the dot, to which according to the grammar rules the *predictor*-operation may be applied. This results in the states

a a. b b

a a. S b b,

both of which are shown by another *scan*-operation to fit the input string.

Next the *completor*-operation moves the dot again one position to the right, resulting in the input string

a a a. b b b

and the states

a a b. b

a a S. b b

Applying the *scan*-operation to the first state does not succeed.

However, applying the *predictor*-operation to the second state results in two new states, namely

a a a. b b b

a a a. S b b b

which are both matched successfully with the input string by another *scan*-operation. Once more the dot is moved one position to the right, producing the input string

  a a a b. b b

and the new states

  a a a b. b b
  a a a S. b b b

This time the *scan*-operation succeeds on the first state.[9]
Again the dot is moved one position to the right, resulting in the input string

  a a a b b. b

and the state

  a a a b b. b

Because the state consists of terminal symbols only, only the *scan*-operations can apply. The first of these happens to be successful, resulting in the input string

  a a a b b b.

and the state

  a a a b b b.

The dot at the end of the input string indicates a successful analysis.

We have seen that the Earley algorithm uses the rules of the grammar, but not directly. Instead, the parsing algorithm disassembles the rules of the grammar successively into their basic elements, whereby the order is determined by the sequence of terminal symbols in the input string – and not by the logical derivation order of the grammatical rule system. Therefore, the relation between the Earley algorithm and the context-free PS Grammars used by it is not type-transparent.

For context-free PS Grammar there exists a considerable number of parsers besides the Earley algorithm, such as the CYK algorithm (Hopcroft and Ullman 1979, pp. 139–141) and the chart parser (Kay 1980). On the positive side, these parsers all interpret arbitrary context-free PS Grammars and analyze any of the associated languages. On the negative side, these parsers all lack type transparency.

Parsers like the Earley algorithm, the CYK algorithm, or the chart parser cannot apply the rules of context-free PS Grammar directly. Instead, they require huge intermediate structures, called *state sets, tables*, or *charts*, in order to correlate the differing derivation orders of the grammar and the parser. As an excuse, it has been pointed out

---

[9] The second state is also still active at this point because it allows a further *predictor*-operation, resulting in the new states

  a a a a. b b b b
  a a a a. S b b b b

The subsequent *scan*-operations on the input

  a a a b. b b

do not succeed, however.

that the user, for example the grammar writer, does not notice the procedural routines of the parser. This is only valid, however, if the PS Grammar is already descriptively adequate.

However, if the parser is used in the *development* of descriptively adequate grammars, the lack of type transparency greatly impedes debugging and upscaling of the grammar. For example, if an error occurs because the parser cannot find a legal grammatical structure for well-formed input, then this error must be found in the complex rule system of the PS Grammar.

The number of rules in context-free PS Grammars used for practical applications often exceeds several thousand. Here, it would be of great help if errors could be localized with the help of parse traces. However, because the parser cannot use the rules of the PS Grammar directly, the parse trace (protocol of states) is about as unreadable as assembler code and therefore of little heuristic value.

One may, of course, write secondary parsers in order to translate the unreadable intermediate structures of the primary parser into a form that can be used by humans for localizing errors. Compared to a type-transparent system like LA Grammar, however, both the construction of the intermediate structures and their reinterpretation for human analysis constitute an essentially superfluous effort, the costs of which show up not only in the programming work required, but also in additional computation and increased use of memory.

9.4 Input-Output Equivalence with the Speaker-Hearer

The nativist approach has attempted to belittle the structural disadvantages of PS grammar as a problem of programming, the solution of which was the job of computer science. They claimed that the real goal was an analysis of the innate language knowledge of the speaker-hearer, and for this the computational unsuitability of PS Grammar was of no concern.

This line of reasoning is not valid, however. Because the form of innate structures follows their function (4.5.3), a minimal requirement for the description of the innate human language capability is that the grammar formalism used be input-output equivalent with the speaker-hearer.

PS Grammar, however, is just as incompatible with the input-output conditions of the speaker-hearer as it is with those of its parsers, as shown by the following PS Grammar for the English sentence Julia read a book.:

9.4.1 CONTEXT-FREE PS GRAMMAR FOR A SIMPLE SENTENCE OF ENGLISH

1.	S	$\rightarrow$ NP VP	5.	V	$\rightarrow$ read
2.	NP	$\rightarrow$ DET N	6.	DET	$\rightarrow$ a
3.	VP	$\rightarrow$ V NP	7.	N	$\rightarrow$ book
4.	NP	$\rightarrow$ Julia			

In the derivation of the associated analysis tree, rule 1 replaces (substitutes) the start symbol S with NP (noun phrase) and VP (verb phrase). Then, rule 4 replaces the node NP with the word Julia, and rule 3 replaces the node VP with the nodes V and NP. Next, rule 5 replaces the node V (verb) with the word read, and rule 2 replaces the node NP with the nodes DET (determiner) and N (noun). Finally, rule 6 replaces the node DET with the word a, and rule 7 replaces the node N with the word book:

9.4.2 PS GRAMMAR ANALYSIS (*top-down* DERIVATION)

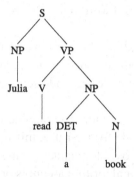

As simple and natural as this derivation may seem from a logical point of view, it is nevertheless in clear contradiction to the time-linear structure of natural language. The discrepancy between the input-output conditions of PS Grammars and the use of language by the hearer/reader is illustrated by the following sketch which attempts a time-linear analysis based on the PS Grammar 9.4.1:

9.4.3 ATTEMPT AT A TIME-LINEAR ANALYSIS IN PS GRAMMAR

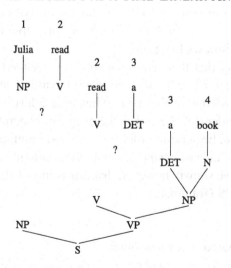

The natural order of reading the sentence Julia read a book is time-linear, i.e., from left to right,[10] one word after the other. After replacing the first two words, Julia and read, by the nodes NP and V (in accordance with rules 4 and 5), the reader's grammar algorithm is looking for a PS rule to replace the node sequence NP V by a higher node. However, since no such rule is provided by the grammar, the subtree consisting of the first word and its category must be set aside for later use.

Next, the reader's grammar algorithm replaces the third word a by its category DET using rule 6, and attempts to combine the category V of the second word with the category DET of the third word by replacing them by a higher node. Again, no suitable rule is provided by the grammar, and the subtree of the second word must also be set aside for later use.

Finally, the reader's grammar algorithm attempts to combine the category of the third word with that of the fourth and final word of the input sentence. Here, at last, the grammar provides a suitable rule, namely rule 2, to combine the node sequence DET N into the higher node NP.

At this point, the reader's grammar algorithm attempts once more to combine the category V of the second word read, which has been set aside for later use, this time with the newly derived NP node. It turns out that this is possible, thanks to rule 3, resulting in the higher node VP. Finally the reader's grammar algorithm attempts once more to combine the category NP of the first word Julia, which has been set aside since the analysis of this four-word sentence first began, this time with the newly derived VP node. This time the attempt is successful due to rule 1, and the analysis is complete.

The analysis sketch 9.4.3 shows that a time-linear interpretation is impossible in a constituent-structure-based context-free PS grammar: the first word of the sentence was the last to be built into the analysis. PS Grammar's lack of type transparency is thus not only an obstacle to the development of systems for the automatic analysis of artificial or natural languages. It is also in conflict with the elementary principle of nature that form – especially innate form – follows function.

But what about the standard nativist reply that their grammars are *not intended*[11] to describe the operations of the speaker-hearer in communication, and that they are intended instead to describe the innate knowledge of the speaker-hearer at a level of abstraction (competence) which is independent of the use of language in concrete communication? This reply cannot convince, because in order for a nativist grammar to be plausible, its basic structures have to be at least *compatible* with the communication mechanism of natural language. We have shown, however, that this is impossible in a nativist theory using the formalism of PS Grammar.

---

[10] According to the writing conventions of the Greco-Roman tradition.

[11] Chomsky has emphasized tirelessly that it was not the goal of his nativist program to model the communication procedure of the speaker-hearer. See for example Chomsky (1965), p. 9.

9.5 Desiderata of Grammar for Achieving Convergence

From the perspective of the history of science, PS Grammar-based nativism may be evaluated in different ways. By means of continuous revision, nativism has achieved over forty years of holding public and scholarly interest, preserving influence, recruiting new followers, and turning internal strife into a source of restoration rather than decline. On the negative side, it is a textbook example of a lack of convergence.[12]

The lack of convergence shows up in at least four ways. First, instead of consolidation there has been a development of ever new derived systems, epitomized by McCawley's (1982) title *Thirty Million Theories of Grammar*.[13] Second, each time an additional mechanism (e.g., transformations, metarules, etc.), regarded as descriptively necessary, was introduced, the mathematical and computational properties were severely degraded compared to the elementary subformalism of context-free PS Grammar. Third, the description of natural language within PS Grammar has led continuously to problems of the type descriptive aporia and embarrassment of riches [14] (Sect. 22.2). Fourth, practical systems of natural language processing either pay only lip service to the theoretical constructs of nativism or ignore them altogether.

There are two main reasons for this lack of convergence. First, nativism is empirically underspecified because it does not include a functional theory of communication. Second, the PS Grammar formalism adopted by nativism is incompatible with the input-output conditions of the speaker-hearer.

---

[12] In the history of science, a field of research is regarded as developing positively if its different areas converge, i.e., if improvements in one area lead to improvements in others. Conversely, a field of science is regarded as developing negatively if improvements in one area lead to a deterioration in other areas.

[13] This number is computed on the basis of the open alternatives within the nativist theory of language. McCawley's calculation amounts to an average of 2 055 different grammar theories a day, or a new theory every 42 seconds for the duration of 40 years.

[14] PS Grammar in combination with constituent structure analysis exhibits descriptive aporia in, for example, declarative main clauses of German such as Peter hat die Tür geschlossen. Because of its discontinuous elements, this sentence cannot be provided with a legal constituent structure analysis within context-free PS Grammar (8.5.1 and 8.5.2).

To resolve this and other problems, transformations were added to context-free PS Grammar (8.5.3). This resulted in many problems of the type embarrassment of riches. For example, there arose the question of whether the main clauses of German should be derived transformationally from the deep structure of subordinate clauses (e.g., weil Peter die Tür geschlossen hat) or vice versa.

The transformational derivation of main clauses from subordinate clauses, championed by Bach (1962), was motivated by the compliance of subordinate clauses with constituent structure, while the transformational derivation of subordinate clauses from main clauses, advocated by Bierwisch (1963), was motivated by the feeling that main clauses are more basic. For a treatment of German main and subordinate clauses without transformations see Chap. 18, especially Sect. 18.5.

Given the long-term consequences of working with a certain formalism,[15] begin-ning linguists interested in (i) modeling the mechanism of natural communication, (ii) verifying their model computationally, and (iii) utilizing their model in practi-cal applications such as human-machine communication, should select their grammar formalism carefully and consciously. As a contribution to a well-educated choice, the properties of PS Grammar are summarized below.

9.5.1 PROPERTIES OF PS GRAMMAR

– *Mathematical:*
Practical parsing algorithms exist only for context-free PS Grammar, which is of a sufficiently low complexity (n^3), but not of sufficient generative capacity for natural language. Extensions of the generative capacity for the purpose of describing natu-ral language turned out to be of such high complexity (undecidable or exponential) that no practical parsing algorithm could exist for them.

– *Computational:*
PS Grammar is not type-transparent. This prevents using the automatic traces of parsers for purposes of debugging and upscaling grammars. Furthermore, the in-direct relation between the grammar and the parsing algorithm requires the use of costly routines and large intermediate structures.

– *Empirical:*
The substitution-based derivation order of PS Grammar is incompatible with the time-linear structure of natural language.

Because bidirectional C Grammar and context-free PS Grammar are weakly equiv-alent (Sect. 9.2), C Grammar cannot serve as an alternative. We must therefore look for yet another elementary formalism with the following properties:

9.5.2 DESIDERATA OF A FORMAL GRAMMAR FORMALISM

1. The grammar formalism should be mathematically well-defined and thus
2. permit an explicit, declarative description of artificial and natural languages.
3. The formalism should be recursive (and thus decidable) as well as

---

[15] Changing from one formalism to another may be costly. It means giving up the hard-earned status of expert in a certain area, implies revising or discarding decades of previous work, and may have major social repercussions in one's peer group, both at home and abroad.

However, fields of science are known to sometimes shift in unexpected ways such that established research groups suddenly find their funds, their influence, and their member-ship drastically reduced. When this happens, changing from one formalism to another may become a necessity of survival.

In light of these possibilities, the best long-term strategy is to evaluate scientific options, such as the choice of grammar formalism, rationally. As in all good science, linguistic research should be conducted with conviction, based on the broadest and deepest possible knowledge of the field.

4. type-transparent with respect to its parsers and generators.
5. The formalism should define a hierarchy of different language classes in terms of structurally obvious restrictions on its rule system (analogous – but orthogonal – to the PS Grammar hierarchy),
6. whereby the hierarchy contains a language class of low, preferably linear, complexity, the generative capacity of which is sufficient for a complete description of natural language.
7. The formalism should be input-output equivalent with the speaker-hearer (and thus should use a time-linear derivation order).
8. The formalism should be suited equally well for production (in the sense of mapping meanings to surfaces) and interpretation (in the sense of mapping surfaces to meanings).

The following chapters will show that LA Grammar satisfies these desiderata. In contradistinction to the formalisms of C Grammar and PS Grammar, the derivations of which are based on the principle of possible *substitutions*, the derivations of LA Grammar are based on the principle of possible *continuations*.

Exercises

Section 9.1

1. What is the origin of the term parser and what are the functions of a parser?
2. What is the relation between morphology, syntax, and semantic parsers, and how do they differ?
3. Describe two different ways of using a formal grammar in a parser and evaluate the alternatives.
4. Explain the notions declarative and procedural. How do they show up in parsers?
5. Is it possible to write different parsers for the same grammatical formalism?

Section 9.2

1. Describe a context-free structure in natural language.
2. Are there context-sensitive structures in natural language?
3. What follows from the assumption that natural language is not context-free? Does the answer depend on the grammar formalism used? Would it be possible to parse natural language in linear time even if it were context-sensitive?
4. Explain the possible equivalence relations between two formalisms of grammar.
5. How is bidirectional C Grammar related to the kinds of PS Grammar?

6. Do artificial languages depend on their formal grammars?
7. Do language classes depend on formalisms of grammar?
8. What impact has the complexity of a language class on the possible existence of a practical parser for it?
9. What is the inherent complexity of a language and how is it determined?

Section 9.3

1. Explain the notion of type transparency.
2. For what purpose did Post (1936) develop his production systems?
3. When are a grammar formalism and a parser input-output equivalent?
4. What is the difference between a top-down and a bottom-up derivation in a context-free PS Grammar?
5. Why is it that a context-free PS Grammar is not input-output equivalent with its parsers? Base your explanation on a top-down and a bottom-up derivation.
6. Explain the functioning of the Earley algorithm using an expression of $a^k b^k$. How does the Earley algorithm manage to get around the substitution-based derivation order of PS Grammar?
7. Explain how the Earley algorithm makes crucial use of the pairwise inverse structure of context-free PS Grammars.
8. Is it possible to parse $a^k b^k c^k$ using the Earley algorithm?
9. Are there type-transparent parsers for context-free PS Grammar?
10. Name two practical disadvantages of an automatic language analysis which is not type-transparent.

Section 9.4

1. Explain why a nativist theory of language based on PS Grammar is incompatible with the principle *form follows function*, using the notion of input-output equivalence.
2. Demonstrate with an example that the derivation order of PS Grammar is incompatible with the time-linear structure of natural language.
3. Does an additional transformational component (Sects. 2.4 and 8.5) diminish or increase the incompatibility between the PS Grammar derivation order and the time-linear order of natural language?

Section 9.5

1. Explain the notion of convergence, as used in the history of science.
2. How does a lack of convergence show up in the historical development of nativism, and what are its reasons?
3. How did McCawley calculate the number in his title *Thirty Million Theories of Grammar*? Does this number indicate a positive development in linguistics?
4. Why can changing to another grammar formalism be costly?

5. Do you see a relation between 'descriptive aporia' and 'embarrassment of riches,' on the one hand, and the proposal of ever new derived formalisms with high mathematical complexity, on the other?

6. Describe the mathematical, computational, and empirical properties of PS Grammar.

7. Which desiderata must be satisfied by a formal grammar in order for it to be suitable for a computational analysis of natural language?

10. Left-Associative Grammar (LAG)

Chapters 7–9 have developed the basic notions for analyzing artificial and natural languages within the historical formalisms of C Grammar (Leśniewski 1929; Ajdukiewicz 1935) and PS Grammar (Post 1936; Chomsky 1957). Chapters 10–12 will apply these notions to the third elementary formalism, namely LA Grammar (Hausser 1985 et seq.).[1] Unlike the other two formalisms, LA Grammar was not borrowed from some other field of research to be adapted to natural language analysis, but was developed from the outset as a time-linear, type-transparent algorithm that is input-output-equivalent with the speaker-hearer.

Section 10.1 explains how the time-linear structure of natural language is modeled by the left-associative derivation order, defines the principle of possible continuations, and shows for C, PS, and LA Grammar the general connection between rule format and conceptual derivation order. Section 10.2 provides an algebraic definition of LA Grammar. Section 10.3 describes formats for representing time-linear derivations. Section 10.4 illustrates the relation between automatic analysis and automatic generation in LA Grammar using the context-sensitive language $a^k b^k c^k$, and demonstrates the type transparency of LA Grammar. Section 10.5 shows how LA-grammatical analyses of natural language are motivated linguistically.

10.1 Rule Kinds and Derivation Order

The name LA Grammar is motivated by the left-associative derivation order on which it is based. The notion *left-associative* is known from logic.

> When we combine operators to form expressions, the order in which the operators are to be applied may not be obvious. For example, a + b + c can be interpreted as ((a + b) + c) or as (a + (b + c)). We say that + is *left-associative* if operands are grouped left to right as in ((a + b) + c). We say it is *right-associative* if it groups operands in the opposite direction, as in (a + (b + c)).
>
> Aho and Ullman (1977), p. 47

---

[1] The 'official', peer-reviewed publication is Hausser (1992) in the journal *Theoretical Computer Science* (TCS).

Left- and right-associative bracket structures have the special property that they may be interpreted as regularly increasing.

10.1.1 INCREMENTAL LEFT- AND RIGHT-ASSOCIATIVE DERIVATION

left-associative:	*right-associative:*

```
        a                                          a
     (a + b)                                     (b + a)
    ((a + b) + c)                           (c + (b + a))
   (((a + b) + c) + d)                 (d + (c + (b + a)))
         . . .                                  . . .
            ⟹                            ⟸
```

Of these two regularly increasing structures, the left-associative one corresponds to the traditional direction of Western (Greco-Roman) writing. It serves as the formalization of time-linearity in LA Grammar.

More specifically, an LA Grammar takes the first word a in an abstract word sequence a b c d e as the sentence start and the second word b as the next word, and combines them into a new sentence start $(a + b)$. This result is combined with the next word c into the new sentence start $((a + b) + c)$, etc. In this way, a sentence start is always combined with a next word into a new sentence start until no new next word is available in the input.

The left-associative derivation order is linear in the sense that it regularly adds one word after the next, and it is time-linear because the direction of growth corresponds to the direction of time 5.4.3. The left-associative derivation order captures the basic structure of natural language in accordance with de Saussure's second law (5.4.4).

Besides the regular left- and the right-associative bracketing structure there is a multitude of irregular structures, e.g.,

```
(((a + b) + (c +d)) + e)
((a + b) + ((c +d)) + e)
(a + ((b + c)) + (d + e))
((a + (b + c)) + (d + e))
(((a + b) + c) + (d +e))
           . . .
```

The number of these irregular bracketings grows exponentially with the length of the string and is infinite if bracketings like (a), ((a)), (((a))), etc., are permitted.

It is these irregular bracketing structures (and corresponding trees) which C and PS Grammar generate via the principle of *possible substitutions*. From the large number of possible trees for a terminal chain, there follows the central task of linguistic description in C and PS Grammar, namely to motivate the 'correct' bracketing structure and the 'correct' phrase structure tree as a constituent structure analysis.

LA Grammar, on the other hand, is based on the principle of *possible continuations*, which is formally reflected in the regular left-associative bracketing structure (10.1.1) and corresponding trees (10.1.6).

10.1.2 THE PRINCIPLE OF POSSIBLE CONTINUATIONS

Beginning with the first word of the sentence, the grammar describes the possible continuations for each sentence start by specifying the rules which may perform the next grammatical composition (i.e., add the next word).

The time-linear derivation order and the structural characterization of possible continuations is formalized in the specific rule schema of LA Grammar.

10.1.3 SCHEMA OF LEFT-ASSOCIATIVE RULES IN LA GRAMMAR

$$r_i : cat_1 cat_2 \Rightarrow cat_3 rp_i$$

The rule consists of the name r_i, the category patterns cat_1, cat_2, and cat_3, and the rule package rp_i. The category patterns define a categorial operation which maps a sentence start ss (matched by cat_1) and a next word nw (matched by cat_2) into a new sentence start ss' (characterized by cat_3). The output of a successful application of rule r_i is a *state* defined as an ordered pair $(ss' \, rp_i)$.

In the next combination, the rules of the rule package rp_i are applied to ss' and a new next word. Because an LA-grammatical analysis starts with the initial words of the input, its conceptual derivation order is *bottom-up left-associative*.

To facilitate comparison, the schemata of C and PS Grammar are restated below.

10.1.4 SCHEMA OF A CANCELING RULE IN C GRAMMAR

$$\alpha_{(Y|X)} \circ \beta_{(Y)} \Rightarrow \alpha\beta_{(X)}$$

This rule schema combines α and β into $\alpha\beta$ by canceling the Y in the category of α with the corresponding category of β. The result is a tree structure in which $\alpha\beta$ of category (X) dominates α and β. The conceptual derivation order of categorial canceling rules is *bottom-up amalgamating*.

10.1.5 SCHEMA OF A REWRITE RULE IN PS GRAMMAR

$$X \rightarrow Y Z$$

Replacing the sign X by Y and Z corresponds to a tree structure in which Y and Z are immediately dominated by X. The conceptual derivation order is *top-down expanding*.

The characteristic derivation orders following from the different rule schemata have the following schematic representation:

10.1.6 THREE CONCEPTUAL DERIVATION ORDERS

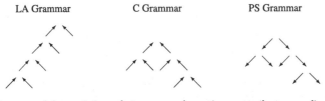

LA Grammar   C Grammar   PS Grammar

bottom-up left-associative   bottom-up amalgamating   top-down expanding

C and PS Grammar, being based alike on the principle of possible substitutions, differ only in the direction of their conceptual[2] derivation order. In C Grammar, two categorized expressions are substituted by one categorized expression (bottom-up). In PS Grammar, one sign is substituted by one, two, or more signs (top-down).

The principle of possible substitutions results in an irregular derivation structure which is reflected in irregular phrase structure trees. From the viewpoint of the SLIM theory of language, a substitution-based derivation order is in conflict with the communicative function of language (no input-output equivalence between the grammar and the speaker-hearer, 9.4.3) and an obstacle to automatic language analysis (no type transparency between the grammar and the parser, 9.3.4).

The principle of possible continuations, in contrast, results in a regular derivation order. The associated tree structure of LA Grammar may seem linguistically uninteresting from the viewpoint of constituent-structure-based C and PS Grammar. From the viewpoint of the SLIM theory of language, however, it (i) models the fundamental time-linear structure of natural language, (ii) allows input-output equivalence between the grammar and the speaker-hearer, and (iii) results in type transparency between the grammar and the parser.

It follows that the formal notion of constituent structure, defined in terms of phrase structure trees (8.4.3), has no place in LA Grammar. In the intuitive discussion of natural language examples, however, this notion may be used informally in the more general sense of a *complex grammatical unit*. In this sense, it is an old concept of classical grammar known as a *syntagma*. For example, when we say that in the English declarative sentence

The little dog surprised Mary.

the verb surprised is in 'second position,' then we do not mean the position of the second word form in the sentence, but rather the position after the first grammatical

---

[2] In C Grammar and PS Grammar, the conceptual derivation order is distinct from the procedural derivation order. For example, the different parsers for context-free PS Grammar use many different derivation orders, some working from left to right, some from right to left, some beginning in the middle (island parsers), some using a left-corner order, others a right-corner order, etc. These alternative orders are intended to improve efficiency by utilizing special properties of the language to be analyzed, and belong to the procedural aspect of the respective systems.

unit, syntagma, or constituent in a nontechnical sense. The complexity of grammatical units may be elementary, e.g., Fido, phrasal, e.g., The little dog, or clausal , e.g., That Fido barked.

10.2 Formalism of LA Grammar

In the following algebraic definition of LA Grammar, we identify positive integers with sets, i.e., $n = \{i \mid 0 \leq i < n\}$, for convenience.[3]

10.2.1 ALGEBRAIC DEFINITION OF LA GRAMMAR

A left-associative grammar (or LA Grammar) is defined as a 7-tuple $<W, C, LX, CO, RP, ST_S, ST_F>$, where

1. W is a finite set of *word surfaces*.
2. C is a finite set of *category segments*.
3. $LX \subset (W \times C^+)$ is a finite set comprising the *lexicon*.
4. $CO = (co_0 \ldots co_{n-1})$ is a finite sequence of total recursive functions from $(C^* \times C^+)$ into $C^* \cup \{\perp\}$,[4] called *categorial operations*.
5. $RP = (rp_0 \ldots rp_{n-1})$ is an equally long sequence of subsets of n, called *rule packages*.
6. $ST_S = \{(cat_s rp_s), \ldots\}$ is a finite set of *initial states*, whereby each rp_s is a subset of n called start rule package and each $cat_s \in C^+$.
7. $ST_F = \{(cat_f rp_f), \ldots\}$ is a finite set of *final states*, whereby each $cat_f \in C^*$ and each $rp_f \in RP$.

A concrete LA Grammar is specified by

(i) a lexicon LX (3),
(ii) a set of initial states ST_S (6),
(iii) a sequence of rules r_i, each defined as an ordered pair (co_i, rp_i), and
(iv) a set of final states ST_F (7).

A left-associative rule r_i takes a sentence start ss and a next word nw as input and tries to apply the categorial operation co_i. If the categories of the input match the patterns of cat_1 and cat_2, the application of rule r_i is successful and an output is produced. The output is the state $(ss' rp_i)$, whereby ss' is a resulting sentence start and rp_i is a rule package. If the input does not match the patterns of cat_1 and cat_2, then the application of rule r_i is not successful, and no output is produced.

---

[3] The algebraic definition of LA Grammar benefited greatly from help by Dana Scott.

[4] For theoretical reasons, the categorial operations are defined as total functions. In practice, the categorial operations are defined as easily recognizable subsets of $(C^* \times C^+)$, where anything outside these subsets is mapped into the arbitrary *"don't care"* value $\{\perp\}$, making the categorial operations total functions.

The rule package rp_i contains all rules which can be applied after rule r_i was successful. A rule package is defined as a set of rule names, whereby the name of a rule is the place number g of its categorial operation co_g in the sequence CO. In practice, the rules are called by more mnemonic names, such as 'Det+N' or 'Fverb+main.'

After a successful rule application, the algorithm gets a new next word (if present) from the input and applies the rules of the current rule package to the (once new) sentence start and the next word. In this way LA Grammar works from left to right through the input, pursuing alternative continuations in parallel. The derivation stops if there is either no grammatical continuation at a certain point (ungrammatical input, e.g., 10.5.5) or if there is no further next word (complete analysis, e.g., 10.5.3).

The general format of LA Grammars is illustrated below with the context-free language $a^k b^k$, previously described within the frameworks of C Grammar (7.4.4) and PS Grammar (7.1.3).

10.2.2 LA GRAMMAR FOR $a^k b^k$

$LX =_{def} \{[a\ (a)], [b\ (b)]\}$
$ST_S =_{def} \{[(a)\ \{r_1, r_2\}]\}$
$r_1: (X)\quad (a)\ \Rightarrow\ (aX)\quad \{r_1, r_2\}$
$r_2: (aX)\quad (b)\ \Rightarrow\ (X)\quad \{r_2\}$
$ST_F =_{def} \{[\varepsilon\ rp_2]\}.$

The lexicon LX contains two words, a and b. Each word, e.g. [a (a)], is an ordered pair, consisting of a surface, e.g. a, and a category, e.g. (a). The categories, defined as lists of category segments, contain here only a single segment,[5] which happens to equal the respective surface.

The initial state ST_S specifies that the first word must be of category (a), i.e., it must be an a. Furthermore, the rules to be applied initially must be r_1 and r_2. Thus, all rules,[6] but not all words, may be used at the beginning of a sentence.

The categorial patterns are based on the sequence variable X, representing zero or more category segments, and the segment constants a and b. Rule r_1 accepts a sentence start of any category (represented by the pattern (X)), and a next word of category (a), i.e., an a. The result of the categorial operation is expressed by the pattern (a X): an a-segment is added at the beginning of the sentence start category.

Rule r_2 accepts a sentence start the category of which begins with an a-segment (represented by the pattern (aX)) and a next word of category (b), i.e., a word b. The result of the categorial operation is expressed by the pattern (X). This means that an a-segment is subtracted from the beginning of the sentence start category.

---

[5] In LA Grammars for more demanding languages, the lexical categories consist of several segments.

[6] In more demanding languages, the initial state specifies a proper subset of the grammar rules.

The rule package of r_1, called rp_1, contains r_1 and r_2. As long as the next word is an a, r_1 is successful, while r_2 fails because it requires a b as the next word. As soon as the first b is reached in the input, r_2 is successful, while r_1 fails because it requires an a as the next word. The rule package rp_2 contains only one rule, namely r_2. Therefore, once the first b has been added, only b is acceptable as a next word.

An analysis is complete when all the a-segments in the sentence start category have been canceled by b-segments. In other words, the analysis ends after an application of r_2 with an empty sentence start category. This is specified by the final state ST_F of 10.2.2, which requires ε (i.e., the empty sequence) as the final result category.

The following LA Grammar generates the context-sensitive language $a^k b^k c^k$:

10.2.3 LA GRAMMAR FOR $a^k b^k c^k$

$LX =_{def} \{[a\ (a)],\ [b\ (b)],\ [c\ (c)]\}$
$ST_S =_{def} \{[(a)\ \{r_1, r_2\}]\}$
r_1: (X)   (a) $\Rightarrow$ (aX) $\{r_1, r_2\}$
r_2: (aX)   (b) $\Rightarrow$ (Xb) $\{r_2, r_3\}$
r_3: (bX)   (c) $\Rightarrow$ (X) $\{r_3\}$
$ST_F =_{def} \{[\varepsilon\ rp_3]\}$.

Compared to the corresponding PS Grammar 8.3.7, this LA Grammar is surprisingly simple. Furthermore, the LA Grammars for context-free $a^k b^k$ and for context-sensitive $a^k b^k c^k$ resemble each other closely.

In LA Grammar, the relation between the rules and their rule packages defines a finite state transition network (FSN). For example, the FSN underlying the LA Grammar for $a^k b^k c^k$ has the following form:[7]

10.2.4 THE FINITE STATE BACKBONE OF THE LA GRAMMAR FOR $a^k b^k c^k$

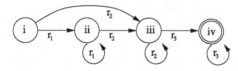

This FSN consists of four states, represented as the circles i–iv. Each state is defined as an ordered pair consisting of a category pattern and a rule package. State i corresponds to the start state ST_S, while the states ii, iii, and iv correspond to the output of rules r_1, r_2, and r_3. State iv has a second circle, indicating that it is a possible final state ST_F.

The application of a left-associative rule to an input pair, consisting of a sentence start and a next word, results in a transition. The transitions are represented graphically as arrows, annotated with the name of the associated rule. The transitions leading into a state represent the categorial operation of the rule associated with this state. The

---

[7] For a more detailed description see CoL, Sect. 8.2.

transitions leading out of a state represent the rule package of the rule common to all the transitions leading into the state.

For example, the transitions leading out of state i are different (namely r_1 and r_2), corresponding to the rule package of the start state in ST_S. The transitions leading into state ii are all the same, representing applications of r_1 from different preceding states. Correspondingly, the transitions leading out of state ii are different, corresponding to the rule package of r_1. The transitions leading into state iii are all the same, representing applications of r_2 from three different preceding states, etc.

An LA Grammar analyzing an input or generating an output navigates through its FSN, from one state to the next, following the transition arrows. Thereby, the generative capacity of LA Grammar resides in the categorial operations of its rules. While the FSN algorithm by itself generates only the regular languages, the algorithm of LA Grammar generates exactly the class of recursive languages (Sect. 11.1).

This enormous generative capacity may be used efficiently, however. For example, the LA Grammars for $a^k b^k$ and $a^k b^k c^k$ are of the lowest possible complexity: they both parse in linear time.[8] Thus, there is no complexity theoretical boundary between the context-free and the context-sensitive languages in LA Grammar. This is a first indication that the formalism of LA Grammar arrives at a hierarchy of language classes different from the formalism of PS Grammar.

10.3 Time-Linear Analysis

The tree structures of LA Grammar may be displayed equivalently as structured lists.

10.3.1 LA TREES AS STRUCTURED LISTS

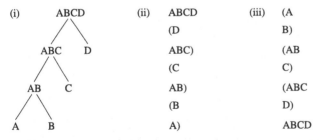

In (i), a left-associative derivation is shown in the form of a tree (10.1.6). In (ii), the same derivation is shown in the equivalent format of a structured list, whereby sentence start, next word, and resulting sentence start each have their own line. Formats (ii) and (iii) differ only in the direction of a time-linear reading: in (ii) it begins at the bottom – in analogy to the tree structure (i) – and in (iii) at the top.

---

[8] The two LA Grammars are unambiguous because their respective rules have incompatible input conditions (they each take different next words). Unambiguous LA Grammars of this kind are called C1 LAGs and parse in linear time (Chap. 11).

Structure (iii) is best suited for displaying derivations on the screen. This format is shown below, based on the LA Grammar 10.2.2, analyzing the expression aaabbb.

10.3.2 LA GRAMMAR DERIVATION OF $a^k b^k$ FOR $k = 3$

```
NEWCAT>  a a a b b

    *START-0
    1
        (A) A
        (A) A
    *RULE-1
    2
        (A A) A A
        (A) A
    *RULE-1
    3
        (A A A) A A A
        (B) B
    *RULE-2
    4
        (A A) A A A B
        (B) B
    *RULE-2
    5
        (A) A A A B B
        (B) B
    *RULE-2
    6
        (NIL) A A A B B B
```

This automatic analysis was generated directly as the formatted protocol (trace) of the LA Parser NEWCAT. Because of the absolute type transparency of LA Grammar, the declarative analysis and the derivation procedure on the computer are merely different realizations of the same left-associative algorithm. The input to be analyzed is typed in after the prompt NEWCAT>. To obtain a better comparison of the input categories, surface and category are printed in inverse order, e.g., (A) A instead of [A (A)].

The first section in begins with the name of the active rule package *START-0. Then follows the composition number 1, the sentence start (consisting of the first word), the next (i.e., second) word, and finally the name of the rule (RULE-1) which combines the sentence start and the next word. After the next composition number follows the result of the (still) current composition:

```
active rule package:        *START-0
composition number:         1
sentence start:             (A) A
next word:                  (A) A
successful rule:            *RULE-1
next composition number:    2
result:                     (A A) A A
```

The rule name ('successful rule') and the resulting sentence start ('result') each have a double function. The rule name simultaneously specifies (i) the rule which is successful in composition n and (ii) the rule package, the rules of which are applied in the next composition n + 1. Correspondingly, the result simultaneously represents (i) the output of composition n and (ii) the sentence start of composition n + 1.

These double functions in a left-associative derivation are clearly visible in the second composition:

```
active rule package:        *RULE-1
composition number:         2
sentence start :            (A A) A A
next word:                  (A) A
successful rule :           *RULE-1
next composition number:    3
result:                     (A A A) A A A
```

The form of the derivation is designed to characterize the categorial operations of the rules. Because it only represents successful continuations, it constitutes a *depth-first* format in LA Grammar. In addition, there is also a *breadth-first* format, which is used in, for example, the morphological analysis of word forms (14.4.2, 14.4.3, and 14.4.4). These output formats have in common that they are simultaneously (i) protocols of the parser and (ii) analyses of the grammar.

10.4 Absolute Type Transparency of LA Grammar

The algorithm of LA Grammar is equally suited for parsing and generation. The structural reason for this is the principle of possible continuations. In parsing, the next word is provided by the input, while in generation the next word is chosen from the lexicon.

The close relation between parsing and generation is illustrated with the following traces. They are based on the same LA Grammar 10.2.3 for the context-sensitive language $a^k b^k c^k$.

For parsing, an arbitrary LA Grammar of the C LAG class is loaded. Then, arbitrary expressions may be put in to be analyzed. The NEWCAT parser includes an automatic rule counter which at the beginning of each derivation shows the rules attempted in each left-associative composition.

10.4.1 PARSING aaabbbccc WITH ACTIVE RULE COUNTER

```
NEWCAT>  a a a b b b c c c
;   1: Applying rules (RULE-1 RULE-2)
;   2: Applying rules (RULE-1 RULE-2)
;   3: Applying rules (RULE-1 RULE-2)
;   4: Applying rules (RULE-2 RULE-3)
;   5: Applying rules (RULE-2 RULE-3)
;   6: Applying rules (RULE-2 RULE-3)
;   7: Applying rules (RULE-3)
;   8: Applying rules (RULE-3)
```

```
; Number of rule applications: 14.

    *START-0
    1
        (A) A
        (A) A
    *RULE-1
    2
        (A A) A A
        (A) A
    *RULE-1
    3
        (A A A) A A A
        (B) B
    *RULE-2
    4
        (A A B) A A A B
        (B) B
    *RULE-2
    5
        (A B B) A A A B B
        (B) B
    *RULE-2
    6
        (B B B) A A A B B B
        (C) C
    *RULE-3
    7
        (B B) A A A B B B C
        (C) C
    *RULE-3
    8
        (B) A A A B B B C C
        (C) C
    *RULE-3
    9
        (NIL) A A A B B B C C C
```

The number of rule applications attempted here is below 2n.

An LA Generator likewise loads an arbitrary LA Grammar of the class of C LAGs. Then the function 'gram-gen' is called with two arguments: the *recursion factor*[9] of the grammar and a list of words to be used in the generation. In this way, the generation procedure is limited to a certain set of words and a certain length. The grammatical analysis of generation is also a direct trace, this time of the LA Generator.

10.4.2 GENERATING A REPRESENTATIVE SAMPLE IN $a^k b^k c^k$

```
NEWCAT> (gram-gen 3 '(a b c))
```

---

[9] CoL, pp. 193f. In another version, 'gram-gen' is called up with the maximal surface length instead of the recursion factor.

```
Parses of length 2:
 A B
   2    (B)
 A A
   1    (A A)

Parses of length 3:
 A B C
   2 3    (NIL)
 A A B
   1 2    (A B)
 A A A
   1 1    (A A A)

Parses of length 4:
 A A B B
   1 2 2    (B B)
 A A A B
   1 1 2    (A A B)
 A A A A
   1 1 1    (A A A A)

Parses of length 5:
 A A B B C
   1 2 2 3    (B)
 A A A B B
   1 1 2 2    (A B B)
 A A A A B
   1 1 1 2    (A A A B)

Parses of length 6:
 A A B B C C
   1 2 2 3 3    (NIL)
 A A A B B B
   1 1 2 2 2    (B B B)
 A A A A B B
   1 1 1 2 2    (A A B B)

Parses of length 7:
 A A A B B B C
   1 1 2 2 2 3    (B B)
 A A A A B B B
   1 1 1 2 2 2    (A B B B)

Parses of length 8:
 A A A B B B C C
   1 1 2 2 2 3 3    (C)
 A A A A B B B B
   1 1 1 2 2 2 2    (B B B B)

Parses of length 9:
 A A A B B B C C C
   1 1 2 2 2 3 3 3    (NIL)
 A A A A B B B B C
   1 1 1 2 2 2 2 3    (B B B)
```

```
Parses of length 10:
A A A A B B B B C C
 1 1 1 2 2 2 2 3 3    (B B)

Parses of length 11:
A A A A B B B B C C C
 1 1 1 2 2 2 2 3 3 3    (B)

Parses of length 12:
A A A A B B B B C C C C
 1 1 1 2 2 2 2 3 3 3 3    (NIL)
```

This systematic generation begins with well-formed but incomplete expressions of length 2 and represents all well-formed intermediate expressions of length up to 12. Complete expressions of the language are recognizable by their result category (NIL).

Each derivation consists of a surface, a sequence of rule names represented by numbers, and a result category. A single derivation is illustrated as follows:

10.4.3 COMPLETE WELL-FORMED EXPRESSION IN $a^k b^k c^k$

```
A A A B B B C C C
 1 1 2 2 2 3 3 3    (NIL)
```

The surface and the rule name sequence are arranged to show which word is added by which rule. The derivation characterizes a well-formed expression because it corresponds to the final state (ε rp$_3$), here written as '3 (NIL),' i.e., an element of the set ST$_F$ of the LA Grammar for $a^k b^k c^k$ defined in 10.2.3.

The relation between this LA Grammar, the LA Parser illustrated in 10.4.1, and the LA Generator illustrated in 10.4.2 demonstrates the notion of absolute type transparency 9.3.1 between a grammar formalism, a parser, and a generator in practice. So far, LA Grammar is the only grammar formalism which achieves absolute type transparency as described by Berwick and Weinberg (1984), p. 41.

10.5 LA Grammar for Natural Language

Before we turn, in the next chapter, to the formal properties of LA Grammar (such as language classes, generative capacity, and complexity), let us illustrate the application of LA Grammar to natural language. The purpose is to show the linguistic motivation of LA Grammar analyses in terms of the traditional notions of valency, agreement, and word order on the one hand, and a time-linear derivation on the other.

The formalism of LA Grammar originated in the attempt to implement the C grammar defined in SCG as a parser (NEWCAT, p. 7). Consider the following C Grammar analysis of the English sentence Mary gave Fido a bone.

10.5.1 CONSTITUENT STRUCTURE ANALYSIS IN C GRAMMAR

```
                    Mary gave Fido a bone
                            (V)
                          /    \
                          /      gave Fido a bone
                         /           (N' V)
                        /            /    \
                       /         gave Fido    a bone
                      /          (N' A' V)     (SNP)
                     /           /    \        /    \
                Mary         gave    Fido    a      bone
                (SNP)     (N' D' A' V) (SNP) (SN' SNP) (SN)
```

This tree is a constituent structure satisfying condition 8.4.3 and could be used in PS as well as in C Grammar. However, because of its complex categories and the concomitant bias towards a bottom-up derivation, it is closer to a C Grammar analysis.

Compared to the algebraic definition of C Grammar 7.4.2, the categories are of an especially simple variety, however. They consist of *lists of category segments*, and not of categorial functor-argument structures based on slashes and multiple parentheses as in traditional C Grammar.

The simplified categories are sufficient to encode the relevant linguistic valency properties. For example, the category (N' D' A' V) of gave indicates a verb V which has valency positions for a nominative N', a dative D', and an accusative A'. Correspondingly, the category (SN' SNP) of the determiner a(n) indicates a functor which takes a singular noun SN' to make a singular noun phrase SNP.

The C grammatical derivation may begin by combining gave and Fido, whereby the SNP segment in the category of Fido cancels the D' segment in the category of gave, resulting in the intermediate expression gave Fido of category (N' A' V). Next, the determiner a and the noun bone must be combined, resulting in the intermediate expression a bone of category (SNP). This cancels the A' segment in the category of gave Fido, resulting in the intermediate expression gave Fido a bone of category (N' V). Finally, the segment SNP in the category of Mary cancels the segment N' in the category of gave Fido a bone, resulting in a complete sentence of category (V).

The lexical categories of the C grammatical analysis 10.5.1 may be re-used in the corresponding left-associative analysis 10.5.2, because their list structure happens to be in concord with the algebraic definition of LA Grammar in 10.2.1.

10.5.2 Time-Linear Analysis in LA Grammar

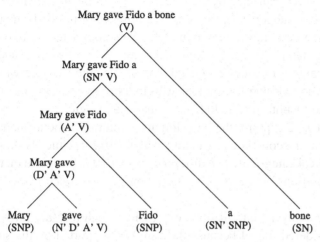

This analysis is based on *LA E2*, an LA Grammar defined in 17.4.1.

In the LA grammar analysis, the same valency positions are canceled by the same fillers as in C grammar analysis. However, the left-associative derivation always combines a sentence start with a next word into a new sentence start, beginning with the first word of the sentence.

The initial combination of Mary and gave is based on the categorial operation

$$(SNP) (N' D' A' V) \Rightarrow (D' A' V).$$

The category segment SNP (for singular noun phrase) of Mary cancels the first segment N' (for nominative) of the category of gave. Linguistically speaking, the nominative valency of the verb is filled here by the category of the first word. The agreement between the segments SNP and N' is defined in the variable definition of 17.4.1.

The result of this first combination is a sentence start of the category (D' A' V), indicating an intermediate expression which still needs a D (dative) and an A (accusative) to become a complete sentence. This new sentence start combines with the next word Fido of category (SNP), whereby the category segment SNP cancels the first segment of the sentence start category (D' A' V).

The result of the second combination is a sentence start of the category (A' V), indicating an intermediate expression which still needs an A (accusative) in order to become complete. This new sentence start combines with the next word, i.e., the determiner a(n) of category (SN' SNP). The categorial operation of the rule used in this combination has the form

$$(A' V) (SN' SNP) \Rightarrow (SN' V).$$

Thus, the result segment SNP of the determiner fills the valency position of the accusative in the category of the sentence start, while the argument position SN' of the determiner is added to the sentence start category, opening a new valency position for a singular noun.

In the next composition of the sentence start Mary gave Fido a and the next word bone, this new valency position is canceled by the category (SN) of the next word. The result is a sentence start of the category (V), for verb. The absence of unfilled valency positions indicates that the expression is now complete. This completeness is only potential, however, because natural language expressions can always be continued – here, for example, by regularly or because she is so fond of this cute little dog which she picked up in Denver when visiting her mother who told her while driving to the cleaners that the Millers had recently moved to Detroit because ..., etc.

The time-linear analysis 10.5.2 captures the same linguistic intuitions about valency, agreement, and word order as the constituent structure analysis 10.5.1, which is shown by their use of the same lexical categories. The difference is that 10.5.1 is based on the principle of possible substitutions, while 10.5.2 is based on the principle of possible continuations.

In a constituent structure analysis, intermediate expressions such as Mary gave or Mary gave Fido a are considered illegal because they are not supported by the substitution (8.4.7) and movement (8.4.8) tests on which constituent structure analysis is based. In a left-associative derivation, on the other hand, they are legitimate intermediate expressions because they may be *continued* into a complete well-formed sentence.

Conversely, expressions like gave Fido or gave Fido a bone will not occur as intermediate expressions in LA Grammar because they cannot be continued to yield complete well-formed sentences. In C and PS Grammar, on the other hand, such expressions are used as intermediate expressions because they are supported by the substitution and movement tests which motivate C and PS Grammar intuitively.

The LA Grammar *LA E2* (17.4.1) underlying derivation 10.5.2 can be used by a parser directly: the parser reads the sentence word form by word form, each time applying the rules of the LA Grammar, always combining a sentence start with a next word into a new sentence start. During the parsing procedure, the evolving trace of the parse may be displayed directly as the grammatical analysis.

The following automatic analysis illustrates the structured list format used in NEW-CAT and CoL, already familiar from the artificial language analyses in 10.3.2 and 10.4.1 above.

10.5.3 LEFT-ASSOCIATIVE PARSING OF EXAMPLE 10.5.2

```
NEWCAT>  Mary gave Fido a bone \.

  *START
  1
      (SNP) MARY
      (N D A V) GAVE
  *NOM+FVERB
  2
      (D A V) MARY GAVE
      (SNP) FIDO
```

```
*FVERB+MAIN
3
    (A V) MARY GAVE FIDO
    (SN SNP) A
*FVERB+MAIN
4
    (SN V) MARY GAVE FIDO A
    (SN) BONE
*DET+NOUN
5
    (V) MARY GAVE FIDO A BONE
    (V DECL) .
*CMPLT
6
    (DECL) MARY GAVE FIDO A BONE .
```

The final combination adds a full stop, which characterizes the expression as a declarative sentence (*LA E3* defined in 17.5.5).[10]

This parsing analysis contains not only all the information of the time-linear tree format 10.5.2, but in addition specifies for each left-associative combination the name of the rule involved – which indicates the name of the currently active rule package at the same time (Sect. 10.3). The structural difference between the linear tree 10.5.2 and the structured list 10.5.3 corresponds to the difference between the equivalent formats (i) and (iii) in 10.3.1.

The next example illustrates the LA Grammar handling of a discontinuous element:

10.5.4 ANALYSIS OF A DISCONTINUOUS ELEMENT

```
NEWCAT>  Fido dug the bone up \.

    *START
    1
        (SNP) FIDO
        (N A UP V) DUG
    *NOM+FVERB
    2
        (A UP V) FIDO DUG
        (SN SNP) THE
    *FVERB+MAIN
    3
        (SN UP V) FIDO DUG THE
        (SN) BONE
    *DET+NOUN
    4
        (UP V) FIDO DUG THE BONE
        (UP) UP
```

---

[10] The distinction between a valency position, e.g. A′, and a valency filler, e.g. SNP, by means of an apostrophe in the valency position is not reflected by the NEWCAT parser.

```
*FVERB+MAIN
5
    (V) FIDO DUG THE BONE UP
    (V DECL) .
*CMPLT
6
    (DECL) FIDO DUG THE BONE UP .
```

The relation between the discontinuous elements dug and up is represented by the segment UP′ in the category (N′ A′ UP′ V) of dug. The final position of up is specified by the order of valency positions (here N′ A′ UP′) in the functor category.

The "problem" of discontinuous elements (8.5.1, 8.5.2) exists only within constituent structure analysis. It is entirely self-inflicted and the result of tests (8.4.8) which are like moving the bones of a lifeless body – instead of (i) recognizing the fundamental role of the time-linear structure of natural language in accordance with the second law (5.4.4) of de Saussure and (ii) broadening the empirical base by modeling the mechanism of living natural language *communication.*

LA Grammar, in contrast, is motivated by the time-linear structure of natural language and the valency, agreement, and word order properties of traditional grammar. The parse trace 10.5.4 shows how discontinuous structures may be treated in a standard way by coding a certain filler position into the relevant functor category and canceling this position at a later point.

In conclusion, consider the handling of an ungrammatical sentence by the NEWCAT parser:

10.5.5 LA ANALYSIS OF UNGRAMMATICAL INPUT

```
NEWCAT>  the young girl give Fido the bone \.

ERROR
Ungrammatical continuation at: "GIVE"

    *START
    1
        (SN SNP) THE
        (ADJ) YOUNG
    *DET+ADJ
    2
        (SN SNP) THE YOUNG
        (SN) GIRL
      *DET+NOUN
    3
        (SNP) THE YOUNG GIRL
```

The derivation begins normally, but breaks off after the third word, because the grammar does not provide a possible continuation for the current sentence start the young girl and the next word give. The reason is that the category segment SNP does not agree with the nominative segment NOM of give. This is specified in the variable definition of *LA E2* in 17.4.1.

LA Parsers analyze the grammatical beginning of ungrammatical input as far as possible, giving a precise grammatical description of the sentence start. This is of practical use for both the debugging and upscaling of a given LA Grammar. In debugging, the break off point and the grammatical structure of the sentence start tell us exactly which rule of the grammar should have fired, what its input categories happen to be, etc. Conversely, if the system accepts input which is ungrammatical (error arising in negative testing), the LA analysis gives an exact grammatical description of the location where the break off should have been.

In upscaling, a new construction may be built up step-by-step from a working sentence start and then led back into the old network of possible continuations as shown by the finite state backbone of the grammars 10.2.4, 17.4.2, 17.5.1, 17.5.6, and 18.5.12. This characteristic property of LA Grammar follows from its time-linear derivation structure and will be used extensively in Part III for developing larger and larger fragments of English (*LA E1* to *LA E3* in Chap. 17) and German (*LA D1* to *LA D4* in Chap. 18).

Exercises

Section 10.1

1. What is meant by a 'left-associative grouping of operands?' What other groupings of operands are possible?
2. Which property of natural language is formally modeled by a left-associative derivation order?
3. Compare the principle of possible continuations to the principle of possible substitutions. How do these different principles relate to the intuitive notions of time linearity and constituent structure? Which elementary formalisms are based on which principle?
4. Explain the relation between different rule formats and conceptual derivation orders in C , PS , and LA Grammar.
5. What is a syntagma?

Section 10.2

1. Explain the algebraic definition of LA Grammar.
2. Which part of a left-associative rule is used for pattern matching?
3. Which part of a left-associative rule participates in the definition of a finite state transition network?
4. Why do the transitions going into a state all represent the same rule, while the transitions going out of a state all represent different rules?

5. Restate the LA Grammar for $a^k b^k$, explain how it works, and compare it with the corresponding C Grammar 7.4.4 and PS Grammar 7.1.3.
6. Define an LA Grammar for $a^{2k} b^k$.
7. Define an LA Grammar for $a^k b^{2k}$.
8. What are the conditions for a left-associative derivation to terminate?

Section 10.3
1. What is the relation between left-associative tree structures and structured lists? Which format is best suited for computational analysis, and why?
2. Describe the numbered sections in the output of a NEWCAT parse and explain their dual function.
3. Why is it remarkable that the LA Grammar for $a^k b^k c^k$ resembles that for $a^k b^k$ so closely? Base your answer on the notions PS hierarchy, language class, complexity, and parsing algorithm.
4. Define LA Grammars for $\{a^k b^k c^k\}^+$, $a^k b^k c^k d^k$, and $a^k b^k c^k d^k e^k f^k$. What is the PS Grammar language class of these languages? What is their LA Grammar complexity?

Section 10.4
1. What is the relation between an LA Parser, an LA Grammar, and an LA Generator?
2. Why does it make sense to specify the maximal length and the specific words to be used when starting an LA Generator? Which of these restrictions is especially useful for artificial languages, and which for natural languages?
3. Explain how the start of a PS Grammar derivation differs from that in LA Grammar. Does the start symbol of PS Grammar have a counterpart in LA Grammar?
4. Do you see a connection between the formal LA analysis 10.4.1 and the schema of language understanding in 5.4.1?
5. Do you see a connection between the formal LA generation 10.4.2 and the schema of language production 5.4.2?
6. Explain the properties of type transparency in LA Grammar.

Section 10.5
1. What are the similarities and differences between the C and the LA Grammar analysis of natural language?
2. How do intermediate expressions differ in a constituent structure analysis and a left-associative analysis of natural language?
3. Why is the handling of discontinuous elements a problem for an analysis based on constituent structure, but not for one based on the time-linear structure of natural language?
4. When does an LA Parser stop the analysis of an ungrammatical expression?
5. Give three different reasons why an LA Parser may stop the analysis before reaching the end of the input.

11. Hierarchy of LA Grammar

In this chapter, different kinds of LA Grammar are defined via natural restrictions of its rule system. Then these kinds of grammar are characterized in terms of their generative capacity and computational complexity.

Section 11.1 shows that LA Grammar in the basic, unrestricted form of its algebraic definition generates the recursive languages exactly. Section 11.2 describes possible restrictions on LA Grammar and defines the hierarchy of A, B, and C LAGs. Section 11.3 describes the origin of nonrecursive and recursive ambiguities and their impact on the number of rule applications. Section 11.4 compares the notions of primitive operation used for determining complexity in context-free PS Grammar and in C LAGs, and explains the relation of the C LAGs to the automata-theoretic concepts of deterministic and nondeterministic automata. Section 11.5 defines the sub-hierarchy of linear C1, polynomial C2, and exponential C3 LAGs within the class of C LAGs, which differ solely in their degrees of ambiguity.

11.1 Generative Capacity of Unrestricted LAG

The generative capacity of a grammar formalism follows from its algebraic definition. It specifies the form of the rules, which in turn determines which structures can be handled by the formalism and which cannot.

According to the algebraic definition of LA Grammar (10.2.1), a rule r_i consists of two parts, a categorial operation co_i and the associated rule package rp_i. The categorial operation co_i is defined as a total recursive function.

A function is recursive if its assignment (7.4.1) can be described as a mechanical step-by-step procedure called an algorithm. A function is total if there exists an algorithm which assigns to each element in the domain a value in the range. In a partial function, in contrast, the assignment is undefined for parts of the domain.

Intuitively, the class of total recursive functions represents those structures which may be computed explicitly and completely. Formally, the total recursive functions characterize the class of recursive languages.

A language is recursive if and only if there is an algorithm (i.e., a total recursive function) which can decide for arbitrary input in finitely many steps whether or not the input belongs to the language. The class of recursive languages comprises all languages which are *decidable*. Thus, the recursive languages constitute the largest class the elements of which have a completely specifiable structure.[1]

LA Grammar in its basic, unrestricted form (definition 10.2.1) has the following generative capacity:

11.1.1 GENERATIVE CAPACITY OF UNRESTRICTED LA GRAMMAR

Unrestricted LA Grammar accepts and generates all and only the recursive languages.

The two parts of this statement are formulated and proven as theorems.[2]

11.1.2 THEOREM 1

Unrestricted LA Grammar accepts and generates *only* the recursive languages.

Proof Assume an input string of finite length n. Each word in the input string has a finite number of readings (> 0).

Combination step 1: The finite set of start states ST_S and all readings of the first word w_1 result in a finite set of well-formed expressions

$$WE_1 = \{(ss'\ rp_S) \mid ss' \in (W^+ \times C^+)\}.$$

Combination step n: Combination step $k - 1$, $k > 1$, produces a finite set of well-formed expressions

$$WE_k = \{(ss'\ rp_i) \mid i \in n,\ ss' \in (W^+ \times C^*) \text{ and the surface of each } ss' \text{ has length k}\}.$$

The next word w_{k+1} has a finite number of readings.

Therefore, the Cartesian product of all elements of WE_k and all readings of the current next word will be a finite set of pairs. Each pair is associated with a rule package containing a finite set of rules. Therefore, combination step k will produce only finitely many new sentence starts. The derivation of this finite set of new sentence starts is decidable because the categorial operations are defined to be total recursive functions. □

Because all possible left-associative analyses for any finite input can be derived in finitely many steps each of which is decidable, there is no halting problem in LA Grammar and associated parsers. Thus LA Grammar satisfies condition 3 of the generative grammar desiderata 9.5.2.

---

[1] In automata theory, the recursive languages are defined as those of which each expression may be recognized by at least one Turing machine in finitely many steps (*'halts on all inputs'*, Hopcroft and Ullman 1979, p. 151). The PS Grammar hierarchy does not provide a formal characterization of the recursive languages – in contrast to the regular, context-free, context-sensitive, and recursively enumerable languages, which have both an automata-theoretic and a PS Grammar definition.

[2] CoL, Theorems 1 and 2, pp. 134f.

11.1.3 THEOREM 2

Unrestricted LA Grammar accepts and generates *all* recursive languages.

Proof[3] Let L be a recursive language with the alphabet W. Because L is recursive, there is a total recursive function $\varrho : W^* \rightarrow \{0, 1\}$, i.e., the characteristic function of L. Let LAG^L be an LA Grammar defined as follows:

The set of word surfaces of LAG^L is W.

The set of category segments $C =_{def} W \cup \{0, 1\}$.

For arbitrary $e, f \in W^+$, [e (f)] $\in$ LX if and only if $e = f$.

$LX =_{def}$ {[a (a)], [b (b)], [c (c)], [d (d)], ... }

$ST_S =_{def}$ {[(seg$_c$) {r_1, r_2}]}, where seg$_c \in$ {a, b, c, d, ... }

r_1: (X) (seg$_c$) $\Rightarrow$ (X seg$_c$)   {r_1, r_2}

r_2: (X) (seg$_c$) $\Rightarrow \varrho$ (X seg$_c$)   { }

$ST_F =_{def}$ {[(1) rp$_2$]}

After any given combination step, the rule package rp_1 offers two choices: application of r_1 to continue reading the input string, or application of r_2 to test whether the input read so far is a well-formed expression of L. In the latter case, the function ϱ is applied to the concatenation of the input categories, which are the same as the input surfaces. If the result of applying r_2 is [(1) rp$_2$],[4] the input surface is accepted; if it is [(0) rp$_2$], it is rejected.

Since the categorial operations of LAG^L can be any total recursive function, LAG^L may be based on ϱ, the characteristic function of L. Therefore, LAG^L accepts and generates any recursive language.   □

In LAG^L, the prefinal combination steps serve only to read the surface into the category. At the final combination step, the complete surface is available in the category and is analyzed in one step by a very complex categorial operation defined as the characteristic function ϱ of the language.

Unrestricted LA Grammars are called A LAGs because they generate exactly *all* recursive (decidable) languages.

11.1.4 DEFINITION OF THE CLASS OF A LAGS

The class of A LAGs consists of unrestricted LA Grammars and generates *all* recursive languages.

In contrast, unrestricted PS Grammars (8.1.1) generate the undecidable set of the recursively enumerable languages. Thus, LA Grammar and PS Grammar are not equivalent in the basic unrestricted form of their respective algebraic definitions.

---

[3] This proof was provided by Dana Scott.

[4] I.e., if ϱ maps the category (X seg$_c$), representing the surface, into the category (1).

11.2 LA Hierarchy of A, B, and C LAGs

The complexity of a grammar formalism – defined as the upper bound on the number of operations required in the analysis of arbitrary input – depends on the following two parameters:

11.2.1 PARAMETERS OF COMPLEXITY

– The *amount* of computation per rule application required in the worst case.
– The *number* of rule applications relative to the length of the input needed in the worst case.

These parameters are independent of each other and apply in principle to any rule-based grammar formalism.

In LA Grammar, the amount parameter depends solely on the categorial operations co_i (10.2.1), while the number parameter is determined completely by the degree of ambiguity. Thus, there are two obvious main approaches to restricting LA Grammars.

11.2.2 MAIN APPROACHES TO RESTRICTING LA GRAMMAR

R1: Restrictions on the form of categorial operations in order to limit the maximal amount of computation required by arbitrary rule applications.
R2: Restrictions on the degree of ambiguity in order to limit the maximal number of possible rule applications.

Approach *R1* in turn suggests two subtypes of restrictions.

11.2.3 POSSIBLE RESTRICTIONS ON CATEGORIAL OPERATIONS

R1.1: Specifying upper bounds for the *length* of categories.
R1.2: Specifying restrictions on *patterns* used in the definition of categorial operations.

These different ways of restricting categorial operations result in two subclasses of A LAGs, called B LAGs and C LAGs. The B LAGs are defined in terms of a *linear bound* on the length of categories relative to the length of the input and correspond to the restriction type *R1.1*.

11.2.4 DEFINITION OF THE CLASS OF B LAGS

The class of *bounded* LA Grammars, or B LAGs, consists of grammars in which for any complete well-formed expression E the length of intermediate sentence start categories is bounded by k · n, where n is the length of E and k is a constant.

The language class generated by the B LAGs is equal to the class of context-sensitive languages in the PS Grammar hierarchy. The proof[5] is analogous to 11.1.3 and based on corresponding restrictions on linearly bound automata, using the LA category of the last combination step as a tape. The B LAGs are a proper subset of the A LAGs because CS $\subset$ REC.[6]

In a B LAG, a categorial operation may be any total recursive function. Therefore, there is no limit on the amount of computation required by a rule application. We define the C LAGs as a subclass of the B LAGs by limiting the amount of computation required by individual categorial operations co_i by a *constant*. This restriction of type *R1.2* is implemented by defining formal patterns which distinguish between constant and nonconstant amounts of computation.

In the following rule schemata, the amount of computation required by the categorial operations is constant, independent of the length of the input categories.

11.2.5 RULE SCHEMATA WITH CONSTANT CATEGORIAL OPERATIONS

$$r_i: (seg_1 \ldots seg_k \; X) \; cat_2 \Rightarrow cat_3 \; rp_i$$
$$r_i: (X \; seg_1 \ldots seg_k) \; cat_2 \Rightarrow cat_3 \; rp_i$$
$$r_i: (seg_1 \ldots seg_m \; X \; seg_{m+1} \ldots seg_k) \; cat_2 \Rightarrow cat_3 \; rp_i$$

These schemata have in common that the pattern matching of the categorial operation has to check exactly k segments in the *ss* category. These patterns of categorial operations are constant because their patterns always check a category from the outer ends $seg_1 \ldots seg_k$, disregarding an arbitrarily large sequence in the middle of the category.

Categorial operations without this property do not provide a constant upper bound on the amount of computation required. A rule schema with a nonconstant categorial operation is illustrated below.

11.2.6 RULE SCHEMA WITH NONCONSTANT CATEGORIAL OPERATION

$$r_i: (X \; seg_1 \ldots seg_k \; Y) \; cat_2 \Rightarrow cat_3 \; rp_i$$

In rules of this form, the pattern matching has to search through an arbitrary number of category segments (represented by X or Y, depending on which side the search begins). Because the length of X and Y may have become arbitrarily long in previous rule applications, the amount of computation needed to perform the categorial operation depends on the overall length of the *ss*-category.

LA Grammars of which the rules use only constant categorial operations constitute the class of C LAGs:

---

[5] CoL, Theorem 5, p. 142.

[6] Hopcroft and Ullman (1979), Theorem 9.8, p. 228. CS stands for the class of context-sensitive languages and REC for the class of recursive languages.

11.2.7 DEFINITION OF THE CLASS OF C LAGS

The class of *constant* LA Grammars, or C LAGs, consists of grammars in which no categorial operation co_i looks at more than k segments in the sentence start categories, for a finite constant k.[7]

The LA Grammar classes considered so far constitute the following hierarchy:

11.2.8 THE HIERARCHY OF A LAGS, B LAGS, AND C LAGS

The class of A LAGs accepts and generates all recursive languages, the class of B LAGs accepts and generates all context-sensitive languages, and the class of C LAGs accepts and generates many context-sensitive, all context-free, and all regular languages.

That all context-free languages are recognized and generated by the C LAGs is proven[8] by C LAGs with categorial operations which modify only the beginning of the cat_1 pattern and thus correspond to the restrictions on pushdown automata. The class of context-free languages is a *proper* subset of the C languages because the C languages contain also context-sensitive languages (e.g., 10.2.3).

The class of regular languages is accepted and generated by C LAGs in which the length of the categories is restricted by an absolute constant k.[9] The regular, context-free, and context-sensitive languages of the PS Grammar hierarchy have thus been reconstructed in LA Grammar.[10]

---

[7] This finite constant will vary between different grammars.

[8] CoL, Theorem 4, p. 138.

A context-free C LAG (cf LAG for short) consists only of rules with the form

r_i: (aX) (b) $\Rightarrow$ (αX) rp_i, with a, b $\in$ C and $\alpha \in C^+$

This restriction on the *ss*- and *ss'*-categories corresponds to the working of a PDA which may write not just one symbol but a sequence of symbols into the stack (Hopcroft and Ullman 1979, Chap. 5.2). The following two assertions have to be proven:

1. For each PDA M, a cf LAG σ may be constructed such that L(M) = L(σ).
This implies CF $\subseteq C_{cf}$.
2. For each cf LAG σ, a PDA M may be constructed such that L(σ) = L(M).
This implies $C_{cf} \subseteq$ CF.

In showing 1 and 2, one has to take into consideration that a cf LAG uses rules while a PDA uses states, which are not entirely equivalent. Thus, it is necessary to provide a constructive procedure to convert states into rules and rules into states – a cumbersome, but not particularly difficult task.

Note with respect to 1 that ε-moves are forbidden in cf LAGs, but not in PDAs (Hopcroft and Ullman 1979, p. 24). However, there exists for each context-free language a PDA working without ε-moves (Harrison 1978, Theorem 5.5.1) and for an ε-free PDA a cf LAG may be constructed.

[9] CoL, Theorem 3, p. 138.

[10] Another possibility for modifying the generative capacity of LA Grammar consists – at least theoretically – in changing clause 4 of the algebraic definition 10.2.1. For example,

11.3 Ambiguity in LA Grammar

The second main approach to restricting LA Grammar (*R2* in 11.2.2) concerns the number of rule applications. This number is determined by the following factors:

11.3.1 FACTORS DETERMINING THE NUMBER OF RULE APPLICATIONS

The number of rule applications in an LA derivation depends on

1. the length of the input;
2. the number of rules in the rule package to be applied in a certain combination to the analyzed input pair (reading);
3. the number of readings[11] existing at each combination step.

Factor 1 is grammar-independent and used as the length n in formulas characterizing complexity (8.2.1).

Factor 2 is a grammar-dependent constant. For example, if the largest rule package of an LAG contains five rules, then the maximal number of rule applications in an unambiguous derivation will be at most $5 \cdot n$, where n is the length of the input.

Only factor 3 may push the total number of rule applications beyond a linear increase. In a given left-associative composition, an additional reading comes about when more than one rule in the current rule package applies successfully to the input. Whether for a given input more than one rule in a rule package may be successful depends on the input conditions of the rules.

---

if the categorial operations had been defined as arbitrary *partial recursive functions*, then LA Grammar would generate exactly the recursively enumerable languages. This would amount to an increase of generative capacity, making LA Grammar weakly equivalent to PS Grammar. Alternatively, if the categorial operations had been defined as arbitrary *primitive recursive functions*, then it could be shown by analogy to Theorem 2 that the resulting kind of LA Grammar generates exactly the primitive recursive languages. This would amount to a decrease in generative capacity compared to the standard definition.

Using alternative definitions of clause 4 in 10.2.1 is not a good method to obtain different subclasses of LA Grammar, however. First, alternating the categorial operations between partial recursive, total recursive, and primitive recursive functions is a very crude method. Secondly, the resulting language classes are much too big to be of practical interest: even though the primitive recursive functions are a proper subset of the total recursive functions, the primitive recursive functions properly contain the whole class of context-sensitive languages. Third, the categorial operations have been defined as total recursive functions in 10.2.1 for good reason, ensuring that basic LA Grammar has the highest generative capacity possible while still being decidable.

[11] For reasons of simplicity, only syntactic causes of ambiguity are considered here. Lexical ambiguities arising from multiple analyses of words have so far been largely ignored in formal language theory, but are unavoidable in the LA Grammatical analysis of natural language. The possible impact of lexical ambiguity on complexity is discussed in CoL, pp. 157f. and 248f.

Between the input conditions of two rules one of the following relations must hold:

11.3.2 POSSIBLE RELATIONS BETWEEN INPUT CONDITIONS

1. *Incompatible* input conditions: two rules have incompatible input conditions if there exist no input pairs which are accepted by both rules.
2. *Compatible* input conditions: two rules have compatible input conditions if there exists at least one input pair accepted by both rules and there exists at least one input pair accepted by one rule, but not the other.
3. *Identical* input conditions: two rules have identical input conditions if it holds for all input pairs that they are either accepted by both rules or rejected by both rules.

Examples of *incompatible* input conditions are (a X) (b) and (c X) (b), as well as (a X) (b) and (a X) (c). If all the rules in a rule package have incompatible input conditions, the use of this rule package cannot be the cause of a syntactic ambiguity.

11.3.3 DEFINITION OF UNAMBIGUOUS LA GRAMMARS

> An LA Grammar is unambiguous if and only if (i) it holds for all rule packages that their rules have *incompatible* input conditions, and (ii) there are no lexical[12] ambiguities.

Examples of unambiguous C LAGs are 10.2.2 for $a^k b^k$ and 10.2.3 for $a^k b^k c^k$.

An example of *compatible* input conditions is (a X) (b) and (X a) (b). Compatible input conditions are the formal precondition for syntactic ambiguity in LA Grammar.

11.3.4 DEFINITION OF SYNTACTICALLY AMBIGUOUS LA GRAMMARS

> An LA Grammar is syntactically ambiguous if and only if (i) it has at least one rule package containing at least two rules with *compatible* input conditions, and (ii) there are no lexical ambiguities.

The number of possible readings produced by a syntactically ambiguous LA Grammar depends on its ambiguity structure, which may be characterized in terms of the two binary features ±global and ±recursive. We begin with the feature ±global.

---

[12] An LA Grammar is lexically ambiguous if its lexicon contains at least two analyzed words with the same surface. A nonlinguistic example of a lexical ambiguity is propositional calculus , e.g., $(x \lor y \lor z) \land (...) ...$, whereby the propositional variables x, y, z, etc., may be analyzed lexically as ambiguous between [x (1)] and [x (0)], [y (1)] and [y (0)], etc. Thereby [x (1)] is taken to represent a true proposition x, and [x (0)] a false one.

While syntactic ambiguities arise in the rule-based derivation of more than one new sentence start, lexical ambiguities are caused by additional readings of the next word. Syntactic and lexical ambiguities can also occur at the same time in an LA Grammar. Furthermore, syntactic ambiguities can be reformulated into lexical ambiguities and vice versa (TCS, pp. 303f.)

In linguistics, a sentence is called syntactically ambiguous if it has more than one reading or structural analysis, as in the following example:

11.3.5 +GLOBAL SYNTACTIC AMBIGUITY

Flying airplanes can be dangerous.

One reading refers to airborne planes, the other to the activity of piloting. This ambiguity is +global because it is a property of the whole sentence.

Besides +global ambiguity there is also −global (or local) ambiguity in the time-linear analysis of language. For example, when reading the following sentence from left to right there are two readings up to and including the word barn:

11.3.6 −GLOBAL SYNTACTIC AMBIGUITY

The horse raced by the barn fell.

The first reading interprets raced by the barn as the predicate of the main clause. This initially dominant reading is −global, however, because it is eliminated by the continuation with fell. The second reading interprets raced by the barn as a reduced relative clause and survives as the only reading of the overall sentence. Such examples are called *garden path sentences* because they suggest an initial interpretation which cannot be maintained.

In LA Grammar, the difference between +global and −global ambiguities consists in whether more than one reading survives to the end of the sentence (11.3.5) or not (11.3.6). Thereby, +global and −global readings are treated alike as parallel time-linear derivation branches. This is in contrast to the substitution-based systems of C and PS Grammar, which recognize only ambiguities which are +global.

The ±global distinction has no impact on complexity in LA Grammar and is made mainly for linguistic reasons. The ±recursive distinction, on the other hand, is crucial for the analysis of complexity, because it can be shown that in LA Grammars with nonrecursive ambiguities the maximal number of rule applications per combination step is limited by a grammar-dependent constant (11.3.7, Theorem 3).

An ambiguity is +recursive if it originates within a recursive loop of rule applications. In other words, a certain state (cat rp_i) has several continuations for a certain next word category, such that one or more of these continuations eventually return to this particular state, thus enabling a repetition of the ambiguity split. Examples of C LAGs with +recursive, −global ambiguities are 11.5.4 for WW^R and 11.5.6 for WW; a C LAG with +recursive, +global ambiguities is 11.5.8 for SubsetSum.

An ambiguity is −recursive if none of the branches produced in the ambiguity split returns to the state which caused the ambiguity. Examples of −recursive ambiguity are the C LAG for $a^k b^k c^m d^m \cup a^k b^m c^m d^k$ (11.5.2), which is +global, and the C LAGs for natural language in Chaps. 17 and 18, which exhibit both +global and −global ambiguities.

11.3.7 THEOREM 3

The maximal number of rule applications in LA Grammar with only −recursive ambiguities is

$$(n - (R - 2)) \cdot 2^{(R-2)}$$

for $n > (R - 2)$, where n is the length of the input and R is the number of rules in the grammar.

Proof Parsing an input of length n requires $(n - 1)$ combination steps. If an LA Grammar has R rules, then one of these rules has to be reapplied after R combination steps at the latest. Furthermore, the maximal number of rule applications in a combination step for a given reading is R.

According to the definition of −recursive ambiguity, rules causing a syntactic ambiguity may not be reapplied in a time-linear derivation path (reading). The first ambiguity-causing rule may produce a maximum of $R - 1$ new branches (assuming its rule package contains all R rules except for itself), the second ambiguity causing rule may produce a maximum of $R - 2$ new branches, etc. If the different rules of the LA Grammar are defined with their maximally possible rule packages, then after $R - 2$ combination steps a maximum of $2^{(R-2)}$ readings is reached. □

Theorem 3 means that in LA Grammars which are not recursively ambiguous the number of rule applications grows only linearly with the length of the input.

11.4 Complexity of Grammars and Automata

The complexity of a grammar kind and its language class is measured in terms of the amount of primitive operations required to process an input in the worst case. Which operation is suitable to serve as the primitive operation and how the number of primitive operations required should be determined, however, is not always obvious.

This holds in particular for grammar formalisms which are not type-transparent. Historically, the complexity of PS Grammar kinds and their language classes was not specified directly in terms of grammar properties, but rather in terms of equivalent abstract automata.[13] These automata each have their own kind of primitive operation.

---

[13] Abstract automata consist of such components as a read/write-head, a write-protected input tape, a certain number of working tapes, the movement of the read/write-head on a certain tape from one cell to another, the reading or deleting of the content in a cell, etc. Classic examples of abstract automata are Turing machines (TMs), linearly bounded automata (LBAs), pushdown automata (PDAs), and finite state automata (FSAa). There is a multitude of additional abstract automata, each defined for the purpose of proving various special complexity, equivalence, and computability properties.

In order to establish the complexity of the Earley algorithm (9.3.4), for example, the primitive operation was chosen first and motivated as follows:

> The Griffith and Petrick data is not in terms of actual time, but in terms of "primitive operations." They have expressed their algorithms as sets of nondeterministic rewriting rules for a Turing-machine-like device. Each application of one of these is a primitive operation. We have chosen as our primitive operation the act of adding a state to a state set (or attempting to add one which is already there). We feel that this is comparable to their primitive operation because both are in some sense the most complex operation performed by the algorithm whose complexity is independent of the size of the grammar and the input string.

Earley (1970), p. 100

Thus, the complexity statement "context-free PS Grammars parse in n^3" does not apply to context-free PS Grammars directly, but to a certain parsing algorithm which takes PS Grammars of this class as input. Accordingly, when Valiant (1975) was able to reduce the complexity of the context-free languages from n^3 to $n^{2.8}$, this was due not to an improvement in PS Grammar, but rather to Valiant's finding an improved parsing algorithm defined as an abstract automaton.

In contrast, the C LAGs make it possible to define the primitive operation (i) directly for the grammar formalism and (ii) transfer it to its parser.

11.4.1 PRIMITIVE OPERATION OF THE C LAGS

The primitive operation of the C LAGs is a rule application (also counting unsuccessful attempts).

Rule applications are suitable as the primitive operation of C LAGs because the computation needed by their categorial operations is limited by a constant. That the primitive operation of C LAGs may double as the primitive operation of its parser is due to the type transparency (9.3.1) of LA Grammar.

It follows that the complexity of C LAGs depends solely on their degree of ambiguity. The linguistic notion of ambiguity is closely related to the automata-theoretic notion of nondeterminism. Before investigating the complexity properties of C LAGs, let us therefore clarify the distinction between deterministic and nondeterministic automata in its relation to LA Grammar.

An automaton is called deterministic if each derivation step of its algorithm permits at most one next step. In this sense, all unambiguous LA Grammars (11.3.3) are deterministic.

An automaton is called nondeterministic if its algorithm has to choose between several (though finitely many) next steps, or equivalently, has to perform several next steps simultaneously. In this sense, all ambiguous LA Grammars (11.3.4) are nondeterministic.[14]

---

[14] In PS Grammar, the notions deterministic and nondeterministic have no counterparts.

A nondeterministic automaton accepts an input if at least one possible path ends in an accepting state. A problem kind has the nondeterministic time complexity NTIME(f(n)) if the longest accepted path requires f(n) operations (where n stands for the length of the input). A problem kind has the nondeterministic space complexity NSPACE(f(n)) if the longest accepted path requires f(n) memory cells.

NTIME and NSPACE complexity are based on the assumption that the nondeterministic automaton can *guess* the longest accepted path. Thus, NTIME and NSPACE must be seen in light of the fact that there may exist many alternative paths which may have to be computed in order to arrive at a solution, but which are not taken into account by these complexity measurements.

In the case of a deterministic automaton, on the other hand, a problem kind is characterized in terms of the time complexity DTIME(f(n)) and the space complexity DSPACE(f(n)). Because by definition there may exist at most one path, DTIME and DSPACE specify the actual amount of time and space units required by a deterministic automaton.

The distinction between the deterministic and the nondeterministic versions of automata has raised the question of whether or not their generative capacity is equivalent. In the case of finite state automata (FSAs) it holds for each language L, that if L is accepted by a nondeterministic FSA then there exists an equivalent deterministic FSA which also accepts L.[15] A corresponding result holds for Turing machines (TMs).[16]

In pushdown automata (PDAs), on the other hand, the deterministic and nondeterministic versions are not equivalent in generative capacity.[17] For example, WW^R (11.5.4) is accepted by a nondeterministic PDA, but not by a deterministic one. In the case of linear bounded automata (LBAs), finally, it is not known whether the set of languages accepted by deterministic LBAs is a *proper* subset of the set of languages accepted by nondeterministic LBAs (LBA problem).

Thus, the following relations hold between deterministic and nondeterministic versions of the automata FSA, PDA, LBA, and TM:

DFSA $=$ NFSA
DPDA $\subset$ NDPA
DLBA ? NLBA
DTM $=$ NTM

Automata in which the deterministic and nondeterministic versions are equivalent raise the additional question of to what degree the space requirement is increased in the transition from the nondeterministic to the deterministic version.

Given the distinction between deterministic (unambiguous) and nondeterministic (ambiguous) LA Grammars, the automata-theoretic notions of complexity, especially

---

[15] Rabin and Scott (1959).

[16] Hopcroft and Ullman (1979), p. 164, Theorem 7.3.

[17] Hopcroft and Ullman (1979), p. 113.

NTIME and DTIME, may be applied to them. It holds in particular that

DTIME complexity of unambiguous C LAGs $= C \cdot (n - 1)$
NTIME complexity of ambiguous C LAG $\quad = C \cdot (n - 1),$

where C is a constant and n is the length of the input.

The reason is that – based on the left-associative derivation structure – each accepted input of length n is analyzed in $n - 1$ combination steps, whereby the rule applications of each combination step take the time required for the constant amount of computation C. In other words, unambiguous C LAGs are of *deterministic linear* time complexity,[18] while ambiguous C LAGs are of *nondeterministic linear* time complexity.

From a theoretical point of view, the applicability of DTIME and NTIME to LA Grammar is of general interest because it facilitates the transfer of results and open questions between automata theory and LA Grammar. For example, the question of whether the class of C LAGs is a *proper* subset of the class of B LAGs may be shown to be equivalent to the LBA problem, i.e., the open question of whether or not DLBA is *properly* contained in NLBA (cf. also Sect. 12.2).

From a practical point of view, however, the automata-theoretic complexity measures have the disadvantage that DTIME applies only to unambiguous LA Grammars and NTIME only to ambiguous ones. Furthermore, the notion of NTIME does not specify the actual amount of computation required to analyze arbitrary new input, but only the amount of computation needed to verify a known result.

In order to employ a realistic method of measuring complexity, which moreover can be applied uniformly to ambiguous and nonambiguous grammars alike, the following complexity analysis of C LAGs will be specified in terms of the total number of rule applications (relative to the length of the input) required to analyze arbitrary new input in the worst case. In LA Grammar, this grammar-based method of measuring complexity is as simple as it is natural.

11.5 Subhierarchy of C1, C2, and C3 LAGs

Compared to the A and B LAGs, the C LAGs constitute the most restricted class of LAGs, generating the smallest LA class of languages. However, compared to the context-free languages (which are properly contained in the C languages), the class of C languages is quite large. It is therefore theoretically interesting and practically useful to differentiate the C LAGs further into subclasses by defining a subhierarchy.

Because the complexity of C LAGs is measured by the number of rule applications, and because the number of rule applications depends solely on the ambiguity

---

[18] Strictly speaking, unambiguous C LAGs have a complexity even better (i.e., lower) than deterministic linear time, namely *real time*.

structure, it is natural to define subclasses of C LAGs in terms of different degrees of ambiguity. These subclasses are called the C1, C2, and C3 LAGs, whereby increasing degrees of ambiguity are reflected in increasing degrees of complexity.

The subclass with the lowest complexity and the lowest generative capacity are the C1 LAGs. A C LAG is a C1 LAG if it is not recursively ambiguous. The class of C1 languages parses in linear time and contains all deterministic context-free languages which can be recognized by a DPDA without ε-moves, plus context-free languages with $-$recursive ambiguities, e.g., $a^k b^k c^m d^m \cup a^k b^m c^m d^k$, as well as many context-sensitive languages, e.g., $a^k b^k c^k$, $a^k b^k c^k d^k e^k$, $\{a^k b^k c^k\}^*$, L_{square}, L^k_{hast}, a^{2^i}, $a^k b^m c^{k \cdot m}$, and $a^{i!}$, whereby the last one is not even an index language.[19]

Another example of an unambiguous context-sensitive C1 LAGs is the following definition for $a^{2^i} =_{def} \{a^i \mid i$ is a positive power of $2\}$:

11.5.1 C1 LAG FOR CONTEXT-SENSITIVE a^{2^i}

$LX =_{def} \{[a\ (a)]\}$
$ST_S =_{def} \{[(a)\ \{r_1\}]\}$
$r_1:$ (a)   (a) $\Rightarrow$ (aa) $\{r_2\}$
$r_2:$ (aX)   (a) $\Rightarrow$ (Xbb) $\{r_2, r_3\}$
$r_3:$ (bX)   (a) $\Rightarrow$ (Xaa) $\{r_2, r_3\}$
$ST_F =_{def} \{[(aa)\ rp_1], [(bXb)\ rp_2], [(aXa)\ rp_3]\}$.

This C1 LAG is unambiguous because r_1 applies only once and r_2 and r_3 have incompatible input conditions. A comparison with corresponding PS Grammars for a^{2^i} illustrates the formal and conceptual simplicity of LA Grammar.[20]

A C1 LAG with a $+$global, $-$recursive ambiguity is 11.5.2 for the context-free language $a^k b^k c^m d^m \cup a^k b^m c^m d^k$. In PS Grammar, this language is called *inherently ambiguous* because there does not exist an unambiguous PS Grammar for it.[21]

11.5.2 C1 LAG FOR AMBIGUOUS $a^k b^k c^m d^m \cup a^k b^m c^m d^k$

$LX =_{def} \{[a\ (a)], [b\ (b)], [c\ (c)], [d\ (d)]\}$
$ST_S =_{def} \{[(a)\ \{r_1, r_2, r_5\}]\}$
$r_1: (X)$ (a) $\Rightarrow$ (a X) $\{r_1, r_2, r_5\}$
$r_2: (a\ X)$ (b) $\Rightarrow$ (X) $\{r_2, r_3\}$
$r_3: (X)$ (c) $\Rightarrow$ (c X) $\{r_3, r_4\}$

---

[19] A C1 LAG for $a^k b^k c^m d^m \cup a^k b^m c^m d^k$ is defined in 11.5.2, for L_{square} and L^k_{hast} in Stubert (1993), pp. 16 and 12, for $a^k b^k c^k d^k e^k$ in CoL, p. 233, for $a^k b^m c^{k \cdot m}$ in TCS, p. 296, and for a^{2^i} in 11.5.1. A C1 LAG for $a^{i!}$ is sketched in TCS, p. 296, footnote 13.

[20] Hopcroft and Ullman (1979) present the canonical context-sensitive PS Grammar of a^{2^i} on p. 224, and a version as an unrestricted PS Grammar on p. 220.

[21] Cf. Hopcroft and Ullman (1979), pp. 99–103.

r_4: (c X)   (d) $\Rightarrow$ (X) $\{r_4\}$
r_5: (X)   (b) $\Rightarrow$ (b X)$\{r_5, r_6\}$
r_6: (b X)   (c) $\Rightarrow$ (X) $\{r_6, r_7\}$
r_7: (a X)   (d) $\Rightarrow$ (X) $\{r_7\}$
$ST_F =_{def} \{[\varepsilon \; rp_4], [\varepsilon \; rp_7]\}$

This C1 LAG contains a syntactic ambiguity in accordance with definition 11.3.4: the rule package rp_1 contains the input compatible rules r_2 and r_5. Nevertheless, the grammar parses in linear time because the ambiguous continuations are not part of a recursion: rp_2 and rp_5 do not contain r_1. In the worst case, e.g., aabbccdd, the grammar generates two analyses based on two parallel time-linear paths which begin after the initial a-sequence.[22]

The kind of C LAG with the second lowest complexity and the second lowest generative capacity are the C2 LAGs. A C LAG is a C2 LAG if (i) it generates +recursive ambiguities and (ii) the ambiguities are restricted by the single return principle.

11.5.3 THE SINGLE RETURN PRINCIPLE (SRP)

A +recursive ambiguity is single return if exactly one of the parallel paths returns to the state resulting in the ambiguity in question.

The class of C2 languages parses in polynomial time and contains certain nondeterministic context-free languages like WW^R and L^∞_{hast}, plus context-sensitive languages like WW, $W^{k \geq 3}$, $\{WWW\}^*$, and $W_1 W_2 W_1^R W_2^R$.[23]

An SR-recursive ambiguity is illustrated by the following C2 LAG for WW^R. As explained in Sect. 8.3, this language consists of an arbitrarily long sequence W of arbitrary words, followed by the inverse of this sequence W^R.

11.5.4 C2 LAG FOR CONTEXT-FREE WW^R

$LX =_{def} \{[a \; (a)], [b \; (b)], [c \; (c)], [d \; (d)] \dots \}$
$ST_S =_{def} \{[(seg_c) \; \{r_1, r_2\}]\}$, where $seg_c \in \{a, b, c, d, \dots\}$
r_1: (X) (seg_c) $\Rightarrow$ $(seg_c \; X)$ $\{r_1, r_2\}$
r_2: $(seg_c \; X)$ (seg_c) $\Rightarrow$ (X) $\{r_2\}$
$ST_F =_{def} \{[\varepsilon \; rp_2]\}$

Each time r_1 has been applied successfully, r_1 and r_2 are attempted in the next composition. As soon, however, as r_2 is successful, the derivation cannot return to r_1 because r_1 is not listed in the rule package of r_2. Therefore, only one branch of the ambiguity (i.e., the one resulting from repeated applications of r_1) can return into the recursion.

---

[22] An explicit derivation is given in CoL, pp. 154f.

[23] A C2 LAG for WW^R is defined in 11.5.4, for L^∞_{hast} in Stubert 1993, p. 16, for WW in 11.5.6, for WWW in CoL, p. 215, for $W^{k \geq 3}$ in CoL, p. 216, and for $W_1 W_2 W_1^R W_2^R$ in 11.5.7.

The worst case in parsing WW^R is inputs consisting of an even number of the same word. This is illustrated below with the input a a a a a a:

11.5.5 DERIVATION STRUCTURE OF THE WORST CASE IN WW^R

rules:	applications:
2	a\$a
122	aa\$aa
11222	aaa\$aaa
11122	aaaa\$aa
11112	aaaaa\$a
11111	aaaaaa\$

The unmarked middle of the intermediate strings generated in the course of the derivation is indicated by $. Of the six hypotheses established in the course of the left-associative analysis, the first two are invalidated by the fact that the input string continues, the third hypothesis correctly corresponds to the input a a a a a a, and the remaining three hypotheses are invalidated by the fact that the input does not provide any more words.

A C2 LAG for a context-sensitive language is illustrated by the following definition:

11.5.6 C2 LAG FOR CONTEXT-SENSITIVE WW

$LX =_{def}$ {[a (a)], [b (b)], [c (c)], [d (d)] ... }
$ST_S =_{def}$ {[(seg$_c$) {r$_1$, r$_2$}]}, where seg$_c$ ∈ {a, b, c, d, ... }
r_1: (X)   (seg$_c$) ⇒ (X seg$_c$)   {r$_1$, r$_2$}
r_2: (seg$_c$ X) (seg$_c$) ⇒ (X)   {r$_2$}
$ST_F =_{def}$ {[ε rp$_2$]}

This grammar resembles 11.5.4 except for the result category of r_1: in context-sensitive WW, r_1 defines the category pattern (X seg$_c$), while in context-free WW^R, r_1 defines the category pattern (seg$_c$ X). The worst case for context-sensitive WW and context-free WW^R is the same. The respective C2 LAGs are both SR-ambiguous, and are both of n^2 complexity. The n^2 increase of readings in the analysis of the worst case of WW^R and WW is clearly visible in 11.5.5.

A C2 LAG of n^3 complexity is the nondeterministic context-sensitive language $W_1W_2W_1^RW_2^R$ devised by Stubert.

11.5.7 C2 LAG FOR CONTEXT-SENSITIVE $W_1W_2W_1^RW_2^R$

$LX =_{def}$ {[a (a)], [b (b)]}
$ST_S =_{def}$ {[(seg$_c$) {r$_{1a}$}], [(seg$_c$) {r$_{1b}$}]}, where seg$_c$, seg$_d$ ∈ {a, b}
r_{1a}: (seg$_c$)   (seg$_d$) ⇒ (# seg$_c$ seg$_d$)   {r$_2$, r$_3$}
r_{1b}: (seg$_c$)   (seg$_d$) ⇒ (seg$_d$ # seg$_c$)   {r$_3$, r$_4$}
r_2: (X)   (seg$_c$) ⇒ (X seg$_c$)   {r$_2$, r$_3$}
r_3: (X)   (seg$_c$) ⇒ (seg$_c$ X)   {r$_3$, r$_4$}

r_4: (X seg_c)   (seg_c) $\Rightarrow$ (X) $\{r_4, r_5\}$
r_5: (seg_c X #)   (seg_c) $\Rightarrow$ (X) $\{r_6\}$
r_6: (seg_c X)   (seg_c) $\Rightarrow$ (X) $\{r_6\}$
$ST_F =_{def} \{[\varepsilon\ rp_5], [\varepsilon\ rp_6]\}$

The exact complexity of this language is $\frac{1}{8}n^3 + \frac{1}{4}n^2 + \frac{1}{2}n$. The degree of polynomial complexity depends apparently on the maximal number of SR-recursive ambiguities in a derivation. Thus, a C2 LAG with one SR-recursive ambiguity can be parsed in n^2, a C2 LAG with two SR-recursive ambiguities can be parsed in n^3, etc.

The subclass with the highest complexity and generative capacity is the C3 LAGs. A C LAG is a C3 LAG if it generates unrestricted +recursive ambiguities. The class of C3 languages parses in exponential time and contains the deterministic context-free language L_{no}, the hardest context-free language HCFL, plus context-sensitive languages like SubsetSum and SAT, which are $\mathcal{NP}$-complete.[24]

A language known to be inherently complex, requiring exponential time irrespective of the algorithm used, is SubsetSum. Its expressions y#a_1#a_2#a_3# ... #a_n# are defined such that y, a_1, a_2, ..., a_n are all binary strings containing the same number of digits. Furthermore, when viewed as binary numbers presenting the least significant digit first, y is equal to the sum of a subset of the a_i.

11.5.8 C3 LAG FOR SUBSETSUM

$LX =_{def} \{[0\ (0)], [1\ (1)], [\#\ (\#)]\}$
$ST_S =_{def} \{[(seg_c)\ \{r_1, r_2\}]\}$, where $seg_c \in \{0, 1\}$
     $seg_c \in \{0, 1\}$

r_1: (X)   (seg_c) $\Rightarrow$ (seg_c X) $\{r_1, r_2\}$
r_2: (X)   (#) $\Rightarrow$ (# X) $\{r_3, r_4, r_6, r_7, r_{12}, r_{14}\}$
r_3: (X seg_c)   (seg_c) $\Rightarrow$ (0 X) $\{r_3, r_4, r_6, r_7\}$
r_4: (X #)   (#) $\Rightarrow$ (# X) $\{r_3, r_4, r_6, r_7, r_{12}, r_{14}\}$
r_5: (X seg_c)   (seg_c) $\Rightarrow$ (0 X) $\{r_5, r_6, r_7, r_{11}\}$
r_6: (X 1)   (0) $\Rightarrow$ (1 X) $\{r_5, r_6, r_7, r_{11}\}$
r_7: (X 0)   (1) $\Rightarrow$ (1 X) $\{r_8, r_9, r_{10}\}$
r_8: (X seg_c)   (seg_c) $\Rightarrow$ (1 X) $\{r_8, r_9, r_{10}\}$
r_9: (X 1)   (0) $\Rightarrow$ (0 X) $\{r_5, r_6, r_7, r_{11}\}$
r_{10}: (X 0)   (1) $\Rightarrow$ (0 X) $\{r_8, r_9, r_{10}\}$
r_{11}: (X #)   (#) $\Rightarrow$ (# X) $\{r_3, r_4, r_6, r_7, r_{12}, r_{14}\}$
r_{12}: (X 0)   (seg_c) $\Rightarrow$ (0 X) $\{r_4, r_{12}, r_{14}\}$
r_{13}: (X 0)   (seg_c) $\Rightarrow$ (0 X) $\{r_{11}, r_{13}, r_{14}\}$
r_{14}: (X 1)   (seg_c) $\Rightarrow$ (1 X) $\{r_{11}, r_{13}, r_{14}\}$
$ST_F =_{def} \{[(X)\ rp_4]\}$

---

[24] A C3 LAG for L_{no} is defined in 12.3.3, for HCFL in Stubert (1993), p. 16, for SubsetSum in 11.5.8, and for SAT in TCS, footnote 19.

This C3 LAG (devised by Applegate) copies y into the category. Then the +recursive ambiguity arises by nondeterministically either subtracting or not subtracting each a_i from y. The grammar is of exponential complexity and enters an accepting state if the result of the subtraction is zero.

In conclusion, let us summarize the different restrictions on LA Grammar, the resulting hierarchy of LA Grammar classes, the associated classes of languages, and their complexity. The LA hierarchy resembles the PS hierarchy (8.1.2) insofar as the subclasses of the LAGs and their languages are defined in terms of increasing restrictions on the rule system.

The language class of the C1 LAGs is a subset of the C2 languages because the −recursive ambiguity structure of the C1 LAGs is more restricted than the SR-recursive ambiguities of the C2 LAGs (11.5.3). The language class of the C2 LAGs is a subset of the C3 languages because the SR-recursive ambiguity structure of the C2 LAGs is more restricted than the +recursive ambiguities of the C3 LAGs. The language class of the C3 LAGs is a subset of the B languages because the category patterns of the C LAGs are more restricted than those of the B LAGs. The language class of the B LAGs is a subset of the A languages because the categories assigned by B LAGs are restricted in length while those of the A LAGs are not.

The restrictions on LA Grammar apply directly to the two complexity parameters *amount* and *number* of rule applications (11.2.1).

11.5.9 KINDS OF RESTRICTION IN LA GRAMMAR

0. LA type A: no restriction
1. LA type B: The length of the categories of intermediate expressions is limited by $k \cdot n$, where k is a constant and n is the length of the input (*R1.1*, amount).
2. LA type C3: The form of the category patterns results in a constant limit on the amount of computation required by the categorial operations (*R1.2*, amount).
3. LA type C2: LA type C3 and the grammar is at most SR-recursively ambiguous (*R2*, number).
4. LA type C1: LA type C3 and the grammar is at most −recursively ambiguous (*R2*, number).

The amount and number parameters are controlled via (1) the length of categories assigned to intermediate expressions, (2) the form of the category patterns in the rules, (3) the possible reapplication of rules as defined by the rule packages, and (4) the input compatibility of rules in the same rule package.

The LA Grammar hierarchy is summarized in 11.5.10. Like the PS Grammar hierarchy 8.1.2, it is based on the structural relation between restrictions on the rule system, kinds of grammar, classes of languages, and degrees of complexity.

11.5.10 LA GRAMMAR HIERARCHY OF FORMAL LANGUAGES

restrictions	types of LAG	languages	complexity
LA type C1	C1 LAGs	C1 languages	linear
LA type C2	C2 LAGs	C2 languages	polynominal
LA type C3	C3 LAGs	C3 languages	exponential
LA type B	B LAGs	B languages	exponential
LA type A	A LAGs	A languages	decidable

Of the five different classes of LA Grammar, only the class of B languages occurs also in the PS Grammar hierarchy, namely as the class of context-sensitive languages. The class of A languages, on the other hand, is properly contained in the class of recursively enumerable languages generated by unrestricted PS Grammars. The classes of C1, C2 and C3 languages have no counterpart in the PS Grammar hierarchy. However, the PS Grammar class of regular languages is properly contained in the class of C1 languages, while the class of context-free languages is properly contained in the class of C3 languages.

Furthermore, compared to the restrictions on PS Grammar, which apply only to the form of the rules, the restrictions on LA Grammar apply to the rule system as a whole. This is because in LA Grammar the application of rules is handled explicitly in terms of the category patterns and rule packages, whereas in PS Grammar it is handled implicitly in terms of the variables contained in the rewrite rules.

Exercises

Section 11.1
1. Explain the notions of *total recursive function* and *partial recursive function*.
2. What is the formal characterization of the class of recursive languages in the hierarchy of PS Grammar?
3. What is the generative capacity of LA Grammar in its basic unrestricted form?
4. Explain the proofs in 11.1.2 and 11.1.3.
5. Describe the difference in generative capacity of unrestricted PS Grammar and unrestricted LA Grammar.

Section 11.2
1. What are possible structural restrictions on LA Grammar?
2. Explain the grammar classes of A LAGs, B LAGs, and C LAGs.

3. What is the difference between a constant and a nonconstant categorial operation?
4. Describe the reconstruction of the PS Grammar hierarchy in LA Grammar.
5. Is there a class of LA Grammar that generates the recursively enumerable languages?
6. Is there a class of PS Grammar that generates the recursive languages?
7. Is there a class of PS Grammar that generates the C languages?

Section 11.3
1. Explain the notions of ±global ambiguities. What is their relation to the notions of ±deterministic derivations in automata theory and the notion of ambiguity in PS Grammar.
2. What determines the number of rule applications in an LA derivation?
3. Describe three different relations between the input conditions of LA Grammar rules.
4. What is the definition of ambiguous and unambiguous LA Grammars?
5. Explain the notions of ±recursive ambiguity in LA Grammar.
6. Define the rule packages of a −recursively ambiguous LA Grammar with seven rules such that it is maximally ambiguous. How many readings are derived by this grammar after 4, 5, 6, 7, 8, and 9 combination steps, respectively?

Section 11.4
1. Explain the complexity parameters of LA Grammar.
2. How is the elementary operation of C LAGs defined?
3. Compare Earley's primitive operation for computing the complexity of his algorithm for context-free PS Grammars with that of the C LAGs.
4. How does Earley compute the amount and number parameters of context-free PS Grammar?
5. Name four notions of complexity in automata theory and explain them.
6. Explain the relation between the deterministic and nondeterministic versions of abstract automata.
7. Explain the application of the notions DTIME and NTIME to the C LAGs. What is the alternative?

Section 11.5
1. Describe the subhierarchy of the C1, C2, and C3 LAGs. What is the connection between ambiguity and complexity?
2. Define a C1 LAG for $a^k b^k c^m d^m \cup a^k b^m c^k d^m$, and explain how this grammar works. Is it ambiguous? What is its complexity?
3. Explain the single return principle.
4. Compare the handling of WW and WW^R in PS Grammar and LA Grammar.
5. Describe the well-formed expressions of SubsetSum, and explain why this language is inherently complex.

6. Explain the hierarchy of LA Grammar.

7. Describe the relation between PS Grammar and the nativist theory of language, on the one hand, and between LA Grammar and the SLIM theory, on the other. Would it be possible to use a PS Grammar as the syntactic component of the SLIM theory? Would it be possible to use an LA Grammar as the syntactic component of the nativist theory?

12. LA and PS Hierarchies in Comparison

Having presented two nonequivalent formalisms of grammar,[1] each with its own fully developed hierarchy of language and complexity classes, we return in this chapter to the formal properties of natural language. Section 12.1 compares the complexity of the LA and PS Grammar language classes. Section 12.2 describes the inclusion relations between language classes in the PS and the LA hierarchy, respectively. Section 12.3 defines a context-free language which is a C3 language. Section 12.4 describes the orthogonal relation between the context-free languages and the classes of C languages. Section 12.5 investigates ambiguity in natural language, and concludes that the natural languages are in the class of C1 LAGs, thus parsing in linear time.

12.1 Language Classes of LA and PS Grammar

A grammar formalism for natural language is like a suit. If the formalism chosen is too small – for example as a regular (type 3) PS Grammar (8.2.3) – there are phenomena which it cannot handle. If it is too large – for example a context-sensitive (type 1) PS Grammar – the characteristic structures of natural language will disappear in a formalism which allows one to describe the most complicated artificial structures as easily as the genuinely natural ones.

Furthermore, the 'larger' a formalism, the more 'expensive' it is in terms of mathematical complexity. Computationally, these costs appear as the amounts of time and memory required for the parsing of language expressions.

A formalism may not only be simply too small or too large for the description of natural language, but also too small and too large at the same time – like a pair of borrowed pants which turn out too short and too wide. For example, the formalism of context-free PS Grammar is too small for the description of natural language, as indicated by the introduction of transformations and similar extensions. At the same time it is too large, as shown by context-free languages like HCFL,[2] the structures of which have no counterpart in natural language.

---

[1] Namely PS Grammar in Chaps. 8 and 9, and LA Grammar in Chaps. 10 and 11.

[2] Hardest Context-Free Language, Greibach (1973).

R. Hausser, *Foundations of Computational Linguistics*,
DOI 10.1007/978-3-642-41431-2_12, © Springer-Verlag Berlin Heidelberg 2014

In principle, there is no theoretical or practical reason why it should not be possible to tailor a formalism of low generative capacity and complexity which really fits natural language. It is just that, despite great efforts, no such subformalism could be found within PS Grammar.

Alternative elementary formalisms are C Grammar and LA Grammar. C Grammar, however, has no fully developed hierarchy with different language classes and degrees of complexity. On the contrary, bidirectional C Grammar is weakly equivalent to context-free PS Grammar (Sect. 9.2).

Therefore, the only language hierarchy orthogonal to that of PS Grammar is that of LA Grammar. Regarding the four basicdegrees of complexity (8.2.1), the language classes of LA and PS Grammar compare as follows:

12.1.1 COMPLEXITY DEGREES OF THE LA AND PS HIERARCHY

	LA Grammar	PS Grammar
undecidable	–	recursively enumerable languages
decidable	A languages	–
exponential	B languages	context-sensitive languages
exponential	C3 languages	
polynomial	C2 languages	context-free languages
linear	C1 languages	regular languages

The nonequivalence of the elementary formalisms of LA and PS Grammar is shown by languages which are in the same class in PS Grammar, but in different classes in LA Grammar, and vice versa. For example, $a^k b^k$ and WW^R are in the same class in PS Grammar (i.e., context-free), but in different classes in LA Grammar: $a^k b^k$ is a C1 LAG parsing in linear time, while WW^R is a C2 LAG parsing in n^2. Conversely, $a^k b^k$ and $a^k b^k c^k$ are in the same class in LA Grammar (i.e., C1 LAGs), but in different classes in PS Grammar: $a^k b^k$ is context-free, while $a^k b^k c^k$ is context-sensitive.

That a language like $a^k b^k c^k$ can be classified into two different language classes (i.e., context-sensitive vs. C1) with different degrees of complexity (i.e., exponential vs. linear) depends on the distinction between the inherent complexity of an individual language and the complexity of its class.

The classification of $a^k b^k c^k$ as context-sensitive in PS Grammar is not because this language is inherently complex, but rather because no lower subclass of PS Grammar happens to fit its structure. It is therefore possible to define an alternative formalism which classifies $a^k b^k c^k$ in a class of linear complexity.

Furthermore, the lower language classes are defined as subsets of the higher language classes. A language like $a^k b^k$, for example, is called context-free in PS Grammar because this is the *smallest* language class containing it. Nominally, however, $a^k b^k$ is also a context-sensitive language, because the class of context-free languages is contained in the context-sensitive class. Therefore, a statement like "$a^k b^k c^k$ is a context-sensitive language which in LA Grammar is a C1 LAG parsing in linear time" is no contradiction: because the class of C1 languages is a subset of the class of B languages, the C1 LAGs are nominally also B LAGs (and thus context-sensitive).

12.2 Subset Relations in the Two Hierarchies

A language class X is a subset of another language class Y (formally $X \subseteq Y$) if all languages in X are also languages in Y. A language class X is a *proper* subset of another language class Y (formally $X \subseteq Y$) if X is a subset of Y and in addition there is at least one language in Y which is not an element of X.

The following subset relations hold for the language classes of the PS hierarchy:

12.2.1 SUBSET RELATIONS IN THE PS HIERARCHY

regular lang. $\subset$ context-free lang. $\subset$ context-sensitive lang. $\subset$ rec. enum. languages

These subset relations follow from decreasing restrictions on the rewrite rules of PS Grammar (Sect. 8.2) and are proper[3] subset relations.

The following subset relations hold for the language classes in the LA hierarchy:

12.2.2 SUBSET RELATIONS IN THE LA HIERARCHY

C1 languages $\subseteq$ C2 languages $\subseteq$ C3 languages $\subseteq$ B languages $\subset$ A languages

These subset relations follow likewise from decreasing restrictions. However, while the B languages are a proper subset of the A languages,[4] the proper inclusion of the other classes can only be surmised. In particular, the question of whether the class of C2 languages is a proper subset of the C3 languages corresponds to an unsolved problem of classic automata theory, namely whether $\mathcal{P} \subset \mathcal{NP}$ or $\mathcal{P} = \mathcal{NP}$ (Sect. 11.4).

The language class $\mathcal{NP}$ contains all languages which can be recognized in nondeterministic polynomial time, while $\mathcal{P}$ contains all languages which be recognized in deterministic polynomial time.

---

[3] Hierarchy lemma, Hopcroft and Ullman (1979), p. 228.

[4] See Hopcroft and Ullman (1979), p. 228, Theorem 9.8. The A LAGs generate the recursive languages while the B LAGs generate the context-sensitive languages, as shown in Sects. 11.1 and 11.2.

The languages recognizable in deterministic polynomial time form a natural and important class, the class $\bigcup_{i \geq 1}$ DTIME(n^i), which we denote by $\mathcal{P}$. It is an intuitively appealing notion that $\mathcal{P}$ is the class of problems that can be solved efficiently. Although one might quibble that an n^{57} step algorithm is not very efficient, in practice we find that problems in $\mathcal{P}$ usually have low-degree polynomial time solutions.

Hopcroft and Ullman (1979), p. 320

A language L is called $\mathcal{NP}$-complete if (i) all languages in $\mathcal{NP}$ can be reduced to L in deterministic polynomial time and (ii) L is in $\mathcal{NP}$. An $\mathcal{NP}$-complete language is designed to represent the worst case of nondeterministic polynomial complexity.

The classic, historically first, example of an $\mathcal{NP}$-complete language is SAT, the problem of Boolean SATisfiability.[5] Consider the following Boolean expression:

12.2.3 A WELL-FORMED EXPRESSION IN 3SAT

$$(x \vee \bar{y} \vee \bar{z}) \wedge (y \vee z \vee u) \wedge (x \vee z \vee \bar{u}) \wedge (\bar{x} \vee y \vee u)$$

The sign $\vee$ stands for the logical or (disjunction), the sign $\wedge$ stands for the logical and (conjunction), the letters represent variables for propositions, and the horizontal bar over some of the variables, e.g., $\bar{z}$, stands for negation. 3SAT is a slight simplification of SAT because 3SAT is restricted to conjunctions in which each conjunct consists of a disjunction containing three variables.

The problem of satisfying this expressions is to find an assignment for the variables which would make the expression true – if such an assignment exists. This problem is inherently complex because the analysis has to keep track of potentially 2^n different assignments. For example, the first variable x may be assigned the values 1 (true) or 0 (false). When the second variable y is encountered, four assignments must be distinguished, namely $(x = 1, y = 1)$, $(x = 1, y = 0)$, $(x = 0, y = 1)$ and $(x = 0, y = 0)$. In other words, each time a new variable is encountered, the number of possible assignments is doubled.

Another example of an $\mathcal{NP}$-complete language is the already familiar Subset Sum. Like 3SAT, Subset Sum is a C3 language, as shown by the definition of the C3 LAG in 11.5.8. Thus, the class of C3 languages contains $\mathcal{NP}$-complete languages. Furthermore, the class of C3 languages is obviously in $\mathcal{NP}$ because C LAGs verify by definition in nondeterministic linear time (Sect. 11.4) – and thus a fortiori in nondeterministic polynomial time.

The C2 languages, on the other hand, are designed to parse in deterministic polynomial time, for which reason they are contained in $\mathcal{P}$. The assumption that the class of C2 languages is not a proper subset of the class of C3 languages would imply that

the class of C2 languages = the class of C3 languages.

---

[5] Hopcroft and Ullman (1979), pp. 324f.

This would mean in turn that there exists a C2 LAG for Subset Sum, for example. Because all $\mathcal{NP}$ languages can be reduced in deterministic polynomial time to Subset Sum, it would follow that

$$\mathcal{P} = \mathcal{NP}.$$

The equivalence of $\mathcal{P}$ and $\mathcal{NP}$ is considered improbable, however, which strengthens the guess that the C2 languages are a proper subset of the C3 languages.[6]

Another open question is whether the class of C3 languages is a proper subset of the class of B languages. Here, one may speculate using the $\mathcal{NP}$-completeness of the C3 LAGs again. It is known that the recognition of context-sensitive languages (CS-recognition) is PSPACE-complete (Hopcroft and Ullman (1979) , pp. 346f.). Because it is improbable[7] that a PSPACE-complete problem is in $\mathcal{NP}$, it is also improbable that the class of C languages is not a proper subset of the set of B languages.

12.3 Nonequivalence of the LA and PS Hierarchy

A language which is context-free in PS Grammar, but a C3 language in LA Grammar, is L_{no} (or *noise* language) devised by Applegate. L_{no} generates expressions which consist of 0 and 1, and which have the structure W'#W^R. The symbol # separates W' and W^R, W^R is the mirror image of W, and W' differs from W by containing an arbitrary number of additional 0s and 1s. These additional words in W' are indistinguishable from those which have a counterpart in W^R and thus function as noise.

A context-free PS Grammar for this language is defined as follows:

12.3.1 PS GRAMMAR OF L_{no}

S → 1S1	S → 1S	S → #
S → 0S0	S → 0S	

The rules in the left column generate corresponding words preceding and following #, while the rules in the middle column generate only noise words in W'.

Traditional parsers for context-free languages like the Earley or the CYK algorithm have no difficulty in analyzing L_{no} in n^3. This is because the parser utilizes the basic inverse pair structure of context-free languages. The following PS Grammar derivation shows the corresponding states produced by the Earley algorithm (9.3.4):

---

[6] Assuming that the proper inclusion of C2 $\subset$ C3 could be shown directly (for example, by means of a pumping lemma for C2 languages), then this would imply $\mathcal{P} \subset \mathcal{NP}$ only if it can be shown that C2 $= \mathcal{P}$, which is improbable.

[7] Not only is a PSPACE-complete problem not likely to be in $\mathcal{P}$, it is also not likely to be in $\mathcal{NP}$. Hence the property whose existence is PSPACE-complete probably cannot even be *verified* in polynomial time using a polynomial length 'guess'.

Garey and Johnson (1979), p. 171

12.3.2 PS GRAMMAR DERIVATION OF 10010#101 IN L_{no}

derivation tree:	generated chains	states:	
S		1.S1	1S1.
1 S 1	1S1	1.S	
		0.S0	0S0.
0 S 0	10S01	0.S	
		0.S0	
0 S	100S01	0.S	0S.
		1.S1	1S1.
1 S 1	1001S101	1.S	
		0.S0	
0 S	10010S101	0.S	0S.
#	10010#101	#.	

The Earley algorithm generates only two states for each terminal symbol preceding # in L_{no}, for example '1.S1' and '1.S'. Thus, if # is preceded by k terminal symbols in the input chain, then the algorithm will produce 2k states by the time # is reached.[8]

In contrast, the categorial operations of the C LAGs reflect the structure of a double-ended queue. This structure is well suited for repetitions of arbitrary number, whereby the repetitions may be modified, e.g., inverted, doubled, halved, etc.

Parsers in general and C LAGs in particular are inefficient if the input contains an unknown number of words such that it can only be determined at the end of the analysis whether later words must correspond to earlier words or not. This is the characteristic property of $\mathcal{NP}$-hard languages, i.e., languages which require $\mathcal{N}$ondeterministic $\mathcal{P}$olynomial time for verification and exponential time for analysis.

For LA Grammar, context-free languages like HCFL[9] and L_{no}, on the one hand, and $\mathcal{NP}$-complete context-sensitive languages like 3SAT and Subset Sum, on the other, are structurally similar. These four languages have in common that in the first half of the input there may occur arbitrarily many words of which it is not known whether or not they are needed as counterparts in the second half.[10]

---

[8] Because L_{no} is a deterministic context-free language, it can be parsed in linear time in PS Grammar. Stubert (1993), p. 71, Lemma 5.1.

[9] HCFL parses in polynomial time in PS Grammar for several reasons:

1. Context-free PS Grammars use a different method of measuring complexity than C LAGs. More specifically, the n^3 time complexity for context-free languages in general depends crucially on the use of multi-tape Turing machines. The complexity of C LAGs, on the other hand, is determined on the basis of the grammars directly.

2. In contrast to abstract automata, no ε-moves are allowed in C LAGs.

[10] The C LAG complexity of context-free L_{no} is the same as that of the context-sensitive language L_{no}^3, which generates expressions of the structure W'#W#W", whereby W' and W" are noisy versions of W. The LA Grammar of L_{no} is in a higher complexity class than the corresponding PS Grammar because C LAGs are not designed to utilize the fixed inverse pair structure of the context-free languages, and because ε-moves are not permitted.

The only way a C LAG can analyze L_{no} is by assigning two interpretations to each word preceding #, one as a 'real' word and one as a 'noise' word. This results in an exponential number of readings for the input chain preceding #, each reading with its own category. For example, if the input is 10010#..., then one reading has the category (10010), representing the hypothesis that all words preceding # are 'real'. Another reading of this input has the category (1001), representing the hypothesis that the last word preceding # is noise, etc.

The following C3 LAG generates these hypotheses systematically from left to right:

12.3.3 C3 LAG FOR L_{no}

$LX =_{def} \{[0\ (0)], [1\ (1)], [\#\ (\#)]\}$

$ST_S =_{def} \{[(seg_c)\ \{r_1, r_2, r_3, r_4, r_5\}]\}$, where $seg_c, seg_d \in \{0, 1\}$.

r_1: $(seg_c)(seg_d)$ $\Rightarrow$ ε $\qquad\{r_1, r_2, r_3, r_4, r_5\}$

r_2: $(seg_c)(seg_d)$ $\Rightarrow$ (seg_d) $\qquad\{r_1, r_2, r_3, r_4, r_5\}$

r_3: $(X)(seg_c)$ $\Rightarrow$ (X) $\qquad\{r_1\ r_2, r_3, r_4, r_5\}$

r_4: $(X)(seg_c)$ $\Rightarrow$ $(seg_c\ X)$ $\qquad\{r_1\ r_2, r_3, r_4, r_5\}$

r_5: $(X)(\#)$ $\Rightarrow$ (X) $\qquad\{r_6\}$

r_6: $(seg_c\ X)(seg_c)$ $\Rightarrow$ (X) $\qquad\{r_6\}$

$ST_F =_{def} \{[\varepsilon\ rp_6]\}$

The +recursive ambiguity of this C3 LAG arises because r_3 and r_4, for example, (i) have compatible (in fact identical) input conditions, (ii) co-occur in rule packages, and (iii) are reapplied in the same analysis path. Rule r_3 ignores the category of the next word, thus treating it as noise. Rule r_4 attaches the category of the next word at the beginning of the new sentence start category, thus requiring that it have a counterpart in the second half of the input.

The C3 LAG for L_{no} is similar to the C3 LAG for $\mathcal{NP}$-complete Subset Sum (11.5.8), where each a_i may be interpreted either as noise or as a 'real' subset. The C3 LAG for Subset Sum is context-sensitive, however, because some rules (e.g., r_5) check the beginning and others (e.g., r_4) the end of the sentence start category. The C3 LAG for L_{no} is context-free because its categorial operations all check only the beginnings of sentence start categories.

12.4 Comparing the Lower LA and PS Classes

Context-free PS Grammar has been widely used because it provides the greatest amount of generative capacity within the PS Grammar hierarchy which is still computationally tractable. There is general agreement in linguistics, however, that context-free PS Grammar does not properly fit the structures characteristic of natural language. The same holds for computer science, where context-free PS Grammar has likewise turned out to be suboptimal for describing the structures of programming languages.

> It is no secret that context-free grammars are only a first order approximation to the various mechanisms used for specifying the syntax of modern programming languages.[11]

Ginsburg (1980), p. 7.

Therefore, there has long been a need for an alternative to better describe the syntax of natural and programming languages. Most attempts to arrive at new language classes have consisted in *conservative extensions*, however, which follow context-free PS Grammar too closely. They are based on adding certain mechanisms and result in additional language classes which fit right into the subset relations of the PS hierarchy. For example, the context-free languages form a proper subset of the tree-adjoining languages (TALs),[12] which form a proper subset of the index languages,[13] which in turn form a proper subset of the context-sensitive languages.

More than five decades of PS Grammar tradition and the long absence of a substantial alternative are no valid reasons, however, to regard the PS Grammar hierarchy of formal languages and its extensions as particularly 'natural'. After all, these language classes are no more than the result of certain restrictions on a certain formalism.

The context-free languages, for example, are defined in terms of restrictions which are suggested only by the formalism of rewrite rules (8.1.2). Similarly, the C1, C2, and C3 languages are defined in terms of restrictions which are suggested only by the formalism of LA Grammar (11.5.9). As a result of these different restrictions, the language hierarchies of PS and LA Grammar are orthogonal to each other:

12.4.1 ORTHOGONAL RELATION BETWEEN C AND CF LANGUAGES

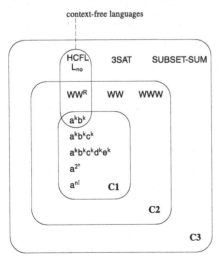

---

[11] See also Harrison (1978), pp. 219f., in the same vein.

[12] Joshi et al. (1975, 1991).

[13] Hopcroft and Ullman (1979), pp. 389f. Hayashi (1973) proved a pumping lemma for index languages.

From a pretheoretical point of view, one would be inclined to classify the language $a^k b^k$ with $a^k b^k c^k$, $a^k b^k c^k d^k$, etc., on the one hand, and WW^R with WW on the other. It is therefore surprising to the untutored that the PS hierarchy puts $a^k b^k$ and WW^R into one class (context-free), but $a^k b^k c^k$, $a^k b^k c^k d^k$, etc., with WW into another class (context-sensitive). The LA hierarchy is intuitively more natural because there a^k, $a^k b^k$, $a^k b^k c^k$, $a^k b^k c^k d^k$, etc. are classified together as linear C1 languages, while WW^R and WW, WW^{R}W and WWW, etc. are classified as polynomial C2 languages.

If the distinction between deterministic context-free languages $\mathcal{L}_{dcf}$ and nondeterministic context-free languages $\mathcal{L}_{cf}$ is made, the orthogonal relation between the PS and the LA hierarchy may be seen even more clearly (Stubert 1993, p. 72):

12.4.2 ORTHOGONAL $\mathcal{L}_{dcf}$, $\mathcal{L}_{cf}$, C$_1$, C$_2$, AND C$_3$ CLASSIFICATIONS

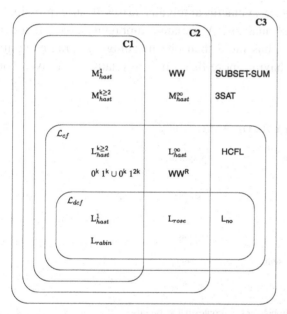

The class of $\mathcal{L}_{dcf}$ cuts across the three subclasses of C in the same way as $\mathcal{L}_{cf}$.

The alternative classifications of LA Grammar provide a new perspective on the theory of formal languages. Furthermore, because the PS Grammar hierarchy may be reconstructed in LA Grammar (Sect. 11.2), open questions of classic automata theory may be transferred directly to LA Grammar (Sect. 12.2).

12.5 Linear Complexity of Natural Language

A context-sensitive language which is not a C language would prove the proper inclusion of the C languages in the B languages (12.2.2). In such a language, the category length would have to grow just within the LBA definition of context-sensitive languages, but grow faster than the pattern-based categorial operations of the C LAGs would permit. That this kind of language would be characteristic for the structure of natural language is improbable.

If the natural languages are contained in the C LAGs, however, then the following two questions are equivalent:

(i) *How complex are the natural languages?*
(ii) *How ambiguous are the natural languages?*

This is because the C LAG subclasses differ solely in their degrees of ambiguity.

An utterance is called ambiguous if more than one meaning$_2$ (PoP-1, 4.3.3) may be derived by the hearer. This may be due to a syntactic, semantic, or pragmatic ambiguity. For complexity analysis – it being concerned with the combinatorial structure of expressions – only syntactic ambiguity is relevant.

In the SLIM theory of language, a syntactic ambiguity arises if an expression is assigned more than one structural analysis. A semantic ambiguity arises if a syntactically unambiguous expression has more than one meaning$_1$. A pragmatic ambiguity is caused by a meaning$_1$ having more than one *use* relative to a given context.

12.5.1 SLIM-THEORETIC ANALYSIS OF AMBIGUITY

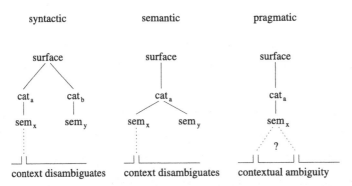

A syntactic ambiguity is characterized by alternative categories of the surface (here, cat$_a$ and cat$_b$), such that each categorial reading has its own meaning$_1$ (here, sem$_x$ and sem$_y$). For example, won is syntactically ambiguous between a noun referring to the currency of Korea and the past tense form of the verb to win. If the context does not disambiguate between sem$_x$ and sem$_y$, the syntactic ambiguity will cause the utterance to have more than one meaning$_2$.

A semantic ambiguity is characterized by a surface having only one syntactic analysis, but more than one meaning$_1$. For instance, the surface perch is semantically ambiguous, one literal meaning standing for a kind of fish, the other for a place to roost. Syntactically, however, perch is not ambiguous because both readings are of the category noun.[14] For internal matching, a semantic ambiguity resembles a syntactic one insofar as in either case the expression used has more than one meaning$_1$.

A pragmatic ambiguity consists in alternative uses of one meaning$_1$ relative to a given context. For example, in a context with two equally prototypical tables right next to each other, the utterance of Put the coffee on the table would be pragmatically ambiguous because it is not clear which of the two tables is meant by the speaker (Sect. 5.2). In contrast to syntactic and semantic ambiguities, a pragmatic ambiguity by its very nature cannot be disambiguated by the context.

An expression is called semantically ambiguous only if it is syntactically *unambiguous* (regarding the particular readings in question). Similarly, an utterance is called pragmatically ambiguous only if the expression used is neither semantically nor syntactically ambiguous. The syntactic or semantic ambiguity of a single word form is also called a lexical ambiguity.

Only syntactic and semantic ambiguities are properties of an expression *type*, while pragmatic ambiguities are properties of utterances in which *tokens* of expressions are used. For determining the complexity of natural language expressions, phenomena of pragmatic ambiguity are irrelevant. This is because pragmatic ambiguities do not affect the type of the expression, but arise in the interaction between the semantic interpretation of the expression and the context (Sect. 4.2).

Phenomena of semantic ambiguity are likewise irrelevant for natural language complexity because semantic ambiguities are by definition associated with syntactically unambiguous surfaces. For example, in light of the fact that the two readings of perch have the same category, it would be superfluous to assign two different syntactic analyses to the sentence The osprey is looking for a perch:

12.5.2 INCORRECT ANALYSIS OF A SEMANTIC AMBIGUITY

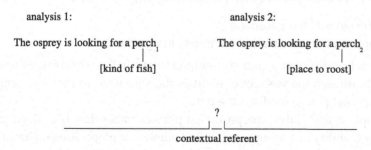

This analysis is misguided because it treats a semantic ambiguity needlessly as a syntactic one.

The correct analysis treats the surface of the sentence in question as syntactically unambiguous, handling the ambiguity instead semantically by assigning two different meanings$_1$ to perch.

---

[14] We are ignoring here the denominal verb to perch which stands for sitting on a place to roost.

12.5.3 CORRECT ANALYSIS OF A SEMANTIC AMBIGUITY

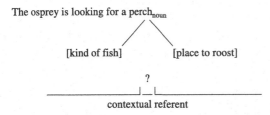

The osprey is looking for a perch_{noun}

[kind of fish]   [place to roost]

?

contextual referent

Even though the syntactic derivation is unambiguous, the semantic interpretation provides two different meanings$_1$, which in turn provide for the possibility of two different meanings$_2$ in the interpretation of the sentence relative to a given context. This method is called semantic doubling.[15]

Semantic doubling is based on the [2 + 1] level structure of natural communication (Sect. 4.2). Assigning the same analyzed surface, here perch$_{noun}$, to more than one meaning$_1$ instantiates the surface compositional insight that it is not always necessary to push semantic distinctions through to the level of syntax.

The use of semantic doubling is highly restricted. It may be applied only if the readings at the semantic level are associated either with *no* (as in 12.5.3) or with a *systematic* distinction (as in 12.5.4) at the syntactic level. Genuine syntactic ambiguity, in contrast, is limited to cases in which different semantic readings are associated with an unsystematic – and thus unpredictable – alternative of syntactic analysis.

As an example of semantic doubling in the case of a systematic alternative, consider prepositional phrases. These permit generally an adnominal and an adverbial interpretation, as shown by the following examples:

12.5.4 MULTIPLE INTERPRETATIONS OF PREPOSITIONAL PHRASES

The man saw the girl with the telescope.
Julia ate the apple on the table behind the tree in the garden.

The first example has two different meaning$_1$ interpretations. In the adverbial reading, the prepositional phrase with the telescope modifies the verb saw. In the adnominal reading, the prepositional phrase modifies the girl.

The second example contains three prepositional phrases rather than one, illustrating the theoretical possibility of adding an unlimited number of prepositional phrases. This raises the question of whether or not the number of syntactic readings should be doubled each time a new prepositional phrase is added. The following analysis illustrates a (mistaken) syntactic treatment of the alternative interpretations of prepositional phrases:

---

[15] First proposed in CoL, pp. 219–232 and 239–247.

12.5.5 RECURSIVE PSEUDO-AMBIGUITY

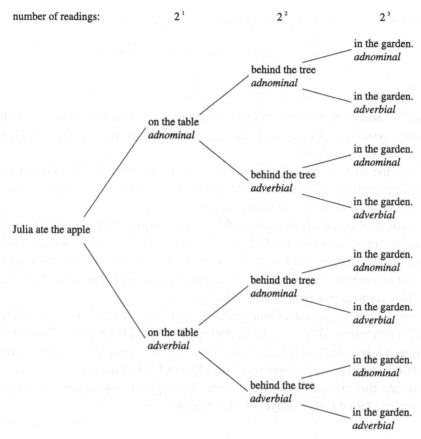

Based on analyses like this, natural language has been argued to be of at least exponential complexity.

For the mechanism of natural communication, however, such a multiplying out of semantic readings in the syntax has no purpose. Anything can be done inefficiently.[16] A good syntactic analysis should aim at finding the absolute minimum of literal meanings sufficient for handling all possible uses.

For communication, an adequate treatment of prepositional phrases requires no more than alternative adverbial and adnominal readings on the *semantic* level. The semantic doubling analysis may be illustrated as follows:

---

[16] Even for unambiguous $a^k b^k$, for example, one may easily write various ambiguous grammars, raising the complexity from linear to polynomial, exponential, or even undecidable.

12.5.6 CORRECT ANALYSIS WITH *Semantic Doubling*

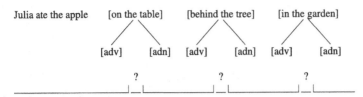

The surface is analyzed as syntactically unambiguous.[17] The semantic interpretation, however, systematically assigns to each prepositional phrase two different literal meanings at the semantic level.

Like 12.5.3, the analysis is based on the $[2 + 1]$ level structure of natural communication. The approach is sufficient for modeling the different meanings$_2$ that may arise in the interpretation relative to different contexts.

The semantic doubling analysis is more efficient and concrete than an analysis based on multiplying out the semantic readings in the syntax. While 12.5.5 is of exponential complexity, the alternative analysis 12.5.6 is linear. This holds for both the level of syntax and of semantics. The number of alternative meanings$_1$ provided by 12.5.6 for matching the interpretation context is well below 2n.

If apparent +recursive syntactic ambiguities of natural language can all be treated as semantic ambiguities, then −recursive ambiguities like 11.3.5 and 11.3.6 remain as the only candidates for a syntactic treatment. Without +recursive syntactic ambiguities, natural languages form a subset of the class of C1 languages.

We formulate this conclusion as the empirical complexity hypothesis for natural language syntax, called CoNSyx hypothesis for short.

12.5.7 CONSYX (COMPLEXITY OF NAT. LANG. SYNTAX) HYPOTHESIS

> The natural languages are contained in the class of C1 languages and parse in linear time.

The linear complexity assigned by CoNSyx to natural language is in agreement with the fact that human speakers and hearers usually have no difficulty in producing and understanding[18] even complicated texts in their native language in real time. The CoNSyx hypothesis will be complemented in Chap. 21 by a corresponding hypothesis for the complexity of semantics, called the CoNSem hypothesis (21.5.2).[19]

---

[17] Syntactically, the prepositional phrases are categorized as (adv&adn) using the multicat notation (see Sect. 15.2).

[18] At least on the syntactic level.

[19] The structural properties assigned by CoNSyx to natural language syntax may and should be tested empirically in the continuing analysis of various different languages. Possible counterexamples to 12.5.7 would be constructions of natural language with +recursive syntactic ambiguities which do not allow an alternative treatment based on semantic dou-

Exercises

Section 12.1

1. Why are the lower classes of a language hierarchy, i.e., those with comparatively low generative capacity, especially interesting for empirical work in linguistics?
2. Describe the complexity degrees of the subclasses in the LA and PS Grammar hierarchy.
3. How is the (non)equivalence of two language classes shown?
4. Compare the inherent complexity of $a^kb^kc^k$ and Subset Sum.
5. What properties of a language determine the language class it belongs to?
6. Explain in what sense the language hierarchies of LA and PS Grammar are orthogonal.

Section 12.2

1. Compare the inclusion relations in the PS and the LA hierarchy.
2. By what method is the proper inclusion of the type 3 language class in the type 2 language class and that of the type 2 language class in the type 1 language class formally proven in PS Grammar?
3. Explain the definition of the languages classes $\mathcal{P}$ and $\mathcal{NP}$.
4. Why is the language 3SAT inherently complex?
5. What unsolved problems of classic automata theory are related to the open questions of whether C2 $\subset$ C3 and whether C3 $\subset$ B?

Section 12.3

1. In which subclass of the C languages is L_{no} and why?
2. Write a PS and an LA Grammar for L_{no}^3, defined as W'#W#W", where W' and W" are noisy versions of W.
3. In which PS Grammar classes are L_{no} and L_{no}^3, respectively?
4. In which LA Grammar classes are L_{no} and L_{no}^3, respectively?
5. Compare the complexity of L_{no} and L_{no}^3 from the viewpoint of the PS Grammar classification of these languages.

Section 12.4

1. What is a conservative extension of context-free PS Grammar? Give two examples and compare their respective classes.
2. Is $a^kb^kc^kd^ke^kf^k$ a TAL? What is the LA class of this language?
3. What is the structural reason that $a^{i!}$ is not an index language? (Consult Hopcroft and Ullman 1979). What is the LA class of this language?
4. Describe the relation between the class of context-free languages and the class of C languages.

bling. Given the mechanism of natural communication within the SLIM theory of language, it seems unlikely that such constructions will be found.

5. Why is the hierarchy of LA Grammar, including the subhierarchy of the C LAGs, more natural than that of PS Grammar ?

6. Explain how the orthogonal relation between the LA and the PS hierarchies also shows up in the subclasses of deterministic and nondeterministic context-free languages.

Section 12.5

1. Why don't the natural languages fit into the class of context-free languages?

2. Why is it likely that the natural languages are a subset of the C languages?

3. If the natural languages are in the class of C languages, what would be the only possible cause for a higher (i.e., nonlinear) complexity degree of natural language?

4. What are the kinds of ambiguity in natural language?

5. Which kinds of ambiguity are irrelevant for the complexity of natural language and why?

6. Explain the method of semantic doubling and its consequence on the degree of complexity of natural language.

7. Are there +recursive syntactic ambiguities in natural language?

8. Explain why the complexity analysis of natural language depends on the theory of grammar, using examples 9.2.1 and 9.2.2.

9. Explain why the complexity analysis of natural language depends on the theory of language, using the second example of 12.5.4.

10. Explain the CoNSyx hypothesis. How can it be disproven empirically?

11. What is the practical importance of the CoNSyx hypothesis?

Part III

Morphology and Syntax

13. Words and Morphemes

Part I analyzed natural communication within the SLIM theory of language. Part II presented formal language theory in terms of methodology, mathematical complexity, and computational implementation. With this background in mind, we turn in Part III to the morphological and syntactic analysis of natural language. This chapter begins with the basic notions of morphology, i.e., the linguistic analysis of word forms.

Section 13.1 describes the principles of combination in morphology, namely inflection,[1] derivation, and compounding, as well as the distinction between the open and the closed word classes. Section 13.2 presents a formal definition of the notions of morpheme and allomorph. Section 13.3 describes two special cases of allomorphy, suppletion, and bound morphemes. Section 13.4 explains the main tasks of automatic word form recognition, namely categorization and lemmatization. Section 13.5 describes the three basic methods of automatic word form recognition, called the word form, the morpheme, and the allomorph methods.

13.1 Words and Word Forms

The words of a natural language are concretely realized as word *forms*. For example, the English word write is realized as the word forms write, writes, wrote, written, and writing. The grammatical well-formedness of a natural language sentence depends not only on the choice of the words, but also on the choice of the correct word forms:

13.1.1 DIFFERENT SYNTACTIC COMPATIBILITIES OF WORD FORMS

    *write
    *writes
    *wrote
John has written *a letter.*
    *writing

In written English, word forms are separated by spaces. For practical purposes, this is sufficient for distinguishing the word forms in a text. Francis and Kučera (1982)

---

[1] For simplicity, we subsume agglutination under the term of inflection.

R. Hausser, *Foundations of Computational Linguistics*,
DOI 10.1007/978-3-642-41431-2_13, © Springer-Verlag Berlin Heidelberg 2014

define a 'graphic' word "as a string of continuous alphanumeric characters with space on either side; may include hyphens and apostrophes, but no other punctuation marks."

Theoretical linguistics, especially American structuralism, has tried to arrive at a watertight structural definition of the notions of word and word form. To establish word forms scientifically, for example in the description of an unknown exotic language, the structuralists proposed using the method of distribution tests, realized as substitution and movement tests.[2]

In contrast, practical work has depended on the fact that native speakers have intuitively a clear notion of what the words and word forms of their language are. As observed by SAPIR (1884–1939), aborigines who do not read or write can nevertheless dictate in their language word form by word form (Sapir 1921, p. 33).

In line with this insight, traditional grammar has avoided turning the scientific definition of words and word forms into a major problem and concentrated instead on the classification of what is intuitively obvious. The results are used in computational linguistics as the theoretical and empirical basis of automatic word form recognition.

In traditional morphology, the following principles of combination are distinguished:

13.1.2 COMBINATION PRINCIPLES OF MORPHOLOGY

1. *Inflection* is the systematic variation of a word which allows it to perform different syntactic and semantic functions, and adapt to different syntactic environments. Examples are learn, learn/s, learn/ed, and learn/ing.
2. *Derivation* is the combination of a word with an affix.[3] Examples are clear/ness, clear/ly, and un/clear.
3. *Compounding* is the combination of two or more words into a new word form. Examples are gas/light, hard/wood, over/indulge, and over-the-counter.

These three processes may also occur simultaneously, as in over/indulg/er/s (16.1.1). Furthermore, these processes are productive in the sense that a new word like infobahning[4] may be inflected in English as a verb (we infobahn, he infobahn/s, we infobahn/ed, ...), may permit derivations like infobahn/er/s, and may participate in compounds, like pseudo-infobahn/er.

The grammarians of ancient Greece and Rome arranged inflectional word forms into paradigms. We define a word[5] abstractly as the set of concrete word forms in its inflectional paradigm.

---

[2] These same tests were also used in the attempt to motivate syntactic constituent structures (8.4.6–8.4.8).

[3] See the distinction between free and bound morphemes in Sect. 13.3.

[4] In analogy to autobahning, coined by Americans stationed in Germany after World War II from 'Autobahn' = highway.

[5] Our terminology is in concord with Sinclair (1991):

13.1.3 DEFINITION OF THE NOTION *word*

word $=_{def}$ {associated analyzed word forms[6]}

The base form of a word is used as its name. In English, the base form of nouns is the nominative singular, e.g., book; of verbs it is the unmarked form of the present tense, e.g., learn; and of adjectives it is the adnominal in the positive, e.g., slow.[7]

For simplicity, the following analysis of word forms is represented as ordered triples[8] consisting of the surface, the syntactic category, and the semantic representation, as in the following example:

13.1.4 EXAMPLE OF AN ANALYZED WORD FORM

[wolves (pn) wolf]

The surface wolves serves as the key for relating the analyzed word form to corresponding unanalyzed surfaces occurring in texts (13.4.7). The category (pn) stands for 'plural noun' and characterizes the combinatorics of the word form. The semantic representation (meaning$_1$ concept) named wolf applies to the word as a whole (rather than to just the word form in question) and serves as the common link between the different forms of the paradigm.[9]

Note that a word form is close to, but not identical to, the usual idea of a word. In particular, several different word forms may all be regarded as instances of the same word. So drive, drives, driving, drove, driven, and perhaps driver, drivers, driver's, drivers', drive's, make up ten different word forms, all related to the word drive. It is usual in defining a word form to ignore the distinction between upper and lower case, so SHAPE, Shape, and shape, will all be taken as instances of the same word form.

Another term for our notion of a word is *lexeme* (see for example Matthews 1972, 1974). Terminologically, however, it is simpler to distinguish between *word* and *word forms* than between *lexeme* and *word forms* (or even *lexeme forms*).

[6] A clear distinction between the notions of *word* and *word form* is not only of theoretical, but also of practical relevance. For example, when a text is said to consist of a '100 000 words' it remains unclear whether the number is intended to refer to (i) the running word forms (tokens), (ii) the different word forms (i.e., the types, as in a word form lexicon), or (iii) the different words (i.e., the types, as in a base form lexicon). Depending on the interpretation, the number in question may be regarded as small, medium, or large.

[7] This holds only for English. In German, it is the adverbial in the positive which is used as the base form for naming adjectives. This is because German adnominals inflect (for example, langsam/er, langsam/e, langsam/es, etc.), whereas in English it is the adverbial which has an additional suffix (for example, slow/ly).

[8] Later work such as NLC and CLaTR uses the format of proplets (Sect. 3.4) instead.

[9] Semantic properties of specific word forms are coded in the third position by means of subscripts. For example, the German verb forms gibst and gabst have the same combinatorics (category), but differ semantically in their respective tense values. NLC and CLaTR use the alternative format of proplets and code such distinctions as values of the sem attribute.

13.1.5 PARADIGM BASED ON A DISTINCTIVE CATEGORIZATION

word   word forms (paradigm)

wolf $=_{def}$ {[wolf (sn) wolf],
        [wolf's (gn) wolf],
        [wolves (pn) wolf],
        [wolves' (gn) wolf]}

The different categories in the second position of the analyzed word forms character-ize their different combinatorial properties.[10]

The paradigm 13.1.5 is based on a *distinctive* categorization, in contradistinction of the *exhaustive* categorization of traditional grammar. For reasons of computational efficiency and linguistic concreteness (surface compositionality), a distinctive cate-gorization takes great care to assign no more than one category (syntactic reading) per word form surface whenever possible.

For comparison, consider the corresponding exhaustive categorization, based on the number of places in a paradigm schema:

13.1.6 PARADIGM BASED ON AN EXHAUSTIVE CATEGORIZATION

word   word forms

wolf $=_{def}$ {[wolf   (nom sg) wolf]   [wolves (nom pl) wolf]
       [wolf's (gen sg) wolf]   [wolves' (gen pl) wolf]
       [wolf   (dat sg) wolf]   [wolves (dat pl) wolf]
       [wolf   (acc sg) wolf]   [wolves (acc pl) wolf]}

A system of automatic word form recognition based on exhaustive categorization will render three readings for input of the unanalyzed surface wolf, while one based on dis-tinctive categorization will render only one. The artificial lexical ambiguities caused by the exhaustive categorization result in an enormous increase in the number of op-erations in syntactic parsing (Sect. 15.2).

The distinction between a word and a word form (13.1.3) applies also to noninflect-ing words like and. That the two may seem to coincide is because in such cases the set of word forms is the unit set.

13.1.7 ANALYSIS OF A NONINFLECTING WORD

word   word form(s)

and $=_{def}$ {[and (cnj) and]}

---

[10] The category (sn) stands for 'singular noun,' (pn) stands for 'plural noun,' and (gn) stands for 'genitive noun.' The distinction between nongenitive singulars and plurals is important for the choice of the determiner, e.g., every vs. all (17.1.1). Because genitives in English serve only as prenominal modifiers, e.g., the wolf's hunger, their number distinction need not be coded into the syntactic category.

The words of a natural language are traditionally divided into parts of speech. There is, however, considerable variation among different grammarians.[11] Of the various options, the SLIM theory uses the following part of speech:

13.1.8 PARTS OF SPEECH

– *verbs*, e.g., walk, read, give, help, teach, ...
– *nouns*, e.g., book, table, woman, messenger, arena, ...
– *adjectives*, e.g., quick, good, low, ...
– *conjunctions*, e.g., and, or, because, after, ...
– *prepositions*, e.g., in, on, over, under, before, ...
– *determiners*, e.g., a, the, every, some, all, any, ...
– *particles*, e.g., only, already, just...

The first three parts of speech form what are called the *open* classes of words, whereas the remaining parts of speech constitute the *closed* classes.

13.1.9 OPEN AND CLOSED CLASSES

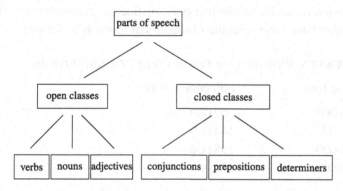

The open classes comprise tens of thousand elements, while the closed classes contain only a few hundred words.

In the open classes, the morphological processes of inflection, derivation, and compounding are productive, for which reason it is difficult to quantify their elements exactly. Also, the use of words is constantly changing, with new ones entering and obsolete ones leaving the current language. The closed classes, on the other hand, show neither a comparable size and fluctuation, nor productive processes of inflection, derivation, or compounding.

The distinction between content words and function words seems problematic in the case of indexical nouns like I, you, he, she, or it, indexical adjectives like here, or now, and proper names nouns like Peter or R2D2. On the one hand, these words don't seem to convey "content" in the usual sense; on the other hand they take the same

---

[11] For a more detailed discussion see CLaTR, Sect. 3.5.

grammatical roles as genuine content words. The SLIM theory takes the position that words which use one of the three mechanisms of reference (6.1.6) are content words (Autosemantika),[12] while words which do not refer on their own are function words (Synsemantika). Accordingly, not only symbols but also indexicals and names are regarded as content words.

13.2 Segmentation and Concatenation

Because a word may have several different word forms, there arises the question of how many forms there are for a given set of words. To get a general idea, let us consider 40 000 of the most frequently used elementary base forms of German.[13]

Elementary base forms are words which are not derived or composed from other words. Of the 40 000 base forms in question, 23 000 happen to be nouns, 6 000 happen to be verbs, and 11 000 happen to be adjectives.

German nouns have two to five different inflectional surfaces (14.5.4) – averaging about four. The verbs have about 24 different forms (14.5.6). The adjectives have normally 18 different inflectional forms. These numbers are based on a distinctive categorization as illustrated in 13.1.5.[14]

Using a maximally concrete, surface compositional, distinctive categorization, the numerical relation between base forms and their inflectional forms is as follows:

13.2.1 RELATION BETWEEN WORDS AND THEIR INFLECTIONAL FORMS

	base forms	inflectional forms
nouns:	23 000	92 000
verbs:	6 000	144 000
adjectives:	11 000	198 000
	40 000	434 000

---

[12] Marty (1908), pp. 205 f.

[13] The morphology of English happens to be simple. For example, compared to French, Italian, or German, there is little inflection in English. Furthermore, much of compounding may be regarded as part of English syntax rather than morphology – in accordance with Francis and Kučera's (1982) definition of a graphic word form cited above. For example, **kitchen table** or **baby wolves** are written as separate words, whereas the corresponding compounds in German are written as one word form, e.g., **Küchentisch** and **Babywölfe**. For this reason, some morphological phenomena will be illustrated in this and the following two chapters in languages other than English.

[14] An exhaustive categorization based on traditional paradigm tables would arrive at much higher numbers. For example, the adjectives of German have 18 inflectional forms per base form according to a distinctive categorization. In contrast, an exhaustive categorization, as presented in the Grammatik-Duden, p. 288, assigns more than eight times as many, namely 147 analyzed inflectional forms per base form, whereby the different analyses reflect distinctions of grammatical gender, number, case, definiteness, and degree, which in most cases are not concretely marked in the surface.

According to this estimate, the relation between words and their inflectional forms in German is about one to ten, on average.

In addition to the inflectional morphology of German, however, there is also derivational and compositional morphology, allowing the formation of new complex words from old ones. Consider, for example, noun-noun compounding, such as Haus/schuh, Schuh/haus, or Jäger/jäger, which is of complexity n^2. This means that from 20 000 nouns 400 000 000 possible compounds of length 2 can be derived (compound base forms which can be inflected).

Furthermore, noun-noun compounds of length 3, such as Haus/schuh/sohle, Sport/schuh/haus, or Jäger/jäger/jäger are of complexity n^3. This means that an additional 8 000 000 000 000 (eight trillion) possible words may be formed. Because there is no grammatical limit on the length of noun compounds, the number of possible word forms in German is infinite. These word forms exist potentially because of the inherent productivity of morphology.

In contradistinction to the possible word forms, the set of actual word forms is finite. There is no limit, however, on the number of 'new' words, i.e., words that have never been used before. These are called *neologisms*, and coined spontaneously by the language users on the basis of known words and the rules of word formation.

A cursory look through Newsweek or The New Yorker will yield English neologisms like the following:

13.2.2 EXAMPLES OF NEOLOGISMS

insurrectionist (inmate)	three-player (set)
copper-jacketed (bullets)	bad-guyness
cyberstalker	trapped-rat (frenzy)
self-tapping (screw)	dismissiveness
migraineur	extraconstitutional (gimmick)

Because new word forms never observed before are constantly being formed, morphological analysis should not merely list as many analyzed word forms as possible. Rather, the goal must be a rule-based analysis of potential word forms on demand.

In traditional morphology, word forms are analyzed by disassembling them into their elementary parts. These are called morphemes and defined as the smallest meaningful units of a language. In contrast to the number of possible words and word forms, the number of morphemes in a language is finite.

The notion of a morpheme is a linguistic abstraction which is manifested concretely in the form of finitely many allomorphs. The term allomorph is of Greek origin and means "alternative shape." For example, the morpheme wolf is realized as the two allomorphs wolf and wolv.

Just as sentences are composed of word forms rather than words, word forms are composed of allomorphs rather than morphemes. By analogy to the definition of a word (13.1.3), a morpheme is defined as the name of the set of associated allomorphs.

13.2.3 DEFINITION OF THE NOTION *morpheme*

morpheme $=_{def}$ {associated analyzed allomorphs}

Like word forms, allomorphs are formally analyzed as ordered triples, consisting of the surface, the category, and the semantic representation. The following examples, based on the English noun wolf, are intended to demonstrate these basic concepts of morphology as simply as possible.[15]

13.2.4 FORMAL ANALYSIS OF THE MORPHEME wolf

morpheme allomorphs

wolf $=_{def}$ {[wolf (sn sr) wolf],
                 [wolv (pn sr) wolf]}

The different allomorphs wolf and wolv are shown to belong to the same morpheme by the common semantic representation in the third position. As the name of the semantic representation (concept, literal meaning$_1$) we use the base form of the allomorph, i.e., wolf, which is also used as the name of the associated morpheme.

Some surfaces, such as wolf, can be analyzed alternatively as an allomorph, a morpheme (name), a word form, or a word (name).

13.2.5 COMPARING THE MORPHEME AND WORD wolf

morpheme	*allomorphs*	*word*	*word forms*
wolf $=_{def}$	{wolf,	wolf $=_{def}$	{wolf,
	wolv}		wolf/'s,
			wolv/es,
			wolv/es/'}

Other surfaces can be analyzed only as an allomorph, e.g., wolv, or only as a word form, e.g., wolves.

Besides the segmentation into morphemes or allomorphs, a word form surface may also be segmented into the units of its realization medium. Thus, written surfaces may be segmented into letters, and spoken surfaces into syllables or phonemes.

---

[15] Nouns of English ending in -lf, such as calf, shelf, self, etc. form their plural in general as -lves. One might prefer for practical purposes to treat forms like wolves, calves, or shelves as elementary allomorphic forms, rather than combining an allomorphic noun stem ending in -lv with the plural allomorph es. This, however, would prevent us from explaining the interaction of concatenation and allomorphy with an example from English. The category segments sn, pn, and sr stand for singular noun, plural noun, and semi-regular (14.1.7), respectively.

13.2.6 ALTERNATIVE FORMS OF SEGMENTATION

allomorphs:	learn/ing
syllables:	lear/ning
phonemes:	l/e/r/n/i/ng
letters:	l/e/a/r/n/i/n/g

The syllables lear and ning do not coincide with the allomorphs learn and ing, and similarly in the case of letters and phonemes. While, for example, syllables are important in automatic speech recognition (Sect. 1.4), morphological analysis and automatic word form recognition aim at segmenting the surface into morphemes or allomorphs, which are independent[16] of the concrete realization in speaking or writing.

13.3 Morphemes and Allomorphs

The number and variation of allomorphs of a given morpheme determine the degree of regularity of the morpheme and – in the case of a free morpheme – the associated word. An example of a regular word is the verb learn, the morpheme of which is defined as a set containing only one allomorph.

13.3.1 THE REGULAR MORPHEME learn

morpheme   allomorphs

learn $=_{def}$ {[learn (n ... v) learn]}

A comparatively irregular word, on the other hand, is the verb swim, the morpheme of which has four allomorphs, namely swim, swimm,[17] swam, and swum. The change of the stem vowel may be found also in other verbs, e.g., sing, sang, sung, and is called *ablaut*.

13.3.2 THE IRREGULAR MORPHEME swim

morpheme   allomorphs

swim $=_{def}$ {[swim (n ... v1) swim],

[swimm (... b) swim],

---

[16] Depending on the modality, there is the distinction between allo*graphs* in written language and allo*phones* in spoken language. Allographs are, for example, happy vs. happi-, and allophones are, for example, the present vs. past tense pronunciation of read.

[17] This allomorph is used in the progressive swimm/ing, avoiding the concatenative insertion of the gemination letter. A psychological argument for handling a particular form nonconcatenatively is frequency. Based on speech error data, Stemberger and MacWhinney (1986) provide evidence that the distinction between rote and combinatorial formation is based not only on regularity, but also on frequency, so that even regular word forms can be stored if they are sufficiently frequent.

> [swam (n ... v2) swim],
> [swum (n ... v) swim]}

The allomorph of the base form is used as the name of the morpheme. Thus, we may say that swam is an allomorph of the morpheme swim.

Cases in which there is no similarity at all between the allomorphs of a given morpheme are called *suppletion*.

13.3.3 EXAMPLE OF SUPPLETION

morpheme allomorphs

> good =$_{def}$ {[good (adv ir) good],
> [bett (cad ir) good],
> [b (sad ir) good]}

While the degree in a regular adjective uses only one allomorph for the stem, e.g., fast, fast/er, fast/est, the irregular adjective good uses three.[18] Their common morpheme is explicitly specified as the last element of each ordered triple.

In structuralism, morphemes of the open and closed classes are called *free* morphemes, in contradistinction to *bound* morphemes. A morpheme is free if it can occur as an independent word form, e.g., *book*. Bound morphemes, on the other hand, are affixes such as the prefixes un-, pre-, dis-, etc., and the suffixes -s, -ed, -ing, etc., which can occur only in combination with free morphemes.

Consider the simplified analysis of the English plural morpheme, which has been postulated in such different forms as book/s, wolv/es, ox/en, and sheep/#.

13.3.4 EXAMPLE OF A BOUND MORPHEME (hypothetical)

morpheme allomorphs

> -s =$_{def}$ {[s (pl1) plural],
> [es (pl2) plural],
> [en (pl3) plural],
> [# (pl4) plural]}

In bound morphemes, the choice of the morpheme name, here -s, and the base form of the allomorph, here 'plural,' is artificial. Also, postulating the 'zero allomorph' # is in violation of the principle of surface compositionality (Sects. 4.5, 21.3).

13.4 Categorization and Lemmatization

Automatic word form recognition of an unknown form consists in principle of the following three steps of morphological analysis. First, the unanalyzed surface is dis-

---

[18] Practically, one may analyze good, better, best as basic allomorphs without concatenation.

assembled into its basic elements[19] (segmentation). Second, the basic elements are analyzed in terms of their grammatical definition (lexical lookup). Third, the analyzed elements are reassembled by means of rules, whereby the overall analysis of the word form is derived (concatenation).

Concatenation applies simultaneously to the surface, the category, and the semantic representation, as shown by the following example based on German:

13.4.1 MORPHOLOGICAL ANALYSIS OF ungelernte

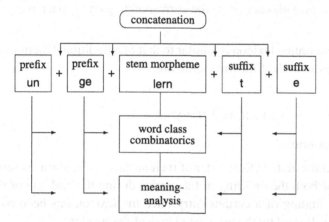

In LA Grammar, the simultaneous concatenation of surface, category, and semantic representation is formally represented by the format of ordered triples:

13.4.2 SCHEMATIC DERIVATION IN LA GRAMMAR

```
("un" (CAT1) MEAN-a) + ("ge" (CAT2) MEAN-b)
  ("un/ge" (CAT3) MEAN-c) + ("lern" (CAT4) MEAN-d)
    ("un/ge/lern" (CAT5) MEAN-e) + ("t" (CAT6) MEAN-f)
      ("un/ge/lern/t" (CAT7) MEAN-g) + ("e" (CAT8) MEAN-h)
        ("un/ge/lern/t/e" (CAT9) MEAN-i)
```

This schematic[20] analysis goes beyond the structure of 13.4.1 in that it is based on the left-associative derivation order .

For automatic word form recognition, the following components are required.

13.4.3 COMPONENTS OF WORD FORM RECOGNITION

– *online lexicon*

For each basic element (i.e., morpheme or allomorph, depending on the approach) a lexical analysis must be defined, which is stored electronically.

---

[19] Depending on the approach, the basic elements of word forms are either the allomorphs or the morphemes.

[20] For simplicity the categories and meanings of the different word form starts and next morphemes are represented as CATn and MEAN-m.

– Recognition algorithm

Using the online lexicon, each unknown word form (e.g., wolves) must be characterized automatically with respect to categorization and lemmatization:

- *Categorization*
  consists in specifying the part of speech (e.g., noun) and the morphosyntactic properties of the surface (e.g., plural); this is needed for syntactic analysis.
- *Lemmatization*
  consists in relating a word form, e.g., wolves, to the corresponding base form[21] (e.g., wolf); the lemma provides access to the corresponding entry in a base form lexicon.

The formal structure of an online lexicon is similar to that of a traditional dictionary. It consists of lexical entries with the following structure:

13.4.4 BASIC STRUCTURE OF A LEXICAL ENTRY

[surface   (lexical description)]

The entries are arranged in the alphabetical order of their surfaces. The surfaces serve as keys which are used for both the ordering of the entries during the building of the lexicon (storage) and the finding of a certain entry once the lexicon has been built (retrieval). The surface is followed by the associated lexical description.

Because traditional and electronic lexica are based on the same structure, traditional dictionaries are well suited for lemmatization in automatic word form recognition, provided they exist online and no copyrights are violated. For example, in Webster's *New Collegiate Dictionary*, the word wolf has the following entry:

13.4.5 ENTRY OF A TRADITIONAL DICTIONARY (*excerpt*)

[1]**wolf** \'wu̇lf\ *n. pl* **wolves** \'wu̇lvz\ *often attributed* [ME, fr. OE *wulf*; akin to OHG *wolf*, L *lupus*, Gk *lykos*] **1** *pl also* **wolf a:** any of various large predatory mammals (genus *Canis* and esp. *C. lupus*) that resemble the related dogs, are destructive to game and livestock, and may rarely attack man esp. when in a pack – compare COYOTE,   JACKAL **b:** the fur of a wolf . . .

The base form surface (lemma) is followed by the lexical description, which specifies the pronunciation, the part of speech (n), the plural form in writing and pronunciation, the etymology, and a number of semantic descriptions and pragmatic uses.

The crucial properties of a lexical entry are the quality of the information contained and the structural consistency of its coding. If these are given online, the information

---

[21] In lexicography, the term lemma refers to the base form surface, which is used as the key for storing or finding a lexical entry.

can be renamed, restructured, and reformatted automatically[22] without losing any of the original information.

The recognition algorithm in its simplest form consists in matching the surface of the unknown word form with the corresponding key (lemma) in the online lexicon, thus providing access to the relevant lexical description.

13.4.6 MATCHING A SURFACE ONTO A KEY

word form surface: wolf
$\quad\quad\quad\quad\quad\quad\quad\quad$| *matching*

lexical entry:$\quad\quad$[wolf (lexical description)]

There exist several computational methods for matching a given surface automatically with the proper lemma in an electronic lexicon.[23]

The simplest is a *linear search*, i.e., going sequentially through the list of entries until there is a match between the unknown surface and the key. In small lexica (containing up to 50 entries) this method is well suited. Possible applications are the formal languages of Part II, where each surface must be assigned a category by way of lexical lookup.

The lexica of natural language are considerably larger, however, containing between 20 000 and 1 000 000 entries, depending on their purpose. Even more importantly, most words are related to several word *forms* which must be categorized and lemmatized. Because in the natural languages

- the number of word forms is considerably larger than the number of words, at least in inflectional and agglutinating languages, and
- the lexical entries normally define words rather than word forms,

it is best to handle categorization and lemmatization, on the one hand, and access to the lexical entry, on the other, in two separate steps.

13.4.7 TWO-STEP PROCEDURE OF WORD FORM RECOGNITION

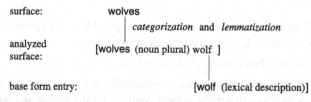

surface:$\quad\quad\quad\quad\quad$wolves
$\quad\quad\quad\quad\quad\quad\quad\quad$| *categorization* and *lemmatization*
analyzed
surface:$\quad\quad\quad\quad$[wolves (noun plural) wolf]

base form entry:$\quad\quad\quad\quad\quad$[wolf (lexical description)]

Automatic word form recognition takes place between surface and analyzed surface. It consists of categorization and lemmatization, and is based on a special analysis lex-

---

[22] For this, special programming languages like AWK (Aho et al. 1988) and Perl (Wall and Schwartz 1990) are available.

[23] See Aho and Ullman (1977), pp. 336–341.

icon. Access to the base form entry, containing the semantic representation common to the whole paradigm, takes place in a second step, using a traditional lexicon.

13.5 Methods of Automatic Word Form Recognition

Possible methods of automatic word form recognition may be distinguished as to whether their analysis lexicon specifies *word forms, morphemes,* or *allomorphs.*[24] Each of the three methods exhibits a characteristic correlation between the recognition algorithm and the associated analysis lexicon.

The *word form method*[25] uses an analysis lexicon consisting of complete word forms.

13.5.1 ANALYZED WORD FORM AS LEXICAL ENTRY

[wolves (part of speech: Subst, num: Pl, case: N,D,A, base form: wolf)]

An analysis lexicon of word forms allows for the simplest recognition algorithm because the surface of the unknown word form, e.g., wolves, is simply matched whole onto the corresponding key in the analysis lexicon.

Of the three steps of morphological analysis, namely (i) segmentation, (ii) lexical lookup, and (iii) concatenation, the word form method omits steps (i) and (iii). Thus, wolves (13.4.7), for example, is treated like and (13.1.7). By obtaining categorization and lemmatization solely from lexical entries of whole word forms, this method is a borderline case of morphological analysis.

The word form method may be useful as a quick and dirty method for toy systems, providing lexical lookup without much programming effort (smart solution, Sect. 2.3). In the long run this method is costly, however, because of the production,[26] the size,[27] and the basic finiteness of its analysis lexicon.

The last point refers to the fact that the word form method is inherently limited to the entries provided by its analysis lexicon. Therefore it cannot recognize neologisms

---

[24] The fourth basic concept of morphology, the *word*, does not provide for a recognition method because words are not suitable keys for a multitude of word forms.

[25] Also known as the *full-form* method based on a *full-form lexicon*.

[26] It is possible to derive much of the word form lexicon automatically, using a base form lexicon and rules for inflection as well as – to a more limited degree – for derivation and compounding. These rules, however, must be written and implemented for the natural language in question, which is costly. The alternative of producing the whole word form lexicon by hand is even more costly.

[27] The discussion of German noun-noun compounds in Sect. 13.2 has shown that the size of a word form lexicon that is attempting to be complete may easily exceed a trillion word forms, thus causing computational difficulties.

during runtime – unless all *possible* word forms are provided by the analysis lexicon. This, however, cannot be done because of the productivity of natural language morphology.

Next consider the *morpheme method*.[28] It uses the smallest analysis lexicon, consisting of analyzed morphemes.[29] Furthermore, neologisms may be analyzed and recognized during runtime using a rule-based segmentation and concatenation of complex word forms into their elements (morphemes). The only requirement is that the elements be lexically known and their mode of composition be handled correctly by the rules.

The disadvantage of the morpheme method is a maximally complex recognition algorithm. The analysis of an unknown surface during runtime requires the steps of (1) segmentation into allomorphs, (2) reduction of the allomorphs to the corresponding morphemes, (3) recognition of the morphemes using an analysis lexicon, and (4) the rule-based concatenation of the morphemes to derive the analyzed word form.

In wolves, for example, step (1) consists in the segmentation into the allomorphs wolv and es. Step (2) reduces these to the corresponding morpheme surfaces wolf and s, enabling lexical lookup as step (3). In step (4), the resulting analyzed morphemes are concatenated by means of grammatical rules which derive the morphosyntactic properties of the word form as a whole, including categorization and lemmatization.

13.5.2 SCHEMA OF THE MORPHEME METHOD

surface:	wolves	
	| |	*segmentation*
allomorphs:	wolv/es	
	⇓ ⇓	*reduction*
morphemes:	wolf+s	base form *lookup* and *concatenation*

Conceptually, the morpheme method is related to transformational grammar. Allomorphs are not treated as fully analyzed grammatical entities, but exist only as the quasi-adulterated surface reflections of the 'underlying' morphemes which are regarded as the 'real' entities of the theory. Concatenation takes place at the level of morphemes – and not at the level of the concretely given allomorphs. For this reason, the morpheme method violates the principle of surface compositionality (S). Also, because the morpheme method tries to compose the morphemes as much as possible as constituents (8.4.3–8.4.6), it violates the principle of time-linear derivation order (L) of the SLIM theory of language.

---

[28] A prototype is the KIMMO-system of *two-level morphology* (Koskenniemi 1983), based on finite state technology.

[29] In light of the morpheme definition 13.2.3, a morpheme lexicon consists strictly speaking of analyzed base form allomorphs.

Mathematically and computationally, the morpheme method is of high complexity ($\mathcal{NP}$-complete)[30] because the system must check the surface for *all possible* phenomena of allomorphy. Faced with English valves, for example, the system would have to consider the nonexisting *valf+s as a possible underlying morpheme sequence. Only after all potential allomorph-morpheme reductions have been checked for a given surface can concatenation begin.

Finally consider the *allomorph method*.[31] It combines the respective advantages of the word form and the morpheme methods by using a simple recognition algorithm with a small analysis lexicon. Based on its rule-based analysis, the allomorph method recognizes neologisms during runtime.

The allomorph method uses two lexica, called the elementary lexicon and the allomorph lexicon, whereby the latter is automatically derived from the former by means of allo rules before runtime. The elementary lexicon consists of (i) the analyzed elementary base forms[32] of the open word classes, (ii) the analyzed elements of the closed word classes, and (iii) the allomorphs of the affixes,[33] as needed in inflection, derivation, and compounding.

During runtime, the allomorphs of the allomorph lexicon are available as precomputed, fully analyzed forms[34] (e.g., 13.2.4, 13.3.1, 13.3.2), providing the basis for a maximally simple segmentation: the unknown surface is matched from left to right with suitable allomorphs – without reducing them to morphemes.

13.5.3 SCHEMA OF THE ALLOMORPH METHOD

```
surface:                    wolves
                            |   |    segmentation
allomorphs:                 wolv/es  allomorph lookup and concatenation
                            ⇑   ⇑    derivation of allomorphs before runtime
morphemes & allomorphs:  wolf  s
```

Concatenation takes place on the level of analyzed allomorphs by means of combi rules. This method is in concord with the principles of surface compositionality (S) and time-linear derivation order (L) of the SLIM theory of language.

The three basic methods may be compared schematically as follows:

---

[30] See Sect. 12.2. The inherent complexity of the morpheme method is shown in detail by Barton et al. (1987), pp. 115–186, using the analysis of spies/*spy+s* in the KIMMO system.

[31] The allomorph method was first presented in Hausser (1989b).

[32] In the case of irregular paradigms, also the suppletive forms are supplied (14.1.8).

[33] Thus, no bound morphemes (13.3.4) are being postulated.

[34] MacWhinney (1978) demonstrates the independent status of lexical allomorphs with language acquisition data in Hungarian, Finnish, German, English, Latvian, Russian, Spanish, Arabic, and Chinese.

13.5.4 SCHEMATIC COMPARISON OF THE THREE BASIC METHODS

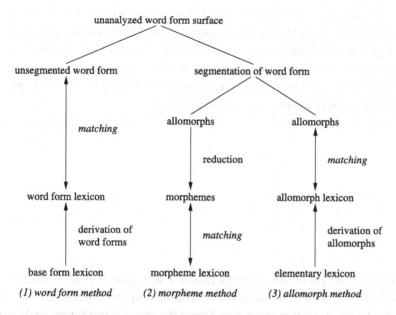

All three methods are based on matching the input surface with a corresponding key of an analysis lexicon characteristic of the method in question. The first alternative consists in whether or not the word form surfaces are segmented into their elements during runtime. This alternative is not only linguistically relevant, but also of practical consequence for the computational implementation.

If the input is not segmented, we obtain the word form method in which the input surface is matched as a whole to corresponding keys of analyzed word forms. In this case the well-known method of hash tables may be used for lexical lookup, as long as the boundaries of each word form are marked, e.g., by spaces.

If the input surface is segmented, the concrete elements are the allomorphs. To automatically determine the allomorph boundaries – which are not orthographically marked – the method of trie structures is suited best (Sect. 14.3). The next question is whether the allomorphs found in the surface should be reduced to morphemes prior to lexical lookup or whether lexical lookup should be defined for allomorphs.

The first option results in the morpheme method, in which both segmentation of the surface into allomorphs and the reduction of the allomorphs into the associated (unanalyzed) morphemes takes place during runtime. The morpheme surfaces obtained in this manner are matched with corresponding keys in a lexicon consisting of analyzed morphemes. Then the analyzed morphemes are put together again by grammatical rules to categorize and lemmatize the word form in question.

The second option results in the allomorph method, in which the input surface is matched onto fully analyzed allomorphs during runtime. The analyzed allomorphs are generated automatically from an elementary lexicon by allo rules before runtime.

During runtime the analyzed allomorphs need only be concatenated by means of left-associative combi rules, which categorize and lemmatize the input.

Of the three methods, the allomorph method is best suited for the task. It is of low mathematical complexity (linear), describes morphological phenomena of concatenation and allomorphy in a linguistically transparent, rule-based manner, handles neologisms during runtime, may be applied easily to new languages, is computationally space and time efficient, and can be easily debugged and scaled up. The allomorph method is described in more detail in the following chapter.

Exercises

Section 13.1

1. Give the inflectional paradigms of man, power, learn, give, fast, and good. Generate new words from them by means of derivation and compounding.
2. Call up LA Morph on your computer and have the above word forms analyzed.
3. Explain the notions word, word form, paradigm, part of speech, and the difference between the open and the closed classes.
4. Why is it relevant to distinguish between the notions word and word form?
5. What is the role of the closed classes in derivation and compounding?
6. Why are only the open classes a demanding task of computational morphology?
7. How do the content and function words relate to the open and the closed classes?

Section 13.2

1. Why is the number of word forms in German potentially infinite?
2. Why is the number of noun-noun compounds n^2?
3. What do the formal definitions of word and morpheme have in common?
4. What is a neologism?
5. Describe the difference between morphemes and syllables.

Section 13.3

1. What is suppletion?
2. Why is a bound morpheme like -ing neither in the open nor the closed classes?
3. What would argue against postulating bound morphemes?

Section 13.4

1. Explain the three steps of a morphological analysis.
2. Why does LA Grammar analyze allomorphs as ordered triples?
3. What are the components of a system of automatic word form recognition?

4. What is a lemma? Are there essential differences between the entries of a traditional dictionary and an online lexicon for automatic word form recognition?
5. How does the surface function as a key in automatic word form recognition?
6. Explain the purpose of categorization and lemmatization.
7. What is an analysis lexicon?

Section 13.5

1. Describe three different methods of automatic word form recognition.
2. Why is there no *word method* of automatic word form recognition?
3. How does the word form method handle categorization and lemmatization?
4. Compare cost and benefit of the word form method.
5. Would you classify the word form method as a smart or as a solid solution?
6. Why is the morpheme method mathematically complex?
7. Why does the morpheme method violate surface compositionality?
8. Why does the morpheme method use surfaces only indirectly as the key?
9. Why is the morpheme method conceptually related to transformational grammar?
10. Why does the allomorph method satisfy the principle of surface compositionality?
11. Why is the runtime behavior of the allomorph method faster than that of the morpheme method?

14. Word Form Recognition in LA Morph

The allomorph method has been developed and implemented as a system called
LA Morph. Linguistically, LA Morph is based on (i) an elementary lexicon, (ii) a set
of allo rules, and (iii) a set of combi rules. The allo rules take the elementary lexicon as input and generate from it a corresponding allomorph lexicon before runtime.
The combi rules control the time-linear concatenation of analyzed allomorphs during
runtime, resulting in the morphosyntactic analysis of complex word forms.

Section 14.1 explains the allo rules and defines four degrees of regularity for inflectional paradigms. Section 14.2 gives an overview of allomorphic phenomena in nouns,
verbs, and adjectives of English, and investigates how many allomorphs a morpheme
has on average (allomorph quotient of English). Section 14.3 describes the computational method of segmenting word forms into their analyzed allomorphs by means of
a tree structure. Section 14.4 explains the combi rules. Section 14.5 gives an overview
of the concatenation patterns of inflectional morphology of English and German.

14.1 Allo Rules

An allo rule takes an entry of the elementary lexicon as input and derives from it one
or more allomorphs. The input and the output are defined in terms of patterns. The
basic structure of the allo rules may be shown as follows:

14.1.1 ABSTRACT FORMAT OF AN ALLO RULE

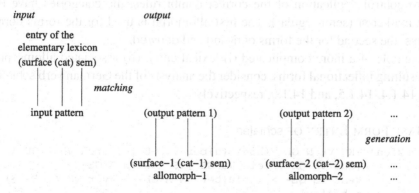

Allo rules apply before runtime and may modify the surface, the category, and the semantic representation of their input.

When the allo rule component is applied to an elementary lexicon, all its entries are run through the allo rules, which are arranged in a fixed order. If an entry matches the input pattern of an allo rule, it is accepted and the associated allomorphs are produced. If an entry is not accepted, it is passed on to the next allo rule. The last allo rule is the default rule. Its input pattern accepts any entry and returns it unchanged.

The output of the allo rules is written sequentially into a file. In this way the elementary lexicon is converted automatically into a lexicon of analyzed allomorphs. Even a lexicon comprising more than 100 000 base forms takes no more than a few seconds to be run through the allo rule component.

Afterwards the allo rule component is not applied again until the allo rules or the elementary lexicon have been modified. Theoretically, the allo rules describe all the morphological regularities and irregularities of the language at hand. Practically, the allo rule software component allows for testing on large amounts of relevant data, which is the basis for incremental upscaling.

Consider the following entry of an elementary lexicon. The format of the entry is that of the LA Morph version programmed by Hausser and Ellis 1990 (15.1.5). The list-based categories of this version are close to the LA Grammars for artificial languages:

14.1.2 EXAMPLE OF A BASE FORM ENTRY

```
("derive" (nom a v) derive)
```

The category (nom a v) characterizes the entry as a verb which takes a nominative and an accusative as arguments (valency fillers).

The allo rules map the base form entry into the following analyzed allomorphs:

14.1.3 RESULT OF APPLYING ALLO RULES TO BASE FORM ENTRY

```
("derive" (sr nom a v) derive)
("deriv" (sr a v) derive)
```

In order to control application of the correct combi rules, the categories have the additional marker sr (semi-regular). The first allomorph is used for the forms derive and derive/s, the second for the forms deriv/ing and deriv/ed.

As an example of a more complicated (i) lexical entry, (ii) associated allomorphs, and (iii) resulting inflectional forms, consider the analysis of the German verb schlafen (sleep) in 14.1.4, 14.1.5, and 14.1.6, respectively.

14.1.4 BASE FORM ENTRY OF schlafen

```
("schla2fen" (KV VH N GE  {hin\"{u}ber VS GE } {durch VH A GE }
              {aus VH GE } {ein VS GE }\$ <be VH A GE- >
              <ent VS GE- > <\"{u}ber VH A GE- > <ver VH A GE- >)
              schlafen)
```

The first element of this lexical entry is the surface in which the characteristic *ablaut* variation of schlafen is specified by the marker '2.' The second element is the category[1] (KV ...>), which is rather long and complex because its description includes four variants with separable prefixes and four variants with nonseparable ones. The third element is the base form *schlafen* without any surface markers.

The allo rules map the base form entry into the analyzed allomorphs schlaf, schläf, and schlief:

14.1.5 OUTPUT OF ALLO RULES FOR schlafen

```
("schlaf" (IV V1 VH N GE { hin\"{u}ber VS GE } { durch VH A GE }
          { aus VH GE } { ein VS GE } $ < be VH A GE- >
          < ent VS GE- > < \"{u}ber VH A GE- > < ver VH A GE- > )
          schlafen)
("schl\"{a}f" (IV V2 _0 N GE { hin\"{u}ber VS GE }
          { durch VH A GE }
          { aus VH GE } { ein VS GE } $ < be VH A GE- >
          < ent VS GE- > < \"{u}ber VH A GE- > < ver VH A GE- > )
          schlafen)
("schlief" (IV V34 _0 N GE { hin\"{u}ber VS GE } { durch VH A GE }
          { aus VH GE } { ein VS GE } $ < be VH A GE- >
          < ent VS GE- > < \"{u}ber VH A GE- > < ver VH A GE- > )
          schlafen_i)
```

Triggered by the surface marker '2' (14.1.4), three different allomorphs without surface markers are derived. To ensure application of the correct combi rules, the first segment KV (Klasse Verb) has been replaced by IV (intransitive verb), and the second

---

[1] The category begins with the segment 'KV', specifying the part of speech, 'verb', The second segment 'VH' indicates that schlafen combines with the auxiliary haben (have) rather than sein (be). The third segment N represents the nominative valency, whereby the absence of additional case segments characterizes the verb as intransitive. Finally, the fourth segment 'GE' indicates that the past participle is formed with ge as in ge/schlaf/en or aus/ge/schlaf/en – in contrast to, for example, ver/schlaf/en.

Then there follow expressions in curly brackets describing the nonseparable prefixes, here hinüberschlafen, durchschlafen, ausschlafen, and einschlafen. These bracketed expressions specify the kind of auxiliary, the kind of past participle, and the valency of each of these variants.

The description of separable prefixes in the base form entry of the stem is necessary for morphological as well as syntactic reasons. The prefix may occur both attached to the verb as in (i) weil Julia schnell einschlief, and separated from the verb as in (ii) Julia schlief schnell ein. In (ii) the prefix in the category of sleep is used by the syntax to identify ein as part of the verb, which is semantically important. In (i) the prefix in the category is used by the morphology to combine ein and schlief into the word form einschlief.

After the separable prefixes there follow the nonseparable prefixes of schlafen marked by angled brackets. Again, the auxiliaries (e.g., hat verschlafen vs. ist entschlafen), the past participle, and the valency structure (e.g., ist entschlafen vs. hat das Frühstück verschlafen) are specified for each prefix variant.

segment VH (combines with "haben") by V1, V2, and V34 in the categories of the respective allomorphs. The remainder of the original category, serving to handle separable and nonseparable prefixes, reappears unchanged in the allomorph categories.

Based on the above allomorphs, the combi rules analyze and generate nine paradigms with 29 forms each. Thus a single base form entry is mapped into a total of 261 different inflectional forms.

14.1.6 THE WORD FORMS OF schlafen (excerpt)

```
("schlaf/e" (S1 {hin\"{u}ber}{durch A}{aus}{ein} V) schlafen_p)
("schlaf/e" (S13 {hin\"{u}ber} {durch A} {aus} {ein} V ) s._k1)
("schlaf/e/n" (P13 {hin\"{u}ber} {durch A} {aus} {ein} V ) s._pk1)
("schlaf/e/st" (S2 {hin\"{u}ber} {durch A} {aus} {ein} V ) s._k1)
("schlaf/e/t" (P2 {hin\"{u}ber} {durch A} {aus} {ein} V ) s._k1)
("schlaf/t" (P2 {hin\"{u}ber} {durch A} {aus} {ein} V ) s._p)
("schlaf/end" (GER ) schlafen)
("schlaf/end/e" (E ) schlafen)
("schlaf/end/en" (EN ) schlafen)
("schlaf/end/er" (ER ) schlafen)
("schlaf/end/es" (ES ) schlafen)
("schlaf/end/em" (EM ) schlafen)
("schlaf/e/st" (S2 {hin\"{u}ber} {durch A} {aus} {ein} V ) s._k1)
("schlaf/e/t" (P2 {hin\"{u}ber} {durch A} {aus} {ein} V ) s._k1)
("schl\"{a}f/st" (S2 {hin\"{u}ber} {durch A} {aus} {ein} V ) s._p)
("schl\"{a}f/t" (S3 {hin\"{u}ber} {durch A} {aus} {ein} V ) s._p)
("schlief" (S13 {hin\"{u}ber} {durch A} {aus} {ein} V ) s._i)
("schlief/e" (S13 {hin\"{u}ber} {durch A} {aus} {ein} V ) s._k2)
("schlief/en" (P13 {hin\"{u}ber} {durch A} {aus} {ein} V ) s._ik2)
("schlief/est" (S2 {hin\"{u}ber} {durch A} {aus} {ein} V ) s._ik2)
("schlief/et" (P2 {hin\"{u}ber} {durch A} {aus} {ein} V ) s._ik2)
("schlief/st" (S2 {hin\"{u}ber} {durch A} {aus} {ein} V ) s._ik2)
("schlief/t" (P2 {hin\"{u}ber} {durch A} {aus} {ein} V ) s._i)
("ge/schlaf/en" (H) schlafen)
("ge/schlaf/en/e" (E) schlafen)
("ge/schlaf/en/en" (EN) schlafen)
("ge/schlaf/en/es" (ES) schlafen)
("ge/schlaf/en/er" (ER) schlafen)
("ge/schlaf/en/em" (EM) schlafen)

("aus/schlaf/e" (S1 V) ausschlafen_pk1)
("aus/schlaf/e" (S13 V ) ausschlafen_k1)
("aus/schlaf/en" (P13 A V ) ausschlafen_pk1)
    . . .
("aus/schl\"{a}f/st" (S2 V) ausschlafen_p)
("aus/schl\"{a}f/t" (S3 V) ausschlafen_p)
    . . .
```

The finite forms of schlafen retain the separable prefixes in their category because they may be needed by the syntax, as in Susanne schlief gestern aus. The nonseparable prefixes, on the other hand, are removed from the categories because the associated surfaces, e.g., verschlafe, verschläfst, etc., have no separable variant. For the same reason the separable prefixes are omitted in the categories of nonfinite forms, e.g., hat ausgeschlafen, wollte ausschlafen.

Depending on whether or not an inflectional paradigm (i) requires exactly one entry in the elementary lexicon, (ii) requires a special marker in the entry's surface, or (iii) derives more than one allomorph per entry, four different degrees of regularity may be distinguished.

14.1.7 FOUR DEGREES OF REGULARITY IN LA MORPH

- *Regular* inflectional paradigm
  The paradigm is represented by one entry without any special surface markings, from which one allomorph is derived, e.g., learn ⇒ learn, or book ⇒ book.
- *Semi-regular* inflectional paradigm
  The paradigm is represented by one entry without any special surface markings, from which more than one allomorph is derived, e.g., derive ⇒ derive, deriv, or wolf ⇒ wolf, wolv.
- *Semi-irregular* inflectional paradigm
  The paradigm is represented by one entry with a special surface marker, from which more than one allomorph is derived, e.g., swlm ⇒ swim, swimm, swam, swum.
- *Irregular* inflectional paradigm
  The paradigm is represented by several entries for suppletive allomorphs which pass through the default rule, e.g., go ⇒ go, went ⇒ went, gone ⇒ gone. Using a suitable categorization, these allomorphs may be processed by the general combi rules, as in go/ing.

The degrees of regularity may be represented as the following table:

14.1.8 TABULAR PRESENTATION OF THE DEGREES OF REGULARITY

	one entry per paradigm	entry without markings	one allomorph per entry
regular	yes	yes	yes
semi-regular	yes	yes	no
semi-irregular	yes	no	no
irregular	no	no	yes

This structural criterion for the classification of (ir)regularities is of general interest insofar as the characterization of regularities and exceptions has always been regarded as a central task of traditional morphology.

14.2 Phenomena of Allomorphy

To get a concrete idea of what the allo rules are needed for, let us consider different instances of allomorphy in English. The following examples of nouns (14.2.1, 14.2.2), verbs (14.2.3, 14.2.4), and adjectives (14.2.5) are presented in a way which resembles the structure of allo rules insofar as the (surface of the) input is listed under the key word LEX and the associated output under the key words ALLO1, ALLO2, etc., in a tabular format. They are only a precursor of the actual allo rules, however, because (i) the structures in question are described by example rather than abstract patterns and (ii) the description is limited to the surfaces.

The *regular* nouns of English occur in four different inflectional forms, namely unmarked singular (book), genitive singular (book/'s), unmarked plural (book/s), and genitive plural (book/s/'). These forms are analyzed and generated concatenatively by combi rules using the base form and the suffixes 's, s, and ' .

The *semi-regular* nouns of English use different allomorphs for the stem in the singular and the plural form. Like the regular nouns, their different forms are analyzed in terms of concatenation. Thereby markers in the category ensure that each allomorph is combined with the proper suffix, for example wolf/'s, but not *wolv/'s, and wolv/es, but not *wolv/s.

14.2.1 ALLOMORPHS OF SEMI-REGULAR NOUNS

LEX	ALLO1	ALLO2
wolf	wolf	wolv
knife	knife	knive
ability	ability	abiliti
academy	academy	academi
agency	agency	agenci
money	money	moni

The *semi-irregular* nouns of English generate their unmarked plural nonconcatenatively by means of allo rules alone. The marked forms (genitives) of singular and plural are handled in a concatenative manner.

14.2.2 ALLOMORPHS OF SEMI-IRREGULAR NOUNS

LEX	ALLO1	ALLO2
analysis	analysis	analyses
larva	larva	larvae
stratum	stratum	strata
matrix	matrix	matrices
thesis	thesis	theses
criterion	criterion	criteria
tempo	tempo	tempi
calculus	calculus	calculi

The *irregular* nouns of English, such as child–children, foot–feet, ox–oxen, and sheep–sheep, are not handled by allo rules, but rather by two entries in the elementary lexicon, one for the unmarked singular and one for the unmarked plural form. In addition there are pluralitantia like scissors and people which are also handled directly in the elementary lexicon. The marked forms of the irregular nouns such as analysis' are handled by special clauses of the relevant combi rules.

The *regular* verbs of English occur in four different inflectional forms, namely unmarked present tense and infinitive (learn), marked present tense (learn/s), past tense and past participle (learn/ed), and progressive (learn/ing). In addition there are derivational forms like learn/er as well as their respective inflectional forms such as learn/er/'s, etc. This set of forms is analyzed and generated by combi rules using the base form and the suffixes ("bound morphemes," 13.3.4) s, ed, ing, and er.

The *semi-regular* verbs of English use two different allomorphs. Like the regular verbs, their inflectional forms are analyzed in terms of concatenation. Thereby markers in the category ensure that each allomorph is combined with the proper suffixes, e.g., derive/s, but not *derive/ing, and deriv/ing, but not *deriv/s (14.1.3).

14.2.3 ALLOMORPHS OF SEMI-REGULAR VERBS

LEX	ALLO1	ALLO2
derive	derive	deriv
dangle	dangle	dangl
undulate	undulate	undulat
accompany	accompany	accompani

The *semi-irregular* verbs of English generate their past tense and past participle nonconcatenatively by means of allo rules alone. The marked form of the present tense, e.g., swim/s, and the progressive, e.g., swimm/ing, are handled by concatenation.

14.2.4 ALLOMORPHS OF SEMI-IRREGULAR VERBS

LEX	ALLO1	ALLO2	ALLO3	ALLO4
swIm	swim	swimm	swam	swum
rUN	run	runn	ran	run
bET	bet	bett	bet	bet

Though the ALLO4 allomorphs of run and bet have the same surface as their base form, these forms differ in their respective categories. ALLO2 handles the gemination needed for the progressive form.

The *irregular* verbs of English, such as arise–arose–arisen, break–broke–broken, give–gave–given, go–went–gone, or seek–sought–sought are not handled by allo rules. Instead the suppletive forms are treated in the elementary lexicon, one entry for the unmarked present tense, one for the past tense, and one for the past participle.

The *regular* adjectives of English occur in four different inflectional forms, namely unmarked (adnominal) positive (e.g., slow), comparative (e.g., slow/er), superlative (e.g., slow/est), and marked (adverbial) positive (e.g., slow/ly). This set of forms is analyzed and generated by combi rules using the base form and the suffixes er, est, and ly.

The *semi-regular* adjectives of English are also analyzed in terms of concatenation, whereby markers in the category ensure that each allomorph is combined with the proper suffixes, e.g., abl/er, but not *able/er, or free/ly, but not *fre/ly.

14.2.5 ALLOMORPHS OF SEMI-REGULAR ADJECTIVES

LEX	ALLO1	ALLO2
able	able	abl
happy	happy	happi
free	free	fre
true	true	tru

Semi-irregular adjectives are not instantiated in English. The *irregular* adjectives of English are exemplified by good–better–best–well.

In light of these examples there arises the question of how many word forms of English are based on allomorphic variants. From the viewpoint of linguistics this question is of interest because the number of allomorphs – compared to the number of base forms – is indicative of the relative degree of (ir)regularity of a natural language in the area of morphology. From the viewpoint of programming it is of interest because the additional number of precomputed allomorphs affects the load on the random access memory (RAM).

If the number of allomorphic variants in natural language turned out to be very large, then the alternative morpheme approach (13.5.2) would have the advantage of computing allomorphs only on demand – for the surface currently analyzed. On the other hand, if this number turned out to be rather small, then the precomputation of allomorphs would require only a modest amount of additional RAM while resulting in a tremendous simplification and speedup of the runtime analysis.

In short, the choice between the allomorph and the morpheme methods depends not only on theoretical and technical considerations, but also on the empirical facts of natural language, namely the number of allomorphs relative to the number of morphemes. We call this numerical correlation the allomorph quotient of a natural language.

14.2.6 DEFINITION OF THE ALLOMORPH QUOTIENT

The allomorph quotient is the percentage of additional allomorphs relative to the number of base form entries.[2]

Because the allomorph method automatically derives all the possible allomorphs to a given elementary lexicon, its application to a certain natural language provides all the data needed for the computation of its allomorph quotient.

---

[2] That is (the number of allomorphs minus the number of morphemes) divided by the number of morphemes and multiplied by 100.

Let us assume that we want to apply LA Morph to a natural language not previously handled, e.g., English. The first step is to look for a traditional lexicon (13.4.5) that is legally available online. Using computational methods, its grammatical information can easily be 'massaged' into a format suitable for the application of allo rules.

Once the format of the traditional lexicon has been adjusted, and the allo- and combi rules have been written for the new language, the system may be tested on free text. Thereby many word forms will turn out to have two analyses. For example, if the traditional lexicon used were Webster's New Collegiate Dictionary, then

pseudoclassic
pseudopregnancy
pseudosalt
pseudoscientific
etc.

would have two analyses, in contrast to

pseudogothic
pseudomigraine
pseudoscientist
pseudovegetarian
etc.

which would have only one. The reason is as follows:

In order to recognize the highly productive compounds involving the prefix pseudo, the LA Morph system must provide a general rule-based analysis. As a consequence, words in Webster's dictionary are recognized twice. The first reading is provided by Webster's as a simplex, for example, pseudoclassic, while the second is provided by LA Morph as a compositional analysis, for example, pseudo/classic based on the known forms pseudo and classic.

One method for avoiding this kind of ambiguity is to remove all base forms with a parallel compositional analysis from the online lexicon. This may be done automatically. First all the key word surfaces in the traditional lexicon are parsed by the LA Morph system. Then all multiple analyses, such as pseudoclassic and pseudo/classic, are collected and their base form entries, here pseudoclassic, are removed.

This approach has the advantage of substantially reducing the size of the elementary lexicon (in German and Italian to about half) while maintaining the original data coverage with respect to categorization and lemmatization. In fact, the data coverage of an LA Morph system based on such a reduced elementary lexicon will be much greater than that of the original lexicon alone, e.g., Webster's, because of the general, rule-based handling of derivation and compounding.

A second method of eliminating the ambiguities in question leaves the non-elementary base forms in the lexicon and selects the most likely reading after the word form analysis. For example, given the choice between an analysis as an elementary form (e.g., pseudoclassic) and as a complex form (e.g., pseudo/classic), the system would normally choose the first. This has the advantage that given the choice between kinship and kin/ship the unlikely compound-interpretation of *water vessel for close relatives* would be filtered out.

The best way is to combine the respective advantages of the two approaches by having two lexica. One is a reduced elementary lexicon which does not contain any base forms which have parallel compositional analyses. This lexicon is used for the categorization and lemmatization of word forms.

The other is a nonreduced base form lexicon of content words, e.g., Webster's. It assigns semantic representations to base forms including composita and derivata established in use. During word form analysis the two lexica are related by matching the result of lemmatization to a corresponding – if present – key word of the base form lexicon (13.4.7).

For example, the word kin/ship resulting from a compositional analysis would be matched to kinship in the nonreduced base form lexicon, accessing the proper semantic description. In this way, (i) maximal data coverage – including neologisms – is ensured by a rule-based analysis using the reduced base form lexicon, (ii) the possibility of noncompositional (non-Fregean) meanings is allowed, and (iii) unnecessary ambiguities are avoided.

LA Morph systems for which traditional lexica were reduced to elementary lexica in the manner described above have resulted in the following allomorph quotients:

14.2.7 THE ALLOMORPH QUOTIENT OF DIFFERENT LANGUAGES

Italian: 37 %

> Wetzel (1996) reduces a traditional lexicon of 91 800 entries into an elementary lexicon of 44 000 entries. These base forms are mapped by allo rules into an analysis lexicon of 60 300 entries. The resulting allomorph quotient of 37 % corresponds to an average of 1.37 allomorphs per morpheme.

German: 31 %

> Lorenz (1996) reduces a traditional lexicon of 100 547 entries into an elementary lexicon of 48 422 entries. These base forms are mapped by allo rules into an analysis lexicon of 63 559 entries. The resulting allomorph quotient of 31 % corresponds to an average of 1.31 allomorphs per morpheme.

English: 8.7 %

> Hausser (1989b) uses an elementary lexicon containing 8 000 of the most frequent base forms, from which allo rules derived an analysis lexicon of 9 500 entries. The resulting allomorph quotient of 19 % corresponds to an average of 1.19 allomorphs per morpheme.

Leidner (1998) uses an elementary lexicon of 231 000 entries, which was extracted from several corpora and extended with additional entries from machine-readable dictionaries. The resulting allomorph quotient of 8.97 % corresponds to an average of 1.09 allomorphs per morpheme.

Spanish: 52.75 %

Mahlow (2000) reduces a traditional lexicon of 98 546 lemmata into an elementary lexicon of 66 103 lemmata. These base forms are mapped by allo rules into an analysis dictionary of 99 297 entries. The resulting allomorph quotient of 50.2 % corresponds to an average of 1.50 allomorphs per morpheme.

Korean: 1.8 %

Kim (2009) reduces a traditional lexicon of 88 086 lemmata into an elementary lexicon of 76 171 lemmata. These base forms are mapped by allo rules into an analysis lexicon of 77 572 entries. The resulting allomorph quotient of 1.8 % corresponds to an average of 1.018 allomorphs.

These preliminary results show that the allomorph quotients resulting from the analysis of different languages (and the analysis style of different linguists) are of the same order of magnitude. Furthermore, they are surprisingly low and therefore of no practical consequence for runtime memory.

In addition, it must be taken into account that the analysis lexicon of allomorphs usually has only half as many entries as the original traditional lexicon. With this reduced lexicon the system analyzes not only all key surfaces (lemmata) of the original traditional lexicon, but also all associated inflectional forms, an unlimited number of derivational and compound forms as well as their inflectional forms.

Because the phenomenon of allomorphy is limited to the high frequency entries of the lexicon,[3] an allomorph quotient will decrease as the size of the lexicon is increased with low frequency items. This is shown by the small and the large systems for English cited in 14.2.7. In order to meaningfully compare the allomorph quotient of different languages it should be normalized by basing the calculation on, for example, the 100 000 most frequent words[4] of the open classes without proper names and acronyms.

14.3 Left-Associative Segmentation into Allomorphs

The construction of an elementary lexicon and the definition of allo rules are language-specific tasks which require the methods and knowledge of traditional linguistics. In order to utilize the analyzed allomorphs computationally, however, there

---

[3] Bybee (1985), pp. 208–209.

[4] In order to determine this set, a representative corpus of the language must be used. See Chap. 15.

must be a procedure which automatically segments any unknown surface, e.g., wolves, into a matching sequence of analyzed allomorphs, i.e., wolv/es. This segmentation algorithm is a language-independent procedure the implementation of which is a task for computer science.

The automatic segmentation of a given word form surface into its allomorphs should work as follows. If the unknown word form begins with, for example, W, any allomorphs not beginning with this letter should be disregarded. If the next letter is an O, any allomorphs not beginning with WO should be disregarded, etc.

14.3.1 LEFT-ASSOCIATIVE LETTER BY LETTER MATCHING

```
attempt 1:   W  O  L  F
             |  |  |  X
surface:     W  O  L  V
             |  |  |  |
attempt2:    W  O  L  V
```

With this method, the possible goal WOLF is eliminated as soon as the fourth letter V is encountered. Thus, in the analysis of wolves the allomorph wolf is never even considered. The theoretical relation between wolf and wolv is established solely in terms of the common base form in the third position of their respective analyses (13.2.4).

If the letter sequence in the unknown surface has been matched successfully by an analyzed allomorph, e.g., wolv, but there are still letters left in the unknown surface, as in, for example, wolves, the next allomorph is looked for. This method of left-associatively matching allomorphs to the unknown surface pursues all possible hypotheses in parallel from left to right. The result is a complete segmentation into all possible allomorph sequences.

As an example in which two alternative segmentations are maintained in parallel (lexical ambiguity), consider the German surface Staubecken:[5]

---

[5] Corresponding hypothetical examples in English are

coverage	grandparent	history	lamp/light	land/s/end
cover/age	grandpa/rent	hi/story	lam/plight	land/send
cove/rage		his/tory		

rampage	rampart	scar/face	sing/able	war/plane
ramp/age	ramp/art	scarf/ace	sin/gable	warp/lane
ram/page	ram/part			

These examples were found computationally by Wetzel at the CL lab of Friedrich Alexander Universität Erlangen Nürnberg (CLUE). Most of them, e.g., 'warp/lane' or 'ramp/art', are not quite real because noun-noun compounds in English are usually written as separate word forms.

14.3.2 ALTERNATIVE SEGMENTATIONS OF A WORD FORM

surface:	Staubecken	Staubecken
segmentation:	Stau/becken	Staub/ecke/n
translation:	*reservoir*	*dust corners*

All that is required for the correct segmentation is to provide the relevant allomorphs stau, staub, becken, ecke, and n, and to systematically match them from left to right onto the unknown surface. This method works even in writing systems in which only the beginning and end of sentences or even texts are marked, as in the *continua* writing style of classical Latin.

Computationally, the left-associative, parallel, letter-by-letter matching of allomorphs is implemented by means of a trie structure[6] or letter tree. A trie structure functions as an index which makes it possible to find an entry (here an analyzed allomorph) by going through the key word letter by letter from left to right. In LA Morph the trie structure is built up automatically when the elementary lexicon is run through the allo rule component.

As an example of a trie structure consider 14.3.3, which shows the storage of the allomorphs swim, swimm, swam, swamp, er, ing, s, and y:

14.3.3 STORING ALLOMORPHS IN A TRIE STRUCTURE

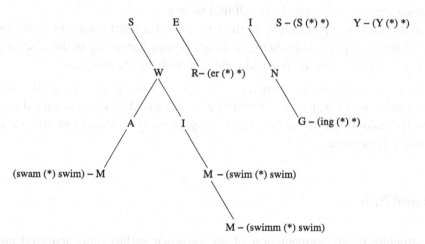

A trie structure consists of several levels, whereby the first level contains all the allomorph initial letters, the second level contains all the allomorph second letters, etc.

---

[6] Knuth (1973), p. 483, attributes the idea of trie structures to de la Briandais (1959). Aho et al. (1983), p. 163, attribute it to Fredkin (1960). The name 'trie' is taken from the middle of the word retrieval. According to Aho et al. (1983) "trie was originally intended to be a homonym of 'tree,' but to distinguish these two terms many people prefer to pronounce trie as though it rhymes with 'pie'."

The '/' and '\' connectors between the different levels in 14.3.3 indicate legal continuations from one level to the next. For example, the attempt to find an allomorph analysis for the input SWQ would break off after SW because in 14.3.3 there is no Q underneath the W on the third level.

The lexical analysis of an allomorph is stored at its last letter in the trie structure. Consider, for example, the search for the analyzed allomorph swim. Because its surface consists of four letters, its lexical analysis is stored at the fourth level of the trie structure. The entry is found by going to the letter S on the first level, then to the letter W underneath the S on the second level, etc.

The search is successful if the navigation through the trie structure arrives at a letter with a lexical analysis. When such an analysis is found, three possibilities arise:

– There are no letters left in the surface of the unknown word form, e.g., SWAM. Then the program simply returns the analysis stored at the last letter, here M.
– There are still letters left in the surface of the unknown word form. Then one of the following alternatives applies:
    • The allomorph found so far *is part* of the word form, as swim in SWIMS. Then the program (i) gives the lexical analysis of swim to the combi rules of the system and (ii) looks for the next allomorph (here, s), starting again from the top level of the trie structure.
    • The allomorph found so far *is not part* of the word form, as swam in SWAMPY. In this case the program continues down the trie structure provided there are continuations. In our example, it will find swamp.

Because it becomes apparent only at the very end of a word form which of these two possibilities applies – or whether they apply simultaneously in the case of an ambiguity (14.3.2) – they are pursued simultaneously by the program.

The downward search in the trie structure is stopped if there is an entry and/or there is no continuation to a lower level. The latter may be caused by ungrammatical input (not a possible allomorph of the language) or by an analysis lexicon of allomorphs which is not yet complete.

14.4 Combi Rules

The trie-structure-based segmentation of an unknown surface into analyzed allomorphs in LA morphology corresponds to automatic word form recognition in LA syntax. Similarly, the time-linear composition of allomorphs into word forms by the combi rules of LA morphology corresponds to time-linear composition of word forms into sentences by rules of LA syntax.

Because the allomorphs of LA morphology and the word forms of LA syntax are similar in structure (ordered triples), their respective time-linear composition is based on the same rule mechanism of abstract LA Grammar (Part II) and the same parser:

14.4.1 COMBI RULE SCHEMA

$$\textit{input} \qquad\qquad \textit{output}$$

$$r_i: \text{(pattern of start) (pattern of next)} \;\Rightarrow\; rp_i \text{ (pattern of new start)}$$

Each time a rule r_i has mapped an input pair into a new word start, a next allomorph is searched for in the trie structure. The next allomorph and the current word start form a new input pair to which all the rules in the rule package rp_i are applied. This is repeated as long as (i) next allomorphs are being provided by a matching between sections of the word form surface and the continuations in the trie structure (14.3.3), and (ii) the process of left-associative combinations is not stopped prematurely because no rule in any of the current rule packages is successful.

While the time-linear combi rules of LA morphology resemble the time-linear rules of LA syntax, they differ from the allo rules of LA morphology as follows:

An *allo rule* takes a lexical entry as input and maps it to one or more allomorphs.

A *combi rule* takes a word form start and a next allomorph as input and maps it to a new word form start.

They differ also in that the allo rules usually modify the surface of their input, whereas the combi rules combine the surfaces of their input expressions without change. Furthermore, the allo rules are applied before runtime, whereas the combi rules apply during runtime.

The combi rules ensure that

1. the allomorphs found in the surface are not combined into ungrammatical word forms, e.g., *swam+ing or *swimm+s (input condition),
2. the surfaces of grammatical allomorph combinations are properly concatenated, e.g., swim+s ⇒ swims,
3. the categories of the input pair are mapped into the correct result category, e.g., (NOM V) + (SX S3) ⇒ (S3 V),
4. the correct result is formed on the level of semantic interpretation, and
5. after a successful rule application the correct rule package for the next combination is activated.

The structure of morphological analysis provided by the LA Morph parser is illustrated with the following trace for the input unduly:

14.4.2 PARSING unduly IN LA MORPH

```
1 +u [NIL . NIL]
2   +n [NIL . (un (PX PREF) UN)]
RP:{V-START N-START A-START P-START}; fired: P-START
3     +d [(un (PX PREF) UN) . (d (GG) NIL)]
       +d [NIL . NIL]
4       +u [(un (PX PREF) UN) . (du (SR SN) DUE (SR ADJ-V) DUE)]
RP:{PX+A UN+V}; fired: PX+A
         +u [NIL . NIL]
```

```
5 L [(un+du (SR ADJ) DUE) . (1 (GG) NIL (ABBR) LITER)]
RP:{A+LY}; fired: none
      +1 [(un (PX PREF) UN) . NIL]
      +1 [NIL . NIL]
6       +y [(un+du (SR ADJ) DUE) . (ly (SX ADV) LY)]
RP:{A+LY}; fired: A+LY
("un/du/ly" (ADV) due)
```

This format of an LA Morph analysis shows the step-by-step search through the trie structure. At the second letter 'n' the allomorph entry un is found, whereby the word form start is NIL. Other allomorphs found are du, l, and ly.

In the analysis we may distinguish between the optional derivation and the obligatory result. The derivation shows which allomorphs were found, which rules were tried, and which were successful. The derivation provides valuable heuristics for debugging and upscaling the system.

The result, i.e., the content of the last line, is used in applications of LA Morph, such as syntactic parsing. In such applications the derivation is of little interest and omitted in the output. The result provides the required categorization and lemmatization. For example, in 14.4.2 the word form unduly is categorized as an adverb and lemmatized as due, whereby the negation is coded in the semantic representation stored underneath the base form.

The combi rules of LA Morph ensure that only grammatically correct forms are recognized or generated. As an example, consider the attempt to combine the legal allomorphs able and ly into an illegal word form:

14.4.3 PARSING UNGRAMMATICAL ablely IN LA MORPH

```
1 +a [NIL . (a (SQ) A)]
2 +b [NIL . NIL]
3   +l [NIL . (abl (SR ADJ-A) ABLE)]
RP:{V-START N-START A-START P-START}; fired: A-START
4   +e [(abl (SR ADJ) ABLE) . NIL]
      +e [NIL . (able (ADJ) ABLE)]
RP:{V-START N-START A-START P-START}; fired: none
5   +l [(abl (SR ADJ) ABLE) . NIL]
ERROR
Unknown word form: "ablely"
NIL
```

The result characterizes the input *ablely as ungrammatical.

Finally, consider the analysis of the simplex undulate, which happens to share the first five letters with unduly (14.4.2).

14.4.4 PARSING THE SIMPLEX undulate IN LA MORPH

```
1 +u [NIL . NIL]
2 +n [NIL . (un (PX PREF) UN)]
RP:{V-START N-START A-START P-START}; fired: P-START
```

```
3      +d [(un (PX PREF) UN) . (d (GG) NIL)]
       +d [NIL . NIL]
4       +u [(un (PX PREF) UN) . (du (SR SN) DUE (SR ADJ-V) DUE)]
RP:{PX+A UN+V}; fired: PX+A
        +u [NIL . NIL]
5       +l [(un+du (SR ADJ) DUE) . (l (GG) NIL (ABBR) LITER)]
RP:{A+LY}; fired: none
        +l [(un (PX PREF) UN) . NIL]
        +l [NIL . NIL]
6       +a [(un+du (SR ADJ) DUE) . NIL]
        +a [NIL . NIL]
7        +t [(un+du (SR ADJ) DUE) . NIL]
         +t [NIL . (undulat (SR A V) UNDULATE)]
RP:{V-START N-START A-START P-START}; fired: V-START
8          +e [(un+du (SR ADJ) DUE) . (late (ADJ-AV) LATE
                                        (ADV) LATE)]
RP:{A+LY}; fired: none
           +e [(undulat (SR A V) UNDULATE) . NIL]
           +e [NIL . (undulate (SR NOM A V) UNDULATE)]
RP:{V-START N-START A-START P-START}; fired: V-START
("undulate" (NOM A V) UNDULATE)
```

Up to the fifth letter the derivation is identical to that of unduly in 14.4.2. These hypotheses do not survive, however, and in the end the word form turns out to be a simplex. At letter 8, the allomorph undulat (as in undulat/ing) is found, but it is superseded by the longer allomorph. The fact that the allomorphs undulat and undulate belong to the same morpheme is expressed solely in terms of their common semantic representation.

14.5 Concatenation Patterns

To get a concrete idea of what the combi rules are needed for, let us consider different instances of inflectional concatenation in English.

14.5.1 CONCATENATION PATTERNS OF ENGLISH NOUNS

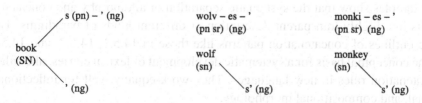

The category (sn) stands for a singular noun, (ng) for noun genitive, and (pn) for plural noun. The example book represents a regular noun. The examples wolf and monkey represent different kinds of semi-regular nouns.

14.5.2 CONCATENATION PATTERNS OF ENGLISH VERBS

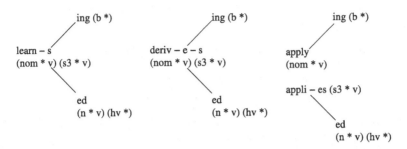

The '*' in the categories of 14.5.2 stands for the oblique (i.e., non-nominative) valency positions, which vary in different verbs, e.g., (sleep (nom′ v) sleep), (see (nom′ a′ v) see), (give (nom′ d′ a′ v) give), or (give (nom′ a′ to′ v) give). The v indicates a finite verb form. b and hv represent the nonfinite present and past participle, respectively, indicating the combination with a form of be or have.

The example learn in 14.5.2 illustrates the concatenation pattern of a regular verb. The examples derive and apply represent different instances of semi-regular verbs. In addition to the forms shown above, there are derivational forms like learn/er and learn/able.

14.5.3 CONCATENATION PATTERNS OF ADJECTIVES

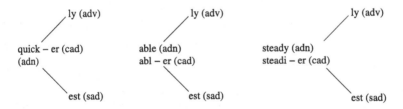

The categories (adj), (adv), (cad), and (sad) stand for adjective, adverb, comparative adjective, and superlative adjective, respectively. The example quick in 14.5.3 illustrates the concatenation pattern of a regular paradigm, while able and steady represent different instances of semi-regular adjectives.

These examples show that the systematic separation of allomorphy and concatenation results in a highly transparent description of different kinds of paradigms. The schematic outlines of concatenation patterns like those in 14.5.1, 14.5.2, and 14.5.3 provide the conceptual basis for a systematic development of lexical entries, allo rules, and concatenation rules in new languages. They work equally well for inflectional, derivational, and compositional morphology.

As an example of a more complicated morphology, consider the nominal and verbal concatenation patterns of German. They will be referred to in the syntactic analysis of German in Chap. 18.

14.5.4 CONCATENATION PATTERNS OF GERMAN NOUNS

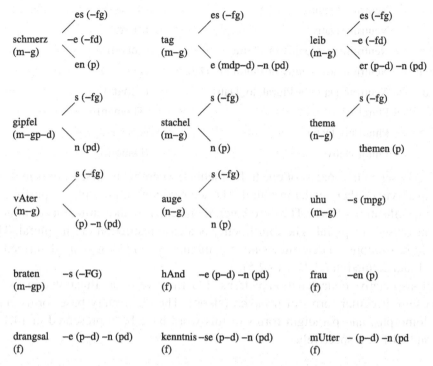

The purpose of the categories in 14.5.4 is to capture the agreement restrictions of the determiner-noun combination as simply and succinctly as possible. While a traditional paradigmatic analysis always assigns eight lexical analyses to a German noun (nominative, genitive, dative, and accusative, in the singular and plural), the distinctive categorization of 14.5.4 assigns only one lexical analysis per distinct surface form. Because there are two to five surface forms per noun, the categorization in 14.5.4 reduces the average number of forms per noun paradigm on average to less than half.

The category segments are explained and illustrated in the following list.

14.5.5 CATEGORY SEGMENTS OF GERMAN NOUN FORMS

mn	= Masculinum Nominativ	(Bote)
m–g	= Masculinum no_Genitiv	(Tag)
–fg	= no_Femininum Genitiv	(Tages, Kindes)
–fd	= no_Femininum Dativ	(Schmerze, Kinde)
m–np	= Masculinum no_Nominativ or Plural	(Boten)
m–gp	= Masculinum no_Genitiv or Plural	(Braten)
mgp	= Masculinum Genitiv or Plural	(Uhus)
m–gp–d	= Masculinum no_Genitiv or Plural no_Dativ	(Gipfel)
f	= Femininum	(Frau)

n–g	= Neutrum no_Genitiv	(Kind)
ng	= Neutrum Genitiv	(Kindes)
nd	= Neutrum Dativ	(Kinde)
n–gp	= Neutrum no_Genitiv or Plural	(Leben)
n–gp–d	= Neutrum no_Genitiv or Plural no_Dativ	(Wasser)
ndp–d	= Neutrum Dativ or Plural no_Dativ	(Schafe)
p	= Plural	(Themen)
p–d	= Plural no_Dativ	(Leiber)
pd	= Plural Dativ	(Leibern)

The category segments consist of one to four letters, whereby the first letter is m, f, –f, n, or p, specifying either gender or plural. The second letter, if present, is a positive or negative specification of case. The third letter, if present, is p, indicating that a singular form is also used for plural. The fourth letter is a case restriction on the plural. The agreement restrictions on determiner-noun combinations in German are described in Sect. 18.1 and defined in *LA D2* (18.2.5).

The left-associative concatenation patterns of German verbs are illustrated in 14.5.6 with the semi-irregular forms of schlafen (sleep). The elementary base forms, analyzed allomorphs, and paradigm forms of this word have been presented in 14.1.4, 14.1.5, and 14.1.6, respectively.

14.5.6 A SEMI-IRREGULAR VERB PATTERN OF GERMAN

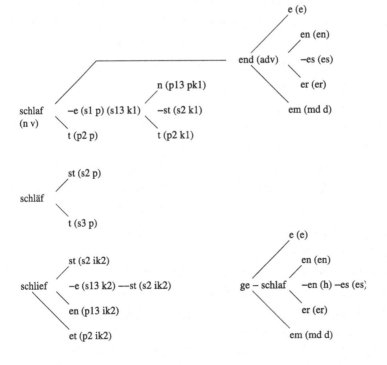

Extensive applications of LA Morph to different languages with fully developed morphology have shown that a strictly time-linear[7] analysis works well for concatenation, even in complicated semi-irregular paradigms with prefixes, suffixes, and several allomorphs. Because the time-linear derivation order is also the basis for a complete segmentation of the unknown surface into analyzed allomorphs, segmentation and concatenation can work incrementally, hand in glove. In addition, a time-linear derivation order corresponds to the empirical situation of word form recognition and synthesis, and is therefore the psychologically most plausible.

Exercises

Section 14.1

1. What is the form and function of allo rules?
2. Why must there be a default rule and where is it ordered among the allo rules?
3. At what point in the development or application of a LA Morph system are the allo rules to be applied?
4. Describe four degrees of regularity in the inflectional paradigms. What structural properties are the basis for these distinctions?

Section 14.2

1. Describe the phenomenon of allomorphy in the nouns, verbs, and adjectives of English.
2. What is the smallest number of allomorphs a morpheme can have?
3. What is the definition of the allomorph quotient?
4. Compare the allomorph quotient of different languages. What does the allomorph quotient say about the word forms of a language?
5. Does the allomorph quotient stay constant when the lexicon is substantially enlarged with low frequency items?
6. Explain the notion of normalizing the allomorph quotients of different natural languages.

---

[7] The time-linear approach of LA Morph is in contradistinction to the popular method of *truncation*. Truncation removes endings from the right to isolate the stem, which is why this method is also called *stemming*. Because truncation does not segment the surface into analyzed allomorphs, but is based on patterns of letters, it provides no detailed morpho-syntactic analysis, works only in morphologically simple languages, and is very imprecise even there. Moreover, the right-to-left direction of truncation is in conflict with the basic time-linear structure of natural language production and interpretation.

Section 14.3

1. How should the segmentation of word forms into allomorphs work conceptually?
2. What is a trie structure and what is its function in automatic word form recognition?
3. What determines the number of levels in a trie structure?
4. Under what conditions is the search for an allomorph in a trie structure discontinued?
5. Under what conditions is the search for an allomorph in a trie structure successful?

Section 14.4

1. What is the relation between the combi rules of LA Morph and the rules of LA Grammar in general?
2. Why is neither the word form nor the morpheme method compatible with the algorithm of LA Grammar?
3. What is the function of the combi rules?
4. What do the allo- and the combi rules have in common, and how do they differ?
5. Describe the linguistic analysis of a complex word form in LA Morph.
6. What is shown by the derivation of an LA Morph analysis? What is this information used for?
7. What is shown by the result of a LA Morph analysis? What is this information used for?
8. How does LA Morph handle ungrammatical input?

Section 14.5

1. Describe the concatenation patterns of the inflectional paradigms of English nouns, verbs, and adjectives.
2. Do left-associative combi rules show a difference in the combination of a prefix and a stem, on the one hand, and a word start and a suffix, on the other? Illustrate your answer with the example un/du/ly.
3. Which reasons support an analysis in morphology from left to right, and what speak against an analysis from right to left, based on truncation (stemming)?
4. Is the method of truncation (stemming) a smart or a solid solution?
5. Compare the distinctive categorization of German nouns with a traditional paradigmatic analysis (Sect. 18.2).

15. Corpus Analysis

This chapter first analyzes the general relation between linguistic analysis and computational method. As a familiar example, automatic word form recognition is used. The example exhibits a number of properties which are methodologically characteristic of all components of grammar. We then show methods for investigating the frequency distribution of words in natural language.

Section 15.1 describes the basic modularity which systems of computational linguistics must satisfy. Section 15.2 presents the method of subtheoretical variants using the example of multicats for lexical ambiguities. Section 15.3 describes the principles of building representative corpora, needed for testing systems of automatic word form recognition. Section 15.4 explains the frequency distribution of word forms in natural language. Section 15.5 describes the method of statistically based tagging and evaluates its accuracy in comparison to rule-based systems.

15.1 Implementation and Application of Grammar Systems

The design of a linguistic component such as word form recognition requires the choice of a general *theory of language* in order to ensure a smooth functional interaction with other components of the system, e.g., syntax and semantics. This decision in turn influences another important choice, namely that of a *grammar system*.

A well-defined grammar system consists of two parts:

15.1.1 PARTS OF A GRAMMAR SYSTEM

– Formal algorithm
– Linguistic method

On the one hand, the algorithm and the method must be independent of each other, in order to enable the formal definition of the algorithm. This in turn is a precondition for mathematical complexity analysis and a declarative specification of the implementation (Sect. 9.1).

R. Hausser, *Foundations of Computational Linguistics*,
DOI 10.1007/978-3-642-41431-2_15, © Springer-Verlag Berlin Heidelberg 2014

On the other hand, the algorithm and the method must fit together well. This is because the linguistic method *interprets* the formal algorithm with respect to an area of empirical phenomena, while the formal algorithm provides a procedural *realization* of the linguistic method.

For example, designing a grammar system of automatic word form recognition presents us with the following options:

15.1.2 OPTIONS FOR A GRAMMAR SYSTEM OF WORD FORM RECOGNITION

- Formal algorithm:
  choice between C (Sect. 7.4), PS (Sect. 8.1), and LA Grammar (Sect. 10.2).
- Linguistic method:
  choice between word form, morpheme, and allomorph method (Sect. 13.5).

For empirical, methodological, and mathematical reasons the allomorph method and the algorithm of LA Grammar were chosen, resulting in the grammar system of LA Morphology, implemented as LA Morph.

The distinction between algorithm and method holds also for syntactic grammar systems. Transformational grammar uses the algorithm of PS Grammar and the method of constituent structure. Montague grammar uses the algorithm of C Grammar and the method of truth conditions. LA Syntax uses the algorithm of LA Grammar and the method of traditional analysis based on valency, agreement, and word order.

A grammar system should be defined in such a way that it can be *implemented* in different manners and *applied* to different languages. This modularity between grammar system, implementation, and application leads to the following standard:

15.1.3 MINIMAL STANDARD OF WELL-DEFINED GRAMMAR SYSTEMS

A grammar system is well-defined only if it simultaneously allows
  1. different *applications* in a given *implementation*, and
  2. different *implementations* in a given *application*.

The first point is necessary for empirical reasons. In order to determine how suitable a grammar system is for the analysis of natural language, it must be tested automatically on large amounts of realistic data. This is the simplest, most straightforward, and most effective scientific strategy to show whether or not its *method* brings out a common core of linguistic principles, and whether or not its *algorithm* has sufficient generative capacity while maintaining low mathematical complexity.

The second point is necessary for practical reasons. In various circumstances the computational implementation of a grammar system will have to be replaced by another one – because of new hardware using a different operating system, a changing preference regarding the programming language, changing demands on the efficiency of the system, changing interface requirements, etc.

Under such circumstances there is no valid theoretical reason why a reimplementation should necessitate changes in its formalism or its applications. On the contrary, different implementations of a grammar system are an excellent way to demonstrate which properties of the grammar system are a *necessary* part of the abstract specification and which result merely from *accidental* properties of the programming.

The essential modularity[1] between a grammar system, its implementations, and its applications may be shown schematically as follows:

15.1.4 MODULARITY OF A GRAMMAR SYSTEM

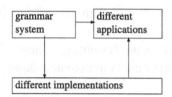

For systems of computational linguistics, this modularity is as important as the functional compatibility[2] of the different components of grammar, and the computational suitability[3] of the algorithm.

Regarding applications, the grammar system of LA Morphology has so far been used for word form recognition of English, German, Korean, Italian, and Spanish (14.2.7), with smaller systems for French, Japanese, and Polish. These successful implementations have strengthened confidence in the approach of LA Morphology.[4]

Regarding implementation, LA Morphology has so far been realized as follows:

---

[1] These considerations should be seen in light of the fact that it is tempting – and therefore common – to quickly write a little hack for a given task. A hack is an ad hoc piece of programming code which works, but has no clear algebraic or methodological basis. Hacks are a negative example of a *smart solution* (Sect. 2.3).

  In computational linguistics, as in other fields, little hacks quickly grow into giant hacks. They may do the job in some narrowly defined application, but their value for linguistic or computational theory is limited at best. Furthermore, they are extremely costly in the long run because even their own authors encounter ever increasing problems in debugging and maintenance, not to mention upscaling within a given language or applications to new languages.

[2] To be ensured by the theory of language.

[3] To be ensured by the principle of type transparency, Sect. 9.3.

[4] Especially valuable for improving the generality of the system was the handling of the Korean writing system Hangul. The various options for coding Hangul are described in Lee (1994).

15.1.5 DIFFERENT IMPLEMENTATIONS OF LA MORPHOLOGY

1988 in Lisp (Hausser and Kaufmann)
1990 in C (Hausser and Ellis)
1992 in C, 'LAMA' (Bröker 1991)
1994 in C, 'LAP' (Lorenz and Schüller 1994)
1995 in C, 'Malaga' (Beutel 1997)

These different implementations are jointly referred to as LA Morph. Though they differ in some ways,[5] they share the following structural principles:

- Specification of the allo rules (14.1.1) and the combi rules (14.4.1) on the basis of patterns which are matched with the input.
- Storage of the analyzed allomorphs in a trie structure and their left-associative lookup with parallel pursuit of alternative hypotheses (Sect. 14.3).
- Modular separation of motor, rule components, and lexicon, permitting a simple exchange of these parts, for example, in the application of the system to new domains or languages.
- Use of the same motor and the same algorithm for the combi rules of the morphological, syntactic, and semantic components during analysis.

Within the general framework, however, the empirical analysis of large amounts of different kinds of data has led to the development of subtheoretical variants.

---

[5] The use of Lisp in the 1988 version allowed for a quick implementation. It employed the same motor for word form recognition and syntax, and was tested on sizable fragments of English and German morphology and syntax. It had the disadvantage, however, that the rules of respective grammars were defined as Lisp functions, for which reason the system lacked an abstract, declarative formulation.

The 1990 C version was the first to provide a declarative specification of the allo- and the combi rules based on regular expressions (RegExp) in a tabular ASCII format, interpreted automatically and compiled in C.

The 1992 reimplementation aimed at improvements in the pattern matching and the trie structure. It did not get wider use, however, because it did not allow for the necessary interaction between the levels of surface and category, and had omitted an interface to syntax.

The 1994 reimplementation repaired the deficiencies of the 1992 version and was tested on sizable amounts of data in German, French, and Korean. These experiences resulted in many formal and computational innovations.

The 1995 implementation of the Malaga system took a new approach to the handling of pattern matching, using attribute-value structures. Malaga provides a uniform framework for simultaneous morphological, syntactic, and semantic parsing and generation.

15.2 Subtheoretical Variants

The algebraic definition of LA Grammar in Chaps. 10–12 aimed at the simplest, most transparent notation for explaining the complexity-theoretic properties of the algorithm in applications to artificial languages. Applications to natural languages, however, encountered empirical phenomena which suggested modifications of the original notation. These resulted in subtheoretical variants. In contrast to a derived formalism (7.1.6 and 7.1.7), a subtheoretical variant does not change the component structure and the theoretical status of the original system.

One phenomenon leading to a modification of the original format was lexical ambiguity in morphology and syntax. Consider, for example, the statistically most frequently used word form of German, the determiner der. As indicated in 15.2.1, it has at least three different sets of agreement properties, which may be represented as three different lexical readings:

15.2.1 COMBINATORICS OF THE GERMAN DETERMINER der

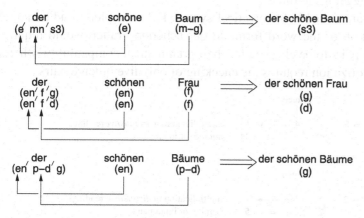

The determiner categories consist of three segments of which the first determines the adjective ending, e.g. e', the second the form of a compatible noun, e.g., mn', and the third the result, e.g., s3. The result category segment s3 stands for singular third person, g for genitive, and d for dative. The specification of number and person in s3 is required only in the nominative, which – as subject – agrees in these parameters with the finite verb form (Sects. 16.2 and 16.3).

Compared to a traditional paradigm analysis, the categorical analysis in 15.2.1 is designed to avoid unnecessary ambiguities. This is motivated both linguistically (concreteness) and computationally (lower combinatorial complexity). For example, the categories (e) and (en) of the adjective forms schöne and schönen do not specify any values for gender, number, case, and definiteness (which would produce seven and 19 lexical readings, respectively), but only the ending, the choice of which depends on the determiner rather than the noun, as shown by the following examples:

15.2.2 AGREEMENT OF ADJECTIVE-ENDING WITH DETERMINER

der	schöne	Baum	$\Longrightarrow$	der schöne Baum	(cf. 15.2.1)
				(s3)	

| ein | schöner | Baum | $\Longrightarrow$ | ein schöner Baum |
| (er mn s3) | (er) | (m–g) | | (s3) |

The point is that der schöne Baum and ein schöner Baum have the same case and number (nominative singular) and use the same noun (Baum). Therefore, the grammatical well-formedness of choosing schöne versus schöner depends solely on the choice of a definite (der) versus indefinite (ein) determiner.

The categorization of the noun forms Baum as (m–g), i.e., masculine minus genitive, Bäume as (p–d), i.e., plural minus dative, and Frau as (f), i.e., feminine, agrees with that of table 14.5.5. This distinctive categorization avoids unnecessary readings and reflects the fact that German nouns either have a grammatical gender, in which case they are singular, or are plural, in which case there is no gender distinction. There is also a possibility of fusing the second and third reading of 15.2.1 by means of the new category segment g&d (for genitive and dative, cf. categorization in 15.2.3), reducing the total number of readings to three.

These reductions are valuable for practical syntax. For example, a traditional, exhaustive categorization of the word forms in der schönen Frauen would require a total of 134 ordered pairs to be checked for their grammatical compatibility, whereas the distinctive categorization requires the checking of only five ordered pairs.

der	schönen			Frauen		
6	*	19 ——▶ 5	*	4 ——▶ 1		multiplication of *exhaustive* readings
	114	+	20	=	134	number of input pairs

der	schönen			Frauen		
3	*	1 ——▶ 2	*	1 ——▶ 1		multiplication of *distinctive* readings
	3	+	2	=	5	number of input pairs

The number after an arrow represents the number of successful compositions, while that below a product sign represents the number of attempted compositions.

In the end, however, there remains the fact that even in a distinctive categorization the most frequently used word form of German, der, has three different categories.[6] From the viewpoint of computational linguistics, this remarkable fact can be handled by means of either three different lexical entries with equal surfaces, as in 15.2.3, or one lexical entry with one surface and three alternative categories, as in 15.2.4. The latter is the so-called multicat notation first explored in the LAP-system (15.1.5).

---

[6] This is commented on by Jespersen (1921), pp. 341–346.

15.2.3 REPRESENTING LEXICAL READINGS VIA DIFFERENT ENTRIES

[der (e′ mn′ s3) def-art]
[der (en′ f′ g&d) def-art]
[der (en′ p–d′ g) def-art]

15.2.4 REPRESENTING LEXICAL READINGS VIA MULTICATS

[der ((e′ mn′ s3) (en′ f′ g&d) (en′ p–d′ g)) def-art]

The multicat solution has the advantage that only one lexical lookup is necessary. Furthermore, instead of branching immediately into three different parallel paths of syntactic analysis, the alternatives coded in the multicat may be processed in one branch until the result segments come into play. There are many other lexical phenomena, e.g., separable and nonseparable prefixes of German verbs (14.1.6), for which multicats provide a simplification of lexical description and syntactic analysis.

The use of multicats requires that format and implementation of the combi rules in morphology and syntax be extended to handle the alternatives coded in the new kind of categories. On the one hand, such an extension of the combi rules capabilities leads to a version of LA Grammar which differs from the original LAP-system as defined for the algebraic definition. On the other hand, an LA Grammar using multicats can always be reformulated as one in the original format using several lexical readings. Thus, the use of multicats is a subtheoretical variant and does not change the theoretical status as compared to a corresponding version without multicats.

15.3 Building Corpora

The empirical testing of a grammar system requires the building of corpora which represent the natural language to be analyzed in terms of a suitable collection of samples. Depending on which aspect of a language is to be documented by a corpus, the samples may consist of printed prose, transcribed dialogue, speeches, personal letters, theater plays, etc., either pure or mixed according to some formula. The samples may be collected either diachronically for a longer period of time or strictly synchronically (usually restricted to samples from a certain domain in a given year).

For German, the first comprehensive frequency analysis was presented 1897/1898 by Wilhelm Kaeding (Meier 1964), intended as a statistical basis for improving stenography. With his small army of 'Zählern' (people who count) Kaeding analyzed texts comprising almost 11 million running word forms (= 20 million syllables) and 250 178 different types.[7] In contrast to the synchronic corpora of today, Kaeding's collection of texts was designed to cover the German language from 1750 to 1890.

---

[7] The size of Kaeding's (1897/1898) corpus was thus more than ten times larger and the number of types twice as large as that of the computer-based 1973 Limas-Korpus (see below).

The arrival of computers provided a powerful tool for new investigations of this kind. Kučera and Francis (1967) took the lead with the Brown corpus[8] for American English. The Brown corpus comprises 500 texts of 1 014 231 running word forms (tokens) and 50 406 different types.

In 1978 there followed the LOB Corpus[9] for British English. Designed as a counterpart to the Brown corpus, it consists of 500 texts, about one million tokens, and 50 000 types. Both corpora were compiled from texts of the following 15 genres:

15.3.1 TEXT GENRES OF THE BROWN AND THE LOB CORPUS

	Brown	LOB
A Press: reportage	44	44
B Press: editorial	27	27
C Press: reviews	17	17
D Religion	17	17
E Skills, trade, and hobbies	36	38
F Popular lore	48	44
G Belle lettres, biography, essays	75	77
H Miscellaneous (government documents, foundation records, industry reports, etc.)	30	38
J Learned and scientific writing	80	80
K General fiction	29	29
L Mystery and detective fiction	24	24
M Science fiction	6	6
N Adventure and western fiction	29	29
P Romance and love story	29	29
R Humor	9	9
Total	500	500

The numbers on the right indicate how many texts were included from the genre in question, indicating slight differences between the Brown and the LOB corpus.

For building the Brown corpus, Kučera and Francis (1967), p. xviii, formulated the following desiderata:

---

[8] Named after Brown University in Rhode Island, where Francis was teaching at the time.

[9] The *Lancaster-Oslo/Bergen* corpus was compiled under the direction of Leech and Johannson. Cf. Hofland and Johannson (1980).

15.3.2 DESIDERATA FOR THE CONSTRUCTION OF CORPORA

1. Definite and specific delimitation of the language texts included, so that scholars using the Corpus may have a precise notion of the composition of the material.
2. Complete synchronicity; texts published in a single calendar year only are included.
3. A predetermined ratio of the various genres represented and a selection of individual samples through a random sampling procedure.
4. Accessibility of the Corpus to automatic retrieval of all information contained in it which can be formally identified.
5. An accurate and complete description of the basic statistical properties of the Corpus and of several subsets of the Corpus with the possibility of expanding such analysis to other sections or properties of the Corpus as may be required.

These desiderata are realized using the mathematical methods of statistics, i.e., the basic equations of stochastics, distributions of independent and dependent frequencies, normalization, computing the margin of error, etc. The goal is to find a theoretical distribution which corresponds to the empirical distribution (invariance of empirical distribution proportions).

The German counterpart to the American Brown Corpus (1967) and the British LOB Corpus (1978) is the Limas Corpus (1973).[10] Like its English analogs, it consists of 500 texts, each containing roughly 2 000 running word forms, amounting to a total of 1 062 624 tokens. Due to the richer morphology of German, the number of types is 110 837, i.e., more than twice that of the corresponding English corpora.

The selection of genres and amounts in 15.3.1 is intended to make the corpora as *representative* and *balanced* as possible.[11] Intuitively these two notions are easy to understand. For example, the editions of a daily newspaper in the course of a year are more representative for a natural language than a collection of phone books or banking statements. And a corpus containing texts from different genres in relative proportions like those indicated in 15.3.1 is better balanced than one which consists of texts from one genre alone.

It is difficult, however, to *prove* a specific quantification like that of 15.3.1 as 'representative' and 'balanced'. According to Oostdijk (1988)

> 'genre' is not a well-defined concept. Thus genres that have been distinguished so far have been identified on a purely intuitive basis. No empirical evidence has been provided for any of the genre distinctions that have been made.

---

[10] See Hess et al. (1983).

[11] Cf. Bergenholtz (1989), Biber (1993), Oostdijk and de Haan (1994).

A representative and balanced corpus ultimately requires knowledge of which genres are used and how often in a given time interval by the language community, in writing and reading as well as speaking and hearing. Because it is next to impossible to realistically determine the correlation of production and reception in written and spoken language in various genres, the building of representative and balanced corpora is more an art than a science. It is based largely on general common sense considerations. Moreover, it depends very much on the purpose for which the corpus is intended.[12]

Today, corpora of one million running word forms are considered far too small for valid natural language statistics. The British National Corpus (BNC), available online since 1995, has a size of 100 million running word forms. Of these, 89.7 million running word forms and 659 270 types[13] are of written language, while 10.34 million running word forms are of spoken language.

15.4 Distribution of Word Forms

The value of a corpus does not reside in the content of its texts, but in its quality as a realistic sample of a natural language.[14] The more representative and balanced the set

---

[12] The difficulties of constructing balanced and representative corpora are avoided in 'opportunistic corpora,' i.e., text collections which contain whatever is easily available. The idea is that the users themselves construct their own corpora by choosing from the opportunistic corpus specific amounts of specific kinds of texts needed for the purpose at hand. This requires, however, that the texts in the opportunistic corpus are preprocessed into a uniform format and classified with respect to their domain, origin, and various other parameters important to different users.

For example, a user must be able to automatically select a certain year of a newspaper, to exclude certain sections such as private ads, to select specific sections such as the sports page, the editorial, etc. To provide this kind of functionality in a fast growing opportunistic corpus of various different kinds of texts is labor-intensive – and therefore largely left undone.

With most of the corpus work left to the users, the resulting 'private corpora' are usually quite small. Also, if the users are content with whatever the opportunistic corpus makes available, the lexically more interesting domains like medicine, physics, law, etc., will be left unanalyzed.

[13] The following type numbers refer to the surfaces of the word forms in the BNC. The numbers published by the authors of the BNC, in contrast, refer to tagged word forms (Sect. 15.5). According to the latter method of counting, the BNC contains 921 073 types.

The strictly surface-based ranking underlying the table 15.4.2 was determined by Marco Zierl at the CL lab of Friedrich Alexander University Erlangen Nürnberg (CLUE).

[14] A language should be continuously documented in corpus linguistics. This may be done by building a *reference corpus* for a certain year. Then each following year, a *monitor*

of samples, the higher the value of the corpus for computing the frequency distribution of words and word forms in the language.

On the most basic level, the statistical analysis is presented as a *frequency* list and an *alphabetic* list of word forms, illustrated in 15.5.1 and 15.5.3, respectively. In the frequency list, the types of the word forms are ordered in accordance with their token frequency. The position of a word form in the frequency list is called its *rank*.

At the beginning of the BNC frequency list, for example, the top entry is the word form the. It occurs 5 776 399 times and comprises 6.4 % of the running word forms (tokens). The low end of the list, on the other hand, contains the word forms which occur only once in the corpus. These are called *hapax legomena*.[15] There are 348 145 hapax legomena in the BNC – amounting to 52.8 % of its types.

Word forms with the same frequency, such as the hapax legomena, may be collected into *frequency classes* (F-classes). An F-class is defined in terms of two parameters, (i) the characteristic frequency of the F-class types in the corpus and (ii) the number of types with that frequency.

15.4.1 Definition of the Notion Frequency Class (F-class)

F-class $=_{def}$ [frequency of types # number of types]

The number of types in an F-class is the interval between the highest and the lowest rank of its elements (15.4.2).

The number of tokens corresponding to an F-class equals the product of its type frequency and its type number. For example, because there are 39 691 word forms (types) which each occur three times in the BNC, the resulting F-class [3 # 39 691] corresponds to a total of 119 073 ($= 3 \cdot 39 691$) tokens.

There are much fewer F-classes in a corpus than ranks. In the BNC, for example, 655 270 ranks result in 5 301 F-classes. Thus, the number of the F-classes amounts to only 0.8 % of the number of ranks. Because of their comparatively small number, the F-classes are well suited to bringing the type/token correlation into focus.

The frequency distribution in the BNC is illustrated below for 27 F-classes – nine at the beginning, nine in the middle, and nine at the end.

---

corpus is built, showing the changes in the language. The reference corpus and the monitor corpora must be based on the same structure. They should consist of a central part for mainstream, average language, as in daily newspapers and other genres, complemented by domain-specific parts for medicine, law, physics, etc., which may be compiled from associated journals.

[15] From Greek, '*said once.*'

15.4.2 TYPE/TOKEN DISTRIBUTION IN THE BNC (*surface-based*)

class	start_r	end_r	types	tokens	types-%	tokens-%	
beginning	(the first 9 F-classes)						
1 (the)	1	1	1	5776399	0.000152	6.436776	
2 (of)	2	2	1	2789563	0.000152	3.108475	
3 (and)	3	3	1	2421306	0.000152	2.698118	
4 (to)	4	4	1	2332411	0.000152	2.599060	
5 (a)	5	5	1	1957293	0.000152	2.181057	
6 (in)	6	6	1	1746891	0.000152	1.946601	
7 (is)	7	7	1	893368	0.000152	0.995501	
8 (that)	8	8	1	891498	0.000152	0.993417	
9 (was)	9	9	1	839967	0.000152	0.935995	
sums			9	19648696	0.001368 %	21.895 %	
middle	(9 samples)						
1000	1017	1017	1	9608	0.000152	0.010706	
2001	2171	2171	1	4560	0.000152	0.005081	tokens
3000	3591	3591	1	2521	0.000152	0.002809	per
3500	4536	4536	1	1857	0.000152	0.002069	type:
4000	5907	5910	4	5228	0.000607	0.005826	1307
4500	8332	8336	5	4005	0.000758	0.004463	801
4750	10842	10858	17	9367	0.002579	0.010438	551
5000	16012	16049	38	11438	0.005764	0.012746	301
5250	44905	45421	517	26367	0.078420	0.029381	51
end	(the last 9 F-classes)						
5292	108154	114730	6577	59193	0.9976520	0.065960	9
5293	114731	122699	7969	63752	1.208763	0.071040	8
5294	122700	132672	9973	69811	1.512736	0.077792	7
5295	132673	145223	12551	75306	1.903775	0.083915	6
5296	145224	161924	16701	83505	2.533260	0.093052	5
5297	161925	186302	24378	97512	3.697732	0.108660	4
5298	186303	225993	39691	119073	6.020456	0.132686	3
5299	225994	311124	85131	170262	12.912938	0.189727	2
5300	311125	659269	348145	348145	52.807732	0.387946	1
sums			551116	1086559	83.595012 %	1.210778 %	

For each F-class the associated rank interval is specified (start_r to end_r). The first nine F-classes each contain only one type, for which reason they each cover only 0.000152 % ($= 100 : 659\,270$) of the types, which adds up to 0.001368 %. The tokens corresponding to these classes, on the other hand, cover 21.895 % of the running word forms of the BNC. The earliest F-class containing more than one type is located between F-classes 3 500 and 4 000. The nine F-classes at the end contain types which occur only one to nine times in the BNC. Together, they cover only 1.2 % of the running word forms, but they comprise 83.6 % of the types.

In other words, 16.4 % of the types in the BNC suffice to cover 98.8 % of the running word forms. Conversely, the remaining 1.2 % of the running word forms require 83.6 % of the types. This corresponds to the interval between rank 659 269 and 108 154, which represents 551 115 types.

The distribution of type and token frequency characterized in 15.4.2 is found generally in corpora of natural language. It may be shown graphically as follows:

15.4.3 CORRELATION OF TYPE AND TOKEN FREQUENCY

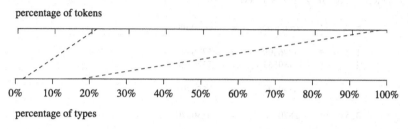

percentage of tokens

percentage of types

The fact that 0.001 % of the types cover almost 22 % of the tokens, and that 16 % of the types cover more than 98 % of the tokens in a corpus, is sometimes misinterpreted as meaning that the small lexica of today's systems of speech recognition (Sect. 1.4) are quite sufficient for practical purposes. This, however, is a serious mistake, because the *semantic significance* of a word increases with decreasing frequency.

For example, the user is benefited little by a system of automatic word form recognition which can lexically recognize the, of, and, and to, but misses on significant BNC hapax legomena like audiophile, butternut, customhouse, or dustheap, to mention only a few, all of which are listed and analyzed in a traditional lexicon like Webster's *New Collegiate Dictionary*.

In addition, there are many significant words contained in a traditional lexicon, such as aspheric, bipropellant, and dynamotor, which occur not even once in the BNC, despite its size and its design as a representative, balanced corpus. Thus, the word form list of a large corpus may help to update a traditional lexicon, but it should not be expected to be equally or more complete.

The correlation of type and token frequency exemplified in 15.4.3 was described most prominently by ZIPF (1902–1950) as a general law of nature.[16] According to Zipf (1935), the frequency distribution of types always follows roughly the same pattern, independent of the text size, the text category, or the natural language, and corresponds to the following formula:[17]

---

[16] Also known as the *Estoup-Zipf-Mandelbrot Law*. The earliest observation of the phenomenon was made by the Frenchman Estoup (1916), who – like Kaeding – worked on improving stenography. After doing a statistical analysis of human speech at Bell Labs, Condon (1928) also noted a constant relation between rank and frequency. Mandelbrot et al. (1957), famous for his work on fractals, worked on mathematical refinements of Zipf's Law. Cf. Piotrovskij et al. (1985).

[17] Criticized, among others, by Joos (1936) on empirical grounds. See also the reply in Zipf (1949).

15.4.4 ZIPF'S LAW

frequency · rank = constant

I.e., the frequency of a given word multiplied by its rank produces a number which is roughly the same as the product of rank and frequency of any other word in the text.[18]

15.4.5 ILLUSTRATION OF ZIPF'S LAW

word form	rank	*	frequency	=	constant
the	1	*	5776399	=	5776399
and	2	*	2789563	=	5579126
...					
was	9	*	839967	=	7559703
...					
holder	3251	*	2870	=	9330370

This shows that Zipf's law holds only roughly, in the sense of the same order of magnitude. To compensate for the curve-like increase and to achieve a better approximation of a constant, logarithmic modifications of the formula have been proposed.[19]

Zipf explained the correlation of frequency and rank he observed in texts as the law of least effort. According to Zipf, it is easier for the speaker-hearer to use a few word forms very frequently than to use the total of all word forms equally often. Zipf observed furthermore that the word forms used most frequently are usually the shortest and that as words get longer their frequency decreases. Zipf also pointed out that the semantic significance of word forms increases with decreasing frequency.

15.5 Statistical Tagging

In the beginning of computational corpus analysis, no systems of automatic word form analysis with sufficient data coverage were available. Therefore corpus analysis was initially purely letter-based. The objects investigated were *unanalyzed word forms*, i.e., sequences of letters between spaces in the online text.

Most online texts contain not only word forms, however, but also a large number of special symbols, such as markups for headlines, footnotes, etc., for example in XML or some other convention, as well as punctuation signs, quotation marks, hyphens, numbers, abbreviations, etc. In order for the statistical analysis of word forms to be linguistically meaningful, these special symbols must be interpreted and/or eliminated by a preprocessor.

---

[18] For simplicity, this example is based on the BNC data. Strictly speaking, however, Zipf's law applies only to individual texts and not to corpora.

[19] The plot of log(frequency) (y axis) vs. log(rank) (x axis) approximates a straight line of slope -1.

The statistical analysis of properly preprocessed online texts results in tables of word forms which specify their frequency relative to the total corpus and usually also relative to its genres. This is illustrated by the frequency list of the Brown Corpus.

15.5.1 TOP OF BROWN CORPUS FREQUENCY LIST

69971-15-500 THE	21341-15-500 IN
36411-15-500 OF	10595-15-500 THAT
28852-15-500 AND	10099-15-485 IS
26149-15-500 TO	9816-15-466 WAS
23237-15-500 A	9543-15-428 HE

The entry 9543-15-428 HE, for example, indicates that the word form HE occurs 9543 times in the Brown corpus, in all 15 genres, and in 428 of the 500 sample texts.

What is missing, however, is the categorization and lemmatization of the word forms. To fill this gap at least partially, Francis (1980) developed TAGGIT, a pattern-based system of categorization which required a lot of post-editing. Building from there (Marshall 1987, pp. 43f.), the CLAWS1-system was developed by Garside et al. (1987), who tried to induce the categorization from the statistical distribution of word forms in the texts. This statistically based *tagging* was developed in part for getting better and quicker results for large corpora than pattern matching.

Statistical tagging is based on categorizing by hand – or half automatically with careful post-editing – a small part of the corpus, called the *core corpus*. The categories used for the classification are called *tags* or *labels*. Their total is called the *tagset*.

The choice of a specific tagset[20] is motivated by the goal of maximizing the statistical differentiation of transitions from one word form to the next (bigrams). For this reason the tagging of the BNC core corpus is based on an especially large tagset, called the *enriched (C7) tagset*, which comprises 139 tags (without punctuation marks).

After hand-tagging the core corpus, the probabilities of the transitions from one word form to the next are computed by means of *Hidden Markov Models* (HMMs).[21] Then the probabilities of the hand-tagged core corpus are transferred to the whole corpus using a simplified tagset. In the BNC this *basic (C5) tagset* comprises 61 labels.

15.5.2 SUBSET OF THE *basic (C5) tagset*

AJ0 Adjective (general or positive) (e.g., good, old, beautiful)
CRD Cardinal number (e.g., one, 3, fifty-five, 3609)
NN0 Common noun, neutral for number (e.g., aircraft, data, committee)
NN1 Singular common noun (e.g., pencil, goose, time, revelation)
NN2 Plural common noun (e.g., pencils, geese, times, revelations)

---

[20] The consequences of the tagset choice on the results of the corpus analysis are mentioned in Greenbaum and Yibin (1994), p. 34.

[21] The use of HMMs for the grammatical tagging of corpora is described in, e.g., Leech et al. (1983), Marshall (1983), DeRose (1988), Sharman (1990), Brown et al. (1991, 1992). See also Church and Mercer (1993).

NP0 Proper noun (e.g., London, Michael, Mars, IBM)
UNC Unclassified items
VVB The finite base form of lexical verbs (e.g., forget, send, live, return)
VVD The past tense form of lexical verbs (e.g., forgot, sent, lived, returned)
VVG The -ing form of lexical verbs (e.g., forgetting, sending, living, returning)
VVI The infinitive form of lexical verbs (e.g., forget, send, live, return)
VVN The past participle form of lexical verbs (e.g., forgotten, sent, lived, returned)
VVZ The -s form of lexical verbs (e.g., forgets, sends, lives, returns)

Once the whole corpus has been tagged in the manner described, the frequency counts may be based on tagged word forms rather than letter sequences. Thereby different instances of the same surface with different tags are treated as different types. This is shown by the following example, which was selected at random from the tagged BNC list available online in 1997.

15.5.3 ALPHABETICAL WORD FORM LIST (SAMPLE FROM THE BNC)

```
1 activ nn1-np0 1              8 activating aj0-nn1 6
1 activ np0 1                  47 activating aj0-vvg 22
2 activa nn1 1                 3 activating nn1-vvg 3
3 activa nn1-np0 1             14 activating np0 5
4 activa np0 2                 371 activating vvg 49
1 activatd nn1-vvb 1           538 activation nn1 93
21 activate np0 4              3 activation nn1-np0 3
62 activate vvb 42             2 activation-energy aj0 1
219 activate vvi 116           1 activation-inhibition aj0 1
140 activated aj0 48           1 activation-synthesis aj0 1
56 activated aj0-vvd 26        1 activation. nn0 1
52 activated aj0-vvn 34        1 activation/ unc 1
5 activated np0 3              282 activator nn1 30
85 activated vvd 56            6 activator nn1-np0 3
43 activated vvd-vvn 36        1 activator/ unc 1
312 activated vvn 144          1 activator/ unc 1
1 activatedness nn1 1          7 activator/tissue unc 1
88 activates vvz 60            61 activators nn2 18
5 activating aj0 5             1 activators np0 1
```

Each entry consists (i) of a number detailing the frequency of the tagged word form in the whole corpus, (ii) the surface of the word form, (iii) the label, and (iv) the number of texts in which the word form was found under the assigned label. Alternatively to the alphabetical order, the entries may be ordered according to frequency, resulting in the BNC frequency list.

15.5.3 illustrates the output of the statistical tagger CLAWS4, which was developed for analyzing the BNC and is generally considered one of the best statistical taggers. The error rate[22] of CLAWS4 is quoted by Leech (1995) at 1.7 %, which at first glance may seem like a very good result.

---

[22] Unfortunately, neither Leech (1995) nor Burnard (ed.) (1995) specify what exactly constitutes an error in tagging the BNC. A new project to improve the tagger was started in June

This error rate applies to the running word forms, however, and not to the types. If we take into consideration that the last 1.2 % of the low frequency tokens requires 83.6 % of the types (15.4.2, 15.4.3), an error rate of 1.7 % may also represent a very bad result – namely that about 90 % of the types are not analyzed or not analyzed correctly. This conclusion is borne out by a closer inspection of the sample 15.5.3.

The first surprise is that of 38 entries, 27 are categorized more than once, namely activ (2), activa (3), activate (3), activated (7), activating (6), activation (2), activator (2), and activators (2). Thereby, activ – which is a typing error – is classified alternatively as nn1-np0 and np0, neither of which makes any sense linguistically. The classification of activate as np0 is also mistaken from the viewpoint of traditional English dictionaries. The typing error activatd is treated as well-formed and labeled nn1-vvb. In activation. the punctuation sign is not removed by the preprocessor, yet it is labeled nn0. In activation/ and activator/ the '/' is not interpreted correctly and they are labeled unc (for *unclassified*), whereby the identical entries for activator/ are counted separately.

In addition to having a high error rate, the frequency counts of the BNC analysis are impaired by a weak preprocessor. For example, by treating different numbers as different word forms, as in

```
1 0.544 crd 1
1 0.543 crd 1
1 0.541 crd 1
```

58 477 additional types are produced, which is 6.3 % of the labeled BNC types. In addition, there are more than 20 000 types resulting from numbers preceded by measuring units like &pound (11 706) and &dollar (8 723). Furthermore, word-form-initial hyphens and sequences of hyphens are counted as separate word forms, producing another 4 411 additional types, which are moreover labeled incorrectly.

Thus, statistical labeling increases the number of types from 659 270 surfaces to 921 074 labeled BNC forms. A proper preprocessing of numbers and hyphens would reduce the number of surface types by an additional 83 317 items to 575 953. All in all, statistical tagging increases the number of types in the BNC by at least 37.5 %.

The BNC tagging analysis is a typical example of the strengths and weaknesses of a smart solution (Sect. 2.3). On the positive side there is a comparatively small effort as well as robustness, which suggests the use of statistical taggers at least in the preparatory phase of building a solid system of automatic word form recognition. On the negative side there are the following weaknesses, which show up even more clearly in languages with a morphology richer than English.

1995, however. Called '*The British National Corpus Tag Enhancement Project*', its results were originally scheduled to be made available in September 1996. Instead, it was apparently superseded by the massive manual postediting effort published as the BNC XML edition (Burnard (ed.) 2007).

15.5.4 WEAKNESSES OF STATISTICAL TAGGING

1. The categorization is too unreliable to support rule-based syntactic parsing.
2. Word forms can neither be reduced to their base forms (lemmatization) nor segmented into their allomorphs or morphemes.
3. The overall frequency distribution analysis of a corpus is distorted by an artificial inflation of types by more than one third.

It is in the nature of statistical tagging that the classification of a surface be based solely on statistical circumstances.[23] Thus, if it turns out that a certain form has been classified incorrectly by a statistical tagger, there is no way to correct this particular error. Even if the tagger is successfully improved as a whole, its results can never be more than probabilistically based conjectures.

The alternative solid solution is a rule- and lexicon-based system of automatic word form recognition. If a word form is not analyzed or is not analyzed correctly in such a system, then the cause is either a missing entry in the lexicon or an error in the rules. The origin of the mistake can be identified and corrected, thus solidly improving the recognition rate of the system.

In addition, the rule-based analysis makes it possible to extend the frequency analysis from letter-based word forms to words and their parts. This is of interest in connection with hapax legomena (i.e., about half of the types). For statistics, the hapax legomena constitute the quasi-unanalyzable residue of a corpus. A rule-based approach, in contrast, can not only analyze hapax legomena precisely, but can reduce their share at the level of elementary base forms by half. In the Limas corpus, for example, word forms like Abbremsung, Babyflaschen, and Campingplatz are hapax legomena, but their parts, i.e., bremse, baby, flasche, camping, and platz, occur more than once.

Exercises

Section 15.1

1. What is the definition of a grammar system?
2. What is the function of the formal algorithm in a grammar system?
3. Why does a grammar system require more than its formal algorithm?
4. Why must a grammar system be integrated into a theory of language?

---

[23] It is for this reason that a surface may be classified in several different ways, depending on its various environments in the corpus.

5. Explain the methodological reason why a grammar system must have an efficient implementation on the computer.
6. Why is a modular separation of grammar system, implementation, and application necessary? Why do they have to be closely correlated?
7. What differences exist between the various implementations of LA Morph, and what do they have in common?

Section 15.2

1. Explain the linguistic motivation of a distinctive categorization, using examples.
2. What are multicats and why do they necessitate an extension of the basic algorithm of LAG?
3. Compare list-based and attribute-based matching in LA Morph.
4. What motivates the development of subtheoretical variants?
5. Why is the transition to a new subtheoretical variant labor-intensive?
6. What is the difference between a subtheoretical variant and a derived formalism?

Section 15.3

1. For which purpose did Kaeding investigate the frequency distribution of German?
2. What is a representative, balanced corpus?
3. List Kučera and Francis' desiderata for constructing corpora.
4. Explain the distinction between the types and the tokens of a corpus.

Section 15.4

1. Describe the correlation of type and token frequency in the BNC.
2. What is the percentage of hapax legomena in the BNC?
3. In what sense are high frequency word forms of low significance and low frequency word forms of high significance?
4. What is Zipf's law?

Section 15.5

1. What motivates the choice of a tagset for statistical corpus analysis?
2. Why is it necessary for the statistical analysis of a corpus to tag a core corpus by hand?
3. What is the error rate of the statistical BNC tagger CLAWS4? Does it refer to types or tokens? Is it high or low?
4. Why does statistical tagging substantially increase the number of types in a corpus? Are these additional types real or spurious?
5. Is statistical tagging a smart or a solid solution?
6. What is the role of the preprocessor in the outcome of the statistical analysis of a corpus? Explain your answer using concrete examples.

16. Basic Concepts of Syntax

This and the following two chapters describe the grammar component of syntax. Section 16.1 analyzes the structural border between the grammar components of morphology and syntax. Section 16.2 discusses the role of valency in the syntactic-semantic composition of natural languages. Section 16.3 explains the notions of agreement and the canceling of valency positions by compatible valency fillers. Section 16.4 demonstrates the handling of free word order with an LA Grammar for a small fragment of German. Section 16.5 demonstrates the handling of fixed word order with an LA Grammar for a corresponding fragment of English.

16.1 Delimitation of Morphology and Syntax

The grammar component of morphology is limited to the analysis of individual word forms, but provides the basis for their syntactic composition in terms of their morphosyntactic categorization. The grammar component of syntax is limited to characterizing the composition of word forms into complex expressions, but depends on their morphological analysis.

Thus, the structural boundary between the morphology and syntax coincides with the boundaries between the word forms in the sentence surface: everything within a word form boundary is in the domain of morphology, while everything dealing with the composition of word forms is in the domain of syntax.

16.1.1 TIME-LINEAR INTERACTION OF LA MORPHOLOGY AND LA SYNTAX

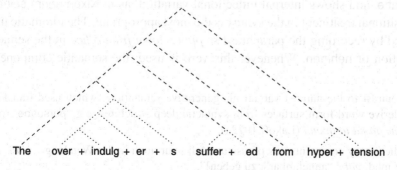

The   over + indulg + er + s   suffer + ed   from   hyper + tension

R. Hausser, *Foundations of Computational Linguistics*,
DOI 10.1007/978-3-642-41431-2_16, © Springer-Verlag Berlin Heidelberg 2014

The tree structures of LA Morphology and LA Syntax each satisfy the SLIM principles of surface compositionality (S) and time-linear composition (L). However, the time-linear adding of a complex word form like over+indulg+er+s in the syntax (dashed lines) presupposes its prior time-linear composition in morphology (dotted lines).

Thus, even though LA Morphology and LA Syntax are based on the same structural principles, their components are separated in a modular fashion[1] because their respective time-linear compositions occur in different phases. This particular correlation of syntactic and morphological composition is in concord with the traditional view according to which complex morphological structures originate historically as "frozen syntactic structures" (Paul 1920, Chap. 19).

The separation of LA Morphology and LA Syntax poses no problem even in borderline cases such as idioms. Critical cases can be handled either lexico-morphologically or syntactically because both components show the same time-linear composition of surfaces and meanings₁. Which grammar component is appropriate should be determined by the structural properties of the phrase in question.

For example, the phrase over-the-counter should be handled in the lexicon, because its use as a unit and its lack of internal variation is expressed orthographically by hyphenation. The variant without the hyphens, on the other hand, should be handled in the syntax.

In German, a phrase like gang und gäbe[2] may at first glance seem to belong in the syntax because the phrase is written as three separate words. However, this particular use of gäbe is like a like a bound morpheme (13.3.4) because it may not occur independently. Therefore the phrase should be handled in the lexicon. Technically, this may be achieved by an internal representation as gang_und_gäbe, treating the phrase as a single word form for the purposes of syntax.

A syntactic treatment is generally motivated in idioms which (i) retain their compositional (Fregean) meaning₁ as an option, (ii) are subject to normal variations of word order, and (iii) exhibit internal inflectional variation. As an example, consider German seinen Hut nehmen, which literally means *to take one's hat*, with the idiomatic meaning of *stepping down from office*.

Because this phrase obeys word order variations, as in nachdem Nixon seinen Hut genommen hatte, and shows internal inflectional variation, as in Nixon nahm seinen Hut, a compositional treatment in the syntax is the most appropriate. The idiomatic use can be handled by recording the paraphrase *stepping down from office* in the semantic representation of nehmen. Whenever this verb is used, the semantic component

---

[1] This is in contrast to the nativist variant of 'generative semantics', which used transformations to derive word form surfaces from syntactic deep structures, e.g., persuade from *cause to come about to intend* (Lakoff 1972a).

[2] Wahrig's's dictionary comments this phrase as "Adj.; nur noch in der Wendung ... *das ist so üblich* [≺ mhd. *gäbe* "annehmbar"; zu geben]".

checks whether the object is Hut. If this is the case, the pragmatic interpretation is provided with the paraphrase *stepping down from office* as an option.

The nature of the morphology-syntax relation may be illuminated further by looking at different kinds of natural languages. This topic belongs in the domain of language typology, in which synthetic languages with a rich morphology are distinguished from analytic languages with a rudimentary morphology.

According to Bloomfield (1933), modern Chinese is an analytic language in which each word (form) is either a morpheme consisting of one syllable, or a compound, or a phrase word. A synthetic language, on the other hand, is Eskimo, in which long chains of morphemes are concatenated into a single word form such as [a:wlis-ut-iss?ar-si-niarpu-na] *I am looking for something suitable for a fish-line* (op.cit., p. 207).

For Bloomfield the distinction between synthetic and analytic is relative, however, insofar as one language can be more synthetic than another in one respect, yet more analytic in another. As an alternative schema of classification he cites the isolating, agglutinative, polysynthetic, and inflectional kinds of morphology:

> Isolating languages were those which, like Chinese, used no bound forms; in agglu-tinative languages the bound forms were supposed to follow one another, Turkish being the stock example; polysynthetic languages expressed semantically important elements, such as verbal goals, by means of bound forms, as does Eskimo; inflec-tional languages showed a merging of semantically distinct features either in a single bound form or in closely united bound forms, as when the suffix ō in a Latin form like amō 'I love' expresses the meanings 'speaker as actor,' 'only one actor,' 'action in present time,' 'real (not merely possible or hypothetical) action.' These distinctions are not co-ordinate and the last three classes were never clearly defined.
>
> Bloomfield (1933), p. 208

Despite the difficulties described,[3] there remains the fact that some natural languages build up meaning$_1$ mainly in the syntax (e.g., Chinese) and others mainly in morphol-ogy (e.g., Eskimo). This alternative exists also within a given natural language. For example, in English the complex concept denoted by the word form overindulgers may roughly be expressed analytically as people who eat and drink too much.

That meaning$_1$ may be composed in morphology as well as in syntax provides no argument against treating these components as separate modules. A reason for their separation, on the other hand, is their being based on different principles of combi-nation. Those of morphology are inflection, derivation, and compounding (13.1.2), whereas those of syntax are the following:

16.1.2 COMBINATION PRINCIPLES OF SYNTAX

1. *Valency* (Sect. 16.2)
2. *Agreement* (Sect. 16.3)
3. *Word order* (Sect. 16.4 for German and 16.5 for English)

---

[3] For an overview of morphological language typology see Greenberg (1954).

In addition to these traditional combination principles there is the higher principle of the left-associative (time-linear) derivation order, which underlies morphological and syntactic composition alike – both in language production (speak mode, 5.4.2) and language interpretation (hear mode, 5.4.1).

16.2 Valency

The notions valency carrier and valency filler go back to the French linguist Tesnière (1959), who borrowed them from the field of chemistry. The valency positions of a carrier must be filled, or canceled, by compatible fillers in order for an expression to be syntactically and semantically complete.

Prototypical valency carriers in the natural languages are the verbs. The verb give, for example, is a three-place carrier because each act of giving necessarily requires (i) a giver, (ii) a receiver, and (iii) something that is given. Even though one may say Susanne has given already in the context of a charity, it follows semantically that there is *something* that Susanne gave and *someone* who received it.[4]

The LA Grammar-specific coding of valency positions and result segments in various different valency carriers of German is illustrated by the following examples:

16.2.1 EXAMPLES OF DIFFERENT VALENCY CARRIERS IN GERMAN

– the one-place verb form schläfst (*sleep*):

[schläfst   (s2' v)   schlafen]
             ↑   ↑
             │   result segment
          valency position

The valency position s2′ indicates that this verb form requires a nominative of second person singular. The result segment v shows that after filling the valency position there results a complete verbal expression (sentence).

---

[4] In addition to the basic valency structure of a word, natural languages allow special uses with secondary valency structures. For example, the English verb to sleep is normally intransitive, but in the sentence This yacht sleeps 12 people it is used transitively. Thereby, the change to the secondary valency structure is accompanied by a profound change in the meaning of the word, which may be paraphrased as provide bunks for.

The number of valency positions may also be reduced (called *Detransitivierung* in German). For example, give in German has a secondary use as a one-place – or arguably two-place – valency carrier, as in Heute gibt es Spaghetti (= today gives it spaghetti/today we'll have spaghetti). Again, the secondary valency structure is accompanied by profound changes in the original word meaning.

The phenomena of *transitivization* and *detransitivization* do not call a systematic analysis of valency structure into question. On the contrary, they throw additional light on the fundamental importance of the valency structure in the analysis of natural language.

– the two-place verb form liest (*read*):

[liest   (s23' a' v)   lesen]

   ↑ ↑ ↑

   | | *result segment*

  valency positions

The valency position s23' indicates that this verb form requires a nominative of second or third person singular. The additional valency position a' indicates that this form requires an additional accusative in order to result in a complete sentence. Specification of the case ensures that ungrammatical oblique fillers, such as a dative or a genitive, are excluded. For example, Der Mann liest einen Roman is grammatical while *Der Mann liest einem Roman is not.

– the two-place verb form hilft (*help*):

[hilft (s3' d' v)   helfen]

   ↑ ↑ ↑

   | | *result segment*

  valency positions

The oblique valency position d' indicates that this form requires a dative (in addition to the nominative). Non-dative valency fillers, as in *Der Mann half die Frau, are not grammatical.

– The three-place verb form gebt (*give*):

[gebt   (p2' d' a' v)   geben]

   ↑ ↑ ↑

   | | | *result segment*

  valency position

The valency position p2' indicates that this form requires a nominative of second person plural. The oblique valency positions d' and a' indicate the need for additional dative and accusative valency fillers.

– The three-place verb form lehrte (*taught*):

[lehrte (s13' a' a' v)   lehren]

   ↑ ↑ ↑ ↑

   | | | *result segment*

  valency position

The valency position s13' indicates that this verb form requires a nominative of first or third person singular. The two oblique valency positions a' indicate the need for two additional accusative valency fillers. Because of this valency structure Der Vater lehrte mich das Schwimmen is grammatical while *Der Vater lehrte mir das Schwimmen is not.

– The one-place preposition nach (*after*):

[nach (d' adp)   nach]

   ↑ ↑

   | *result segment*

  valency position

The preposition *nach* requires a dative noun phrase as argument, as indicated by the valency position d′. The result segment adp (for ad-phrase) expresses that filling the valency position results in an expression which functions as an adverbial or adnominal modifier (12.5.4–12.5.6).

As shown by the last example, there are other valency carriers besides verbs in the natural languages, such as prepositions and determiners (15.2.1).

In LA Grammars for natural languages, the syntactic categories have at least one category segment – in contrast to LA Grammars for artificial languages, which also use empty lists as categories, especially in final states (e.g., 10.2.2, 10.2.3, 11.5.2, 11.5.4, 11.5.7). Syntactic categories consisting of one segment can serve only as valency fillers or as modifiers, e.g.:

[Bücher (p-d) buch]   (*books*)
[ihm (d) er]   (*him*)
[gestern (adv) gestern]   (*yesterday*)

Valency carriers may also function as valency fillers using their result segment, e.g., v, as the filler segment. In this case, the segments representing valency positions are attached at the beginning of the category resulting from the composition.

16.3 Agreement

The second combination principle of natural language syntax besides valency is agreement. Agreement violations are among the most obvious and most serious grammatical mistakes one can make in a natural language, even though the intended meaning of the utterance is usually not really jeopardized. Consider the following example:

16.3.1 AGREEMENT VIOLATION IN ENGLISH

*Every girls need a mother.

In grammatical expressions, agreement interacts with valency in that a potential valency filler can only cancel a structurally compatible valency position.

As a simple example of the functional interaction between a valency carrier and compatible fillers consider the following analysis of the sentence he gives her this, which shows the successive filling (canceling) of valency positions in a left-associative derivation. Agreement is shown by using the same letter for the category segments representing (i) the valency position and (ii) the associated filler:

16.3.2 A SIMPLE ANALYSIS IN LA SYNTAX

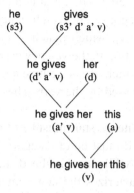

The bottom-up left-associative derivation order (10.1.6) is represented as a tree struc-ture growing downward from the terminal string (input).[5] The step-by-step canceling of valency positions is specified in the category of the sentence start, which shows at each step how many valency positions remain to be filled.

A maximally simple LA Grammar for the derivation is *LA plaster*.[6] On the positive side, it is written just like the LA Grammars for artificial languages in Chaps. 10–12. On the negative side, it is intentionally primitive insofar as no variables are used in the rule patterns.

16.3.3 AN LA GRAMMAR FOR 16.3.2 (*LA plaster*)

LX $=_{def}$ { [he (s3) *], [her (d) *], [this (a) *], [gives (s3′ d′ a′ v) *]}

$ST_S =_{def}$ { [(s3) {MAIN+FV}] }

MAIN+FV:	(s3) (s3′ d′ a′ v)	$\Rightarrow$	(d′ a′ v)	{FV+MAIN1}
FV+MAIN1:	(d′ a′ v) (d)	$\Rightarrow$	(a′ v)	{FV+MAIN2}
FV+MAIN2:	(a′ v) (a)	$\Rightarrow$	(v)	{ }

$ST_F =_{def}$ { [(V) rp$_{FV+MAIN2}$] }

For simplicity, the lexicon LX is defined as a word form lexicon (13.5.1). In this way the grammar is independent of a component of automatic word form recognition. LX contains only the word forms occurring in the example.[7]

---

[5] This format corresponds to the derivation structure (iii) in 10.3.1 as well as the automatic parsing analyses 10.3.2, 10.4.1, 10.5.3, 10.5.4, and 10.5.5. The equivalent format of LA trees growing upward from the terminal string, illustrated in 10.5.2 and 16.1.1, on the other hand, has served only for the comparison with corresponding constituent structures, and is of no further use.

[6] In German, this grammar is called LA Beton. The English translation of Beton as *concrete* has a misleadingly positive ring, hence the name *LA Plaster*.

[7] The third position is indicated by a '*' because the base forms are not referred to by the rules.

According to the start state ST_S, the derivation must begin with a word of category (s3) and the rule MAIN+FV (main constituent plus finite verb). The input condition of this rule requires that the sentence start must be of category (s3), which matches *he*, and that the next word must be of category (s3′ d′ a′ v), which matches *gives*. The categorial operation of MAIN+FV cancels the s3′ position in the valency carrier. The result category (d′ a′ v) characterizes a sentence start which needs a dative and an accusative in order to complete the semantic relation expressed by the verb. The rule package of MAIN+FV activates the rule FV+MAIN1.

According to the input condition of FV+MAIN1, the sentence start must be of category (d′ a′ v), which matches *he gives*, and the next word must be of category (d), which matches *her*. The categorial operation of FV+MAIN1 cancels the d′ position in the sentence start. The result category (a′ v) characterizes the new sentence start *he gives her* as requiring an accusative in order to complete the semantic relation expressed by the verb. The rule package of FV+MAIN1 activates the rule FV+MAIN2.

According to the input condition of FV+MAIN2, the sentence start must be of category (a′ v), which matches *he gives her*, and the next word must be of category (a), which matches *this*. The categorial operation of FV+MAIN2 cancels the a′ position in the sentence start. The result category (v) characterizes the new sentence start *he gives her this* as an expression which does not have any open valency positions. FV+MAIN2 activates the empty rule package. The final state ST_F characterizes the output of FV+MAIN2 as a complete sentence of the 'language' described by *LA Plaster*. At this point the derivation shown in 16.3.2 is completed successfully.

In an extended grammar, the sentence start *he gives her this* could be continued further, for example by a concluding full stop, an adverb like *now*, a subordinate clause like *because she asked for it*, or a conjoined clause like *and she smiled happily*. Thus, whether a given sentence start is a complete expression or not requires not only that its analysis constitute a final state, but also that the surface be analyzed completely.

Even though *LA Plaster* lacks the flexibility and generality that LA Grammars for natural languages normally strive for, it is fully functional as a parser, strictly time-linear, and descriptively adequate insofar as it accepts the example in 16.3.2. Furthermore, because the input and output patterns of the rules refer to categories, the grammar would analyze many additional sentences if the lexicon LX were extended with additional word forms of the categories (s3), (d), (a), and (s3′ d′ a′ v), respectively.

In all three combination steps of the example there is agreement between the filler segment and the canceled valency position. In the first combination, s3′ is canceled by s3, in the second, d′ by d, and in the third, a′ by a. Thus, agreement is formally handled here as the *identity* of the filler segment and the associated valency position. Violations of identity-based agreement show up clearly in the input categories.

16.3.4 EXAMPLE OF AN ERROR IN IDENTITY-BASED AGREEMENT

I   +   gives   ⟶   Error: ungrammatical continuation
(s1)   (s3' s' a' v)

That the first person pronoun I does not agree with gives is obvious at the level of
the respective categories because the filler segment s1 has no corresponding valency
segment in the carrier category (s3' d' a' v).

16.4 Free Word Order in German (*LA D1*)

The third combination principle of natural language syntax besides valency and agreement is word order. Just as natural languages may be distinguished typologically with
respect to their relative degree of morphological marking (specifying case, number,
gender, tense, verbal mood, honorifics, etc.), they may also be distinguished typologically with respect to their relative degree of word order freedom.

In natural language, grammatical functions may be coded by their morphology, by
means of function words, or by their word order. Furthermore, Greenberg (1963) observed that languages with a rich morphology have a free word order, while languages
with a simple morphology have a fixed word order.

This is because the richer the morphology, the fewer grammatical functions are
left for the word order to express – allowing it to be free.[8] Conversely, the simpler
the morphology, the more must grammatical functions be expressed by means of the
word order – thus limiting its freedom.

A language with a relatively free word order is German. The position of the verb is
fixed, but the order of fillers and modifiers is free. This is illustrated by a declarative
main clause with a three-place verb: the finite verb is fixed in second position, while
the three fillers allow six variations of word order.

16.4.1 WORD ORDER VARIATIONS IN A DECLARATIVE MAIN CLAUSE

Der Mann gab der Frau den Strauß.
(the man gave the woman the bouquet.)
Der Mann gab den Straußder Frau.
(the man gave the bouquet the woman.)
Der Frau gab der Mann den Strauß.
(the woman gave the man the bouquet.)
Der Frau gab den Straußder Mann.
(the woman gave the bouquet the man.)
Den Straußgab der Mann der Frau.
(the bouquet gave the man the woman.)
Den Straußgab der Frau der Mann.
(the bouquet gave the woman the man.)

---

[8] This freedom is utilized for other aspects of communication, such as textual cohesion.

These all translate into English as the man gave the woman the bouquet. Which variant is chosen by the speaker depends on the purpose and the circumstances of the
utterance context.[9]

In contrast to the grammatically correct examples, the following example is ungrammatical because it violates the verb-second rule of declarative main clauses in
German.

16.4.2 Word Order Violation in German

   *Der Mann der Frau gab einen Strauß.
   (the man the woman gave the bouquet.)

In LA Grammar, the free word order of German is formally captured by allowing
the canceling of arbitrary valency positions in the carrier category, and not just the
currently first segment.

16.4.3 Free Canceling of Valency Positions in a Carrier of German

Der Mann	+	gab	⟶	Der Mann gab
(s3)		(s3' d' a' v)		(d' a' v)

Der Frau	+	gab	⟶	Der Frau gab
(d)		(s3' d' a' v)		(s3' a' v)

Den Strauß	+	gab	⟶	Den Strauß gab
(a)		(s3' d' a' v)		(s3' d' v)

The arrow indicates the canceling of a valency position (marked by ') by a suitable
(here identical) valency filler. Which of the available valency positions is to be canceled is decided here by the case-marked filler. In all three examples, the resulting sentence start can be continued into a complete well-formed sentence, e.g., Den Straußgab der Mann der Frau.

How can *LA Plaster* (16.3.3) be generalized in such a way that the free word order
characteristic of German declarative main clauses is handled correctly? The obvious
first step is to fuse FV+MAIN1 and FV+MAIN2 of *LA Plaster* into one rule.

16.4.4 German LA Grammar with Partial Free Word Order

   LX $=_{def}$ { [er (s3) *], [ihr (d) *], [das (a) *], [gab (s3' d' a' v) *]}
   Variable definition: NP $\in$ {d, a}, with *NP'* correspondingly d' or a'
                        X, Y = .?.?.?.? (i.e., an arbitrary sequence up to length 4)

---

[9] Given the isolation of these variants from discourse contexts, some may seem less natural
than others. The reason for this, however, is not grammar, but that for some it is more
difficult to imagine utterance situations suitable for their topic-comment structures.

$$\text{ST}_S =_{def} \{ \, [(s3) \, \{MAIN+FV\} \,] \, \}$$

MAIN+FV: (s3) (s3' d' a' v) $\Rightarrow$ (d' a' v) {FV+MAIN}

FV+MAIN: (X NP' Y v) (NP) $\Rightarrow$ (X Y v) {FV+MAIN}

$$\text{ST}_F =_{def} \{ \, [(V) \, \text{rp}_{FV+MAIN} \,] \, \}$$

This extension of *LA Plaster* translates the English word form lexicon LX of 16.3.3 into German. Furthermore, the variables X, Y, and NP are used to fuse the rules FV+MAIN1 and FV+MAIN2 of 16.3.3. The variables X and Y are *unspecified*, standing for a sequence of zero, one, two, three, or four arbitrary category segments, while NP is a *specified* variable, the range of which is explicitly limited to the category segments d and a (see variable definition).

The variables in a rule are assigned values by matching the rule's input patterns with the input's categories. Thereby the value for a given variable must be the same throughout the rule, i.e., the variable is *bound*. Consider the following example:

16.4.5 FV+MAIN Matching a Next Word Accusative

input/output:	er	gab	+	das	er gab das
	(d' a'	v)		(a)	(d' v)
FV+MAIN–pattern:	(X NP' Y	v)		(NP)	→ (X Y v)

On the level of the input, the sentence start has category (d' a' v) and the next word has the category (a). Therefore, the next word variable NP at the level of the rule is bound to the constant value a. Accordingly, everything preceding the a' in the sentence start category at the input level is matched by (and assigned to) the variable X – here the sequence <d'> – while everything between the a' and the v is matched by (and assigned to) the variable Y – here the empty sequence < >. These bound variables, together with the constant v, are used for building the output category – here (d' v). The categorial operation cancels the segment a' in the sentence start category because the variable NP' does not occur in the output category pattern.

The new rule FV+MAIN of 16.4.4 generates and analyzes not only the variant er gab das (ihr), but also er gab ihr (das) (i.e., the single sentence of *LA Plaster*, though this time in German). The reason is that the input pattern of FV+MAIN accepts an accusative (16.4.5) as well as a dative (16.4.6) after the verb:

16.4.6 FV+MAIN Matching a Next Word Dative

input/output:	er	gab	+	ihr	er gab ihr
	(d'	a' v)		(d)	(a' v)
FV+MAIN pattern:	(X NP' Y	v)		(NP)	→ (X Y v)

The variable NP' is bound to the category segment d' for the duration of this rule application because the next word category is d. Everything before the d' in the sentence start is represented by X, while everything between the d′ and the v is represented by Y. Thus, X is bound to the empty sequence < >, while Y is bound to the sequence <a′>. With these bound variables the output of the rule application is specified.

Another important aspect of FV+MAIN in 16.4.4 as compared to 16.3.3 is the fact that FV+MAIN calls itself via its rule package. This provides for a possible recursion which can proceed as long as the categorial states of the input permit. For example, the output of 16.4.6 fits the input pattern of FV+MAIN one more time:

16.4.7 REAPPLICATION OF FV+MAIN

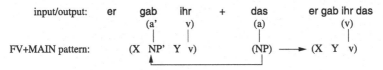

After this second application of FV+MAIN, the category is not suitable for further applications. Thus the content of the current rule package provides options, but whether these options are realized or not is controlled by the content of the current categories.

It is only a short step from the tentative LA Grammar 16.4.4 to an LA Grammar which handles the syntactic structures in question simply and adequately.

16.4.8 GERMAN LA GRAMMAR WITH FREE WORD ORDER (*LA D1*)

LX $=_{def}$ { [er (s3) *], [ihr (d) *], [das (a) *], [gab (s3′ d′ a′ v) *]}

Variable definition: NP $\in$ {s3, d, a}, with NP′ correspondingly s3′, d′ or a′
                            X, Y = .?.?.?.? (i.e., an arbitrary sequence up to length 4)
ST$_S$ $=_{def}$ { [(NP) {MAIN+FV}] }
MAIN+FV: (NP) (X NP′ Y v) $\Rightarrow$ (X Y v) {FV+MAIN}
FV+MAIN: (X NP′ Y v) (NP) $\Rightarrow$ (X Y v) {FV+MAIN}
ST$_F$ $=_{def}$ { [(V) rp$_{FV+MAIN}$] }

Compared to the tentative LA Grammar 16.4.4, the range of the variable NP is extended to s3. While the rule FV+MAIN is unchanged, the rule MAIN+FV has a new formulation: its input patterns now resemble those of FV+MAIN except that the patterns for the sentence start and the next word are in opposite order.

The required verb second position is ensured in *LA D1* by the start state which activates only one initial rule, MAIN+FV, and by the fact that MAIN+FV is not called by any other rule. The otherwise free word order of *LA D1* is based on the variables in the input patterns of MAIN+FV and FV+MAIN. Using the specified word form lexicon, the following sentences can be analyzed/generated:

16.4.9 WORD ORDER VARIANTS OF *LA D1*

er gab ihr das	das gab er ihr	ihr gab er das
er gab das ihr	das gab ihr er	ihr gab das er

LA D1 works also with an extended lexicon, such as the following:

[ich (s1) *], [du (s2) *], [wir (p1) *], [schlafe (s1′ v) *], [schläfst (s2′ v) *], [schläft (s3′ v) *], [schlafen (p1′ v) *], [lese (s1′ a′ v) *], [liest (s2′ a′ v) *], [las (s3′ a′ v) *], [helfe (s1′ d′ v) *], [hilfst (s2′ d′ v) *], [half (s3′ d′ v) *], [lehre (s1′ a′ a′ v) *], [lehrst (s2′ a′ a′ v) *], [lehrt (s3′ a′ a′ v) *], [gebe (s1′ d′ a′ v) *], [gibst (s2′ d′ a′ v) *].

For empirical work, this ad hoc way of extending the lexicon should be replaced by a general component of automatic word form recognition (Chaps. 13–15). For the theoretical explanation of certain syntactic structures, however, the definition of small word form lexica is sufficient.

After the indicated extension of the word form lexicon and extending the range of NP to include the segments s1 and s2, *LA D1* will also accept, e.g., ich schlafe:

16.4.10 IDENTITY-BASED SUBJECT-VERB AGREEMENT IN GERMAN

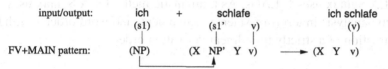

This example shows that the identity-based handling of agreement in *LA D1* works correctly for nominatives in different persons and numbers, and verbs with different valency structures. Ungrammatical input like *ich schläfst will not be accepted:

16.4.11 AGREEMENT VIOLATION IN GERMAN

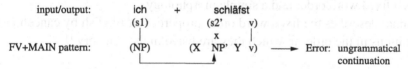

The handling of free word order in German is illustrated by the following derivation of a declarative main clause with a topicalized dative (see 16.3.2 for comparison):

16.4.12 DERIVATION IN *LA D1* (identity-based agreement)

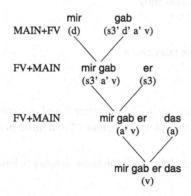

LA D1 handles agreement between the nominative and the finite verb in all possible person-number combinations. Only valency fillers of the correct case are accepted. Sentences with superfluous valency fillers, e.g., Susanne schläft das Buch, are rejected. If the rule name FV+MAIN is added to the (rule package of the) start state, *LA D1* is extended to yes/no-interrogatives, e.g., gab er ihr diesen. The tiny two-rule grammar of *LA D1* thus handles 18 different word order patterns of German.[10]

If the lexicon is extended to lexical ambiguities which lead to syntactic ambiguities – as in sie mag sie, then these are presented correctly as multiple analyses by the parser. Because LA Grammar computes possible continuations *LA D1* can be used equally well for analysis and generation, both in the formal sense of Sect. 10.4 and the linguistic sense of language production described in Sect. 5.4. Because *LA D1* has no recursive ambiguities it is a C1 LAG and parses in linear time.

LA D1 exemplifies a syntactic *grammar system* (Sect. 15.1) called LA Syntax. As an algorithm, LA Syntax uses C LAGs. As a linguistic method, LA Syntax uses traditional syntactic analysis in terms of valency, agreement, and word order – with the additional assumption of a strictly time-linear derivation order.

16.5 Fixed Word Order in English (*LA E1*)

As in all natural languages, the verbs of English have an inherent valency structure. For example, by assigning the verb form gave the category $(n'\ d'\ a'\ v)$ we express that this carrier requires a nominative, a dative (indirect object), and an accusative (direct object) to complete the semantic relation expressed. Compared to German, however, English has a fixed word order and a simple morphology.

LA Grammar describes the fixed word order properties of English by canceling the valency positions in the order in which they are listed in the category.[11]

16.5.1 FIXED CANCELING OF VALENCY POSITIONS IN A CARRIER OF ENGLISH

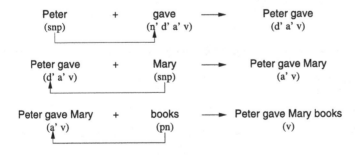

---

[10] Two basic sentence patterns correspond to a one-place verb: one declarative and one interrogative. Accordingly, four patterns correspond to a two-place verb, and 12 to a three-place verb.

[11] Accordingly, the variant of gave used in, for example, John gave the book to Mary is based on the alternative lexical category $(n'\ a'\ to'\ v)$.

In contrast to the German example 16.4.3, only the currently first position in the carrier category may be canceled. This simple principle results in a fixed word order. It is formalized by the rules[12] of *LA E1*, an English counterpart to *LA D1* (16.4.8).

16.5.2 ENGLISH LA GRAMMAR WITH FIXED WORD ORDER (*LA E1*)

LX $=_{def}$ { [Peter (snp) *], [Mary (snp) *], [books (pn) *],
    [gave (n' d' a' v) *]}
Variable definition: NP $\in$ {snp, pn}, NP' $\in$ {n', d', a'},
        X = .?.?.?.? (i.e., an arbitrary sequence up to length 4)

$ST_S =_{def}$ { [(X) {NOM+FV}] }
NOM+FV: (NP) (NP' X v) $\Rightarrow$ (X v) {FV+MAIN}
FV+MAIN: (NP' X v) (NP) $\Rightarrow$ (X v) {FV+MAIN}
$ST_F =_{def}$ { [(V) rp$_{FV+MAIN}$] }

Here, agreement is *definition-based* rather than identity-based. Because English nouns are usually not marked for case, the valency fillers are represented by the variable NP and the valency positions by the variable NP'. According to the variable definition, NP is defined to range over the category segments snp (singular noun phrase) or pn (plural noun), while NP' is defined to range over n', d', and a'.

The valency position to be canceled is decided by the carrier: it is the currently first valency position.[13] In this way, case is *assigned* to the English fillers by the respective valency positions they cancel. Consider the following example:

16.5.3 DERIVATION IN *LA E1* (definition-based agreement)

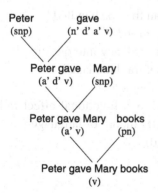

```
Peter        gave
(snp)       (n' d' a' v)


     Peter gave   Mary
      (a' d' v)   (snp)


     Peter gave Mary   books
        (a' v)         (pn)


     Peter gave Mary books
            (v)
```

This derivation is the English counterpart to the German derivation 16.4.12 with its *identity-based* agreement and free word order.

LA D1 and *LA E1* demonstrate that the elementary formalism of C LAGs handles different instances of agreement as well as variations and restrictions of word order

---

[12] For a reformulation using the proplet format see Sect. 22.5.

[13] For a complete description of the agreement restrictions of English see the variable definition of *LA E2* in 17.4.1.

on a high level of generality, in linear time, and without a counterintuitive proliferation of rules, lexical readings, or additional components like transformations. The efficiency, flexibility, and parsimony of LA Grammar is due to its novel technique of matching variable-based rule patterns onto categorially analyzed input expressions using a strictly time-linear derivation order.

Exercises

Section 16.1

1. Explain the boundary between the components of morphology and syntax.
2. What do morphology and syntax have in common? How are they related in the long-term history of a language?
3. Why are idioms a borderline phenomenon between morphology and syntax? Why don't they pose a problem for grammar? Give examples with explanations.
4. Describe some characteristics of synthetic and analytic languages.
5. Compare the combination principles of morphology with those of syntax.

Section 16.2

1. Explain the valency structure of the verb give.
2. What are secondary valency structures and how can they be handled?
3. What is meant by *transitivization* and *detransitivization*?
4. Do secondary valency structures call the concept of valency into question?
5. Are there other valency carriers besides verbs in natural language?
6. How are valency carriers and modifiers similar/different?
7. Explain how syntactic well-formedness is treated as a functional effect rather than a primary object of description within the SLIM theory of language.
8. Explain the interpretation of the category (a$'$ b$'$ c$'$ d).

Section 16.3

1. What is agreement, and how can it be violated?
2. How do valency and agreement interact?
3. What is identity-based agreement?
4. Write a variant of *LA Plaster* (16.3.3) for he sees her.
5. What is good about *LA Plaster*, and in which respects is it deficient?

Section 16.4

1. Is there a relation between free word order and a rich morphology?
2. What is the word order of declarative main clauses in German?

3. Explain the use of variables in the rule patterns of LA Grammar.
4. What is necessary for a recursive rule application, and how is it stopped?
5. Explain why er ihr gab das is not accepted by *LA D1*. Go through the derivation and show where and why it fails.
6. Why does adding the rule name FV+MAIN to the rule package of the start state result in an extension of *LA D1* to German yes/no-interrogatives?
7. What algorithm and what method define the grammar system LA Syntax?

Section 16.5

1. Compare the patterns for the valency carrier *(X NP' Y v)* in the rules of *LA D1* and *(NP' X v)* in those of *LA E1*, and explain how they provide for the different word order properties of German and English.
2. Why would it be inefficient to use identity-based agreement in English?
3. Are *LA D1* and *LA E1* surface compositional, time-linear, and type transparent?
4. What is the complexity of *LA D1* and *LA E1*, respectively?
5. Explain the inherent difficulties that basic C and PS Grammar have with the handling of (i) word order variation and (ii) agreement.
6. Write and test a C and a PS Grammar for the 18 sentence patterns and associated agreement phenomena handled by *LA D1*. Are the three grammars strongly or weakly equivalent?

17. LA Syntax for English

This chapter extends the simple LA Syntax for English called *LA E1* (16.5.2) to the time-linear derivation of complex valency fillers, complex verb forms, and yes/no-interrogatives. The emphasis is on explaining the descriptive power of the categorial operations in combination with the finite state backbone defined by the rule packages.

Section 17.1 describes the left-associative derivation of complex noun phrases in pre- and postverbal positions, showing that the categorial patterns of the rules involved are the same in both positions. Section 17.2 develops a system for distinguishing nominal fillers to handle agreement with the nominative and the oblique valency positions in the verb. Section 17.3 shows that the system works also for the nominative positions in the auxiliary be. Section 17.4 formalizes the intuitive analysis as *LA E2*, and describes the finite state backbone of the expanded system. Section 17.5 explains why upscaling the LA Syntax for a natural language is simple, and demonstrates the point by upscaling *LA E2* to yes/no-interrogatives in *LA E3*.

17.1 Complex Fillers in Pre- and Postverbal Position

Noun phrases require a treatment of *external agreement*, i.e., restrictions which apply to the combination of nominal fillers and verbal valency carriers. Complex noun phrases require in addition a treatment of *internal agreement*, i.e., restrictions which apply to the grammatical composition of complex noun phrases from smaller parts.[1]

---

[1] One could argue that another possible aspect of internal agreement in noun phrases is the choice between the relative pronouns who and which. This choice, however, is not really an instance of grammatical agreement in English, but is motivated semantically. It expresses whether the referent is considered to be human or not, similar to the choice of the pronouns he/she vs. it. For example, in some contexts a dog will be referred to as it or which. In other contexts, however, the dog may be referred to as he, she, or who. Because the choice of relative pronouns depends on the speaker's viewpoint, the human/nonhuman distinction is not coded into the syntactic category of English nouns. For an alternative treatment see CoL, p. 366.

R. Hausser, *Foundations of Computational Linguistics*,
DOI 10.1007/978-3-642-41431-2_17, © Springer-Verlag Berlin Heidelberg 2014

For the sake of simplicity, the LA Syntax[2] for English has so far avoided a treatment of internal agreement by using only elementary valency fillers like Peter, Mary, and books. The extension to complex nominal fillers like every child or all children must not only handle internal agreement, but also the time-linear derivation of complex valency fillers positioned before and after their valency carrier.

Internal determiner-noun agreement in English is restricted in terms of *number*. For example, every child is grammatical, while *every children is not. Furthermore, the noun phrases resulting from a determiner-noun combination must be marked for number because they have an external agreement restriction in relation to the finite verb. For example, every child sleeps is grammatical, while *all children sleeps is not.

Using an identity-based handling of agreement (Sect. 16.3), these restrictions may be represented by the following categories of determiners and nouns:

17.1.1 DETERMINER AND NOUN CATEGORIES OF ENGLISH

categories	*surfaces*	*samples of lexical entries*
singular and plural determiners:		
(sn′ snp)	a, an, every, the	[a (sn′ snp) *]
(pn′ pnp)	all, several, the	[all (pn′ pnp) *]
singular and plural nouns:		
(sn)	man, woman, book, car	[woman (sn) *]
(pn)	men, women, books, cars	[men (pn) *]

According to this categorization, the derivation of a noun phrase is based on canceling the argument position, i.e., sn′ or pn′, in the determiner with an identical noun segment, resulting in a singular (snp) or plural (pnp) noun phrase.[3]

If a complex noun phrase like the girl precedes the verb, the time-linear derivation requires that the noun phrase first be put together and then combined with the verb. This is illustrated in the following sample derivation:

---

[2] See the definition of *LA E1* in 16.5.2, which illustrates the handling of word order in basic declarative main clauses of English.

[3] The number of a phrasal noun is often assigned by the determiner, for example, every child vs. all children. In phrasal nouns with a definite article, however, number is assigned by the common noun filler, for example, the child vs. the children. This can be accommodated in an analysis of word forms as feature structures (proplets), but causes a complication in the style of formal analysis used here. For the sake of simplicity, the determiner the is treated in 17.1.1 as two lexical entries, one for singular and one for plural. The same would hold, for example, for no, my, your, his, her, our, their.

17.1.2 COMPLEX NOUN PHRASE BEFORE THE VALENCY CARRIER

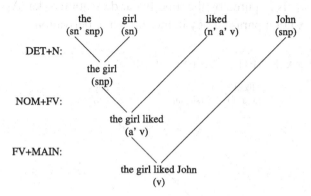

The rules DET+N, NOM+FV, and FV+MAIN used in the derivation plus DET+ADJ and AUX+NFV are discussed below. They constitute the grammar *LA E2*, formally defined in 17.4.1 as an extension of *LA E1* (16.5.2).

The preverbal application of DET+N is based on the following categorial operation:

17.1.3 PREVERBAL APPLICATION OF DET+N

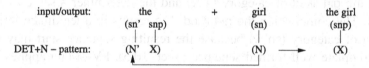

Next NOM+FV applies, which is based on the following categorial operation:

17.1.4 APPLICATION OF NOM+FV TO COMPLEX NOMINATIVE NP

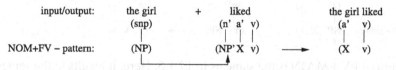

The derived noun phrase the girl of category (snp) cancels the nominative position in the valency carrier, resulting in the sentence start the girl liked of category (a' v).

Finally, the rule FV+MAIN fills the accusative position with the name John, resulting in a sentence start of category (v) – with no open valency positions left:

17.1.5 FV+MAIN ADDING ELEMENTARY OBJECT NP

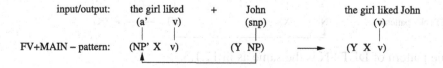

In contrast, if a complex noun phrase follows the verb, the parts of the noun phrase must be added step by step. This is required by the time-linear derivation order. As an example, consider the complex noun phrase a boy in the following derivation.

17.1.6 COMPLEX NOUN PHRASE AFTER VALENCY CARRIER

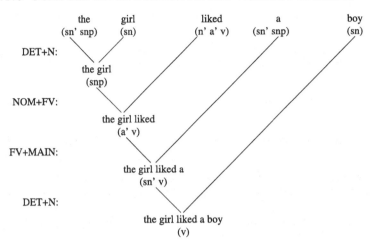

The sentence start the girl liked of category (a' v) and the determiner a serve as input to FV+MAIN. The combination the girl liked + a results in a legitimate intermediate expression of category (sn' v) because the resulting sentence start may be continued into a complete well-formed sentence (Sect. 10.5). FV+Main applies as follows:

17.1.7 FV+MAIN ADDING BEGINNING OF COMPLEX OBJECT NP

	input/output:	the girl liked	+	a		the girl liked a
		(a' v)		(sn' snp)		(sn' v)
FV+MAIN – pattern:		(NP' X v)		(Y NP)	⟶	(Y X v)

The rule pattern of FV+MAIN is the same as in 17.1.5. Here, it results in the sentence start the girl liked a. The nominal segment sn' at the beginning of the result category specifies the number of the following noun. This satisfies the input condition of the rule DET+N to be applied next.

17.1.8 POSTVERBAL APPLICATION OF DET+N

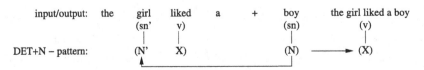

The rule pattern of DET+N is the same as in 17.1.3.

A simple extension of derived noun phrases is the addition of one or more adjectives between the determiner and the noun. In English, adjectives are morphologically unmarked and there is no agreement between either the determiner and the adjective(s) or between the adjective(s) and the noun. Unlike C Grammar (7.5.3), the semantic function of adjectives as modifiers of the noun is not reflected in the category.

The LA rule for adding adjectives is called DET+ADJ. It requires that the sentence start category begin with a noun segment sn′ or pn′ (like DET+N) and that the next word, i.e., the adjective, have the category (adj).

17.1.9 DET+ADJ RECURSIVELY ADDING ADJECTIVES

input/output:	the	+	beautiful	the beautiful	+	young	...
	(sn′ snp)		(adn)	(sn′ snp)		(adn)	(sn′ snp)
DET+ADJ pattern:	(N′ X)		(ADJ) ⟶ (N′ X)		(ADJ) ⟶ (N′ X)		

DET+ADJ produces an output category which is the same as the sentence start category – here (sn′ snp). Thus the rule may apply to its own output with no categorially-induced upper limit (in contrast to 16.4.5). The recursive reapplication of DET+ADJ in a pre- and a postverbal noun phrase is illustrated below.

17.1.10 COMPLEX NOUN PHRASES WITH ADJECTIVES

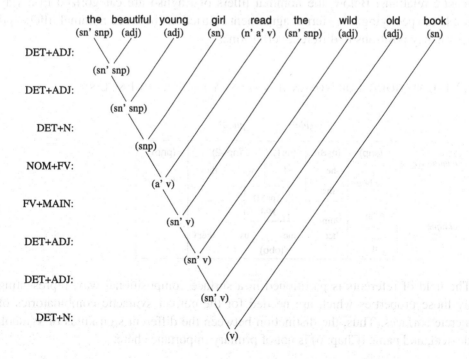

Because the number of adjectives between a determiner and a noun is unrestricted there is no grammatical limit on the length of noun phrases.

In summary, even though complex noun phrases in preverbal position are composed first and then fill the valency position in the verb as a whole, while complex noun phrases in postverbal position first fill the valency position and then are assembled step by step, the categorial patterns of the rules building complex noun phrases, namely DET+N and DET+ADJ, are the same in both instances. Furthermore, the categorial pattern of FV+MAIN accepts the beginning of oblique fillers irrespective of whether they are basic, e.g., it, or complex, e.g., the wild old book.

17.2 English Field of Referents

Having described the internal agreement restrictions of complex noun phrases in pre- and postverbal position, we next analyze the external agreement restrictions between nominal valency fillers and their valency positions in the verb. The set of nominal fillers includes personal pronouns, proper names, and complex noun phrases. Their external agreement restrictions apply to distinctions of *case* (nominative or oblique), *number* (singular or plural), and *person* (first, second, or third).

From a cognitive point of view, the nominal fillers form an abstract *field of referents* comprising the kinds of agents and objects which may serve as the arguments of semantic relations. Below, the nominal fillers of English are categorized in a way suitable to specifying all external agreement restrictions between nominal fillers and their valency positions in different verb forms.

17.2.1 CATEGORIES OF NOMINAL VALENCY FILLERS IN ENGLISH

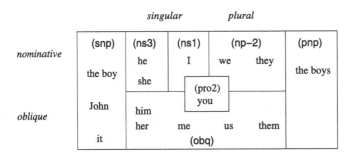

The field of referents is partitioned in a surface compositional way, representing only those properties which are needed for the correct syntactic combinatorics of concrete surfaces. Thus, the distinction between the different sign kinds of symbol, indexical, and name (Chap. 6) is not of primary importance here.

For example, the pronoun it is categorized as an (snp) because it behaves combinatorially like a proper name or a singular noun phrase. The pronouns I (ns1) and he/she (ns3) are distinguished from singular noun phrases (snp) because they cannot fill oblique valency positions, in contrast to the latter. For the same reason, we and they of category (np-2) are distinguished from plural noun phrases (pnp).

Noun phrases of third person singular nominative, i.e., (snp) and (ns3), are distinguished from other noun phrases of the categories (ns1), (np-2), and (pnp) because the nominative valency of verb forms like sleeps is restricted to third person singular, while that of verb forms like sleep is restricted to the other five. The reason for providing I with the special category (ns1) is that the nominative valency position of the auxiliary verb form am is uniquely restricted to it.

The pronouns me, him, her, us, them of category (obq) can fill only oblique (i.e., non-nominative) valency positions. For this reason they are distinguished from their nominative counterparts and are unmarked for number or person in their category.

The pronoun you of category (pro2), finally, is special in that it may fill both nominative and oblique valency positions, in both singular and plural. you is restricted only with respect to *person* in that it may not fill valency positions specified for first (*you am) or third (*you is, *you sleeps) person.

The arrangement of fillers in the field of referents follows their categories. The upper half is occupied by the nominatives (agents). The lower half is occupied by the oblique fillers. The left half contains the singular fillers while the right half contains the plural fillers. All in all, the field of referents is divided into seven different classes.[4]

The vertical peripheries are occupied by the filler categories (snp) and (pnp), which are unrestricted with respect to case. The category (pro2), representing the partner in discourse you, is in the center because it is unrestricted with respect to case *and* number. In this way the horizontal sequence s3 s1 sp2 p1 p3 is fixed, with s standing for singular, p for plural, and 1, 2, 3 for person.

Though the categorization and associated grouping of nominal fillers in 17.2.1 arises from grammatical considerations of a strictly surface compositional method, it is also quite telling in terms of cognition. Note that it is not universal, as shown by the analogous analysis 18.2.2 of the German field of referents.

The correlation between the nominal filler categories of 17.2.1 and compatible valency positions in finite main verbs of English may be shown as follows, using give as our example. Thereby a total of five different valency positions must be distinguished,

---

[4] On the number seven see Miller (1956).

There is in fact one additional class of nominal fillers, namely the pronominal noun phrases mine, yours, his, hers, ours, and theirs. They are restricted in that they may not fill valency positions of first person singular, e.g., *mine am here, *yours am here. Other than that they may fill any nominative valency positions, e.g., mine is here, mine are here, and oblique ones, e.g., she ate mine, of either number. This agreement pattern may be expressed by the category np-s1 (noun phrase minus first person singular nominative).

namely the nominative positions n-s3' (in give), n' (in gave), and ns3' (in gives) as well as the oblique positions d' (for dative) and a' (for accusative).

17.2.2 AGREEMENT OF FILLERS AND VALENCY IN MAIN VERBS

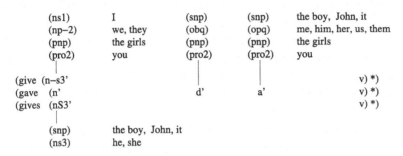

The valency position n-s3' may only be canceled by the category segments ns1, np-2, pnp, and pro2, while the valency position ns3' may only be canceled by the category segments snp and ns3. Thus, the possible fillers of n-s3' and ns3' are in complementary distribution. The valency position n' accepts elements from the union of the n-s3' and ns3' fillers. The oblique valency positions d' and a' accept all filler segments which are not explicitly marked as a nominative, namely snp, obq, pnp, and pro2.

All main verbs of English have the three finite forms illustrated in 17.2.2, including the irregular ones, and they all share the same pattern of nominative agreement. Also, the agreement restriction between fillers and oblique valency positions is the same for all main verbs. The only variation between different kinds of main verbs arises in the number of oblique argument positions, which may be zero, e.g., [sleep (n-s3' v) *], one, e.g., [see (n-s3' a' v) *], or two, e.g., [give (n-s3' d' a' v) *].

17.3 Complex Verb Forms

In addition to the English main verbs there are three auxiliary verbs, do, have, and be, and a larger number of modals, such as can, could, may, might, must, shall, could, will, would, and ought. The modals are morphologically parallel to the past tense form of main verbs, e.g., [gave (n' d' a' v) *] in that they have no special forms and therefore have no special agreement restrictions regarding their nominative fillers.

The auxiliaries do and have, on the other hand, have three finite forms do, does, did, and have, has, had, respectively, which are morphologically parallel to the forms of the main verbs and share their pattern of nominative agreement. The auxiliary be, finally, has the five finite forms am, is, are, was, and were, which require a special pattern for nominative agreement, described schematically as follows:

17.3.1 NOMINATIVE AGREEMENT OF THE AUXILIARY be

		(pnp)	the girls
(ns3)	he, she	(np13)	we, they
(ns1) I	(snp) the boy, John, it	(pro2)	you

[am (ns1' be' v) *]   [is (ns3' be' v) *]   [are (n–s13' be' v) *]
[were (n–s13' be' v) *]

(snp)   the boy, John, it
(ns1)   I

[was (ns13' be' v) *]

The categorization of the fillers is that of 17.2.1, already used in 17.2.2. Regarding the corresponding valency positions, on the other hand, the additional segments ns1', ns13', and n-s13' are needed for handling the special restrictions of am, was, and are/were.

The finite forms of the auxiliaries combine with the nonfinite forms of the main verbs into complex verb forms. In accordance with traditional grammar, the nonfinite forms of English main verbs are the infinitive, e.g., give, the past participle, e.g., given, and the present participle, e.g., giving.

The infinitive has no form of its own, but coincides with the unmarked present tense of the verb.[5] The past participle is marked in some irregular verbs, e.g., given, but usually coincides with the past tense, e.g., worked. The present participle, finally, is always marked, as in giving or working.

The infinitive combines with the finite forms of do into the emphatic, e.g., does give. The past participle combines with the finite forms of have into the present perfect, e.g., has given. The present participle combines with the finite forms of be into the progressive, e.g., is giving.[6]

The finite auxiliary forms all have variants with integrated negation, namely don't, doesn't, didn't, haven't, hasn't, hadn't, isn't, aren't, wasn't, and weren't. They have the same combinatorial properties as their unnegated counterparts.

The basic categorial structure of combining a finite auxiliary with a nonfinite main verb may be shown schematically as follows:

---

[5] For reasons of surface compositionality, the ultimately correct way is to categorize a form like give only once, namely as [give (n-s3' d' a' v) *] (CLaTR, Sect. 15.4). However, to bring out the parallel nature of complex verb forms built with the auxiliaries do, have, and be, as in does give, has given, and is giving shown in 17.3.2, we adopt temporarily two categories, e.g., (n-s3' d' a' v) for the use as a finite form and (d' a' do) for the use as an infinitive.

[6] In addition there are complex verb forms like is given and has been given (passive) and has been giving (present perfect progressive), which we leave aside. Cf. CoL, pp. 100f.

17.3.2 COMPLEX VERB FORMS OF ENGLISH

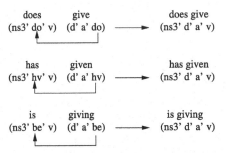

The nominative agrees with the finite auxiliary, for which reason its valency position (here ns3′) is located in the auxiliary category. The oblique valencies, on the other hand, are contributed by the respective nonfinite main verb (here d′ and a′). That the above auxiliaries are finite is marked by the presence of the v segment in their categories. That the main verb forms are nonfinite is shown correspondingly by the absence of a v segment. There is an identity-based agreement between the finite auxiliary and the nonfinite main verb, which is expressed in terms of the auxiliary segments do (for do), hv (for have), and be (for be), respectively.

The combination of an auxiliary with a nonfinite main verb form, e.g., has given, results in a complex verb form which has the same properties in terms of nominative agreement and oblique valency positions as the corresponding finite form of the main verb in question, here gives. This holds also in a strictly time-linear derivation, as shown by the following examples.

17.3.3 COMPARING BASIC AND COMPLEX VERB FORMS OF ENGLISH

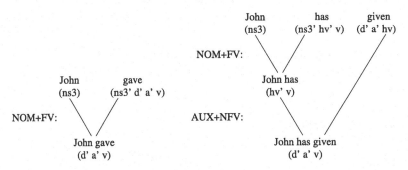

The nonfinite main verb is added by a new rule called AUX+NFV, illustrated below. The two partial derivations end in the same state and may be continued in the same way.

17.3.4 AUX+NFV ADDING A NONFINITE VERB

This application of AUX+NFV shows the identity-based agreement between the finite auxiliary and the nonfinite main verb as well as the canceling of the auxiliary segment, here hv′.

17.4 Finite State Backbone of LA Syntax (*LA E2*)

The handling of (i) complex noun phrases in pre- and postverbal position, (ii) external nominal agreement, and (iii) complex verb forms described intuitively in Sects. 17.1–17.3 will now be formalized as the grammar *LA E2*, which extends *LA E1* (16.5.2) in terms of a larger lexicon, a more detailed variable definition, and the three additional rules DET+ADJ, DET+N, and AUX+NFV. Also, the *nw* pattern of FV+MAIN will be adjusted to handle complex noun phrases.

17.4.1 *LA E2*: AN ENGLISH LA SYNTAX WITH COMPLEX NPS

LX $=_{def}$ {[Julia (snp) *], [John (snp) *], [Susanne (snp) *], [it (snp) *],
  [boy (sn) *], [boys (pn) *], [girl (sn) *], [girls (pn) *], [book (sn) *],
  [books (pn) *], [a (sn′ snp) *], [every (sn′ snp) *], [the (sn′ snp) *],
  [all (pn′ pnp) *], [several (pn′ pnp) *], [the (pn′ pnp) *]
  [i (ns1) *], [you (pro2), [he (ns3) *], [she (ns3) *], [it (snp) *],
  [we (np-2) *], [they (np-2) *], [me (obq) *], [him (obq) *],
  [her (obq) *], [us (obq) *], [them (obq) *]
  [am (ns1′ be′ v) *], [is (ns3′ be′ v) *], [are (n-s13′ be′ v) *]
  [was (ns13′ be′ v) *], [were (n-s13′ be′ v) *]
  [have (n-s3′ hv′ v) *], [has (ns3′ hv′ v) *], [had (n′ hv′ v) *]
  [do (n-s3′ do′ v) *], [does (ns3′ do′ v) *], [did (n′ do′ v) *]
  [give (n-s3′ d′ a′ v) *], [gives (ns3′ d′ a′ v), [gave (n′ d′ a′ v) *],
  [give (d′ a′ do) *], [given (d′ a′ hv) *], [giving (d a be) *]
  [like (n-s3′ a′ v) *], [likes (ns3′ a′ v), [liked (n′ a′ v) *]
  [like (a′ do) *], [liked (a′ hv) *], [liking (a′ be) *]
  [sleep (n-s3′ v) *], [sleeps (ns3′ v) *], [slept (n′ v) *]
  [sleep (do) *], [slept (hv) *], [sleeping (be) *]}
variable definition:
  NP′ ∈ {n′, n-s3′, ns1′, ns3′, ns13′, n-s13′, d′, a′}, (valency positions)
  NP ∈ {pro2, ns1, ns3, np-2, snp, pnp, pn, obq} (valency fillers), and
    If NP = pro2, then NP′ ∈ {n′, n-s3′, n-s13′, d′, a′},
    if NP = ns1, then NP′ ∈ {n′, n-s3′, ns1′, ns13′},
    if NP = ns3, then NP′ ∈ {ns3′, ns13′},
    if NP = np-2, then NP′ ∈ { n′, n-s3′},
    if NP = snp, then NP′ ∈ { n′, ns3′, ns13′, d′, a′},
    if NP = pnp, then NP′ ∈ {n′, n-s3′, n-s13′, d′, a′},

if NP = obq, then NP' ∈ {d', a'},

N ∈ {sn, pn} and N' correspondingly sn' or pn',

AUX ∈ {do, hv, be} and aux' correspondingly do', hv' or be'

X, Y = .?.?.?.? (arbitrary sequence up to length 4)

ST$_s$ =$_{def}$ { [(X) {1 DET+ADJ, 2 DET+N, 3 NOM+FV}] }

DET+ADJ:	(N' X) (ADJ)	⇒ (N' X)	{4 DET+ADJ, 5 DET+N}
DET+N:	(N' X) (N)	⇒ (X)	{6 NOM+FV, 7 FV+MAIN}
NOM+FV:	(NP) (NP' X v)	⇒ (X v)	{8 FV+MAIN, 9 AUX+NFV}
FV+MAIN:	(NP' X v) (Y NP)	⇒ (Y X v)	{10 DET+ADJ, 11 DET+N, 12 FV+MAIN}
AUX+NFV:	(AUX' v) (X AUX)	⇒ (X v)	{13 FV+MAIN}

ST$_F$ =$_{def}$ { [(v) rp$_{nom+fv}$], [(v) rp$_{aux+nfv}$], [(v) rp$_{fv+main}$], [(v) rp$_{det+n}$] }

The categories of the word forms in LX correspond to those developed in the previous three sections. The specified variables NP, NP', N, N', AUX, and AUX' characterize the category segments of valency positions for – and valency fillers consisting of – noun phrases, nouns, and auxiliaries, respectively.

The conditional clauses relating NP and NP' in the variable definition provide a definition-based characterization of the external agreement restrictions between nominal fillers and their valency positions (Sect. 17.2).[7] Empirical investigations have shown that a definition of agreement restrictions will use a smaller set of agreeing elements (and will thus be more efficient) if for each filler segment the compatible valency positions are defined, instead of the other way around.

As shown by the LA Grammar defined in 10.2.3 for $a^k b^k c^k$, the relation between rules and their rule packages defines a finite state transition network (10.2.4). The FSNs of LA Grammars of artificial languages are usually too simple to be of particular interest. The FSNs for LA Grammars for natural languages, on the other hand, may be quite illuminating for the empirical work.

The FSN of *LA E2* has six different states, namely the start state ST$_S$ (i) and the output states of the five rules DET+ADJ (ii), DET+N (iii), NOM+FV (iv), FV+MAIN (v), and AUX+NFV (vi).

---

[7] The variable definition in this and the following LA Grammars is designed for maximal brevity in a complete description of the complex agreement restrictions of English and German. Alternatively, one could define an equivalent LA Syntax using typed feature structures and unification. However, translating the definition-based agreement restrictions in 17.4.1 between noun phrases and their verbal positions into typed feature structures would result in an artificially inflated representation on the level of the lexicon without making the rules any simpler. Furthermore, in order to handle the categorial operations, unification alone would not be sufficient, but would have to be supplemented by operations for canceling and building up valencies, defined in terms of deleting and adding parts of the feature structures. NLC and CLaTR use nonrecursive feature structures with ordered attributes, called proplets, and define the categorial operations of the rules in terms of proplet patterns.

17.4.2 THE FINITE STATE BACKBONE OF *LA E2*

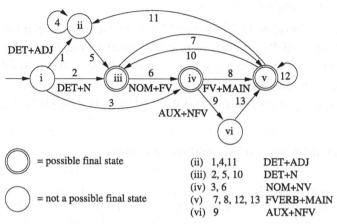

(ii)	1,4,11	DET+ADJ
(iii)	2, 5, 10	DET+N
(iv)	3, 6	NOM+NV
(v)	7, 8, 12, 13	FVERB+MAIN
(vi)	9	AUX+NFV

⚪ = possible final state

⚪ = not a possible final state

As in 10.2.4, the states are represented by circles and the transitions by arrows. The additional circles in the states (iii), (iv), (v), and (vi) indicate that they may also serve as final states (ST_F in 17.4.1).

All transitions going into a state correspond to the categorial operation of the *same rule* – though from different preceding states. All transitions leading out of a state, on the other hand, correspond to *different rules* and represent the (content of the) rule package of the rule leading into the state.

A transition corresponds to a successful rule application and thus combines a sentence start with a next word. The possible transitions which a certain rule may perform are defined explicitly by the rule packages which name the rule in question.

The FSNs for natural languages may be quite complex.[8] To make them more transparent it is recommended to number the transitions in the rule packages of the LA Grammar (in *LA E2* from 1 to 13). These numbers may then be used to name the transition arrows in the FSN. Given that the rules leading into a state are all the same, it is sufficient, and less cluttering, if rule names are added to only *one* transition arrow leading into a state (compare 17.4.2 and 10.2.4).

If each transition of an LA Syntax is given a unique name (e.g., a number), then grammatical derivations within that grammar may be characterized by writing the respective transition names in front of each next word, as in the following examples:

17.4.3 SPECIFYING THE TRANSITION NUMBERS IN THE INPUT

Peter 3 gave 8 Mary 12 a 11 book

the 1 beautiful 4 young 5 girl 6 is 9 reading 13 a 10 wild 4 old 5 book

---

[8] Especially in the step-by-step extension of an LA Grammar for a natural language, the associated FSNs provide a transparent representation of the increase in transitional connections between states. This is shown by the extension of *LA E1* via *LA E1.5* (FSNs in 17.5.1) and *LA E2* (FSN 17.4.2) to *LA E3* (FSN 17.5.6).

the 2 boy 6 gave 8 the 11 girl 7 a 11 book
Peter 3 gave 8 Mary 12 Susanne

The numbers correspond to those in 17.4.1 and in 17.4.2. The names assigned to the transitions in an FSN are essentially arbitrary – instead of numbers one could also use letters or the names of cities. The numbers in 17.4.2 and 17.4.3 are chosen to follow the sequence of rule names in the rule packages of *LA E2*.

The FSN aspect of left-associative analysis is illustrated in more detail below.

17.4.4 SYNTACTIC ANALYSIS WITH TRANSITION NUMBERS

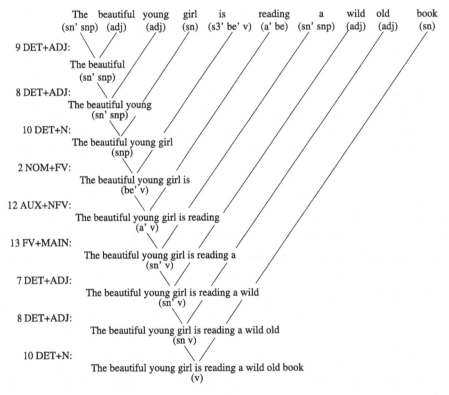

This example has the familiar form of left-associative derivations (e.g., 17.1.2, 17.1.6, 17.1.10) except that the transition numbers of 17.4.2 are specified in front of the rule names. Note that, for example, DET+ADJ occurs with three different transition numbers, namely 1, 4, and 10, indicating that this rule is called by the rule packages of the start state, of DET+ADJ, and of FV+MAIN. And similarly for DET+N.

The five rules of *LA E2* fulfill the pattern requirement for C LAGs (11.2.5–11.2.7). Furthermore, the five rules have incompatible input conditions (11.3.3). Therefore, *LA E2* is a C1 LAG and parses in linear time.

17.5 Yes/No-Interrogatives (*LA E3*) and Grammatical Perplexity

The extension of a simple LA Syntax, e.g., *LA E1*, to a descriptively more powerful system, e.g., *LA E2*, is facilitated by the fact that each new construction is realized as an additional sequence of transitions within the existing FSN. In the simplest case, a new transition requires no more than adding an existing rule name to an existing rule package. Sometimes the categorial operation of a rule has to be generalized in addition (compare for example FV+MAIN in *LA E1* and *LA E2*). At worst, a new rule has to be written and integrated into the network by adding its name to existing rule packages and by writing the names of existing rules into its rule package.

As an example of an extension requiring the definition of new rules consider the addition of complex noun phrases to *LA E1* (16.5.2). The finite state backbone of *LA E1* and its extension into the intermediate system *LA E1.5* is given below.

17.5.1 EXPANDING *LA E1* TO *LA E1.5* HANDLING COMPLEX NPS

LA–E1

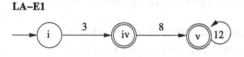

LA–1.5

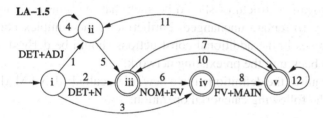

To facilitate comparison, the FSNs of *LA E1* and *LA E1.5* use the same names for corresponding states and transitions as the FSN of *LA E2* (17.4.2). The grammar *LA E1.5*, which is omitted here, is like *LA E2* without the rule AUX+NFV.

To extend *LA E1* to the handling of complex noun phrases, two locations in the network have to be taken care of. One corresponds to the preverbal position of complex noun phrases in the sentence, the other to the postverbal position(s).

Adding complex noun phrases in a preverbal position requires definition of the new rules DET+ADJ and DET+N, resulting in the additional states **ii** and **iii**. Furthermore, the additional transitions 1 and 4 (DET+ADJ), 2 and 5 (DET+N), and 6 (NOM+FV) must be defined. This is done by writing the rule names DET+ADJ and DET+N into the rule packages of START and DET+ADJ, and the rule name NOM+FVERB into the rule package of DET+N.

Adding complex noun phrases in a postverbal position re-uses the just added rules DET+N and DET+ADJ without any need for additional state definitions or changes in their categorial operations. All that is required are three additional transitions, namely 7 (FV+MAIN), 10 (DET+ADJ), and 11 (DET+N). These are implemented by writing the rule name FV+MAIN into the rule package of NOM+FV, and the rule names DET+ADJ and DET+N into the rule package of FV+MAIN.

In the development and extension of LA Grammars, existing rules may be re-used in additional transitions if the patterns of their categorial operations have been designed with sufficient generality (Sects. 17.1 and 17.3). The debugging of rules is greatly facilitated by the fact that LA Syntax is (i) type-transparent (9.3.1) and (ii) time-linear (10.5.2). For this reason, errors in the parsing follow directly from errors in the grammar specification. The first occurrence of an error usually causes the time-linear derivation to break off immediately (10.5.5), whereby the cause is displayed explicitly in the category or the rule package of the last sentence start.

As another example of a possible extension consider adding yes/no-interrogatives to *LA E2*. In English, this construction is based on inverting the order of the nominative and the finite auxiliary compared to that of the corresponding declarative.

17.5.2 COMPARING DECLARATIVES AND YES/NO-INTERROGATIVES

Susanne does enjoy the book.   Does Susanne enjoy the book?
Susanne has enjoyed the book.   Has Susanne enjoyed the book?
Susanne is enjoying the book.   Is Susanne enjoying the book?

The extension to the interrogative structures should be such that the transitions following the nonfinite main verb remain unchanged. Furthermore, the complex noun phrases serving as nominatives in the additional constructions should be derived by feeding the new transitions back into the preexisting network.

The planned extension requires the definition of two new rules, called AUX+MAIN and IP. AUX+MAIN has the following categorial operation:

17.5.3 CATEGORIAL OPERATION OF AUX+MAIN

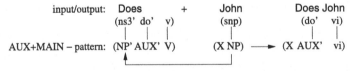

The variable X in the next word pattern (X NP) anticipates complex nominatives beginning with a determiner, e.g., [every (sn′ snp) *] as in Does every + child (sleep). Changing the verb segment from v to vi ensures that the other new rule IP (for interpunctuation, cf. 17.5.4) adds a question mark rather than a full stop.

Next we have to integrate AUX+MAIN into *LA E2*. Because AUX+MAIN handles the beginning of interrogative sentences it must be written into the rule package of the start state ST_S. If the nominative is a complex noun phrase, as in Does the girl or Does the beautiful young girl, AUX+MAIN should be continued with DET+NOUN or DET+ADJ, the names of which are therefore written into its rule package.

If the nominative is elementary, on the other hand, AUX+MAIN should be continued with the existing rule AUX+NFV. Because complex nominatives following AUX+MAIN must also continue with AUX+NFV, the name AUX+NFV must be written not only into the rule package of AUX+MAIN, but also into those of DET+ADJ and DET+N. Once the already existing rule AUX+MAIN has been reached, the derivation continues as in *LA E2*.

The new rule IP adds a question mark to sentence starts of category (vi), and a question mark or a full stop to sentence starts of category (v). Thus the new system will handle, e.g., Susanne sings., Susanne sings?, and Is Susanne singing?, while *Is Susanne singing. will be rejected. The categorial operation of IP is illustrated below, whereby the variable VT stands for 'V type.'

17.5.4 CATEGORIAL OPERATION OF IP

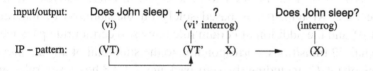

The name of IP must be added to the rule packages of DET+N (e.g., Susanne ate the apple + .), NOM+FV (e.g., Susanne sings + .), FV+MAIN (e.g., Susanne saw Mary + .), and AUX+NFV (e.g., Susanne is singing + . or Is Susanne singing + ?).

These extensions are formally captured by the following definition of *LA E3*:

17.5.5 *LA E3* FOR ENGLISH YES/NO-INTERROGATIVES

LX = LX of *LA E2* plus {[. (v' decl) *], [? (v' interrog) *], [? (vi' interrog)*]}
Variable definitions = that of *LA E2* plus VT ∈ {v, vi},
$ST_S =_{def}$ { [(X) {1 DET+ADJ, 2 DET+N, 3 NOM+FV, 4 AUX+MAIN}] }
DET+ADJ: (N′ X) (adj)   ⇒   (N′ X)   {5 DET+ADJ, 6 DET+N}
DET+N: (N′ X) (N)   ⇒   (X)   {7 NOM+FV, 8 FV+MAIN, 9 AUX+NFV, 10 IP}
NOM+FV: (NP) (NP′ X v)   ⇒   (X v)   {11 FV+MAIN, 12 AUX+NFV, 13 IP}
FV+MAIN: (NP′ X VT) (Y NP)
          ⇒   (Y X VT)   {14 DET+ADJ, 15 DET+N, 16 FV+MAIN, 17 IP}
AUX+NFV: (AUX′ VT) (X AUX)   ⇒   (X VT)   {18 FV+MAIN, 19 IP}
AUX+MAIN: (NP′ AUX′ v) (x NP)
          ⇒   (X AUX′ vi)   {20 AUX+NFV, 21 DET+ADJ, 22 DET+N}
IP: (VT) (VT′ X)   ⇒   (X)   {}
$ST_F =_{def}$ { [(decl) rp_{ip}], [(interrog) rp_{ip}]}

The finite state backbone of *LA E3* has the following structure:

17.5.6 THE FINITE STATE BACKBONE OF *LA E3*

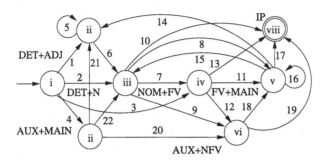

(ii)	1, 5, 14, 21	DET+ADJ	(v)	8, 11, 16, 18	FVERB+MAI
(iii)	2, 6, 15, 22	DET+N	(vi)	9, 12, 20	AUX+NFV
(iv)	3, 7	NOM+FV	(vii)	4	AUX+MAIN
			(viii)	10, 13, 17, 19	IP

The extension of *LA E2* to *LA E3* in order to handle yes/no-interrogatives required no revision of the older system, but is based solely on the addition of the rules AUX+MAIN and IP, and the addition of certain rule names to certain rule packages.

The FSN 17.5.6 has 22 transitions, corresponding to the sum total of all rule names in all rule packages of *LA E3* including the start package. *LA E3* has seven rules and one start state for which reason the FSN consists of a total of eight states (i–viii). The new interpunctuation rule IP has the special property that its rule package is empty. Furthermore, the definition of the final states in *LA E3* treats IP as the only 'completing rule' of the grammar.[9]

The seven rules of *LA E3* have incompatible input conditions for which reason *LA E3* – like its predecessors – is a C1 LAG and parses in linear time. When parsing with *LA E3*, any kind of input is analyzed from left to right, until either the whole input has been analyzed or the derivation fails because of ungrammatical continuation.

If the input is parsed to the end and at least one of the last states turns out to fulfill a final state definition of the grammar, the input is classified as a *complete grammatical* sentence. If the input is parsed to the end and none of the last states turns out to fulfill a final state definition, the input is classified as an *incomplete well-formed* expression. If the input is not parsed to the end, on the other hand, the input is classified as *ungrammatical*.

The step-by-step extension of *LA E1* to *LA E3* has resulted in increasingly denser transitions in the FSNs. Nevertheless, the use of rule packages with *selected* rules is still far more efficient than a hypothetical system in which all rule packages blindly list all the rules of the grammar. In the latter case, an LA Grammar with one start state

---

[9] *LA E3* and its predecessors are conventional in that their derivation stops at the end of a sentence. The rule IP may be extended, however, to attach the beginning of the next sentence, as shown in NLC and CLaTR. In this way, time-linear parsing may be extended from sentences to text.

and seven rules (analogous to *LA E3*) would result in $7 + (7 \cdot 7) = 56$ transitions – in contrast to *LA E3*, which has only 22 transitions.

The total number of transitions divided by the number of states provides a general measure for the *perplexity* of C1 LAGs. In statistical language recognition, perplexity represents the average number of possible continuations at any point.

> Perplexity is, crudely speaking, a measure of the size of the set of words from which the next word is chosen given that we observe the history of the spoken words.
>
> Roukos (1995)

In the word sequence The early bird gets the, for example, it is statistically highly probable that the next word will be worm. Thus, for statistical language recognition the set from which the next word is chosen is very small here and the perplexity therefore very low. Correspondingly, the perplexity of a scientific paper on, e.g., radiology, will be higher than in the above example, but still lower than in general English. An example of general English is the Brown corpus, which has been claimed to have a perplexity of 247.

While statistical language recognition determines perplexity probabilistically with respect to the sequences of word forms observed in a corpus, the notion of *grammatical* perplexity represents the average number of attempted rule applications in an LA Grammar. For example, in the hypothetical LA Grammar with nonselective rule packages mentioned above, the grammatical perplexity would be 56 : 8, i.e., seven attempted rule applications per composition. In *LA E3*, on the other hand, the grammatical perplexity is only $2.75(= 22 : 8)$.

The use of selective rule packages results not only in lower grammatical perplexity and thus in higher efficiency, however. Equally important is the fact that selective rule packages (i) provide a descriptively more adequate linguistic description and (ii) allow simpler definitions of the categorial input patterns of the rules.[10]

---

[10] Point (ii) refers to the fact that the categorial operations need to provide pattern-based *distinctions* relative to only those rules which they share a rule package with. In practice, one will find that specifying the categorial operations for an LA Grammar with an average of 2.75 rules per package is considerably easier than for an equivalent LA Grammar with an average of seven rules per package.

Exercises

Section 17.1

1. Explain the LA categorization of English determiners. Does this categorization use a definition-based or an identity-based handling of agreement?
2. Describe the LA derivations of John gave Mary Fido, the boy gave the girl the dog, and the old boy gave the young girl the big dog, and give detailed explanations of the pattern matching and the categorial operations of the rules involved.
3. Why is the recursive application of DET+ADJ unrestricted? What causes the recursion of FV+MAIN to be restricted to at most two applications?
4. Explain why the time-linear derivations of complex noun phrases in pre- and post-verbal position are asymmetric, yet can be handled by the same rules.

Section 17.2

1. What are the seven classes of nominal fillers in English? In what sense do they constitute the field of referents characteristic of the English language?
2. Why is the analysis of nominal fillers in 17.2.1 strictly surface compositional? Why would it be unjustified to transfer this analysis to other languages?
3. Describe the agreement restrictions of nominal fillers and verbal valency positions in English main verbs.
4. What are the agreement restrictions of you, I, he, him, and she?

Section 17.3

1. What special agreement restrictions are required by the auxiliary to be?
2. What is the categorial structure of English auxiliaries?
3. Describe the nonfinite verb forms of English. To what degree are they marked morphologically, and how are they categorized?
4. Explain the categorial operation of the rule AUX+NFV.

Section 17.4

1. Describe the finite state backbone of *LA E2* and explain where in 17.4.1 it is defined.
2. Why must the transitions going into a state all have the same rule name, while the transitions going out of a state must all have different rule names?
3. Which components of an LA Grammar determine the exact total number of its transitions?
4. Which component of an LA Grammar determines the choice of transitions at any step of a derivation during analysis?
5. What do LA Grammars have in common with finite automata and which formal aspect of LA Grammars raises their generative power from the class of regular languages to the class of recursive languages?
6. Which complexity-theoretic property makes the C LAGs especially suitable for the description of natural languages?

Section 17.5

1. What may be required for the extension of an existing LA Syntax to new constructions? Illustrate your explanation with examples.

2. Write an explicit LA Grammar for the finite state backbone of *LA E1.5* provided in 17.5.1.

3. Explain the categorial operation of AUX+MAIN. Give a linguistic reason why AUX+MAIN applies only at the beginning of a sentence and show how this is realized in the formal LA Grammar *LA E3*.

4. How is the derivation of ungrammatical '*Does Susanne sing.' prevented in *LA E3*? Explain the categorial operation of IP.

5. Expand *LA E3* to handle sentences like There is a unicorn in the garden.

6. On what grounds is the analysis of an input expression classified as in/complete or un/grammatical? Are the principles of this classification limited to natural languages or do they apply to formal languages as well?

7. Give three reasons why selective rule packages are preferable to nonselective rule applications. By what means can a rule be prevented from applying successfully if the system does not use selective rule packages?

8. Explain the notion of grammatical perplexity as a meaningful measure for the efficiency of C LAGs. Could it be applied to B LAGs and A LAGs as well?

9. Why is it possible to compute the grammatical perplexity of C1 LAGs, but not of C2 or C3 LAGs?

18. LA Syntax for German

The LA Grammar analysis of natural languages should not only provide a formal description of their syntactic structure, but also explain their communicative function. To advance a functional understanding of different kinds of natural language syntax within a strictly time-linear derivation order, the LA Syntax of a fixed word order isolating language (English, Chap. 17) will be complemented with the LA Syntax of a free word order inflectional language (German).

Section 18.1 describes the pre- and postverbal derivation of complex noun phrases in German, based on a distinctive categorization of determiners. Section 18.2 analyzes the external agreement restrictions of nominal fillers based on a field of referents and formalizes the results in *LA D2*. Section 18.3 illustrates the far-reaching differences between English and German word order regarding complex verb forms, interrogatives, and subordinate clauses. Section 18.4 presents a detailed categorial analysis of complex verb forms and formalizes the results in *LA D3*. Section 18.5 expands *LA D3* to interrogatives and adverbial subclauses, and concludes with the formal definition of *LA D4* and its finite state transition network.

18.1 Standard Procedure of Syntactic Analysis

All natural languages are based on the same time-linear derivation order. The only differences between individual languages arise in their handling of *agreement*, *word order*, and *lexicalization*, whereby the latter may result in differences in valency structure. Because of this profound similarity, the SLIM theory of language provides a standard procedure for the grammatical description of any natural language.

To determine the typological properties of a natural language, the first step of its syntactic analysis should be the formal treatment of declarative main clauses with elementary finite verbs and elementary nominal fillers. This is because (i) the position of the finite verb and its nominal fillers and (ii) the agreement restrictions between the nominal fillers and verbs of differing valency structure determine the basic word order and agreement properties of the language. This step has been illustrated with *LA D1* for a free word order inflectional language (German, Sect. 16.4) and *LA E1* for a fixed word order isolating language (English, Sect. 16.5).

R. Hausser, *Foundations of Computational Linguistics*,
DOI 10.1007/978-3-642-41431-2_18, © Springer-Verlag Berlin Heidelberg 2014

The second step is the extension to complex nominal fillers. This requires treatment of the internal and the external agreement restrictions of complex noun phrases, and the time-linear derivation of complex fillers in pre- and postverbal position. Apart from their more complicated internal structure, the addition of complex noun phrases to the initial grammar should result in the same kinds of sentences as before. This is illustrated by the transition from *LA E1* (16.5.2) to *LA E2* (17.4.1).

The third step is the extension to complex verb phrases to treat complex tenses and modalities. This may lead to new variants of word order. Otherwise, depending on the language type, the number of different sentence frames handled by the formal grammar may still be rather small. Yet all aspects of valency, agreement, and word order applicable to these sentence frames should now have their completely detailed and general final treatment. This step is illustrated by the transition from *LA E2* (17.4.1) to *LA E3* (17.5.5).

After this initial three-step phase one may well be tempted to explore the syntactic territory further by adding additional constructions. This is not recommended, however. What has to be done first, at this point, is the definition of a theoretically well-founded semantic and pragmatic interpretation for the syntactic analysis developed so far, which must be demonstrated to be functionally operational.

Only then follows the second phase of expanding the grammar. There are many topics to choose from: (i) the addition of basic and complex modifiers ranging from adnominal and adverbial adjectives to prepositional phrases to adnominal and adverbial subclauses, (ii) the treatment of sentential subjects and objects, (iii) infinitive constructions, (iv) different syntactic moods like the interrogative including unbounded dependencies, (v) different voices of the verb like passive, (vi) conjoined sentences, and (vii) gapping constructions.

Syntactically, the extensions of the second phase should build on the structures of the first phase without any need for revisions in the basic valency and agreement structures. The syntactic analyses of the second phase should be developed directly out of the semantic and pragmatic interpretation, and should be provided for both the speak and the hear mode (Chaps. 19, 22–24).

Having illustrated the initial three-step phase of grammar development with the definition of *LA E1*, *LA E2*, and *LA E3* for English, let us turn now to German. The free word order of German in declarative main clauses with elementary fillers has already been described in Sect. 16.4. Let us therefore take the second step, i.e., the extension to complex noun phrase fillers in pre- and postverbal position.

Complex noun phrases in German resemble those in English in that their structure consists of a determiner, zero or more adjectives, and a noun. They differ from those in English, however, in that they (i) are marked for case and (ii) show a wide variety of inflectional markings resulting in complicated internal agreement restrictions between the determiner and the noun. Furthermore, (iii) adjectives have inflectional endings which result in agreement restrictions between determiners and adjectives (15.2.2).

The definite and the indefinite determiners in German have a total of 12 distinct surfaces. Using the distinctive categorization of nouns in 14.5.4 for a definition-based determiner-noun agreement, an identity-based determiner-adjective agreement (18.1.2), and a fusion of cases whenever possible (e.g., (S3&A) for das Kind), a total of 17 different categories for the 12 determiner surfaces is sufficient for a complete treatment of the internal and external agreement restrictions of complex noun phrases in German.

18.1.1 DISTINCTIVE CATEGORIZATION OF DETERMINERS

definite article   *indefinite article*

[der	(e' mn' s3)			[ein	(er' mn' s3)	
	(en' f' g&d)				(es' n-g' s3&a)	indef-art]
	(en' p-d' g)	def-art]		[eines	(en' -fg' g)	indef-art]
[des	(en' -fg' g)	def-art]		[einem	(en' -fd' d)	indef-art]
[dem	(en' -fd' d)	def-art]		[einen	(en' m-n' a)	indef-art]
[den	(en' m-n' a)			[eine	(e' f' s3&a)	indef-art]
	(en' pd' d)	def-art]		[einer	(en' f' g&d)	indef-art]
[das	(e' n-g' s3&a)	def-art]				
[die	(e' f' s3&a)					
	(en' p-d' p3&a)	def-art]				

As explained in Sect. 15.2, the proper treatment of German adjective agreement is very simple, and consists in matching the ending of the adjective with a corresponding segment of the determiner. This is illustrated by the following examples showing the pattern matching of the rules DET+ADJ and DET+N. They are part of the German LA Grammar *LA D2* defined in 18.2.5.

18.1.2 CATEGORIAL OPERATION OF DET+ADJ

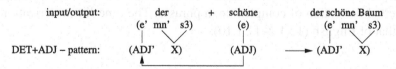

The categorial operation of DET+ADJ leaves the adjective segment in place to allow recursion (compare 17.1.9).

18.1.3 CATEGORIAL OPERATION OF DET+N

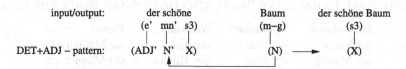

The categorial operation of DET+N removes both the adjective and the noun segment from the category because they can no longer be used.

The time-linear derivation of complex noun phrases in pre- and postverbal position may be shown as follows, using the transition numbers of *LA D2* (18.2.5).

18.1.4 PRE- AND POSTVERBAL DERIVATION OF NOUN PHRASES

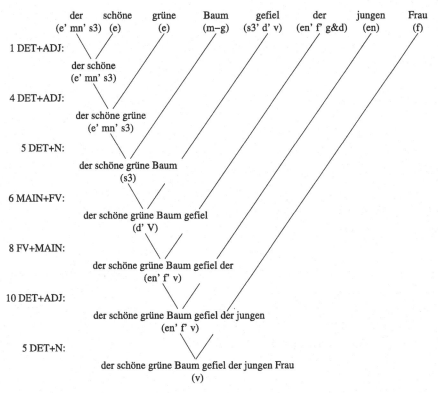

The categorial patterns of DET+ADJ and DET+N are suited equally well for the pre- and the postverbal derivation of complex noun phrases. The time-linear derivation is analogous to that of English (17.1.2–17.1.10).

18.2 German Field of Referents (*LA D2*)

Because German is an inflectional language, its noun phrases and verbs are traditionally represented in the form of exhaustive paradigms such as the following:

18.2.1 TRADITIONAL EXHAUSTIVE PARADIGMS OF GERMAN NOUN PHRASES

	Masculinum	*Femininum*	*Neutrum*	*Plural*
Nominative	der Mann	die Frau	das Kind	die Männer, etc.
Genitive	des Mannes	der Frau	des Kindes	der Männer, etc.

Dative	dem Mann	der Frau	dem Kind	den Männern, etc.
Accusative	den Mann	die Frau	das Kind	die Männer, etc.

Developed by the grammarians of classic Greek and Latin, exhaustive paradigms characterize all the forms of a word or phrase kind in terms of certain parameters such as case, gender, and number in noun prases; person, number, tense, voice, and mood in verbs; case, gender, number, and degree in adjectives; etc.

A paradigm table results from multiplying the relevant parameter values. In 18.2.1, for example, there are 24 slots resulting from multiplying four cases, three genders, and two numbers. Note that only 18 distinct surfaces are distributed over the 24 slots. Surfaces which occur in more than one slot are treated as ambiguous.

Exhaustive paradigms are misleading for the description of German because they disguise the fact that feminine, neuter, and plural noun phrases of German always have the same surface for the nominative and the accusative. Furthermore, feminine noun phrases of German always have the same surface for the genitive and dative. Thus, a crucial property of German is that the surfaces of some nominal fillers are *not marked* for grammatical properties that are *relevant* for an unambiguous specification of the associated valency position.

Exhaustive paradigms are misleading also in another respect: they *mark* nominal fillers for properties that are *not relevant* for an unambiguous specification of compatible valency positions. For example, while the distinction of singular and plural in the genitive, dative, and accusative is important semantically, it is combinatorially irrelevant because the oblique valency positions of German verbs – like their English counterparts – are not restricted for number. The same holds for the gender distinction, which is combinatorially irrelevant in all grammatical cases.

A surface compositional categorization of nominal fillers in German is shown below. It includes complex noun phrases, personal pronouns, and proper names, and forms an abstract field of referents analogous to that of English (cf. 17.2.1).

18.2.2 DISTINCTIVE CATEGORIES OF NOMINAL FILLERS (GERMAN)

					Singular	**Plural**		
N	du (s2)	ich (s1)	er (s3)	Peter (s3& a& d)	das Kind es die Frau (s3&a)	sie (s3&p3&a)	die Männer die Frauen die Kinder	wir (p1)	*ihr* (p2)
A	dich mich ihn (a) den Mann							uns (d&a)	euch
							(p2&a)		
D	dir mir ihm (d) dem Mann				*ihr* ihnen		den Männern den Frauen den Kindern		
				der Frau (g&d)					
G	deiner meiner seiner			des Mannes	ihrer (g)		der Männer der Frauen der Kinder	unserer eurer	

Certain surfaces which an exhaustive paradigm would present in several slots are analyzed here as lexical units occurring only once.[1] For example, Peter occurs only once in the field with the category (s3&d&a). And correspondingly for das Kind, es, die Frau (s3&a), sie (s3&p3&a), die Männer, die Frauen, die Kinder (p3&a), uns, euch (d&a), and der Frau (g&d).

Furthermore, certain forms of different words with the same distinctive category are collected into one subfield. Thus, dir, mir, ihm, ihr, dem Mann, ihnen, den Männern, den Frauen, and den Kindern have the same category (d) even though they differ in person or number. This is because these differences do not affect agreement with valency positions specified for oblique cases.

Like the English counterpart shown in 17.2.1, the order of the fields is based on the horizontal distinction between number and the vertical distinction between case with the levels n (nominative), a (accusative), d (dative), and g (genitive). The center is formed by a nominal filler which happens to be unrestricted with respect to number and combines the nominative and accusative case. This is the pronoun sie with the category (s3&p3&a), serving simultaneously as (i) feminine singular nominative and accusative, (ii) plural nominative and accusative, and (iii) the formal way of addressing the partner(s) of discourse in the nominative and accusative.

To the left and right of the center are placed the other third person singular and plural noun phrases, respectively. Then follow the personal pronouns of second and first person, symmetrical in singular and plural. Different fields are distinguished in terms of person and number only on the level N, because only the nominative fillers are restricted in these parameters.

The horizontal levels of cases N, A, D, and G are ordered in such a way that fields covering more than one case, such as s3&p3&a (e.g., Peter), s3&a (e.g., es, das Kind, die Frau), g&d (e.g., der Frau), and d&a (e.g., uns, euch) can be formed. The vertical columns are arranged symmetrically around the center, forming the horizontal sequence

s2, s1, sp3, p1, p2

in German, as compared to the English sequence

s3, s1, sp2, p1, p3

with s for singular, p for plural and 1, 2, 3 for person. Accordingly, the center sp2 of English stands for second person singular and plural (you), while the center sp3 of German stands for third person singular and plural (sie).

The distinctions between first person (I, we), second person (you), and third person (he, she, it) may be interpreted as increasing degrees of distance D1, D2, and D3. Combined with the different centers sp2 (you) of the English field of referents and sp3 (sie) of its German counterpart, there result the following correlations:

---

[1] There is one exception, ihr, which has two uses differing in person, case, and number. These may be expressed in the common category (p2&d), but not graphically in terms of a single occurrence.

18.2.3 CENTERING AND DISTANCE IN FIELDS OF REFERENCE

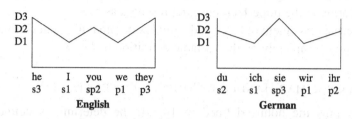

The center of the English field of referents is focussed onto the medium distance D2, while in German it is focussed onto the maximal distance D3. The peripheries are focussed in English onto the maximal distance D3, and in German onto the medium distance D2. The intermediate positions between center and peripheries are focussed in both languages onto the minimal distance D1.

A strictly surface compositional analysis of different natural languages may thus provide insight into their different coding methods – which would be obscured by blindly multiplying out paradigm slots as in an exhaustive analysis like 18.2.1. Even if one prefers to refrain from interpreting the fields of referents 17.2.1 and 18.2.2 cognitively as different language-inherent conceptualizations, there remains the fact that the distinctive categorization is more concrete and combinatorially more efficient[2] than corresponding exhaustive categorizations.

For the 14 kinds of nominal fillers there are 11 valency positions in German, represented as s1′, s13′, s2′, s23′, s13′, s2p2′, s3′, p13′, p2′, g′, d′, and a′:

18.2.4 AGREEMENT OF NOMINAL FILLERS AND VERBAL VALENCIES

```
         (s&d&a)                                    (s3&p3&a)
           (d&a)                                    (s3&d&a)
        (p2&d)  (s3&p3&a)                           (s3&a)
     (s1)   (d)   (a)              (s2)             (s3)
      |      |     |                |                |
(gebe (s1'  d'    a'   v)  *)   (gibst (s2' * v) *)  (gibt (s3' * v) *)
                                (gabst (s2' * v) *)
```

```
                                                   (s3&p3&a)
                                                   (s3&d&a)
                                                   (s3&a)
     (p3&a)                       (p2&d)           (s3)
      (p1)                         (p2)            (s1)
       |                            |               |
(geben (p13'*  v) *)          (gebt (p2' * v) *)   (gab (s13 * v) *)
(gaben (p13'*  v) *)          (gabt (p2' * v) *)
```

---

[2] The distinctive analysis uses only 14 different categories, in contrast to the 72 categories of the exhaustive paradigm analysis. 72 is the product of three genders, two numbers, four cases, and three persons.

The valency positions in the finite verb forms of German fuse the first and third person plural forms in the present and imperfect tense, represented as p13′, and the first and third person singular forms of the imperfect tense, represented as s13′.

The internal and external agreement of basic and complex nominal fillers in German are handled explicitly and completely by the variable definition of *LA D2*.

18.2.5 GERMAN LA GRAMMAR HANDLING COMPLEX FILLERS (*LA D2*)

LX = LX of LA D1 plus the nouns defined in 14.5.4, the determiners defined in 18.1.1, and the following pronouns

[ich (s1) *], [du (s2) *], [er (s3) *], [es (s3&a) *], [wir (p1) *],
[ihr (p2&d) *], [sie (s3&p3&a) *], [deiner (g) *], [uns (d&a) *],
[euch (d&a) *], [mir (d) *], [dir (d) *], [ihm (d) *], [mich (a) *],
[dich (a) *], [ihn (a) *]

plus adjectives in various degrees

[schöne (e) *]	[schönere (e) *]	[schönste (e) *]
[schönen (en) *]	[schöneren (en) *]	[schönsten (en) *]
[schöner (er) *]	[schönerer (er) *]	[schönster (er) *]
[schönes (es) *]	[schöneres (es) *]	[schönstes (es) *]

plus finite main verb forms of differing valency structures

[gebe (s1′ d′ a′ v) *]	[lese (s1′ a′ v) *]	[schlafe (s1′ v) *]
[gibst (s2′ d′ a′ v) *]	[liest (s23′ a′ v) *]	[schläfst (s2′ v) *]
[gibt (s3′ d′ a′ v) *]	[lesen (p13′ a′ v) *]	[schläft (s3′ v) *]
[geben (p13′ d′ a′ v) *]	[lest (p2′ a′ v) *]	[schlafen (p13′ v) *]
[gebt (p2′ d′ a′ v) *]	[las (s13′ a′ v) *]	[schlaft (p2′ v) *]
[gab (s13′ d′ a′ v) *]	[last (s2p2′ a′ v) *]	[schlief (s13′ v) *]
[gabst (s2′ d′ a′ v) *]	[lasen (p13′ a′ v) *]	[schliefst (s2′ v) *]
[gaben (p13′ d′ a′ v) *]		[schliefen (p13′ v) *]
[gabt (p2′ d′ a′ v) *]		[schlieft (p2′ v) *]

variable definition
NP ∈ {s1, s2, s3, p1, p2, p2&d, g, g&d, d, a, s3&a, s3&d&a, d&a, p3&a, s3&p3&a}
NP′ ∈ {s1′, s13′, s2′, s23′, s2p2′, s3′, p13′, p2′, g′, d′, a′}
and if NP ∈ {g, d, a}, then NP′ is correspondingly g′, d′, or a′
    if NP = p1, then NP′ = p13′
    if NP = s1, then NP′ ∈ {s1′, s13′}
    if NP = s2, then NP′ ∈ {s2′, s23′}
    if NP = s3, then NP′ ∈ {s3′, s23′}
    if NP = p3&a, then NP′ ∈ {p13′, a′}
    if NP = p2&d, then NP′ ∈ {p2′, d′}
    if NP = g&d, then NP′ ∈ {g′, d′}
    if NP = d&a, then NP′ ∈ {d′, a′}

if NP = s3&a, then NP′ ∈ {s3′, s23′, a′}
if NP = s3&d&a, then NP′ ∈ {s3′, s23′, d′, a′}
if NP = s3&p3&a, then NP′ ∈ {s3′, s23′, p13′, a′}
N ∈ {mn, m-g, m-np, m-gp, mgp, m-gp-d, f, n-g, -fg, -fd, n-gp, n-gp-d,
      ndp-d, p, p-d, pd},
N′ ∈ {mn′, m-n′, f′, n-g′, -fg′, -fd′, p-d′, pd′}, and
  if N ∈ {mn, -fg, -fd, f, p-d, pd}, then N′ is corresponding
  if N = m-g, then N′ ∈ {mn′, m-n′}
  if N = m-np, then N′ ∈ {-fg′, -fd′, p-d′, pd′ }
  if N = m-gp, then N′ ∈ {mn′, -fd′, m-n′, p-d′, pd′}
  if N = mgp, then N′ ∈ {-fg′, p-d′, pd′}
  if N = m-gp-d, then N′ ∈ {mn′, -fd′, m-n′, p-d′}
  if N = n-g, then N′ ∈ {n-g′, -fg′, -fd′}
  if N = n-gp, then N′ ∈ {n-g′, -fg′, -fd′, p-d′, pd′}
  if N = n-gp-d, then N′ ∈ {n-g′, -fg′, -fd′, p-d′}
  if N = ndp-d, then N′ ∈ {-fd′, p-d′}
  if N = p, then N′ ∈ {p-d′, pd′}
ADJ ∈ {e, en, es, er} and ADJ′ is corresponding
    X, Y = .?.?.?.? (arbitrary sequence up to length 4)
$ST_S =_{def} \{[(X) \{1\ DET+ADJ, 2\ DET+N, 3\ MAIN+FV\}] \}$
DET+ADJ: (ADJ′ X) (ADJ)   ⇒   (ADJ′ X)   {4 DET+ADJ, 5 DET+N}
DET+N: (ADJ′ N′ X) (N)   ⇒   (X)   {6 MAIN+FV, 7 FV+MAIN}
MAIN+FV: (NP) (X NP′ Y v)   ⇒   (X Y v)   {8 FV+MAIN}
FV+MAIN: (X NP′ Y v) (Z NP)   ⇒   (Z X Y v)   {9 FV+MAIN, 10 DET+ADJ,
                                                    11 DET+N}
$ST_F =_{def} \{[(v)\ rp_{MAIN+FV}], [(v)\ rp_{FV+MAIN}], [(v)\ rp_{DET+N}] \}$

LA D2 handles the same 18 word order patterns as *LA D1*, but with the additional capacity for complex nominal fillers. The categorial pattern of the rule FV+MAIN, defined in *LA D1* as (X NP′ Y v) (NP) ⇒ (X Y v), is generalized in *LA D2* to (X NP′ Y v) (Z NP) ⇒ (Z X Y v). In this way FV+MAIN can handle continuations with elementary fillers (e.g., pronouns or proper names) as well as continuations with (the beginning of) complex noun phrases.

18.3 Verbal Positions in English and German

The word order of English and German differs in the position of the finite – main or auxiliary – verb in declarative main clauses. English has the verb in *post-nominative* position, whereby the nominative is always the first valency filler. German has a *verb-second* structure in declarative main clauses, whereby fillers, including the nominative, may be placed freely. This difference is illustrated by the following examples:

18.3.1 FINITE VERB POSITION IN DECLARATIVE MAIN CLAUSES

English: post-nominative	*German*: verb-second
1. Julia *read* a book	Julia *las* ein Buch
2. *a book *read* Julia	Ein Buch *las* Julia
3. Yesterday Julia *read* a book	*Gestern Julia *las* ein Buch
4. *Yesterday *read* Julia a book	Gestern *las* Julia ein Buch
5. Julia quickly *read* a book	*Julia schnell *las* ein Buch
6. *While Mary slept, *read* Julia a book	Als Maria schlief, *las* Julia ein Buch
7. While Mary slept, Julia *read* a book	*Als Maria schlief, Julia *las* ein Buch

In clauses with a finite main verb and beginning with a nominative, English and German may be alike, as shown by 1. In German, the positions of the nominative and the accusative may be inverted (2), however, leading to a dissimilarity between the two languages described in Sects. 16.4 and 16.5. The structure of 2 violates the post-nominative rule of English, but satisfies the verb-second rule of German.

The word order difference in question shows up also in clauses with initial modifiers, such as elementary adverbs (3, 4, 5) and adverbial clauses (6, 7). In English, the preverbal nominative may be preceded (3, 7) or followed (5) by an adverbial, which in German leads to a violation of the verb-second rule. In German, adverbials are treated as constituents filling the preverbal position (4, 6), which in English leads to a violation of the post-nominative rule.

In other words, adverbials occupy the preverbal position of declarative main clauses *exclusively* in German, but *non-exclusively* in English. Because in German nominal fillers may occur freely in postverbal position there is no reason to squeeze one of them into a preverbal spot already occupied by a modifier. English, in contrast, marks the nominative grammatically by its preverbal position. Rather than being prevented from occurring in preverbal position, modifiers may share it with the nominative.

A second difference arises in the positions of finite auxiliaries and nonfinite main verbs. In English, the parts of complex verb forms like is reading or has given must be in *contact position*, i.e., contiguous. In German, they are typically separated, which is known as *distance position*: in this case adverbs and/or nominals occur between the finite auxiliary in second position and the nonfinite main verb at the end of the clause.

18.3.2 NONFINITE MAIN VERB POSITION IN DECLARATIVE MAIN CLAUSES

English: contact position	*German*: distance position
1. Julia *has slept*	Julia *hat geschlafen*
2. Julia *has read* a book	*Julia *hat gelesen* ein Buch
3. *Julia *has* a book *read*	Julia *hat* ein Buch *gelesen*
4. Today Julia *has read* a book	*Heute Julia *hat gelesen* ein Buch
5. *Today *has* Julia a book *read*	Heute *hat* Julia ein Buch *gelesen*

6. Julia *has given* M. a book today   *Julia *hat gegeben* M. ein Buch heute
7. *Julia *has* M. today a book *given*   Julia *hat* M. heute ein Buch *gegeben*

In declarative main clauses with a complex one-place verb, English and German may be alike, as shown by 1. In the case of complex two- and three-place verbs, however, the two languages diverge. The word orders in 2, 4, and 6 are grammatical in English, but violate the distance position rule in German, whereby 4 also violates the verb-second rule of German. The word orders 3, 5, and 7 are grammatical in German, but violate the contact position rule of English.

The distance position of complex verb forms in declarative main clauses of German is also called *Satzklammer* (sentential bracket).[3] From the viewpoint of communication, the clause-final position of the nonfinite main verb serves, first, to mark the end of the clause. Second, it keeps the attention of the hearer, whose interpretation has to wait for the main verb. Third, it gives the speaker more time to select the main verb. As a case in point, consider the following example:

> Julia has the offer of the opposing party today this afternoon
> Julia hat das Angebot der Gegenseite heute nachmittag   *abgelehnt.*   (declined)
>   *verworfen.*   (refused)
>   *kritisiert.*   (criticized)
>   *zurückgewiesen.*   (rejected)

In English, the choice of the main verb must be decided very early, as shown by the corresponding example Julia has *declined/refused/criticized/rejected* the offer of the opposing party this afternoon.

A third word order difference between English and German arises in the position of the – basic or complex – finite verb in subordinate clauses. In English, the position of the verb in subordinate clauses is the same as in declarative main clauses, namely *post-nominative*. In German, on the other hand, the verb is in *clause-final* position, whereby in complex verb forms the nonfinite main verb precedes the finite auxiliary.

18.3.3 VERB POSITION IN SUBORDINATE CLAUSES

English: post-nominative	*German*: clause final
1. before Julia *slept*	bevor Julia *schlief*
2. before Julia *had slept*	*bevor Julia *hatte geschlafen*
3. *before Julia *slept had*	bevor Julia *geschlafen hatte*
4. before Julia *bought* the book	*bevor Julia *kaufte* das Buch
5. *before Julia the book *bought*	bevor Julia das Buch *kaufte*
6. before Julia *had bought* the book	*bevor Julia *hatte gekauft* das Buch
7. *before the book a man *bought*	bevor das Buch ein Mann *kaufte*

---

[3] The Satzklammer is one of many structures of natural language syntax which systematically violate the (defunct) principles of constituent structure analysis (Sect. 8.4).

In subordinate clauses with a basic one-place verb, English and German may be alike, as shown by 1. However, in the case of complex verb forms of arbitrary valencies (2, 3, 6) and basic verbs of more than one valency (4, 5, 7), the two languages diverge. The word orders in 2, 4, and 6 are grammatical in English, but violate the clause-final rule for the position of the finite verb in subordinate clauses of German. The word orders 3, 5, and 7 are grammatical in German, but violate the postnominative rule of English, whereby 7 also violates the fixed order of nominative and accusative.

From the viewpoint of communication, the clause-final position of the finite verb in subordinate clauses has a function similar to that of the clause-final position of the nonfinite main verb in declarative main clauses. It serves to mark the end of the clause, keeps the hearer's attention, and gives the speaker maximal time for selecting the main verb.

18.4 Complex Verbs and Elementary Adverbs (*LA D3*)

German has two auxiliaries, haben (*have*) and sein (*be*), as well as a number of modals, such as werden (*will*), können (*can*), wollen (*want*), dürfen (*may*), sollen (*should*), and müssen (*must*). Their nominative restrictions in the present and imperfect are the same as those of German main verbs.[4]

18.4.1 LA PARADIGMS OF GERMAN AUXILIARIES AND MODALS

[bin (s1′ s′ v) *]	[habe (s1′ h′ v) *]	[kann (s13′ m′ v) *]
[bist (s2′ s′ v) *]	[hast (s2′ h′ v) *]	[kannst (s2′ m′ v) *]
[ist (s3′ s′ v) *]	[hat (s3′ h′ v) *]	[können (p13′ m′ v) *]
[sind (p13′ s′ v) *]	[haben (p13′ h′ v) *]	[könnt (p2′ m′ v) *]
[seid (p2′ s′ v) *]	[habt (p2′ h′ v) *]	[konnte (s13′ m′ v) *]
[war (s13′ s′ v) *]	[hatte (s13′ h′ v) *]	[konntest (s2′ m′ v) *]
[warst (s2′ s′ v) *]	[hattest (s2′ h′ v) *]	[konnten (p13′ m′ v) *]
[waren (p13′ s′ v) *]	[hatten (p13′ h′ v) *]	[konntet (p2′ m′ v) *]
[wart (p2′ s′ v) *]	[hattet (p2′ h′ v) *]	

The segments s′ (*sein*), h′ (*haben*), and m′ (*modal*) control the identity-based agreement between the finite auxiliary and a suitable nonfinite form of the main verb. As shown in 18.4.2, s and h agree with the past participles of different verbs (e.g., ist begegnet, but hat gegeben), while modals combine with the unmarked form of the verb (infinitive), e.g., will sehen.

---

[4] Cf. 18.2.5; compare also 17.3.1. For simplicity, the 'Konjunktiv' (subjunctive) is omitted in 18.2.5.

Whether a past participle agrees with the auxiliary h (*have*) or s (*be*) is a lexical property of the main verb and is related to the semantic phenomenon of aspect. Some verbs may combine with either h or s, e.g., ist ausgeschlafen (emphasizing the state of having slept enough) versus hat ausgeschlafen (emphasizing the completion of the process).

The unmarked form of the verb, e.g., sehen, is used for the first and third person plural of the present tense and as the infinitive, with one exception: the infinitive of the auxiliary sein differs from the finite form in question, i.e., sind.[5] To bring out the parallel nature of complex verbs built with auxiliaries and modals, we provide the infinitive temporarily with its own category, based on the modal category segment m, in analogy to English (17.3.2).

18.4.2 COMPLEX VERB FORMS OF GERMAN

To explain the special structure of German auxiliary constructions in a strictly time-linear derivation order, let us first consider declarative main clauses with a finite main verb. There, the valency carrier is in second position, such that for incoming fillers all the valency positions are available from the beginning. For example, in

Die Frau *gab* dem Kind den Apfel

or

Dem Kind *gab* die Frau den Apfel,

the initial nominal filler cancels a compatible position in the adjacent main verb, then the following nominal fillers cancel the remaining positions postverbally.

In corresponding auxiliary constructions, on the other hand, the valency carrier is not present from the beginning, with the result that incoming fillers may be without suitable valency positions for a while. For example, in

Die Frau *hat* dem Kind den Apfel *gegeben*

the first filler cancels the nominative position in the auxiliary, but the dative and the accusative have no corresponding valency positions until the nonfinite main verb arrives

---

[5] The corresponding exception of the English auxiliary be is the form am for the first person singular present tense.

at the end. Furthermore, if the first filler is not a nominative, as in

Dem Kind *hat* die Frau den Apfel *gegeben*,

no valency position at all can be canceled in the combination of the initial nominal filler and the auxiliary.

Thus, in auxiliary constructions the fillers often have to be remembered in the sentence start category until the valency carrier is added. This requires the following extensions of *LA D2*: (i) the combination of the first syntagma and the auxiliary (MAIN+FV revised as **+FV**), (ii) the combination of the sentence start ending in the auxiliary and the next constituent(s) (FV+MAIN revised as **+MAIN**), and (iii) adding the nonfinite main verb in clause final position, whereby the collected fillers must cancel the corresponding positions in the nonfinite main verb (new rule **+NFV**).

In step (i) the following case distinctions must be made:

18.4.3 +FV ALTERNATIVES OF ADDING THE AUXILIARY

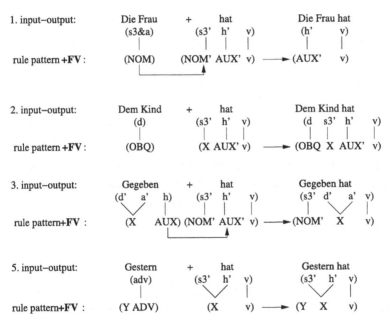

In clause 1, the nominative filler cancels the nominative valency in the finite auxiliary. In clause 2, the presence of the auxiliary segment triggers the oblique filler to be added to the category. In clause 3, a topicalized nonfinite main verb cancels the agreeing auxiliary segment and adds its valency positions, resulting in a category equivalent to a corresponding finite main verb. In clause 5, the combination of an adverb and a finite auxiliary leaves the category of the latter unchanged.

It would be possible to treat each clause as a separate rule. However, because the clauses are linguistically related and share the same rule package we introduce a notation for combining several clauses into a complex categorial operation. This notation, illustrated below, is a subtheoretical variant like multicats. It is equivalent to the standard notation of the algebraic definition and does not change the formal status of the grammars with respect to their complexity.

18.4.4 EXTENDING MAIN+FV INTO +FV USING CLAUSES

+FV: 1. (NOM) (NOM' AUX' v) $\Rightarrow$ (AUX' v)
2. (OBQ) (X AUX' v) $\Rightarrow$ (OBQ X AUX' v)
3. (X AUX) (NOM' AUX' v) $\Rightarrow$ (NOM' X v)
4. (NP) (X NP' Y v) $\Rightarrow$ (X Y v)
5. (Y ADV) (X v) $\Rightarrow$ (Y X v)   {+MAIN, +NFV, +FV, +IP}

The input conditions of the clauses are applied sequentially to the input. When a clause matches the input, the associated output is derived and the rule application is finished.[6] Clauses 1, 2, 3, and 5 correspond to those in 18.4.3. Clause 4 handles the standard combination of a nominal filler and a finite main verb inherited from MAIN+FV in *LA D2* (18.2.5).

Next consider step (ii), i.e., the continuations after the finite auxiliary.

18.4.5 +MAIN ALTERNATIVES AFTER THE AUXILIARY

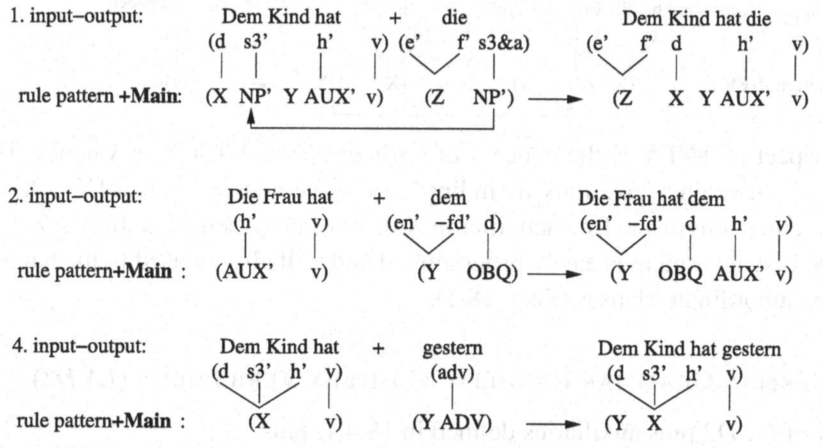

In clause 1, the auxiliary is followed by a nominative which cancels the nominative valency position in the auxiliary. In clause 2, the auxiliary is followed by an oblique filler, whereby the presence of the auxiliary segment triggers the addition of the next word category segments to the sentence start. In clause 4, the continuation with an adverb has no effect on the syntactic category of the sentence start.

These alternatives are joined with the FV+MAIN combination of a finite main verb and a nominal filler (clause 3) into the new rule **+MAIN**.

---

[6] There is the additional possibility of bracketing several clauses to indicate that they apply in parallel, which may result in more than one continuation path.

18.4.6 EXTENDING FV+MAIN INTO +MAIN USING CLAUSES

+MAIN: 1. (X NOM' Y AUX' v) (Z NOM) ⇒ (Z X Y AUX' v)
    2. (X AUX' v) (Y OBQ) ⇒ (Y OBQ X AUX' v)
    3. (X NP' Y v) (Z NP) ⇒ (Z X Y v)
    4. (X V) (Y ADV) ⇒ (Y X v) {+ADJ, +N, +MAIN, +NFV, +FV, +IP}

Clause 2 of **+MAIN** allows the addition of arbitrarily many oblique fillers. The resulting sentence is only grammatical, however, if the nonfinite main verb added at the end happens to provide a corresponding set of valency positions.

Step (iii) consists in adding the nonfinite main verb concluding the clause. It is handled by the new rule **+NFV**, which checks identity-based agreement between the auxiliary and the nonfinite main verb illustrated in 18.4.2. Furthermore, the oblique fillers collected in the sentence start cancel all the oblique valency positions in the nonfinite main verb (the nominative is already canceled at this point). The categorial operation of **+NFV** may be illustrated as follows:

18.4.7 CATEGORIAL OPERATION OF +NFV

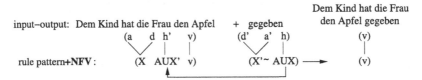

A novel aspect of **+NFV** is the concept of *agreeing lists*. A list X of valency fillers and a list X'~ of valency positions are in linguistic agreement, written as [X = X'~], if they are of equal length and for each filler in X there is an agreeing position in X'~ and vice versa. List agreement is easily programmed and will also be used in the handling of German subordinate clauses (Sect. 18.5).

18.4.8 GERMAN GRAMMAR HANDLING COMPLEX VERB FORMS (*LA D3*)

LX = LX of *LA D2* plus auxiliaries defined in 18.4.1, plus
    nonfinite main verb form of 18.4.2, plus adverbials
    [gestern (adv) *], [hier (adv) *], [jetzt (adv) *], plus punctuation signs
    [. (v' decl) *], [? (vi' interrog) *], [? (v' interrog) *]
variable definition = variable definition of *LA D2* plus
    NOM ∈ NP \ {d, a, d&a}   nominative filler[7]
    NOM' ∈ NP \ {d, a}   nominative valency positions

---

[7] If Y is a subset of X, then the notation X\Y (X minus Y) stands for the set of elements of X without the elements of Y. This notation should not be confused with the definition of categories in C Grammar (7.4.3).

OBQ $\in$ {d, a, d&a}   oblique filler

AUX $\in$ {h, b, m},   auxiliaries and modals

VT $\in$ {v, vi},   mood marker

SM $\in$ {decl, interrog},   sentence mood

$ST_S =_{def}$ {[(X) {1 +ADJ, 2 +N, 3 +FV, 4 +NFV}] }

+ADJ: (ADJ′ X) (ADJ) $\Rightarrow$ (ADJ X)   {5 +ADJ, 6 +N}

+N: (ADJ′ N′ X) (N) $\Rightarrow$ (X)   {7 +FV, 8 +MAIN, 9 +NFV, 10 +IP}

+FV: (NOM) (NOM′ AUX′ v) $\Rightarrow$ (AUX′ v)

            (OBQ) (X AUX′ v) $\Rightarrow$ (OBQ X AUX′ v)

            (X AUX) (NOM′ AUX′ v) $\Rightarrow$ (NOM′ X v)

            (NP) (X NP′ Y v) $\Rightarrow$ (X Y v)

            (ADV) (X v) $\Rightarrow$ (X v)   {11 +MAIN, 12 +NFV, 13 +IP}

+MAIN: (X NOM′ Y AUX′ v) (Z NOM) $\Rightarrow$ (Z X Y AUX′ v)

            (X AUX′ v) (Y OBQ) $\Rightarrow$ (Y OBQ X AUX′ v)

            (X NP′ Y v) (Z NP) $\Rightarrow$ (Z X Y v)

            (X v) (Y ADV) $\Rightarrow$ (Y X v)   {14 +ADJ, 15 +N, 16 +MAIN,

                                        17 +NFV, 18 +FV, 19 +IP}

+NFV: (X AUX′ v) (X′$^{\sim}$ AUX)

            (X = X′$^{\sim}$) $\Rightarrow$ (v)   {20 +IP}

+IP: (VT) (VT′ SM) $\Rightarrow$ (SM)   {}

$ST_F =_{def}$ {[(SM) rp$_{+ip}$]}

While **+FV** and **+MAIN** show the use of *clauses*, **+NFV** shows the use of a *subclause*. If the pattern of the main clause of **+NFV** is matched by the input, then the indented subclause checks whether the list agreement between the values of X and the values of X′$^{\sim}$ is satisfied. Only if this is the case is an output derived. Especially in larger applications, subclauses allow a natural structuring of LA rules into main conditions and subconditions, improving both linguistic transparency and computational efficiency.

The rule **+IP** adds full stops or question marks to declarative main clauses, as in Julia hat gestern ein Buch gelesen? In *LA D4*, **+IP** will be adopted without change. Other sentence moods are based on *prefinal* derivation steps (Sect. 18.5).

LA D3 provides a complete treatment of word order variations and word order restrictions in German declarative main clauses with and without auxiliaries. It handles all internal and external agreement restrictions and valency phenomena arising in 980 kinds of clauses which differ with respect to the valency structure of the verb, basic vs. complex noun phrases, basic vs. complex verb forms including topicalized nonfinite main verbs, and declarative vs. interrogative mood. If the possible adding of adverbs in various positions is taken into account, the number of constructions handled by *LA D3* is theoretically infinite.

The application of **+NFV** with the canceling of agreeing lists is illustrated by the following derivation, the transition numbers of which are those of *LA D3*.

18.4.9 DECLARATIVE WITH DATIVE PRECEDING AUXILIARY

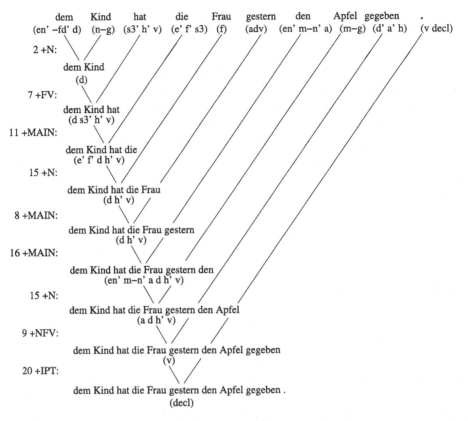

Whether a nominal argument is added to the sentence start category or used to cancel a valency position is determined by the presence/absence of an AUX segment, i.e., h', b', or m', in the carrier and by whether the filler is a nominative or not.

18.5 Interrogatives and Subordinate Clauses (*LA D4*)

The distance position of auxiliary and main verb in declarative sentences arises in similar form in interrogatives with auxiliaries and in subordinate clauses. Consider the following examples of interrogatives with the verbal components in italics:

18.5.1 INTERROGATIVE WITH AND WITHOUT AUXILIARY

1. *Hat* die Frau   dem Kind gestern   den Apfel *gegeben*?
    (*Has the woman the   child yesterday the   apple given   ?*)
2. *Hat* dem Kind gestern die Frau den Apfel *gegeben*?
3. *Hat* gestern die Frau dem Kind den Apfel *gegeben*?

4. *Gab* die Frau   dem Kind gestern   den Apfel ?
    (*Gave the woman the   child yesterday the   apple?*)
5. *Gab* gestern die Frau dem Kind den Apfel?

A sentential bracket (Satzklammer) is formed in 1, 2, and 3 by the initial auxiliary and the final nonfinite main verb. The auxiliary is followed in 1 by the nominative, in 2 by an oblique filler, and in 3 by an adverb. The examples 4 and 5 begin with a finite main verb, followed by a nominal filler and an adverb, respectively. The initial finite verb is combined with a main component by the new rule **?+MAIN**.

18.5.2 **?+MAIN** STARTING AN INTERROGATIVE MAIN CLAUSE

1. input–output:
$$
\begin{array}{ccccc}
& \text{hat} & + & \text{die} & \text{hat die} \\
(\text{s3'} & \text{h'} & \text{v}) \quad (\text{e'} & \text{f'} \quad \text{s3\&a}) & (\text{e'} \quad \text{f'} \quad \text{h'} \quad \text{vi}) \\
\end{array}
$$

rule pattern **?+Main**: (NOM' AUX' v)   (Z NOM) ⟶ (Z   AUX' vi)

?+MAIN is similar to **+MAIN** except for changing the verb segment from v to vi, thus enforcing the addition of a question mark at the end. By including **?+MAIN**, but not **+MAIN**, in the start state's rule package, a sentence-initial finite verb is treated obligatorily as the beginning of an interrogative.

After the application of **?+MAIN**, the derivation of interrogatives is based on existing rules. For example, sentence 1 in 18.5.1 is based on the rule sequence **?+MAIN, +N, +MAIN, +N, +MAIN, +MAIN, +N, +NFV, +IP**, while sentence 5 is based on the rule sequence **?+MAIN, +MAIN, +N, +MAIN, +N, +MAIN, +N, +IP**.

Another kind of sentential bracket is formed by subordinate clauses. As illustrated below, the bracket begins with the subordinating conjunction, to the category of which the subsequent nominal fillers are added. The end of the bracket is the verb. It requires list agreement to cancel the fillers collected in the sentence start.

18.5.3 SUBORDINATE CLAUSES WITH AND WITHOUT AUXILIARY

1. *Als*   die Frau   dem Kind gestern   den Apfel *gegeben hat*
    (*When the woman the   child yesterday the   apple given   has*)
2. *Als* dem Kind gestern die Frau den Apfel *gegeben hat*
3. *Als* gestern die Frau dem Kind den Apfel *gegeben hat*
4. *Als*   die Frau   dem Kind gestern   den Apfel *gab*
    (*When the woman the   child yesterday the   apple gave*)
5. *Als* gestern die Frau dem Kind den Apfel *gab*

The beginning of adverbial subclauses is handled by an extension of **+MAIN**:

18.5.4 +MAIN STARTING AN ADVERBIAL SUBCLAUSE

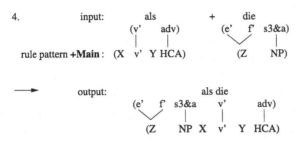

4.   input: als   +   die
                              (v'   adv)   (e'   f'   s3&a)
        rule pattern +Main : (X   v'   Y   HCA)   (Z   NP)

        ⟶   output: als die
                          (e'   f'   s3&a   v'   adv)

                          (Z   NP X   v'   Y   HCA)

The variable HCA (for higher clause attachment) is specified for the values v, vi, and adv. The addition of nominal fillers to the sentence start category is triggered by the presence of the nonfinal v', provided here by the subordinating conjunction. The clause-final finite main verb is added by an extension of +FV.

18.5.5 +FV CONCLUDING SUBCLAUSE WITH FINITE MAIN VERB

2.   input: als die Frau dem Kind den Apfel   +   gab
                          (a   d s3&a v'   adv)   (s13'   d'   a' v)
        rule pattern +FV :   (X   v' Y HCA)   (X'~   v)

        ⟶ output: als die Frau dem Kind den Apfel gab
                              (adv)

                        (Y HCA)

If the adverbial clause has a preverbal position in the higher sentence, the adv segment in the category of the subordinating conjunction serves as the result segment. Once the derivation of the adverbial subclause is completed, it has the category (adv) and is treated like an elementary adverb (e.g., gestern in 18.4.3, 5). If the adverbial clause has a postverbal position in the higher clause, the adv-segment is deleted in the process of adding the subordinating conjunction (cf. 18.5.6).

Adverbial clauses in any position use the v' segment of the subordinating conjunction category as the main node for the duration of the subclause derivation. This means that the preverbal nominal fillers are attached to the left of the current v' segment. The v' segment of the current subclause is always positioned leftmost in the category of the sentence start.

18.5.6 BEGINNING OF AN ADVERBIAL SUBCLAUSE IN POSTVERBAL POSITION

Julia las + als   Julia las, als + Maria   Julia las, als Maria
(a' v)   (v' adv) ⟶ (v' a' v)   (s3&d&a) ⟶ (s3&d&a v' a' v)

The next combination finishes the subordinate clause with the finite main verb. Thereby everything up to and including the first non-final v' is canceled and the category is the same as before the adverbial subclause was started.

18.5.7 COMPLETION OF AN ADVERBIAL SUBCLAUSE IN POSTVERBAL POSITION

Julia las, als Susanne + schlief   Julia las, als Susanne schlief
   (s3&d&a v' a' v)   (s3' v) $\longrightarrow$ (a' v)

In this manner, adverbial subclauses may also be nested, allowing center embedding of arbitrary depth.

18.5.8 NESTING OF ADVERBIAL SUBCLAUSES IN PREVERBAL POSITION

Als Maria, obwohl Julia die Zeitung + las   Als Maria, obwohl Julia die Zeitung las
  (a s3&d&a v' s3&d&a v' adv)   (s3' a' v) $\longrightarrow$ (s3&d&a v' adv)

The nesting is indicated by the presence of more than one v' segment in the sentence start category, but only as long as the nested clauses have not been completed.

Subclauses with complex verb phrases are handled in the same way, except that the nonfinite main verb and the finite auxiliary are added in two steps.

18.5.9 +NFV ADDS NONFINITE MAIN VERB TO SUBCLAUSE

```
1.              input:   als dem Kind die Frau den Apfel    +     gegeben
                         (d  s3&a   d   v'     adv)             (d'  a'  h)
                          |    |    |   |       |               \__/   |
          rule pattern +NFV :  (X1  NOM  X2  v'  Y  HCA)          (X'~  AUX)


    ──────▶     output:   als dem Kind die Frau den Apfel gegeben
                             (s3&a    h    v'      adv)
                               |      |    |        |
                             (NOM   AUX   v'    Y  HCA)
```

This example illustrates that the nominative filler may be positioned between oblique fillers. To achieve list agreement between the oblique fillers and their valency positions in the nonfinite verb, the sublists X1 and X2 are concatenated, written as (X1 ∘ X2). With this notation, the desired list agreement may be formulated as $[(X1 \circ X2) = X'^{\sim}]$ (cf. +NFV in *LA D4*, defined in 18.5.11).

The second and final step of concluding a subordinate clause with a complex verb is adding the finite auxiliary.

18.5.10 +FV CONCLUDES SUBCLAUSE WITH FINITE AUXILIARY

```
1.              input:  als dem Kind die Frau den Apfel gegeben   +      hat
                            (s3&a   h    v'        adv)                (s3'  h'  v)
                             |      |    |          |                   |    |   |
          rule pattern +Main :   (NOM  AUX  v'   Y  HCA)           (NOM'  AUX'  v)


    ──────▶     output:  als dem Kind die Frau den Apfel gegeben hat
                                            (adv)
                                              |
                                          (Y  HCA)
```

The nominative segments have to agree.

The handling of interrogatives and adverbial subclauses is formalized as the LA Syntax *LA D4* for German.

18.5.11 LAG HANDLING INTERROGATIVE AND ADVERBIAL CLAUSES (*LA D4*)

LX = LX of *LA D3* plus subordinating conjunctions

[als (v′ adv) *], [nachdem (v′ adv) *], [obwohl (v′ adv) *]

variable definition = variable definition of *LA D3* plus HCA ∈ {v, vi, adv}

$ST_S =_{def}$ {[(X) {1 +ADJ, 2 +N, 3 +FV, 4 +MAIN, 5 ?+MAIN}] }

+N: (ADJ′ N′ X) (N) ⇒ (X)   {6 +FV, 7 +MAIN, 8 +NFV, 9 +IP}

+ADJ: (ADJ′ X) (ADJ) ⇒ (ADJ′ X)   {10 +ADJ, 11 +N}

?+MAIN: (NOM′ AUX′ v)(z NOM) ⇒ (Z AUX′ vi)

           (NOM′ AUX′ v)(Y OBQ) ⇒ (Y OBQ NOM′ AUX′ vi)

           (X NP′ Y v)(Z NP) ⇒ (Z X Y vi)

           (X v)(Y ADV) ⇒ (Y X vi)   {12 +ADJ, 13 +N, 14 +MAIN,

                                    15 +NFV, 16 +IP}

+FV: (NOM AUX v′ Y HCA) (NOM′ AUX′ v) ⇒ (Y HCA)

           (X v′ Y HCA)(X′~ v)

              [X = X′~] ⇒ (Y HCA)

           (NOM) (NOM′ AUX′ v) ⇒ (AUX′ v)

           (OBQ) (X AUX′ v) ⇒ (OBQ X AUX′ v)

           (X AUX) (NP′ AUX′ v) ⇒ (X NP′ v)

           (NP) (X NP′ Y v) ⇒ (X Y v)

           (ADV) (X v) ⇒ (X v)   {17 +MAIN, 18 +NFV, 19 +FV, 20 +IP}

+MAIN: (X NOM′ Y AUX′ VT) (Z NOM) ⇒ (Z X Y AUX′ VT)

           (X AUX′ VT) (Y OBQ) ⇒ (Y OBQ X AUX′ VT)

           (X NP′ Y VT) (Z NP)   ⇒ (Z X Y VT)

           (X VT′ y HCA) (Z NP) ⇒ (Z NP X VT′ Y HCA)

           (X VT) (Y ADV) ⇒ (Y X VT)   {21 +ADJ, 22 +N, 23 +MAIN,

                                    24 +NFV, 25 +FV, 26 +IP}

+NFV: (X1 Nom X2 VT′ Y HCA) (X′~ AUX)

              [(X1 ∘ X2) = X′~] ⇒ (NOM AUX *vt*′ y HCA)

           (X AUX′ VT) (x′~ AUX) ⇒ (VT)   {27 +FV, 28 +IP}

+IP: (VT) (VT′ SM) ⇒ (SM) {}

$ST_F =_{def}$ {[(*sm*) rp$_{+ip}$]}

LA D4 extends *LA D3* to yes/no-interrogatives and adverbial subclauses, each with simple and complex verb forms, whereby the adverbial subclauses may take various positions, including center embedding.

LA D4 has the following finite state transition network:

18.5.12 THE FINITE STATE BACKBONE OF *LA D4*

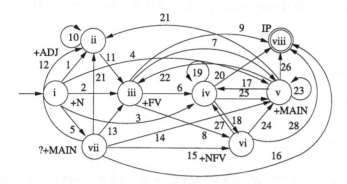

(ii)	1, 10, 12, 21	+ADJ	(vi)	8, 15, 18	+NFV
(iii)	2, 11, 13, 22	+N	(vii)	5	?+MAIN
(iv)	3, 6, 17, 19, 27	+FV	(viii)	9, 16, 20, 26	+IP
(v)	4, 7, 14, 23, 24, 25	+MAIN			

Extending *LA D3* to *LA D4* requires only one additional rule, **?+MAIN**, and one additional clause in **+NFV**. The extension consists primarily in adding transitions, implemented by writing additional rule names into rule packages. While *LA D3* has six rules and 19 transitions, *LA D4* has seven rules and 28 transitions. The handling of agreement and word order variation of *LA D3* is preserved in *LA D4*. Like its predecessors, *LA D4* is a C1 LAG and parses in linear time.

At this point the syntactic coverage of English and German could easily be extended further and further. For the methodological reasons explained in Sect. 18.1, however, the existing grammars should first be *verified* in the following areas:

1. *Syntactic verification*
   The formal grammars for English and German developed so far should be implemented as parsers and tested automatically on increasing sets of positive and negative test sentences.
2. *Morphological and lexical verification*
   The word form recognition of these grammars should be changed from the preliminary full-form lexica LX to suitable applications of LA Morph and be tested on corpus-based word lists in order to provide extensions with sufficient data coverage of the lexicon and the morphology.
3. *Functional verification in communication*
   The formal grammars and parsers for natural languages should be supplemented with an automatic semantic and pragmatic interpretation that is (i) in line with the basic assumptions of the SLIM theory of language and (ii) demonstrated to be functional in automatic applications.

Verification steps 1 and 2 have been provided by the extensive LA Grammars for English and German described in NEWCAT and CoL, from which *LA E1 – LA E3* and *LA D1* – *LA D4* were abstracted. The details of verification step 3, on the other hand, require a closer theoretical description, which will be the topic of Part IV.

Exercises

Section 18.1

1. Explain the three steps and two phases of developing an LA Grammar for the syntactic description of a new language.
2. What is the structure of complex noun phrases in German and how does it differ from English?
3. Describe the agreement of German adjectives.
4. Which rule in *LA D1* must be slightly generalized for the derivation of 18.1.4, and how?
5. Give derivations like those of 18.1.4 for the sentences der jungen Frau gefiel der schöne grüne Baum, die junge Frau gab dem kleinen Kind einen Apfel, dem kleinen Kind gab die junge Frau einen Apfel, and einen Apfel gab die junge Frau dem kleinen Kind. Explain why the time-linear derivation of complex nominal fillers in pre- and postverbal position can be handled by the same rules.

Section 18.2

1. Explain in what two respects traditional paradigms, e.g., of German noun phrases, are misleading from a syntactic point of view. Why are traditional paradigms not surface compositional?
2. Compare the abstract field of referents of German (18.2.2 and 18.2.4) and English (17.2.1). Explain their surface compositional motivation and relate them to traditional paradigms.
3. Because the genitive case is becoming obsolete in its function as a nominal filler/valency position, you may simplify 18.2.2 for the purposes of modern German. How many fields are there after eliminating the genitive?
4. Describe the agreement between nominal fillers and finite verbs in German.
5. Explain the handling of external and internal agreement of complex noun phrases in *LA D2*.
6. Provide a finite state backbone – analogous to 17.4.2 – for *LA D2* using the transition numbers given in 18.2.5.

Section 18.3

1. What is the difference between a post-nominative and a verb-second word order? Give examples from English and German.

2. Do adverbials play a role in the word order specification of English or German?
3. What is the difference between contact and distance positions in complex verb constructions? Give examples from English and German.
4. Explain why the sentential bracket (*Satzklammer*) in German is in systematic conflict with the principles of constituent structure 8.4.3.
5. Is it possible to motivate distance position in terms of communicative function?
6. Compare the word order of subordinate clauses in English and German.
7. Why does the word order of auxiliary constructions in declarative main clauses and in subordinate clauses of German pose an apparent problem for the time-linear filling of valency positions?

Section 18.4

1. Describe the categorial structure of complex verb forms in German.
2. Explain the five categorial alternatives which arise from adding a finite auxiliary in declarative main clauses of German and describe how they are formalized in the rule +FV.
3. Explain the four categorial alternatives which arise from continuing after a finite auxiliary in declarative main clauses of German and describe how they are formalized in the **+MAIN**.
4. Describe the role of list agreement in the rule **+NFV**.
5. Why does the variable definition of *LA D3* specify the variables NOM and NOM′ in addition to NP and NP′?
6. Provide a finite state backbone – analogous to 17.5.5 – for *LA D3* using the transition numbers given in 18.4.8.

Section 18.5

1. Explain why German yes/no-interrogatives with auxiliaries are the maximal form of a *sentential bracket*.
2. Why is there a new rule **?+MAIN** for the beginning of yes/no-interrogatives rather than handling its function by existing **+MAIN**?
3. Compare the categorial operations of **?+MAIN** and **+MAIN** in 18.5.11.
4. Why is *LA D4* a C1 LAG?
5. Determine the grammatical perplexity of *LA D4*. Does the use of rule clauses and subclauses affect the perplexity value?
6. Extend *LA D4* to a handling of prepositional phrases in postnominal position as in der Apfel + auf dem Tisch, and in adverbial position as in Auf dem Tisch + lag. Take into account the semantic analysis of prepositional phrases presented in Section 12.5. Adapt the finite state backbone 18.5.12 to your extension.

Part IV

Semantics and Pragmatics

19. Three Kinds of Semantics

Part I presented the basic mechanism of natural communication using the example of a talking robot. Part II explained the complexity-theoretic aspects of syntactic analysis. Part III developed detailed morphological and syntactic analyses of natural language surfaces. Based on these foundations, we turn in Part IV to the semantic and pragmatic interpretation of syntactically analyzed expressions in natural language interpretation and production.

First, traditional approaches to semantic interpretation will be described in Chaps. 19–21, explaining basic notions, goals, methods, and problems. Then a semantic and pragmatic interpretation of LA Grammar within the SLIM theory of language will be developed in Chaps. 22–24. The formal interpretation is implemented computationally as a content-addressable database system called a word bank.

Section 19.1 explains the structure common to all systems of semantic interpretation. Section 19.2 compares three different kinds of formal semantics, namely the semantics of the logical languages, the programming languages, and the natural languages. Section 19.3 illustrates the functioning of logical semantics with a simple model-theoretic system and explains the underlying theory of Tarski. Section 19.4 shows why the procedural semantics of the programming languages is independent of Tarski's hierarchy of metalanguages and details the special conditions a logical calculus must fulfill in order to be suitable for an implementation as a computer program. Section 19.5 explains why a complete interpretation of natural language within logical semantics is impossible and describes Tarski's argument to this effect, based on the Epimenides paradox.

19.1 Basic Structure of Semantic Interpretation

The term semantics is used in various fields of science. In *linguistics*, semantics is a component of grammar which derives representations of meaning from syntactically analyzed natural surfaces. In *philosophy*, semantics assigns set-theoretic denotations to logical formulas in order to characterize truth and to serve as the basis for certain methods of proof. In *computer science*, semantics consists in executing commands of a programming language automatically as machine operations.

R. Hausser, *Foundations of Computational Linguistics*,
DOI 10.1007/978-3-642-41431-2_19, © Springer-Verlag Berlin Heidelberg 2014

Even though the semantics in these different fields of science differ substantially in their goals, their methods, their applications, and their form, they all share the same basic two level structure consisting of syntactically analyzed language expressions and associated semantic structures. The two levels are systematically related by means of an assignment algorithm.

19.1.1 THE TWO LEVEL STRUCTURE OF SEMANTIC INTERPRETATION

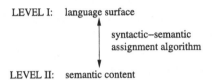

LEVEL I: language surface

                    syntactic–semantic
                    assignment algorithm

LEVEL II: semantic content

For purposes of transmission and storage, semantic content is coded into surfaces of language (representation). When the content is needed, any speaker of the language may reconstruct it by analyzing the surface.[1] The reconstruction consists in (i) syntactic analysis, (ii) retrieval of word meanings from the lexicon, and (iii) deriving the meaning of the whole by assembling the meanings of the parts as specified by the syntactic structure of the surface.

The expressive power of semantically interpreted languages resides in the fact that the inverse procedures of representing and reconstructing content are realized *automatically*: a semantically interpreted language may be used correctly without the user having to be conscious of these procedures, or even having to know or understand their details.

For example, the programming languages summarize frequently used sequences of elementary operations as higher functions, the names of which the programmer may then combine into complex programs. These work in the manner intended even though the user is not aware of – and does not care about – the complex details of the machine or assembler code operations.

A logical language may likewise be used without the user having to go through the full details of the semantic interpretation. One purpose of a logical syntax is to represent the structural possibilities and restrictions of the semantics in such a way that the user can reason truly[2] on the semantic level based solely on the syntactic categories and their combinatorics.

---

[1] For example, it is much easier to handle the surfaces of an expression like $36 \cdot 124$ than to execute the corresponding operation of multiplication semantically by using an abacus. Without the language surfaces one would have to slide the counters on the abacus 36 times 124 'semantically' each time this content is to be communicated. This would be tedious, and even if the persons communicating were to fully concentrate on the procedure it would be extremely susceptible to error.

[2] In the sense of always going from true premises to true conclusions.

The natural languages are also used by the speaker-hearer without conscious knowledge of the structures and procedures at the level of semantics. In contradistinction to the artificial languages of programming and logic, for which the full details of their semantics are known at least to their designers and other specialists, the exact details of natural language semantics are not known directly even to science.

19.2 Logical, Programming, and Natural Languages

The two level structure common to all genuine systems of semantics allows one to control the structures on the semantic level by means of syntactically analyzed surfaces. In theory, different semantic interpretations may be defined for one and the same language, using different assignment algorithms. In practice, however, each kind of semantics has its own characteristic syntax in order to achieve optimal control of the semantic level via the combination of language surfaces.

The following three kinds of semantics comply with the basic structure of semantic interpretation shown in 19.1.1:

19.2.1 THREE DIFFERENT KINDS OF SEMANTIC SYSTEMS

1. *Logical languages*
   These originated in philosophy.[3] Their complete expressions are called *propositions*. The logical languages are designed to determine the truth value of arbitrary propositions relative to arbitrary models. They have a *metalanguage-based semantics* because the correlation between the two levels is based on a metalanguage definition.

2. *Programming languages*
   These are motivated by a practical need to simplify the interaction with computers and the design of software. Their expressions are called *commands*, which may be combined into complex programs. They have a *procedural semantics* because the correlation between the levels of syntax and semantics is based on the principle of execution, i.e., the operational realization of commands on an abstract machine which is usually implemented electronically.

3. *Natural languages*
   These evolve naturally in their speech communities and are the most powerful and least understood of all semantically interpreted systems. Their expressions are called *surfaces*. Linguists analyze the preexisting natural languages syntactically by reconstructing the combinatorics of their surfaces explicitly as formal grammars. The associated semantic representations have to be deduced via the general principles of natural communication because the meanings₁

---

[3] An early highlight is the writing of Aristotle, in which logical variables are used for the first time.

(4.3.3), unlike the surfaces, have no concrete manifestation. Natural languages have a *convention-based* semantics because the word surfaces (types) have their meaning₁ assigned by means of conventions (de Saussure's first law, 6.2.2).

On the one hand, the semantic interpretations of the three kinds of languages all share the same two level structure. On the other hand, their respective components differ in all possible respects: they use (i) different language expressions, (ii) different assignment algorithms, and (iii) different objects on the semantic level:

19.2.2 THREE KINDS OF SEMANTIC INTERPRETATION

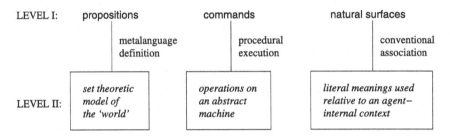

The most important difference between the semantic interpretation of artificial and natural languages consists in that the interpretation of artificial languages is limited to the two level structure of their semantics, whereas the interpretation of natural languages is based on the [2+1] level structure (4.2.2) of the SLIM theory of language.

Thus, in logical and programming languages the interpretation is completed on the semantic level. The natural languages, in contrast, have an additional interpretation step which is as important as the semantic interpretation. This second step is the pragmatic interpretation in communication. It consists in matching the structures of the semantic level with corresponding structures of an appropriate context of use.

In the abstract, six relations may be established between the three basic kinds of semantics:

19.2.3 MAPPING RELATIONS BETWEEN THE THREE KINDS OF SEMANTICS

We represent these relations as N→L, N→P, L→N, L→P, P→N, and P→L, where N stands for the natural languages, L for the logical languages, and P for the programming languages.

In reality, there has evolved a complicated diversity of historical, methodological, and functional interactions between the three systems. These relations may be characterized in terms of the notions *replication, reconstruction, transfer*, and *composition*:

(a) *Replication*

The logical languages evolved originally as formal replications of selected natural language phenomena (N→L). Programming languages like Lisp and Prolog were designed to replicate selected aspects of the logical languages procedurally (L→P). The programming languages replicate phenomena of natural language also directly, such as the concept of 'command' (N→P).

(b) *Reconstruction*

When an artificial language has been established for some time and has achieved an independent existence of its own, it may be used to reconstruct the language it was originally designed to replicate in part. A case in point is the attempt in theoretical linguistics to reconstruct formal fragments of natural language in terms of logic (L→N). Similarly, computational linguistics aims at reconstructing natural languages by means of programming languages (P→N). One may also imagine a reconstruction of programming concepts in a new logical language (P→L).

(c) *Transfer*

The concentrated efforts to transfer methods and results of logical proof theory to programming languages (L→P)[4] have led to important results. A simple, general transfer is not possible, however, because these two kinds of language use different methods, structures, and ontologies for different purposes.[5] Attempts in philosophy of language to transfer the model-theoretic method to the semantic analysis of natural language (L→N) have been only partially successful as well.[6]

(d) *Combination*

Computational linguistics aims at modeling natural communication with the help of programming languages (P→N), whereby methods and results of the logical languages play a role in both the construction of programming languages (L→P) and the analysis of natural language (L→N). This requires a functional overall framework for combining the three kinds of language in a way that utilizes their different properties while avoiding redundancy as well as conflict.

The functioning of the three kinds of semantics will be explained below in more detail.

19.3 Functioning of Logical Semantics

In logical semantics, a simple sentence like Julia sleeps is analyzed as a proposition which is either true or false. Which of these two values is denoted by the proposition depends on the state of the world relative to which the proposition is interpreted.

---

[4] Scott and Strachey (1971).

[5] The transfer of logical proof theory to an automatic theorem prover necessitates that each step – especially those considered 'obvious' – be realized in terms of explicit computer operations (Weyhrauch 1980). This requirement has already modified modern approaches to proof theory profoundly (P→L reconstruction).

[6] Sect. 19.4.

The state of the world, called the model, is defined in terms of sets and set-theoretic operations.

19.3.1 INTERPRETATION OF A PROPOSITION

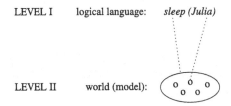

LEVEL I   logical language: *sleep (Julia)*

LEVEL II   world (model):

By analyzing the surface Julia sleeps formally as *sleep (Julia)* the verb is characterized syntactically as a functor and the name as its argument.

The lexical part of the associated semantic interpretation (word semantics) assigns denotations to the words – here the set of all sleepers to the verb and the individual Julia to the proper name. The compositional part of the semantics derives denotations for complex expressions from the denotations of their parts (4.4.1). In particular, the formal proposition *sleep (Julia)* is assigned the value true (or 1) relative to the model if the individual denoted by the name is an element of the set denoted by the verb. Otherwise, the proposition denotes the value false (or 0).

A logical language requires definition of (1) a lexicon in which the basic expressions are listed and categorized, and (2) a syntax which provides the rules for combining the basic expressions into well-formed complex expressions. Its semantic interpretation requires in addition definition of (3) a model, (4) the possible denotations of syntactic expressions in the model, and (5) a semantic rule for each syntactic rule.

These five components of model theory are illustrated by the following definition, which in addition to the usual propositional calculus also handles example 19.3.1 in a simple manner.[7]

19.3.2 DEFINITION OF A MINIMAL LOGIC

1. **Lexicon**
   Set of one-place predicates: {sleep, sing}
   Set of names: {Julia, Susanne}
2. **Model**
   A model $\mathcal{M}$ is a tuple (A, F), where A is a non-empty set of entities and F a denotation function (see 3).
3. **Possible Denotations**
   (a) If P_1 is a one-place predicate, then a possible denotation of P_1 relative to a model $\mathcal{M}$ is a subset of A. Formally, $F(P_1)\mathcal{M} \subseteq A$.

---

[7] For simplicity, we do not use here a recursive definition of syntactic categories with systematically associated semantic types à la Montague (CoL, pp. 344–349).

(b) If α is a name, then the possible denotations of α relative to a model $\mathcal{M}$ are elements of A. Formally, $F(\alpha).\mathcal{M} \in A$.

(c) If ϕ is a sentence, then the possible denotations of ϕ relative to a model $\mathcal{M}$ are the numbers 0 and 1, interpreted as the truth values 'true' and 'false.' Formally, $F(\phi).\mathcal{M} \in \{0, 1\}$.

Relative to a model $\mathcal{M}$ a sentence ϕ is a true sentence if and only if the denotation ϕ in $\mathcal{M}$ is the value 1.

4. **Syntax**

(a) If P_1 is a one-place predicate and α is a name, then $P_1(\alpha)$ is a sentence.

(b) If ϕ is a sentence, then $\neg\phi$ is a sentence.

(c) If ϕ is a sentence and ψ is a sentence, then $\phi \ \& \ \psi$ is a sentence.

(d) If ϕ is a sentence and ψ is a sentence, then $\phi \vee \psi$ is a sentence.

(e) If ϕ is a sentence and ψ is a sentence, the $\phi \rightarrow \psi$ is a sentence.

(f) If ϕ is a sentence and ψ is a sentence, then $\phi = \psi$ is a sentence.

5. **Semantics**

(a) '$P_1(\alpha)$' is a true sentence relative to a model $\mathcal{M}$ if and only if the denotation of α in $\mathcal{M}$ is an element of the denotation of P_1 in $\mathcal{M}$.

(b) '$\neg\phi$' is a true sentence relative to a model $\mathcal{M}$ if and only if the denotation of ϕ is 0 relative to $\mathcal{M}$.

(c) '$\phi \ \& \ \psi$' is a true sentence relative to a model $\mathcal{M}$ if and only if the denotations of ϕ and of ψ are 1 relative to $\mathcal{M}$.

(d) '$\phi \vee \psi$' is a true sentence relative to a model $\mathcal{M}$ if and only if the denotation of ϕ or ψ is 1 relative to $\mathcal{M}$.

(e) '$\phi \rightarrow \psi$' is a true sentence relative to a model $\mathcal{M}$ if and only if the denotation of ϕ is 0 relative to $\mathcal{M}$ or the denotation of ψ is 1 relative to $\mathcal{M}$.

(f) '$\phi = \psi$' is a true sentence relative to a model $\mathcal{M}$ if and only if the denotation of ϕ relative to $\mathcal{M}$ equals the denotation of ψ relative to $\mathcal{M}$.

The rules of syntax (4) define the complex expressions of the logical language; those of the semantics (5) specify the circumstances under which these complex expressions are true.

The simple logic system establishes a semantic relation between the formal language and the world by defining the two levels as well as the relation between them in terms of a *metalanguage*. The theory behind this method was presented by the Polish-American logician Alfred TARSKI (1902–1983) in a form still valid today.

In the formal definition of an interpreted language, Tarski (1935) distinguishes between the object language and the metalanguage. The object language is the language to be semantically interpreted (e.g., quoted expressions like '$\phi \ \& \ \psi$' in 19.3.2, 5), while the definitions of the semantic interpretation are formulated in the metalanguage. It is assumed that the metalanguage is known by author and reader at least as well or even better than their mother tongue because there should be no room at all for differing interpretations.

The metalanguage definitions serve to formally interpret the object language. In logical semantics the task of the interpretation is to specify under what circumstances the expressions of the object language are true. Tarski's basic metalanguage schema for characterizing truth is the so-called T-condition. According to Tarski, the T stands mnemonically for *truth*, but it could also be taken for *translation* or *Tarski*.

19.3.3 SCHEMA OF TARSKI'S T-CONDITION

T: x is a true sentence if and only if p.

The T-condition as a whole is a sentence of the metalanguage, which quotes the sentence x of the object language and *translates* it as p. Tarski illustrates this method with the following example:

19.3.4 INSTANTIATION OF TARSKI'S T-CONDITION

'Es schneit' is a true sentence if and only if it is snowing.

This example is deceptively simple, and has resulted in misunderstandings by many non-experts.[8] What the provocative simplicity of 19.3.3 and 19.3.4 does not express when viewed in isolation is the exact nature of the *two level structure* (19.1.1), which underlies all forms of semantic interpretation and therefore is also exemplified by the particular method proposed by Tarski.

A closer study of Tarski's text shows that the purpose of the T-condition is not a redundant repetition of the object language expression in the metalanguage translation. Rather, the T-condition has a twofold function. One is to construct a systematic connection between the object language and the world by means of the metalanguage: thus, the metalanguage serves as the means for realizing the *assignment* (19.1.1) in logical semantics. The other is to characterize truth: the truth value of x in the object language is to be determined via the interpretation of p in the metalanguage.

Both functions require that the metalanguage can refer directly (i) to the object language and (ii) to the correlated state of affairs in the world (model). The connection between the two levels of the object language and the world established by the metalanguage may be shown schematically as follows:

19.3.5 RELATION BETWEEN OBJECT AND METALANGUAGE

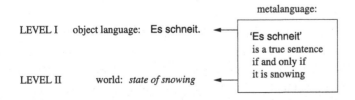

---

[8] Tarski (1944) complains about these misunderstandings and devotes the second half of his paper to a detailed critique of his critics.

The direct relation of the metalanguage to the world requires the possibility of *verification*, i.e., the ability to actually determine whether p holds or not. For example, in order to determine whether Es schneit is true or not, it must be possible to determine whether or not it is actually snowing. Without the possibility of verifying p, the T-condition is (i) vacuous for the purpose of characterizing truth and (ii) dysfunctional for the purpose of assigning semantic objects.

That Tarski calls the p in the T-condition the 'translation' of the x is misleading because translation in the normal sense of the word is not concerned with truth at all. Instead a translation is adequate, if the speaker meaning₂ of the source and the target language expressions happen to be *equivalent*. For example, translating Die Katze ist auf der Matte as The cat is on the mat is adequate simply because the German source and the English target expression mean the same thing. There is obviously neither the need nor even the possibility of verification outside a theory of truth.

Tarski, however, took it to be just as obvious that within a theory of truth the possibility of verification must hold. In contradistinction to 19.3.4, Tarski's scientific examples of semantically interpreted languages do not use some natural language as the metalanguage – because it does not ensure verification with sufficient certainty. Rather, Tarski insisted on carefully *constructing* special metalanguages for certain well-defined scientific domains for which the possibility of verification is guaranteed.

According to Tarski, the construction of the metalanguage requires that (i) all its basic expressions are explicitly listed and that (ii) each expression of the metalanguage "has a clear meaning" (op.cit., p. 172). This conscientious formal approach to the metalanguage is exemplified in Tarski's (1935) analysis of the calculus of classes, which illustrates his method in formal detail. The only expressions used by Tarski in this example are notions like not, and, is contained in, is an element of, individual, class, and relation. The meaning of these expressions is immediately obvious insofar as they refer to the most basic mathematical objects and set-theoretic operations. In other words, Tarski limits the construction of his metalanguage to the elementary notions of a fully developed (meta-)theory, e.g., a certain area in the foundations of mathematics.

The same holds for the semantic rules in our example 19.3.2, for which reason it constitutes a well-defined Tarskian semantics. The semantic definition of the first rule[9] as a T-condition like 19.3.5 may shown as follows:

---

[9] Compared to 19.3.5, 19.3.6 is more precise because the interpretation is explicitly restricted to a specific state of affairs, specified formally by the model $\mathcal{M}$. In a world where it is snowing only at certain times and certain places, on the other hand, 19.3.5 will work only if the interpretation of the sentence is restricted – at least implicitly – to an intended location and moment of time.

19.3.6 T-Condition in a Logical Definition

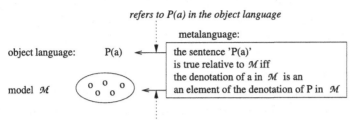

The possibility of verifying the T-condition 19.3.6 is guaranteed by no more and no less than the fact that for any given model $\mathcal{M}$ anyone who speaks English and has some elementary notion of set theory can *see* (in the mathematical sense of "unmittel-bare Anschauung" or "immediate obviousness") whether the relation specified in the translation part of T holds in $\mathcal{M}$ or not.

In the history of mathematics, the appeal to immediate obviousness has always served as the ultimate justification, as formulated by Blaise PASCAL (1623–1662):

> En l'un les principes sont palpables mais éloignés de l'usage commun de sorte qu'on a peine à tourner la tête de ce côté-la, manque d'habitude: mais pour peu qu'on l'y tourne, on voit les principes à peine; et il faudrait avoir tout à fait l'esprit faux pour mal raisonner sur des principes si gros qu'il est presque impossible qu'ils échappent.
>
> [In [the mathematical mind] the principles are obvious, but remote from ordinary use, such that one has difficulty to turn to them for lack of habit: but as soon as one turns to them, one can see the principles in full; and it would take a thoroughly unsound mind to reason falsely on the basis of principles which are so obvious that they can hardly be missed.]

Pascal, Pensées (1951:340)

In summary, Tarski's theory of truth and logical semantics is clearly limited to the domains of mathematics, logic, and natural science insofar as only there are sufficiently certain methods of verification available.

19.4 Metalanguage-Based or Procedural Semantics?

In contrast to the semantic definitions in 19.3.2, which use only immediately obvious logical notions and are therefore legitimate in the sense of Tarski's method, the following instantiation of the T-conditions violates the precondition of verifiability:

19.4.1 Example of a Vacuous T-Condition

'A is red' is a true sentence if and only if A is red.

The example is formally correct but vacuous because it does not relate the meaning of red in the object language to some verifiable concept of the metalanguage.

Instead the expression of the object language is merely repeated in the metalanguage.[10]

Within the boundaries of its set-theoretic foundations, model-theoretic semantics has no way of providing a truth-conditional analysis for a content word like red such that its meaning would be characterized adequately in contradistinction to, for example, blue. There exists, however, the possibility of *extending the metatheory* by calling in additional sciences such as physics.

From such an additional science one may select a small set of new basic notions to serve in the extended metalanguage. The result functions properly if the meaning of the additional expressions is verifiable within the extended metatheory.

In this way we might improve the T-condition 19.4.1 as follows:

19.4.2 IMPROVED T-CONDITION FOR red

'A is red' is a true sentence if and only if A refracts light in the electromagnetic frequency interval between 430–480 THz.

Here the metalanguage translation relates the object language expression red to more elementary notions (i.e., the numbers 430 and 480 within an empirically established frequency scale and the notion of refracting light, which is well understood in the domain of physics) and thus succeeds in characterizing the expression in a nonvacuous way which is moreover objectively verifiable.

Example 19.4.1 shows that the object language may contain expressions for which there are only vacuous translations in the metalanguage. This does not mean that a sentence like 'x is red' is not meaningful or has no truth value. It only means that the metalanguage is not rich enough to provide a verification of the sentence. This raises the question of how to handle the semantics of the metalanguage, especially regarding the parts which go beyond the elementary notions of its metatheory.

Tarski's answer is the construction of an infinite hierarchy of metalanguages:

19.4.3 HIERARCHY OF METALANGUAGES

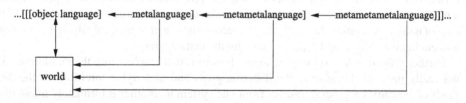

---

[10] Tarski's own example 19.3.4 is only slightly less vacuous. This is because the metalanguage translation in Tarski's example is in a natural language *different* from the object language. The metalanguage translation into another natural language is misleading, however, because it omits the aspect of verification, which is central to a theory of truth. The frequent misunderstandings which Tarski (1944) so eloquently bewails may well have been caused in large part by the 'intuitive' choice of his examples.

Here, some vacuous T-conditions of the metalanguage, e.g., 19.4.1, are repaired by nonvacuous T-conditions, e.g., 19.4.2, in the metametalanguage. Some holes in the metametalanguage are filled in turn by means of additional basic concepts in the metametametalanguage, and so on. That an infinite hierarchy of metalanguages makes total access to truth ultimately impossible, at least for mankind, is not regarded as a flaw of Tarski's construction – on the contrary, it constitutes a major part of its philosophical charm.

For the semantics of programming and natural languages, however, a hierarchy of metalanguages is not a suitable foundation.[11] Consider for example the rules of basic addition, multiplication, etc. The problem is not to provide an adequate metalanguage definition for these rules, similar to 19.3.2. Rather, the road from such a metalanguage definition to a working calculator is quite long and in the end the calculator will function mechanically – without any reference to the metalanguage definitions and without any need to understand the metalanguage.[12]

This simple fact has been called *autonomy from the metalanguage*.[13] It is characteristic of all programming languages. Autonomy from the metalanguage does not mean that computers would be limited to uninterpreted, purely syntactic deduction systems, but rather that Tarski's method is not the only one possible. Instead of the Tarskian method of assigning semantic representations to an object language by means of a metalanguage, computers use an operational method in which the notions of the programming language are executed automatically as electronically realized operations.

Because the semantics of programming languages is procedural (i.e., metalanguage-independent), while the semantics of logical calculi is Tarskian (i.e., metalanguage-dependent), the reconstruction of logical calculi as computer programs is at best difficult.[14] If it works at all, it usually requires profound compromises on the side of the

---

[11] The discussion of Tarski's semantics in CoL, pp. 289–295, 305–310, and 319–323, was aimed at bringing out as many similarities between the semantics of logical, programming, and natural languages as possible. For example, all three kinds of semantic interpretation were analyzed from the viewpoint of truth: whereas logical semantics *checks* whether a formula is true relative to a model or not, the procedural semantics of a programming language *constructs* machine states which 'make the formula true', – and similarly in the case of natural semantics. Accordingly, the reconstruction of logical calculi on the computer was euphemistically called 'operationalizing the metalanguage'.

Further reflection led to the conclusion, however, that emphasizing the similarities was not really justified: because of the differing goals and underlying intuitions of the three kinds of semantics a general transfer from one system to another is ultimately impossible. For this reason the current analysis first presents what all semantically interpreted systems have in common, namely the basic two level structure, and then concentrates on bringing out the formal and conceptual differences between the three systems.

[12] See in this connection also 3.4.5.

[13] CoL, pp. 307f.

[14] With the notable exception of propositional calculus. See also *transfer* in 19.2.3.

calculus – as illustrated, for example, by the computational realization of predicate calculus in the form of Prolog.

Accordingly, there are many logical calculi in existence which have not been and never will be realized as computer programs. The reason is that their metalanguage translations contain parts which may be considered immediately obvious by their designers (e.g., quantification over infinite sets of possible worlds in modal logic), but which are nevertheless unsuitable to be realized as empirically meaningful mechanical procedures.

Thus, the preconditions for modeling a logical calculus as a computer program are no different from nonlogical theories such as physics or chemistry: the basic notions and operations of the theory must be sufficiently clear and simple to be realized as electronic procedures which are empirically meaningful and can be computed in a matter of minutes or days rather than centuries (8.2.2).

19.5 Tarski's Problem for Natural Language Semantics

Because the practical use of programming languages requires an automatic interpretation in the form of corresponding electronic procedures they cannot be based on a metalanguage-dependent Tarski semantics. But what about using a Tarski semantics for the interpretation of natural languages?

Tarski himself leaves no doubt that a complete analysis of natural language is in principle impossible within logical semantics.

> The attempt to set up a structural definition of the term 'true sentence' – applicable to colloquial language – is confronted with insuperable difficulties.
>
> Tarski (1935), p. 164

Tarski proves this conclusion on the basis of a classical paradox, called the Epimenides, Eubulides, or liar paradox.

The paradox is based on self-reference. Its original 'weak' version has the following form: if a Cretan says All Cretans (always) lie there are two possibilities. Either the Cretan speaks truly, in which case it is false that *all* Cretans lie – since he is a Cretan himself. Or the Cretan lies, which means that there exists at least one Cretan who does not lie. In both cases the sentence in question is false.[15]

Tarski uses the paradox in the 'strong' version designed by Leśniewski and constructs from it the following proof that a complete analysis of natural language within logical semantics is necessarily impossible:

> For the sake of greater perspicuity we shall use the symbol 'c' as a typological abbreviation of the expression 'the sentence printed on page 391, line 2 from the bottom.' Consider now the following sentence:
>
> c is not a true sentence
>
> Having regard to the meaning of the symbol 'c', we can establish empirically:

---

[15] For a detailed analysis of the weak version(s) see Thiel (1995), pp. 325–327.

(a) 'c is not a true sentence' is identical with c.
For the quotation-mark name of the sentence c we set up an explanation of type (2) [i.e., the T-condition 19.3.3]:
(b) 'c is not a true sentence' is a true sentence if and only if c is not a true sentence.
The premise (a) and (b) together at once give a contradiction:
c is a true sentence if and only if c is not a true sentence.

Tarski (1935)

In this construction, self-reference is based on two preconditions. First, a sentence located in a certain line on a certain page, i.e., line 2 from the bottom on page 391 in the current Chap. 19, is abbreviated as 'c'.[16]

Second, the letter 'c' with which the sentence in line 2 from the bottom on page 391 is abbreviated also occurs in the unabridged version of the sentence in question. This permits one to substitute the c in the sentence by the expression which the 'other' c abbreviates. The substitution may be described schematically as follows:

19.5.1 Leśniewski's Reconstruction of the Epimenides Paradox

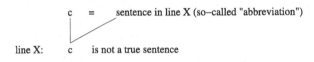

substitution of the c–abbreviation: sentence in line X is not a true sentence

If sentence c in line X is true, then what sentence c says, namely that 'c is not a true sentence', holds. Thus, 'c is not a true sentence' (as the original statement) and 'c is a true sentence' (as obtained via substitution and its interpretation) both hold.

To prove that a logical semantics for natural language is impossible, Tarski combines Leśniewski's version of the Epimenides paradox with his T-condition. In this way he turns an isolated paradox into a contradiction of logical semantics.

19.5.2 Inconsistent T-Condition Using Epimenides Paradox

There are three options to avoid this contradiction in logical semantics.

The first consists in forbidding the abbreviation and the substitution based on it. This possibility is rejected by Tarski because "no rational ground can be given why substitution should be forbidden in general."

---

[16] The page and line numbers have been adjusted here from Tarski's original text to fit those of this chapter. This adjustment is crucial in order for self-reference to work.

The second possibility consists in distinguishing between the predicates 'true^o' of the object language and 'true^m' of the metalanguage.[17] Accordingly, the formulation

c is true^m if and only if c is not true^o

is not contradictory because true$^m \neq$ true^o. Tarski does not consider this possibility, presumably because the use of more than one truth predicate runs counter to the most fundamental goal of logical semantics, namely a formal characterization of *the* truth.

The third possibility, chosen by Tarski, is to forbid the use of truth predicates in the object language. For the original goals of logical semantics the third option poses no problem. Characterizing scientific theories like physics as true relations between logical propositions and states of affairs does not require a truth predicate in the object language. The same holds for formal theories like mathematics.

Furthermore, for many mathematical logicians the development of semantically interpreted logical calculi was motivated by the desire to avoid what they called the vagueness and contradictions of natural language. For example, Frege (1892) expresses this sentiment as follows:

> Der Grund, weshalb die Wortsprachen zu diesem Zweck [d.h. Schlüsse nur nach rein logischen Gesetzen zu ziehen] wenig geeignet sind, liegt nicht nur an der vorkommenden Vieldeutigkeit der Ausdrücke, sondern vor allem in dem Mangel fester Formen für das Schließen. Wörter wie >also<, >folglich<, >weil< deuten zwar darauf hin, daßgeschlossen wird, sagen aber nichts über das Gesetz, nach dem geschlossen wird, und können ohne Sprachfehler auch gebraucht werden, wo gar kein logisch gerechtfertigter Schlußvorliegt.

> [The reason why the 'word-languages' are little suited for this purpose [i.e., draw inferences based on purely logical laws] is not only the existing ambiguity of the expressions, but above all the lack of clear forms of inference. Even though words like 'therefore,' 'consequently,' 'because' indicate inferencing, they do not specify the rule on which the inference is based, and they may be used without violating the well-formedness of the language even if there is no logically justified inference.]

This long-standing, widely held view provides additional support to refraining from any attempt to apply a Tarskian semantics to natural language.

If logical semantics is nevertheless applied to natural language, however, the third option does pose a serious problem. This is because the natural languages *must*[18] contain the words true and false. Therefore a logical semantic interpretation of a natural (object) language in its entirety will unavoidably result in a contradiction.

Tarski's student Richard Montague (1930–1970), however, was undaunted by Tarski's proof and insisted on applying logical semantics to natural language:

---

[17] The second option will be explored in Chap. 21, especially Sect. 21.2, for the semantics of natural language.

[18] This follows from the role of natural languages as the pretheoretical metalanguage of the logical languages. Without the words true and false in the natural languages a logical semantics couldn't be defined in the first place.

> I reject the contention that an important theoretical difference exists between formal and natural languages. ... Like Donald Davidson I regard the construction of a theory of truth – or rather the more general notion of truth under an arbitrary interpretation – as the basic goal of serious syntax and semantics.
>
> Montague (1970), *"English as a formal language"*[19]

We must assume that Montague knew the Epimenides paradox and Tarski's related work. But in his papers on the semantics of natural languages Montague does not mention this topic at all. Only Davidson, whom Montague appeals to in the above quotation, is explicit:

> Tarski's ... point is that we should have to reform natural language out of all recognition before we could apply formal semantic methods. If this is true, it is fatal to my project.
>
> Davidson (1967)

A logical paradox is fatal because it destroys a semantic system. Depending on which part of the contradiction an induction starts with, one can always prove both a theorem and its negation. This is not acceptable for a theory of truth.[20]

Without paying much attention to Tarski's argument, Montague, Davidson, and many others insist on using logical semantics for the analysis of natural language. This is motivated by the following parochial prejudices and misunderstandings:

For one, the advocates of logical semantics for natural language have long been convinced that their method is the best-founded form of semantic interpretation. Because they see no convincing alternatives to their metalanguage-dependent method – despite calculators and computers – they apply logical semantics in order to arrive at least at a partial analysis of natural language meaning.

A second reason is the fact that the development of logic began with the description of selected natural language examples. After a long independent evolution of logical systems it is intriguing to apply them once more to natural languages,[21] in order to show which aspects of natural language semantics can be easily modeled within logic.

---

[19] Montague (1974), p. 188.

[20] As a compromise, Davidson suggested limiting the logical semantic analysis of natural language to suitable consistent fragments of natural language. This means, however, that the project of a complete logical semantic analysis of natural languages is doomed to fail.

Attempts to avoid the Epimenides paradox in logical semantics are Kripke (1975), Gupta (1982), and Herzberger (1982). These systems each define an artificial object language (first-order predicate calculus) with truth predicates. That this object language is nevertheless consistent is based on defining the truth predicates as *recursive valuation schemata*.

Recursive valuation schemata are based on a large number of valuations (transfinitely many in the case of Kripke 1975). As a purely technical trick, they miss the point of the Epimenides paradox, which is essentially a problem of reference: a symbol may refer on the basis of its meaning and at the same time serve as a referent on the basis of its form.

[21] As an L→N reconstruction (19.2.3).

A third reason is that natural languages are often viewed as defective because they can be misunderstood and – in contrast to the logical calculi – implicitly contradictory. Therefore, the logical analysis of natural language has long been motivated by the goal of systematically exposing erroneous conclusions in rhetorical arguments in order to arrive at truth. What is usually overlooked, however, is that the interpretation of natural languages works quite differently (19.2.2) from the interpretation of metalanguage-dependent logical languages.

Exercises

Section 19.1

1. What areas of science deal with semantic interpretation?
2. Explain the basic structure common to all systems of semantic interpretation.
3. Name two practical reasons for building semantic structures indirectly via the interpretation of syntactically analyzed surfaces.
4. Explain the inverse procedures of representation and reconstruction.
5. How many kinds of semantic interpretation can be assigned to a given language?
6. Explain in what sense axiomatic systems of deduction are not true systems of semantic interpretation.

Section 19.2

1. Describe three different kinds of formal semantics.
2. What is the function of syntactically analyzed surfaces in the programming languages?
3. What principle is the semantics of the programming languages based on and how does it differ from that of the logical languages?
4. What is the basic difference between the semantics of the natural languages, on the one hand, and the semantics of the logical and the programming languages, on the other?
5. Why is a syntactical analysis presupposed by a formal semantic analysis?
6. Discuss six possible relations between different kinds of semantics.
7. What kinds of difficulties arise in the replication of logical proof theory in the form of computer programs for automatic theorem proving?

Section 19.3
1. Name the components of a model theoretically interpreted logic and explain their functions.
2. What are the goals of logical semantics?
3. What is Tarski's T-condition and what is its purpose for semantic interpretation?
4. Why is verification a central part of Tarski's theory of truth?
5. What is the role of translation in Tarski's T-condition?
6. Why does Tarski *construct* the metalanguage in his example of the calculus of classes? What notions does he use in this construction?
7. What does immediate obviousness do for verification in mathematical logic?

Section 19.4
1. Explain a vacuous T-condition with an example.
2. What is the potential role of non-mathematical sciences in Tarski's theory of truth?
3. For what purpose does Tarski construct an infinite hierarchy of metalanguages?
4. Why is the method of metalanguages unsuitable for the semantic interpretation of programming languages?
5. What is the precondition for realizing a logical calculus as a computer program?
6. In what sense does Tarski's requirement that only immediately obvious notions be used in the metalanguage have a counterpart in the procedural semantics of the programming languages?

Section 19.5
1. How does Tarski view the application of logical semantics to the analysis of natural languages?
2. Explain the Epimenides paradox.
3. Explain the three options for avoiding the inconsistency of logical semantics caused by the Epimenides paradox.
4. What is the difference between a false logical proposition like 'A & ¬A' and a logical inconsistency caused by a paradox?
5. What difference does Montague see between the artificial and the natural languages, and what is his goal in the analysis of natural languages?
6. Give three reasons for applying logical semantics to natural languages. Are they valid?

20. Truth, Meaning, and Ontology

This chapter further explores the relation between a theory of truth and a theory of natural language meaning. The classic problems of intensional contexts, propositional attitudes, and vagueness are related to the different possible ontologies underlying theories of semantics.

Section 20.1 describes natural language phenomena which have motivated expansions of logical semantics, in particular Frege's distinction between sense and reference. Section 20.2 explains Carnap's reconstruction of Frege's sense as formal functions called intensions. Section 20.3 shows why the phenomenon of propositional attitudes is incompatible with the ontological assumptions of logical truth conditions. Section 20.4 explains why there are in principle four basic kinds of ontology for theories of semantic interpretation. Section 20.5 describes the basic concepts of many-valued logics and shows how the choice of a particular ontology can greatly influence the outcome of a formal analysis, using the phenomenon of vagueness as an example.

20.1 Analysis of Meaning in Logical Semantics

The application of logical semantics to natural language is intended to characterize meaning. It is not obvious, however, how a theory of truth is supposed to double as a theory of meaning. To indirectly motivate the logical semantics of natural language as a theory of meaning, the following principle is used:

20.1.1 THE MEANING PRINCIPLE OF LOGICAL SEMANTICS

> If a speaker-hearer knows the meaning of a sentence, he can say for any state
> of affairs whether the sentence is true or false with respect to it.

This principle equates the intuitive knowledge of a natural sentence meaning with the knowledge of its truth conditions. In logical semantics, the meanings of natural language sentences are characterized by explicitly defining their truth conditions.

However, if the meanings of the natural (meta-)language are used to define the truth conditions of logical semantics, and the truth conditions of logical semantics are used to define the meanings of the natural (object) language, then there arises the danger of a vicious circle. Such a circle can only be avoided if the meaning analysis within logical semantics is limited to *reducing* complex natural language meanings to elementary logical notions.

For this purpose, the logical notions must be restricted explicitly to a small, well-defined arsenal of elementary meanings which are presupposed to be immediately obvious – in accordance with Tarski's requirement for the metalanguage (Sect. 19.3). The natural language fragment (object language) is analyzed semantically by translating it into the logical language with the goal of bringing out the truth-conditional aspects of the natural language as much as possible.[1]

The logical analysis of natural language has repeatedly brought to light properties which seemed puzzling or paradoxical from a logical point of view. This has evoked ambivalent reactions in the logicians involved.

On the one hand, they felt confirmed in their view that natural languages are imprecise, misleading, and contradictory.[2] On the other hand, some of these phenomena were taken as a challenge to expand logical systems so that they could handle selected natural language puzzles and explain them in terms of their extended logical structure (N→L reconstruction, Sect. 19.2).

The discrepancies between the intuitive assumptions of logical semantics and the meaning structures of natural language, as well as attempts at overcoming them at least in part, are illustrated by a classical example from the history of logic. The example is based on two rules of inference developed from Aristotelian logic by medieval scholasticists, namely *existential generalization* and *substitutivity of identicals*.

According to the rule of existential generalization it follows from the truth of a proposition F(a, b) that a exists and that b exists. For example, the sentence Julia kissed Richard is analyzed semantically as a *kiss* relation between the entities Julia and Richard. If Julia kissed Richard is true, then it must be true that Julia exists and Richard exists.

The rule of substitutivity of identicals says that, given the premises F(a, b) and b = c, F(a, b) implies F(a, c). For example, if Richard = Prince of Burgundy, then the truth of the sentence Julia kissed Richard implies the truth of the sentence Julia kissed the Prince of Burgundy. This substitutivity of Richard and Prince of Burgundy *salva*

---

[1] Thereby it was initially considered sufficient to assign logical translations informally to suitably selected examples, based on intuition. For example, Quine (1960) presented the formula $\wedge x[\text{raven}(x) \rightarrow \text{black}(x)]$ as the semantic representation of the sentence All ravens are black, using his native speaker understanding of English and his knowledge of logic (informal translation).

A rigorously formal method of analyzing the truth-conditional aspect of natural languages was pioneered by Richard Montague. In Montague grammar, syntactically analyzed expressions of natural language are mapped systematically into equivalent logical formulas by means of a well-defined algorithm (formal translation).

[2] It would be a worthwhile topic in history of science to collect and classify statements to this effect in the writings of Frege, Russell, Tarski, Quine, and many others.

veritate, i.e., preserving the truth value, is based on the fact that these two different expressions denote the same object.

But what about the following pairs of sentences?

20.1.2 VALID AND INVALID INSTANCES OF EXISTENTIAL GENERALIZATION

(1) Julia finds a unicorn. > A unicorn exists.

(2) Julia seeks a unicorn. ≯ A unicorn exists.

The symbols > and ≯ represent *implies* and *doesn't imply*, respectively. The premises in these two examples have exactly the same syntactic structure, namely F(a, b). The only difference consists in the choice of the verb. Yet in (1) the truth of the premise implies the truth of the consequent, in accordance with the rule of existential generalization, while in (2) this implication does not hold.

Example (2) raises the question of how a relation can be established between a subject and an object if the object does not exist. How can Julia seeks a unicorn be grammatically well-formed, meaningful, and even true under realistic circumstances? Part of the solution consisted in specifying certain environments in natural sentences in which the rule of existential generalization does not hold, e.g., in the scope of a verb like seek. These environments are called the *uneven* (Frege 1892), *opaque* (Quine 1960), or *intensional* (Montague 1974) *contexts*.

This solves only part of the puzzle, however. If the meaning of a unicorn is not an object existing in reality, what else could it be? And how should the difference in the meaning of different expressions for nonexisting objects, such as square circle, unicorn, and Pegasus, be explained within the framework of logic?

The necessity of distinguishing between these meanings follows from the second inference rule, the substitutivity of identicals. For example, if we were to use the empty set as the referent of square circle, unicorn, and Pegasus in order to express that no real objects correspond to these terms, then the truth of Julia seeks a unicorn would imply the truth of Julia seeks Pegasus and Julia seeks the square circle because of the substitutivity of identicals. Such a substitution would violate the intuitive fact that the resulting sentences have clearly nonequivalent meanings – in contrast to the earlier the Richard/Prince of Burgundy example.

The nonequivalence of Julia seeks a unicorn and Julia seeks a square circle leads to the conclusion that in addition to the real objects in the world there also exist natural language meanings which are independent of their referents. This was recognized in Frege's (1892) distinction between *sense* (Sinn) and *reference* (Bedeutung).

Frege concluded from examples like 20.1.2 that all expressions of language have a meaning (sense), even square circle and Pegasus. Based on their meaning some of these expressions, e.g., Julia, refer to real objects (referents), whereas others, e.g., a unicorn, happen to have no referent.[3] In this way a sentence like Julia seeks a

---

[3] Frege proposed using the empty set as the referent for nonreferring expressions – to make referring a total function. This was declared *plainly artificial* by Russell (1905).

unicorn can be properly explained: the proposition establishes a relation between the real individual denoted by Julia and the meaning (sense) of a unicorn.

Frege's move to distinguish the meaning of language expressions (sense) and the object referred to (referents) is correct from the viewpoint of natural language analysis, but dangerous for the main concern of analytic philosophy, i.e., the characterization of truth. Whereas (i) the signs of language (surfaces) and (ii) the objects in the world are real, concrete, and objective, this does not hold in the same way for the entities called meaning (sense). As long as it is not completely clear in what form these meanings exist they pose an ontological problem.

From the ontological problem there follows a methodological one: how can a logical theory of truth arrive at reliable results if it operates with concepts (senses) the nature of which has not been clearly established? Doesn't the everyday use of language meanings show again and again that utterances may be understood in many different ways? This 'arbitrariness' of different speaker-hearer meanings threatens to compromise the main concern of philosophical logic.

Frege's way out was to attribute a similar form of existence to the meanings of natural language as to the numbers and their laws in mathematical realism. Mathematical realism proceeds on the assumption that the laws of mathematics exist even if no one knows about them; mathematicians *discover* laws which are eternally valid.[4] Frege supposed the meanings of natural language to exist in the same way, i.e., independently of whether there are speakers-hearers who have discovered them and use them more or less correctly.

20.2 Intension and Extension

Frege's proposal for making language meaning 'real' was successful insofar as it rekindled interest in solving puzzles of natural language. On the one hand, there were attempts to handle the phenomena treated by Frege without postulating a sense (Russell 1905; Quine 1960). On the other hand, there were attempts to reconstruct the notion of sense logically.

A highlight among the efforts of the second group is Carnap's reconstruction of Frege's sense as formal intensions. Carnap (1947) proceeds on the assumption that the meaning of sleep, for example, is the set of sleepers (as in 19.3.1). In addition, Carnap uses the fact that the elements of this set may vary in time: two individuals awake, another one falls asleep, etc. Also, the set of sleepers may vary from one place to another.

Using the set I of different places and the set J of different points in time, Carnap constructs an index (i, j), with $i \in I$ and $j \in J$. Then he defines the *intension* of a word or expression as a function from $I \times J$ into 2^A, i.e., from an ordered pair (i, j) to the

---

[4] The counterposition to mathematical realism is constructivism, according to which a mathematical law begins to exist only at the point when it has been constructed from formal building blocks and their inherent logic by mathematicians.

power set over the set of entities A. Carnap calls the value of an intension at an index (i, j) the *extension*. The set-theoretic kind of an extension depends on whether the expression is a sentence, a proper name, or a predicate.

20.2.1 EXAMPLES OF CARNAP'S *Intensions*

$$\underset{extension}{\overset{intension}{\text{proposition:}\quad I \times J \to \{0,1\}}}$$

proposition:
intension
$I \times J \to \{0,1\}$
extension

proper name:
intension
$I \times J \to a \in A$
extension

1-pl. predicate:
intension
$I \times J \to \{a_1, a_2, \dots\} \subseteq A$
extension

The notion of intension refers to the function as a whole (7.4.1). Its domain is $I \times J$ and its range is called the extension. The extensions of propositions are the truth values defined as elements of $\{0, 1\}$, the extensions of proper names are objects defined as elements of A, and the extensions of predicates are relations defined as subsets of A.

Carnap's systematic variation of denotations relative to different indices required an extended definition of the logical language (as compared to, e.g., 19.3.2). For this purpose the model $\mathcal{M}$ is expanded into a so-called model structure $\mathcal{MS}$. A model structure consists of a set of models such that each index (i, j), $i \in I$ and $j \in J$, is associated with a model specifying the extension of all words of the logical language at that index.

In order to determine the truth value of a sentence relative to a model structure and an index, the model structure must be explicitly defined. Even for a very small model structure this definition is extremely cumbersome and complex. Moreover, the formal interpretation of a sentence relative to such a definition produces nothing that isn't already known to begin with: the truth value of the sentence is an exact reflection of what the logician defined in the model structure at the index in question.

That model structures have no practical purpose is not regarded as a drawback by model-theoretic semanticists, however. Their goal is not to define a complete model of the world in order to determine the actual truth value of sentences, but rather to design a logical semantics in which the truth value of arbitrary well-formed sentences *could in principle* be determined formally if the model structure were defined.

From this viewpoint, Carnap's formal intensions fulfill many desiderata of Frege's sense. Intensions characterize the meaning (sense) of an expression insofar as anyone who knows the metalanguage definition of the model structure and the metalanguage definition of the logical language can determine the extension of the expression at any index. Furthermore, intensions serve as denotations in intensional contexts: the sentence Julia seeks an apple, for example, may be analyzed as a *seek* relation between the extension of Julia and the intension of an apple, irrespective of whether or not there are any apples at the index in question.

In addition, Carnap uses the index parameters I and J for the definition of modal and temporal operators. Based on the temporal parameter J, the past operator H is defined as follows: a proposition H(p) is true relative to a model structure $\mathcal{MS}$ and an index (i, j) if there exists an index j', j' < j, and p is true relative to $\mathcal{MS}$ and (i, j'); and accordingly for the future operator W (temporal logic).

Furthermore, by generalizing the location parameter I to range over 'possible worlds', Carnap defines the modal operators for necessity $\square$ and possibility $\lozenge$. In modal logic, two expressions are treated as necessarily equivalent, iff their extensions are the same in *all* possible worlds; two expressions are possibly equivalent, iff there is *at least one* possible world in which they have the same extension.

By defining intensions in this way, Carnap managed to avoid some of the problems with substitution *salva veritate*. Assume, for example, that neither apples nor pears exist at an index (i, j), such that the extensions of the notions apple and pear are the same at (i, j), namely the empty set. Because the distribution of apples and pears is not necessarily (i.e., not in all possible worlds) the same, they have different intensions. Therefore the truth of Julia seeks an apple relative to (i, j) does not imply the truth of Julia seeks a pear relative to (i, j) – provided that substitutivity of identicals applies here at the level of intensions, as it should in the intensional context created by seek.

This kind of analysis has been extended to prevent expressions for fictitious objects such as unicorn or Pegasus from having the same meaning. While admitting that neither unicorn nor Pegasus exists in the real world, it is argued that their nonexistence is not *necessary* (i.e., does not hold in *all* possible worlds). Thus, given that the expressions in question have meaning it may be assumed that there is at least one 'non-actual' possible world in which unicorns and Pegasus exist and have different extensions, ensuring different intensions. It is this use of possible worlds which was especially offensive to Quine (1960) on ontological grounds – and justly so.

Even though Carnap's formal notion of intension[5] exhibits properties with regard to substitutivity of identicals and existential generalization which are similar to Frege's notion of sense, the two underlying theories are profoundly different, in terms of both structure and content. This difference is characterized schematically using the binary feature [±sense]:

---

[5] Carnap's formal notion of intensions plays a central role in Montague grammar, in which analyzed language expressions are formally translated into a typed lambda calculus. This *intensional logic* was designed by Montague to accommodate many traditional and new puzzles of natural language in a clean formal fashion within logical semantics.

For example, in his "Proper treatment of quantification in ordinary English" (PTQ), Montague presents and solves the new puzzle The temperature is 30 and rising: the extension of temperature equals the extension of a certain number, here 30; because a number like 30 cannot increase, the predicate rise is applied not to the extension of temperature, but to the intension!

20.2.2 Two Approaches to Meaning

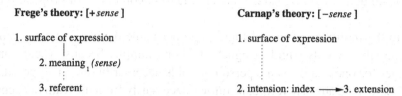

Frege's approach is [+sense] because it uses a separate level for the meaning₁ of language. The surface and the meaning₁ of expressions form a fixed unit which faces the level of referents.[6] In this respect, Frege's approach and the [2+1] level structure of the SLIM theory of language are similar.

Carnap's approach is [−sense] because expressions refer directly to the 'world.' Apart from the definition of a few additional operators, the only difference between Carnap's intensional logic and the extensional system defined in 19.3.2 consists in the fact that for Carnap the world is represented not just by a single model $\mathcal{M}$ but rather by a model structure $\mathcal{MS}$. The model structure represents different states of the world as a multitude of models which have different indices. The indices provide the formal domain for functions which Carnap calls intensions.

Though the relation between intensions and the intended referents is treated in Carnap's system, it is by metalanguage definition only. The meaning (intension) refers to a referent at a given index by using the index as the argument of the intension function, thus rendering the associated extension as the value. Because Carnap defines extensions solely in terms of set-theoretic structures, he does not characterize the meaning of expressions like square (4.2.2), triangle, red, or blue any more than does Frege.

20.3 Propositional Attitudes

Despite the successful treatment of intensional contexts, temporal and modal operators, and other puzzles in logical semantics, there remain two basic problems which in principle cannot be solved within the truth-conditional frameworks, namely

– the Epimenides paradox (Sect. 19.5) and
– propositional attitudes.

Propositional attitudes are expressed by sentences which describe the relation between a cognitive agent and a propositional content. For example, the sentence

Susanne believes that Cicero denounced Catiline.

---

[6] According to Frege, expressions of language refer by means of their sense. Frege never specified how the meaning (sense) of an expression should be defined exactly and how reference to the intended object should be guided by the properties of the meaning. But the main point is that his general approach provides a certain structural correlation between the surface, the meaning, and the referent.

expresses the propositional attitude of *belief* as a relation between Susanne and the proposition Cicero denounced Catiline. What are the truth conditions of propositional attitudes?

According to the intuitions of modal logic, a proper name denotes the same individual in all possible worlds (rigid designator).[7] For example, because Cicero and Tullius are names for one and the same person, it holds necessarily (i.e, in all possible worlds) that Cicero = Tullius. Therefore, it follows necessarily from the truth of Cicero denounced Catiline that Tullius denounced Catiline.

However, if one of these sentences is embedded under a predicate of propositional attitude, e.g., believe, the substitution *salva veritate* is not valid even for proper names. Thus, according to intuition, Susanne believes that Cicero denounced Catiline does not imply that Susanne believes that Tullius denounced Catiline. Even though the referent of Cicero is necessarily identical with the referent of Tullius, it could be that Susanne is not aware of this. Accordingly, a substitution *salva veritate* would require in addition the truth of Susanne believes that Cicero is Tullius.

Because different human beings may have different ideas about reality, a treatment of propositional attitudes in the manner of Carnap and Montague would have to model not only the realities of the natural sciences, but also the belief structures of all individual speaker-hearers.[8] Such an attempt at handling this particular natural language phenomenon by yet another extension of model-theoretic semantics, however, would violate the basic assumptions of a theory of truth.

As shown in connection with Tarski's semantics in Sect. 19.3, a theory of truth is concerned not only with a formal definition of implications, but equally with the verification of the premises of those implications. Only if the second aspect is fulfilled is it possible to establish a true relation between a language and the world.

In order to determine what an individual believes, however, one is dependent on what the individual chooses to report, whereby it cannot be checked objectively whether this is true or not. For this reason, individual 'belief-worlds' have justly been regarded as a prime example of what lies outside any scientific approach to truth.[9]

The phenomenon of propositional attitudes raises once more the fundamental question of logical semantics for natural language (Sect. 20.1), namely

---

[7] Compare Kripke's (1972) model-theoretic treatment of proper names with their SLIM-theoretic treatment in terms of internal name markers (Sects. 6.1, 6.4, and 6.5).

[8] In purely formal terms one could define a 'belief-operator' $\mathcal{B}$ as follows:

$$\mathcal{B}(x, p)^{\mathcal{M}S, i, j, g} \text{ is 1 iff } p^{\mathcal{M}S, b, j, g} \text{ is 1, whereby } b \text{ is a belief-world of x at index i, j.}$$

However, one should not be fooled by this seemingly exacting notation which imitates Montague's PTQ. This T-condition is just as vacuous as 19.4.1 as long as it is not clear how the metalanguage definition should be verified relative to belief-worlds.

[9] In logical semantics, an ontological problem similar to individual belief-worlds is created by individual sensations, like a toothache, which do not exist in the same way as real objects

'Definition of truth (conditions) by means of meaning or
definition of meaning in terms of truth (conditions)?'

though in a different form relating to ontology:

20.3.1 THE BASIC ONTOLOGICAL PROBLEM OF MODEL THEORY

Is the speaker-hearer part of the model structure or
is the model structure part of the speaker-hearer?

If the goal of logical semantics is to characterize truth, then one may use only logical meanings which are presupposed to be immediately obvious and eternal. In this
approach the speaker-hearer must be part of the model structure, just like all the other
objects. Thereby, the relation of truth between expressions and states of affairs exists
independently of whether it is discovered by this or that speaker-hearer or not.[10]

Yet if the goal is the analysis of language meaning, then the logical system, which
was developed originally for the characterization of truth based on logical meanings,
is used for a new purpose, namely the description of language meanings in the form
of truth conditions. This new purpose of bringing out the logical aspect of natural
language meanings brings about a profound change in the original ontological assumptions.

In order for the meanings of language to be used in communication by the speaker-
hearer they must be part of cognition. The cognitive (re-)interpretation of the model
as part the speaker-hearer is incompatible with the goals and methods of traditional
theories of truth. Conversely, the 'realistic' interpretation of the model within a theory
of truth is incompatible with an analysis of natural language meanings which are used
in communication.[11]

---

in the world. The so-called *double aspect theory* attempts to make such sensations 'real' to
the outside observer by means of measuring brain waves. By associating the phenomenon
pain with both, (i) the individual sensation and (ii) the corresponding measurement, this
phenomenon is supposed to obtain an ontological foundation acceptable to logical semantics. A transfer of this approach to the truth-conditional analysis of belief would require
infallible lie detectors.

[10] The mainstream view in philosophical logic does not require that a representation of scientific truth include the speaker-hearer as part of the model. The only reason why a speaker-
hearer is sometimes added to a model-theoretic logic is the treatment of special phenomena
characteristic of natural language, especially the interpretation of indexical pronouns like I
and you. Thereby the speaker-hearer is in principle part of the model structure – making it
impossible to provide an adequate truth-conditional treatment of propositional attitudes, for
the reasons given above. A detailed critique of the outmoded 'received view' in the theory
of science, as well as its alternatives, may be found in Suppe (ed.) (1977).

[11] Early examples of the misguided attempt to reinterpret the model structure as something
cognitive inside the speaker-hearer are Hausser (1978, 1979a,b, 1983), and SCG.

There are examples known in mathematics where a basic formal theory happens to allow more than one interpretation, e.g., geometry. This does not mean, however, that any formal theory may in general be used for any new interpretation desired. A case in point is logical semantics, the formalism of which cannot be interpreted simultaneously as a general description of truth and a general description of natural language meaning – as shown by the phenomenon of propositional attitudes.

The alternative stated in 20.3.1 may characterized schematically in terms of the binary feature [±constructive]:

20.3.2 Two Ontological Interpretations of Model Theory

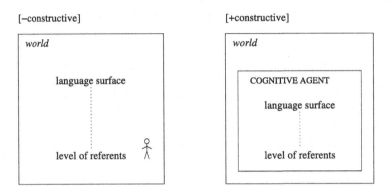

[−constructive]   [+constructive]

The [−constructive] interpretation establishes the relation between the language surfaces and the level of referents outside the cognitive agent out there in the real world. The agent is itself an object at the level of referents, who may observe this somehow god-given relation between language and the objects of the world.

The [+constructive] interpretation, on the other hand, establishes the relation between the language surfaces and the level of referents solely inside the cognitive agent. What the agent does not perceive in the world plays no role in his reference procedures, though what he feels, wishes, plans, etc., does.

The most fundamental difference between the two ontologies consists in the fact that they require different kinds of semantics:

– Any system based on a [−constructive] ontology must have a metalanguage-based semantics. This is because scientific statements believed to be eternally true and independent of any speaker-hearer cannot be meaningfully operationalized. The only option remaining for establishing the external relation between the expression and the state of affairs is in terms of metalanguage definitions.

– Any system based on a [+constructive] ontology must have a procedural semantics. This is because such systems would be simply useless without a procedural semantics. Neither a computer nor a cognitive agent could function practically on the basis of a metalanguage-based semantics.

For different phenomena of logical analysis, the distinction between a [−constructive] and a [+constructive] ontology has different implications. In propositional calculus, the difference between the two ontologies happens to make no difference. In first-order predicate calculus, quantification over infinite sets (universal quantifier) will differ within the two ontologies. In intensional logic, the treatment of opaque contexts and modality is incommensurable with their alternative treatment in a [+constructive] cognitive model. A treatment of propositional attitudes, finally, is incompatible with a [−constructive] ontology, but poses no problem in a [+constructive] system.

20.4 Four Basic Ontologies

The features [±sense] (20.2.2) and [±constructive] (20.3.2) are independent of, and can be combined with, each other. This results in four kinds of semantic interpretations based on four basic ontologies, namely [−sense, −constructive], [+sense, −constructive], [−sense, +constructive], and [+sense, +constructive]:

20.4.1 ONTOLOGIES OF SEMANTIC INTERPRETATION

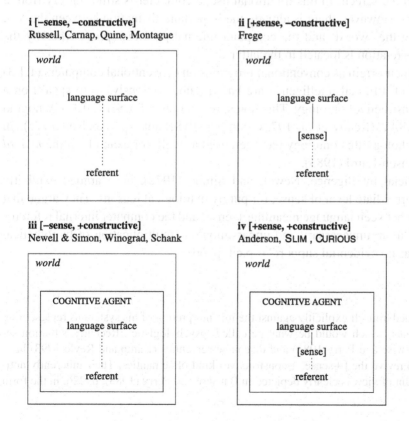

i [−sense, −constructive]
Russell, Carnap, Quine, Montague

> *world*
>
> language surface
>
> referent

ii [+sense, −constructive]
Frege

> *world*
>
> language surface
>
> [sense]
>
> referent

iii [−sense, +constructive]
Newell & Simon, Winograd, Schank

> *world*
>
> COGNITIVE AGENT
>
> language surface
>
> referent

iv [+sense, +constructive]
Anderson, SLIM , CURIOUS

> *world*
>
> COGNITIVE AGENT
>
> language surface
>
> [sense]
>
> referent

Each of these ontologies has been adopted at one time or another by different schools of semantic interpretation.

The [−sense, −constructive] ontology (i) is presumed by the mainstream of analytic philosophy, from Russell via the early Wittgenstein, Carnap, Quine, Montague, to Putnam. Anxious for a solid foundation for truth, it uses only referents which are considered to be ontologically real. In nominalism, these are the concrete signs of language and the states of affairs built up from concrete objects in the world. In mathematical realism, the ontology is extended to include abstract objects like sets and numbers. Both have in common that the semantics is defined as a direct, external relation between language and the world.

The [+sense, −constructive] ontology (ii) was used by Frege in his attempt to analyze uneven (opaque, intensional) readings in natural language. For modeling the mechanism of natural language communication, this kind of semantics is only half a step in the right direction. As a theory of truth, any [−constructive], metalanguage-based semantics is necessarily incompatible with representing cognitive states.[12]

The [−sense, +constructive] ontology (iii) underlies the semantics of programming languages. The user puts commands (surfaces of a programming language) into the computer which turns them directly into corresponding electronic procedures. When a result has been computed it is communicated to the user by displaying language expressions on the screen. In this traditional use, a computer is still a far cry from a cognitive agent. However, there is already the important distinction between the *task environment* in the 'world' and the computer-internal *problem space*, whereby the semantic interpretation is located in the latter.

Because of their origin as conventional programs on conventional computers (1.1.3) most systems of artificial intelligence are based (subconsciously, so to speak) on a [−sense, +constructive] ontology. This holds, for example, for SHRDLU (Winograd 1972), HEARSAY (Reddy et al. 1973), and SAM (Schank and Abelson 1977). In cognitive psychology this ontology has been used as well, for example in the *mental models* of Johnson-Laird (1983).

Within artificial intelligence, Newell and Simon (1972), have argued explicitly against an intermediate level of sense, for purely ontological reasons. They argue that the distinction between language meanings (sense) and the computer internal referents would result "in an unnecessary and unparsimonious multiplication of hypothetical entities that has no evidential support" (op.cit, p. 66).

---

[12] Frege defended himself explicitly against the misinterpreting of his system as representing cognitive states, which would be what he called 'psychologistic'. Recently, situation semantics (Barwise and Perry 1983) and discourse semantics (Kamp and Reyle 1993) have attempted to revive the [+sense, −constructive] kind of semantics. Their inherently anti-cognitive point of view is clearly depicted in Barwise and Perry (1983), p. 226, in the form of comics.

A direct connection between language expressions and their referents, however, prevents any autonomous classification of new objects in principle. Therefore, a [−sense, +constructive] kind of semantics is limited to closed toy worlds created in advance by the programmer.[13] It is by no means accidental that these systems have no components of artificial perception: because they lack the intermediate level of concepts (sense) they could not utilize perception (e.g., artificial vision) to classify and to automatically integrate new objects of a known kind into their domain (Sect. 4.3).

The [+sense, +constructive] ontology (**iv**), finally, underlies the SLIM theory of language. SLIM bases its [+sense] property structurally on the matching of the literal meaning and the context of use, while its [+constructive] property is based on the fact that this matching occurs inside the cognitive agent. In cognitive psychology, this kind of semantics has been used by Anderson and Bower (1973, 1980). They present a general psychological model of natural language understanding, which may be interpreted as an internal matching between language concepts and a context structure, and to that extent resembles the functioning of CURIOUS as described in Chap. 4.

The theoretical relation between the four alternative kinds of semantics may be analyzed by emphasizing either their ontological difference or their formal similarities. In the latter case, one will present one's semantics as a purely formal structure which may be assigned different interpretations without affecting the formal essence. For this, one may relate the different ontologies in terms of different degrees of specialization or generalization.

The difference between a [+sense] and a [−sense] ontology may be minimized by interpreting the latter as a simplification of the former. Assume that (i) the world is closed such that objects can neither appear nor disappear,[14] (ii) the relation between language expressions and their referents is fixed once and for all, and (iii) there is no spontaneous use of language by the speaker-hearer. Then there is no reason for postulating a level of senses, thus leading to a [−sense] system as a special case of a [+sense] system.

Because of this simplification one might view the [−sense] system as more valid or more essential than the [+sense] system. One should not forget, however, that there are empirical phenomena which simply cannot be handled within a [−sense] ontology, such as the reference to new objects of a known kind.

The difference between a [+constructive] and a [−constructive] ontology may also be minimized in terms of a simplification. Assume that the cognitive agent has perfect recognition, such that the distinction between the external objects (i.e., language ex-

---

[13] Examples are the chessboard (Newell and Simon 1972; Reddy et al. 1973) and the blocks world (Winograd 1972).

[14] This is represented formally by the definition of the sets A, I, and J of a model structure $\mathcal{MS}$.

pressions and referents) and their internal cognitive representations may be neglected. Then there is no reason to distinguish between the external reality and its internal cognitive representation, thus leading to a [−constructive] ontology as a special case of a [+constructive] ontology.

Because of this simplification, one might view the [−constructive] system as more valid and more essential than the [+constructive] system. One should not forget, however, that there are empirical phenomena which simply cannot be handled within a [−constructive] ontology, such as propositional attitudes.

The choice between the four different kinds of semantics depends on the intended application. Therefore, when (i) *expanding* a given semantics to a new application or when (ii) *transferring* partial analyses from one application to another, one should be as well informed about the structural differences between the four basic ontologies as about the potential formal equivalences based on simplifying abstractions.

20.5 Sorites Paradox and the Treatment of Vagueness

The importance of ontology for the empirical results of semantic analysis is illustrated by the phenomenon of vagueness. In logical semantics, the treatment of vagueness takes a classic paradox from antiquity as its starting point, namely the Sorites paradox or paradox of the heap:

> One grain of sand does not make a heap. Adding an additional grain still does not make a heap. If n grains do not form a heap, then adding another single grain will not make a heap either. However, if this process of adding grains is continued long enough, a genuine heap will eventually result.

The Sorites paradox has been carried over to the logical semantics of natural language by arguing as follows: consider the process of, for example, a slowly closing door. Does it not raise the question about at what point the sentence The door is open is still true and at what point it is false? Then one goes one step further by asking to what *degree* the sentence is true in the various stages of the door closing.

> Sensitive students of language, especially psychologists and linguistic philosophers, have long been attuned to the fact that natural language concepts have vague boundaries and fuzzy edges and that, consequently, natural-language sentences will very often be neither true, nor false, nor nonsensical, but rather true to a certain extent and false to a certain extent, true in certain respects and false in other respects.
>
> Lakoff (1972b), p. 183

Another situation which has been presented as an example of truth-conditional vagueness is the classification of colors. If an object is classified as *red* in context a, but as *non-red* in context b, does it not follow that the natural language concept *red* must be vague? If the predicate x is red is applied to the transition from red to orange in a color spectrum, the situation resembles the slowly closing door.

If these assumptions are accepted and sentences are true or false only to certain degrees, then the traditional two-valued (bivalent) logic must be changed to a many-valued logic.[15] Such systems evolved originally in connection with the question of whether a proposition must always be either true or false.

> Throughout the orthodox mainstream of the development of logic in the West, the prevailing view was that every proposition is either true or else false – although which of these is the case may well neither be *necessary* as regards the matter itself nor *determinable* as regards our knowledge of it. This thesis, now commonly called the "Law of Excluded Middle," was, however, already questioned in antiquity. In Chap. 9 of his treatise *On Interpretation (de interpretatione)*, Aristotle discussed the truth status of alternatives regarding "future-contingent" matters, whose occurrence – like that of the sea battle tomorrow – is not yet determinable by us and may indeed actually be undetermined.
>
> Rescher (1969), p. 1

Nonbivalent systems exceed the founding assumptions of logic, as shown by the remarkable term 'future-contingent'. While standard logic takes the viewpoint of an omniscient being and is concerned with the interpretation of absolute propositions, future-contingent propositions are concerned with more mundane situations. For example, the question of what truth value the sentence Tomorrow's sea battle will be lost by the Persians has *today* is obviously not asked by an all-knowing being. Furthermore, the content of this proposition is neither mathematical nor scientific in nature, and therefore cannot be verified.

In modern times, nonbivalent logics began with the Scotsman Hugh MacColl (1837–1909), the American Charles Sanders Peirce (1839–1914), and the Russian Nikolai A. Vasil'ev (1880–1940). The nonbivalent logics may be divided into two basic groups, namely the *three-valued* logics, in which a proposition can be true (1), false (0), or undetermined (#), and the *many-valued* logics, in which truth values are identified with the real numbers between 0 and 1, e.g., 0.615.

The three-valued logics and the many-valued logics all suffer from the same basic problem:

> What truth value should be assigned to complex propositions based on component propositions with nonbivalent truth values?

Thus, a three-valued system raises the question: What should be the value of, for example, $A \wedge B$, if A has the value 1 and B has the value #? Similarly in a many-valued system: if the component proposition A has the truth value 0.615 and B has the value 0.423, what value should be assigned to $A \wedge B$?

---

[15] Besides vagueness, nonbivalent logics have been motivated by semantic presuppositions (see for example Hausser (1973, 1976)).

There is an discomfiting wealth of possible answers to these questions. Rescher (1969) describes 51 different systems of nonbivalent logics proposed in the literature up to that date. Of those, only a few will be briefly described here.

Łukasiewicz (1935) assigns the following truth values to logical conjunction: if both A and B are 1, then A ∧ B is 1; if one of the conjuncts is 0, then A ∧ B is 0; but if one of the conjuncts is 1 and the other is #, then A ∧ B is #. This assignment reflects the following intuitions: if it turns out that one conjunct of A ∧ B is 0, then the other conjunct need not even be looked at because the whole conjunction will be 0 anyhow. But if one conjunct is 1 and the other is #, then the whole is indeterminate and assigned the value #. The same reasoning is used by Łukasiewicz regarding logical disjunction: if one of the two disjuncts is 1, then A ∨ B is 1; if both disjuncts are 0, then A ∨ B is 0; but if one disjunct is 0 and the other is #, then the conjunction A ∨ B is #.

A different value assignment is proposed by Bochvar (1939), who proceeds on the assumption that a complex proposition is always # if one of its components is #. Thus, if A is 0 and B is #, then Bochvar does not assign 0 to A ∧ B (as in the system of Łukasiewicz), but rather #. And similarly for A ∨ B. Bochvar justifies this assignment by interpreting # as *senseless* rather than unknown.

A third method of assigning nonbivalent truth values is *supervaluations* by van Fraassen (1966, 1968, 1969), whose concern is to maintain the classic tautologies and contradictions in a three-valued system. According to van Fraassen, it should not matter, for example, in the case of A ∨ ¬A (tautology) or A ∧ ¬A (contradiction), whether A has the value 1, 0, or #, because according to the classic view tautologies *always* have the value 1 and contradictions *always* have the value 0.

Supervaluations are basically a complicated motivational structure which allows assigning bivalent truth values to tautologies and contradictions while treating contingent propositions similarly to Łukasiewicz's system. The motivation is based on the ontologically remarkable assumption that the truth value of an elementary proposition may be checked repeatedly (as in scientific measuring).[16]

In multi-valued systems, the problem of justifying the choice of a certain value assignment is even worse than in three-valued ones. For example, if the component proposition A has the truth value 0.615 and B has the truth value 0.423, what should be the value of A ∧ B? 0.615? 0.423? the average 0.519? 1? 0? And similarly for

---

[16] The appeal of van Fraassen's construction resides in the fact that multiple value assignments are essentially a hidden procedural component. This procedural component is coached within the overall metalanguage-based approach and partial in that it is limited to elementary propositions. The use of a procedural component is ironic insofar as van Fraassen aims at saving the bivalence of logical tautologies and contradictions as compared to, e.g., Łukasiewicz (1935).

A ∨ B. For each of these different assignments one may find a suitable application. In the majority of the remaining cases, however, the principle chosen will turn out to be counterintuitive or at best artificial.

From a history of science point of view such a multitude of more than 50 different alternatives is a clear case of an *embarrassment of riches* in combination with *descriptive aporia* (Sect. 22.2). These two syndromes are an infallible sign that there is something seriously wrong with the basic premises of the approach in question.

In multi-valued logic systems, the mistake resides in the premise formulated in the above quotation from Lakoff, that propositions may obviously have nonbivalent truth values. Once this premise has been accepted, one is stuck in a futile search for adequate value assignments to complex propositions, e.g., the question of which truth value should be assigned to 'A ∧ B' if A has the truth value 0.615 and B has the truth value 0.423.

Instead of accepting this premise we should ask how such peculiar truth values as 0.615 come about in the first place. And with this question we come back to the issue of the underlying ontology. More precisely: what impact does the structural difference between the [−sense, −constructive] and the [+sense, +constructive] ontology have on the formal analysis of vagueness?

We begin with the analysis of an example within the [−sense, −constructive] ontology of logical semantics. Let's assume that 'A ∧ B' is a proposition with A = [The door is open] and B = [The door is red]. Furthermore, let A have the truth value 0.615 and B the truth value 0.423. Then the conjunction has the following structure:

20.5.1 Vagueness in [−sense, −constructive] Semantics

world				
language surfaces:	[The door is open]	and	[the door is red]	
referents:	0,615		0,423	

Assigning the truth values 0.615 and 0.423 to the propositions A and B may be motivated by giving a long story about how the door is slightly non-open and how its color is slightly non-red. Such stories, though not part of logical theory, are intended to make us accept the peculiar, artificial values assigned to A and B. Once these assignments have been accepted, attention is focussed on the question of which truth value should be assigned to the complex proposition A ∧ B.

A completely different analysis of this example is obtained within a [+sense, +constructive] ontology. Its structure contains four different positions which may be postulated as a source of vagueness. They are marked by the letters a–d:

20.5.2 VAGUENESS IN [+SENSE, +CONSTRUCTIVE] SEMANTICS

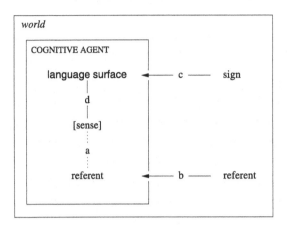

Position d corresponds to the vertical dotted lines in 20.5.1, because there the meanings are assigned to the language surfaces. The places a, b and c have been added by the transition to a [+sense, +constructive] ontology. In contradistinction to position d, they have in common that they are interfaces based on pattern matching.

Within a [+sense, +constructive] ontology, the most natural place for handling vagueness is a. This is because in a a language meaning$_1$, e.g., the concept of red, is matched with a restricted set of potential contextual referents. This procedure is based on the principle of *best match* within a restricted subcontext.

For example, the word red may be used to refer to a pale pink stone, provided that the other objects in the subcontext are, for example, grey. As soon as a bright red stone is added, however, the candidate for best match changes and the pale pink stone will now be counted among the non-red objects. This is not due to a special 'vagueness'-property of the color concept *red*, but rather to a change in the context of use (see also the handling of metaphoric reference in 5.2.1).

Other places where vagueness may arise naturally are b and c. In b, vagueness is caused by imprecise perception of the task environment. In c, it is caused by imprecise recognition of language expressions. In either case, vagueness originates in the interaction of the cognitive agent with the external environment and may influence communication by affecting the matching procedure a.

Thus, the alleged vagueness of the color words does not stem from their semantics. Instead it is a normal consequence of matching a language concept and a contextual referent in the pragmatics, a procedure based on the principle of best match in a restricted context of use. This analysis of the semantics and pragmatics of the color terms can easily be realized operationally within the construction of a robot by defining concepts like red as intervals of electromagnetic frequency.

Exercises

Section 20.1
1. What principle is used to apply the logical characterization of truth indirectly to the analysis of natural language meanings?
2. How can a *circulus vitiosus* (vicious circle) be avoided, if truth is defined in terms of meanings and meanings are defined in terms of truth?
3. Describe the rules of existential generalization and substitutivity of identicals, and explain them with examples.
4. Describe the properties of intensional contexts. What other names have they been called?
5. Why would it not suffice to let terms for which no referents exist, like unicorn and Pegasus, denote the empty set?
6. Read Frege (1892) in Frege (1967), pp. 143–162, and explain the distinction between sense and reference using his morning/evening star example.
7. What does Frege accomplish with this distinction, why is it ontologically problematic, and how does mathematical realism help him in overcoming this problem?

Section 20.2
1. Explain Carnap's formal reconstruction of Frege's notion of sense.
2. What is an intension? Specify the domain/range structure of intensions for expressions of different categories.
3. What is the relation between a logical model and a model structure?
4. Define a formal model structure for six verbs, five nouns, and four adjectives using the definition of intensional logic in SCG, pp. 81f. The sets A, I, and J should each contain ten elements. For a simplified example see 22.2.1. Describe and evaluate the experience.
5. Name two modal operators and explain their formal definition within model theory.
6. What is the formal basis for defining the tense operators H and W?
7. What are possible worlds used for in model theory?

Section 20.3
1. Explain in what sense the treatments of intensional contexts by Frege and Carnap achieve similar results, and in what sense they differ ontologically.
2. What is Montague's main accomplishment in the logical analysis of natural language?
3. Name two problems which are in principle unsolvable for a logical semantics of natural language.
4. What is a propositional attitude?
5. Explain in detail why a formal treatment of propositional attitudes in logical semantics would be incompatible with the goals of a theory of truth.

6. Why is it impossible to operationalize a semantics based on a [−constructive] ontology?

7. Why would a semantics based on a [+constructive] ontology be pointless if it is not operationalized?

Section 20.4

1. Describe four different kinds of ontology for systems of semantics.

2. Explain which kinds of ontology the semantics of logical, programming, and natural language are based on.

3. Explain how a [−sense, −constructive] ontology may be viewed as both a special case of a [+sense, +constructive] ontology and a higher form of abstraction.

4. Name a phenomenon which can be handled only in systems with a [+sense] ontology.

5. Name a phenomenon which can be handled only in systems with a [+constructive] ontology.

6. Which ontological property limits systems of classic AI, such as SHRDLU, in principle to toy worlds?

Section 20.5

1. Explain the Sorites Paradox. How does it relate to the alleged vagueness of natural language?

2. Explain the notion of semantic presuppositions (CoL, pp. 333–344). How may they be used to motivate nonbivalent logic?

3. What is the *law of excluded middle*?

4. What are future-contingent propositions?

5. Name two different interpretations of the third truth value #.

6. Look up the three-valued system of Kleene in Rescher (1969) and compare it with those of Łukasiewicz and Bochvar.

7. How are the truth values of complex propositions computed from the component propositions in a many-valued logic? Use the example A ∨ B, where A = 0.37 and B = 0.48.

8. How many different systems are described in Rescher's (1969) account of nonbivalent logics? Does this number reflect positively or negatively on nonbivalent approaches to logic? What could be the reason behind the invention of so many alternative solutions?

9. Explain how the treatment of vagueness differs in systems with a [−sense, −constructive] and a [+sense, +constructive] ontology.

10. What is the role of pragmatics in the analysis of vagueness?

11. Why is it desirable from the viewpoint of classic logic to handle vagueness without a many-valued logic?

21. Absolute and Contingent Propositions

The ontology of a semantic theory can influence empirical analysis profoundly. This has been demonstrated with the phenomenon of vagueness, which leads to an embarrassment of riches within the [−sense, −constructive] ontology of logical semantics, but falls into the spectrum of normal pragmatic interpretation within the [+sense, +constructive] ontology of the SLIM theory of language.

It is therefore promising to reanalyze other classical problems of logical semantics within the [+sense, +constructive] ontology in order to disarm them. Of special interest is the Epimenides paradox, which Tarski (1935, 1944) used to prove that a complete analysis of natural language is impossible within truth-conditional semantics. Will a [+sense, +constructive] reanalysis of the Epimenides paradox enable an object language to contain the words true and false without becoming inconsistent?

Section 21.1 develops a distinction between the logical truth values 1 and 0 and the contingent truth values $true^c$ and $false^c$, based on a comparison of absolute and contingent propositions. Section 21.2 reconstructs the Epimenides paradox in a [+sense, +constructive] system. Section 21.3 strengthens Montague's notion of a homomorphic semantic interpretation into a formal version of surface compositionality. Section 21.4 shows that the strictly time-linear derivation of LA Grammar is not in conflict with a homomorphic semantic interpretation. Section 21.5 explains why the mathematical complexity of a system may be greatly increased by a semantic interpretation and how this is to be avoided.

21.1 Absolute and Contingent Truth

In logic, the term proposition has acquired a specialized use, representing sentences which do not require knowledge of the utterance situation for their semantic interpretation. Such propositions are usually obtained by translating selected natural language examples into formulas of logic. Compared to the natural language originals, the formal translations are partly simplified and partly supplemented, depending on what the logical language provides and requires for a proper logical proposition.

R. Hausser, *Foundations of Computational Linguistics*,
DOI 10.1007/978-3-642-41431-2_21, © Springer-Verlag Berlin Heidelberg 2014

From the viewpoint of the SLIM theory of language, this specialized use of the term proposition[1] (German 'Aussage') is problematic because it constitutes a hybrid between an *utterance* (i.e., a pragmatically interpreted or interpretable token) and an *expression* (i.e., a pragmatically uninterpreted type). The suppressed distinction between utterance token and expression type may be brought to light by investigating the difference between absolute and contingent propositions.

Absolute propositions express scientific or mathematical contents. These are special in that they make the interpretation largely independent of the usual role of the speaker. For example, in the proposition

In a right-angled triangle, it holds for the hypotenuse A and the catheti B and C that $A^2 = B^2 + C^2$

the circumstances of the utterance have no influence on the interpretation and the truth value of the sentence in question, for which reason they are ignored.

The special properties of absolute propositions are reflected in logical truth. This notion is formally expressed by the metalanguage words false and true, referring respectively to the abstract set-theoretic objects $\emptyset$ (empty set) and $\{\emptyset\}$ (set of empty set) of the model structure.[2]

Thereby, logical truth is based on the system of truth conditions of the language at hand. The referential objects $\emptyset$ and $\{\emptyset\}$ serve merely as model-theoretic fix points into which the denotations of propositions are mapped by the metalanguage rules of the formal interpretation (e.g., 19.3.2).

Contingent propositions, on the other hand, are based on sentences with everyday content such as

Your dog is doing well.

Contingent propositions can only be interpreted – and thereby evaluated with respect to their truth value – if the relevant circumstances of the utterance situation are known and are systematically entered into the interpretation.

This requires that the parameters of the STAR be known, i.e., the spatial location S, the time T, the author A, and the intended recipient R (Sect. 5.3). The characteristic properties of contingent propositions correspond to a natural notion of truth, represented by the contingent truth values true^c and false^c. Intuitively, a proposition such as

The Persians have lost the battle

may be regarded as true^c, if the speaker is an eyewitness who is able to correctly judge and communicate the facts, or if there is a properly functioning chain of communication between the speaker and a reliable eyewitness.

Within the SLIM theory of language, the contingent truth values true^c and false^c have a procedural definition. A proposition – or rather a statement – uttered by, for

---

[1] See Sect. 3.4 for a description of propositions proper.

[2] Instead of $\emptyset$ and $\{\emptyset\}$, other notations use 0 and 1, $\bot$ and $\top$, no and yes, etc.

example, a robot is evaluated as true^c, if all procedures contributing to communication work correctly. Otherwise it is evaluated as false^c.[3]

What follows from this distinction between logical and contingent truth? Using two different notions of truth for absolute and contingent propositions would clearly be suboptimal from both the viewpoint of philosophical logic and the SLIM theory of language. Instead, the goal is an overall system with a uniform semantics which can correctly interpret any utterance of the form C is true no matter whether C happens to be a contingent or an absolute sentence.

A straightforward way of unifying the semantics of absolute and contingent statements is treating one kind as a special case of the other. For a [−constructive, −sense] approach it would thus be desirable if logical semantics would allow a complete treatment of contingent statements as a special case of absolute statements. Conversely, for a [+constructive, +sense] approach it would be desirable if natural semantics would allow a treatment of absolute statements as a special case of contingent statements. Given the choice between the two possibilities, the one applicable with greater generality is to be preferred.

In logical semantics, the handling of absolute statements may be extended to contingent statements in many instances – as shown by Montague's model-theoretic analysis of English.[4] The phenomenon of propositional attitudes (Sect. 20.3) has shown, however, that a proper semantic interpretation – that is, an ontologically justified assignment of the values 1 or 0 – is *not always* possible. Furthermore, according to Tarski, sentences of the form C is (not) true are forbidden in the object language. For these two reasons a general treatment of contingent statements as a special case of absolute statements is impossible.

In natural semantics, on the other hand, absolute statements may always be treated as a special case of contingent statements. For the SLIM theory of language, absolute statements are special only insofar as (i) they can be interpreted independently of their STAR and (ii) the cognitive responsibility for their content is transferred from the individual speaker to society and its historically evolved view of the world.

Thus, an absolute statement like The chemical formula of water is H_2O is true^c if there is a correctly functioning chain of communication between the speaker and the responsible experts.[5] The true sentences of absolute scientific and logically mathe-

---

[3] A limiting case of this approach is the possibility that two errors accidentally cancel each other such that a statement happens to be true despite faulty processing. The crucial fact here is not that an isolated statement turns out to be true by accident, but rather the combination of errors. Statistically, this special case will occur very rarely and a doubly faulty cognition of a robot will reveal itself in the obvious defects of the vast majority of its utterances.

[4] See the sample analyses at the end of PTQ (Chap. 8 in Montague 1974).

[5] The notion of a 'causal chain' from one speaker to the next is emphasized in Kripke (1972), especially with regards to proper names and natural classes. The central role of 'experts' in

matical systems are thus reconstructed contingently by interpreting them as cognitive accomplishments of the associated human – and thus fallible – society.

From this anthropological point of view it is quite normal that an absolute statement may be considered true^c at certain times – due to the majority opinion of the experts – yet later turn out to be false^c. Such mishaps have happened and still happen quite frequently in the history of science, as shown by statements like Fire is based on the material substance of phlogiston or, closer to home, The surface is determined by repeated application of certain formal operations called "grammatical transformations" to [base phrase markers].[6]

The differences in the truth predicates of natural and logical semantics derive directly from the structural difference between their respective [−sense, −constructive] and [+sense, +constructive] ontologies:

21.1.1 ONTOLOGICAL FOUNDATION OF CONTINGENT AND LOGICAL TRUTH

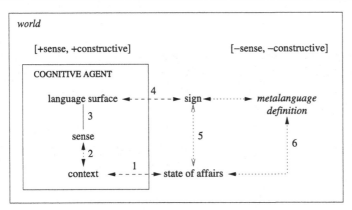

Both systems treat truth as relation 5 between the external sign and the external state of affairs. But they use different methods and concepts to realize this relation.

The [−sense, −constructive] system defines relation 5 directly by means of a suitable metalanguage definition 6. The state of affairs and the language expression are defined by the logician, who – in accordance with the ontology presumed – abstracts away all interpersonal aspects of communication.[7] The set-theoretic model and the metalanguage-based interpretation of the expression are designed to realize formally

---

the scientific specification of certain meanings in the language community – e.g., analyzing water as H_2O – is stressed in Putnam (1975), but with the absurd conclusion *that meanings just ain't in the head* (op. cit., p. 227). These authors investigate meaning and reference as a precondition for the foundation of truth, but they fail to make the necessary distinctions between the semantics of logical and natural languages, between a [−sense, −constructive] and a [+sense, +constructive] ontology, and between absolute and contingent truth.

[6] See 4.5.2 and 8.5.6.

[7] For the logician, the state of affairs is not given by nature, but must be defined as a specific formal model $\mathcal{M}$. Strictly speaking, logic does not define relation 5 in the world, but only in a formal system designed to resemble the world.

what is assumed as obvious to begin with. The purpose is the explicit derivation of truth values based on if-then clauses.

In a [+sense, +constructive] system, on the other hand, the real world surrounding the cognitive agent naturally provides a state of affairs. It must be analyzed automatically via the agent's external interfaces in certain relevant aspects in order to construct a corresponding agent-internal context of use. Relation 5 between the external sign and the external state of affairs is thus established solely in terms of cognitive procedures based on the components 1 (contextual recognition/action), 2 (pragmatic interpretation), 3 (semantic interpretation), and 4 (language-based recognition/action). The purpose is communicating contextual contents by means of natural language between cognitive agents.

In summary, the contingent truth values $true^c$ and $false^c$ concentrate on the cognitive functions of concrete speaker-hearers in the evaluation of concrete utterances. The logical truth values 1 and 0, on the other hand, leave these aspects aside, taking the view of an omniscient being who evaluates the relation between expression types and states of affairs independently of (the existence of) concrete speaker-hearers.

21.2 Epimenides in a [+sense, +constructive] System

Based on the contingent truth values $true^c$ and $false^c$, let us reanalyze the Epimenides paradox. In contradistinction to Tarski's analysis (Sect. 19.5), the following [+sense, +constructive] analysis permits an object-language to contain the words true and false without causing its semantics to be inconsistent.

In preparation for this reanalysis, consider a nonparadoxical use of the expression C is not a true sentence. This expression, used by Tarski to derive the Epimenides paradox, consists of a language-based abbreviation, C, and a negative truth statement. Its legitimate use within a [+sense, +constructive] system is based on the following structure:

21.2.1 BENIGN CASE OF A LANGUAGE-BASED ABBREVIATION

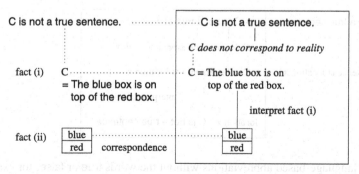

C abbreviates the expression The blue box is on the red box. The abbreviation is shown in the external task environment as fact (i). In addition, the task environment contains the state of affairs described by the sentence abbreviated as C, shown as fact (ii).

When the expression C is not a true sentence is processed by a [+sense, +constructive] system, e.g., CURIOUS, the semantics assigns to the surface a meaning$_1$ which may be paraphrased as *C does not correspond to reality*. For this semantic representation the pragmatics attempts to supply a matching contextual structure.

Thereby it turns out that C is defined as an abbreviation of the expression The blue box is on top of the red box according to fact (i). The remaining part of the input expression, i.e., is not a true sentence, is processed by the pragmatic component by checking whether the content of the long version of C corresponds to reality. The meaning$_1$ of The blue box is on top of the red box is matched with the corresponding subcontext, namely fact (ii), whereby it turns out that they *do* correspond. Thus the original input C is not a true sentence is evaluated as false^c.

This result may cause a suitably developed robot to react in various different ways. If it is in a righteous mood, it may protest and argue that C is in fact true. If it is forbearing, it might quietly register that the speaker was joking, cheating, or plain wrong. If it is cooperative, it will discuss the facts with the speaker to discover where their respective interpretations diverge, in order to arrive at an agreement.

There are many language-based abbreviations in combination with contingent truth statements which are as benign as they are normal.[8] For example, the position of the boxes in fact (ii) of 21.2.2 may be inverted, in which case the input sentence would be evaluated as true^c. Or fact (ii) may be removed from the task environment of CURIOUS, in which case the robot could not check the truth of the input sentence on its own. Whether the robot will use unverified hearsay should depend on whether the speaker providing it has earned the status of a reliable partner or not (CoL, p. 280 f).

A special case of a language-based abbreviation is the Epimenides paradox. Its [+sense, +constructive] reanalysis has the following structure:

21.2.2 RECONSTRUCTION OF THE EPIMENIDES PARADOX

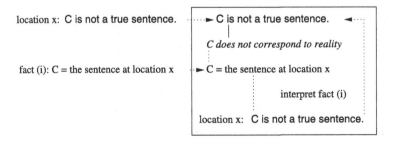

---

[8] They also include language-based abbreviations without the words true or false, for example, C consists of eight words or C consists of seven words. Relative to the situation 21.2.1 these sentences would be evaluated as true^c and false^c, respectively. See Quine (1960).

In a clearly marked location x, the robot reads C is not a true sentence and assigns to it the meaning$_1$ *C doesn't correspond to reality*. As in 21.2.1, the pragmatics attempts to supply a context of use corresponding to this meaning$_1$.

Taking into account fact (i), it turns out that C is defined as an abbreviation of The sentence at location x. The remaining part of the input sentence, i.e., is not true, is processed by the pragmatics by checking whether the content of what C abbreviates corresponds to reality. For this, the meaning$_1$ of The sentence at location x is matched with a corresponding subcontext. In contrast to 21.2.1, where the meaning$_1$ of The blue box is on the red box is matched with the contextual (nonlanguage) fact (ii), the meaning$_1$ of The sentence at location x in 21.2.2 leads to the language-based referent (sign) C is not true.

At this point, the pragmatics may treat the referential object C is not true as an uninterpreted or as an interpreted sign. Treating it as an uninterpreted sign would be reasonable in combination with, for example, *is printed in sans serif*. In 21.2.2, however, treatment as an uninterpreted sign would make no sense. Rather, the most natural action would seem to interpret the sign, and this starts the semantic-pragmatic interpretation procedure all over again.

Thus, if the external circumstances bring a [+sense, +constructive] system into the special situation of the Epimenides paradox, it will get into a cycle and – without additional assumptions – will remain there. As shown schematically in 21.2.2, the C in C is not true will be replaced again and again with the corresponding sentence at location x.

Our ontologically based reanalysis of the Epimenides paradox does not result in its resolution, but rather in its transformation. What appears as a logical contradiction on the level of the semantics in Tarski's [−sense, −constructive] system (Sect. 19.5) reappears as an infinite recursion of the semantic-pragmatic interpretation. The [+constructive, +sense] reanalysis disarms the Epimenides paradox, both on the level of the semantics and the theory of communication, because

- the words true^c and false^c may be part of the object language without causing a logical contradiction in its semantics, and
- the recursion caused by the Epimenides paradox can be recognized in the pragmatics and taken care of as a familiar[9] kind of failing interpretation without adversely affecting the communicative functioning of the system.

The reanalysis avoids Tarski's contradiction in the semantics because the metalanguage distinguishes between (i) the logical truth values 1 and 0 of the T-condition, (ii) the contingent truth values true^c and false^c of the object language, and replaces the

---

[9] It holds in general of pragmatic interpretation that a continuous repetition in the analysis of one and the same contextual object should be prevented, for example, by means of a counter. In this way the recursion caused by the Epimenides paradox may be recognized and stopped. Discontinuing a particular interpretation attempt in order to choose an alternative scheme of interpretation or to ask for clarification are normal parts of pragmatics.

metalanguage phrase is (not) a true sentence with the (iii) procedural correlate *does (not) correspond to reality*.

If we were to assume that the semantic component of CURIOUS was a truth-conditional semantics like Montague grammar, then the [+sense, +constructive] reanalysis of the Epimenides paradox would not result in Tarski's contradiction

a. C is 1 if and only if C is not 1

but rather in the contingent statement

b. C is 1 if and only if C does not correspond to reality.

In contrast to version *a*, version *b* does not contain a logical contradiction.

For the SLIM theory of language, the reanalysis of the Epimenides paradox is important. The reanalysis opens the way to define a *complete* semantics of natural language because it avoids contradiction even if the language to be modeled contains the words true and false.

For the logical semantics of natural language, on the other hand, the reanalysis is of little help. This is because the procedural notion of contingent truth – essential for avoiding Tarski's contradiction – can be neither motivated nor implemented outside a [+constructive, +sense] ontology.

21.3 Frege's Principle as Homomorphism

In artificial languages, the form of the syntax and its associated semantics is decided by the language designers. Their job is to *construct* the artificial language as best as possible for a given task. The natural languages, on the other hand, are given in all their variety as the historically evolved conventions of their speech communities.

Computational linguistics has the task of functionally *reconstructing* the mechanism of natural language communication as realistically as possible (reverse engineering). The starting point of this reconstruction is the natural surfaces, because they are manifested in the acoustical or visual modality as concrete signs.

The meanings, on the other hand, are of a cognitive nature. They lie in the dark for the outside observer (4.3.2), and can only be deduced from (i) the lexical and syntactic properties of the surfaces and (ii) their use in different contexts of interpretation.

At the most basic level, the deduction is based on Frege's principle (4.4.1), according to which the meaning of a complex expression results from the meaning of its parts and the mode of their composition. Thus the purpose of natural syntax is the composition of semantic representations by putting together the associated surfaces.

The building up of complex meanings$_1$ via syntactic composition is achieved by defining (i) for each word form a semantic counterpart and (ii) for each syntactic operation a simultaneous semantic operation. Montague formalized this structural correlation between syntax and semantics mathematically as a *homomorphism*.[10]

---

[10] The formal definitions may be found in Montague's paper *Universal Grammar*, Montague (1974), especially pp. 232–233.

The notion of a homomorphism captures the intuitive concept of a *structural simi-larity* between two complex objects. A structural object so is homomorphic to another structural object SO if for each basic element of so there is a (not necessarily basic) counterpart in SO, and for each relation between elements in so there is a correspond-ing relation between corresponding elements in SO.

To express the structural similarity between the semantic level and the surface level, Montague defined a homomorphism formally as a relation between two (uninter-preted) languages.

21.3.1 FORMAL DEFINITION OF A HOMOMORPHISM

Language-2 is homomorphic to language-1 if there is a function T which

- assigns to each word of category a in language-1 a corresponding expression of category A in language-2, and
- assigns to each n-place composition f in language-1 a corresponding n-place com-position F in language-2, such that
- $T(f(a, b)) = F((T(a))(T(b)))$.

According to this definition, the following are equivalent: either (i) combining a and b first in language-1 via f(a,b) after which the result a_b is translated by T into A-B of language-2, or (ii) translating a and b first via T(a) and T(b) into A and B, respectively, and then combining them in language-2 via F(A,B) into A-B:

21.3.2 SCHEMATIC REPRESENTATION OF MONTAGUE'S HOMOMORPHISM

```
language–1:              f (a, b)  ────►  a _ b
                    T       │ │                │
language–2:             F (A, B)  ────►   A–B
```

A grammar in which the semantics (i.e., language-2) is homomorphic to the syntax (i.e., language-1) satisfies the so-called homomorphism condition. In such a system (i) each word form (basic element) in the syntax must be assigned a semantic counterpart (meaning$_1$) and (ii) each syntactic composition of word forms and/or expressions must be assigned a corresponding composition on the semantic level:

21.3.3 SYNTACTIC COMPOSITION WITH HOMOMORPHIC SEMANTICS

```
analyzed surfaces:      a * b  ────►  ab
                        │  │             │
meanings₁:              A * B  ────►  AB
```

The homomorphism condition by itself, however, is not sufficient as a formalization of Frege's principle, insofar as it is defined for *analyzed* surfaces (Sect. 4.4), whereas natural language communication is based on *unanalyzed* surfaces.

The problem is that the transition from unanalyzed to analyzed surfaces (interpreta-tion) and vice versa (production) has been misused to enrich the levels of the analyzed surface and/or the meaning$_1$ by means of zero elements or identity mappings. From the viewpoint of the SLIM theory of language, this is strictly illegal because it violates the methodological principle of surface compositionality.

The use of zero elements and identity mappings is illustrated schematically in 21.3.4 and 21.3.5, respectively, in which the zero elements are written in italics (\it).

21.3.4 USE OF THE ZERO ELEMENT *b* (illegal)

1. Smuggling in during interpretation (↓) – Filtering out during production (↑)

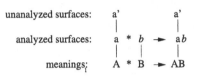

2. Filtering out during interpretation (↓) – Smuggling in during production (↑)

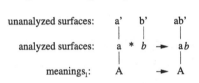

Zero elements of kind 1 are postulated whenever the unanalyzed surface does not provide what the grammar theory at hand would like to find. Examples are the postulation of a 'zero determiner' in

Peter drank *det* wine

or a 'zero subject' in the imperative

you help me!

Zero elements of kind 2 are postulated whenever the surface contains something which the grammar theory at hand would not like to find. Examples are (i) the conjunctions *that* in sentential objects, e.g.,

Peter believes *that* Jim is tired.

and (ii) *to* in infinitives. They are regarded as superfluous and called 'syntactic sugar.'
The two kinds of zero elements are also combined, as in the passive

det wine *was* ordered *by* Peter

or in infinitives

Peter promised Jim *to Peter* sleep
Peter persuaded Jim *to Jim* sleep.

Being at the core of nativism's "linguistic generalizations," zero elements continue to be popular. They are usually supported with elaborate linguistic argumentations, as for example by Chomsky, who calls his zero elements 'traces.'

Because zero elements are not marked in the unanalyzed surface or the meaning$_1$, they must be inferred by the parser. This is done by (i) adding them hypothetically into all possible positions and (ii) testing each case by attempting a derivation.

As soon as a formal theory of grammar admits a single zero element, any given unanalyzed surface or meaning$_1$ raises the question of where and how often this zero element should be postulated. For this reason the use of zero elements pushes the complexity of such systems sky-high, making them either $\mathcal{N}P$-complete or undecidable (Chaps. 8, 12).

Equivalent to the problem caused by zero elements is the one caused by identity mappings of the form x ∘ y → x. This is shown by the schematic examples in 21.3.5, which use no zero elements in the input to the composition rules, yet have the same outputs as in 21.3.4. The reason is that the rule of composition suppresses the contribution of b in the surface (kind 1) or in the meaning (kind 2).

21.3.5 USE OF AN IDENTITY MAPPING (illegal)

1. Filtering out during production (↑) – Smuggling in during interpretation (↓)

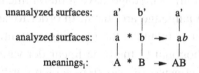

2. Smuggling in during production (↑) – Filtering out during interpretation (↓)

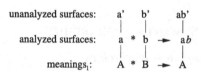

It has been argued that zero elements and identity mappings do not violate the homomorphism definition 21.3.1.[11] This requires, however, that the choice between treating the element marked by italics as part of the homomorphism (as required by the kind 1 structures) or not (as required by the kind 2 structures) is left open. Not making the choice explicit is a clear violation of mathematical method.

In short, zero elements and identity mappings alike (i) destroy the systematic correlation between syntax and semantics, (ii) have a devastating effect on mathematical complexity, and (iii) fail to maintain the minimal methodological standard of concreteness. To ensure a proper functioning of the homomorphism condition and to prevent the use of zero elements and identity mappings, we present a formally oriented variant of the SC-I principle (4.5.1).

---

[11] Even Montague used quasi-transformational derivations of anaphoric pronouns and a syncategorematic treatment of logical operators, thus violating the spirit of Frege's principle and the homomorphism condition. A detailed account may be found in SCG.

21.3.6 SURFACE COMPOSITIONALITY II (SC-II PRINCIPLE)

A semantically interpreted grammar is surface compositional if and only if

- the syntax is restricted to the composition of concrete word forms (i.e., no zero elements and no identity mappings),
- the semantics is homomorphic to the syntax (as defined in 21.3.1), and
- objects and operations on the level of semantics which correspond to the syntax in accordance with the homomorphism condition may not be realized by zero elements or identity mappings.

The SC-I principle applies Frege's principle to concrete surfaces of language in order to arrive at (i) a strictly compositional syntax and (ii) a clear separation of semantics and pragmatics. The SC-II principle makes this goal more precise by defining surface compositionality as a formal strengthening of the homomorphism condition.

21.4 Time-Linear Syntax with Homomorphic Semantics

The functor-argument constructions of natural language have a hierarchical semantic structure, while the surfaces of natural language are linear. In order to supply the time-linear derivation with a homomorphic semantics, the resulting semantic hierarchy must be built in a manner that is orthogonal to the time-linear derivation structure.[12] This comparatively new method[13] consists of two steps which correspond to the conditions of the homomorphism condition:

21.4.1 TIME-LINEAR BUILDING UP OF SEMANTIC HIERARCHIES

Step 1: *Translation of word forms into component hierarchies*
Each word form is mapped into a semantic component hierarchy (tree). The structure of the tree is determined by the syntactic category of the word form.

---

[12] This is different from the traditional method of building semantic hierarchies by means of possible substitutions. As shown in 10.1.6, PS Grammar derives semantically motivated hierarchies (constituent structures at the level of deep structure) by substituting elementary nodes with more complex structures (top-down branching); C Grammar derives such hierarchies by substituting complex structures with elementary nodes (bottom-up amalgamating).

In other words, the formalisms of PS and C Grammar in their respective context-free forms are alike in that their linguistic applications are (i) conceptually based on constituent structure (Sects. 8.4, 8.5) and (ii) achieve the buildup of the constituent structure hierarchies by using syntactic derivations which directly reflect the structure of the underlying semantic intuitions. This method is not compatible with a time-linear derivation order and therefore unsuitable for semantically interpreting an LA Grammar.

[13] An informal description was first presented in CoL, pp. 42f., and illustrated with an LA parser for a semantically interpreted fragment of English (op.cit., pp. 345–402).

Step 2: *Left-associative combination of component hierarchies*
For each combination of the left-associative syntax there is defined a corresponding combination of component hierarchies on the level of the semantics.

Step 1 is illustrated below with the analyzed word forms the and man.

21.4.2 DERIVATION OF COMPONENT HIERARCHIES FROM WORD FORMS

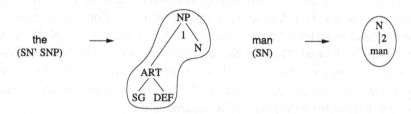

The two subtrees are derived automatically from the categories (SN′ SNP) and (SN), respectively. The subtree of content words contains the associated concept type, represented by the base form of the surface (here man). Next consider step 2:

21.4.3 TIME-LINEAR COMPOSITION WITH HOMOMORPHIC SEMANTICS

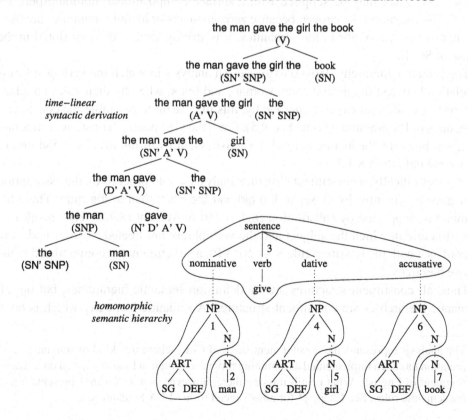

For each word form in the syntax there is a corresponding elementary component tree and for each left-associative composition in the syntax there is a composition of component trees in the semantics. To indicate the strictly compositional nature of the semantic hierarchy, the elementary component trees are outlined graphically and each is marked with the position number of the word form from which it was derived.

For example, component tree 1 (for the in position 1) is a functor, which takes the component tree 2 (for man in position 2) as its argument. The resulting (complex) component tree 1+2 (i.e., the NP representing the man) is a sentence start which serves as the argument for the (elementary) component tree 3. Component tree 3 is derived from the third word form gave, whereby the syntactic category (N′ D′ A′ V) determines the form of the tree. The resulting complex tree 1+2+3 is then combined with the elementary component tree 4, which serves as an argument derived from the determiner the. The complex component tree 1+2+3+4 in turn takes the elementary component tree 5 derived from the noun girl as argument, etc.

The category-based derivation of elementary subtrees from the word forms is handled by automatic word form recognition (LA Morph). The time-linear combination of the semantic component trees is handled by semantic clauses in the combination rules of LA Syntax.

The simultaneous syntactic-semantic derivation shows in principle[14] how a time-linear LA Syntax may be supplied with a surface compositional, homomorphic semantic interpretation. Moreover, because zero-elements or identity mappings are used neither in the syntax nor in the semantics, it is strictly surface compositional in the sense of SC-II.

The semantic hierarchy derived expresses an analysis in which the verb give forms a relation between the actants man, woman, and book, whereby their roles are characterized by different cases. Superficially, this may seem to resemble the constituent structures of PS-grammar (Sects. 8.4–9.5). From the viewpoint of constituent structure analysis, however, the hierarchy in 21.4.3 satisfies neither its intuitive assumptions nor its formal definition 8.4.3.

More specifically, a constituent structure analysis would proceed on the assumption that gave is semantically closer to the girl and the book than to the man. These assumptions, supported by substitution (8.4.7) and movement (8.4.8) tests, result in a tree structure in which the subject and the verb phrase are treated as sister nodes (in accordance with the rewriting rule S → NP VP), a structure not accommodated in the above hierarchy.

Thus, all constituent structures are by definition semantic hierarchies, but not all semantic hierarchies are constituent structures. A semantic hierarchy which is not a

---

[14] The analysis represents the development stage of CoL, where this kind of semantic interpretation has been implemented as a running program written in Lisp and tested on a sizable fragment of English. What is still missing there, however, is a *declarative* presentation of the semantic rules. See Chap. 24 for an advanced form of LA Semantics.

constituent structure is illustrated in 21.4.3. It is motivated linguistically in terms of two general principles, namely (i) the functor-argument structure and (ii) the time-linear derivation order of natural language.

21.5 Complexity of Natural Language Semantics

According to the CoNSyx hypothesis 12.5.7, the natural languages fit into the class of C1 languages (Sect. 11.5) and parse in linear time. The benefits of an efficient syntax are wasted, however, if its semantic interpretation has mathematical properties which push the overall system into a complexity class higher than that of the syntax alone. For this reason a formal semantic interpretation of an LA Syntax for natural language is empirically suitable only if the semantic interpretation does not increase the complexity of the resulting overall system as compared to the syntax alone.

That the low complexity of a syntactic system may easily be pushed sky-high by the semantic interpretation is illustrated by the following examples from mathematics:

(a) π (b)   1:3
        | |
    3,14159265...   1' :' 3' = 0,333...

Both examples satisfy the homomorphism condition. In example (a), the word form π (Pi), standing for the ratio of the circumference of a circle to its diameter, denotes an infinitely long transcendental number. In example (b), the simple syntactic structure 1:3 denotes an infinitely long periodic number.

These examples show that an elementary word form or a very simple composition can denote infinitely long numbers in mathematics or nonterminating procedures in computer programs. Thereby, the semantic interpretation pushes the complexity from linear in the original syntax to exponential or undecidable in the overall system.

How can natural language semantics retain low complexity if it includes mathematical objects which are infinite and thus of high complexity? The crucial structural basis for this is the principled distinction between (i) the meaning$_1$ of language expressions, (ii) the internal subcontext providing the contextual referents, and (iii) the external counterparts of the contextual referents.

According to the SLIM-theoretic analysis of natural communication, one function of meaning$_1$ is as a *key* to information which is stored in the intended 'files' of the internal subcontext (Sect. 5.3). To perform this function, minimal meanings$_1$ suffice. They must be differentiated only to the degree that the correct contextual referents and relations can be matched. This process is supported by preselecting and restricting the relevant subcontext using the pragmatic circumstances of the interpretation (especially the STAR, 5.3.2).

The basic accessing function of natural language meaning shows up in the example Suzanne is writing a thesis on the Trakhtenbrot Theorem. We have no trouble understanding this sentence even if we have no idea of the mathematical content referred to with the noun phrase Trakhtenbrot Theorem. The relation between the key, the context file, and the mathematical content may be represented schematically as follows:

21.5.1 INTERPRETATION OF 'TRAKHTENBROT THEOREM'

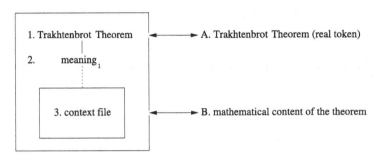

The left-hand side shows the speaker-hearer's internal processing of language while the right-hand side shows the external situation with (A) the sign Trakhtenbrot Theorem and (B) the corresponding mathematical content. Analogous to 20.5.2 and 21.1.1, the internal analysis is based on the [+sense, +constructive] ontology of the SLIM theory of language, while the associated external analysis represents the [−sense, −constructive] ontology of mathematical realism.

In accordance with mathematical realism, the content of the theorem is located in the external real world, outside the cognitive agent.[15] The meaning$_1$ of the expression Trakhtenbrot Theorem in natural semantics, in contrast, is a cognitive, speaker-hearer-internal concept. It may be paraphrased roughly as *mathematical theorem discovered by a person named Trakhtenbrot*. This minimal semantic representation is sufficient as the key to contextual files the content of which may vary widely from one speaker-hearer to another, depending on their knowledge of mathematics in general and Trakhtenbrot's Theorem in particular.

For example, if a speaker-hearer encounters the expression Trakhtenbrot Theorem for the first time, a new contextual file is opened which contains no more than the expression and the circumstances of the utterance situation. An average speaker-hearer may nevertheless be said to understand the expression in such a situation – as shown by the fact the he would be able to, for example, procure literature on the theorem.

A more demanding task would be to recognize the theorem solely on the basis of its content, as when choosing it from a collection of unnamed theorems. For this, the relevant contextual file of the speaker-hearer would have to contain specialized

---

[15] This example shows clearly that the difficulties of logical semantics with the Epimenides paradox (Sect. 19.5), the analysis of propositional attitudes (Sect. 20.3), and the treatment of vagueness (Sect. 20.5) do not argue against mathematical realism and its [−sense, −constructive] ontology at all. Rather, the described difficulties of logic result solely from the misguided attempt to transfer a [−sense, −constructive] semantics designed for the treatment of mathematical and natural science to the meaning analysis of natural language.

mathematical knowledge. The acquisition of this knowledge does not affect the literal meaning of the expression Trakhtenbrot Theorem, however, but only the associated contextual file of an individual speaker-hearer.[16]

Structures of high mathematical complexity have no place in the semantic component (2) of natural language. Like the vastness of the universe, the laws of physics, or real beer mugs, they exist outside of the cognitive agent in position B and in a secondary way as contextual structures in position 3 of 21.5.1. Even contextual referents which do not originate in the external reality, like the acute individual toothache[17] of a cognitive agent, should not be treated in position 2 but located instead in the relevant internal subcontext 3.

The functioning of language meanings as keys for accessing the potentially complex – though always finite – contents of the internal context does not require that the semantics be of any higher complexity than the associated syntax. This conclusion is summarized as the **Complexity of Natural language Semantics** hypothesis, or CoNSem hypothesis for short:

21.5.2 CoNSem (Complexity of Nat. Lang. Semantics) Hypothesis

The semantic interpretation of a natural language syntax within the C LAGs is empirically adequate only if there is a finite constant k such that

– it holds for each elementary word form in the syntax that the associated semantic representation consists of at most k elements, and

– it holds for each elementary composition in the syntax that the associated semantic composition increases the number of elements introduced by the two semantic input expressions by maximally k elements in the output.

This means that the semantic interpretation of syntactically analyzed input of length n consists of maximally $(2n - 1) \cdot k$ elements.

A semantic interpretation which complies with the CoNSem hypothesis will increase the complexity of the overall system – as compared to the syntax alone – by only a constant. For example, if $k = 5$, then the semantic interpretation of a syntactically analyzed input of length 3 will consist of maximally $(2 \cdot 3 - 1) \cdot 5 = 25$ elements:

21.5.3 Illustration of the CoNSem Hypothesis

$$a \quad * \quad b \quad \longrightarrow \quad ab \quad * \quad c \quad \longrightarrow \quad abc$$

$$[1–5] \quad \& \quad [6–10] \qquad [1–15] \quad \& \quad [16–20] \qquad [1–25]$$

---

[16] A similar analysis holds for the expression π. From the viewpoint of mathematical realism, the referent of π may be regarded as an infinitely long number in position B of 21.5.1. Its internal, cognitive counterpart in position 3, on the other hand, is a finite approximation, contained in a context file which may be accessed by a minimal meaning$_1$ (position 2).

[17] Cf. footnote 9 in Sect. 20.3.

In other words, CoNSem systems are in the same overall complexity class as their C LAG syntax alone.

The CoNSem hypothesis is applicable to the whole class of C LAGs. This is because (i) C LAGs limit the complexity of syntactic composition by a finite constant and (ii) different degrees of complexity within the C LAGs are caused solely by different degrees of ambiguity.[18] For the analysis of natural languages, however, the CoNSem hypothesis is of special interest in connection with the CoNSyx hypothesis 12.5.7, which puts the syntax of natural languages into the linear class of C1 LAGs.

CoNSyx and CoNSem are empirical hypotheses and as such they can neither be proven nor refuted through logic alone. Instead they serve as formal constraints. Their joint fulfillment guarantees any empirical analysis of natural language to be of linear complexity.

To refute the two hypotheses one would have to present constructions of natural language which clearly cannot be analyzed within the boundaries of CoNSyx and CoNSem. Conversely, to support the two hypotheses it must be shown in the long run that maintaining them does not create unsurmountable difficulties – in contradistinction to, for example, the historical precedent of constituent structure.[19]

Whether or not the empirical analysis of a problematic construction will satisfy CoNSyx and CoNSem depends not only on the skill of the person doing the syntactic-semantic analysis, but also on the question of whether the problem in question is really of a syntactic-semantic nature (cf. 12.5.5 and 12.5.6 as well as 20.5.1 and 20.5.2). Therefore the possibility of maintaining the CoNSyx and CoNSem hypotheses can only be properly evaluated relative to a functioning overall model of natural language communication.

Exercises

Section 21.1
1. Explain the notion of a logical proposition in comparison to the notions 'utterance' and 'expression.'
2. Describe the difference between absolute and contingent propositions using examples.

---

[18] Sects. 11.4 and 11.5.

[19] The principle of constituent structure turned out to be incompatible with the empirical facts because of the discovery – or rather the belated recognition – of discontinuous structures. See Sects. 8.4 and 8.5.

3. How are logical truth values represented formally?
4. What is the difference between the notions of logical and contingent truth?
5. What are the preconditions for the interpretation of contingent propositions, and why is it that absolute propositions seem to be free from these preconditions?
6. Why is it impossible for logical semantics to treat contingent propositions generally as a special case of absolute propositions?
7. How is the status of truth affected by the reanalysis of absolute propositions as special cases of contingent propositions?
8. What role is played by the 'experts' in determining the contingent truth value of absolute propositions?
9. Describe how [+sense, +constructive] and [−sense, −constructive] systems differ in their respective methods for establishing a relation between language expressions and states of affairs.
10. What is meant by the words true and false in everyday communication?

Section 21.2

1. Explain the interpretation of the sentence C is not true within the framework of a [+sense, +constructive] system using the analysis of a benign example.
2. Explain the reanalysis of the Epimenides paradox in a [+sense, +constructive] system.
3. Why does the reanalysis of the Epimenides paradox require a change of Tarski's ontology?
4. What is the difference between treating a given language expression as an uninterpreted vs. an interpreted sign? Explain the difference using examples from Quine (1960).
5. Is the Epimenides paradox based on a contingent or an absolute proposition?
6. In what sense is the Epimenides paradox preserved in the [+sense, +constructive] reanalysis and in what sense is it disarmed?
7. Why is the introduction of contingent truth values crucial for the definition of an object language which can contain the words true and false without making the overall semantics inconsistent?
8. To what degree is a transfer of logical semantic analyses to the semantics of natural language possible?
9. Why is the reanalysis of the Epimenides paradox of little help to the logical semantics of natural language?
10. What kinds of errors in the cognitive processing of a [+sense, +constructive] system result in false statements? When does the system produce true statements?

Section 21.3

1. How do the artificial and the natural languages differ from the viewpoint of a language designer?

2. What is the connection between Frege's principle, surface compositionality, and Montague's use of a homomorphism to relate syntax and semantics?
3. Explain the formal definition of a homomorphism and illustrate it with a formal example.
4. Explain why the use of zero elements and identity mappings makes the homomorphism condition vacuous.
5. What mathematically dubious assumption is needed for arguing that zero elements and identity mappings do not formally violate the homomorphism condition?
6. Why does the use of zero elements increase the mathematical complexity of a system?
7. Why does the use of zero elements violate the most minimal methodological standard of concreteness?

Section 21.4
1. Explain the SC-II principle in comparison with SC-I.
2. Why is the fixed surface compositional connection between the semantics and the syntax functionally necessary in natural communication?
3. Describe three different methods of building up a semantic hierarchy.
4. Why is a time-linear building up of semantic hierarchies compatible with maintaining a homomorphic semantics?
5. What is meant by the 'functor-argument structure' of a semantics?

Section 21.5
1. What is the complexity class of an LA Syntax for natural language?
2. Show with examples why a semantic interpretation can increase the complexity of a syntactic system.
3. Explain the functioning of natural language meanings using the Trakhtenbrot Theorem example.
4. Summarize why the underlying theory of language has a direct impact on the complexity of syntax and semantics, using the example of PP-attachment (Sect. 12.5) for syntax and the example π for semantics.
5. Summarize why the underlying theory of language has a direct impact on the way in which relevant phenomena are analyzed, using the examples of the Epimenides paradox, propositional attitudes, vagueness, intensional contexts, and semantic presuppositions.
6. Why is a [−sense, −constructive] ontology appropriate for mathematical realism, but not for the analysis of natural language?
7. What is the CoNSem hypothesis and what would be required to refute it?

22. Database Semantics

The SLIM[1] theory of language outlined in Chaps. 3–6 serves as the theoretical foundation for a computational model of natural language communication, called Database
Semantics (DBS).[2] Database Semantics models the transfer of information from the
speaker to the hearer by representing the knowledge of speaker and hearer, respectively, in the form of agent-internal databases. Natural language communication is
successful if a certain database content, encoded by the speaker into natural language
signs, is reconstructed analogously in the database of the hearer.

Section 22.1 illustrates the database metaphor of natural communication with a simple example. Section 22.2 explains that logical models and frame-theoretic knowledge
bases lead to problems of *descriptive aporia* and *embarrassment of riches*, making
them unsuitable for representing the agent-internal context of use. Section 22.3 provides the NEWCAT rule format (used in Chaps. 16–18) with a semantic interpretation.
The resulting contents are shown in Sect. 22.4 to be suitable for modeling reference
as a pattern matching between the language and context levels. Section 22.5 discusses
an instant in which adding the semantic interpretation simplifies the NEWCAT syntax.

22.1 Database Metaphor of Natural Communication

A computational model of natural language communication must do without postulating an external relation between the sign and the referent, as in [−sense, −con-
structive] systems (Sect. 20.4). Using a [+sense, +constructive] ontology instead,
SLIM treats reference as an agent-internal, cognitive process, based on matching

---

[1] As explained in the Introduction, Sect. XI, the acronym SLIM abbreviates **S**urface compositional, time-**L**inear, **I**nternal **M**atching, which are the methodological, empirical, ontological, and functional principles of the approach. When the acronym is viewed as a word, SLIM
indicates low mathematical complexity, resulting in the computational efficiency required
for real-time processing.

[2] As the name of a specific scientific theory, the term Database Semantics is capitalized. DBS
is distinct from the generic use of the term in the sense of "semantics of databases." For
example, Bertossi et al. (eds.) (2003) discuss semantic constraints on databases.

between language meanings and contextual counterparts. This basic principle of Internal Matching[3] is illustrated below with the schematic structure of a talking robot:[4]

22.1.1 IMMEDIATE REFERENCE BASED ON INTERNAL MATCHING

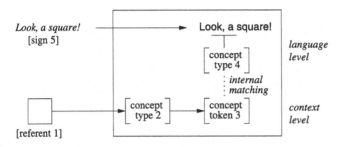

The schema shows the core values (concepts) without their embedding into proplet shells (Sect. 3.4). The robot recognizes the referent [1] by applying the concept type [2] (3.3.1) to the incoming parameter values (3.2.3) and instantiating the referent as a concept token [3] (3.3.3). The sign [5] is recognized in a similar way. The lexicon assigns to the sign square the concept type [2] as its literal meaning [4].[5]

The relation between the levels of language and context is established by matching the (language) concept type [4] and the (context) concept token [3] (4.2.2). A concept type used as a literal meaning may be matched with any number of referential tokens. This models the flexibility which distinguishes the natural from the logical and programming languages (Sects. 19.1 and 19.2).

Internal matching with an isolated content word, here square, may be extended to full-blown natural language communication. According to the database metaphor, the speaker's and the hearer's knowledge are contained in agent-internal databases. Communication is successful if the speaker encodes a certain content into language, and the hearer reconstructs this content analogously in his database – in terms of (i) a correct decoding and (ii) a correct storage at a corresponding location.

The speaker's selection of content and the hearer's analogous reconstruction in successful communication constitute a storage and retrieval problem. Its nature may be explained by comparing the interaction between a user and a conventional database (DB interaction), and between a speaker and a hearer (NL communication):

---

[3] Internal matching is represented by the letters IM in the SLIM acronym.

[4] See also Chaps. 3 and 4, especially 4.3.2.

[5] This general component structure will be used in Sect. 23.5 for the ten SLIM states of cognition. To facilitate comparison, the SLIM states are shown uniformly with their external interfaces on the left.

22.1.2 CONVENTIONAL DATABASE INTERACTION

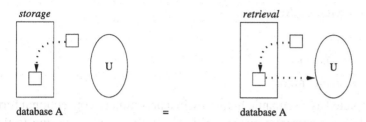

The interaction takes place between two different entities, the user (ovals) and the database (large boxes). The small boxes represent the language signs serving as input and output. The user controls the storage and retrieval operations of the database with a programming language, the commands of which are executed as electronic procedures.

Next consider the transfer of content between a speaker and hearer:

22.1.3 INTERACTION BETWEEN SPEAKER AND HEARER

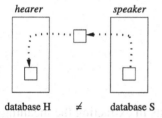

Here the large boxes represent cognitive agents which may be natural or artificial. There is no user. Instead, the interaction takes place between two similar and equal cognitive agents, which control each other's flow of information by alternating in the speak and hear modes (turn-taking). The speaker controls language production as an autonomous agent. The hearer's interpretation is controlled by the incoming language expressions. In contrast to a conventional database, e.g., an RDBMS, no separate index is needed by the hearer to reconstruct the storage location the content had in the speaker's database or to retrieve relevant content for inferencing.

The database metaphor may be applied to statements, questions, and requests alike. In statements, the content encoded by the speaker must be decoded by the hearer and stored in an analogous location. In questions and requests, the hearer must locate the content and the task, respectively, to derive adequate responses.

The database metaphor assumes from the outset that the communicating databases are embedded in cognitive agents, natural or artificial, with language-based as well as nonlanguage-based recognition and action. The latter provide the context of use relative to which the language expressions are interpreted. As an example consider the interpretation of the sentence Fido likes Zach.

Prior to the interpretation we specify a suitable context of use:[6]

22.1.4 SKETCH OF A SIMPLE SUBCONTEXT

The subcontext is depicted as a semantic hierarchy in a preliminary conventional form familiar from knowledge representations in artificial intelligence. According to this representation, Fido is a dog, Felix and Fritz are his friends, and Zach and Eddie are his brothers.

In the hear mode, the pragmatic interpretation of the expression Fido likes Zach consists in embedding the expression's meaning$_1$ into the context structure. This means that the context is extended to contain the additional relation like between Fido and Zach, as illustrated below.

22.1.5 ADDING THE CONTENT OF *Fido likes Zach* TO 22.1.4

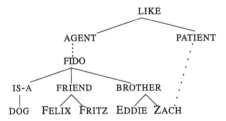

In the speak mode the pragmatic interpretation consists in extracting the meaning$_1$ of Fido likes Zach from the subcontext. This means that the speaker copies a relevant part of the contextual substructure and maps it into natural language.

The task of the pragmatics is to describe the embedding (5.4.1) and extraction (5.4.2) between the semantic representation and the context in terms of explicit, programmable rules. This requires the definition of (i) a grammar including syntax and semantics, (ii) an internal context of use, and (iii) a pragmatics defined as a matching procedure between the semantic representation and the context of use.

22.2 Descriptive Aporia and Embarrassment of Riches

To facilitate implementation of the matching procedure between language meanings and the context of use, the representation of the two levels should be defined in terms of the same formalism. What formalism would be suitable for this purpose? We begin by investigating two well established systems from different traditions, namely (a) formal logic and (b) frame theory.

---

[6] Based on Carbonell and Joseph (1986).

The logical analysis of natural language is exemplified by Montague grammar, which is widely admired for its high standard of formal explicitness and differentiation of content. Within this framework, the information contained in 22.1.4 may be represented equivalently as follows (following Montague (1974), Chap. 8, PTQ):

22.2.1 MODEL-THEORETIC DEFINITION OF THE CONTEXT 22.1.4

Let $\mathcal{MS}$ be a model structure $(A, I, J, \leq, F)$, where A, I, J are sets, and F is a denotation function.

$A, I, J,$ and F have the following definition:

$A = \{a_0, a_1, a_2, a_3, a_4\}$

$I = \{i_1\}$

$J = \{j_1\}$

$F(\text{fido'})(i_1, j_1) = a_0$

$F(\text{felix'})(i_1, j_1) = a_1$

$F(\text{fritz'})(i_1, j_1) = a_2$

$F(\text{zach'})(i_1, j_1) = a_3$

$F(\text{eddie'})(i_1, j_1) = a_4$

$F(\text{dog'})(i_1, j_1) = \{a_0\}$

$F(\text{fido-friend'})(i_1, j_1) = \{a_1, a_2\}$

$F(\text{fido-brother'})(i_1, j_1) = \{a_3, a_4\}$

At the index (i_1, j_1) the proper names fido, felix, zach, and eddie denote the model-theoretic individuals $a_0, a_1, a_2, a_3,$ and a_4, respectively, while the properties fido-friend and fido-brother denote the sets $\{a_1, a_2\}$ and $\{a_3, a_4\}$, respectively.

The original purpose of such a definition is to serve in the explicit interpretation of logical propositions (Sect. 19.3). For example, the semantic interpretation of fido-friend'(felix') relative to the formal model would render the truth value 1, whereas fido-friend'(zach') would be evaluated as 0.

This metalanguage-based derivation of truth values presupposes a [−sense, −constructive] ontology and treats the formal model as a representation of the external real world. It is possible, however, to ontologically reinterpret the formal model structure:

Instead of defining the model as a set-theoretic description of the real, external world in a [−sense, −constructive] approach, we may choose to view it as a specification of the cognitive, internal subcontext in a [+sense, +constructive] system.[7] This instantiates the strategy – used frequently in science – of specifying a new construct (here: the agent-internal context of use) in terms of a known, well-defined formalism (here: model theory).

The reinterpretation uses truth conditions to *build* models which make specific propositions true. These models are used to represent (i) the meaning of language and (ii) the context of use. The goal is to realize internal matching pragmatics by

---

[7] This approach was explored in SCG.

embedding meaning models into context model structures and by extracting meaning models from context model structures in a rhetorically meaningful way.

For example, extending the hearer context to the meaning of a new sentence such as Fido likes Zach would require that the formula

$$F(like)(i_1, j_1) = \{(a_0, a_3)\}$$

be added automatically to 22.2.1, thus asserting the additional relation like between a_0 (Fido) and a_3 (Zach) at (i_1, j_1). Programming this as a hear mode procedure requires inferring the intended referents and the correct index from the sign and its utterance situation (5.3.4), which turns out to be impossible (descriptive aporia).[8]

Another method to formally define a content is frame theory. Based on the programming language Lisp, it has been widely used in artificial intelligence. A frame is an abstract data type consisting of a frame name, an arbitrary number of slots, and for each slot an arbitrary number of fillers. A larger collection of frames is called a knowledge base. Frame systems provide a simple method for adding new information into – and for retrieving specific data from – the knowledge base.

Using the command `(make-frame FRAME (SLOT (value FILLER ...) ...)`, the subcontext 22.1.4 may be defined equivalently as the following frame:

22.2.2 FRAME-THEORETIC DEFINITION OF THE CONTEXT 22.1.4

```
(fido
  (is-a (value dog))
  (friend (value felix fritz))
  (brother (value zach eddie))
)
```

The frame name is fido. It has the slots is-a, friend, and brother. The slot is-a has the value dog, the slot friend has the values felix and fritz, and the slot brother has the values zach and eddie as fillers.

The original purpose of such a definition is storing information which may later be retrieved using commands[9] like `(get-values FRAME SLOT)`. For example, the command

```
(get-values 'FIDO 'FRIEND)
```

would retrieve the values

```
(FELIX FRITZ)
```

assuming that the frame FIDO is defined as in 22.2.2. This retrieval of slot values can be surprisingly useful in larger knowledge bases.[10]

---

[8] For this reason volume II of SCG was never written.

[9] The names of the commands vary between the numerous different implementations of frames. As an introduction, see, for example, Winston and Horn (1984), pp. 311f.

[10] Frame systems usually offer a wealth of additional operations and options, such as for removing information, inheritance, defaults, demons, and views. Despite these additional

It is possible, however, to ontologically reinterpret the frame definition 22.2.2. Instead of viewing it as a [+constructive, −sense] knowledge base to be manipulated by the commands of a programming language, we may choose to view it as an internal subcontext within a [+constructive, +sense] approach.[11] This instantiates once more the strategy of specifying a new concept (here: agent-internal context of use) in terms of a known, implemented formalism (here: frame theory).

The reinterpretation uses frame definitions to represent (i) the meaning of natural language and (ii) the context of use. The goal is to realize internal matching pragmatics by automatically embedding language frames into the context frame and by extracting language frames from the context frame as the basis of rhetorically meaningful utterances.

For example, extending the hearer context to the meaning of a new sentence such as Fido likes Zach would require representing this information as a frame, e.g.,

```
(fido
    (like (value Zach)))
```

and automatically adding the part

```
(like (value Zach)
```

as a new slot to the Fido frame name of 22.2.2.

The problem is that a given piece of information, e.g., a set of propositions, may be represented in many alternative ways in frame theory. For example, instead of making fido the frame name in 22.2.2, we could have arranged the information equivalently by using dog, friend, or brother as frame names. Each of these alternatives requires that the rules for adding and retrieving information be formulated accordingly.

The original [+constructive, −sense] design of a knowledge base expects the *user* to maintain a systematic structuring of the data by operating directly on the knowledge base with the commands of a programming language. Such a structuring is necessary to ensure proper storage and retrieval of the data.

The problem with the [+constructive, +sense] reinterpretation of frame theory for internal matching is that it is impossible to (i) restrict the format as required for the purposes of storage and retrieval, and at the same time (ii) accommodate the variable structures occurring in the interpretation and production of natural language. Thus, effective storage and retrieval is prevented by the structural variety of natural language, which leads to many alternative ways of structuring the same data (embarrassment of riches).[12]

---

structural possibilities, or perhaps because of them, frame systems typically suffer from uncontrolled growth combined with a lack of transparency and difficulties in checking consistency.

[11] This approach was explored in CoL using the FrameKit+ software by Carbonell and Joseph (1986).

[12] For this reason the frame-theoretic approach of CoL was abandoned.

The problems encountered with the reinterpretation of model theory and frame theory, respectively, lead to the conclusion that using the same formalism for defining the meaning of language and the context of interpretation is a necessary, but not a sufficient condition for realizing internal matching pragmatics. Furthermore, the attempts at reinterpreting these traditional formalisms fail ultimately for the same reason:

Because both formalisms are originally based on a [−sense] ontology, their reinterpretation in the [+sense, +constructive] environment of the SLIM theory of language results in the juxtaposition of two levels never designed to interact with each other. The holistic presentation of the two levels as separate, closed entities may be in line with the conceptual explanation of internal matching pragmatics (Chaps. 3–6), but fails to suggest an abstract algorithm for embedding meaning$_1$ into the context (hear mode) and for extracting meaning$_1$ out of the context (speak mode).

The underlying difficulty manifests itself as descriptive aporia in the model-theoretic approach and as an embarrassment of riches in the frame-theoretic approach. These problem types are symptomatic of situations in which a given formal method is inherently unsuitable for the description of the empirical phenomena at hand.

Descriptive aporia arises in situations in which the adopted grammar system does not suffice for the analysis of the phenomena: the alternatives all seem to be equally bad. Embarrassment of riches arises in situations in which the phenomena to be addressed may be analyzed in several different ways within the adopted system: the alternatives all seem to be equally good. Descriptive aporia and embarrassment of riches may also occur simultaneously (Sects. 9.5 and 20.5).

22.3 Combining Categorial Operation and Semantic Interpretation

Unsuitable for reconstructing reference as a pattern matching between the language and the context level inside the cognitive agent, logical formulas (model theory, SCG) and tree structures (frame theory, CoL) raise the question of what else could be done with them. In SCG, the formulas of predicate calculus serving as the semantic representation of English examples are (i) small in number and (ii) based on hand-crafted lambda reductions. When it turned out that this formal system is impossible to program, we designed and programmed the NEWCAT system.

Its extension into the CoL software provided the automatic time-linear generation of trees designed as the semantic representations for 421 grammatical constructions of English (21.4.3). In an age when hundreds of tree banks were and still are constructed all over the world, the trees generated automatically by the CoL method would surely be of some use. Unfortunately, however, none were to be found.

Instead, we discovered additional requirements for a linguistically well-founded semantic representation suitable for building a talking robot – apart from surface compositionality, a time-linear derivation order, and support of internal matching (SLIM). One of these was the storage of content in a database as part of the hear mode and the retrieval of content from the database as part of the speak mode. This resulted in the transition from the SLIM theory of language to Database Semantics (DBS).

DBS does not require any changes of the SLIM theory of language. It only requires the following definitions:

22.3.1 ADDITIONAL CONSTRUCTS REQUIRED BY DBS

1. Basic items: data structure of *proplets*
2. Database schema: content-addressable *word bank*
3. Primary key for storage and retrieval: core and prn value

Let us begin by showing how the linguistic analyses of English (Chap. 17) and German (Chap. 18) syntax can be interpreted semantically by combining (i) the categorial operations and (ii) the semantic interpretations in the rules of an LA Hear grammar.

Consider the syntactic analysis of the example

Field contains triangle and field contains square

shown as a content defined as set of proplets in 3.4.3 and as a DBS graph in 3.4.4. The first derivation step is based on the rule NOM+FV defined in 17.1.4:

22.3.2 APPLICATION OF NOM+FV TO COMPLEX NOMINATIVE NP

input/output:	field	+	contains		field contains
	(snp)		(n' a' v)		(a' v)
NOM+FV – pattern:	(NP)		(NP' X v)	⟶	(X v)

Here the nominative valency position n' of the verb is canceled by the cat value snp of the initial noun. While maintaining an autonomous syntax, a semantic interpretation based on cross-copying the core values of proplets may be added as follows:

22.3.3 HEAR MODE INTERPRETATION OF field contains (COMBINATION STEP 1)

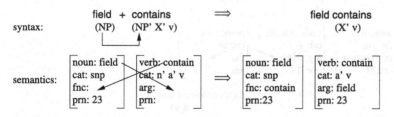

Finally, the syntactic operation based on categorial valency buildup and canceling, and the semantic interpretation based on cross-copying may be fused into one rule, called Nom+FV, using pattern proplets:

22.3.4 PATTERN MATCHING BETWEEN THE RULE AND THE CONTENT LEVEL

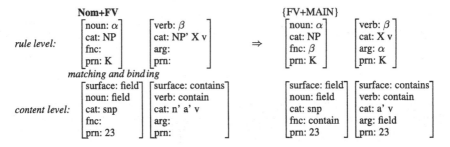

Note how the categorial operation used in 22.3.2 and 22.3.3 reappears at the cat level of the rule and its language input. In addition, cross-copying shown by arrows in 22.3.3 is coded by binding the core value α to field and the core value β to contain.

The second combination step is based on the rule FV+MAIN defined in 17.1.5:

22.3.5 FV+MAIN ADDING ELEMENTARY OBJECT NP (COMBINATION STEP 2)

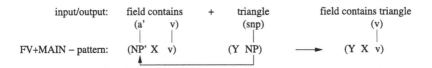

Here the oblique valency position a′ of the verb is canceled by the cat value snp of the second noun. While maintaining an autonomous syntax, a semantic interpretation (based on cross-copying the core values of proplets) may be added as follows:

22.3.6 HEAR MODE INTERPRETATION OF field contains triangle

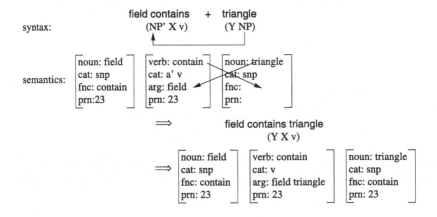

Again, the syntactic operation based on categorial valency buildup and canceling, and the semantic interpretation based on cross-copying core values, may be fused at the rule level by using pattern proplets:

22.3.7 RECODING THE SECOND RULE OF *LA E1* IN THE PROPLET FORMAT

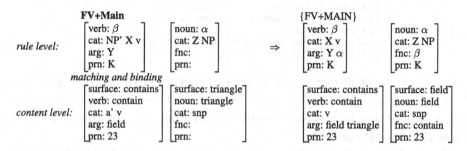

The extension of the purely syntactic rules in Chaps. 16–18 to the format of pattern proplets and an interpretation based on cross-copying is used to implement the semantic relations of structure in natural language. They are the subject/verb, object\verb, adverbial|verb, adnominal|noun, and conjunct−conjunct relations.

22.4 Reference as Pattern Matching

The definition of proplets as flat[13] (nonrecursive) feature structures is the key to simple, efficient, computational pattern matching in DBS. Pattern matching is used (i) in the application of LA Grammar rules to input content in the hear, think, and speak modes and (ii) for modeling reference.

The pattern matching between the rule level and the content level is based on pattern proplets at the rule level, e.g. 22.3.7. Pattern proplets are characterized by containing variables as values, the domains of which may be restricted. Pattern matching between the language level and the context level, in contrast, is based on (i) the type/token relation (4.2.2) and (ii) the presence versus absence of a sur(face) value.

The following example illustrates the pattern matching of agent-internal reference:

---

[13] In earlier editions, proplets were structured into sub-feature structures for separating syntactic and semantic properties. This was intended for better readability and did not affect their nonrecursive nature. It had the disadvantage, however, of complicating the pattern matching (i) between language proplets and context proplets in reference and (ii) between the pattern proplets of rules and the content proplets serving as the input to the rules. Therefore, the structuring into sub-feature structures has been abandoned.

22.4.1 REFERENCE AS INTERNAL MATCHING

language level:
$$\begin{bmatrix} \text{surface: Feld} \\ \text{noun: field} \\ \text{cat: snp} \\ \text{fnc: contain} \\ \text{prn: 23} \end{bmatrix} \begin{bmatrix} \text{surface: enthält} \\ \text{verb: contain} \\ \text{cat: v} \\ \text{arg: field triangle} \\ \text{prn: 23} \end{bmatrix} \begin{bmatrix} \text{surface: Dreieck} \\ \text{noun: triangle} \\ \text{cat: snp} \\ \text{fnc: contain} \\ \text{prn: 23} \end{bmatrix}$$

internal matching

context level:
$$\begin{bmatrix} \text{surface:} \\ \text{noun: field} \\ \text{cat: snp} \\ \text{fnc: contain} \\ \text{prn: 23} \end{bmatrix} \begin{bmatrix} \text{surface:} \\ \text{verb: contain} \\ \text{cat: v} \\ \text{arg: field triangle} \\ \text{prn: 23} \end{bmatrix} \begin{bmatrix} \text{surface:} \\ \text{noun: triangle} \\ \text{cat: snp} \\ \text{fnc: contain} \\ \text{prn: 23} \end{bmatrix}$$

The values of the sur attributes are language-dependent word *forms*, here in German.[14] The type/token distinction is not explicitly indicated, but implied by the proplets' level. Type/type matching is also possible as a limiting case, for example, in generic sentences like A cat likes mice.

In the speak mode, the proplets at the context level are matched by language proplets; their sur values are used for realizing a modality-dependent unanalyzed external surface. In the hear mode, the language proplets are embedded into the context.

Example 22.4.1 shows the literal use of a natural language expression. As an example of a nonliteral use, consider the expression Put the coffee on the table, with table intended to refer to an orange crate (5.2.1). How should such a matching between the concepts *table* and *orange crate* be programmed? There are two possibilities, one based on a weakened type/token relation, the other based on inferencing:

22.4.2 TWO PROPOSALS TO TREAT NONLITERAL REFERENCE

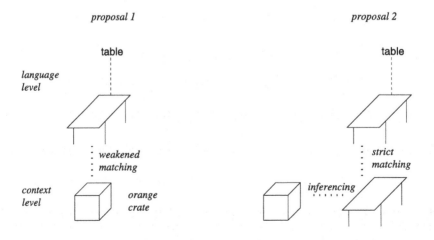

According to proposal 1, the nonliteral use is treated by overextending the standard type/token relation to include a matching between the core values *table* and *orange crate*.

Proposal 2, in contrast, preserves the standard type/token relation and relocates the figurative interpretation of *table* into contextual inferencing.[15] In the speak mode, inferencing precedes the context/language matching; in the hear mode, it follows language/context matching. The kind of inferencing carrying the burden of a nonliteral interpretation occurs also outside of language use (independent motivation). An example of such nonliteral nonlanguage use is employing a screwdriver as a can opener or a doorstop (Sect. 5.2).

An important factor for successful nonliteral use inferencing is delimiting the context of interpretation. In immediate reference (4.3.1), this delimitation is provided by the external situation, in mediated reference by the content preceding the utterance. The following example of a nonliteral mediated reference is from a TV program (Nat-Geo Wild 2011) on the change of seasons in a South American jungle and shows a whole network of nonliteral uses:

22.4.3 EXAMPLE OF A NONLITERAL USE (METAPHOR)

The river awoke thirsty, waiting for the deluge.

The text preceding this example happens to coactivate "change of seasons," which is concordant with *awake* as a change from sleep to alertness, "dry season," which is concordant with a state of being *thirsty*, and "rainy season," which is concordant with "deluge." The verbs *wait for* and *awake* treat the river as a sentient being.

The literature on figurative language use is divided on whether or not the nonliteral interpretation must proceed from a literal coding. Formulating such a literal variant for example 22.4.3 is difficult at best. A more promising approach is to apply the inferences for constructing the analogies inherent in the figurative use directly to the content activated at this point in the agent's cognition.

Many words are inherently figurative, for example, the verb dovetail. Also, numerous nonliteral uses in spoken and written language consist of frozen metaphors, figures of speech, and idioms. There are, however, new nonliteral uses arising every day, which an adequate theory of natural language communication must be able to handle on the fly.

22.5 Repercussion of the Semantic Interpretation on the DBS Syntax

Combining the categorial operation and the semantic interpretation of an LA Grammar rule by using pattern proplets (22.3.4, 22.3.7) allows to semantically interpret the

---

[15] In the terminology of Richards (1936), crate serves as the tenor and table as the vehicle.

original "autonomous" NEWCAT syntax. As an example consider adding a phrasal noun in postverbal position. The first step is an application of FV+Main, defined in 17.1.7 and repeated for convenience:

22.5.1 APPLYING FV+MAIN (17.1.7) IN THE NEWCAT RULE FORMAT

input/output: the girl liked + a the girl liked a
(a'   v) (sn' snp) (sn'   v)

FV+MAIN – pattern: (NP' X v) (Y NP) ⟶ (Y X v)

Because a syntax in NEWCAT format defines the sentence start as a single categorized surface, the sentence_start-determiner combination takes place between the category (a′v) of a verbal sentence start expression and the next word category (sn′ snp), resulting in another verbal expression of category (sn′v).

The version of rule FV+Main which unifies the categorial operation and the semantic interpretation (22.3.7), in contrast, defines the sentence start as a set of content proplets. This allows adding the next word, i.e., the determiner a(n), as another proplet to the resulting sentence start:

22.5.2 COMBINING (The girl) liked + a IN THE UNIFIED RULE FORMAT

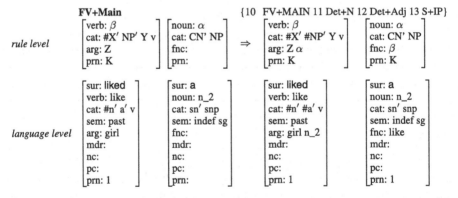

Next let us compare the two rule formats in the combination step adding the common noun. We begin with the NEWCAT rule 17.1.8:

22.5.3 APPLYING DET+N (17.1.8) IN THE NEWCAT RULE FORMAT

input/output: the girl liked a + boy the girl liked a boy
(sn') (v) (sn) (v)

DET+N – pattern: (N' X) (N) ⟶ (X)

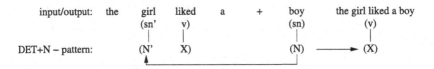

The NEWCAT format of Det+N combines the verbal sentence start of category (sn′v) and the common noun category (sn), resulting in the category (v).

The corresponding left-associative combination using the unified rule format, in contrast, takes place between the proplet of the determiner proplet and the common noun proplet:

22.5.4 COMBINING (The girl liked) a + boy IN THE UNIFIED RULE FORMAT

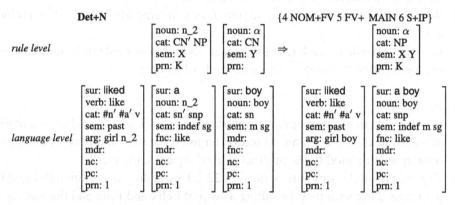

The verb proplet is affected only insofar as the substitution value n_2 is replaced by the core value of the common noun (simultaneous substitution). Once the relevant values of the common noun proplet have been copied into the proplets of the determiner and the verb, it is discarded.

In summary, the NEWCAT format uses semantically motivated valency buildup and canceling for time-linear LA Hear derivations which accept grammatically well-formed input surfaces and reject ungrammatical ones. However, there is no derivation of a semantic representation, i.e., a content.

The unified format based on proplets, in contrast, not only uses the categorial operation of the NEWCAT format to distinguish between grammatical and ungrammatical input, but also derives semantic representations as sets of concatenated proplets, based on cross-copying. The hear mode storage of these sets in the content-addressable database of a word bank and their speak mode retrieval will be the topic of the following chapter.

Exercises

Section 22.1

1. Explain how an agent's internal context of use may be viewed as a database.
2. Describe the storage and retrieval problem for modeling natural language communication.
3. How does the interaction between a user and a conventional database differ from the interaction between a speaker and a hearer?
4. Why is there no turn-taking in the user's interaction with a conventional database?
5. Explain the basic procedures of the speak and the hear mode in natural language communication by using a simple example of a context.

Section 22.2

1. Is it possible to reinterpret model-theoretic semantics as a formal representation of the context of use? What would be required for this, and how would such a reinterpretation modify the original goal of logical semantics?
2. Expand the model structure defined in 22.2.1 by adding one more index and the predicate sleep such that the falling asleep of Felix and Fritz and the waking up of Zach and Eddie are being modeled. Write an evaluation of your experience.
3. Describe the basic principles of frame theory and compare it with model theory.
4. Is it possible to reinterpret frame-theoretic semantics as a computational representation of the context of use? How would such a reinterpretation modify the original purpose of frame-theoretic semantics?
5. Why does the use of a frame-theoretic semantics within the SLIM theory of language necessitate a change of the original ontology?
6. Is the use of a uniform formalism for representing the levels of (i) the language meaning$_1$ and (ii) the context of interpretation a necessary or a sufficient condition for the successful definition of an internal matching pragmatics?
7. Is it a good idea to construct a [+sense] system by combining two instantiations of a [−sense] system? What kinds of problems are likely to occur?
8. Why is the format of 21.4.3 unsuitable for the storage and retrieval task of natural language communication.

Section 22.3

1. What are the requirements on a semantics in addition to being suitable for a modeling of reference as an agent-internal pattern matching?
2. What is the difference between the variables NP and NP′?
3. Explain the difference between the format of uninterpreted NEWCAT rules (e.g., 22.3.2, 22.3.5) and the format of unified DBS rules (e.g., 22.3.4, 22.3.7).
4. How are lexical meanings like *field, triangle,* or *contain* coded in DBS?
5. How are the lexical meanings composed into propositions?

6. How are propositions composed into complex content?
7. How are semantic relations between proplets coded by the unified DBS rules in the hear mode?

Section 22.4
1. Does the definition of content as a(n order-free) set of proplets help or hinder pattern matching between the language and the context level (reference)?
2. How does pattern matching between the language and the context level differ from the pattern matching between a rule pattern and a content?
3. Explain two ways for handling nonliteral use.
4. Why are the inferences for interpreting nonliteral uses of natural language expressions independently motivated?

Section 22.5
1. How does a sentence start in the unified rule format differ from a sentence start in the NEWCAT format?
2. How does this difference affect the role of the verb in time-linear addition of a postverbal phrasal noun?
3. Does a similar difference occur also in the combination of a preverbal phrasal noun with the finite verb?
4. What is the database aspect in the cycle of natural language communication and why is the unified rule format essential for this aspect?

23. Semantic Relations of Structure

This chapter continues the description of DBS constructs. Section 23.1 shows the uniform coding of content at the elementary, the phrasal, and the clausal levels of grammatical complexity as sets of proplets. Section 23.2 uses the order-free nature of proplets for their storage in a content-addressable word bank and shows the selective activation of content by means of navigating along the semantic relations between proplets. Section 23.3 introduces the graphical representation of semantic relations in DBS, and compares paratactic and hypotactic clausal constructions. Section 23.4 discusses the handling of alternative surfaces for a given content. Section 23.5 presents the ten SLIM states of cognition as different constellations of a DBS robot.

23.1 Coding Content at the Elementary, Phrasal, and Clausal Levels

Coding interproplet relations solely by means of proplet-internal values, defined as addresses and implemented as pointers, works for all semantic relations of natural language. In contradistinction to the semantic relations of meaning such as synonymy, the semantic relations of structure are the functor-argument relations of subject/predicate, object\predicate, adnominal|noun, adverbial|verb, and the coordination relation of conjunct−conjunct, at the elementary, the phrasal, and the clausal level.

23.1.1 SEMANTIC RELATIONS OF STRUCTURE AT THE ELEMENTARY LEVEL

Yesterday Mary bought a book and a cookie.

$$
\begin{bmatrix} \text{adj: yesterday} \\ \text{cat: adv} \\ \text{sem: pad} \\ \text{mdd: buy} \\ \text{prn: 7} \end{bmatrix}
\begin{bmatrix} \text{noun: Mary} \\ \text{cat: snp} \\ \text{sem: nm f sg} \\ \text{fnc: buy} \\ \text{prn: 7} \end{bmatrix}
\begin{bmatrix} \text{verb: buy} \\ \text{cat: \#n' \#a' decl} \\ \text{sem: past} \\ \text{arg: Mary book} \\ \text{mdr: yesterday} \\ \text{prn: 7} \end{bmatrix}
\begin{bmatrix} \text{noun: book \&} \\ \text{cat: snp} \\ \text{sem: def sg} \\ \text{fnc: buy} \\ \text{nc: cookie} \\ \text{prn: 7} \end{bmatrix}
\begin{bmatrix} \text{noun: cookie} \\ \text{cat: snp} \\ \text{sem: def sg} \\ \text{fnc:} \\ \text{pc: book} \\ \text{prn: 7} \end{bmatrix}
$$

The adverbial use of the adj proplet *yesterday* is specified by the adv value of the cat attribute, while the modified is specified by the mdd value buy.

The noun proplet *Mary* is specified as an snp (singular noun phrase) in the cat attribute and as nm (name), f (feminine[1]), and sg (singular) in the sem attribute. The relation to the verb is specified by the value buy of the fnc (functor) attribute.

The form bought of the verb proplet *buy* is indicated by the value past of the cat attribute. The first value of the arg attribute Mary is the subject, while the second value book is the direct object. The mdr (modifier) slot contains yesterday.

The core value of the noun *book* is marked as an initial conjunct by &. The next conjunct is specified as the value cookie of the nc (next conjunct) attribute, just as book is specified as the previous conjunct by the value of the pc attribute of *cookie*.

The five proplets characterizing the content coded by the English surface are held together by the common prn value 7. The semantic relations *Mary/buy* (subject/ predicate) and *book\buy* (object\predicate) are obligatory, while the relations *yesterday|buy* (adverbial|verb) and *book−cookie* (conjunct−conjunct) are optional. The adverbial and the conjuncts are included because they are themselves elementary, though they create phrasal structures by being concatenated with their modified.

The modifiers creating phrasal relations at the content level are optional. They are integrated into the attribute-value structure of the elementary content, as in the following example:

23.1.2 SEMANTIC RELATIONS OF STRUCTURE AT THE PHRASAL LEVEL

The young girl has bought a little book and a large cookie.

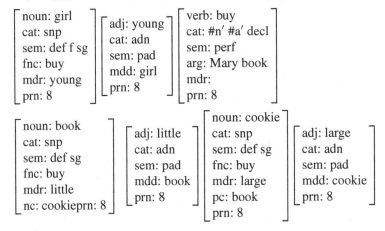

---

[1] The gender specification in the singular is needed for agreement with a possible coreferential pronoun.

The elementary noun *girl* is made phrasal by adding the modifier *young* using the respective mdr and mdd attributes, and similarly for *book* and *cookie*. Thereby the elementary relations of 23.1.1 remain unaffected.[2]

Upscaling to clausal relations is based on sentential subjects, objects, adnominals, and adverbials, as well as extrapropositional coordination. Consider the following example with a sentential subject:

23.1.3 SEMANTIC RELATIONS OF STRUCTURE AT THE CLAUSAL LEVEL

That Bill bought a book surprised Mary.

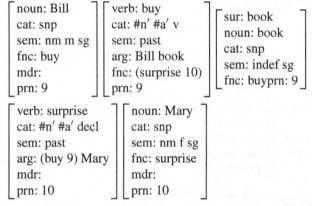

The relation between the verb *buy* of the subject sentence and the matrix verb *surprise* is coded by the additional fnc attribute with the address value (surprise 10) of *buy* and the initial arg value (buy 9) of *surprise*. Relations which require additional attributes, here fnc of *buy*, and elementary relations coded as extrapropositional addresses, here (buy 9), are called opaque, in contradistinction to the relations in 23.1.1 and 23.1.2, which are transparent.

23.2 Storing Content in a Word Bank

The contents coded in 23.1.1, 23.1.2, and 23.1.3 are shown in an order corresponding to that of the surface. However, because the interproplet relations are coded solely by means addresses, the proplets are in fact order-free. This allows their storage in a new kind of content-addressable database, called a word bank (NLC, CLaTR):

---

[2] The function words the, has, a, and a in the surface of 23.1.2 are absorbed into the associated content word proplets and represented as certain values such as def(inite). In as much as the girl, for example, is regarded as phrasal at the surface level, but as elementary at the corresponding content level, the notion 'phrasal' is used differently at the two levels.

23.2.1 A WORD BANK CONTAINING CONCATENATED PROPLETS

PROPLET TOKENS   NOW FRONT   PROPLET TYPES

$$
\begin{bmatrix}
\text{noun: Bill} \\
\text{cat: snp} \\
\text{sem: nm m sg} \\
\text{fnc: buy} \\
\text{mdr:} \\
\text{prn: 9}
\end{bmatrix}
\qquad
\begin{bmatrix}
\text{noun: Bill} \\
\text{cat: snp} \\
\text{sem: nm m sg} \\
\text{. . .} \\
\text{prn:}
\end{bmatrix}
$$

$$
\begin{bmatrix}
\text{noun: book \&} \\
\text{cat: snp} \\
\text{sem: indef sg} \\
\text{fnc: buy} \\
\text{nc: cookie} \\
\text{prn: 7}
\end{bmatrix}
\begin{bmatrix}
\text{noun: book} \\
\text{cat: snp} \\
\text{sem: indef sg} \\
\text{fnc: buy} \\
\text{mdr: little} \\
\text{nc: cookie} \\
\text{prn: 8}
\end{bmatrix}
\begin{bmatrix}
\text{sur: book} \\
\text{noun: book} \\
\text{cat: snp} \\
\text{sem: indef sg} \\
\text{fnc: buy} \\
\text{prn: 9}
\end{bmatrix}
\qquad
\begin{bmatrix}
\text{noun: book} \\
\text{cat: snp} \\
\text{. . .} \\
\text{prn:}
\end{bmatrix}
$$

$$
\begin{bmatrix}
\text{verb: buy} \\
\text{cat: \#n}' \text{ \#a}' \text{ decl} \\
\text{sem: past} \\
\text{arg: Mary book} \\
\text{mdr: yesterday} \\
\text{prn: 7}
\end{bmatrix}
\begin{bmatrix}
\text{verb: buy} \\
\text{cat: \#n}' \text{ \#a}' \text{ decl} \\
\text{sem: perf} \\
\text{arg: Mary book} \\
\text{mdr: yesterday} \\
\text{prn: 8}
\end{bmatrix}
\begin{bmatrix}
\text{verb: buy} \\
\text{cat: \#n}' \text{ \#a}' \text{ v} \\
\text{sem: past} \\
\text{arg: Bill book} \\
\text{fnc: (surprise 10)} \\
\text{prn: 9}
\end{bmatrix}
\qquad
\begin{bmatrix}
\text{verb: buy} \\
\text{cat: n}' \text{ a}' \text{ v} \\
\text{. . .} \\
\text{prn:}
\end{bmatrix}
$$

$$
\begin{bmatrix}
\text{noun: cookie} \\
\text{cat: snp} \\
\text{sem: def sg} \\
\text{fnc: buy} \\
\text{pc: book} \\
\text{prn: 7}
\end{bmatrix}
\begin{bmatrix}
\text{noun: cookie} \\
\text{cat: snp} \\
\text{sem: def sg} \\
\text{fnc: buy} \\
\text{mdr: large} \\
\text{pc: book} \\
\text{prn: 8}
\end{bmatrix}
\qquad
\begin{bmatrix}
\text{noun: cookie} \\
\text{cat: snp} \\
\text{. . .} \\
\text{prn:}
\end{bmatrix}
$$

$$
\begin{bmatrix}
\text{noun: girl} \\
\text{cat: snp} \\
\text{sem: def f sg} \\
\text{fnc: buy} \\
\text{mdr: young} \\
\text{prn: 8}
\end{bmatrix}
\qquad
\begin{bmatrix}
\text{noun: girl} \\
\text{cat: snp} \\
\text{sem: f sg} \\
\text{. . .} \\
\text{prn:}
\end{bmatrix}
$$

$$
\begin{bmatrix}
\text{adj: large} \\
\text{cat: adn} \\
\text{sem: pad} \\
\text{mdd: cookie} \\
\text{prn: 8}
\end{bmatrix}
\qquad
\begin{bmatrix}
\text{adj: large} \\
\text{cat: adn} \\
\text{. . .} \\
\text{prn:}
\end{bmatrix}
$$

$$
\begin{bmatrix}
\text{adj: little} \\
\text{cat: adn} \\
\text{sem: pad} \\
\text{mdd: book} \\
\text{prn: 8}
\end{bmatrix}
\qquad
\begin{bmatrix}
\text{adj: little} \\
\text{cat: adn} \\
\text{. . .} \\
\text{prn:}
\end{bmatrix}
$$

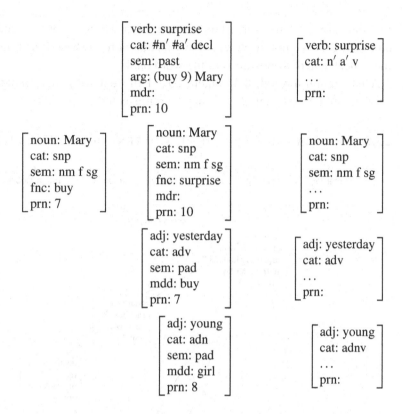

The proplet types in the column on the right are like lexical entries. They are ordered alphabetically according to their core value, i.e., the value of the core attribute noun, verb, or adj. A proplet type may also contain values for other lexical properties, such as the cat or sem values, or have attributes which have no value, e.g. prn.

Each proplet type is preceded by an open number of proplet tokens, thus forming a *token line*. Proplets in the same token line have the same core value. Incoming proplets are stored at the now front, resulting in the temporal structure of *sediment*.

Proplet tokens belonging to the same proposition are held together across token lines by a common proposition number (prn value). The prn values reflect the temporal order of arrival. The attributes concatenating proplets with semantic relations of structure, i.e., fnc, arg, mdr, mdd, nc, and pc, are called *continuation attributes*.

The structure of a word bank resembles a classic network database (Elmasri and Navathe 2010). A network database defines a 1:n relation between two kinds of records, the owner records and the member records. However, instead of records (1.1.1) a word bank uses the equivalent data structure of proplets. In the above example, the proplet types are the owners and the proplet tokens are the members. The primary key for the storage and retrieval of a proplet is its core and its prn value.

A word bank goes beyond a classic, i.e., record-based, database because it defines the semantic relations of functor-argument and coordination between proplets. These relations are the basis for a kind of operation which a conventional database, e.g., an RDBMS, does not provide, namely an autonomous time-linear navigation through the concatenated propositions in the word bank.

A navigation through the content 23.1.1 of Yesterday Mary bought a book and a cookie. in the word bank 23.2.1 may be represented graphically as follows:

23.2.2 NAVIGATING THROUGH THE CONTENT OF THE WORD BANK 23.2.1

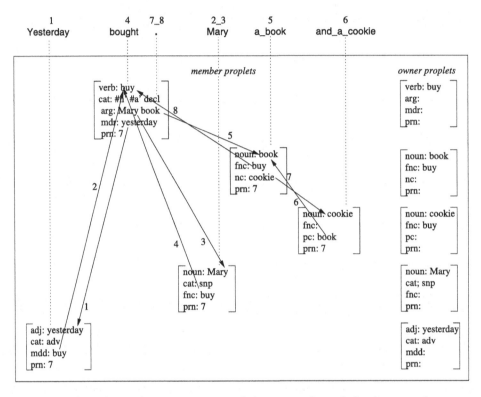

Using the continuation value yesterday and the prn value of the *buy* proplet as an address, navigation step 1 goes from *buy* to *yesterday*. Similarly, navigation steps 2_3 go from *yesterday* to *buy* and from *buy* to *Mary*, 4 from *Mary* to *buy*, 5 from *buy* to *book*, 6 from *book* to *cookie*, and 7_8 from *cookie* back to *buy*.

Navigating along the semantic relations between proplets in a word bank may be used for (i) the selective activation of content and (ii) the realization of the activated content in language. Language surfaces are always realized from the core value of the goal proplet of a navigation step, as indicated by the vertical dotted lines. The realization of a surface may require more than one navigation step, e.g., the 2_3 navigation realizing Mary, and a navigation step may realize more than one surface, e.g., the navigation step 6 realizing and_a_cookie.

The navigation through a word bank content is driven by an LA Think grammar. Consider the rule application performing the navigation step from *buy* to *Mary*:

23.2.3 THE LA THINK RULE V+N NAVIGATING FROM *buy* TO *Mary*

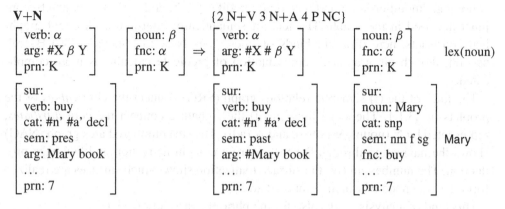

V+N {2 N+V 3 N+A 4 P NC}

$$\begin{bmatrix} \text{verb: } \alpha \\ \text{arg: \#X } \beta \text{ Y} \\ \text{prn: K} \end{bmatrix} \begin{bmatrix} \text{noun: } \beta \\ \text{fnc: } \alpha \\ \text{prn: K} \end{bmatrix} \Rightarrow \begin{bmatrix} \text{verb: } \alpha \\ \text{arg: \#X \# } \beta \text{ Y} \\ \text{prn: K} \end{bmatrix} \begin{bmatrix} \text{noun: } \beta \\ \text{fnc: } \alpha \\ \text{prn: K} \end{bmatrix} \text{lex(noun)}$$

$$\begin{bmatrix} \text{sur:} \\ \text{verb: buy} \\ \text{cat: \#n' \#a' decl} \\ \text{sem: pres} \\ \text{arg: Mary book} \\ \dots \\ \text{prn: 7} \end{bmatrix} \begin{bmatrix} \text{sur:} \\ \text{verb: buy} \\ \text{cat: \#n' \#a' decl} \\ \text{sem: past} \\ \text{arg: \#Mary book} \\ \dots \\ \text{prn: 7} \end{bmatrix} \begin{bmatrix} \text{sur:} \\ \text{noun: Mary} \\ \text{cat: snp} \\ \text{sem: nm f sg} \\ \text{fnc: buy} \\ \dots \\ \text{prn: 7} \end{bmatrix} \text{Mary}$$

The first rule pattern matches the input proplet. Its variables occur also in the second proplet. Binding the variable β to the continuation value Mary and the variable K to the prn value 7 of the input proplet *buy* allows navigation to (retrieval of) the goal proplet *Mary*. To prevent a relapse or a loop, the continuation value used for the navigation is #-marked in the output, here the arg value #Mary in the *buy* proplet. As an LA Speak option, the function lex(noun) may realize the core value of the goal proplet, here Mary.

23.3 Representing the Semantic Relations of Structure Graphically

While the proplet-based representations 23.2.1 and 23.2.2 show the database aspect of a content precisely and may be produced automatically, they are difficult to read. Therefore, we developed a graphical analysis which consists of four different views on a DBS content. Consider the following example showing the graphical analysis of the content 23.1.1 (elementary grammatical complexity):

23.3.1 GRAPHICAL ANALYSIS OF Yesterday Mary bought a book and a cookie.

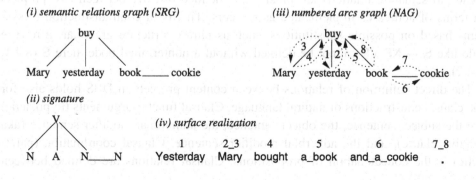

(i) semantic relations graph (SRG)

(iii) numbered arcs graph (NAG)

(ii) signature

(iv) surface realization

The lines distinguishing the relations of subject/predicate, object\predicate, "|" for adnominal_modifier|noun and adverbial_modifier|verb, and "−" for conjunct−conjunct are used in the graph. The idea of semantically interpreting different graphical constructs, here different kinds of lines, goes back to Frege's (1889) Begriffsschrift, though his graphical representation of predicate calculus is more complicated.

The lines of the (i) semantic relations graph (SRG) connect the core *values* of the proplets in 23.1.1. The same lines in (ii) the signature connect the core *attributes*, represented by N (noun), V (verb), and A (adj). The (iii) numbered arcs graph (NAG) shows the navigation through the SRG during content activation and language production. The numbers in (iv) the surface realization show which surfaces are realized form the goal node of which numbered arc.

This kind of analysis works also for the phrasal construction 23.1.2:

23.3.2 The young girl has bought a little book and a large cookie.

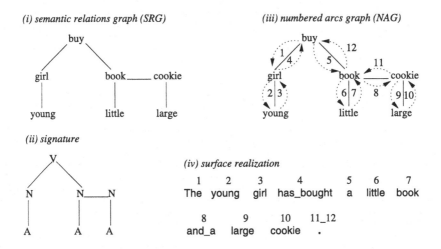

DBS graph analyses like 23.3.1 and 23.3.2 do not use any nonterminal nodes. Instead, all semantic relations are binary, i.e., defined directly between two proplets in terms of addresses implemented as pointers. This is in contradistinction to systems based on possible substitutions, such as phrase structure grammar: a rewrite rule like S → NP VP cannot be defined without a nonterminal node, here S (8.4.1, 8.4.2).

The direct definition of relations between content proplets in DBS holds also for the clausal constructions of natural language. Clausal functor-arguments (hypotactic) are the subject sentence, the object sentence, the adnominal modifier sentence (aka relative clause), and the adverbial modifier sentence. Clausal coordination (paratactic) is the concatenation of propositions. Clausal relations are defined between the verb proplets of two propositions. This is shown by the graphical analysis of the subject sentence 23.1.3, which is an extrapropositional intrasentential functor-argument:

23.3.3 HYPOTACTIC: That Bill bought a book surprised Mary. (ACTIVE VOICE)

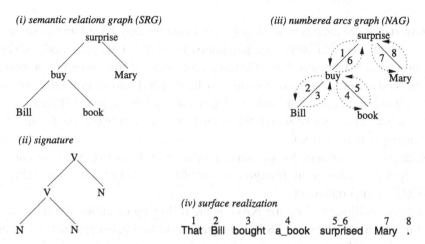

As in all subclause constructions of natural language, the semantic relation between the subclause and the main clause is opaque: even though the function of the subclause is that of a subject, as shown by the "/" line between *buy* and *surprise*, the node representing the subclause is V. The double function of *buy* as the verb of the subclause and the subject of the main clause is handled at the proplet level (23.1.3) with the additional (non-lexical) fnc attribute, which is normally (lexically) reserved for nouns. The other opaque property of this construction is the use of the verbal address (buy 9) as the first argument of *surprise*.

Finally consider an extrasentential extrapropositional coordination.

23.3.4 PARATACTIC: Peter leaves the house. Then Peter crosses the street.

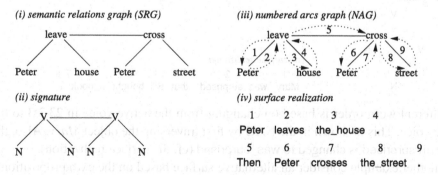

As in clausal relations in general, the coordination is defined between the verb proplets of the conjuncts. In contradistinction to extrapropositional (clausal) functor-arguments, which are always intrasentential, extrapropositional coordination may be intra- or extrasentential.

23.4 Paraphrase and the Universalist/Relativist Dichotomy

For different rhetorical purposes, a propositional content may have various surfaces which are semantically equivalent, i.e., paraphrases (4.4.6). In the hear mode, several different surfaces may be mapped into the same propositional content (set of proplets). In the speak mode, a propositional content may be mapped into several different surfaces. Though applied here to alternative surfaces in a given language (English), the following considerations apply also to the coding of a given propositional content in different languages (translation).

In DBS, alternative surfaces for the same content may have two different causes. One is an alternative navigation through a given SRG. The other is the possibility of different SRGs being equivalent.

The first cause is illustrated by the NAG of the following example of a hypotactic construction, which uses the same SRG and signature as 23.3.3, but realizes a different surface based on a different navigation order:

23.4.1 HYPOTACTIC: Mary was surprised that Bill bought a book. (PASSIVE)

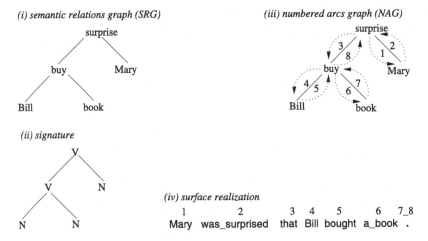

The different word order is based on changing from the active voice in 23.3.3 to the passive voice. This is shown in the NAG by first traversing the object *Mary*. Also, the verb form surprised is changed to was_surprised (cf. the surface realization).

As another example consider an alternative surface based on the extrapropositional coordination 23.3.4. Here the different word order is based on changing from a forward to a backward navigation:

23.4.2 PARATACTIC: Peter crosses the street. Before that he leaves the house.

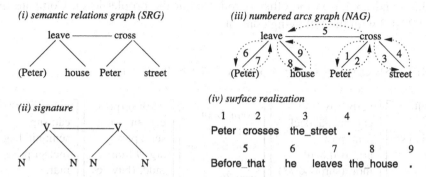

The alternative navigations through the same SRG, here 23.3.4 (forward navigation) and 23.4.2 (backward navigation), are semantically equivalent because the SRG is an abstract representation of the content defined as a set of proplets.

Now let us turn to the second possible cause of paraphrase in DBS, i.e., the possibility of different SRGs being equivalent. The following example changes the subclause of 23.3.3 into the main clause, and the main clause into an adverbial subclause:[3]

23.4.3 Bill bought a book, which surprised Mary.

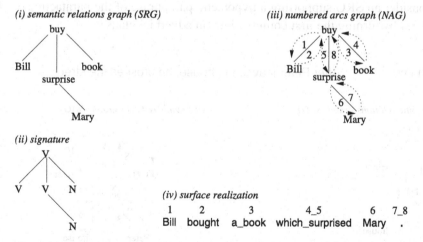

Leaving aspects of foregrounding aside, this construction has the same meaning as that in 23.3.3, despite the difference between the semantic constructions.

In addition, a paraphrase based on an alternative navigation may be constructed, though it is somewhat laborious:

Bill bought a book, by which Mary was surprised

---

[3] For the corresponding treatment of adnominal subclauses, aka relative clauses, see CLaTR, Sect. 9.3.

The difference between the semantic relations of 23.3.3 and 23.4.1 on the one hand and of 23.3.3 and 23.4.3 on the other is reflected at the proplet level. Compare the proplet set 23.1.3 with the following content:

23.4.4 REPRESENTATION OF 23.4.3 AS A SET OF PROPLETS

$$
\begin{bmatrix} \text{noun: Bill} \\ \text{cat: snp} \\ \text{sem: nm m sg} \\ \text{fnc: buy} \\ \text{mdr:} \\ \text{prn: 76} \end{bmatrix}
\begin{bmatrix} \text{verb: buy} \\ \text{cat: \#n' \#a' decl} \\ \text{sem: past} \\ \text{arg: Bill book} \\ \text{mdr: (surprise 77)} \\ \text{prn: 76} \end{bmatrix}
\begin{bmatrix} \text{noun: book} \\ \text{cat: snp} \\ \text{sem: indef sg} \\ \text{fnc: buy} \\ \text{prn: 76} \end{bmatrix}
\begin{bmatrix} \text{verb: surprise} \\ \text{cat: \#n''\#a' v} \\ \text{sem: past} \\ \text{arg: \# Mary} \\ \text{mdd: (buy 76)} \\ \text{prn: 77} \end{bmatrix}
\begin{bmatrix} \text{noun: Mary} \\ \text{cat: snp} \\ \text{sem: nm f sg} \\ \text{fnc: surprise} \\ \text{mdr:} \\ \text{prn: 77} \end{bmatrix}
$$

The constructions 23.3.3, 23.4.1, and 23.4.3 have the following counterparts in German, showing substantially different word orders (Sect. 18.3):

23.3.3: Dass Bill ein Buch kaufte, überraschte Maria.

23.4.1: Maria war überrascht, dass Bill ein Buch kaufte.

23.4.3: Bill kaufte ein Buch, was Maria überraschte.

The alternative word orders of the English examples and their German translations are treated solely by alternative navigation orders through the same signature.

Next consider an SRG supporting a hypotactic paraphrase of the paratactic coordination 23.3.4 by turning the first conjunct into an adverbial clause:

23.4.5 HYPOTACTIC: After Peter leaves the house, he crosses the street.

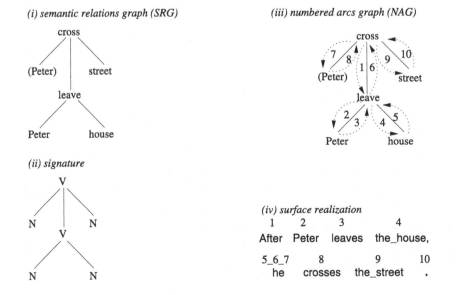

(i) semantic relations graph (SRG)

(ii) signature

(iii) numbered arcs graph (NAG)

(iv) surface realization

1	2	3	4
After	Peter	leaves	the_house,

5_6_7	8	9	10
he	crosses	the_street	.

Like the previous hypotactic examples, this construction is opaque because the modifier, i.e., the adverbial clause After Peter leaves the house, is represented by a V rather than an A. The coreferential interpretation of the pronoun he is represented by the address (Peter) pointing at the antecedent.

Basing some paraphrases on different SRGs, here 23.3.4/23.4.2 and 23.4.5, may be related to the choice between linguistic universalism (represented by nativism) and linguistic relativism (represented by the Humboldt-Sapir-Whorf hypothesis). Universalism would presumably base the equivalences on deriving all the paraphrases from a single underlying SRG, while a moderate relativism may derive some paraphrases from different SRGs as long as the SRGs may be *inferred* to be equivalent.

For a computational reconstruction of the speak and the hear mode, this choice has practical consequences. A single, universal, underlying SRG establishes a "permanent" equivalence between the alternative surfaces, but requires heavy inferencing to relate the surface and the content every time one of the paraphrases is produced or interpreted. A construction-dependent representation (as shown in 23.3.3/23.4.1 and 23.4.3 as well as 23.3.4/23.4.2 and 23.4.5), in contrast, provides a greatly simplified mapping between the surface and the content with the possibility of inferring equivalence when needed.

23.5 The Ten SLIM States of Cognition

In this section, we turn from the grammatical analysis of the speak and the hear mode to language communication. This requires the additional distinctions between nonlanguage recognition and action, and between immediate and mediated reference. Using the component structure 22.1.1, the analysis results in the ten SLIM states of cognition. They represent alternative functional flows in the agent's cognition, with ❋ indicating the activation point of a constellation.

23.5.1 SLIM 1: RECOGNITION (contextual)

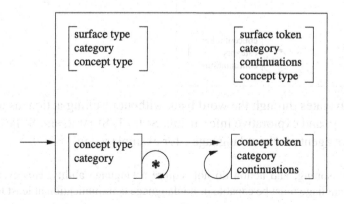

SLIM 1 represents a cognitive agent observing its external environment. Contextual parameter values are matched with concept types provided by memory, resulting in proplets with concept tokens as core values, which are combined into concatenated propositions (Sects. 3.3, 3.4). The activation is indicated by the circular arrow on the left. When the proplets are read into the word bank, the sequence of their storage mirrors the sequence of their recognition and concatenation (represented by the right-hand circular arrow).

23.5.2 SLIM 2: ACTION (contextual)

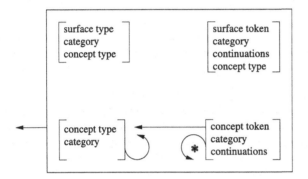

SLIM 2 represents a cognitive agent acting in its external environment using stored blueprints or freshly derived inferences. When these are traversed by LA Think (right-hand circular arrow), copies are passed to the agent's action components to be realized (left-hand circular arrow).

23.5.3 SLIM 3: INFERENCE (contextual)

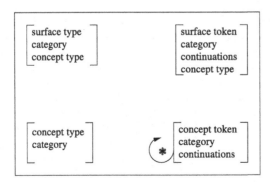

In SLIM 3, LA Think navigates through the word bank without resulting action, as in free association, dreaming, and explorative inferencing. SLIM 1, SLIM 2, and SLIM 3 function also in cognitive agents without language,[4] for example a dog.

---

[4] In DBS, recognition, reasoning, and action do not require a language ability. However, natural agents without language must be capable of nonlanguage communication at least to

23.5.4 SLIM 4: INTERPRETATION OF LANGUAGE (mediated reference)

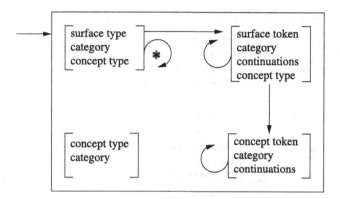

SLIM 4 represents a hearer interpreting natural language without accompanying nonlanguage recognition (circular upper left arrow), as when reading a letter (5.3.4). SLIM 4 is powered by an LA Hear grammar which connects the incoming proplets (24.1.1) resulting from lexical lookup. When the proplets are read into the word bank, the sequence of their storage mirrors the sequence of their recognition and concatenation (represented by the circular lower arrow).

23.5.5 SLIM 5: PRODUCTION OF LANGUAGE (mediated reference)

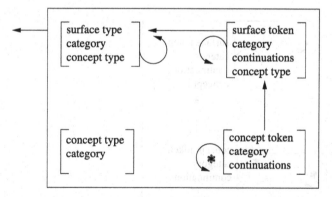

SLIM 5 represents a speaker reporting content stored in memory or derived by inferences without using current recognition. SLIM 5 is powered by LA Think's navigation through the word bank. The proplets traversed are matched by corresponding language proplets. These are input to an LA Grammar for language production which provides language-specific word order, lexicalization including function word precipitation, inflection, etc. (represented by the circular upper right arrow).

---

the degree that reproduction is ensured.

23.5.6 SLIM 6: LANGUAGE-CONTROLLED ACTION (immediate reference)

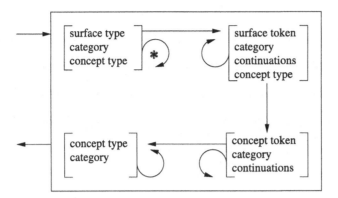

The constellation of SLIM 6 describes an agent interpreting an order, a request, or an instruction (language recognition) and obeying it (nonlanguage action). As such, SLIM 6 is a combination of language-based SLIM 4 and contextual SLIM 2. An example would be an instruction like Peel the potatoes and put them in boiling water. Note that SLIM 4 and SLIM 5 are instances of mediated reference, while SLIM 6 to SLIM 9 are instances of immediate reference (4.3.1).

23.5.7 SLIM 7: COMMENTED RECOGNITION (immediate reference)

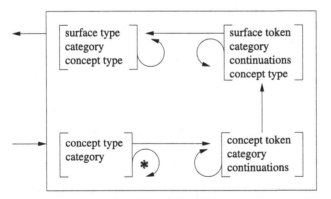

The constellation of SLIM 7 describes an agent observing a current event and reporting it. SLIM 7 is a combination of contextual SLIM 1 and language-based SLIM 5. The procedure is driven by contextual recognition (circular arrow at lower left). When the proplets are read into the word bank, the sequence of their storage mirrors the sequence of their recognition and concatenation (represented by the circular arrow at lower right). The incoming context proplets are matched by language proplets, and turned into a sequence of connected proplets (circular arrow at upper right). The surfaces of these are passed to the action component for realization. An example is life reporting as in Now a man with a violin case is showing up.

23.5.8 SLIM 8: LANGUAGE-CONTROLLED RECOGNITION (immediate reference)

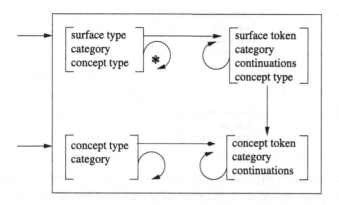

SLIM 8 is a constellation in which incoming language directs the agent's recognition. An example is an instruction like In the upper drawer you will find a silver key. SLIM 8 is a combination of language-based SLIM 4 and contextual SLIM 1. It is driven by language recognition (circular arrow in upper left). Language interpretation is matched by context proplets (circular arrow in lower right) which are used to control the agent's recognition (circular arrow in lower left).

23.5.9 SLIM 9: COMMENTED ACTION (immediate reference)

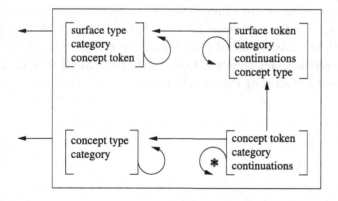

SLIM 9 is a constellation in which self-performed nonlanguage action is reported directly. An example is a comment like I now operate the lever of the door lock and open it. SLIM 9 is powered by the autonomous navigation through the propositions of the contextual word bank (circular arrow at lower right). This navigation is simultaneously put into contextual action and into words. SLIM 9 may be analyzed as a combination of language-based SLIM 5 and contextual SLIM 2.

23.5.10 SLIM 10: COGNITIVE STILLSTAND

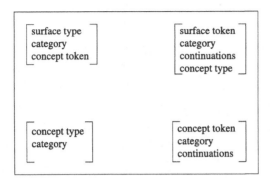

While in natural cognitive agents there is always a minimum of cognitive activity (SLIM 3) as long as they are alive and well, in artificial agents the time-linear navigation may be halted without jeopardizing the database contents. For this reason, SLIM 10 is included as a legitimate cognitive state (limiting case).

The typology of SLIM 1 to SLIM 10 is basic because it systematically represents constellations of the SLIM machine which are structurally obvious. It is real because each of the ten constellations is supported by natural examples. It is also useful because it allows us to define important theoretical notions as simple variations of the same well-motivated structure.

More specifically, *context-based* cognition is represented by SLIM 1 to SLIM 3, and *language-based* cognition is represented by SLIM 4 and SLIM 5, while simultaneous context- and language-based cognition is represented by SLIM 6 to SLIM 9. Context-based cognition distinguishes between *recognition* (SLIM 1), *action* (SLIM 2), and *inferencing* (SLIM 3). Language-based cognition distinguishes between the *hear mode* (SLIM 4, SLIM 6, SLIM 8), and the *speak mode* (SLIM 5, SLIM 7, SLIM 9). *Mediated* reference (SLIM 4, SLIM 5) is distinguished from *immediate* reference (SLIM 6 to SLIM 9). In immediate reference, language-based *control* (SLIM 6, SLIM 8) is distinguished from context-based *commenting* (SLIM 7, SLIM 9).

Exercises

Section 23.1
1. Give an example of an elementary and a phrasal noun, adj, and verb.
2. Name the clausal relations of natural language.
3. Why are the clausal relations opaque?
4. Explain the relation between the sentential subject and the matrix verb in 23.1.3. Describe the relevant attributes and values.
5. Define a corresponding proplet set for a sentential object construction.
6. Define a corresponding proplet set for a sentential adverb construction.

Section 23.2
1. Compare a classic network database and a word bank.
2. What is the primary key for storage and retrieval in a word bank?
3. What is the difference between an owner proplet and a member proplet?
4. What is the storage location for a new proplet?
5. Explain the core and the continuation attributes in a proplet.
6. Why are the proplets of a proposition stored in different token lines?
7. How does a content navigation use the retrieval mechanism of the word bank?

Section 23.3
1. Explain how the semantic relations subject-predicate, object-predicate, adnominal-noun, adverbial-verb, and conjunct-conjunct are represented in an SRG.
2. Compare an SRG and a corresponding signature.
3. How are coreferential pronouns represented in a signature?
4. Are NAGs defined for the speak mode or for the hear mode?
5. Explain surface realizations in which a surface requires more than one traversal step and in which one traversal step realizes more than one surface.
6. How are paratactic and hypotactic constructions represented in an SRG?
7. Explain why systems based on the principle of possible substitution cannot define relations between content words directly.

Section 23.4
1. Explain the two reasons why a propositional content may have alternative surfaces.
2. In what sense is a mapping between alternative surfaces and a propositional content in the same language analogous to a mapping between a given content and equivalent surfaces in different languages?
3. Describe the tasks of the mapping between a content and a surface in the speak and in the hear mode.
4. What are the respective advantages and disadvantages of postulating a universal representation of a propositional content, within a language and across languages.
5. What relations allow the construction of contents which are unlimited in size?

Section 23.5

1. Describe the ten SLIM states of cognition.
2. What are the three possible activation points of a SLIM machine?
3. Compare the SLIM states of language-based and context-based cognition.
4. Compare the SLIM states of immediate and mediated reference.
5. How do the speak and the hear mode differ in a SLIM machine?
6. Why is immediate reference a special case of mediated reference?

24. Conclusion

This chapter returns to the robot CURIOUS introduced in Chap. 3 and shows how the software constructs designed above work in this basic cognitive machine. Section 24.1 characterizes the hear mode schematically with the interpretation of a declarative sentence. Section 24.2 shows the production of the example in the speak mode and illustrates the mechanism of natural language communication in its most basic form. Section 24.3 extends this mechanism to the querying and query answering in natural language, using the database schema of a word bank and the data structure of pattern proplets. Section 24.4 explains the need for an autonomous control based on the principle of maintaining the agent's balance vis-à-vis constantly changing internal and external environments. Section 24.5 discusses the dependence of a content's coherence on whether DBS is implemented on a standard computer or as a robot.

24.1 Hear Mode

Let us summarize the cycle of natural language communication by showing the cognitive agent's speak and hear modes with the robot CURIOUS, using the simple examples 3.4.2–3.4.4. The environment of CURIOUS is a flat floor divided into fields containing colored geometric objects of different sizes, like a big blue square or a small black triangle. The hardware of CURIOUS consists of a video camera moving on the ceiling to visit and analyze one field after another (3.5.2).

CURIOUS differs from a standard computer in that the interfaces of the latter are essentially for transporting alphanumerical characters in and out. CURIOUS, in contrast, provides the core values field, contain, triangle, and square with procedural definitions based on matching concept types on raw data (bitmap outlines, 3.2.3).

Initially, the cognitive operations keeping track of CURIOUS's task environment do not involve language. They may be extended to language, however, by providing (i) the proplets' sur attributes with suitable values as well as (ii) LA Grammars for the interpretation and production of modality-dependent unanalyzed external surfaces.

The following extension to language begins with the hear mode in order to fill the agent's word bank for subsequent speak mode productions. For simplicity, the following analysis shows only the first sentence of the example. The complete example,

R. Hausser, *Foundations of Computational Linguistics*, 475
DOI 10.1007/978-3-642-41431-2_24, © Springer-Verlag Berlin Heidelberg 2014

including the handling of extrapropositional coordination, is shown in 3.4.3 as a set of proplets. The spatio-temporal specifications of the original example are omitted.

24.1.1 HEAR MODE INTERPRETATION OF Field contains triangle...

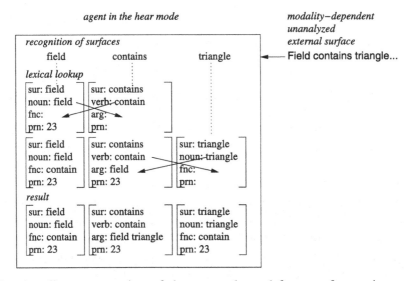

The time-linear perception of the external word form surfaces triggers the agent's surface recognition. The recognized surfaces are used for lexical lookup, provided by automatic word form recognition. It maps each recognized surface into a proplet.

Automatic word form recognition is incrementally intertwined with the syntactic-semantic parsing provided by the agent's LA Hear grammar: the time-linear derivation looks up the current next word, combines it with the current sentence start into a new sentence start (left-associative combination), turns the new sentence start into the current sentence start, does lexical lookup of a new next word, and continues in this way until no next word is available or the derivation hits an ungrammatical continuation.

The syntactic-semantic interpretation in 24.1.1 is simplified in that it shows the buildup of content only by means of cross-copying, but omits the categorial operations. The resulting proplets are suitable for storage in the agent's word bank.

24.2 Speak Mode

Having shown how a sample sequence of natural language sentences is automatically read into the word bank, we turn next to natural language production. This task has to solve the following problems:

1. conceptualization (*what to say*)
2. coherence (*how to say it*, macro structure)
3. cohesion (*how to say it*, micro structure)

Important aspects of cohesion are:

  a. serialization (how to order the content)
  b. lexicalization (which words to choose)

Recent and current systems of natural language generation (NLG) come in three kinds of architecture: (i) pipeline (McDonald 1983; McKeown 1985; Reiter et al. 1997), (ii) interactive (Hovy 1988; Reithinger 1992), and (iii) integrated (Appelt 1985). Pipeline systems move in only one direction, from a complete selection of content via planning to realization. Interactive systems provide interfaces for a bidirectional decision procedure regarding the choice of topic, sentence content, and sentence structure. Integrated systems do not use the distinction between 'what to say' and 'how to say it', but treat generation instead in terms of a planning procedure based on a single hierarchy involving both language knowledge and contextual knowledge (Busemann 2000).

The Database Semantics approach to language production differs from these in that it does not use any planning hierarchy. Instead, conceptualization is based on a general notion of thought, implemented as (i) a navigation along the semantic relations between proplets, complemented by (ii) inferencing. The navigation provides essential aspects of cohesion, namely the basic serialization of the language expressions and some aspects of lexicalization. In this way, the traditional distinction between content (*what to say*) and form (*how to say it*) is minimized. Furthermore, coherence is achieved by feeding the word bank with coherent contextual information (Sect. 24.5).

The structural basis for the navigation through a complex propositional content are the core and the continuation values of the order-free proplets stored in a word bank:

24.2.1 STORING THE PROPOSITIONS DERIVED IN 24.1.1 IN A WORD BANK

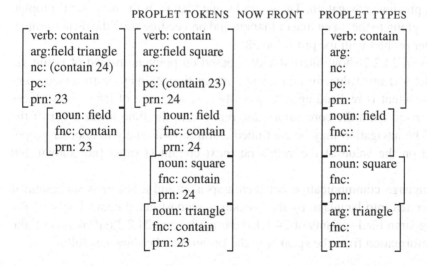

By using the continuation value of a present proplet as a core value, the navigation utilizes the retrieval mechanism of the word bank for finding a next proplet, as shown by the following example:

24.2.2 SPEAK MODE PRODUCTION OF field contains triangle

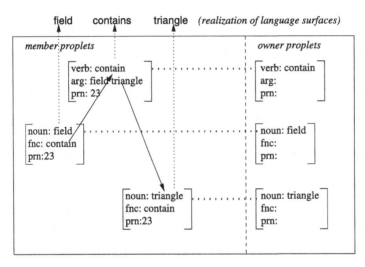

Compared to the NAG navigations in Sects. 23.3–23.5, the navigation is simplified in that it is more direct. Instead of beginning with the verb, it takes the noun proplet *field* with the prn value 23 as its start proplet.

Access to a next proplet may be external using the address or internal using the implementation of the address as a pointer. Based on the start proplet's continuation feature, here [fnc: contain], external access looks for the token line of contain and proceeds from the owner proplet to the member proplet with the prn value 23. The proplet *contain* has the continuation feature [arg: field triangle]. The first value, field, confirms the previous navigation. The second value triangle is the new 'next' proplet. It is found by going to the token line of triangle and proceeding from the owner proplet to the member proplet with the prn value 23.

The arrows in 24.2.2 show internal access based on pointers instead of going via owner proplet and prn value. In either way, proposition 23 may be traversed completely. The content is realized agent-externally as a sequence of language surfaces which are derived from the core values and realized in the time-linear order of the navigation. The navigation may be continued extrapropositionally to another proposition, based on the value of the verb's nc (next conjunct) value (not shown, but see 24.2.1).

Natural language communication between a speaker and a hearer is successful if the content coded into language by the speaker is reconstructed equivalently by the hearer. Using simplified variants of 24.1.1 (hear mode) and 24.2.2 (speak mode), the transfer of information from the speaker to the hearer may be shown as follows:

24.2.3 Transfer of Information from the Speaker to the Hearer

The speaker's navigation (24.2.2) serves as the conceptualization (*what to say*) and as the basic serialization (*how to say it*) of natural language production. The hearer's interpretation (24.1.1) consists in deriving a corresponding set of proplets. The time-linear order of the sign induced by the speaker's navigation is eliminated in the hear mode, allowing storage of the proplets in accordance with the database schema of a word bank. When the agent switches from the hear mode to the speak mode, the order may be reconstructed by navigating along the semantic relations of structure.

24.3 Questions and Answers

In addition to using natural language for reading the content of declarative sentences into and out of the word bank, the SLIM machine permits querying the content using natural language questions and providing natural language answers. The terms question and answer refer to a kind of utterance, like statement and request, in contradistinction to the terms interrogative and responsive, which refer to a sign kind like declarative and imperative.

Just as declaratives may be used (PoP-1, 4.3.3) not only for statements, interrogatives may be used not only for questions. For example, I am asking you if you ate my cookie. is a declarative used as a question, while Could you pass the salt? is an interrogative used as a request. These are indirect uses (22.4.2) which require inferencing. Let us consider the simplest case, namely interrogatives used as questions.

There are two basic kinds of interrogative, called (i) WH Interrogative and (ii) Yes/No Interrogative:

24.3.1 BASIC KINDS OF INTERROGATIVE IN NATURAL LANGUAGE

WH Interrogative	**Yes/No Interrogative**
Who entered the restaurant?	Did Peter enter the restaurant?

The interpretation of a WH Interrogative results in a functor proplet in which the value occupied by the WH word is represented by a variable σ_1 and the value of prn is represented by a variable σ_2. The interpretation of a Yes/No Interrogative results in a functor proplet in which only the prn attribute contains a variable as its value:

24.3.2 SEARCH PROPLETS OF THE TWO BASIC KINDS OF INTERROGATIVES

WH Interrogative	**Yes/No Interrogative**
$\begin{bmatrix} \text{fnc: enter} \\ \text{arg: } \sigma_1 \text{ restaurant} \\ \text{prn: } \sigma_2 \end{bmatrix}$	$\begin{bmatrix} \text{fnc: enter} \\ \text{arg: Peter restaurant} \\ \text{prn: } \sigma_2 \end{bmatrix}$

An interrogative is answered by attempting to match the search proplet with the last (most recent) proplet of the corresponding token line. If the continuation value(s) of this last proplet match the search proplet, the answer is found and there is no need for further search. Otherwise, the token line is systematically searched, proceeding backwards from the last (rightmost) proplet. Consider the following example:

24.3.3 APPLYING QUERY PATTERN OF A WH QUESTION TO A TOKEN LINE

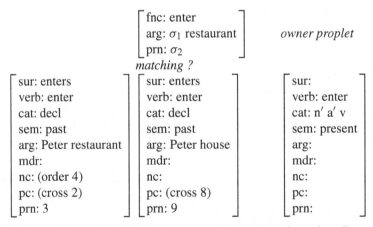

The fnc value enter of query pattern determines the token line to be searched. The initial attempt at matching fails because the second argument restaurant of the query proplet and its counterpart house in the token line are not compatible. Therefore, the search is continued by moving the pattern proplet one step to the left. This time pattern matching will be successful, σ_1 will be bound to the value Peter and σ_2 to 3. The resulting answer will be Peter.

The search with a WH query proplet is based on the following LA Grammar:

24.3.4 DEFINITION OF *LA Q1* FOR WH INTERROGATIVES QUERYING SUBJECT

ST_S: $\{([\alpha]\{rule_1, rule_2\})\}$

rule$_1$ $\qquad\qquad\qquad\qquad\qquad\qquad$ $\{rule_1\ rule_2\}$

$$\begin{bmatrix} \text{verb: } \alpha \\ \text{ňarg: } \sigma_1\ X \\ \text{prn: } \sigma_2 \end{bmatrix} \begin{bmatrix} \text{verb: } \alpha \\ \text{ňarg: } \sigma_1\ Y \\ \text{prn: } \sigma_2 - 1 \end{bmatrix} \Rightarrow \begin{bmatrix} \text{verb: } \alpha \\ \text{ňarg: } \sigma_1\ Y \\ \text{prn: } \sigma_2 - 1 \end{bmatrix}$$

rule$_2$ $\qquad\qquad\qquad\qquad\qquad\qquad$ $\{rule_3\}$

$$\begin{bmatrix} \text{verb: } \alpha \\ \text{ňarg: } \sigma_1\ X \\ \text{prn: } \sigma_2 \end{bmatrix} \begin{bmatrix} \text{verb: } \alpha \\ \text{arg: } \sigma_1\ Y \\ \text{prn: } \sigma_2 - 1 \end{bmatrix} \Rightarrow \begin{bmatrix} \text{verb: } \alpha \\ \text{arg: } \sigma_1\ Y \\ \text{prn: } \sigma_2 - 1 \end{bmatrix}$$

rule$_3$ $\qquad\qquad\qquad\qquad\qquad\qquad$ $\{\ \}$

$$\begin{bmatrix} \text{verb: } \alpha \\ \text{arg: } \sigma_1\ X \\ \text{prn: n} \end{bmatrix} \begin{bmatrix} \text{noun: } \sigma_1 \\ \text{fnc: } \alpha \\ \text{prn: n} \end{bmatrix} \Rightarrow \begin{bmatrix} \text{noun: } \sigma_1 \\ \text{fnc: } \alpha \\ \text{prn: n} \end{bmatrix} \{\ \}$$

ST_F: $\{([\text{noun: } \sigma_1]\ rp_3)\}$

The prn patterns follow the convention that $\sigma_2 - 1$ (for σ_2 minus one) stands for the proplet immediately preceding the current proplet in the token line. The ň operator is negation. For example, ňarg: σ_1 X means that the value which X has been bound to in the query pattern does not match the input proplet.

The first two *LA Q1* rules apply if their first input pattern does *not* match the continuation predicates of the current input proplet. If the proplet preceding the current proplet does not match the second input pattern either, rule$_1$ fires and the search continues with rule$_1$ and rule$_2$ using the preceding proplet as the new sentence start. This procedure is repeated until the preceding proplet does match, or the (left) end of the token line is reached. If the preceding proplet matches, rule$_2$ fires and the variable σ_1 is bound to the value searched for. Then rule$_3$ navigates to the proplet of the queried continuation value and returns this noun proplet as the desired answer.

For example, applying the pattern of the WH Interrogative in 24.3.2 to the rightmost member proplet of the token line *enter* in 24.3.3 will result in failure because the continuation feature [arg: Peter house] does not match the search pattern [arg: σ_1 restaurant]. Thus, the input conditions of rule$_1$ and rule$_2$ of *LA Q1* are satisfied.

When applying rule$_1$ and rule$_2$ to the preceding proplet (here with the prn value 3), rule$_2$ happens to be successful. Thereby the variable σ_1 is bound to the answer of the query (i.e., Peter). Rule rule$_3$ navigates to this value (i.e., the proplet *Peter* of proposition 3). It is turned into a responsive and uttered as the answer.

A query based on a Yes/No Interrogative is handled in a similar manner, using the following LA Grammar:

24.3.5 DEFINITION OF *LA Q2* FOR YES/NO INTERROGATIVES

ST_S: $\{([\alpha]\{\text{rule}_1, \text{rule}_2\})\}$

rule$_1$ $\qquad\qquad\qquad\qquad\qquad$ $\{\text{rule}_1\ \text{rule}_2\}$

$$\begin{bmatrix} \text{verb: } \alpha \\ \text{ňarg: X} \\ \text{prn: } \sigma_2 \end{bmatrix} \begin{bmatrix} \text{verb: } \alpha \\ \text{ňarg: Y} \\ \text{prn: } \sigma_2 - 1 \end{bmatrix} \Rightarrow \begin{bmatrix} \text{verb: } \alpha \\ \text{ňarg: Y} \\ \text{prn: } \sigma_2 - 1 \end{bmatrix}$$

rule$_2$ $\qquad\qquad\qquad\qquad\qquad$ $\{\ \}$

$$\begin{bmatrix} \text{verb: } \alpha \\ \text{ňarg: X} \\ \text{prn: } \sigma_2 \end{bmatrix} \begin{bmatrix} \text{verb: } \alpha \\ \text{arg: Y} \\ \text{prn: } \sigma_2 - 1 \end{bmatrix} \Rightarrow \begin{bmatrix} \text{verb: } \alpha \\ \text{arg: Y} \\ \text{prn: } \sigma_2 - 1 \end{bmatrix}$$

ST_F: $\{([\text{fnc: } \alpha]\ \text{rp}_1)\ ([\text{fnc: } \alpha]\ \text{rp}_2)\}$

In *LA Q2*, the responsives are based on the final states ST_F, the first of which represents the answer no and the second the answer yes. For example, in the attempt to answer the Yes/No Interrogative Did Peter enter the restaurant? relative to the token line 24.3.3, the left-most proplet will match, resulting in the final state ([fnc: α] rp$_2$), which is realized as the answer yes. In contrast, if there are no preceding proplets left in the token line, *LA Q2* terminates in the final state ([fnc: α] rp$_1$), which is realized linguistically as the answer no.

The correct answering of interrogatives interacts closely with inferencing. For example, even if the agent's word bank contains the episodic proposition *Peter eat salad*, the interrogative Did Peter eat some food? would be answered with no. After adding the absolute proposition *salad is food* to the word bank, the answer to the interrogative Did Peter eat some food? would still be no – which is counterintuitive. What is needed is a non-monotonic inference which, based on the premises *Peter eat salad* and *salad is food*, results in the system's answering Did Peter eat some food? with yes.

The formal nature of inferences depends on the kind of semantics (19.2.2), i.e., whether the semantics is based on metalanguage definitions (as in logical languages), procedural execution (as in programming languages), or the assignment of bidirectionally connected proplets in a database (as in natural languages in accordance with the SLIM theory of language). This raises the question of whether and how the inferences of classical as well as modern systems[1] should be recreated within Database Semantics.

As a first step towards answering this question let us consider some classic inferences of propositional calculus.

---

[1] Cf. Bibel (1993).

24.3.6 INFERENCE SCHEMATA OF PROPOSITIONAL CALCULUS

1. $\dfrac{A, B}{\vdash A \wedge B}$ 2. $\dfrac{A \vee B, \neg A}{\vdash B}$ 3. $\dfrac{A \rightarrow B, A}{\vdash B}$ 4. $\dfrac{A \rightarrow B, \neg B}{\vdash \neg A}$

5. $\dfrac{A \wedge B}{\vdash A}$ 6. $\dfrac{A}{\vdash A \vee B}$ 7. $\dfrac{\neg A}{\vdash A \rightarrow B}$ 8. $\dfrac{\neg\neg A}{\vdash A}$

These inference schemata consist of propositions which may be either basic, e.g., A, or complex, e.g., $A \vee B$. A single premise (5–8) or two premises (1–4) appear above the horizontal line, the latter separated by commas. The conclusion appears below the horizontal line and is preceded by '$\vdash$' (turnstile).

The first inference is called conjunction and says that the truth of two arbitrary propositions A and B implies the truth of the complex proposition $A \wedge B$. A transfer of this inference into Database Semantics would amount to an operation which establishes new extrapropositional relations based on the conjunction *and*. This operation may be realized by the following SLIM inference (hypothetical):

24.3.7 HYPOTHETICAL INFERENCE RULE inf_{conj} FOR CONJUNCTION

$$\text{inf}_{conj}\colon \begin{bmatrix} \text{fnc: } \alpha \\ \text{prn: } m \end{bmatrix} \begin{bmatrix} \text{fnc: } \beta \\ \text{prn: } n \end{bmatrix} \implies \begin{bmatrix} \text{fnc: } \alpha \\ \text{nc: } (\beta\ n) \\ \text{prn: } m \end{bmatrix} \begin{bmatrix} \text{fnc: } \beta \\ \text{pc: } (\alpha\ m) \\ \text{prn: } n \end{bmatrix}$$

This inference rule produces a new extrapropositional relation between two arbitrary propositions by means of the address values $(\alpha\ m)$ and $(\beta\ n)$, enabling a navigation from any proposition to any other proposition asserted in the word bank.

In its logical interpretation, the inference expresses a conjunction of truth and is as such intuitively obvious. Under these circumstances it is not relevant *which* propositions are conjoined as long as they are true.

In its Database Semantic interpretation, however, the inference raises the question of *why* two – up to now unconnected – propositions should be concatenated. Even though the concatenation would not result in asserting a falsehood, an uncontrolled application of inf_{conj} would destroy coherence (Sect. 24.5). This shows that the inferences of classical logic change their character when transferred to Database Semantics, for which reason they should not be adopted blindly.[2]

24.4 Autonomous Control

While the navigation through the content of an agent's word bank is enabled and constrained by the semantic relations between proplets, it is not determined completely

---

[2] The problems of logical inference systems have been clearly identified in the literature. See for example Russell and Norvig (1995).

by them. First, each proplet usually provides several possible continuations. Second, inferences connect antecedents with consequents, thus providing another method of moving through content. Therefore, the agent requires an autonomous control for connecting (i) recognition, (ii) content stored in memory, and (iii) action.

To maintain the agent in a continuous equilibrium vis-à-vis constantly changing internal and external environments, autonomous control relates current recognition to relevant past experiences and derives appropriate actions by evaluating their outcome in relation to the present. In this way, changes in the environment are used as the motor driving the agent's cognitive operations, including the processing of natural language.

Achieving balance may be based on concatenated propositions in the agent's word bank, which are individuated into recognition-action-recognition (rac) sequences.[3] These store past experiences relating to, for example, feeling hungry. When the cognitive agent's internal recognition reads *CA feels hungry* into CA's word bank once more, this proposition is used to retrieve and highlight all earlier rac sequences beginning with it:

24.4.1 RECOGNITION HIGHLIGHTING ASSOCIATED RAC SEQUENCES

CA feels hungry
|
CA feels hungry–CA searches at place X–CA finds no food
|
CA feels hungry–CA searches at place Y–CA finds a little food
|
CA feels hungry–CA searches at place Z–CA finds lots of food

Each rac sequence consists of an antecedent, a consequent, and an evaluation. The retrieval of rac sequences with the antecedent *CA feels hungry* is based on the word bank's data structure, using the core values as the key. LA Think navigates through these rac sequences, jumping throughout the word bank from proplet to proplet by following their continuation values.

The evaluation is expressed by means of need vectors, pointing up or down at various degrees, including 'no change'. When a rac sequence is activated later by an incoming recognition, its need vector is related to the current parameter values. If one of the parameters is out of normal range, the rac sequence with a need vector most likely to regain balance for that parameter and with the least cost is highlighted most. In this way, (i) the rac sequence most appropriate to regain balance is chosen, and (ii) the associated action is realized.

---

[3] Our notion of a rac sequence is reminiscent of Skinner's stimulus-response model (Skinner 1957, 1974), though he would probably object to our representation of content in terms of concatenated propositions. Furthermore, in contrast to Skinner, a rac sequence does not require repeated training.

For example, if CA's need parameter for energy has dropped a little out of range, the proposition *CA feels hungry* is read into the word bank. If the state of the energy parameter corresponds best to the second rac sequence, it would be highlighted most, causing CA to search at place Y. The first and the third rac sequence would come into play only if CA's search at place Y is unsuccessful.

Similarly, if CA's need parameter for temperature has risen out of range by a lot, *CA feels hot* is read into the word bank. This results in highlighting rac sequences beginning with that proposition, e.g., (1) *CA feels hot–CA moves into the shade–CA cools down a little*, (2) *CA feels hot–CA moves into the basement–CA cools down a lot*, and (3) *CA feels hot–CA moves into the sun–CA feels hotter*. Here the need vector of the second rac sequence is best suited to regain balance, resulting in the corresponding action.

But what about situations never encountered before, such that there are no rac sequences in the word bank to be activated by current recognition? In this case, predefined ('innate') open rac sequences provide options for action. Consider the following example:

24.4.2 OPEN RAC SEQUENCES FOR UNKNOWN SITUATIONS

CA meets unknown animal
|
1. *CA meets unknown animal–CA approaches– ?*
|
2. *CA meets unknown animal–CA waits– ?*
|
3. *CA meets unknown animal–CA flees– ?*

These rac sequences are open because due to lack of experience no evaluation is known (represented by '?'). However, there may be predefined need vectors relating to the fear parameter

For example, appearance of the unknown animal as small and cuddly will lower the fear parameter, resulting in agreement with the first rac sequence. Appearance as big and ferocious will increase the fear, resulting in agreement with the third rac sequence. If the animal's appearance is uncertain, CA chooses the second rac sequence.

Provided that CA survives the encounter, a new complete rac sequence evaluating CA's action towards this particular animal or kind of animal will be stored in CA's word bank. Thus, a situation without the agent having an appropriate rac sequence available will rarely occur, because as soon as this situation arises again there will be a rac sequence in the agent's database.

If there are no external or internal demands activating specific navigation patterns appropriate to the situation at hand, the navigation of LA Think may take the form of a random, aimless motion through the contents of a word bank analogous to free association in humans. Thereby, two problems requiring a general solution may arise, namely relapse and split. A relapse arises if an LA navigation continues to traverse the same proplet sequence in a loop. A split arises if a given START proplet is accepted by more than one navigation rule in an active rule package.

Relapse and split are avoided by tracking principles. Their technical basis are counters indicating for each proplet when it was traversed. Adding traversal counters gives the static nature of a word bank a dynamic aspect insofar as they make the course of the navigation visible as a track in terms of (positive or negative) highlighting.

24.4.3 TRACKING PRINCIPLES OF LA NAVIGATION

1. *Completeness*
   Within an elementary proposition, proplets already traversed during the current navigation are marked with # (negative highlighting).
2. *Uniqueness*
   If several START or NEXT proplets are available, only one is selected, whereby the choice is based on an activated rac sequence or at random.
3. *Recency*
   In extrapropositional navigations, propositions which have been most recently traversed receive negative highlighting.
4. *Frequency*
   When entering a new subcontext, the paths most frequently traversed in previous navigations are highlighted.

The first principle prevents intrapropositional relapses and premature extrapropositional continuations. The second principle prevents an LA navigation from traversing several thought paths simultaneously. The third principle prevents extrapropositional relapses and ensures that a subcontext is traversed as completely as possible in the course of a free navigation. According to the fourth principle, the free navigation of a new subcontext first traverses the propositions which have been traversed most frequently in the past – whereby it is assumed that under the normal circumstances of everyday life the most important navigation patterns are activated most often.

24.5 Coherence

In order for the agent to survive and prosper in its environment, the content in its word bank must be coherent. This requires adequate recognition and action performance of the agent's external interfaces. Today's standard computers, however, provide mainly a keyboard and a screen for moving alphanumerical sequences in and out, which is not sufficient.

Until the necessary recognition and action interfaces become available, one might consider simulating contextual cognition as a virtual reality (1.1.3). This would allow the user to control movement through an artificial world (automated cinematography;

Funge et al. 1999) and to communicate with artificial agents which interact with their virtual task environment (Rickel and Johnson 1999; Loyall and Bates 1993).

It turns out, however, that virtual reality and Database Semantics pursue different goals: virtual reality designs artificial worlds containing artificial agents for the interaction with natural agents (i.e., the users), while Database Semantics designs artificial agents for the interaction with the natural world containing natural agents. Reliance on virtual reality is problematic for Database Semantics for the following reasons:

First, it is a misdirection of effort; rather than grounding coherence in real interaction with the external world, the programming work is directed mostly toward simulating convincing 3-D environments with animated agents. Second, an artificial model of the world is not credible as a procedural foundation of word semantics. Third, a simulation of reference is of little help for arriving at real reference.

There are both practical and theoretical reasons why the cognitive agent's interaction with the real world in terms of artificial recognition and action should be neither simulated nor avoided. Regarding practical applications, an absence of such real interaction makes it impossible for the system to translate natural language commands into real-world actions or to report real-world observations in natural language.

Regarding theoretical development, such an absence deprives the system of two essential foundations: One is a procedural definition of elementary concepts, needed for the autonomous buildup of contextual content and re-used as the literal meanings of language. The other is the grounding of cognitive coherence in contextual content.

A propositional content such as *field contain triangle* (3.4.4) may be read into the word bank either directly via immediate perception, or indirectly via spoken or written language, film, etc. (4.3.1). When content is read in directly by a well-functioning system, the content's coherence follows from the coherence of the external world, i.e., the temporal and spatial sequencing of events, the part-whole relations, etc.

Content stored on media, in contrast, allows for the possibility that an author has reordered and reconnected elements familiar from immediate recognition and action. This is why mediated content may be incoherent.

For example, a swimmer standing at the poolside, diving into the water, and disappearing with a splash is coherent. In contrast, a pair of feet appearing in the foaming water with a swimmer flying feet first into the air and landing at the poolside would be incoherent – unless it is specified in addition that the content is represented by means of a medium, e.g., a backward running movie.

Similarly, for people to be conversing in English is coherent. In contrast, a deer conversing in English with a skunk would be incoherent – unless it is specified that the content is represented by means of a medium, e.g., a piece of fictional language.

An agent's idea of what is coherent and what is not influences whether a content is evaluated as possible, plausible, or even true. Other factors are whether it happens to be a mediated or a direct content. The value of a mediated content, acquired via language, film, and the like, depends on how the agent evaluates the reliability of the source, e.g, the speaker. An immediate content, acquired via the agent's direct observation, in contrast, is usually regarded as the most reliable. Nevertheless, immediate content is not infallible, as shown by optical illusions, conflicting eyewitness reports, and changing ideas in the history of science of what is coherent and what is true.

Exercises

Section 24.1

1. Does the hear mode of DBS apply automatic word form recognition and syntactic-semantic parsing in separate phases?
2. Why is the derivation in 24.1.1 surface compositional?
3. Why is the derivation in 24.1.1 time-linear?
4. Why is the content derived in 24.1.1 suitable for a handling of reference as an agent internal pattern matching?
5. Why is the content derived in 24.1.1 suitable for storage in a word bank?
6. Why is a word bank content-addressable?
7. Explain the difference between extrapropositional and intrapropositional relations. Does this distinction affect storage of the associated contents in a word bank?

Section 24.2

1. Why does language production require conceptualization?
2. Explain the notions of coherence and cohesion.
3. What is the database schema of a word bank and why is it essential for implementing an autonomous navigation through stored content?
4. What is a token line?
5. What is the key for the storage and retrieval of proplets in a word bank?
6. Which database procedures require finding the token line for a particular core value? Explain possible computational techniques for finding the token line for *rabbit*.
7. Describe the mechanism of navigating from a given proplet to a next proplet.
8. How does the navigation contribute to the speak mode?
9. Which proplet values are used for realizing a surface?

Section 24.3

1. Describe the difference between pipeline, interactive, and integrated systems of natural language generation and compare them with natural language production within the SLIM theory of language. How do they handle conceptualization?

2. What is the difference between a statement and a declarative sentence? How does this relate to PoP-1?
3. What is the difference between a question and an interrogative sentence?
4. What is the difference between an answer and a responsive?
5. What are indirect language uses and what is required for their production and interpretation?
6. How many kinds of WH Interrogatives are there in English?
7. Compare the responsives for answering WH questions and Yes/No questions.
8. Explain the DBS mechanism for finding the answer to a question.
9. Describe the differences between the query proplets for the different kinds of interrogatives. Why do they contain variables?
10. Explain the different functioning of *LA Q1* and *LA Q2*.
11. Explain which aspect of a word bank's database schema supports the automatic answering of natural language interrogatives.
12. What is the role of inferences for adequate query answering?

Section 24.4

1. What is the task of an agent's autonomous control?
2. How is the agent's memory involved in providing adequate behavior?
3. What are the agent's options in a situation never encountered before?
4. Explain the tracking principles of DBS.

Section 24.5

1. Can the DBS system be used on a standard computer?
2. Discuss the possible contribution of virtual reality (VR) to the goal of constructing a talking robot.
3. What is the contribution of a robot's recognition and action capabilities to the semantics of DBS?
4. Who is responsible for the veracity of the data in an agent's word bank? Discuss different setups.
5. How does the external environment determine the agent's notion of coherence?

Bibliography

Ackermann, W. (1928) "Zum Hilbertschen Aufbau der reellen Zahlen," *Mathematische Annalen* 99:118–133

Aho, A.V., and J.D. Ullman (1977) *Principles of Compiler Design*, Reading: Addison-Wesley

Aho, A.V., J.E. Hopcroft, and J.D. Ullman (1983) *Data Structures and Algorithms*, Reading: Addison-Wesley

Aho, A.V., B.W. Kernighan, and P. Weinberger (1988) *The AWK Programming Language*, Reading: Addison-Wesley

Ajdukiewicz, K. (1935) "Die syntaktische Konnexität," *Studia Philosophica* 1:1–27

Anderson, J.R. (1990) *Cognitive Psychology and Its Implications*, 3rd edn. New York: W.H. Freeman and Company

Anderson, J.R., and G.H. Bower (1973) *Human Associative Memory*, Washington: V.H. Winston

Anderson, J.R., and G.H. Bower (1980) *Human Associative Memory: A Brief Edition*, Hillsdale: Lawrence Erlbaum Associates

Appelt, D. (1985) *Planning English Sentences*, Cambridge: Cambridge University Press

Austin, J.L. (1962) *How to Do Things with Words*, Oxford: Clarendon Press

Bach, E. (1962) "The Order of Elements in a Transformational Grammar of German," *Language* 38:263–269

Bar-Hillel, Y. (1953) "Some Linguistic Problems Connected with Machine Translation," *Philosophy of Science* 20:217–225

Bar-Hillel, Y. (1964) *Language and Information. Selected Essays on Their Theory and Application*, Reading: Addison-Wesley

Bar-Hillel, Y. (1971) "Out of the Pragmatic Waste-Basket," *Linguistic Inquiry* 2:401–407

Barcan-Marcus, R. (1960) "Extensionality," *Mind* 69:55–62, reprinted in L. Linsky (ed.), 1971

Barthes, R. (1986) *The Rustle of Language*, New York: Hill and Wang

Barton, G., R.C. Berwick, and E.S. Ristad (1987) *Computational Complexity and Natural Language*, Cambridge: MIT Press

Barwise, J., and J. Perry (1983) *Situations and Attitudes*, Cambridge: MIT Press

Bergenholtz, H. (1989) "Korpusproblematik in der Computerlinguistik. Konstruktionsprinzipien und Repräsentativität," in H. Steger (ed.)

Berkeley, G. (1710) *A Treatise Concerning the Principles of Human Knowledge*, reprinted in Taylor, 1974

Berwick, R.C., and A.S. Weinberg (1984) *The Grammatical Basis of Linguistic Performance: Language Use and Acquisition*, Cambridge: MIT Press

Bertossi, L., G. Katona, K.-D. Schewe, and B. Thalheim (eds.) (2003) *Semantics in Databases*, Berlin: Springer

Beutel, B. (1997) *Malaga 4.0*, CLUE-Manual, CL Lab, Friedrich Alexander Universität Erlangen Nürnberg

Bibel, W. (1993) *Wissensrepräsentation und Inferenz*, Braunschweig-Wiesbaden: Vieweg

Biber, D. (1993) "Representativeness in Corpus Design," *Literary and Linguistic Computing* 8.4

Bierwisch, M. (1963) *Grammatik des deutschen Verbs*, Studia Grammatica II, Berlin: Akademie-Verlag

Blair, D.C., and M.E. Maron (1985) "An Evaluation of Retrieval Effectiveness for a Full-Text Document-Retrieval System," *Communications of the ACM* 28.3:289–299

Bloomfield, L. (1933) *Language*, New York: Holt, Rinehart, and Winston

Bochvar, D.A. (1939) "Ob Odnom Tréhznačnom Isčislénii i Égo Priménénii k Analizu Paradoksov Klassičéskogo Rasšsirennogo Funkcional'nogo Isčisléniá" (On a 3-Valued Logical Calculus and Its Application to the Analysis of Contraditions), *Matématičéskij Sbornik* 4:287–308. Reviewed by Alonzo Church, *The Journal of Symbolic Logic* 4:98–99, and 5:119

Book, R.V. (ed.) (1980) *Formal Language Theory: Perspectives and Open Problems*, New York: Academic Press

Brady, M., and R.C. Berwick (eds.) (1983) *Computational Models of Discourse*, Cambridge: MIT Press

Bray, T., J. Paoli, C.M. Sperberg-McQueen, E. Maler, and F. Yergeau (eds.) (2008) *Extensible Markup Language (XML) 1.0*, 5th edn., W3C Recommendation. `http://www.w3.org/XML/Core/#Publications`

Bresnan, J. (ed.) (1982) *The Mental Representation of Grammatical Relation*, Cambridge: MIT Press

de la Briandais, R. (1959) *Proc. Western Joint Computer Conf.*, Vol. 15, 295–298

Bröker, N. (1991) *Optimierung von LA-Morph im Rahmen einer Anwendung auf das Deutsche*, CLUE-betreute Diplomarbeit der Informatik, Friedrich Alexander Universität Erlangen Nürnberg

Brooks, R.A. (1986) "A Robust Layered Control System for a Mobile Robot," *IEEE Journal of Robotics and Automation* 2.1:14–23

Brooks, R.A. (1990) "Elephants Don't Play Chess," *Robotics and Autonomous Systems* 6.1–2, reprinted in P. Maes (ed.), 1990, 3–15

Brown, P., S. Della Pietra, V. Della Pietra, and R. Mercer (1991) "Word Sense Disambiguation Using Statistical Methods," *Proceedings of the 29th Annual Meeting of the Association for Computational Linguistics*, Berkeley, CA, 1991, 264–270

Brown, P., V. Della Pietra, et al. (1992) "Class-based n-gram Models of Natural Language," Paper read at the Pisa Conference on European Corpus Resources

Bühler, K. (1934) *Sprachtheorie: die Darstellungsfunktion der Sprache*, Stuttgart: Fischer

Burnard, L., and C.M. Sperberg-McQueen (1995) *TEI Lite: An Introduction to Text Encoding Interchange*, `http://www-tei.uic.edu/orgs/tei/intros/teiu5.tei`

Burnard, L. (ed.) (1995) *Users Reference Guide British National Corpus Version 1.0*, Oxford: Oxford University Computing Services

Burnard, L. (ed.) (2007) *Reference Guide for the British National Corpus (XML Edition)*, Oxford: Oxford University Computing Services

Busemann, S. (2000) "Generierung natürlichsprachlicher Texte," in G. Görz, C.-R. Rollinger, and J. Schneeberger (eds.)

Bybee, J.L. (1985) *Morphology: A Study of the Relation Between Meaning and Form*, Amsterdam/Philadelphia: John Benjamins

Carbonell, J.G., and R. Joseph (1986) *FrameKit+: A Knowledge Representation System*, Carnegie Mellon University, Department of Computer Science

Carnap, R. (1947) *Meaning and Necessity*, Chicago: The University of Chicago Press

Casanova de Seingalt, J. (1963) *Histoire de Ma Vie, Suivie de Textes Inèdit, Vols. I–III*, Bouquins, Robert Laffont

Chafe, W. (1970) *Meaning and the Structure of Language*, Chicago: The University of Chicago Press

Chen, Y. (1988) *Bianji Chuban Cidian* (Lexicon for Editors and Publishers, p. 221), Beijing Kexuejishu Chubanshe

Chomsky, N. (1957) *Syntactic Structures*, The Hague: Mouton

Chomsky, N. (1965) *Aspects of the Theory of Syntax*, Cambridge: MIT Press

Chomsky, N. (1981) *Lectures on Government and Binding*, Dordrecht: Foris

Church, A. (1956) *Introduction to Mathematical Logic, Vol. I*, Princeton: Princeton University Press

Church, K., and R.L. Mercer. (1993) "Introduction to the Special Issue on Computational Linguistics Using Large Corpora," *Computational Linguistics* 19.1:1–24

Cole, R. (ed.) (1998) *Survey of the State of the Art in Human Language Technology*, Edinburgh: Edinburgh University Press

Collins, A.M., and E.F. Loftus. (1975) "A Spreading-Activation Theory of Semantic Processing," *Psychological Review* 82.6:407–428

Condon, E.U. (1928) "Statistics of Vocabulary," *Science* 68.1733:300

Date, C.J. (2003) *An Introduction to Database Systems*, 8th edn. Reading: Addison-Wesley

Davidson, D. (1967) "Truth and Meaning," *Synthese* VII:304–323

Davidson, D., and G. Harman (eds.) (1972) *Semantics of Natural Language*, Dordrecht: D. Reidel

Denning, K., and S. Kemmer (eds.) (1990) *On Language, Selected Writings of Joseph H. Greenberg*, Stanford: Stanford University Press

DeRose, S. (1988) "Grammatical Category Disambiguation by Statistical Optimization," *Computational Linguistics* 14.1:31–39

Dretske, F. (1981) *Knowledge and the Flow of Information*, Cambridge: Bradford Books/MIT Press

Dreyfus, H. (1981) "From Micro-Worlds to Knowledge Representation: AI at an Impasse," in J. Haugeland (ed.)

Earley, J. (1970) "An Efficient Context-Free Parsing Algorithm," *Communications of the ACM* 2:94, reprinted in B. Grosz, K. Sparck Jones, and B.L. Webber (eds.), 1986

Eco, U. (1975) *A Theory of Semiotics*, Bloomington: Indiana University Press

Elmasri, R., and S.B. Navathe (2010) *Fundamentals of Database Systems*, 6th edn. Redwood City: Benjamin-Cummings

Estoup, J.B. (1916) *Gammes Sténographiques*, 4th edn. Paris: Institut Sténographique

van Fraassen, B. (1966) "Singular Terms, Truth-Value Gaps, and Free Logic," *The Journal of Philosophy* 63:481–495

van Fraassen, B. (1968) "Presupposition, Implication, and Self-reference," *The Journal of Philosophy* 65:136–152

van Fraassen, B. (1969) "Presuppositions, Supervaluations, and Free Logic," in K. Lambert (ed.), *The Logical Way of Doing Things*, New Haven: Yale University Press

Francis, W.N. (1980) "A Tagged Corpus: Problems and Prospects," in S. Greenbaum, G. Leech, and J. Svartvik (eds.), 192–209

Francis, W.N., and H. Kučera (1982) *Frequency Analysis of English Usage: Lexicon and Grammar*, Boston: Houghton Mifflin

Fredkin, E. (1960) "Trie Memory," *Communications of the ACM* 3.9:490–499

Frege, G. (1892) "Über Sinn und Bedeutung," *Zeitschrift für Philosophie und philosophische Kritik* 100:25–50

Frege, G. (1967) *Kleine Schriften*, edited by Ignacio Angelelli, Darmstadt: Wiss. Buchgesellschaft

Funge, J., X. Tu, and D. Terzopoulos (1999) *Cognitive Modeling: Knowledge, Reasoning and Planning for Intelligent Characters*, Los Angeles, CA: SIGGRAPH99

Gaifman, C. (1961) *Dependency Systems and Phrase Structure Systems*, P-2315, Santa Monica: Rand Corporation

Garey, M.R., and D.S. Johnson (1979) *Computers and Intractability: A Guide to the Theory of NP-Completeness*, San Francisco: W.H. Freeman

Garside, R., G. Leech, and G. Sampson (1987) *The Computational Analysis of English*, London: Longman

Gazdar, G. (1981) "Unbounded Dependencies and Coordinate Structure," *Linguistic Inquiry* 12.2:155–184

Gazdar, G. (1982) "Phrase structure grammar," in P. Jacobson and G.K. Pullum (eds.)

Gazdar, G., E. Klein, G. Pullum, and I. Sag (1985) *Generalized Phrase Structure Grammar*, Cambridge/Oxford: Harvard University Press/Blackwell

Geach, P. (1972) "A Program for Syntax," in D. Davidson and G. Harman (eds.), 483–497

Ginsburg, S. (1980) "Formal Language Theory: Methods for Specifying Formal Languages – Past, Present, Future," in R.V. Book (ed.), 1–22

Girard, R. (1972) *La Violence et le Sacré*, Paris: Bernard Grasset

Givón, T. (1985) "Iconicity, Isomorphism, and Non-arbitrary Coding in Syntax," in J. Haiman (ed.), 1985a

Goldfarb, C.F. (1990) *The SGML Handbook*, Oxford: Clarendon Press

Greenbaum, S., and N. Yibin (1994) "Tagging the British ICE Corpus: English Word Classes," in N. Oostdijk and P. de Haan (eds.)

Greenberg, J. (1954) "A Quantitative Approach to the Morphological Typology of Language," reprinted in K. Denning and S. Kemmer (eds.), 1990

Greenberg, J. (1963) "Some Universals of Grammar with Particular Reference to the Order of Meaningful Elements," in J. Greenberg (ed.)

Greenberg, J. (ed.) (1963) *Universals of Language*, Cambridge: MIT Press

Greibach, S. (1973) "The Hardest Context-Free Language," *SIAM Journal on Computing* 2:304–310

Grice, P. (1957) "Meaning," *Philosophical Review* 66:377–388

Grice, P. (1965) "Utterer's Meaning, Sentence Meaning, and Word Meaning," *Foundations of Language* 4:1–18

Griffith, T., and S. Petrik (1965) "On the Relative Efficiencies of Context-Free Grammar Recognizers," *Communications of the ACM* 8:289–300

Grosz, B., K.S. Jones, and B.L. Webber (eds.) (1986) *Readings in Natural Language Processing*, Los Altos: Morgan Kaufmann

Groenendijk, J.A.G., T.M.V. Janssen, and M.B.J. Stokhof (eds.) (1980) *Formal Methods in the Study of Language*, University of Amsterdam: Mathematical Center Tracts, Vol. 135

Gupta, A. (1982) "Truth and Paradox," *Journal of Philosophical Logic* 11:1–60

Haiman, J. (ed.) (1985a) *Iconicity in Syntax*, Typological Studies in Language, Vol. 6, Amsterdam/Philadelphia: John Benjamins

Haiman, J. (1985b) *Natural Syntax, Iconicity, and Erosion*, Cambridge: Cambridge University Press

Halliday, M.A.K. (1985) *An Introduction to Functional Grammar*, London: Edward Arnold

Harman, G. (1963) "Generative Grammar Without Transformational Rules: A Defense of Phrase Structure," *Language* 39:597–616

Harris, Z. (1951) *Method in Structural Linguistics*, Chicago: University of Chicago Press

Harrison, M. (1978) *Introduction to Formal Language Theory*, Reading: Addison-Wesley

Haugeland, J. (ed.) (1981) *Mind Design*, Cambridge: MIT Press

Hausser, R. (1973) "Presuppositions and Quantifiers," *Papers from the Ninth Regional Conference*, Chicago: Chicago Linguistics Society

Hausser, R. (1976) "Presuppositions in Montague Grammar," *Theoretical Linguistics* 3:245–279

Hausser, R. (1978) "Surface Compositionality and the Semantics of Mood," reprinted in J. Searle, F. Kiefer, and M. Bierwisch (eds.), 1980

Hausser, R. (1979a) "A Constructive Approach to Intensional Contexts," *Language Research* 18.2, Seoul, Korea, 1982

Hausser, R. (1979b) "A New Treatment of Context in Model-Theory," *Sull' Anaphora, Atti del Seminario Accademia della Crusca*, Florence, Italy, 1981

Hausser, R. (1980) "The Place of Pragmatics in Model-Theory," in J.A.G. Groenendijk et al. (eds.)

Hausser, R. (1983) "On Vagueness," *Journal of Semantics* 2:273–302

Hausser, R. (1984) *Surface Compositional Grammar*, Munich: Wilhelm Fink Verlag

Hausser, R. (1985) "Left-Associative Grammar and the Parser NEWCAT," Center for the Study of Language and Information, Stanford University, IN-CSLI-85-5

Hausser, R. (1986) *NEWCAT: Parsing Natural Language Using Left-Associative Grammar*, Lecture Notes in Computer Science, Vol. 231, Berlin: Springer

Hausser, R. (1989a) *Computation of Language, An Essay on Syntax, Semantics and Pragmatics in Natural Man-Machine Communication*, Symbolic Computation: Artificial Intelligence, Berlin: Springer

Hausser, R. (1989b) "Principles of Computational Morphology," Laboratory of Computational Linguistics, Carnegie Mellon University

Hausser, R. (1992) "Complexity in Left-Associative Grammar," *Theoretical Computer Science* 106.2:283–308

Hausser, R. (ed.) (1996) *Linguistische Verifikation. Dokumentation zur Ersten Morpholympics*, Tübingen: Max Niemeyer Verlag

Hausser, R. (2001c) "Database Semantics for Natural Language," *Artificial Intelligence* 130.1:27–74

Hausser, R. (2006) *A Computational Model of Natural Language Communication: Interpretation, Inferencing, and Production in Database Semantics*, pp. 365, Berlin: Springer

Hausser, R. (2010) "Language Production Based on Autonomous Control – A Content-Addressable Memory for a Model of Cognition," *Language and Information* 11:5–31, Seoul: Korean Society for Language and Information

Hausser, R. (2011) *Computational Linguistics and Talking Robots: Processing Content in Database Semantics*, pp. 286, Berlin: Springer

Hayashi, T. (1973) "On Derivation Trees of Indexed Grammars: An Extension of the uvwxy Theorem," *Publications of the Research Institute for Mathematical Sciences* 9.1:61–92

van Herwijnen, E. (1990) *Practical SGML*, Dordrecht: Kluwer, 2nd edn., 1994

Herzberger, H. (1982) "Notes on Naive Semantics," *Journal of Philosophical Logic* 11: 61–102

Hess, K., J. Brustkern, and W. Lenders (1983) *Maschinenlesbare deutsche Wörterbücher*, Tübingen: Max Niemeyer Verlag

Hockett, C.F. (1958) *A Course in Modern Linguistics*, New York: Macmillan

Hofland, K., and S. Johansson (1980) *Word Frequencies in British and American English*, London: Longman

Hopcroft, J.E., and J.D. Ullman (1979) *Introduction to Automata Theory, Languages, and Computation*, Reading: Addison-Wesley

Hovy, E. (1988) *Generating Natural Language under Pragmatic Constraints*, Hillsdale: Lawrence Erlbaum

Howell, P.R. (ed.) (1990) *Beyond Literacy: The Second Gutenberg Revolution (Mind Age)*, Dallas: Saybrook Publishing Company

Hubel, D.H., and T.N. Wiesel (1962) "Receptive Fields, Binocular Interaction, and Functional Architecture in the Cat's Visual Cortex," *Journal of Physiology* 160:106–154

Hume, D. (1748) *An Enquiry Concerning Human Understanding*, reprinted in Taylor, 1974

Hurford, J., M. Studdert-Kennedy, and C. Knight (1998) *Approaches to the Evolution of Language*, Cambridge: Cambridge University Press

Hutchins, W.J. (1986) *Machine Translation: Past, Present, Future*, Chichester: Ellis Horwood

Illingworth, V. et al. (eds.) (1990) *Dictionary of Computing*, Oxford: Oxford University Press

Jackendoff, R. (1972) *Semantic Interpretation in Generative Grammar*, Cambridge: MIT Press

Jacobson, P. and G.K. Pullum (eds.) (1982) *The Nature of Syntactic Representation*, Dordrecht: D. Reidel

Jespersen, O. (1921) *Language. Its Nature, Development, and Origin*, reprinted in the Norton Library 1964, New York: W.W. Norton and Company

Johnson-Laird, P.N. (1983) *Mental Models*, Cambridge: Harvard University Press

Joos, M. (1936) "Review of G.K. Zipf: The Psycho-biology of Language," *Language* 12:3

Joshi, A.K., L.S. Levy, and M. Takahashi (1975) "Tree Adjunct Grammars," *Journal of Computer and Systems Sciences* 10:136–163

Joshi, A.K., K. Vijay-Shanker, and D.J. Weir (1991) "The Convergence of Mildly Context-Sensitive Grammar Formalisms," in P. Sells, S. Shieber, and T. Wasow (eds.)

Jurafsky, D., and J. Martin (2000) *Speech and Language Processing: An Introduction to Natural Language Processing, Computational Linguistics, and Speech Recognition*, Upper Saddle River: Prentice Hall

Kaeding, W. (1897/1898) *Häufigkeitswörterbuch der deutschen Sprache*, Steglitz

Kamp, J.A.W., and U. Reyle (1993) *From Discourse to Logic, Parts 1 and 2*, Dordrecht: Kluwer

Katz, J., and P. Postal (1964) *An Integrated Theory of Linguistic Descriptions*, Cambridge: MIT Press

Kay, M. (1980) "Algorithmic Schemata and Data Structures in Syntactic Processing", reprinted in Grosz, Sparck Jones, Webber (eds.), 1986

Kim, D.-C. (1981) *Hankwuk-ko-insway-kiswul-sa*, Tham-ku-tang [A History of Old Typography in Korea]

Kim, S. (2009) *Automatische Wortformanalyse für das Koreanische*, Inaugural Dissertation, CLUE, Friedrich Alexander Universität Erlangen Nürnberg

Kleene, S.C. (1952) *Introduction to Metamathematics*, Amsterdam

Knuth, D.E. (1973) *The Art of Computer Programming: Vol. 3. Sorting and Searching*, Reading: Addison-Wesley

Knuth, D.E. (1984) *The TEX Book*, Reading: Addison-Wesley

Koskenniemi, K. (1983) *Two-Level Morphology*, University of Helsinki Publications, Vol. 11

Kripke, S. (1972) "Naming and Necessity," in D. Davidson and G. Harmann (eds.), 253–355

Kripke, S. (1975) "Outline of a Theory of Truth," *The Journal of Philosophy* 72:690–715

Kučera, H., and W.N. Francis (1967) *Computational Analysis of Present-Day English*, Providence: Brown University Press

Lakoff, G. (1968) "Pronouns and Reference," University of Indiana Linguistics Club, Bloomington, Indiana

Lakoff, G. (1972a) "Linguistics and Natural Logic," in D. Davidson and G. Harman (eds.), 545–665

Lakoff, G. (1972b) "Hedges: A Study in Meaning Criteria and the Logic of Fuzzy Concepts," in P.M. Peranteau, J.N. Levi, and G.C. Phares (eds.), *Papers from the Eighth Regional Meeting of the Chicago Linguistic Society*, 183–228, Chicago, Illinois

Lamb, S. (1996) *Outline of Stratificational Grammar*, Washington: Georgetown University Press

Lambek, J. (1958) "The Mathematics of Sentence Structure," *The American Mathematical Monthly* 65:154–170

Lamport, L. (1986) *LaTeX, A Document Preparation System*, Reading: Addison-Wesley

Langacker, R. (1969) "Pronominalization and the Chain of Command," in D.A. Reibel and S.A. Shane (eds.), 160–186

Langacker, R. (1987/1991) *Foundations of Cognitive Semantics*, Vols. 1/2, Stanford: Stanford University Press

Lawson, V. (1983) "Machine Translation," in C. Picken (ed.), 203–213

Lee, K.-Y. (1994) "Hangul, the Korean Writing System, and Its Computational Treatment," *LDV-Forum* 11.2:26–43

Leech, G., R. Garside, and E. Atwell (1983) "The Automatic Grammatical Tagging of the LOB Corpus," *ICAME Journal* 7:13–33

Leech, G. (1995) "A Brief User's Guide to the Grammatical Tagging of the British National Corpus," http://www.natcorp.ox.ac.uk/docs/gramtag.html, September 7 (2013)

Lees, R.B. (1960) "The Grammar of English Nominalizations," *International Journal of American Linguistics, Part 2*, 26.3

Leidner, J. (1998) *Linksassoziative morphologische Analyse des Englischen mit stochastischer Disambiguierung*, Magisterarbeit, CLUE, Friedrich Alexander Universität Erlangen Nürnberg

Leśniewski, S. (1929) "Grundzüge eines neuen Systems der Grundlagen der Mathematik," *Fundamenta Mathematicae* 14:1–81

Levinson, S.C. (1983) *Pragmatics*, Cambridge: Cambridge University Press

Lieb, H.-H. (1992) "The Case for a New Structuralism," in H.-H. Lieb (ed.), *Prospects for a New Structuralism*. Amsterdam/Philadelpia: John Benjamins

Linsky, L. (ed.) (1971) *Reference and Modality*, London: Oxford University Press

Locke, J. (1690) *An Essay Concerning Human Understanding*, In Four Books, printed by Elizabeth Holt for Thomas Basset, London, reprinted in Taylor, 1974

Lorenz, O., and G. Schüller. (1994) "Präsentation von LA-MORPH," *LDV-Forum* 11.1:39–51, reprinted in R. Hausser (ed.), 1996

Lorenz, O. (1996) *Automatische Wortformerkennung für das Deutsche im Rahmen von Malaga*, Magisterarbeit, CLUE, Friedrich Alexander Universität Erlangen Nürnberg

Loyall, A.B., and J. Bates (1993) "Real-Time Control of Animated Broad Agents," *Proceedings of the Fifteenth Annual Conference of the Cognitive Science Society*, Boulder, Colorado

Luce, R., R. Bush, and E. Galanter (eds.) (1963) *Handbook of Mathematical Psychology*, Vol. 2, New York: John Wiley

Łukasiewicz, J. (1935) "Zur vollen dreiwertigen Aussagenlogik," *Erkenntnis* 5:176

Lyons, J. (1968) *Introduction to Theoretical Linguistics*, Cambridge: Cambridge University Press

MacWhinney, B. (1978) *The Acquisition of Morphophonology*, Monographs of the Society for Research in Child Development, No. 174, Vol. 43

MacWhinney, B. (1999) "The Emergence of Language from Embodiment," in B. MacWhinney (ed.)

MacWhinney, B. (ed.) (1999) *The Emergence of Language*, Mahwah: Lawrence Erlbaum

Maes, P. (ed.) (1990) *Designing Autonomous Agents*, Cambridge/Amsterdam: MIT/Elsevier.

Mahlow, C. (2000) *Automatische Wortformanalyse für das Spanische*, Magisterarbeit, CLUE, Friedrich Alexander Universität Erlangen Nürnberg

Mandelbrot, B., L. Apostel, and A. Morf (1957) "Linguistique Statistique Macroscopique," in J. Piaget (ed.), *Logique, Langage et Théorie de L'information*, Paris: Bibliothèque scientifique internationale, Études d'épistémologie génétique

Marr, D. (1982) *Vision*, New York: W.H. Freeman and Company

Marshall, I. (1983) "Choice of Grammatical Word-Class Without Global Syntactic Analysis: Tagging Words in the LOB Corpus," *Computers and the Humanities* 17:139–150

Marshall, I. (1987) "Tag Selection Using Probabilistic Methods," in Garside et al. (eds.)

Marty, A. (1908) *Untersuchungen zur Grundlegung der allgemeinen Grammatik und Sprachphilosophie*, Vol. 1, Halle: Niemeyer, reprint Hildesheim, New York: Olms (1976)

Matthews, P.H. (1972) *Inflectional Morphology. A Theoretical Study Based on Aspects of Latin Verb Conjugation*, Cambridge: Cambridge University Press

Matthews, P.H. (1974) *Morphology. An Introduction to the Theory of Word Structure*, Cambridge Textbooks in Linguistics, Cambridge: Cambridge University Press

McCawley, J.D. (1982) *Thirty Million Theories of Grammar*, Chicago: The University of Chicago Press

McDonald, D. (1983) "Natural Language Generation as a Computational Problem: An Introduction," in M. Brady and R.C. Berwick (eds.)

McKeown, K. (1985) *Text Generation: Using Discourse Strategies and Focus Constraints to Generate Natural Language Text*, Cambridge: Cambridge University Press

Meier, H. (1964) *Deutsche Sprachstatistik*, Vol. 1, Hildesheim

Miller, G. (1956) "The Magical Number Seven, Plus or Minus Two: Some Limits on our Capacity for Processing Information," *Psychological Review* 63.2:81–97

Miller, G., and N. Chomsky (1963) "Finitary Models of Language Users," in R. Luce, R. Bush, and E. Galanter (eds.)

Montague, R. (1974) *Formal Philosophy*, New Haven: Yale University Press

Nakayama, K., H. Zijiang, and S. Shimojo (1995) "Visual Surface Representation: A Critical Link Between Lower-Level and Higher-Level Vision," in S. Kosslyn and D. Osherson (eds.)

Neisser, U. (1967) *Cognitive Psychology*, New York: Appleton-Century-Crofts

Newell, A., and H.A. Simon (1972) *Human Problem Solving*, Englewood Cliffs: Prentice-Hall

Newell, A., and H.A. Simon (1975) "Computer Science as Empirical Inquiry: Symbols and Search," in J. Haugeland (ed.)

Norman, D.A., and D.E. Rumelhart (eds.) (1975) *Explorations in Cognition*, San Francisco: W.H. Freeman and Company

Ogden, C.K., and I.A. Richards (1923) *The Meaning of Meaning*, London: Routledge and Kegan Paul

Oostdijk, N. (1988) "A Corpus Linguistic Approach to Linguistic Variation," in G. Dixon (ed.), *Literary and Linguistic Computing*, Vol. 3.1

Oostdijk, N., and P. de Haan (1994) *Corpus-based Research into Language*, Amsterdam-Atlanta: Editions Rodopi

Palmer, S. (1975) "Visual Perception and World Knowledge: Notes on a Model of Sensory-Cognitive Interaction," in D.A. Norman and D.E. Rumelhart (eds.), *Explorations in Cognition*, 279–307

Park, Y.-W. (1987) *Koryo-sitay-sa (Ha)*, ilcisa [A History of the Koryo Dynasty, Vol. II]

Pascal, B. (1951) *Pensées sur la Religion et sur Quelques Autre Sujets*, Paris: Éditions du Luxembourg

Paul, H. (1920) *Grundzüge der Grammatik*, Halle, 1880, 5th edn., 1920

Peirce, C.S. (1871) "Critical Review of Berkeley's Idealism," *North American Review* 93:449–472

Peirce, W.S. (1931–1958) *Collected Papers of Charles Sanders Peirce*, edited by C. Hartshorne and P. Weiss, 6 Vols. Cambridge: Harvard University Press

Peters, S., and R. Ritchie (1973) "On the Generative Power of Transformational Grammar," *Information and Control* 18:483–501

Picken, C. (1989) *The Translator Handbook*, 2nd edn., London: Aslib

Piotrovskij, R.G., K.B. Bektaev, and A.A. Piotrovskaja (1985) *Mathematische Linguistik*, translated from Russian, Bochum: Brockmeyer

Pollard, C., and I. Sag (1987) *Information-Based Syntax and Semantics Vol. I, Fundamentals*, Stanford University: CSLI Lecture Notes, Vol. 13

Pollard, C., and I. Sag (1994) *Head-Driven Phrase Structure Grammar*, Stanford/Chicago: CSLI Stanford/The University of Chicago Press

Post, E. (1936) "Finite Combinatory Processes – Formulation I," *The Journal of Symbolic Logic* I:103

Pustejovsky, J. (1995) *The Generative Lexicon*, Cambridge: MIT Press

Putnam, H. (1975) "The Meaning of 'Meaning'," in Putnam, H. (ed.), *Mind, Language, and Reality* 2, 215–271, Cambridge: Cambridge University Press

Quine, W.v.O (1960) *Word and Object*, Cambridge: MIT Press

Rabin, M.O., and D. Scott. (1959) "Finite Automata and Their Decision Problems," *IBM Journal of Research* 3.2:115–125

Reddy, D.R., L.D. Erman, R.D. Fennell, and R.B. Neely (1973) "The Hearsay Speech Understanding System: An Example of the Recognition Process," *Proceedings of the Third International Joint Conference on Artificial Intelligence*, Stanford, CA

Reibel, D.A., and S.A. Shane (eds.) (1969) *Modern Studies of English*, Englewood Cliffs: Prentice-Hall

Reiter, E., A. Cawsey, L. Osman, and Y. Roff (1997) "Knowledge Acquisition for Content Selection," *Proceedings of the 6th European Workshop on Natural Language Generation (ENGLGWS-97)*, Duisburg, 117–126

Reithinger, N. (1992) *Eine parallele Architektur zur inkrementellen Generierung multimodaler Dialogbeiträge*, St. Augustin: Infix

Rescher, N. (1969) *Many-Valued Logic*, New York: McGraw-Hill

Richards, I.A. (1936) *The Philosophy of Rhetoric*, Oxford: Oxford University Press

Rickel, J., and W.L. Johnson (1999) "Animated Agents for Procedural Training in Virtual Reality: Perception, Cognition, and Motor Control," *Applied Artificial Intelligence* 13:343–382

Roukos, S. (1995) "Language Representation," in R. Cole (ed.), 35–41

Rumelhart, D.E. (1977) *Human Information Processing*, New York: John Wiley and Sons

Rumelhart, D.E., J.L. McClelland et al. (eds.) (1986a) *Parallel Distributed Processing*, Cambridge: MIT Press

Rumelhart, D.E., P. Smolensky, J. McClelland, and G.E. Hinton. (1986b) "Schemata and Sequential Thought Processes in PDP Models," in Rumelhart, D.E., J.L. McClelland et al. (eds.), Vol. II, 7–57

Russell, S.J. (1905) "On Denoting," *Mind* 14:479–493

Russell, S.J., and P. Norvig (1995) *Artificial Intelligence, a Modern Approach*, Englewood Cliffs: Prentice Hall

Salton, G. (1989) *Automatic Text Processing: The Transformation, Analysis, and Retrieval of Information by Computer*, Reading: Addison-Wesley

Salminen, A., and F. Tompa (2011) *Communicating with XML*, Berlin: Springer

Sapir, E. (1921) *Language, an Introduction to the Study of Speech*, New York: Harvest Books – Harcourt, Brace, and World

Saussure, F. de (1967) *Grundfragen der Allgemeinen Sprachwissenschaft*, Berlin: Walter de Gruyter

Saussure, F. de (1972) *Cours de Linguistique Générale*, Édition Critique Préparée par Tullio de Mauro, Paris: Éditions Payot

Schank, R.C., and R. Abelson (1977) *Scripts, Plans, Goals, and Understanding*, Hillsdale: Lawrence Erlbaum

Scott, D., and C. Strachey (1971) "Toward a Mathematical Semantics of Computer Languages," Technical Monograph PRG-6, Oxford University Computing Laboratory, Programming Research Group, 45 Branbury Road, Oxford, UK

Searle, J.R. (1969) *Speech Acts*, Cambridge: Cambridge University Press

Searle, J.R. (1992) *The Rediscovery of the Mind*, Cambridge: MIT Press

Searle, J., F. Kiefer, and M. Bierwisch (eds.) (1980) *Speech Act Theory and Pragmatics*, Dordrecht: D. Reidel

Searle, J.R., and D. Vanderveken (1985) *Foundations of Illocutionary Logic*, Cambridge: Cambridge University Press

Sells, P. (1985) *Lectures on Contemporary Syntactic Theory*, Stanford University: CSLI Lecture Notes, Vol. 3

Sells, P., S. Shieber, and T. Wasow (eds.) (1991) *Foundational Issues in Natural Language Processing*, Cambridge: MIT Press

Shannon, C.E., and W. Weaver (1949) *The Mathematical Theory of Communication*, Urbana: University of Illinois Press

Sharman, R. (1990) *Hidden Markov Model Methods for Word Tagging*, Report 214, IBM UK Scientific Centre, Winchester

Shieber, S. (1985) "Evidence Against the Non-Contextfreeness of Natural Language," *Linguistics and Philosophy* 8:333–343

Shieber, S., S. Stucky, H. Uszkoreit, and J. Robinson (1983) "Formal Constraints on Metarules," *Proceedings of the 21st Annual Meeting of the Association for Computational Linguistics*, Cambridge, Mass

Sinclair, J. (1991) *Corpus, Concordance, Collocation*, Oxford: Oxford University Press

Skinner, B.F. (1957) *Verbal Behavior*, New York: Appleton-Century-Crofts

Skinner, B.F. (1974) *About Behaviorism*, New York: Alfred A. Knopf

Sperling, G. (1960) "The Information Available in Brief Visual Processing," *Psychological Monographs* 11. Whole No. 498

St. Laurent, S. (1998) *XML. A Primer*, Cambridge: MIT Press

Steger, H. (ed.) (1989) *Handbücher zur Sprach- und Kommunikationswissenschaft*, Vol. IV, Berlin: de Gruyter

Stemberger, P.J., and B. MacWhinney. (1986) "Frequency and Lexical Storage of Regularly Inflected Forms," *Memory & Cognition* 14.1:17–26

Stubert, B. (1993) *"Einordnung der Familie der C-Sprachen zwischen die kontextfreien und die kontextsensitiven Sprachen,"* CLUE-betreute Studienarbeit der Informatik, Friedrich Alexander Universität Erlangen Nürnberg

Suppe, F. (ed.) (1977) *The Structure of Scientific Theories*, Urbana: University of Illinois Press

Tarr, M.J., and H.H. Bülthoff (eds.) (1998) *Image-Based Object Recognition in Man, Monkey, and Machine*, special issue of *Cognition* 67.1–2:1–208

Tarski, A. (1935) "Der Wahrheitsbegriff in den formalisierten Sprachen," *Studia Philosophica* I:262–405.

Tarski, A. (1944) "The Semantic Concept of Truth," *Philosophy and Phenomenological Research* 4:341–375

Tesnière, L. (1959) *Éléments de syntaxe structurale*, Paris: Editions Klincksieck

Thiel, C. (1995) *Philosophie und Mathematik*, Darmstadt: Wissenschaftliche Buchgesellschaft

Turing, A.M. (1950) "Computing Machinery and Intelligence," *Mind* 59:433–460

Uszkoreit, H., and S. Peters (1986) "On Some Formal Properties of Metarules," Report CSLI-85-43, Stanford University: Center for the Study of Language and Information

Valiant, L.G. (1975) "General Context-Free Recognition in Less than Cubic Time," *Journal of Computer and System Sciences* 10.2:308–315

Wahrig, G. (1986/1989) *Deutsches Wörterbuch*, Munich: Mosaik Verlag

Wahlster, W. (1993) "Verbmobil, Translation of Face-to-Face Dialogs," *Proceedings of the Fourth Machine Translation Summit*, Kobe, Japan, 127–135

Wall, L., and R.L. Schwartz (1990) *Programming Perl*, Sebastopol: O'Reilly and Associates

Webber, B., and N. Nilsson (eds.) (1981) *Readings in Artificial Intelligence*, Los Altos: Morgan Kaufmann

Wheeler, P., and V. Lawson (1982) "Computing Ahead of the Linguists," *Ambassador International*, 21–22

Weizenbaum, J. (1965) "ELIZA – A Computer Program for the Study of Natural Language Communications Between Man and Machine," *Communications of the ACM* 9.1 (11)

Wetzel, C. (1996) *Erstellung einer Morphologie für Italienisch in Malaga*, CLUE-betreute Studienarbeit der Informatik, Friedrich Alexander Universität Erlangen Nürnberg

Wexelblat, A. (ed.) (1993) *Virtual Reality, Applications and Explorations*, Boston: Academic Press Professional

Weyhrauch, R. (1980) "Prolegomena to a Formal Theory of Mechanical Reasoning," *Artificial Intelligence*, reprint in Webber and Nilsson (eds.), 1981

Winograd, T. (1972) *Understanding Natural Language*, San Diego: Academic Press, Harcourt Brace Jovanovich

Winston, P.H., and B.K. Horn (1984) *LISP*, 2nd edn., Reading: Addison-Wesley

Wittgenstein, L. (1921) "Logisch-philosophische Abhandlung," *Annalen der Naturphilosophie* 14:185–262

Wittgenstein, L. (1953) *Philosophical Investigations*, Oxford: Blackwell

Wloka, D.W. (1992) *Roboter-Systeme 1*, Berlin: Springer

Zipf, G.K. (1935) *The Psycho-biology of Language*, Oxford: Houghton, Mifflin

Zipf, G.K. (1949) *Human Behavior and the Principle of Least Effort*, Oxford: Addison-Wesley

Zue, V., R. Cole, and W. Ward (1995) "Speech Recognition," in R. Cole (ed.), 1998

Name Index

R. Hausser, *Foundations of Computational Linguistics*,
DOI 10.1007/978-3-642-41431-2, © Springer-Verlag Berlin Heidelberg 2014

Subject Index

A LAGs, 211, 214
A-language, 154
Abacus, 380
Abbreviation, 421–423
Ablaut, 257, 271
Aborigines, 250
Absolute type transparency, 174, 197
Abstract automata, 146, 173, 218
Abstract ideas, 55
Ackermann function, 152, 154
Action, 52
Action component, 60, 68
Ad hoc solutions, 141
Adjective, 56, 140, 254
   agreement, 333, 353
   allomorphs, 276
   inflection, 286
Adnominal, 56
Adverb, 56
Agglutination, 249
Agglutinative language, 313
Agreeing lists, 366
Agreement, 140, 201, 204, 295, 313, 316,
   334
   definition-based, 340
   external, 330
   identity-based, 318, 330
   internal, 329
   violation, 316
Algebraic definition, 130
   LA Grammar, 193
   C Grammar, 135
   PS Grammar, 144
Allo rule, 269, 271
Allograph, 257
Allomorph, 255–257

Allomorph method, 264, 265, 269
Allomorph quotient, 276, 278
Allomorph reduction, 263
Allophon, 257
Alphabet, 128
Alphabetical word form list, 20, 306
Ambiguity syntactic, 38
Ambiguity of natural language, 240
Ambiguity structure, 216
Amount parameter, 212, 226
Analogous reconstruction, 438
Analytic language, 313
Analytic philosophy, 58, 69, 72, 105
Analyzed surface, 75, 380
Anaphoric interpretation, 111
Antecedent, 111
Application, 292
Arbitrariness of signs, 108
Argument, 56
Artificial intelligence, 3
Assignment, 135, 139, 386
Assignment algorithm, 380
Astronomy, xxvi
Automata theory, 210
Automated cinematography, 486
Automatic word form recognition, 9, 257,
   259–261, 264, 307, 323
Autonomous agent, 6, 61
Autonomy from the metalanguage, 390
Autosemantika, 254
Auxiliary
   English, 337
   German, 362, 364
Average sentence length, 147
AWK, 261
Axiomatization, xxv

R. Hausser, *Foundations of Computational Linguistics*,
DOI 10.1007/978-3-642-41431-2, © Springer-Verlag Berlin Heidelberg 2014

Printed in the United States
By Bookmasters